PC Graphics
UNLEASHED

SAMS PUBLISHING

201 West 103rd Street
Indianapolis, IN 46290

Trademarks

Publisher
Richard K. Swadley

Acquisitions Manager
Stacy Hiquet

Managing Editor
Cindy Morrow

Acquisitions Editor
Grace Buechlein

Development Editor
Dean Miller

Software Development Editor
Keith Davenport

Senior Editor
Sandy Doell

Production Editor
Deborah Frisby

Editors
Cherie Clark
Charles Hutchinson
Rosie Piga
Ryan Rader
Tonya Simpson
Angie Trzepacz

Editorial Coordinator
Bill Whitmer

Editorial Assistants
Carol Ackerman
Sharon Cox
Lynette Quinn

Technical Reviewer
Brad Pillow

Marketing Manager
Gregg Bushyeager

Cover Designer
Jay Corpus

Book Designer
Alyssa Yesh

**Director of Production
and Manufacturing**
Jeff Valler

Imprint Manager
Juli Cook

Manufacturing Coordinator
Paul Gilchrist

Production Analysts
Angela D. Bannan
Dennis Clay Hager
Mary Beth Wakefield

Proofreading Coordinator
Joelynn Gifford

Indexing Coordinator
Johnna VanHoose

Graphics Image Specialists
Becky Beheler
Brad Dixon
Jason Hand
Clint Lahnen
Cheri Laughner
Michael Reynolds
Dennis Sheehan
Craig Small
Jeff Yesh

Production
Katy Bodenmiller
Mary Ann Cosby
Judy Everly
Shawn MacDonald
Stephanie J. McComb
Casey Price
Susan Shepard
Scott Tullis
Dennis Wesner

Proofreaders
Georgiana Briggs
Mona Brown
Kimberly K. Hannel
Donna Harbin
Brian-Kent Proffitt
Holly Wittenberg

Indexer
Jeanne Clark

Overview

Contents

Part II Digital Image Manipulation

Part IV Blobs

Part V Ultra-Realistic 3-D

About the Authors

Scott Anderson, president of Wild Duck software of Rohnert Park, California, created the popular commercial animation package *FantaVision*. He also wrote *Morphing Magic*, a book on animation special effects from Sams Publishing (1993), and several other graphics programs.

Steve Anger had his introduction to computer graphics when he downloaded the DKB ray tracer from a local BBS; he has been hooked on ray tracing ever since. Although he does some occasional modeling and rendering, he prefers to write code. He currently works on the POV-Ray ray tracer as well as his own ray tracer utilities 3DS2POV, RAW2POV, and FRGEN. Steve spends his working hours designing industrial computer vision systems.

W. Andrew Bass is a biomedical engineering graduate student at Vanderbilt University in Nashville, TN. Andy is a member of the Stereotactic Neurosurgical Apparatus Research Lab and is the author of the present software used in the Interactive Image-Guided Surgical Navigation System.

Truman Brown is a programmer analyst for the City of Los Angeles, providing technical support in Distributed Technologies. He is also the sysop for the City's bulletin board, CityLINK. His academic background includes an A.A. in photo-offset lithography (Pasadena City College, 1977) and a B.S. in business information systems (California State University, Los Angeles, 1989, *magna cum laude*). Somewhere between the A.A. and the B.S., he became a Marine and then an ex-Marine. The extent of his computer graphics experience has been purely as a hobby. He enjoys creating abstract art in the ray trace medium using popular freeware and shareware ray tracers such as POV-Ray and Vivid. Hundreds of his images and animations can be found on CompuServe and other online services. His programming background includes formal studies in FORTRAN, Pascal, and COBOL. He is also self-taught in C, C++, Z80 Assembly, and BASIC. He has written several freeware and shareware utilities including CTDS (Connect The Dots System), CM (CircleMaster), Hype, Zoom, and FWheel. All of these programs are tools designed to make working with freeware/shareware ray tracers easier, and they can be found online. He lives in Pasadena, California with his wife, three daughters, two ducks, and a cat.

Martin Crumpton is 430 years old, married, with three children, three cats, two dogs, and one pony. He runs a one-man computer consultancy in England and is currently working for IBM as a developer for their Removable Media Manager (DFSMSrmm) tape management system. Thus are 23 years in computing (nine as a mainframe MVS operator and the rest as a systems programmer) rewarded. He says IBM is still the best company in the world to work for. He speaks Assembler and mutters in C. He has vowed never to work for the Civil Service ever again. When the lure of real life fades into the background, he writes science fiction and fantasy—or programs, which is much the same thing.

Harry Dusenberg was born in Philadelphia on October 28, 1943. After attending high school in Media, Pennsylvania, he became a musician and spent 15 years on the road playing lead guitar. He has been working in the computer industry for about 15 years but has been playing around with computers for about 20 years. His other hobbies are music, oil painting, fishing, and computer programming.

Spyro Gumas is an electrical engineer by day, and a graphics programmer by night, living in Fullerton, California. He is the author of the leading shareware VSA256 and TIFF256 graphics libraries for C programmers, and he specializes in image-processing and photographic-manipulation software. In addition to this book, Spyro also co-authored *Tricks of the Graphics Gurus*, from Sams Publishing (1993).

Jim Hawkins is a multimedia programmer/artist consultant, specializing in C, C++, Grasp, and POCO languages with artistic experience in 3D Studio and Animator Pro images and animations. His work has been used for television, commercial presentations, Disney World, and CD-ROM titles. He has been in the computer field for 20 years, working in the UNIX and DOS environments with major programming accomplishments in graphics, automatic control systems, and language interpreters. His CompuServe ID is 76520,3356 or Internet 76520,3356@compuserve.com.

Alfonso Hermida has a B.S. and M.S. in mechanical engineering from the University of Puerto Rico and an M.S. in mechanical engineering from The George Washington University in Washington, D.C. He currently works with NASA/Goddard Space Flight Center as an aerospace engineer. He is also an adjunct professor in the mathematics department at Capitol College in Laurel, MD. He is the author of *Adventures in Ray Tracing* published by Que, and co-author of *Hidden Images: Making Random Dot Stereograms*, published by Que, 1994. He also has written various articles for *3D Artist Magazine*.

Sandeep Jolly holds a B. Tech. in electrical engineering from RECK, India, and an M.S. in computer science from Mississippi State University. His major interests include 3-D graphics, GUI design, system programming, image processing, and data communication. He is currently involved in satellite image processing.

Rob McGregor is the founder of Screaming Tiki, a software development company specializing in interactive multimedia programs for Microsoft Windows. He has worked as a software consultant and has written programs for Microsoft and numerous other smaller companies. He writes a column on Visual Basic tricks and tips for the CD-ROM virtual magazine *Synapse* and in his free time enjoys ray tracing, writing, and playing classical guitar. His CompuServe ID is 73122,3125 (Internet 73122.3125@CompuServe.Com)

Gregory MacNicol has been actively involved with computer graphics for the last 14 years, specializing in computer animation for the last decade. His first computer-generated film was created in the early 1980s on an Apple II on motion picture film. Since then, he has worked as a computer graphics programmer, consultant, writer, and animator.

Mr. MacNicol is a contributing editor for *Computer Graphics World*—since the magazine's birth over 10 years ago—and writes for dozens of magazines focusing on computer graphics. The periodicals include *New Media, Desktop Video World, PC Graphics* (formerly *Hi-Color*), *Publish, Mac World, Videomaker, Cadence, Byte, Iris, Imaging, Computer Technology Review*, and *Step-By-Step Graphics*. He has been the Western Editor of *Digital Design Magazine* for two years.

He has also been an international consultant working with computer graphics software and hardware developers, in addition to technical direction for computer graphics production companies involved with creating special effects for the film and video industry. Mr. MacNicol has taught computer animation at the University of California, Santa Cruz and currently lectures at other universities and conferences covering computer graphics, animation, virtual reality, video, HDTV, computer-generated holography, and special effects production in the entertainment business. He holds a patent on automated digital scanning, which is used in the fashion industry.

His background is based in the sciences, specifically physics and electronics, having attended Massachusetts Institute of Technology, RIT, and New Mexico Tech, where he also worked as Director of Information. He currently works in Santa Cruz, California, where he has a multiplatform computer animation facility.

William Newhall is a recording engineer and computer programmer who lives and works in Washington, DC. He has been conducting research in systems programming, ray tracing, and radiosity at the American University. In Chapter 1, William addresses the hardware and software issues of the PC graphics workstation. The radiosity method of photorealistic image synthesis and PC software is explored by William in Chapter 18. In addition, William compiled the computer graphics resource appendix. William has written articles for *3D Artist Magazine* and *3D Graphics: From Ray Tracing to Radiosity*, a book on photorealistic PC graphics forthcoming from Sams Publishing.

Chikai J. Ohazama is currently a graduate student in biomedical engineering at Duke University. He is an NSF/ERC Pre-Doctoral Fellow and is working under Dr. Olaf von Ramm and Dr. George Stetten doing research in the field of ultrasound imaging. He received his bachelor's degree in biomedical engineering at Vanderbilt University and graduated *summa cum laude*. Chikai is also a composer, singer/songwriter, poet, and playwright.

Dick Oliver has written several commercial graphics programs, articles, and books, including the world's best-selling 3-D fractal design system and Sams Publishing's *FractalVision* book and software. Dick is president of Cedar Software of Morrisville, Vermont, which specializes in new approaches to advanced graphics and 3-D modeling.

George Stetten received a bachelor's degree from the Department of Engineering and Applied Physics at Harvard University in 1976, an M.S. from the Department of Biology at N.Y.U. in 1986, concentrating in neuroscience, and an M.D. from the S.U.N.Y. at Syracuse in 1991. From 1980 to 1984 he helped develop the onboard data and navigation systems for *Deep Submersible Alvin.* He is currently Director of the Visualization and Image Analysis Laboratory at Duke University, and Assistant Research Professor in the Department of Biomedical Engineering at Duke University.

Introduction: State of the Art

by Dick Oliver

If you have watched TV or gone to a movie in the last 10 years, you've almost certainly seen advanced computer graphics in action. And you know that, on a scale from "yawn" to "WOW!" fancy graphics sure rate better than plain old numbers and text. If you picked up this book, you might also want to create some computer graphics of your own—preferably registering as high on the WOW-o-meter as possible.

Alas, until recently, state-of-the-art computer graphics was chained to exotic and expensive workstations. Unless your initials happened to be ABC or NBC, you probably didn't have a spare $100,000 to blow on an advanced graphics system—no matter how much fun it might be. That's just as well, too, because programming that big-bucks workstation once you got it would have meant combing through reams of obtuse technical manuals and academic computer science papers. What joy.

Now all that has changed. Computer graphics have been unleashed from dedicated workstations. Even the lowliest PC comes with a snazzy graphics card, and a screaming, state-of-the-art, graphics monster machine will take less out of your wallet than the average used car. Graphics programming has also been let out of its cage—cheap, fast, and easy-to-use graphics programming tools come with every major compiler. And you'll encounter a pack of even more powerful tools on the CD-ROM included with this book.

With killer graphics on the loose, all you need is the know-how to take command of the raging graphics beast on your desktop. This book gives you detailed, plain-English explanations of how to pull off the latest, most impressive graphics stunts—along with tons of working C code and a CD-ROM packed with ready-to-run graphics programs, images, and animations.

In the next thousand pages, a baker's dozen of graphics experts will give you a real-world, plain-English introduction to the best that contemporary PC graphics has to offer. You'll run the graphics gamut, from choosing the graphics hardware and software you need to creating your own photorealistic, animated 3-D worlds. Along the way, you'll learn how to do advanced morphing, computer video, computer painting, digital image processing and composition, image and video compression, interactive 3-D modeling, free-form deformation, 2-D and 3-D "blob" sculpting, ultra-realistic ray traced and radiosity rendering, 3-D data visualization and imaging, and even how to make those nifty random dot stereograms you've seen in malls. But first, I'll take you on a flyby of the world of PC graphics, and introduce you to each of the graphics techniques you'll explore in subsequent chapters.

One caveat: This book is written in English, not techno-babble, so almost anyone will be able to read it without the severe brain hemorrhaging that can result from exposure to some advanced computer books. However, it is really intended for programmers, so a working knowledge of C and/or C++, as well as a general familiarity with basic PC operation and graphics programming, will certainly help you get the most out of it. If you need an introduction to computer graphics with an eye toward gearing up quickly for the kind of advanced topics covered in this book, we humbly recommend *Tricks of the Graphics Gurus* (Sams Publishing, 1993), by several of the same authors who went on to write *PC Graphics Unleashed*.

Graphics Freedom at Last

Media pundits everywhere are heralding the liberation of sophisticated computer graphics from academic ivory towers and multimillion-dollar television networks. Liberation in general is a nice idea, but exactly what new freedoms do you have on your desktop? After all, color graphics adapters have been around for years, and most of the graphics programs included with this book will even run on an aging 386. Before we dance in the aisles and whoop too loudly about graphics emancipation, perhaps I'd better introduce the new technologies and techniques that have recently been unleashed.

The graphics revolution is winning us five basic freedoms:

1. **True 3-D.** Old-style PC graphics were restricted to the two dimensions of paper or a computer screen. Thanks to increased speed, improved interface design, and advanced programming techniques, your computer screen can now become a window into truly three-dimensional worlds. The freedom to create 3-D objects and explore 3-D universes literally brings PC graphics into a whole new dimension. Fancy tricks such as SIRDS (single-image random dot stereograms) can add true stereoscopic perception as well.

2. **True photorealism.** Let's face it. Sixteen colors—the standard palette for most pre-1990s computer graphics—are not enough. When you're rendering complex 3-D objects with light sources, you can squeak by with a bare minimum of 256 colors, but you really want all the colors the eye can see. Now that true-color and "high-color" video cards are widely available for under $200, you are free to employ sophisticated photorealistic rendering techniques such as ray tracing and radiosity on your own PC.

3. **Real-time animation and video.** As impressive as computer-generated images can be, they kinda lose their "oomph" if they just *sit there*. Nothing in the real world stays still for very long these days, and the new breed of hardware and software can flip frames up onto your computer monitor fast enough to simulate

seamless motion. So now your computer graphics are finally free to move and to perform wild stunts—like morphing monsters into heros and combining ray-traced creatures with footage of live actors.

4. **Real-world visualization.** Exploring the new universe of computer-generated "cyberspace" worlds is exciting. But perhaps even more liberating is the ability to bring information from the real world into our computers, where the magic of graphics can reveal secrets that eyes alone could never see. From advanced image processing to 3-D medical visualization, you can use your computer to expose hidden truths and get creative with reality itself.

5. **True interactivity.** The most fundamental freedom that computer graphics can deliver has also been the most long-awaited and technically challenging. What good are all these new graphics technologies if you can't control them? And the only way to really keep control in a world of moving visual images is to interact with the graphical objects on your screen in real time. Even though the most advanced rendering techniques such as ray tracing and radiosity are still too slow to permit direct interaction, programs like the 3-D modeler and the blob modeler included with this book enable you to interactively set up scenes for the ray tracer to render at its leisure. This represents a giant step toward the graphics Holy Grail of photorealistic, real-time interactivity.

The rest of this chapter explains the current state of these new graphics capabilities. You'll find out what you can do now that you couldn't do before, and what still remains beyond the reach of current PC-based technology. Of course, you'll also get a visual tour of the state of the art, with computer-generated illustrations of each technique.

New Dimension, New Reality

Programming and working with two-dimensional graphics is simple. Using x and y coordinates, you specify where points, lines, and shapes should appear on the screen. The common mouse provides an ideal way to "point and click" on each x-y location, and filling areas with colors or patterns is also relatively straightforward.

Add another dimension, however, and things quickly get complex. The flat computer screen and two-axis mouse can no longer relate directly to your graphical objects, so depth must be specified and represented by some indirect method. Possible methods of indicating depth include hidden surface removal, light-source shading, specular highlights and other lighting effects, shadows, and 3-D animated rotation. None of these is trivial to execute or quick to compute.

Figures IN.1 and IN.2 compare a subject rendered with 2-D graphics versus 3-D graphics.

FIGURE IN.1.

Even when you use perspective drawing and shading tricks, 2-D computer graphics look a bit flat.

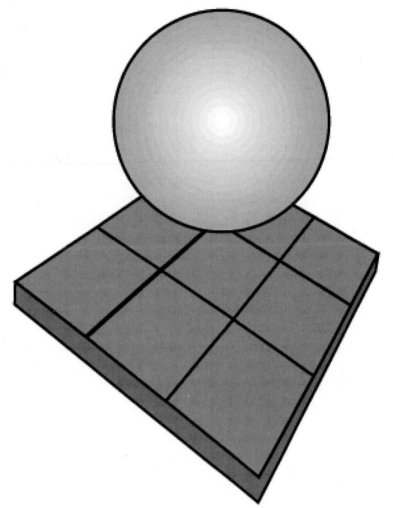

FIGURE IN.2.

Rendering a similar scene with true 3-D geometry gives it far more visual impact and realism.

The problem of giving users the ability to "point and click" in 3D can be even more daunt-ing, because they would ideally like to be able to point at any graphical object, even those hidden by other objects in front of them. Consequently, interfaces for 3-D software are notoriously difficult to learn. Though many creative programmers have tried their hands at interactive 3-D graphics, no one has found a way to provide the kind of intuitiveness and ease of use that 2-D graphics users take for granted. The fact that 3-D objects can move, scale, and rotate in six independent directions doesn't make life in 3-D space any easier.

Figures IN.3 and IN.4 show the user interface of Autodesk 3D Studio (a popular com-mercial 3-D modeling program), and POVCAD (an equally popular but far less expen-sive shareware modeler included with this book). Both tackle the problem of working with 3-D objects on a 2-D screen by giving the user multiple views of a scene, interactive mouse controls, and a mind-boggling array of menu choices for 3-D transformations and opera-tions. Both programs show only a rough "wire frame" view of objects for interactive edit-ing, simply because PCs have until recently been far too slow to render anything more realistic fast enough for mouse-based interaction.

FIGURE IN.3.

Autodesk 3D Studio is the most popular—and one of the most expensive—3-D modeling and rendering tools available.

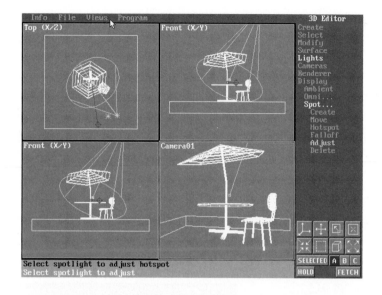

FIGURE IN.4.

POVCAD is a less sophisticated—and far less expensive—modeling program. A shareware copy is on the CD-ROM in this book.

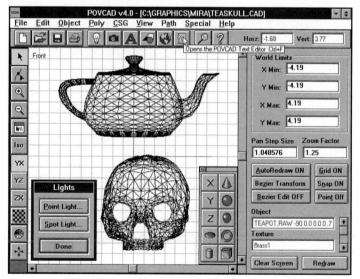

A few recent entries into the 3-D software arena, such as Caligari's trueSpace, are being heavily promoted as a radical step forward in 3-D interface design, trueSpace uses essentially the same display and interaction techniques as the older programs, with the addition of some limited real-time surface rendering.

Despite the inherent difficulties of representing and manipulating three-dimensional objects on a two-dimensional screen, the thirst for 3-D is intense. Almost everything that human beings know and love—and might want to represent on a computer screen—is three-dimensional. Vast regions of our brains are dedicated to interpreting and interacting with spatial information. It's no wonder that flat 2-D graphics created by non-artists tend to look, at best, stylistic or cartoony and, at worst, a bit brain-dead. Even not-so-well-done 3-D graphics, on the other hand, can look excitingly real. In fact, 3-D graphics pros usually give their renderings a surreal shininess, cleanliness, and geometric perfection that no Hollywood cinematographer could ever match. Realism often exceeds reality, as Figure IN.5 demonstrates.

FIGURE IN.5.

Staging this scene for a photographer would be tricky at best. 3-D computer graphics makes all things possible.

So 3-D is key, but creating and using a 3-D interface can be a major headache. What can you do? One popular solution is to forego an interactive interface and define 3-D objects and scenes using a text-based *scene description language.* This approach is especially popular for ultra-sophisticated rendering techniques that usually have so many object types and surface-texture options that a tangled maze of menu choices would be required to access them all. Rendering programs that use a text-based language range from freeware and shareware ray tracers (such as Polyray, included with this book) to Pixar's Renderman, the leading high-end, photorealistic commercial rendering system. Listing IN.1 and Figure IN.6 show a Polyray scene description and the resulting image.

Listing IN.1. The Polyray ray tracer discussed in Chapter 10 reads scene descriptions like this.

```
// Simple sample POLYRAY scene description

viewpoint {                  //first, set up the camera
    from <0, 0, -40>         //location of the eye
    at <0, 0, 0>             //where the eye is looking
    up <0, -1, 0>            //which way is up
    angle 40                 //vertical view angle
    resolution 640, 480      //size of the image in pixels
    aspect 4/3               //aspect ratio of image (x/y)
    }

background <0.5, 0.5, 1>  //make the background light blue
light <30, -100, -100>    //a point light and a spotlight
spot_light <0, -100, 10>, <0, 0, 0>, 3, 5, 20

define shiny_red          //define the word shiny_red
  texture {               //to mean a surface texture and color
    surface {
      color <1, 0, 0>     //you could also say "color red" here
      ambient 0.2         //a little red color everywhere
      diffuse 0.8         //a lot of red wherever light hits
      specular white, 0.9 //and a shiny white highlight
      }
    }

define mirror             //define a mirror texture
  texture {
    surface {
      color white         //eqivalent to "color <1, 1, 1>"
      ambient 0.1         //a little white all over
      diffuse 0.1         //a little more where light hits
      specular 0          //no shiny highlights at all
      reflection 1        //totally reflective
      }
    }
```

continues

Listing IN.1. continued

```
object {                  //first object is a sphere
   sphere <0, 0, 0>, 4    //centered at 0,0,0 with radius 4
   shiny_red              //give it the texture defined above
      }

object {                  //next object is a disc
   disc <0, 0, 0>, <0, 1, 0>, 1   //center, normal, radius
   scale     <20, 1, 20>  //enlarge it 20 times along x and z
   rotate    <0, 45, 0>   //spin 45 degrees around the y axis
   rotate    <15, 0, 0>   //then tilt 15 degrees around x
   translate <0, 6, 0>    //move it down 6
   texture {              //red squares and mirrored squares
     checker shiny_red, mirror
     scale <0.3, 0.3, 0.3>  //textures can be scaled, too!
     }
   }

   object {               //a compound dumb bell object
      object {
         sphere <-7, 0, 0>, 4
         } +
      object {
         sphere <7, 0, 0>, 4
         } +
      object {
         cylinder <-5, 0, 0>, <5, 0, 0>, 2
         }
      scale <0.5, 0.5, 0.5>
      rotate <0, 60, 0>
      translate <20, -2, 5>
      mirror                //give it the mirror texture
      }
```

FIGURE IN.6.

Polyray turns text like the preceding listing into realistic images like this.

Both the cheap and the expensive text-based renderers can usually interface with a separate modeler *front end.* The POVCAD program included with this book is one such modeler. Graphics gurus often use their favorite interactive modeler to lay out a scene and define objects, and then use a text editor to edit the resulting scene description file for "handcrafted" texture definitions, complex transformations, and other tricky stuff.

Nearly universal 3-D file exchange formats such as AutoCAD's DXF or ASCII listings of 3-D data point coordinates are frequently used to bring a 3-D object from your favorite modeler into your favorite renderer. You may also find it handy to combine elements created with two or more different modelers for use in a single rendered scene or animation. For example, you would want to use the 3-D blob modeler included with this book for sculpting irregular or complex forms such as creature faces. But for most other types of objects, the POVCAD modeler would be your tool of choice. Using a text editor, you can easily combine your creature face with the other elements of a scene for rendering with the Polyray ray tracer.

Graphics-oriented online services, such as The Graphics Alternative BBS (510-524-2780) or the GRAPHDEV and GRAPHSUP forums on CompuServe, have a large selection of specialized utilities for creating and manipulating text-format 3-D data files before rendering. The FFD3D program presented in Chapter 21, "Free Form Deformation," is one example of this sort of routine—it reads a set of 3-D data points, applies a freeform deformation to warp and twist the model, and then writes a new set of data points to a file. Creating small utility programs like FFD3D is a great way to implement your own graphics tricks without having to reinvent the wheel and write your own full-blown modeler and renderer.

To create Figure IN.7, I used a 3-D fractal modeler of my own creation (available from Cedar Software—see the order form in the back of the book), combined the data with a model made with POVCAD, and fed the results into Polyray for rendering. Finally, I used a utility called DTA by Dave Mason to find the best palette of 256 colors (shown here in grayscales) for the true-color image. This type of creative graphics design, combining your own custom programs and your choice of modelers, renderers, and utilities, is becoming commonplace as the number of 3-D-literate graphics users and programmers skyrockets.

The largest obstacle you'll face in working with 3-D graphics today is slow speed. While commercial programs can render some reasonably simple photorealistic 3-D images in seconds, more complex images often take hours—or even days—to render. Ray tracers are especially slow, because they actually trace the path of each light ray that reaches a pixel on the screen. But the spectacular reflections and crisp shadows that ray tracers provide are worth the wait if you're looking for state-of-the-art image quality. Figure IN.8 took nearly 24 hours to render on a 50 Mhz 486, even at this relatively modest (640×480) resolution. A renderer using hidden surface removal and texture mapping instead of ray tracing could have completed the image much sooner (probably in an hour or so), but it would have left out the detailed reflections of the mountain in the ellipsoid saucers.

FIGURE IN.7.

Using graphics programs of your own creation, in conjunction with programs written by others, gives you unlimited creative potential.

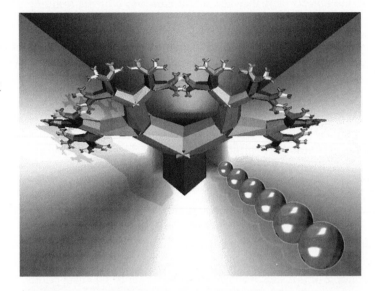

FIGURE IN.8.

Unidentified Ray-traced Objects (UROs) over a fractal mountain.

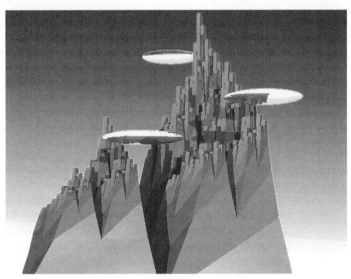

Ironically, most 3-D computer graphics images don't take advantage of our innate sense of depth perception, known as stereoscopic vision. Why? Because computer and video screens (and printed paper) deliver the same image to both eyes. This short-circuits your natural ability to decipher depth information from the differences between what your two eyes see.

Calculating stereo image pairs for two eye views is quite easy—you simply move one viewpoint slightly to the side of the other. The tough part is getting each of your eyes to see only one image of the stereo pair. One approach is to display the images side-by-side and use some type of lens system to guide the appropriate image to each eye. (Many people can also "free view" small stereo pairs by focusing their eyes past the plane of the screen or page where the images appear.) Figure IN.9 is a stereo pair generated in 3D Studio by moving the rendering "camera" a few inches.

Red/green "anaglyph" glasses are another solution. To get it to work well, however, you need to match the colors on the screen closely to the color filters in the glasses, and write both the left-eye image and right-eye image on top of one another in two different colors. This limits the technique to monochrome images.

Lately, there has been a flurry of interest in a stereoscopic rendering technique called *single-image random dot stereograms* (SIRDS), or simply RDS. These images appear to be a field of random dots or repetitive arrays of abstract designs until you focus past the printed page or computer screen. Then a dramatic three-dimensional picture pops out. Figure IN.10 shows a SIRDS image, and Chapter 16, "Stereoscopic 3-D Stunts," reveals the secret (but simple) technique for making them yourself.

Researchers are developing techniques for displaying true stereoscopic images on relatively inexpensive monitors without the need for special glasses or eyeball calisthenics. "Virtual reality" *head-mounted displays* (HMDs) are also coming down in price to the commercial market. (If you'd like to see the latest low-cost stereoscopic gadgets, call 3DTV Corporation at 415-479-3516 and ask for a catalog.) Meanwhile, stereoscopic 3-D imaging remains largely a specialized tool for medical, scientific, and military systems in which depth perception can help discern information that would otherwise be missed.

With or without stereoscopic enhancement, photorealistic 3-D computer graphics is becoming a standard tool for video and CD-ROM producers, as well as for film and print publishers.

FIGURE IN.9.

To view this stereo pair, try holding a white card up between the images, placing your nose on the edge of the card and focusing your eyes past the page. (It may take a couple minutes for the 3-D effect to kick in.)

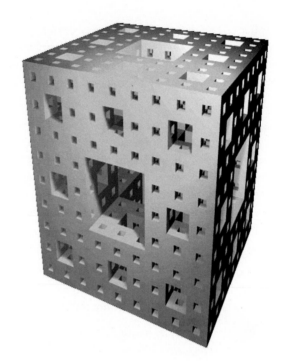

FIGURE IN.10.

To view this random dot stereogram, relax your eyes and try to look beyond the surface of the page. (Looking far away and then quickly placing the book in front of you sometimes helps.)

Graphics on the Move

If you asked me to describe the state of PC graphics today in 10 words or less, I'd say, "We're poised on the edge of full-motion video." Millions of ordinary PCs are now equipped to play back full-screen video at several frames per second, and thousands upon thousands of CD-ROM and software titles include movie or animation sequences. Multimedia upgrade kits, which add CD-ROM, sound, and sometimes video playback enhancement hardware, are selling like hotcakes. Video cards that take NTSC input from your VCR and digitize it into reasonably clear digital images don't cost much more than run-of-the-mill Super-VGA cards. Still, despite the omnipresence of ads in computer magazines for multimedia-this and multimedia-that, even TV-quality video remains just beyond the grasp of the common PC.

Instead, you get jerky 320×200 resolution, 256-color video (see Figure IN.11), usually reduced to a tiny window so that the abysmal quality doesn't frighten you out of your chair (see Figure IN.12). And even at that resolution, you'll need an expensive quad-speed CD-ROM drive and accelerated video card to get near the 30 frames-per-second that your VCR pumps out. What's more, a CD-ROM holds far fewer frames than a videotape, and you can't put any of your own animated video on the CD-ROM because the RO in the middle stands for Read Only. Fairly casual experimentation with computer-generated animation can fill up your 200 MB hard drive in a single afternoon's jaunt of creativity. Multi-gigabyte hard drives (a multi-kilobuck investment) are essential for serious computer video work.

FIGURE IN.11.

Current PC video is limited to low-resolution frames like this one. Individual pixels are easily visible when played back using the full screen area.

FIGURE IN.12.

To make low-resolution video look acceptable, it is often played back in a small window.

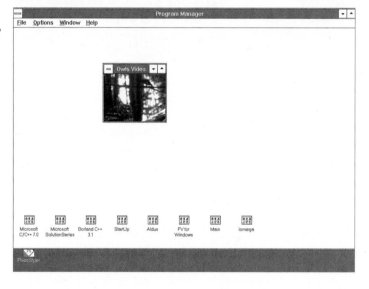

Although I wouldn't dare to predict a magical month or year when PC video will suddenly rule the desktop, hope shines bright on the near horizon. MPEG compression (named after its originators, the Motion Picture Experts Group) has become a *de facto* standard for drastically reducing the amount of space needed to store motion video, and it can significantly improve the playback speed on slower drives as well. The aging but still dominant FLIC animation file standard is slowly being upstaged by more compact and sophisticated video formats such as Microsoft's AVI and Apple's QuickTime. Best of all, gigabyte hard drives are on the verge of becoming far more affordable, thanks to advances such as IBM's new high-capacity, promised-to-be-low-cost-Real-Soon-Now 2.5-inch laptop drives.

Now that realistic digital video is almost here, what can you do with it? Lots. Photorealistic 3-D absolutely begs to be animated so that hidden surfaces can come into view (see Figure IN.13), realistic objects and characters can come to life, and computer-generated landscapes can be explored. Add the capability to bring in cinematographic footage from a video camera, and special effects from Hollywood and MTV will start appearing in your home videos.

Newtek's Video Toaster has revolutionized video production by offering superb real-time digital video effects and 3-D rendering on the Amiga. The revolution hasn't yet spread to PCs, but rumors of a PC-Toaster product are exchanged with hushed awe behind the doors of small video-production houses everywhere. Regardless of Newtek's development and marketing strategy, you can expect an explosion of video-in, video-out, and video-effects cards for PCs in the next few years. As Chapter 2, "Video for Computer Graphics," shows, dealing with video signals on a PC isn't the rocket science it's sometimes made out to be, and Chapters 5, "Advanced Image Processing," and 6, "Digital Composition," also demonstrate how easy it can be to do some snazzy image processing and compositing. As the PC market leaps the hurdles of speed and storage capacity, product developers will follow quickly to pick up the coins falling out of its pockets.

Many animation-oriented add-ons and enhancements have recently appeared for commercial image-processing software such as Adobe Photoshop and Aldus Photostyler. Many video producers and editors already use these programs to pull off spectacular image enhancements and effects like those in Figures IN.14 through IN.17.

The much-ballyhooed merger of computer and TV is still a few years away. Gimmicky attempts at combining these technologies, such as the Mac-TV, will continue to meet with a lukewarm reception in the marketplace until technology advances beyond the TV-in-a-window approach to support true digital video editing for low-end PC prices. Nevertheless, we will all soon be invited to the preordained marriage of graphics and video—we just need to wait for the bride and groom to mature a bit first.

FIGURE IN.13.

Animation sequences of multiple frames bring out the excitement of 3-D computer graphics.

FIGURE IN.14.

Today's photo-editing software lets you scan in an ordinary backyard snapshot...

FIGURE IN.15.

...add MTV-like effects like posterization, whirlpools, and 3-D transformations...

FIGURE IN.16.

...change the race and location of the subject...

FIGURE IN.17.
*…or automatically simulate
a hand-drawn artwork.*

You Are There: Interactive Visualization

Given a choice between your favorite video and your favorite video game, which one would you spend the next hour with? If you're under 20, odds are pretty good that you'll pick the game. The fact that many adults would pick the movie or TV show is an indication of how good some video production has gotten, and how bad the general quality of interactive computer simulations still is. What if your favorite TV show were an interactive, participatory experience? Only elder members of the rocking-chair crowd would rather sit back and watch the show.

In fact, the whole point of computers is interactivity. Word processors wouldn't be much good if you couldn't interactively edit the text (paper's easier to read than a computer screen!). Read-only databases are handy at times, but most businesses need interactive access and control over their data. The spreadsheet revolution of the early 1980s took database interactivity to new heights and made a billion-dollar industry out of the interactive ledger book. Figure IN.18 shows a text-based suite of interactive software.

FIGURE IN.18.

Interactive software is nothing new. Even text-based word processors, databases, and spreadsheets rely on direct user interaction for their utility.

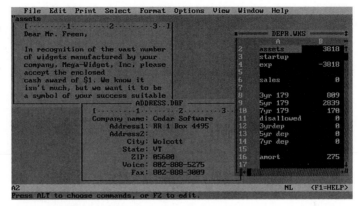

When the first interactive graphics programs (such as the legendary PC Paintbrush in Figure IN.19) appeared, they became the fourth basic category of PC software. The latest generation of painting programs for the PC adds the capability to simulate a wide variety of natural artistic media and tools (Figure IN.20), as well as the freedom to bring in and manipulate scanned photographic images (Figure IN.21). Chapter 4, "Computer Painting Techniques," highlights some artistic techniques for making the most of the power to paint on your PC.

FIGURE IN.19.

PC Paintbrush was one of the first interactive graphics programs for the PC, and remains one of the best-selling software applications of all time.

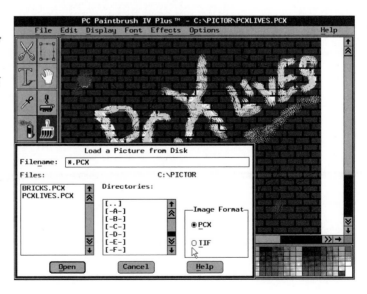

FIGURE IN.20.

Newer painting programs give you the ability to simulate natural media and work in true color.

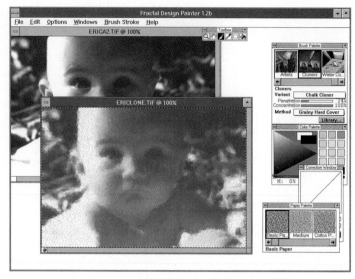

FIGURE IN.21.

Many contemporary 2-D graphics programs also enable you to manipulate scanned images of reality.

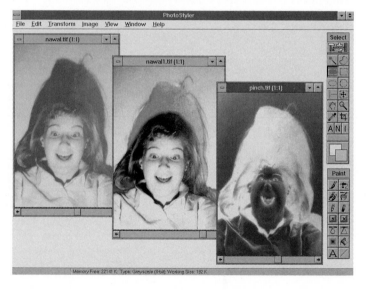

We are experiencing the infancy of a new category of software, at least as fundamental to computing in the next century as the "big four" applications of word processing, database, spreadsheets, and 2-D graphics software are today. To date, the most advanced graphics applications have had only the most limited interactivity due to the vast numbers of computations needed to process graphical data. We've suffered with a pen-and-paper level of interactive editing when working with photorealistic 3-D renderings, large true-color scanned images, or digital video. The ability to work with these data types at all has been welcomed as revolutionary, but genuine real-time interactivity will even more dramatically alter the way we work with sophisticated graphics.

One key to bringing 3-D, photorealism, and video together is the ability to acquire massive amounts of graphical data from the physical world. You'll need not only scanned images and captured video, but actual 3-D volumetric and vector descriptions of real-world objects as well. Traditionally, scientists used computer visualization as a tool for exploring information such as the topographical data depicted in Figure IN.22. Nowadays, you might see a similar data set in a computer-generated science fiction movie set (Figure IN.23). As advanced 3-D graphics charges into the mainstream, ever more complex real-world data sets are showing up everywhere from the arcade to the classroom. Data visualization has evolved from an obscure and expensive technique used by oil companies and mathematicians to an essential tool for nearly every graphics user.

FIGURE IN.22.

Visualization was once just a tool for geologists and engineers working with complex data sets.

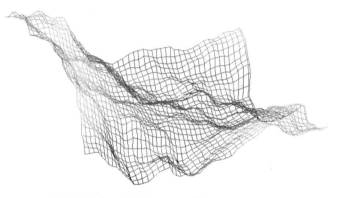

FIGURE IN.23.

Today, visualization of complex real-world data is an essential part of almost all advanced graphics.

Unfortunately, the single most in-demand data set—the human body—is also one of the most complex and difficult to acquire or model. Photorealistic, computer-generated architecture and scenes are nice, but when was the last time you watched (or wanted to watch) a feature-length video with no people in it? Surrealistic humans (see Figure IN.24) can be reconstructed from 3-D scans of the human form (see Figure IN.25), but nobody has successfully created a truly photorealistic, animated human that could actually fool you into thinking it was a familiar actor. However, an increasing number of "clip-model" companies such as Noumenon Labs (214-688-4100) and Syndesis (414-674-5200) do offer complete libraries of 3-D objects, including reasonably detailed human bodies and faces.

FIGURE IN.24.

Computer models of humans have become almost—but not quite—realistic enough to fool the public.

FIGURE IN.25.

You can now buy off-the-shelf geometric data sets for everything from faces to Ferraris.

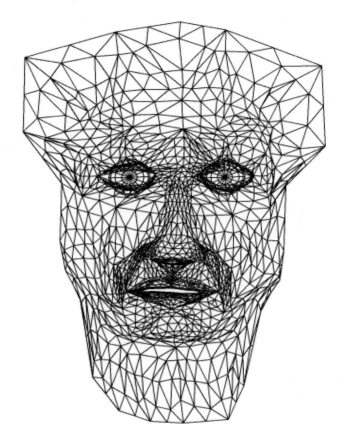

Not surprisingly, medical technology has led the way in human-body data acquisition and analysis. In Chapters 19, "Basic 3-D Data Visualization Techniques," and 20, "3-D Medical Imaging," three cutting-edge medical researchers share their know-how (and some of their data) to help you explore human-body data acquisition and rendering. They also offer a solid introduction to dealing with any type of graphical data that must be handled as an array of 3-D pixels (called *voxels*) rather than a mathematical description of lines and surfaces.

The PC Graphics of Tomorrow

The history of desktop publishing may give us a glimpse of what's in store for advanced graphics. Ten years ago, desktop publishing was possible, but PCs lacked the speed and storage to make it commonplace. Only when easy-to-use applications such as Aldus PageMaker and Ventura Publisher met a new generation of PCs with the power to run them interactively did DTP truly revolutionize the publishing industry. Now, literally millions of individuals and small companies publish their own professional-quality documents, and even traditional publishing houses increasingly rely on PC-based production to speed their time to market and streamline their efficiency.

The first truly interactive and economical 3-D graphics, image processing, digital video, and real-time visualization products are now hitting the streets. And the latest generation of accelerated local-bus video cards and high-capacity, high-speed storage devices are ready to make these applications sing. Just as the printed page is no longer "read-only" for millions of DTP-equipped publishers, the world of graphics and video are about to become accessible to everyone with a personal computer. It's an exciting time to be involved with PC graphics.

The rest of this book will give you hands-on, practical techniques for entering and exploring the new world of advanced graphics. Enjoy, and welcome to the future.

PART

Cool Stuff to Start

Computer Graphics Systems Issues

1

by William Parsons Newhall, Jr.

IN THIS CHAPTER

- Components of a Computer Graphics System
- Microprocessor Design Issues
- Bus Architecture Issues
- Operating System Issues
- Graphics Display Architecture Issues
- Computer Graphics Software Interface Standards
- Future Systems Issues: Development, Support, and Evolution

Introduction

The field of computer graphics has always been in the forefront of computer technology. Each year, the leaps and bounds made through technical innovation are matched by newer applications requiring even more power. In computer graphics applications, there can never be too much memory, and there is no such thing as a processor that is too fast. The unique demands of computer graphics applications require special consideration. Although the personal computers produced by today's corporations are extremely fast and powerful, very few of them are designed to be graphics workstations. Thanks to the open architecture of the modern PC, however, you can determine how much power you *really* need and, more importantly, where you need it most. If you are building a graphics workstation or if you are considering enhancing the capabilities of your PC for graphics applications, there are many hardware and software issues that affect your system's capabilities. Only you can build the computer that meets your needs best.

Set Practical Goals

The design of a computer graphics workstation is determined by a set of decisions that take into account how the system will be used. The plethora of options offered by the large personal computer market allows the designer to tailor the system to suit the needs of the user. This way, more money can be spent on critical components and less money can be spent on components that are necessary but not primary. The "power user" mentality that calls for the maximum amount of performance and the latest technology you can afford has a great deal of foundation in computer graphics. Not many applications are more demanding of high performance. It is far better to spend money where it is needed, rather than simply to attempt to blindly buy the best. Only careful consideration of hardware and software issues—along with a clear understanding of what you really want from the system—can successfully determine the best course for building or upgrading a computer graphics workstation.

Most graphics workstations are designed to perform all of the tasks in the computer graphics production process: texture design with 2-D paintbox applications, modeling with 3-D CAD software, rendering with ray tracing or other shading algorithms, image processing, animation composition, and playback or output to a videotape recording. The hardware and software you choose dramatically affects each of these processes (see Figures 1.1 and 1.2). If you are looking for a system to perform all the tasks of computer graphics production, ask yourself what tasks are most important to you. If you do not feel you can afford to buy the newest, high-end computer equipment, consider buying secondhand equipment or upgrading your present system. Computer systems have extremely long life spans (except for moving-part components like disk drives and printers), and secondhand equipment is usually a very good value. With a little creativity, older technology can be effectively and inexpensively employed to outperform the latest technology. You can make many simple and inexpensive changes—such as adding memory, a new operating system, or a coprocessor—that have a significant impact on the capabilities of any system in graphics applications.

FIGURE 1.1.

A low resolution image of a ray traced scene.

FIGURE 1.2.

The same image at higher resolution.

As an example, consider what you would do if you had to build a commercial computer animation system for a television station with Autodesk 3D Studio 4.0. In this situation, the most important design goal is to be able to put out finished work quickly. Within a realistic budget, you could purchase a 90 MHz Pentium system, or you could purchase an entire network of 80386 systems with coprocessors. Autodesk 3D Studio incorporated a feature in version 3.0 (and carried it over to version 4.0) that allows the task rendering to be spread across multiple machines in a network. With this distributed rendering feature, the network of 80386s will be just as effective as the Pentium (if not more so), but at less cost. Another advantage of the network is that one 80386 can be used to model another segment of animation while the rest of the network works on the rendering. In a professional market such as commercial animation, where rapid results and flexibility are required, creative solutions like this require an under-the-hood understanding of the hardware and software issues that are at stake.

Components of a Computer Graphics System

The design of computer graphics workstations has evolved considerably in the last ten years. Since the first computer graphics workstations appeared, significant improvements have been made in display technology, input devices, computer architecture, and software design and interfacing (see Figure 1.3). Some simple fundamental design issues are universal, even today:

- Software base
- Computer architecture
- Input devices
- Display architecture
- Hardware acceleration
- Output medium

FIGURE 1.3.

*Computer graphics
workstation components.*

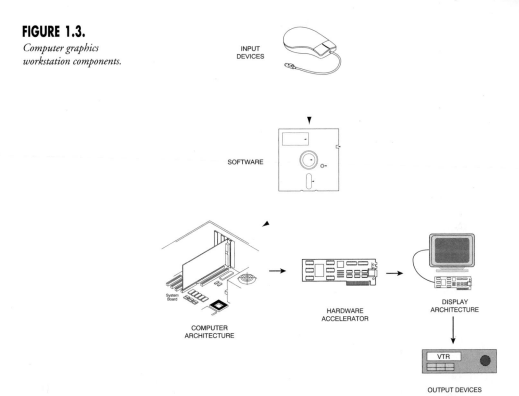

INPUT
DEVICES

SOFTWARE

COMPUTER
ARCHITECTURE

System
Board

HARDWARE
ACCELERATOR

DISPLAY
ARCHITECTURE

VTR

OUTPUT DEVICES

Software Base

Before considering any aspects of computer graphics workstation hardware, think about what software you will want to run on the system. Have any applications been selected already? Will you be developing your own graphics software? The answers to these questions are helpful in determining which operating systems and user interfaces will be employed and which computer architectures are most viable. If specific applications will definitely be employed, the best results can be obtained if the system is built *around* the application. Software corporations can be extremely helpful in providing information about their products; they can even tell you what hardware works best with their software.

If a software application is not available for a certain hardware platform or operating system, it may be possible to port the application. For example, a number of applications have been developed—specifically for the Silicon Graphics Iris and Indigo systems—that make extensive use of SGI's OpenGL graphics library. Microsoft and IBM have announced that in the next releases of the Windows NT and OS/2 operating systems, OpenGL will be supported. Many public domain applications (the Radiance radiosity system, for example) will be extremely easy to port, and many SGI developers may port their software to Windows NT. In the computer industry, one should take promises and predictions (also called "vaporware") with a grain or a bag of salt, but keep an ear firmly planted to the ground anyway.

Computer Architecture

At the heart of any computer system there are three elemental parts: the microprocessor, the memory, and input/output devices. Connecting these elements is a set of busses (see Figure 1.4). Information (called *data*) enters the system through input components such as the keyboard, mouse, network interface, or disk drive. The microprocessor can perform operations on the data, retain it in memory, or send it to an output device such as the screen, disk drive, network interface, or printer. The flow of information and the actions of the microprocessor are dictated by a program that contains a sequence of instructions for the microprocessor to follow. Programs are loaded into and out of memory through an operating system that manages the interaction between programs and input/output devices. The user interacts with the operating system through a shell or user interface. An understanding of how these components interact can help you make intelligent decisions in how you build your system.

FIGURE 1.4.

Basic computer architecture.

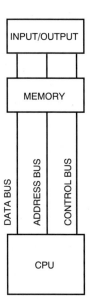

Personal computers are built around a motherboard upon which the microprocessor, memory, and busses reside. Expansion slots that cross the busses like railroad ties enable the user to add peripheral expansion cards, such as graphics adapters, disk controllers, network interfaces, and dozens of other devices, to the system. There are many kinds of motherboards supporting different types of microprocessors and expansion architectures. With careful selection of components, a powerful graphics workstation can be built around an Intel 32-bit processor (such as an 80386, 80486, or Pentium) or one of the clone chips from companies such as Cyrix or AMD.

Input Devices

In any classic text on computer graphics, input devices are explained as devices employed by the user to obtain graphics data. Typical input devices are keyboards, mice, digitizer tablets, frame grabbers, image scanners, and spaceballs. Another input device that bears consideration is a CD-ROM drive: a wide variety of computer graphics clip art, object and scene data, surface texture maps, and other valuable graphics materials can be obtained on compact disc. As of late, a considerable amount of graphics data can also be obtained through computer bulletin board systems and Internet FTP sites, and a network interface card or modem should be considered just as seriously as a mouse or digitizer as a means of obtaining graphics data.

A *keyboard* is used for basic user input and precise numeric data.

A *mouse* allows a simple and intuitive interface for manipulating graphical objects and rapid navigation within the graphical user interface.

A *digitizer tablet* with a stylus or puck offers a more accurate and intuitive drawing interface than does a mouse, but is more expensive.

A *frame grabber* enables the user to record video digitally in real time by converting the composite NTSC information into monochrome or color digital graphics data.

An *image scanner* can convert printed pages, photographs, and illustrations into color or monochrome digital graphics data.

A *spaceball* is like a mouse, but a spaceball works in three dimensions instead of only two.

Display Architecture

The first computer graphics display systems were vector systems that displayed images by sweeping an electron beam across the phosphor screen according to an ordered list of lines and geometric primitives. Vector systems were costly, did not handle color very well, and caused visible flicker when a large number of lines needed to be drawn. Vector systems do draw lines, circles, and curves very precisely, however, without suffering from many artifacts (such as jagged edges and intensity variations) present in modern raster display systems.

All modern computer graphics systems display images on raster screens with electron beams or liquid crystal displays. *Raster displays* represent images with small colored dots called picture elements, or *pixels*. Typically, a raster display has a rectangular array of pixels of a defined resolution that determines how fine the dots are. Typical resolutions for modern display screens range from 320×200 pixels to 1600×1024 pixels. The *refresh rate* of the display screen represents how many times per second the image is updated. The human eye has a persistence of vision that temporally blurs rapidly changing still images into continuous fluid animation. Thus, screens with high refresh rates (72 Hz and higher) tend to produce "crisp" and "flicker-free" imagery.

The image displayed on the screen is determined by the signal generated by the graphics display hardware. The signal represents the image one pixel at a time in an ordered sequence: left to right, top to bottom. In some cases, the image is displayed by *interlacing*— or sending the odd horizontal scanlines lines first, followed by the even horizontal scanlines. Interlacing cuts the required transmission bandwidth down significantly (bringing higher resolutions at lower prices), but it has been proven to cause headaches. Whenever possible, noninterlaced modes with high refresh rates should be used.

The color of each pixel is represented by three analog voltages representing the red, green, and blue intensity. A white pixel will have high voltages in each color band, representing the presence of all colors. A black pixel will have no voltages in any of the three wires. Shades of gray will have all three channels at the same voltage, and colors are represented by varying proportions between the three voltages. Older graphics systems used digital signals, which have defined limitation built into the architecture. For example, a system that has two bits of red, two bits of green, and two bits of blue can display only 2^6 shades of color (sixty-four colors), whereas an analog signal theoretically can have an infinite number of shades because it is not limited to a defined wordlength.

To generate an analog signal to drive the screen, the graphics adapter hardware has a digital-to-analog converter (DAC) (see Figure 1.5). The DAC has a defined wordlength and the inherent limitations that come with one. Most SuperVGA systems come with DACs with wordlengths of at least eight bits per pixel. Eight bits per pixel enables the user to display 256 colors on the screen simultaneously. Highcolor systems have 15-bit and 16-bit wordlengths to support 32,768 and 65,536 colors respectively. Truecolor systems have 24-bit DACs that can produce 16,777,216 shades of color, which exceeds the visual acuity of the human eye.

Before the image can be displayed on the monitor, it must be composed within the computer. The graphics display hardware has a block of memory called the *frame buffer* where the image is stored before it is transmitted. Typically, graphics adapters have between 64K and 8 MB of RAM set aside for the frame buffer. Larger frame buffers allow for higher resolutions. A typical SuperVGA mode of 1024×768 in 256 colors requires a DAC with a minimum of eight bits per pixel and a frame buffer of at least 786,432 bytes (1024×768×1 byte per pixel = 786,432 bytes). A not-so-typical SuperVGA mode of 1024×768 in 16,777,216 colors requires a 24-bit DAC and a frame buffer of at least 2,359,296 bytes.

FIGURE 1.5.
*Signal flow of a
SuperVGA system.*

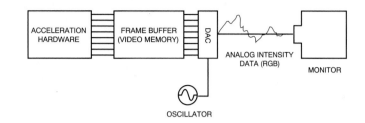

Hardware Acceleration

Whenever a line is drawn, a polygon is filled, or a frame of animation is displayed, the contents of the frame buffer must be updated with the new graphics data one pixel at a time. Images involving many lines or polygons can consume a great deal of processing time and cause a serious bottleneck when other tasks need processing. Many of the UNIX workstations developed in the early 1980s included special display processors that were connected to I/O ports and accepted symbolic instructions for drawing graphics primitives such as lines, circles, and polygons. Thus, menial tasks like line drawing and polygon filling could be performed by the graphics display processor while the central processing unit went about its business. Three-dimensional workstations from companies such as Silicon Graphics and Sun began incorporating object transformations and also surface-shading algorithms as well.

In the late 1980s, the proliferation of Microsoft Windows with its scalable fonts, icons, and device-independent graphics interface wrought graphics bottlenecks in the personal computer market ("I hate that #%@* hourglass!"), and SuperVGA adapter cards from companies such as ATI, S3, Orchid, and Weitek came with graphics display processors on the card and special windows drivers for accessing them. In recent years, PC graphics adapters from Matrox and Silicon Graphics have incorporated three-dimensional support and surface-shading as well.

One of the primary advantages of hardware-accelerated graphics is that the interface between the graphics display processor and the frame buffer can be wider than the system's data bus, allowing rapid transfers of data. At the time of this writing, graphics adapters from Media Vision, ATI, and Matrox have 64-bit busses between the graphics display processors and frame buffers, while the bus architectures of PCI 1.0 and VESA 1.0 can only transfer data 32 bits at a time. Thus, not only is the processor freed of the menial task of copying pixel data, but the display processor can copy twice as much data per instruction.

> **NOTE**
>
> As of this writing, the future of Media Vision is not clear. In late 1994, Media Vision filed for Chapter Eleven and was placed under federal investigation for altering financial statements. Most of the PC industry and Wall Street have taken a "wait and see" attitude towards the company.

Output Medium

Some consideration must be made as to what medium will be used for the finished product and how the product will be obtained. A wide variety of output mediums are available: film, videotape, and even digital animation recorders. Brute-force methods, like photographing a screen with a 35mm camera or recording animation with a non-frame-accurate VCR in real time, can produce workable results with some minor side effects. For example, Autodesk 3D Studio 4.0 and Topas can produce 256-color animation files ("flics") that can be played back in real time through an RGB to NTSC encoder and recorded on a VHS videotape recorder. Unfortunately, the frame rate at playback can be unstable (depending on the speed of the system) and the color depth is limited to 256 colors. There are other "flic" encoders that can work with 16-bit hicolor images, but the results do not match the results obtained by recording the animation one frame at a time on a frame-accurate videotape recorder. If you are just getting started or do not foresee creating enough work to warrant expensive equipment purchases, you can try service bureaus that support multiple mediums and formats with very rapid turnaround.

What must be considered in building your graphics workstation is the means of transmitting or transporting your images to your output media, whether it is a frame-accurate video recorder or a service bureau. Many graphics adapters feature (or have as an option) RGB to NTSC conversion, and advanced graphics architectures such as MGA (Matrox Graphics Architecture) can lock up with and control single-frame videotape recorders not only for recording animation but also for character generation, chroma-key, and other basic video effects.

Microprocessor Design Issues

The basic architecture of any computer system has as its three primary components the central processing unit (CPU), the memory, and input/output devices. We have already seen that in a computer graphics workstation there is a plethora of input and output devices, and the amount of information required to represent simple graphics images requires a considerable amount of memory as well.

The microprocessor is able to direct the flow of data between input devices, memory, and output devices because every byte of memory has a unique memory address, and every input/output device has at least one input/output port number. The microprocessor interfaces three main busses to transfer information and to access input/output and memory devices. The data bus carries any information being transferred, and the address bus represents where the data is coming from or going to. The control bus contains a number of wires or "lines" for regulating or indicating what kind of information transaction is going on. The most important of the control lines is the system clock, which oscillates at a set frequency like a pulse to keep the entire system in sync. Because the components are located at different positions throughout the system and the flow of electrons has a finite speed (although this speed is 186,000 MPH—the speed of light), it important for all the components to work cooperatively. If one or more fell out of sync, data could be lost or misdirected, causing the system to crash.

Inside the microprocessor is a set of registers (see Figure 1.6). There are several kinds of registers that have different purposes. Connected to the address bus is a memory address register that holds the memory address or port number where a piece of data or an instruction will be read or written. Connected to the data bus is the memory data register that holds the piece of data or instruction that was just read or is about to be written to memory. System registers keep track of information vital to the operation of the microprocessor. For example, the program counter register points to the memory address of the current instruction being processed. The instruction register contains the actual instruction being processed, and the flags register indicates the status of the microprocessor and the results of the last instruction operation. General registers are used as "scratch pads" for temporary storage of data during transfer, arithmetic, or comparison operations.

Most of the parameters that define a microcomputer system are dependent upon the design of the microprocessor. The size of the memory data register determines the size of the data bus, which determines the maximum amount of information that can be transferred to or from the microprocessor in one clock cycle. The size of the memory address register determines the size of the address bus, which determines the maximum amount of memory that can be directly addressed within a system. The 80386 DX and 80486 DX microprocessors support a 32-bit data bus and a 32-bit address bus, which means that these processors can transfer four bytes at a time and can directly address up to 2^{32} (4,294,967,296) bytes of memory. The Pentium microprocessor has a 64-bit data bus and a 32-bit address bus, which means it can transfer eight bytes at a time and can address memory segments up to 2^{32} (4,294,967,296) bytes in length. The 80386 SX and 80486 SX microprocessors have only a 16-bit data bus, and as such, they can only transfer two bytes at a time. (The 80486 SX also comes without a floating point unit, which makes it not a very practical choice for computer graphics systems.)

FIGURE 1.6.
Microprocessor/bus interfacing.

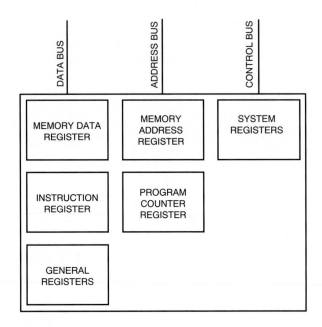

Real and Protected Modes

When an 80386, 80486, or Pentium system is first turned on, the microprocessor is not running at its fullest potential. All three microprocessors power up in "real mode," which disables a majority of the key features of these processors so that they can emulate the operating parameters of the 16-bit 8086 microprocessor. In real mode, the larger register set of the 32-bit processors is still supported, but memory addressing is restricted to the antiquated addressing system of the 8086 for compatibility reasons. The 8086 addressing system makes use of 16-bit segment registers and 16-bit offset registers, which divide the one megabyte of directly addressable RAM into 64K overlapping segments placed at 16-byte segment boundaries. Large arrays, which appear *very often* in computer graphics applications, are extremely clunky and difficult to handle in real mode.

The 80386, 80486, and Pentium processors also have a 32-bit "protected mode" that supports variable length segments that can be up to four gigabytes (4,294,967,296 bytes) in length, privilege protection, hardware multitasking, memory paging, and virtual memory. Privilege protection allows segments to have "restricted access," where each segment is defined with a "privilege level" that determines whether the segment can be read, written to, or executed. Hardware multitasking allows multiple programs (or even operating systems) to be executing independently and simultaneously on the same machine. Memory paging allows memory access to be redirected, and virtual memory makes use of paging to swap unused blocks of memory out to the disk to give the illusion of having more memory than is physically present.

Microprocessor Operation Issues

The operation of the microprocessor is controlled by a set of routines built into the system's microcode. Each instruction is handled as a set of operations that occur both inside and outside of the microprocessor. When a program is run by the computer, the microprocessor reads an instruction from the code in memory and handles the instruction with the operations specified within its microcode. For example, to add two integers and store the result in memory, the microprocessor must perform the following steps:

1. Fetch an instruction opcode from memory (the "copy the first number variable into the AX register" instruction).

   1a. Place the address of the program counter on the address bus via the memory address register.

   1b. Set the control bus to "read from memory" (MEMR).

   1c. Increment the program counter to point to the next instruction or operand.

   1d. Copy the contents of the memory data register into the instruction register.

2. Fetch the instruction operand (the contents of the first number variable) from memory.

   2a. Place the contents of the program counter on the address bus via the memory address register.

   2b. Set the control bus to "read from memory" (MEMR) to obtain the address of the first number variable.

   2c. Increment the program counter to point to the operand.

   2d. Copy the operand from the memory data register into the memory address register.

   2e. Set the control bus to "read from memory" (MEMR) to copy the contents of the first number variable into the memory data register.

   2f. Execute the microcode to copy the contents of the memory data register into the AX register.

3. Fetch an instruction opcode from memory (the "copy the second number variable into the BX register" instruction).

   3a. Place the address of the program counter on the address bus via the memory address register.

   3b. Set the control bus to "read from memory" (MEMR).

   3c. Increment the program counter to point to the next instruction or operand.

   3d. Copy the contents of the memory data register into the instruction register.

4. Fetch the instruction operand (the contents of the second number variable) from memory.

   4a. Place the contents of the program counter on the address bus via the memory address register.

   4b. Set the control bus to "read from memory" (MEMR) to obtain the address of the second number variable.

   4c. Increment the program counter to point to the operand.

   4d. Copy the operand from the memory data register into the memory address register.

   4e. Set the control bus to "read from memory" (MEMR) to copy the contents of the second number variable into the memory data register.

   4f. Execute the microcode to copy the contents of the memory data register into the BX register.

5. Fetch an instruction opcode from memory ("Add the AX and BX registers together and store the result in the BX register").

   5a. Place the address of the program counter on the address bus via the memory address register.

   5b. Set the control bus to "read from memory" (MEMR).

   5c. Increment the program counter to point to the next instruction or operand.

   5d. Copy the contents of the memory data register into the instruction register.

6. Execute the microcode for adding the contents of the AX register into the BX register.

   6a. Copy the contents of the AX register "A" into the accumulator register.

   6b. Add the contents of the BX register into the accumulator register.

   6c. Copy the contents of the accumulator into the BX register.

7. Fetch the next instruction from memory ("Copy the contents of the BX register to the variable in memory that is to hold the answer").

   7a. Place the address of the program counter on the address bus via the memory address register.

   7b. Set the control bus to "read from memory" (MEMR).

   7c. Copy the contents of the memory data register into the instruction register.

   7d. Increment the program counter to point to the next instruction or operand.

8. Fetch the operand from memory (get the address of where the result will be stored).

   8a. Place the address of the program counter on the address bus via the memory address register.

8b. Set the control bus to "read from memory" (MEMR).

8c. Increment the program counter to point to the next instruction or operand.

9. Execute the microcode for storing the contents of a register to a memory address.

   9a. Copy the target address from the memory data register into the memory address register.

   9b. Copy the contents of the BX register (the result of the addition) into the memory data register.

   9c. Set the control bus to "write to memory" (MEMW).

   9d. Increment the program counter to point to the next instruction.

10. Fetch the next instruction from memory.

   10a. Place the address of the program counter on the address bus via the memory address register.

   10b. Set the control bus to "read from memory"(MEMR).

   10c. Increment the program counter to point to the next instruction or operand.

Here is the equivalent assembly code for the preceding set of operations:

```
MOV   AX, FirstNumber    ;copy the first number into the AX register
MOV   BX, SecondNumber   ;copy the second number into the BX register
ADD   BX, AX             ;BX=BX+AX
MOV   Sum, BX            ;store the result in the Sum variable
```

Here is the equivalent C source code for the preceding set of operations:

```
Sum=SecondNumber+FirstNumber;
```

You can easily see that more complicated operations, such as rapidly playing back frames of animation and drawing three-dimensional shaded polygons, are very complex operations at the machine level. Machine operations could be made more efficient is many ways, either by reducing the number of instructions required to complete a task or by reducing the number of clock cycles required by each instruction. The evolution of microprocessor technology has been towards the goal of maximum performance. Many microprocessor design parameters have been developed to increase performance.

Clock Speed

The clock speed of a microprocessor determines how many clock cycles occur per second. Clock speed is largely determined by the tolerance of the microcomponents to the buildup of heat caused by the rapid changes in electrical current. The microprocessors of today are extremely stable, and recent microprocessor designs use a logic level of +3.3 volts instead of 5.0 volts, producing less heat and having higher clock speeds. When the IBM PC debuted in 1981, it ran with an Intel 8088 processor at 4.77 MHz and was considered fast for its time (most microcomputers in 1981 ran at speeds below 1 MHz). Recently developed Pentium systems can run at clock speeds of 90 MHz, and Intel claims that even faster clock speeds will be available in December 1994.

Register Count

In any computer application, a number of variables will need to be frequently used. Programs that are efficiently coded or compiled will try to keep as many of the frequently used variables stored in general registers inside the microprocessor. This way, data does not have to be fetched from memory as often, and a great many unnecessary clock cycles are eliminated. The C programming language allows variables to be specified with the REGISTER type identifier. For example,

```
register int index;
```

will automatically place the contents of the variable index into a free register. The larger and more generalized a register set is, the easier it is for a compiler to generate efficient code.

Bus/Register Wordlength

There are many applications in computer graphics where large blocks of contiguous data are moved from memory to memory, memory to I/O, and vice versa. If you consider the data bus to be a pipe through which the information is pumped, it makes sense that more information can be transmitted in less time if you "get a bigger pipe." An 8-bit data bus allows one byte of data to be moved by each data transfer instruction. A 32-bit data bus allows four bytes of data to be moved by each data transfer instruction. To accommodate the data bus wordlength, the microprocessor must have at least one register of equal wordlength. Consider also that it is inefficient to have an expansion bus that can transmit only sixteen bits of data at a time, when the microprocessor it interfaces can support 32 or even 64 bits of data.

Instruction Complexity

One way to cut down on the number of instructions required to perform a task is to have a microprocessor with sophisticated instructions that can rapidly combine the tasks which were once accomplished with multiple instructions. For example, there was a time in the ancient era of 8-bit microprocessors when there were no instructions for performing integer multiplication. Instead, multiplication was accomplished through repeated addition. By cutting down on the number of instruction fetches and incorporating a large number of sophisticated addressing modes (that is, "multiply this number by this register," "multiply this register by the number at this address," "multiply the number in this register by the number in this other register," and so on), the multiply instruction is easier to code and requires "fewer" instructions to accomplish the same task.

In computer graphics, a considerable amount of arithmetic involves floating point or "real" numbers, which are difficult to represent and even more difficult to process in software. Math coprocessors that implement floating point procedures and automate the process of representing and converting floating point values with their own instruction set appeared in the late 1970s and were standardized under the IEEE-754 guidelines. Intel designed the 80387 coprocessor around the IEEE-754 guidelines and began incorporating floating point instructions into the instruction sets of their main processors, starting with the 80486 DX. When you consider that a simple floating point multiplication requires approximately forty regular instructions and can be accomplished with only one floating point instruction, it is almost pointless to compare (in any application like computer graphics) the performance of systems lacking floating point support with those that have it.

The Intel Pentium microprocessor has perhaps the most complex instruction set of any microprocessor on the planet. Complex instruction set computers are often referred to as CISC machines, and much research has gone into the effects of large instruction sets on performance. On a CISC machine, an instruction can take 1 to 20 clock cycles to complete execution, and there are issues of cost and efficiency. Many interesting questions and anecdotes have come out on the issue of complex instruction sets: "Do I really need to have an instruction that calculates the cube root of an integer? Why don't they have an instruction that makes coffee for me while they're at it? Do I want to pay for instructions that I will never use?"

An alternative called RISC, or "reduced instruction set computing," architecture was developed in hopes of producing powerful, efficient microprocessors. RISC architecture was designed to take advantage of the latest innovations in microprocessor manufacturing and design techniques and works within very tight constraints. A typical RISC processor (such as the MIPS R4400 or the Motorola PowerPC) has less than 100 instructions and a small number of addressing modes.

In reducing the number of instructions, RISC architecture frees up a considerable amount of "chip real estate" for optimizations and enhancements such as instruction pipelining, branch prediction, and out-of-order instruction execution. Pipelining allows multiple operations (instruction decoding, microcode execution, arithmetic and logic) to be performed simultaneously instead of sequentially. Branch prediction looks ahead at the instruction queue and starts preparing for conditional jumps and calls before the condition is evaluated. Lastly, out-of-order instruction execution prevents slower instructions from causing bottlenecks for faster instructions. Thanks to these enhancements, processors designed with RISC enhancements can execute a majority of their instructions within one clock cycle.

Although the Intel Pentium has about 158 instructions and dozens of addressing modes, it has co-opted many RISC enhancements without losing its backward compatibility. Both the Intel Pentium and the NexGen NX586 (a RISC processor that emulates the Pentium at equivalent speed) are superscalar designs (incorporating more than one pipeline), offering a majority of the advantages of RISC systems. The Intel processor is designed with compatibility as the primary issue because most of its user base has already invested in "shrink wrapped" (pre-compiled) software for older 80x86 processors. RISC processors were developed for engineering and graphics workstations running custom-compiled applications under UNIX. Because the Pentium offers compatibility with many RISC enhancements, the modern desktop PC can compete with the specialized designs of RISC systems without sacrificing 80x86 compatibility.

Clock Multiplying

Many of the operations performed by a microprocessor while executing an instruction are performed entirely internally, without involving the bus, memory, or input/output devices. Significant performance gains can be made if two or three internal operations are performed for every one system clock pulse. Intel has designed special 80486 DX2 processors that internally clock at 50 MHz or 66 MHz but interface with a system clock running at 25 MHz or 33 MHz respectively. The Intel Overdrive chip is an inexpensive upgrade that brings clock doubling to standard 25 MHz or 33 MHz motherboards. Recently, IBM and Intel released 80486 processors (dubbed "Blue Lightning" and "80486 DX4") that internally clock at 100 MHz but interface to a 25 MHz system clock. Clock multiplying is a cost-effective enhancement because none of the memory, input/output devices, or system components must be replaced.

Internal Cache

In any microcomputer system, a large number of clock cycles are spent fetching code or data from memory. Because the memory is external to the microprocessor, this time cannot effectively make use of clock multiplying; instead, the microprocessor must idly wait until the next system clock cycle. An internal cache is a small amount of extremely fast memory (usually 8 KB) built into the microprocessor (see Figure 1.7). As the microprocessor executes a program, the cache memory is filled with a carbon copy of the code and data. Whenever a memory fetch occurs, the index of the internal cache is checked to see whether the information sought by the microprocessor is available immediately without bus access. Caching program code gives significant performance gains because most machine language programs "drop through" long segments of sequential instructions and don't usually jump beyond a range of 128 bytes. Caching data reaps some gains when data is sequential, such as in large arrays, but dynamic linked-list data structures (used a majority of the time) scatter data, which makes it difficult for data caching to be efficient at all.

FIGURE 1.7.

Cache design.

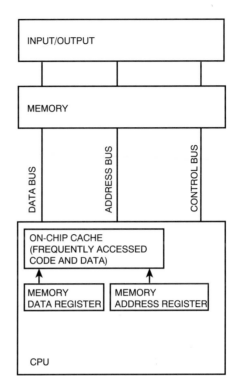

Bus Architecture Issues

It should be apparent that the performance and capabilities of a computer graphics workstation are directly affected by how much information can be carried between the microprocessor, memory, and input/output components and how fast the information can be transferred. Through larger register sets and cache memory, this can be affected by good microprocessor design, but the real difference is made in the design architecture of the bus that carries the information. Until recently, the bus architecture of personal computers was a real bottleneck, and even today it is possible (if you don't know what you're doing) to purchase systems with 32-bit or 64-bit processors running as fast as 100 MHz interfaced to 16-bit system busses that run as slow as 8 MHz. For many components—such as modems, mice, printers, and digitizers—that do not require much bandwidth to begin with, 8 MHz and 16 bits are good enough, but for other components—graphics adapters, frame grabbers, and hard disk controllers—this just will not do. As of this writing, no less than five different bus architectures are available. It is even possible to obtain motherboards that incorporate four of them on the same motherboard.

The Industry Standard Architecture (ISA)

Originally designed by IBM for the PC/AT, the ISA architecture has a 24-bit address bus and a 16-bit data bus. It was designed to run synchronously (in lock step with) an 8 MHz 80286. This architecture was built on top of the expansion architecture of the original IBM PC and is the most commonly employed system architecture in the world. IBM published the specifications of its PC/AT architecture in hopes that a large number of third-party expansion boards would become available. The ancient Chinese curse "May you get everything you want and more" has never had a better example. Within a few very short years, a billion dollar industry emerged to compete directly with IBM, offering more powerful systems at lower cost. In an effort to circle its wagons, IBM redesigned its Personal Computer and came up with the Microchannel architecture. The clone industry rallied around the status quo architecture and renamed it the Industry Standard Architecture (ISA), throwing 25 MHz and 33 MHz 80386 and 80486 processors onto the 8 MHz asynchronous bus.

The Microchannel Architecture (MCA)

The Microchannel architecture represented a significant leap forward in technology. It was designed around the 80386, had wider data and address busses, and supported powerful bus mastering capabilities. Microchannel never really took off because IBM was very strict in its licensing practices, not wanting to get burned again. A few companies built MCA systems and network servers, but very few MCA peripherals have been produced, and as a result, the cost of microchannel peripherals is slightly more than that of other architectures.

The Extended Industry Standard Architecture (EISA)

Developed shortly after Microchannel, EISA was designed to incorporate many of the advances offered by Microchannel but at a lower cost. EISA has a 32-bit data bus, a 32-bit address bus, and four different kinds of bus mastering. EISA is also backward compatible with ISA. EISA was the preferred architecture for network servers and CAD stations in the late 1980s, and it is still available today; however, its base has been eroded by the proliferation of VESA and PCI architectures, which offer more speed at less cost.

The VESA Local Bus Architecture

The proliferation of Microsoft Windows in the late 1980s brought out a need for a new bus architecture. Many people bought top-of-the-line 80386 and 80486 systems that ran at fast clock speeds but were not yielding a fast enough performance in Windows. The problem was that a large amount of processing time was being spent pushing graphics data through an 8 MHz bus that was only 16 bits wide. A number of clever clone manufacturers built motherboards that integrated graphics display architecture connected to the processor via the 32-bit 33 MHz synchronous local bus which interfaced the system memory. The Video Electronics Standards Association (VESA) gathered together and drafted an expansion architecture specification that could be built on top of the ISA architecture with an additional connector. The VESA architecture quickly gained momentum and became the expansion architecture of choice.

The Peripheral Component Interconnect Architecture (PCI)

In designing its Pentium processor, Intel designed a new bus architecture with many auspicious aims. The VESA local bus architecture has many advantages but also has many disadvantages. It offers good support for graphics applications, but because it is synchronous, it actually slows down the operation of the microprocessor when it is interfaced to slower input/output devices. The VESA architecture is also tied into the 80x86 architecture, and Intel wanted an architecture that could be employed by a variety of microprocessors. The resulting PCI architecture is an asynchronous mezzanine bus architecture that does not directly connect to the microprocessor, but instead interfaces to bridge circuitry that sits between the processor and the bus. PCI is also designed to be a glueless architecture—adapter boards configure themselves, avoiding address conflicts and other nightmares.

PCI has proliferated significantly. Apple has avowed that it will be producing PCI-based PowerMacs in the near future. Digital Equipment Corporation has produced a number of UNIX workstations with Alpha processors, and a number of companies have announced systems that can interface with a variety of microprocessors. The original design, PCI 1.0, has a 32-bit data bus and runs asynchronously at 33 MHz. The latest design, PCI 2.0, has a 64-bit data bus. Because the PCI architecture has been brought to the market only recently, motherboards and expansion adapters built around it are still more expensive than their VESA counterparts.

Operating System Issues

The performance of a computer graphics workstation is only partially dependent upon its hardware. No matter how fast a processor is or how much memory a system has, it will not perform at its maximum capacity if the software does not take full advantage of the hardware. Because the operating system serves as the interface between the software and the hardware, the choice of operating system should be taken just as seriously as the choice of hardware. In selecting your operating system, you choose not only how much of your hardware you are taking advantage of, but also what software applications you will be able to run.

Microsoft MS-DOS/Windows 3.1

Microsoft's MS-DOS is the most popular operating system in the world. A wide variety of software is available, including some very powerful graphics applications. MS-DOS does not take advantage of the Intel 32-bit protected mode, but a number of compilers (such as Watcom, DJGPP, and others) have DOS Extenders that allow 32-bit applications to be coded and run from MS-DOS. MS-DOS can be interfaced with Microsoft Windows to support a standardized graphical user interface (GUI) and multitasking; this choice does not, however, offer the maximum efficiency because the operating system calls are made through MS-DOS. Windows is a fair GUI, and a number of powerful graphics applications have been written for it, such as TrueSpace and Microstation. MS-DOS with Windows is easy on the wallet as well. It is usually bundled with systems (and is inexpensive to buy) and does not require as much memory or disk space, although Windows does chew through memory very quickly and runs best with a minimum of eight megabytes.

Microsoft soon will be releasing Windows 95, which will bridge the gap between Windows NT and Windows 3.1. Windows 95 (given the working title "Chicago") will be a 32-bit protected mode stand-alone operating system, with support for Windows 3.1 and MS-DOS applications.

The future of MS-DOS as a computer graphics operating system is not very clear. MS-DOS has been able to survive because of numerous add-ons, such as expanded memory (XMS), DOS Extenders, the DOS Protected Mode Interface (DPMI), and operating environments like Windows 3.1. With the release of Windows 95, MS-DOS will have effectively been sold down the river. Computer graphics software companies like Autodesk appear to be hedging on what operating systems they will be supporting.

IBM OS/2

IBM's OS/2 is a true 32-bit operating system that is inexpensive and powerful. OS/2 can run Microsoft MS-DOS applications and is compatible with Windows. Not as many applications are available for OS/2 as for Microsoft Windows, and there are not many computer graphics applications compiled for OS/2. IBM has announced that it is porting Silicon Graphics Inc.'s OpenGL graphics library to OS/2, which may make OS/2 a serious contender as an inexpensive operating system for computer graphics. OS/2 is not as demanding of system resources as Windows NT, but OS/2 is the most seasoned 32-bit operating system available for the 80x86 family.

Microsoft Windows NT

Unlike Microsoft Windows 3.1 and its other predecessors, Windows NT is a true 32-bit operating system independent of MS-DOS. Windows NT is considerably more expensive and requires more resources. Windows NT requires 16 megabytes of RAM and 50 megabytes of disk space just to get up and running. Like the PCI bus architecture, Windows NT is designed to work with multiple platforms and has been ported to a number of RISC systems already. Windows NT was originally received as a powerful operating system good for network server applications, but impractical for desktop computer users. There has been considerable talk in the computer graphics community that Microsoft will soon be porting Silicon Graphics Inc.'s OpenGL graphics library to Windows NT. Microsoft also recently acquired SoftImage, a corporation that produced 3-D graphics software for high-end UNIX workstations. It is not certain whether Windows 95 will have equivalent graphics support or whether it will be available as an option.

Linux

One of the best-kept secrets in the computer industry and the graphics community is Linux. Linux is a *free* 32-bit port of the UNIX operating system for 80386, 80486, and Pentium systems. Linux includes the X Window graphical user interface and has demonstrated considerable prowess in the domain of computer graphics. Linux is somewhat miraculous because it was written by hundreds of programmers around the world in their free time. It is extremely stable, and it has received rave reviews in the computer graphics community because many computer graphics applications that were considered out of reach for the desktop (such as Greg Ward's Radiance radiosity system) are now within reach, and DOS applications (such as the Persistence of Vision ray tracer) run up to 25 percent faster under Linux.

Linux is available for downloading from several bulletin board systems around the country and is available via anonymous FTP on the Internet as well. Linux can be purchased on CD-ROM in several configurations, with a variety of applications precompiled. On CD-ROM, Linux costs about $15–25 and requires resources of 386SX and 2 MB or better. Linux is still very young. It has been developed through the last four years and has only been used in practice for the last year. One of the strengths of Linux is that it is continually being improved and enhanced. At present, two very impressive public-domain emulators for Linux are in development: WINE is a windows emulator, and DOSEMU is a DOS emulator. Beta versions of both can be downloaded from the Internet.

In choosing an operating system, you should consider what kind of software you plan to run, how much of your hardware is being used to its fullest potential, and how much headroom you will have to run your software after the operating system has been loaded. If you plan to run only commercial DOS and Windows applications that you already own or will soon be purchasing, you may want to stick with DOS and Windows. OS/2 appears to be the best value in commercial operating systems at the present, because it is inexpensive and it does not require much in system resources. Windows NT is extremely costly in terms of resources, but considering recent actions by Microsoft, it may become the new operating system for computer graphics. If you plan to write your own applications or to compile public domain programs such as Persistence of Vision, Radiance, and

YART, you will probably get the best performance out of Linux; and you can't beat its price. Linux, OS/2, and Windows NT all feature "multiboot" utilities that enable the user to select from multiple operating systems at powerup, so you can easily work with more than one operating system, if you have the patience and the disk space.

Graphics Display Architecture Issues

When the IBM PC was originally designed in 1981, the expectations for the personal computer did not call for much investment in high-resolution color graphics technology. Until the Apple Macintosh and Commodore Amiga came on the scene in 1984, the only significant personal computer graphics market was computer-aided drafting, and at the time, the 16-color Enhanced Graphics Adapter (EGA) was adequate. The Macintosh and Amiga brought about the desktop publishing and desktop video revolutions, and IBM responded by developing the MCGA, VGA, 8514, and most recently the XGA graphics architectures. These architectures support higher resolutions and more color. Microsoft Windows provided a device-independent graphics interface that supported all of IBM's graphics architectures (except monochrome, of course) and allowed equipment manufacturers to develop their own drivers. A number of third-party hardware developers began offering "super" VGA adapters with proprietary expanded modes with higher resolutions and even more color.

The Video Electronics Standards Association (VESA), which consisted of the third-party hardware developers, came up with a set of standard modes, a methodology for defining proprietary modes, and a uniform interface for programming graphics through software interrupt 10h. Each manufacturer wrote interrupt handling routines for their graphics cards and either burned them into on-board ROM or included a DOS Terminate-Stay-Resident program that loaded them into memory. The VESA interface provides a simple way for programmers to develop applications that can be run on almost any SuperVGA graphics adapter. The VESA SuperVGA graphics architecture has gained nearly universal acceptance for DOS applications. VESA has recently been extended to include support for a variety of audio products and pointing devices as well.

If you plan to use a large number of windows applications, you should take graphics acceleration hardware into account. To cut costs, a number of clone manufacturers may throw in a simple unaccelerated SuperVGA card. In applications such as Fractal Design Painter, Coreldraw, TrueSpace, Visual Reality, and Adobe Illustrator, working is much easier when you do not have to wait long for objects to be redrawn or windows resized. Inexpensive windows accelerator cards are available from OEMs who make use of chipsets from Tseng Labs and Cirrus Logic. Boards from S3, Media Vision, and ATI tend to be more expensive but have special capabilities, such as hardware support for fonts.

Since the mid-1980s, a number of special-application graphics architectures have come and gone. Texas Instruments introduced the TIGA (Texas Instruments Graphics Architecture), which was based around the TI 34010 and 34020 graphics coprocessors. The TIGA architecture had built-in support for drawing lines, circles, and polygons without the aid of the microprocessor. Truevision introduced its Targa family of enhanced graphics adapters for such applications as desktop video and computer animation. Silicon Graphics briefly supported a product that featured real-time shaded polygon display for CAD and rendering applications, and companies such as Matrox incorporated similar designs into their high-end "MGA architecture." Matrox systems come with drivers for Windows, OS/2, Autodesk applications, and other software. The MGA architecture can work cooperatively with SuperVGA systems but is not VGA compatible in its own right.

Recent trends in graphics accelerator design have shown that the future of PC graphics has significant improvements coming in the near future. A considerable amount of research has gone into ways of bringing full screen full motion video to the desktop PC. To accomplish the task, a number of manufacturers have included hardware video decompression chips that can play back MPEG and AVI video "flics" full screen at 30 frames per second. The Media Vision Pro Graphics 1024 and Pro Graphics 1280 already support this capability. Weitek, ATI, Tseng Labs, and S3 all have video playback coprocessors in the works as well. In addition, graphics accelerators from Media Vision, Matrox, and ATI feature 64-bit graphical data busses between the acceleration hardware and the frame buffer memory.

In selecting graphics hardware, you should determine first what applications are most important. Then contact the manufacturers *directly* and find out whether the display adapter supports your bus architecture operating system and applications. For some operating systems (especially Linux), third-party public-domain display drivers are available from bulletin board systems or Internet FTP sites and are not from the manufacturer. If you plan to develop your own software, find out whether the display adapter is compatible with the VESA BIOS extensions or whether a developer's kit is available.

Computer Graphics Software Interface Standards

As the task of interfacing between software and hardware becomes more centralized by the evolution of PC operating systems, graphics interface libraries are becoming increasingly important in the development of 3-D graphics software. Standardized graphics interfaces use a uniform, device-independent function interface. When a graphics library has been ported to an operating system or GUI, the user does not have to become familiar with the intricacies of the hardware or operating system. The graphics interface will take care of setting the graphics modes and sending commands to the acceleration hardware. This way, a program written in C or C++ can be ported from one platform to another with minimal effort, if the platform supports the graphics library.

Graphics standards are implemented as machine code or high-level language libraries that make calls to operating system drivers or hardware graphics accelerators. Originally, graphics interfaces took care of two-dimensional functions, such as drawing lines, curves, and polygons. The Graphics Kernel System was an interface adopted by the American National Standards Institute (ANSI) in 1985 and was restricted to two-dimensional graphics. It was followed in 1988 by GKS-3D, which extended GKS to include lines, polygons, and other 3-D primitives. The Programmers Hierarchical Interactive Graphics System (PHIGS) allowed 3-D objects to be grouped hierarchically and transformed. Both PHIGS and GKS have been ported to numerous platforms.

Many other standards have emerged from the computer graphics industry and academic research. The PostScript page description language developed by Adobe, the X Window System developed by MIT, Ithaca Software's HOOPS 3-D graphics interface, and Silicon Graphics Inc.'s Open GL are all standards that, at one time or another, caught on despite the presence of GKS and PHIGS. OpenGL has shown considerable promise because a number of high-level computer graphics applications have been written with it, and it has been adopted by both IBM and Microsoft for their OS/2 and Windows NT operating systems. Silicon Graphics proudly boasts that it has licensed development of OpenGL to the corporations that make up 95 percent of the computer graphics marketplace.

A number of 3-D acceleration chipsets have been developed for different markets and applications. The GLiNT chipset from 3DLabs, Inc., is designed to work with OpenGL implementations in Windows NT (and other operating systems to come) for high-end real-time 3-D graphics workstation applications. The 3D Game Open Alliance is developing a 3-D real-time architecture for DOS games, and Intel's 3DR architecture is being developed to perform basic rendering assistance in DOS and Windows applications. Keep a watchful eye on hardware and software graphics standards in 1995. In particular, watch the direction taken by major graphics software companies such as Autodesk.

Future Systems Issues: Development, Support, and Evolution

Ideally, you should design and build your system to suit your needs not just for today, but for the years to come. One often-made mistake, however, is to accept the belief that a particular system is "obsolete." As long as the hardware and software are capable of meeting your needs with timely, professional results, the system is not obsolete.

Through outreach, participation, and involvement, you can help your investment maintain its value. Through computer bulletin boards, user groups, and Internet mailing lists, you can develop ties with others who have invested in the hardware and software you have purchased. By contacting the corporations that make the software and hardware, you can give them suggestions and feedback as to how they can improve their products. By sharing tips in magazines such as *3D Artist*, distributing the software you develop through bulletin board systems like The Graphics Alternative, and participating in discussion groups on BBS's and USENET groups, you are broadening and strengthening the base of support.

Unfortunately, the same competitive element that drives computer companies to excel can also kill them off. Recently, Commodore International announced that it would be going into liquidation. The future of the Commodore Amiga is not certain. The system brought desktop video and multimedia to the fore, but in recent years it fell short because of poor marketing. Owners of the Commodore Amiga now must rely on each other and the third-party companies such as NewTek (which developed the Video Toaster desktop video system and the Lightwave computer graphics software) to continue support for their systems. Although there will always be support for the 80x86 systems because no single company controls their production, individual hardware and software systems can come and go. By participating in the computer graphics community, you can protect and enrich the investment you have made in your computer graphics workstation.

Video for Computer Graphics

2

by Gregory MacNicol

IN THIS CHAPTER

- What Is Video?
- Video Encoders and Sync Maintenance
- Waveform Monitors and Other Support Equipment
- Time Base Correctors
- Video Recording Formats for Animation
- Recording Computer-Generated Images on Video
- VTR Selection, Usage, and Maintenance
- Striping a Videotape

Video is a pervasive, worldwide phenomenon. It is now clearly the most popular of all the viewing media, having eclipsed both film and print as the dominant vehicle for the provision of entertainment and information. Yet, unlike the media it supplants, video depends on a dauntingly complex technology. Even technicians well-trained in electronics have trouble fully understanding the principles that make it work. Luckily, viewers have little need to trifle with the technology that underlies the video programming they enjoy—that is, unless they want to get in on the creative end of the medium.

The need to understand video technology exists certainly for animators who envision video as their destination medium. They have little choice but to acquaint themselves with the technology and procedures that allow for the transfer of computer-generated animations to videotape. In this chapter, I'll focus on video as it relates to the production of computer graphics. After reading this overview, you should have a working understanding of current video technology and how it influences the animation process.

Despite its utility and flexibility, video is not conducive to the placement of single images of animation on tape. Thus, desktop computer animators must get some technical grounding in video technology if they want to achieve dependable results.

You should be warned right now that video gear can get expensive. In fact, video support equipment may exceed the cost of your desktop computer animation system—just one more inducement to evaluate your animation needs carefully. If you have a clear idea about the level of quality you require for output, you'll have a much easier time deciding what you need and what you can get by without.

At any rate, before we explore the process of recording on video, let's first look at how video works. After laying down a suitable groundwork, I'll focus on tape formats, equipment, and interfacing issues—especially those factors that affect computer/video compatibility.

What Is Video?

A good place to start this discussion is with an ordinary computer's display system. In a standard color graphics display, five discrete signals are generated and sent from the desktop computer. These consist of three color signals—red, green, and blue (RGB)—and two additional synchronization signals that coordinate horizontal and vertical positioning. These five signals (typically routed via five separate cables combined in a pack) are designed to connect directly to what's called an RGB monitor. If properly generated, the signal produces an accurate image on any standard RGB display screen. So transferring the RGB image should be a simple, straightforward procedure, right?

You'd think so. Transferring the image sounds easy enough: just reroute the same five individual video signals to a VCR/VTR and record. Unfortunately, in the real world of video, it's not that easy. Graphics display signals are not usually compatible with standard video gear, and thus video signals must be converted—*encoded*, that is—to produce a standardized video signal. This standardized, everyday form of video is referred to as *composite video.*

Actually, composite video is a factor in almost every household in the country. Technicians refer to it as NTSC (National Television Standards Committee) or as RS-170A, but you and I know it as ordinary TV. It's the standard that has become the basis for the broadcast television communications industries. Because composite video uses only one cable to channel all video information (a clear advantage, logistically, over RGB), all RGB and sync signals are combined in their transport through the cable. There are, however, penalties to pay for this convenience. Although composite video is easier to manage, it is, signal-quality wise, inherently inferior to RGB.

Two important additional components affect the quality of a composite video signal: the black-and-white information (called *luminance* or *Y*), and the color information, called *chrominance* or *chroma* (also called *C*). In order for a single wire to convey all video information, the luminance and chrominance (Y/C) signals are combined in a particular way, based on certain subjective viewing assumptions.

When the NTSC color standard was adopted in 1953, the NTSC committee observed that human vision is most sensitive to green, least sensitive to blue, and somewhat sensitive to red. They also observed that human vision does not rely entirely on color information to resolve detail in a scene. Based on these assumptions and desiring to standardize video signal transmission using current (1953) equipment capabilities and a limited bandwidth (amount of available signal space), the NTSC color format was formulated. Because of these assumptions, the format is biased and, of necessity, compromised. Yet, despite its notable limitations, the standard prevails to this day in the United States and in many other countries throughout the world. Minor improvements have been made, however. In 1957, the Electronics Industry of America refined the NTSC monochrome standard, calling it RS-170, and in 1977 added the RS-170A specification for color.

Figure 2.1 shows a simplification of an NTSC waveform when colorbars are displayed on the video screen. The exact details of the waveform should adhere exactly to the FCC specification.

With this in mind, let's return to the computer desktop. If you want your computer to "talk" video, the graphics display information generated by your computer system must be compatible with the composite video standard; that is, the RGB signals must also include correct timing information to satisfy NTSC requirements.

In other words, all signals must be in "sync." Specifically, the horizontal frequency, or scan rate, must be calibrated at 15.7 kHz (kilohertz) with a vertical scan rate of 30 Hz (hertz). You understand why synchronization is so important when you consider that one single frame of video is made up of 525 vertical lines. These lines produce about 350 lines of resolution on a standard monitor. Where did the other lines go, you ask? The answer is overhead. Some 41 are used for the delay during the vertical retrace, showing one field leaving 484 lines that overlap slightly to produce the 350 viewable lines. Although these numbers are the standard, many monitors will accept deviations. Professional video equipment, however, often fails beyond slight variations of the signal specifications.

FIGURE 2.1.

An NTSC waveform.

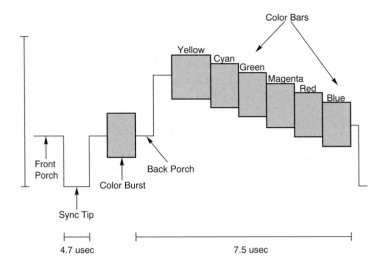

From Figure 2.2, you can see that the timing of the NTSC video signal consists of overhead that is used for sweeping the beam back to the screen's other side. You can also see that the video timings must be exactly the same for video boards, VCRs, monitors, and all other video devices to work correctly.

FIGURE 2.2.

Video scanning process and timing.

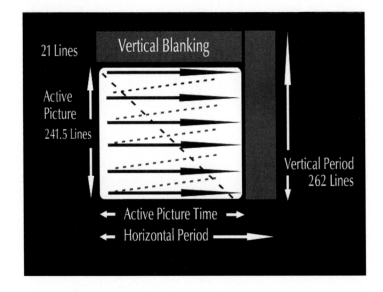

> **NOTE**
>
> ### Like Numbers?
>
> The specification for composite video may seem like a jumble of arbitrary numbers, particularly if you write them down and try to figure them out. At any rate, if you like numbers, try these on for size.
>
> The scanning rate of composite video is 15,734.25 horizontal scans per second. The vertical sweep is 59.94 times per second. The chrominance subcarrier is specified as 3,579,545.4545 Hz and controls color accuracy. The voltage levels have a negative 0.286 volts for the sync, and pure black should be 0.053 volts. Pure white is 0.661 volts. The other timings are detailed in TV handbooks and are specified to the nanosecond. Don't attempt to understand these numbers unless you have a thirst for arcane history. Instead, I recommend that you accept the specs and rely on quality equipment to deliver the dictated performance.

To prevent noticeable flicker (which would otherwise be distractingly apparent), an interesting technical strategy is employed. Instead of refreshing the display with a new image 30 times a second, first the odd and then the even horizontal lines (called scanlines) are displayed alternately. That's why each frame of NTSC video is composed of two fields: the odd and even fields are alternately displayed every 1/60th of a second, whereas every frame is displayed every 1/30th of a second. This odd/even display technique is called *interlacing*.

New Math: 60=59+

Technically, the 60 Hz field rate isn't really 60 Hz but 59.94. In 1953, when the NTSC introduced color to the monochrome standard and wanted to maintain compatibility with existing TV electronics, they discovered that the new color encoding format interfered slightly with the old standard. To eliminate this, the scanning rate was shifted a tad from 60 to 59.94 Hz.

NTSC is just one of a number of video format standards that have been defined in the last 40 years. The PAL (Phase Alternating Lines) standard is used throughout most of Europe—except France, which is standardized on the SECAM format, although French production studios do use PAL.

If you have access to European videotapes, you'll quickly discover that although they may appear on the outside to be identical to U.S. tapes, your VCR will be unable to read or record the "foreign" videotape. The European video formats (theoretically) allow for improved color quality. Both the PAL and SECAM formats display the image 25 times a second instead of 30 and provide for 625 vertical scan lines instead of the NTSC's 525. However, those accustomed to NTSC often notice flickering when they view European video—a distraction directly related to the lower scan rate.

Sadly, the color limitations of all video are severe. Figure 2.3 is a chromaticity diagram where pure white is in the center. From this, you can see the difference between the available colors on TV and what you can see in real life.

FIGURE 2.3.

Chromaticity chart.

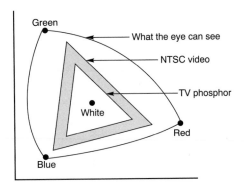

CIE Chart of Chromaticity

Video Encoders

So how do you get your animation to play out on broadcast grade (NTSC) video? Here's another way of asking the same question: How do you convert the computer's separate RGB signals into a composite NTSC video that's compatible with your standard video gear? The answer is that you use a device called an *encoder*. Encoders take two general forms. You can purchase them as an integrated feature on your computer's graphics display circuit board, or you can buy them housed in a stand-alone box. One somewhat useful index of encoder capability is cost.

You'll find that a considerable range of capability is built into the electronics of the stand-alone converters. Prices, which roughly reflect performance, range from $100 to $20,000. Various levels of output quality (broadcast, special color filters, and so on) are supported, and a host of features influence the degree of control afforded the operator for the manipulation of various signal attributes.

The RGB input timings must be accurate for an encoder to work properly. That is, the original RGB signals must arrive ready for encoding at the correct horizontal and vertical scanning rate (interlaced, of course) in addition to the proper voltage levels. Because this is such a critical factor, encoders first access input scanning frequencies to verify accuracy before they do the conversions.

Low-cost encoders may be acceptable for industrial-grade video, but they are not dependable generators of broadcast-quality output. If your objective is to produce broadcast-level quality, sync signal controls (such as delay and chroma offset) are highly desirable features. You'll find, not surprisingly, that the better (and usually more expensive) encoders produce superior NTSC signal quality by using electronic filters to remove unwanted frequencies and, thus, unwanted visual artifacts. They also address the problem of *chroma crawl*, which is perhaps the most obvious of NTSC "artifacts" (see Figure 2.4).

FIGURE 2.4.

If you look closely at the borders, you can see the "chroma crawl" effect, which, on a TV screen, moves or crawls. The only way to avoid this ugly artifact is to avoid the colors that produce it.

Another feature incorporated in better encoders is the conversion of thin horizontal lines that otherwise might flicker. The encoder translates these automatically to lines that are more viewable and more pleasing—an especially helpful feature when text must be displayed.

Chroma crawl is an insidious problem endemic to NTSC video. If you were to display a typical set of colorbars, you would notice an area between the more or less distinct bars where colors are visibly distorted. Look closer and you will notice that the lines appear to crawl along the color border (see Figure 2.4).

This artifact is prevalent on everyday broadcast video. You might have noticed, for example, a weird lightshow happening on the chest of a news broadcaster wearing a striped tie. Likewise, you may have seen the patterned clothing of a TV show's guest appear to self-animate. These are chroma crawl effects. A good encoder can reduce not only chroma crawl problems but also other artifacts of NTSC video, such as colored moire effects, which result from tightly spaced black-and-white lines.

All encoders, even low-cost units, should include a feature called "loop-through." A device with loop-through capability enables you to, in effect, bypass a device so that, in the case of an encoder's circuitry, both processed (encoded) and unprocessed output is available to other devices. This feature enables you to connect and "daisy-chain" devices. The result is more versatile and flexible configurations. You might, for example, want to connect an additional VTR or monitor to your system. Regardless of the cost and independent of loop-through, all encoders should provide for a simple electrical process called *termination.* This capability enables you to switch on a 75-ohm resistor, which serves notice to the signal source that the wire connection has ended its transmission. In other words, regardless of system configuration, the last unit (monitor, VCR encoder, or whatever) deployed in a chain of connected components needs a termination switch and the termination signal needs to be switched ON (terminated).

Conversely, all other devices in the chain should have their termination signals switched OFF. If termination is not properly signaled on all pieces of equipment in the chain, the signal quality produced by any or all of the devices in the system will be seriously impaired.

Some encoders provide additional video outputs (such as SVHS) that require different kinds of plug-and-socket configuration. In fact, some VCR manufacturers employ variations on the so-called standard type of SVHS connectors, so an adaptor may be necessary.

Some encoders may incorporate their counterpart function—that is, decoder function. A decoder accepts NTSC input and separates out the red, green, and blue components of the video signal. Decoders are typically used for video capture from a camera, VTR, or other device. This provides the animator with a new source of raw material. The separated signals can be digitized in the computer for image processing or whatever. Remember, however, that the RGB products of this process are dependent on input quality—which are inferior. At best, the visual quality can be no better in quality than the original inherently poor-quality NTSC signal (see Figure 2.5).

Some newer and more expensive encoders incorporate a process called *scan conversion,* and so they are often called scan converters. These units handle a larger range of scanning frequencies, and as you might expect, they are also more expensive. As the name implies, these devices can convert one scan rate (usually the computer's) to another. Typically, these devices are used to translate the images generated by high-resolution computer display screens, such as 1024×768 pixels (non-interlaced), so that the output is video recordable.

The better encoders are also adept at managing substandard input—especially relative to pixels and lines that are below the resolution of video. You'll discover that the manufacturers of scan converters handle these kinds of problems in different ways and their solutions can be expensive—some of these devices cost $10,000 or more. Good units may offer a number of additional features that enable you to tailor the output in various ways. Some are designed to reduce flicker; others allow for adjustment of the video size and the aspect ratio, provide for advanced color filtering, and enable video or computer graphics overlays.

FIGURE 2.5.

Colors on video are different than on paper. Although many colors disappear or look bleached out, the combination of certain colors can look absolutely hideous.

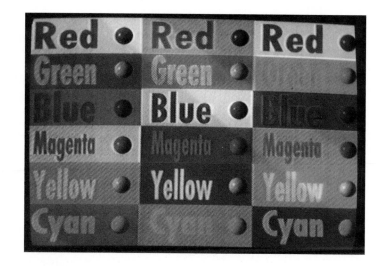

Sync Maintenance

Synchronization is absolutely essential to video quality and device compatibility. In order to produce usable output, all components in a video system must be in sync with one another. The sync signal provides a reference point for all the devices in a system. For example, the sync informs the video equipment when a video scan begins and ends. If there were no sync, devices (such as a VCRs/VTRs, cameras, graphics boards, and the like) would display video images that conflict with other video gear. The resulting visual stew would be a jumble of useless output. Even minor variations from sync can cause serious problems. In fact, if sync timing is only slightly off, many processes are adversely affected, and the resultant images are likely to appear distorted or worse.

Video Cables

Video sync is so sensitive that seemingly the insignificant time spans of only a few nanoseconds are problematic. For example, subtle delays caused by different cable lengths can result in video mistiming. Because different cable lengths cause differences in the rate of delivery of video signal pulses (by a few nanoseconds), they can adversely affect video timing. If the red wire from an RGB monitor is longer than the green and blue cables, the red part of the image will be slightly offset relative to the other colors. Color problems are noticed first. The color of composite video is determined by the phase of the chroma signal (also known as the subcarrier) and runs at 3.58 MHz. A delay of only a few nanoseconds caused by a mismatched cable causes a color shift. For this reason, always use cables of the same type and length to connect video equipment.

A master sync signal is used to control synchronization and forestall a Pandora's box of potential problems engendered by subtle timing lapses. Professional studios establish what's called "house sync" by using a special video sync generator.

Studios use professional-grade sync generators to provide stable oscillation and other timing-related capabilities. Some of these devices enable controllable delays and other adjustments that allow studios to fine-tune sync output and compensate for errors caused by cables or for other minor errors introduced by additional equipment. For example, the phase of the chroma that controls hue can be offset to compensate for long cables. Alternatively, you can use other video sources, including a video camera.

Genlock

A video board's capability to accept and operate within the confines of another system's sync is called *genlocking*. If you're looking to create high-quality video, it's an essential feature. Without genlocking, the video board free-runs its RGB signal timing without reference to other units that must be coordinated in time with the video. Improperly synced video recordings are typically identifiable because of a jumpy video image.

A reliable solution to head off sync problems is to use an external sync signal source, such as an RGB-to-NTSC encoder. In this configuration, the encoder acts as the master source and controls the sync of the VTR and the (genlocking) video board. Using this method, the board's sync signal is timed exactly with the VCR and any other video devices. This means you can be sure that the VCR will properly accept the video signal that the board provides. Also, for video capture, the board will be timed so that when it captures a frame, the timing will be frame-accurate.

Without genlocking, the image on your monitor may appear satisfactory and you may think that the video is being recorded correctly. In marginal situations, the VCR may indeed be recording properly—with the exception of an occasional missing frame. Worse yet, you may be able to play back the video, only to realize that the video signal was not true enough for another VCR to properly record your playback.

Figure 2.6 shows the most basic layout of a video recording setup. A more refined setup includes a TBC and interconnecting cables for improved synchronization for superior video quality and single-frame accuracy.

FIGURE 2.6.

Setup of sync/board/VTR.

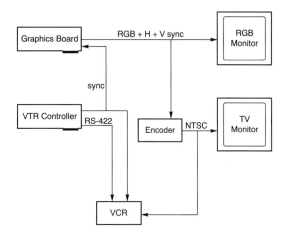

Display Size

The terms *underscanning* and *overscanning* are sometimes confused even by video professionals. In this context, the scanning refers to the area that's viewable on your video screen. Ordinary home TVs use less than the full picture transmitted to them; some of the picture is not visible because it extends beyond the viewable borders of the picture tube. On an ordinary TV screen, the image is cropped, or *overscanned* (see Figure 2.7).

FIGURE 2.7.

Showing underscan and overscan.

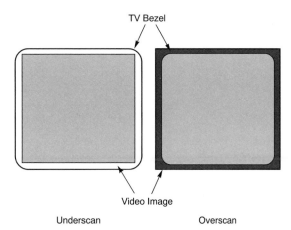

Video and computer monitors often have a convenient switch for overscan and underscan. Switching back and forth enables you to get a good idea of the complete frame and to compare that to what the viewers will see.

When you create an animation using a good RGB monitor, a viewer can see the whole image on the screen, including the black border surrounding the image. There is no question about where the image begins and ends. This working image, which includes the border surround, is said to be *underscanned.* It is seen and manipulated by the animator in its entirety. However, when this same image is viewed on a composite monitor—the typical viewing medium for most animations—parts of the image are likely to be cropped, that is, overscanned. This is the way most animations are actually viewed, and thus it's a view that the animator needs to be aware of. Fortunately, this need has been anticipated by equipment manufacturers who have designed some monitors (both RGB and composite) so that they can switch-select either overscanning or underscanning. Built-in scan switches configure the video output so that it either scans all the lines making the image or else overshoots them.

Because of monitor-to-monitor differences, the video industry has developed a standard called the *safe titling area* (STA). Anything within the safe titling area is definitely viewable. Image information outside this proscribed area may or may not be viewable, depending on the degree of a given monitor's overscanning. This is important information for the animator. For example, when creating text, you would want to be sure that the words are placed within the STA boundaries (see Figure 2.8).

FIGURE 2.8.

The safe titling area (STA).

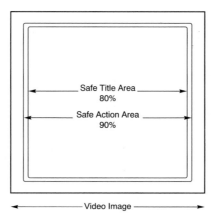

Safe Title Area
80%

Safe Action Area
90%

Video Image

For video work, it is essential that you adhere to the limits of the safe title area. Anything around it will probably be obscured by the monitor bezel.

Waveform Monitors and Other Support Equipment

How can you tell if your video quality is meeting spec? For broadcast applications, where this is a critical question, two oscilloscope-like devices are used to help find the answer. Waveform monitors and vectorscopes are the tools professional animators use to help them meet exacting video standards (see Figure 2.9).

FIGURE 2.9.

The waveform monitor and vectorscope are essential tools for visualizing and evaluating the video signal. (Courtesy of Tektronix, Inc.)

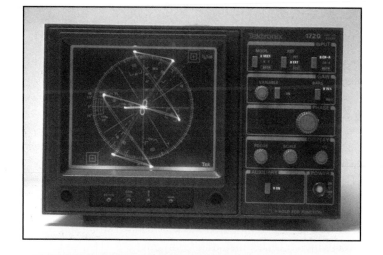

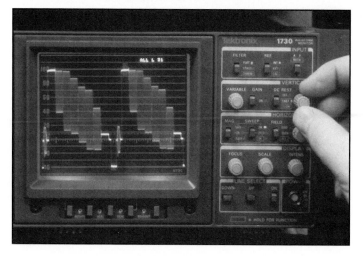

The *waveform monitor* is similar in appearance to an oscilloscope but is specially designed to monitor specific video format signals. Here's how it works. A depiction of the video signal is displayed on the monitor screen. The lower, rectangularly shaped sync pulse is portrayed in conjunction with the remaining horizontal scanlines.

The waveform monitor's controls enable you to zoom into specific parts of the signal—for example, the chroma burst, which displays a signal's color configuration. Basically, this device enables you to see what, if anything, is wrong with the signal you produce. Armed with the necessary information (regarding noise or chroma jitter, for example), you can make whatever adjustments are necessary. You may find that, for example, you need to repair or change cables or replace faulty equipment.

A signal's voltage levels may need to be adjusted so the signal meets FCC-specified NTSC levels. You should be warned that even when video equipment has not been moved and temperature is stable, voltage levels tend to drift with time. They require periodic checking and, occasionally, adjustment.

In a typical setup at a professional animation studio, next to the waveform monitor you will find a vectorscope. Round in shape like a radar screen, the vectorscope's electronics produce markings on the screen for the colors as seen on a standard display of colorbars. In an ideal reading, when colorbars are displayed, the vectors displayed on the monitor should have their "elbows" positioned within each of the marked positions. Adjusting the "hue" on the encoder rotates the "elbows" to the correct position. As you might expect, there are specially configured waveform and vector monitors that are designed for use with other video formats, including component, SVHS, and PAL formats.

With a board such as Truevision's VIDI/O Analyser, you can closely evaluate the NTSC signal making sure it is "legal video."

Time Base Correctors

To assure reliable results when videotaping, a time base corrector (TBC) is used. The TBC adjusts timing offsets that result from the actual process of video recording. Subtle variations are introduced by the mechanics of tape recording. For example, videotape has a tendency to stretch. Also, the VTR motors that move the tape across the recording heads tend to fluctuate slightly, thus introducing minor errors. These discrepancies may be undetectable—to you—and your productions may appear to be entirely satisfactory on the monitor. Only later will you discover that downstream video equipment (such as video editors) can't accept the timing variations generated by your VTR. You may discover that your perfectly presentable animation sequence has been reduced to a series of broken-up images. It happens. In short, you will have discovered why TBCs are essential in the production of dependable high-quality video animation.

Until recently, TBCs were large and prohibitively expensive devices found only in professional post-production facilities. Today's units, however, are relatively compact and considerably less expensive than they were only a few years ago. Now they are integral to a VCR. To produce broadcast-quality video, the exacting specifications of the NTSC signal must be adhered to by all related video equipment. Given the proliferation of cables and the variation in even the most spartan of equipment setups, this can sometimes seem like an almost superhuman task.

Make no mistake about it: dependable, quality work requires the oversight and adjustments provided by a TBC. You need to be able to ensure absolutely correct timing even when the video source output varies or is slightly unstable. Using a TBC, all sorts of potential timing snags can be sidestepped. For instance, you may be able to record and play back an animation on a VCR with a slightly offset sync; yet, when you want to duplicate the animation onto another VCR, you'll be faced with unwanted surprises, such as color changes or jumpiness. It can get worse: you may discover that your video is not even playable on another VCR.

This is where the TBC comes in. A TBC takes an "unclean" video signal and electronically rebuilds it so that output signal timing and amplitude are absolutely perfect. It strips the sync off the original video signal and then reconstructs the signal based on another sync source (often self-generated). After this process is complete, you can be sure that the VTR will dependably and accurately record the computer-generated image.

The TBC has another very desirable feature. If you have produced an "industrial quality" video and later decide that you want to upgrade it so that it satisfies NTSC broadcast standards, a good TBC sometimes can be used to "fix up" the level of quality. Good practice, however, suggests that you start with a clean signal.

Video Recording Formats for Animation

Before selecting a VTR, you will need to make some determination regarding video format. Be forewarned. This is a topic that requires constant re-evaluation because the technology and equipment are seemingly in perpetual flux. Keep in mind that the tape format you choose must properly match your other video equipment. Furthermore, consider this. Your videotaped animation will most likely be shipped off to a video post-production facility for final editing. You'll need to provide that facility with a format they can work with.

A number of tape formats are available to the beginning and professional animator. You will need to select the one that best satisfies your creative, technical, and financial requirements and expectations. What follows is a short description of the more popular VTR formats that are suitable for desktop computer animation. Not all formats will be discussed, especially those that do not fit into the low-cost/high-quality category. Others are not discussed because some important factor precludes their use, such as the lack of a controller or having a format that is undependable with reference to single-frame accuracy.

Because of the ongoing video format wars (based on cost, convenience, and technology "updates"), evaluation of and selection from the available formats can be difficult even for experienced and technically sophisticated professionals. Indeed, even for animators who, constrained by budget considerations, need usable low-cost equipment, the options are numerous. You'll quickly discover certain limits, however. For example, any VTR/VCR worth buying new is, regardless of format, expensive—but essential for quality production.

With this in mind, let's survey the format options. The primary focus will be on the features of the constantly evolving, lower-cost VTR equipment, starting with the least costly format.

VHS and Hi-8

The least costly recorder format suitable for serious animation work is VHS, which uses standard 1/2-inch tape. Both JVC and Panasonic make high-end VHS VCRs with cast aluminium frames that make for stable, reliable operation. The problem you may run into here is finding a suitable controller. Currently, there are only a few controllers that support these recorders because of the format's inherent weakness when it comes to reliable single-frame control.

Another drawback to be considered when contemplating the use of VHS is that the resolution is only 240 lines and the color bandwidth (and hence, quality) is limited. Thus, the level of quality, particularly when making copies for editing, makes this format acceptable only for low-quality, first-generation animations or for work that will not require duplicating.

Hi-8 is a popular, and in many ways, superior video format. Its small size has both blessings and shortcomings. Single-frame controllers and editors are available that provide animators with a low-cost solution to reasonable-quality video. Because of the small size of the tape and mechanics, however, it is vulnerable to minor failures that are unacceptable for animation. Furthermore, its color encoding method limits its capability to display fully saturated colors, which are typical of computer graphics.

Super VHS

One level up on the scale of format quality is Super VHS, also called S-video or SVHS. This format offers color quality comparable to VHS, but the resolution is significantly enhanced. SVHS generates better than twice the black-and-white resolution of VHS.

SVHS requires special tape with higher *coercivity* (magnetic density). The SVHS VTR is downward compatible with VHS. In other words, it can play back or record in VHS mode; however, SVHS tape cannot be played on a VHS deck. SVHS equipment uses a different video signal and requires special connectors that are not VHS compatible. The format separates the chroma from the luminance and, as a result, offers a much better signal quality than VHS. For optimal viewing quality, you will want to use an SVHS-compatible monitor that can display the video without mixing the chroma and luminance. The quality is something between that of NTSC and of RGB.

Make note, however, that in all probability the viewer will see your animation in composite mode—which produces the artifacts SVHS can remove. The SVHS format was (and is) marketed as a low-cost alternative to the still-popular mainstay 3/4-inch format. But even though SVHS quality is comparable to that of 3/4-inch, the ubiquity of 3/4-inch equipment and its industry-wide acceptance and support represent considerable momentum; thus 3/4-inch is still a considerable rival for the newer 1/2-inch SVHS format. In-dustrial-quality editing SVHS VTRs, also made by JVC and Panasonic, are very reliable continuous-operation machines. There is a range of suitable controllers, TBCs, and advanced editing machines currently on the market that support SVHS machines.

The SVHS format is not without its drawbacks, some of which may preclude its satisfactory use for a particular computer animation usage. One of these is the color encoding method. Some VTRs produce a chroma delay as a by-product of improving the quality of the color. The color processing appears as though the colors have been shifted upward one scan line. Although this may not be perceivable in a first-generation playback, it becomes more noticeable with each generation and is pronounced on a third-generation copy. The good news is that a competent TBC (one specially matched to the deck) will correct this problem. Panasonic, for example, now includes a TBC in its high-end SVHS video recorder.

Based on color quality, it's hard to say categorically whether the SVHS or the popular industrial-standard 3/4-inch format is superior. Highly saturated SVHS colors do not retain color accuracy as well as do 3/4-inch color images. Computer-generated images typically possess highly saturated colors that can be troublesome using the SVHS format. On the other hand, the higher black-and-white resolution of an SVHS image makes color contrast appear clearer in low color-saturated images.

3/4-Inch

The 3/4-inch or "U" format has been around and improving for more than a decade. Predictable performance and mid-range cost have made it popular, and its use is widespread. Despite the better characteristics of other formats, when it comes to finishing, you can be sure that a 3/4-inch editing facility is close by. This may be a compelling consideration for you. Many animators need to be assured of the availability of quick and complete services after an animation segment has been created.

The 3/4-inch format uses the standard method for displaying color and luminance information. This means that you can expect to see the pervasive artifacts of NTSC, such as chroma crawl and colored moire patterns caused by the proliferation of fine black-and-white lines. Yet, despite these drawbacks, with good tape and a reliable VTR, your finished quality should be acceptable for editing.

An improvement in the 3/4-inch lineup is Sony's SP series. Both variations of the format are compatible with one another, except that SP recording requires SP editing VTRs. SP, for "Superior Performance," relies on improved circuitry and tape, which Sony claims makes about a 30 percent improvement in overall quality. Because the resolution is enhanced and color interference has been reduced, the improvement over the 3/4-inch U format is noticeable.

Betacam and M-II

The next level up represents a significant improvement—a jump up that is echoed by a comparable boost in equipment costs. Sony's Betacam and Betacam SP VTRs are expensive, but they offer excellent quality. The reason for the marked improvement in video quality is that Betacam and M-II uses the component video format and an improved method for recording the signal onto the videotape. This, along with superior tape, provides for seamless dupes and edits at multiple generations.

Betacam recorders, in contrast to less expensive VHS series and 3/4-inch VTRs, use a serial port (technically, an RS-422) for the remote control of the VTR. Betacam is an increasingly popular format and, in terms of overall video quality, is considered by many professionals to be superior to top-of-the-line broadcast 1-inch machines costing in the $100,000 range. In other words, even for broadcast applications, Betacam is more than adequate.

M-II is another fine choice in a component-based format that also offers excellent quality. Although not as popular as Betacam and not so often supported in post-production facilities, M-II offers solid reliability and is supported by many single-frame VCR controller vendors.

Digital Formats

Although digital formats are growing in popularity, they are still out of the price range of most low-cost computer animation facilities. The most common digital formats, D-1 and D-2, have a clear advantage over other formats because each generation (copy of the original) maintains the quality of the original: there is no image degradation. For the animator, this means that multiple overlays and composited images can be repeatedly integrated into an image or an animation without having to pay the usual price in image attrition.

The D-1 format compresses a component signal into 4 bits of luminance and two channels of chrominance at 2 bits each. Thus, it is sometimes referred to as 4:2:2, or

CCIR 601, which is an international standard that defines this format. Because of its perfect reproducibility, the format is used in video post-production facilities, especially those that create special effects. D-1 enables you to composite numerous layers of video, add effects, edit, copy, and edit—again without any losses in image quality. As a result, it is the most popular digital standard.

Although D-1 video recorders are likely to stretch even a relaxed budget, your work may still be compatible for use by a facility that uses D-1 equipment. Converting to D-1 is easy. Elastic Reality offers a program that converts RGB images into the component D-1 format. Once converted, the images can then be stored on an Exabyte tape drive (typically used in D-1 facilities). Thus D-1 represents an easy-to-manage and straightforward path from your computer system to top-of-the-line video post-production.

Table 2.1 shows a comparison of videotape formats. Note that "Color Under" is the method that the color information gets onto the video signal, meaning that its frequency is "under" or lower than the video frequency. The AZ in "Color Under" indicates that the method used for recording color suffers from a vertical shift because of its being based on azimuth recording.

Table 2.1. Comparison of videotape formats.

Format	Luminance	Color Method
D-1	450	4:2:2
D-2	500	Direct
Betacam	300	Component
Betacam SP	360	Component
M-II	360	Component
U-format	240	Color Under
U-format SP	340	Color Under
VHS	220	Color Under (AZ)
SVHS	400	Color Under (AZ)
Hi-8	400	Color Under (AZ)

Digital Recorders

Digital recording devices are an excellent choice for animators. They range from $2,000 to more than $40,000, depending on features and quality. Digital recording systems offer many advantages over mechanically-oriented VTRs. One of the obvious improvements is the elimination of preroll. This alone saves 15 seconds per frame, as well as the waits that occur during the VTR's progress from standby, start, record, stop, and standby. A secondary advantage is that the mechanical problems associated with VCRs are bypassed. (What remains in the realm of mechanics is potential hard-disk failures.)

Low-cost units, such as the Personal Animation Recorder from Digital Processing Systems, compact the RGB files into a stream of compressed video (JPEG). Formats supported include VHS, component (Betacam), or 752×480 resolution at a full 24 bits of color. The level of quality is very good—far beyond SVHS. A system such as this is well suited to the constant interactive processing that is typical of computer animation production.

Top-of-the-line units, such as an Abacas A-60, digitally store the images on fast hard disks for real-time playback, forwards, backwards, or slow motion. Although these units are very expensive and are found in high-quality video post-production facilities, they offer a comprehensive range of real-time special effects and produce superior output.

Video Disk Recorders

Until recently, optical media has been, in cost, out of range for most animators, yet the price keeps dropping. Rewriteable optical disk recorders—such as those made by JVC, Sony, and Pioneer—cost $12,000 and more. However, with optical media, you get a lot of bang for your video buck. A single disk provides 57,600 video frames (32 minutes) in either high-quality RGB, SVHS, or standard composite video. Another advantage of the optical recorders is that the units do not require preroll, and their lack of complex mechanics translates into long lifetimes. Accessing a particular video frame is also fast—0.3 seconds. Regarding quality, the output is a notch below Betacam, so it's not suitable for use in broadcast applications. Still, because of its ease-of-use and relatively low cost, the video disk recorder is an excellent contender for single-frame or live video recording of everyday applications.

Recording Computer-Generated Images on Video

There are two ways to record computer-generated animation on video: you can record live video from the computer display, or you can place individual frames on videotape. Each method has its advantages and drawbacks, and the methods differ considerably in regards to overall process, required equipment, and quality of output. Regardless of method, you should know that VTRs, by format definition, have remarkably poor resolution: so-called "industrial-quality" 3/4-inch video formats produce about 330 lines of resolution, and VHS is even less refined, generating only 240 lines. This means that even though the resolution may appear acceptable when the tape is running at normal speed, a single frame is likely to appear noticeably degraded when it's isolated. Despite this drawback, for the computer animator, the VTR is still the most popular vehicle.

You'll find that recording an animation sequence "live" from the display board is the easiest and the least expensive way to go. The level of quality, however, is marginal, and so the "real-time" method is best suited to noncommercial applications where viewers will not expect top-notch video quality. Let's take a look at these two recording methods in more detail, starting first with the real-time method.

Real-Time Video Recording

Recording an animated sequence as it is displayed on the computer (in "real time") may seem like the most obvious way of getting your work onto video, but several technical hurdles must be overcome. First, the signals from the computer must mesh with the video compatibility requirements of videotape recorders. Second, assuming complete NTSC compatibility, the computer system must be fast enough to display the animation in real time, that is, at the rate it is intended be to viewed.

Desktop computers are still not fast enough to calculate and display complex, high-quality 3-D animation in real time. Even if your computer system can display single frames a 1/30th of a second (to accommodate video's rate of 30 frames-per-second), you would still be unable to record your animation on a VTR unless the signal were converted to standard NTSC video.

Even though real-time animation quality isn't ready for network-level TV, it has its uses. If you can work with the compromises, you can produce very effective computer-to-video recordings. The trade-offs have to do with the quality of the finished product. Typically, you must be ready to accept reduced resolution, limited colors, no anti-aliasing, or the animation of small regions or parts. These compromises can be very acceptable in certain situations (especially those that don't require full resolution or full-color animation). For example, real-time animations are often well suited to animated scientific presentations or for architectural fly-throughs. Likewise, animated business graphics or accident simulations can convey a wealth of information via moving graphics, without any need for the polish of top-notch, broadcast-level quality.

Single-Frame Video Recording

The other recording method, which is considerably more time-consuming and produces a superior end-product, is called "single-frame recording." Even using today's most advanced hardware, most computers are simply incapable of processing or displaying high-quality 3-D animation in real time. That's why computer animation is usually created one frame at a time and later placed onto videotape.

To produce successful single-frame animation, you need video interfacing equipment, including a high-quality videotape recorder (VTR or VCR), and detailed knowledge about how to properly connect and operate the computer-interfaced video equipment. Single-frame animation's payoff is first-rate quality, the kind of output you're used to seeing in the best TV work.

Assembling single images on videotape is a complex business—and a potentially troublesome one. However, after a system has been properly set up, you will find that you can automate many steps in the animation process, streamlining many time-consuming operations. After your system is properly set up, you'll be able to direct your focus to the more creative aspects of your work, while your equipment cranks out the frames.

Video Cassette and Video Tape Recorders (VCRs/VTRs)

We'll start the discussion of single-frame animation techniques by taking a close-up look at the operations of a typical videotape recorder (VTR/VCR). First of all, let's examine exactly what you want your VTR to be doing, repeatedly. Most VTRs are designed to run continuously. In other words, they are *not* designed to stop and to start on demand, as they must do to produce each single frame of an animated sequence. The apparently simple procedure whereby a single frame is recorded on tape is actually a complex operation. In order to get a single frame recorded on video in the right place at the right time, the VTR is put through an arduous and repeated routine.

This is how it works (see Figure 2.10). First, the tape is run backwards a small measured amount, stopped, and then run forward in order to reach correct recording speed. This mechanical procedure is called *preroll* and is essential to the correct timing of a video recording. At exactly the right moment, the desired frame is recorded on the videotape at an exact position on the tape. Incidentally, a high-quality videotape recorder is essential to this process. Unlike home VCRs, a higher-quality "VTR" can be directed to a particular location on a tape and there record a single frame of video. This feature is referred to as *single-frame accuracy.*

FIGURE 2.10.

The process of single-frame animation is based on preroll, the basic, time-consuming process of waiting, starting, going, stopping, and waiting again. In addition to being hard on mechanical devices such as VTRs, preroll takes up about 15 seconds per frame.

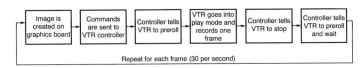

Image is created on graphics board → Commands are sent to VTR controller → Controller tells VTR to preroll → VTR goes into play mode and records one frame → Controller tells VTR to stop → Controller tells VTR to preroll and wait

Repeat for each frame (30 per second)

A VTR suitable to the animation process will have a range of other features that facilitate the single-frame animation process and ensure a high level of quality. The VTR should be able to accept different types of sync inputs and outputs and provide at least two audio channels. A competent VTR will facilitate later downstream processes as well. You will probably need to use the same VTR during editing when it is connected to an editing device, and you will probably want a unit that can be remotely controlled by the animator or by another piece of equipment.

VTR Selection

VTRs and VCRs range widely in capability and cost ($3,000 to $140,000), so selecting one for use in animation warrants careful consideration. You'll find that, beyond a determination of format, selection is complicated by the continual introduction of "improvements" and by the attempts of manufacturers to launch new standards as they "update" features. Given such a fluid marketplace, no guide (including this one) is adequate to the task of assessing the latest VTR capabilities.

When shopping for a VTR to be used for animation applications in your chosen format, you can ask yourself the following key questions to help you gather relevant information about a unit's capabilities:

- Can the VTR handle continuous operation? Remember, during recording, it will be running 24 hours a day.
- Is the unit completely dependable? Can you expect it to be consistently frame-accurate and color-accurate?
- Are the heads designed to withstand the countless prerolls that characterize single-frame animation?
- Is the format compatible with available editing facilities and your (or your client's) usual preferences?
- Is output quality (including multiple generation) acceptable?
- What professional features does it offer? TBC, External Sync, display in frames, and so on?

For up-to-date information, consult the video magazines for trends, and ask professionals at video facilities—particularly ones you are likely to work with—about the attributes, benefits, and characteristic problems of units currently on the market. Although you may not find much consensus regarding a unit's technical virtues, the process will sharpen your awareness of what is available and make you more adept at cutting through the jargon and sales hype.

Of course, the VTR you select not only must support your particular format and animation needs—based on features currently available—it must also be affordable. Here you may discover that, depending on the quality of the animation you wish to produce, this is a tall order, especially if you are also shopping for durability.

VTR Usage and Maintenance

Single-frame animation is particularly hard on the recording equipment. For every second of animation (30 frames), the VTR must be on constant standby, waiting for the next rendered frame. This pause may last a minute or it may extend 45 minutes between frames. Then, on signal, the VTR goes into action: it turns on the drive-motors switch and the unit prerolls, plays up to speed, records a frame, stops and goes into operational limbo again, waiting for the next rendered frame. So, if preroll takes 15 seconds, one second of rendered animation represents about seven or eight minutes of stop-start VTR operation. It's a mechanical strain on the hardware—wear and tear that takes a toll even on the stoutest equipment, particularly the video heads, the components that make direct contact with the videotape.

To ensure dependable quality, VTRs must be maintained and serviced on a regular basis. VTRs are for the most part mechanical devices; they are, therefore, vulnerable to wear, heat, and dirt. First of all, set up the unit in the workspace where it will remain cool, well ventilated, and dust free. In operation, look for shortcuts that maximize the mechanical efficiency of the recording process. Programs exist (from Diaquest, for example) that use a system's RAM to hold several images at once and so can facilitate the recording of several frames in one sweep.

Effective maintenance involves cleaning the heads properly, carefully, and regularly. It is a good practice to log usage in hours and note the kind of use. Then, after a manufacturer-rated span, you can have the recorder professionally checked and recalibrated.

Degraded recording is subtle and usually goes unnoticed at first. You may not notice a fall-off in performance in the first generation, but you can be sure that it will be noticed as multiple generations accumulate. Things to look for are individually offset colors (the object and its color may be shifted), washed-out colors, image position offset, poor resolution, and noise.

Magnetic Tape

Regardless of format and VTR used, high-quality tape is essential to the production of a quality animation. Because each frame of an animated sequence requires stopping and starting of the tape's transport mechanism, the tape you use must endure repeated stretching, hitting, and flexing while still maintaining its specified physical characteristics. That's why, as a general rule, tape used for animation is used only once. If you re-use it, be prepared for dropouts caused by the flaking of tiny magnetic particles imbedded in the tape. Dropouts appear as blemishes that are small but momentarily visible on-screen. Get the best tape possible.

VTR and VCR Controllers

Now let's shift our focus to another device that must be included on the list of essential equipment for the computer animator—the VTR controller. This crucial component interprets instructions sent by the animation software, in effect translating the instructions into video commands. Thus, the controller tells the VTR when, how, and where to record a frame. In order for the VTR and the controller to know the exact location of any frame of animation on the videotape, a time code is superimposed on the videotape. The time code provides essential reference points for video control and editing.

Based on instructions issued through the computer's software, the controller sits between the computer and the VTR and mediates instructions from the animation program. The VTR positions the tape for the recording of each individual frame, turns record mode on and off, and then repositions for the next frame. Controllers are manufactured either as stand-alone units or as circuit boards designed to plug into the computer's motherboard.

Most professional grade VTRs and VCRs are engineered so that they can be controlled externally—that is, remotely. Communications from a remote device such as an editor (or some other piece of equipment) to the recording equipment is managed via a standard communications port that may operate either serially (RS-422) or parallel. Note that this particular kind of serial port is not usually configured as a typical RS-232 computer serial port and so is not compatible with a standard RS-232 interface. This may be changing, however. Some of the newer computer-oriented recorders on the market are RS-232 compatible, but there's a drawback. The interface is intended only for real-time recording and is unable to support the level of accuracy required of single-frame recording.

Although there is no functional advantage to either a parallel or a serial communications setup as far as the animator is concerned, you should make sure that the controller (board or unit) is compatible with your VTR's communications setup. For parallel operation, this also means that specific and sometimes unusual cables are required to connect to a given VTR. Generally, the more sophisticated (and usually more expensive) VTRs/VCRs operate via a serial RS-422 port and so are not cable-specific.

Because a VCR/VTR controller is essential equipment for single-frame recording and because the features that are bundled with one can considerably shorten your workday, be sure to evaluate the options carefully. Here are a few of the more important options that are worthy of consideration:

■ Has internal sync generator

■ Accepts external sync source

■ Interfaces with a variety of graphics signals

■ Has complete documentation for installation and troubleshooting

■ Has software or on-board diagnostic capabilities

■ Has an internal time code reader/generator

■ Has interfacing with a variety of VTRs

■ Has all necessary cables for interfacing

Some controllers have the capability to control two recorders at once. This is useful when you want to read in a video frame for image capture, render another image over it, and then save the composited image (using the second recorder). Alternatively, the second recorder can be used for rotoscoping, where a video-captured sequence from the VTR is saved digitally and then altered. As you might expect, the more advanced controllers are more versatile. For example, they have features such as the availability of an "advanced sync" signal and "black burst," which control the signal timing into the VTR.

Time Code

As already mentioned, the controller is oriented with reference to the tape by means of time code; because of time code calibration, the controller knows the current position on the videotape, when to start a preroll, and where exactly to place the next frame. Time code is an essential attribute for video production. It's a utility that unifies the entire video industry. With time code, you have the following advantages:

■ Precise time reference results in accurate information regarding length of animated sequences, video programs, and elapsed times.

■ Time code enables synchronized tape recorder operation. Video information can therefore be accurately transferred.

■ Video information can be accessed repeatedly, as needed.

Two methods have been developed to encode timing information on videotape. The most common method places coded sounds on one of the two available audio channels (usually channel 2). This code, established by the SMPTE (Society of Motion Picture and Television Engineers), identifies hours, minutes, seconds, and frames on a given length of tape. The SMPTE standard is used in virtually every editing and production studio.

The other time code standard uses neither of the audio tracks on a standard videotape. Called VITC (Vertical Interval Time Code), this method instead relies on the sync timing between video frames, which is known as the *vertical interval*. The main advantage of this method of time referencing (aside from the freeing of an audio channel) is that tracking of video fields (one half of a video frame) is more accurate.

Another notable advantage to the use of VITC is that it enables consistent VCR orientation to tape location even while the VCR is holding on a single frame. In contrast, audio-based SMPTE time code requires the shuttling of tape back and forth over the heads of the VTR in order to read the code embedded on the audio channel. Still, despite the limitations of audio-based time code, it is by far the more prevalent time coding method.

Formatting a Videotape with Time Code

Just as floppy disks must be formatted before they can be used, videotape must be initiated with time code. In other words, the tape has to be formatted before it is usable. In its raw state, out of the box, new videotape lacks SMPTE time code on either of its audio tracks, and so it must be "striped" before single-frame videotaping.

If your VTR/VCR controller doesn't incorporate an internal time code reader/generator as one of its features, then an external unit must be used to put the time code onto one of the audio tracks. First, a blank video signal ("video black") is recorded along with the time code for each tape prior to its use in production.

A few features are of special interest when you look at time code reader/writers. The so-called "jam-sync" capability enables you to use another time code generator to resynchronize the time code already on a videotape. Another feature, Tach Pulse Operation, automatically and continuously maintains time code information during "drop out" periods when there is temporarily no information on the tape, due to tape flaws.

Striping a Videotape

When an SMPTE time code generator is used, it is common practice to put the time code into audio channel 2. Then the level of the signal is set to 3 dB, as seen on the meter's display, above the 0 reference level on the VTR's audio meter. This ensures a correct signal level that is readable on other VTRs with varying audio levels. You should be sure the Automatic Gain Control (AGC) is OFF to prevent potential distortion artifacts. Finally, be sure to allow enough header, at least 20 seconds of black. This ensures sufficient time for most VTRs to reach a stable speed.

Conclusion

As you have seen, if you want video to be in your production picture, you need a good working understanding of the available equipment and of the various video options that will inevitably influence your production decisions. Knowing how video works and how to manipulate the equipment can make the difference between a professional-quality product and what, to even the most casual observer, will be seen as an amateur's handiwork. This introduction should get you headed in the right direction.

Advanced Morphing

3

by Scott Anderson

Introduction

Morphing is an abused child. It is only six years old and it has already been exploited shamelessly to sell everything from gasoline to granola. Terminators from the future morph across our movie screens; shape-shifting aliens are commonplace on *Star Trek* and *Deep Space Nine*. Rock stars can't wait to be warped and morphed into everything from panthers to sea horses.

Morphing got its first job in 1988, metamorphosing a witch in the movie *Willow*, but it has been relentlessly employed since then in countless other movies, rock videos, television shows, and commercials. Especially commercials. With 15 to 30 seconds to get the point across, hang the expense and get some morphing.

There is a reason for this madness: morphing works. It grabs your eyeballs and won't let go. And this is only the beginning—morphing has still more tricks up its youthful sleeve. Morphing seems magical, and you can use it in surprising ways. The software wizards have been wearing out their wands creating new programs. Now you can be the sorcerer's apprentice and try your own hand with some digital alchemy.

Morphing used to be expensive. These days, anyone with a personal computer can do it, so you can expect to see a lot more morphing in the years to come. That may be a mixed blessing.

As you might remember, the advent of desktop publishing brought mind-boggling documents that looked like ransom notes—every font known to man was on every page. Similarly, expect to see some amazing overkill on morphing effects when people get their hands on some of this inexpensive software. Prepare yourself for the onslaught.

Does this mean that morphing will become a cliché? Perhaps, but there are many legitimate uses for morphing—and some not-so-obvious applications that will keep morphing happily employed for years to come. This chapter looks at the expanding world of morphing and how you can use your home PC to create novel morphing sequences.

First, a Few Words

Before going any further, it's important to clarify some terminology: *morphing* is a combination of *warping*, *tweening*, and *dissolving*. Are there any questions?

Actually, as strange as that sounds, it's really very simple.

Warping is the mathematical trick of stretching and squashing an image as if it were painted on rubber. A great example of warping was Meryl Streep's severely twisted neck in *Death Becomes Her*. Clever people have created numerous warping routines over the last thirty years. The process is usually accomplished with a series of hundreds of dots to outline eyes, lips, noses, or other parts of an image. The dots have only a local effect, so you need a lot of them to cover the scene. Managing all these dots can be tedious, and it is easy to misplace one, creating a very strange warp.

This chapter discusses an implementation of a newer method that uses lines to control the warping. Lines make the warping specification much easier than using points, giving the artist a break.

Tweening is short for in-betweening, the process of smoothly going from one image to the next by automatically adding extra frames in between them. Long before computerized tweening was invented, animators at Disney used a manual tweening method to squeeze a little extra realism into their cartoons. Mathematically speaking, automatic tweening interpolates between two images to yield a smooth-flowing animation. Tweening is typically done with points, lines, or polygons.

Because the warping algorithm presented in this chapter is line-oriented, tweening fits right in. By tweening the position of the control lines, you can smoothly warp an image around.

With warping and tweening alone, you can create photo-real animations from single photographs, and it's simple to do. Animators, take note. This principle is illustrated at greater length in my book *Morphing Magic*.

Dissolving, or cross-dissolving, is Hollywood-speak for fading out one scene while fading in the next. In the middle, you have a double exposure. This powerful effect was used in the early Wolfman movies. While poor Lon Chaney Jr. stuck his head in a vise, makeup people swarmed about, adding hair and putty. After each little change in makeup was completed, another few frames of film were squeezed off. Each short take was cross-dissolved with the previous one to complete the illusion.

These three tricks are great special effects by themselves, but put them all together and you get a mesmerizing morph.

The words morphing and warping are often used interchangeably—and they are related—but the two are quite different. One of the differences is that morphing needs two images (called keyframes) to work its sorcery, whereas warping needs only one. Warping is the more basic concept and has many applications of its own, beyond its association with morphing.

The simplest morphing method involves matching up the significant features—such as the eyes, nose, and lips—of two keyframes. This is usually done with control points that are placed on one keyframe and moved to the corresponding spot on the other. Then you tell the computer how many in-between frames you want, and it crunches the data. For each in-between frame, the program warps the two images into alignment while simultaneously cross-dissolving them. As the sequence proceeds, the result looks less like the original image and more like the final image.

Imagine you want to morph yourself into a tiger. On the first frame, your own magnificent self-portrait, you mark the key areas with lines. You might place a control line from one eye to the other, down that noble nose, and across the lips. These three lines capture the most important aspects of a face.

Then, on the tiger's ferocious countenance, you would draw control lines on the same features: eyes, nose, and mouth.

That's enough information for the computer to morph the two. To create a single morph in the middle, the control lines are tweened halfway and the images are warped to follow the new lines. The algorithm warps your face midway to the tiger, and warps the tiger midway to you. This is the 50-50 interpolation between the two sets of control lines—the central tween. It is also simply the average of the two sets.

After creating the two warped images, the routine cross-dissolves them, finally producing the morph. If you use more tweens, such as 10 interpolations between you and the tiger, you can make a smoothly animated sequence of you turning into the tiger.

Here's how it works: The first frame uses 10 percent of the tiger mixed with 90 percent of you. The second frame has 20 percent of the tiger with 80 percent of you. The ninth frame is 90 percent tiger, and you have faded out to 10 percent.

This method creates footage that you can output to video, but the source images are both static. The next step up in morphing is to move beyond those still pictures and morph two movie clips. Called dynamic morphing, this requires a whole slew of new techniques, but the results justify the hassle. These are great effects to add to your video productions, but they are only the tip of the special effects iceberg. Today's morphing programs are multitalented and powerful. They can make the impossible not only do-able, but relatively easy.

History

Warping has a long (for computers anyway) history, going back to the 1960s when the U.S. had a working space program. After sending up LandSat, NASA was snapping shots of the earth like an eager tourist. But when it came time to put all the pictures together, they discovered that nothing quite lined up correctly. Due to the different altitudes, angles, times, and optics for each shot, it's amazing that they even tried to stitch them together.

But try they did, and they succeeded. The folks at NASA developed algorithms that treated the digitized data as points on a polynomial surface that could be stretched to fit a set of reference points. They called their endeavor *image registration*. I would call it the first warp program. By using major landmarks for registration and stretching the images around, they made everything fit perfectly into a big quilt of pictures blanketing the globe. This was a great start for a little warping routine.

Warping was dusted off again in the mid-seventies when Viking 2 landed on Mars. Viking had a very clever, compact, cylindrical camera. Unfortunately, it came to rest at an angle, with the camera angling down. This skewed the optics of the device; the landscape it depicted looked like the Big Valley, with the horizon strongly curved. To correct this twisted vista, the images of Mars were pushed through a warping algorithm that corrected for the odd optics before the public ever saw them.

Other uses are being discovered for morphing and warping every day. One of them is in the medical field: digital subtraction angiography. This mouthful describes a method of looking at someone's arteries by taking an x-ray before and after the injection of a dye. The first x-ray is digitally subtracted from the second, leaving only the parts that are different. That should be the dyed artery. This uncluttered image is of great value to the diagnostician.

However, there is a problem: patients move. Doctors like that in a patient, but it's a nuisance nonetheless. If the patient moves, the effect is wrecked.

That's where warping comes in. Warping is used to register the two x-rays before subtraction, making the final image razor sharp.

These are not exactly home applications of morphing, obviously. And yet, you can be enjoying the fruits of these high-powered routines if you have a hand scanner. Some of these useful devices come with software to match up different swipes of the scanner to create a larger image. Again, the registration problem is solved by warping.

New Technology

Using directed lines (vectors) instead of dots to specify the features makes the life of the morphing artist considerably easier. Instead of hundreds of dots, you may need only a dozen or so lines. The majority of commercial programs use dots, although some have started to incorporate lines as well.

The algorithms used in my book, *Morphing Magic*, all use a line algorithm. It leads to a very intuitive interface. However, being a global instead of local algorithm, it can take longer to calculate the morph.

One of the interesting aspects of this global algorithm is that you can specify squashes, rotations, and skews with just one line. For instance, start by drawing a horizontal line on the screen. When you move it, all the screen pixels move with it. If you make the line vertical, the whole picture rotates by 90 degrees. This can be a very useful feature in its own right.

Lines make many warping and morphing jobs a lot easier. Warping can pull your picture around so much that the edges are no longer straight. But using lines to control the warp simplifies things: you just draw four lines to define the border, and that pins it down.

Morphing Programs

There are morphing programs on every popular computer platform. For the Amiga, there is ImageMaster from Black Belt Systems, (800) TK-AMIGA. ImageMaster can do more than morph. It is a complete image-processing program that also happens to include morphing. The morphing can be done full screen or just in a specified area of the screen.

For the Macintosh, there is Morph 2.0 from Gryphon Software Corp., (619) 536-8815. This program enables dynamic morphing, where two different *moving* images are morphed together. All the other software described in this chapter is used to morph two *still* images. Morph 2.0 lets you warp as well as morph, so you can create caricatures, as described later.

Elastic Reality, from Elastic Reality, Inc., (608) 273-6585, also for the Mac, is one of the most capable of the morph programs, introducing the ability to "fold" an image over a background, solving a problem discussed later in this chapter. Elastic Reality also enables dynamic morphing, but the best part of Elastic Reality is its use of splines to define the shapes you want to morph. Splines, which are curved lines, allow you to morph with much greater ease and precision.

MetaFlo', from the Valis Group, (800) VALIS04, is another Mac program that enables warping and morphing. It takes a different tack from the other programs in this genre, creating warps in a user-defined area, rather than using lines or dots to move parts around. For instance, you can enlarge an eye by drawing a closed curve around it and then drawing a bigger target curve. The eye will instantly swell to fit the new area. Although it is not as precise as Elastic Reality, MetaFlo' is a fun, freeform program that provides fast feedback, perfect for the artist who wants to try a lot of experiments.

For the IBM PC and clones, there is Morph for Windows, also from Gryphon Software. This program allows lines to be used in the morphing specification. The results are saved in the FLI format or can be output as a Video for Windows movie. The individual images can be saved in TIFF or GIF formats.

Also for the PC is PhotoMorph from North Coast Software Inc., (603) 664-6000. In addition to morphing, this package provides some picture-editing tools like cropping, rotating, and scaling. Different clips can be chained together to make longer movies. Output is saved in the AVI, FLC, or Video for Windows format.

In addition to the programs mentioned previously, consider PhotoMorph from North Coast Software and WinImages:morph from Black Belt Systems. They are both competent and reasonably priced morphing packages. And of course, for the budget-minded, there is the software that comes with *Morphing Magic* (from Sams Publishing). It isn't strong on the user interface (it's a DOS program), but all the source code is included so that programming-oriented morphophiles can customize it. The images are saved in the PCX file format. A small part of that code is included with this book and is discussed later in this chapter.

New Tricks

Animation

One unexpected use for warping and tweening—and one you can do on your PC—is animation. Given any image, such as a drawing or a photograph, you can warp it into motion. If you have ever produced 30 frames of animation only to see them fly by in one second, you can appreciate the assistance of a computer.

Warping lets you animate cartoons or photographs with minimal hassle. Just a few mouse strokes can produce a gratifying amount of animation. *Morphing Magic* has several examples of animation produced by moving only six lines. Animation adds immeasurably to a training film or commercial but is rarely used because of its difficulty. Warping lowers the barrier.

For instance, warping makes it possible to make an animal talk. First the animal is photographed on the set, as usual. Then each frame of the movie is manipulated to make the lips move, and the fur comes along for the ride. This effect was used on a recent episode of *Northern Exposure* titled "Mr. Sandman." Fitting right in with the surrealistic nature of the series, there is a dream sequence featuring a talking dog in a taxi-cab. The dog delivers his lines in perfect lip-sync—with a French accent yet! This animation was created by VisionArt using the warp mode of Elastic Reality. Similarly, a cat was made to talk with this technique in the movie *Hocus Pocus*.

As another example, look at the animated dance sequence I created with MetaFlo' from the Valis Group. When it comes to animation, MetaFlo' is a standout program, offering isolated warps and multiple image layers. For the original picture, I scanned in a caricature of Isadora Duncan, circa 1904—placing it safely out of copyright. I brought it into MetaFlo' and used the warping tools to pull the arms and legs around. MetaFlo' uses free-form borders to limit the range of the warping, so I could isolate the leg, say, from the rest of the body.

I created three keyframes this way (see Figures 3.1, 3.2, and 3.3), and they became the basis of an animated dance. MetaFlo' automatically tweens from one keyframe to the next, creating a QuickTime movie or a numbered sequence of frames.

FIGURE 3.1.

Isadora's original image from a 1904 cartoon.

FIGURE 3.2.

Isadora kicks up her heels.

What is great about this technique is that more elaborate animations can be attempted. With the computer as your partner, you just specify the basic movement, and the computer makes sure all the details (like Isadora's dress or the dog's fur) are attended to automatically.

This is a long-standing problem in cartoon animation. It's just too much work to track detail from frame to frame. When animation was born, certain rules were quickly formulated. The most important one, from the artistic point of view, was to forego detail and use flat, solid coloring. This is so entrenched that you don't even notice it—that's just what cartoons look like. Not any more. Prepare yourself for a whole new look in animation as computer tools find their way into the hands of animators.

FIGURE 3.3.

Another frame from Isadora's dance.

The Seamless Cut

Another interesting use for morphing is the seamless cut. You might not have seen this effect before—but that's because you aren't supposed to. This is an effect that succeeds only when it's invisible. Why bother?

Imagine you are filming your great American epic and for one scene there are 10 takes. The next day, while viewing the rushes, you discover that the beginning of take 3 is great but the ending stinks. Similarly, the end of take 10 is great but the start stinks. Unfortunately, it was a stormy outdoor location scene, and it's almost impossible to match the lighting for another shoot.

Morphing is the medicine to cure this common illness. Simply morph the beginning of take 3 into the end of take 10—the perfect take, without reshooting. It also saves money, which pleases the accountants. This simple remedy is another reason that morphing will be around to doctor films for a long time to come.

Texturing

It's not obvious that morphing could be used as a texturing tool, but by now, you shouldn't be surprised at anything morphing can do. The technique here is to warp a texture pattern and superimpose it on another object. For instance, you could take a leopard, warp its head to fit human proportions, and then superimpose it on a woman's face to make a cat-woman. The result adds perfectly contoured leopard spots to the face, without warping it.

To do this, start with the woman (see Figure 3.4) and define the control lines for her face and the corresponding lines for the leopard (see Figure 3.5). Then use these lines to warp the leopard into the shape of the woman's face (see Figure 3.6). Finally, use a dissolve to blend the two images, as shown in Figures 3.7, 3.8, and 3.9. Notice that unlike a traditional morph, the shape of the woman's face doesn't change. Instead, the leopard texture slowly dominates her features.

FIGURE 3.4.

A woman about to be leopardized, with lines to define her features.

FIGURE 3.5.
A leopard to be used as a texture, with corresponding lines.

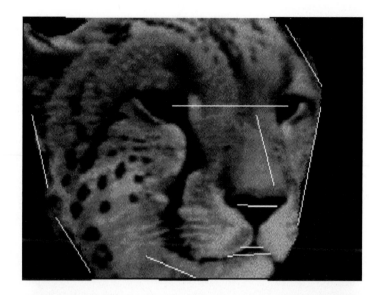

FIGURE 3.6.
The leopard warped to match up with the woman.

FIGURE 3.7.

The first tween in the dissolving sequence puts just a hint of the leopard in the cheeks of the model.

FIGURE 3.8.

The next tween shows even more cat texture.

As another example, you can use a painting as a texture. I used this technique to get my portrait painted by Van Gogh. First I scanned in Van Gogh's portrait and a photo of myself (see Figures 3.10 and 3.11). Using Elastic Reality, I put myself in the A-roll and Van Gogh in the B-roll. Then, using the Bézier curves that are the hallmark of this program, I defined the features to correlate.

FIGURES 3.9.

The third tween completes the transition into the cat-woman. Who needs makeup when you have morphing?

FIGURE 3.10.

A rare shot of the author with his mouth closed.

FIGURE 3.11.

Vincent Van Gogh on one of his better days.

After drawing the outline of my face, eyes, and mouth, I copied them to the B-roll. There I moved the outlines until they corresponded to Van Gogh's features.

The key to texturing in Elastic Reality is adjusting the motion curve. Motion curves allow you to vary the speed of the control points. They are primarily used to put some extra life into the warps, but this is another use for them.

The motion curves should be adjusted so that the A-roll *doesn't* warp and the B-roll *stays* warped until the very last minute. When the morph is executed, Van Gogh is immediately warped and cross-dissolved with my face, which doesn't warp at all. The result is a sequence where the texture of the Van Gogh painting is gradually cross-dissolved with my face. For the final product, I picked a composite that was about two-thirds of the way through the sequence (see Figure 3.12).

FIGURE 3.12.

The author, as painted by Van Gogh.

Notice how my dark shirt contributed little to the final composite, bringing Van Gogh's smock to the foreground. Although this example is with a still image, the same technique can be applied to a movie sequence. Elastic Reality has some handy tools to deal with such a dynamic morph.

This can be a very useful effect, even taking over for some makeup jobs. You can give your sasquatch a furry face, or give a lagoon creature an alligator complexion—all without any putty or greasepaint.

Caricatures

Another non-obvious use for warping is to create photo-real caricatures. Scan in a picture of Ross Perot and make his ears even bigger (if your monitor is large enough). Or take a picture of Ted Kennedy and enlarge his jowls. It takes an artistic eye to catch the key features of a person, but with warping, you can exaggerate those features even more. Photo-real caricatures are a little disconcerting, but very interesting.

3-D Animation

An unexpected bonus of morphing is the ability to simulate a 3-D world. Given an object photographed from two different angles, morphing lets you re-create the angles in between. The trick is to match up the features as seen from each angle. When the morph is completed, the object appears to rotate in perfect 3-D.

For a convincing effect, the warping routines must be capable of correctly interpolating the intermediate angles. To do this with the utmost mathematical rigor, you would need elliptical interpolation. Most morphing programs provide only linear interpolation, but for small enough angles, this is sufficient.

As an example, consider the Mt. Shasta sequence. The two end frames, or keyframes, are computer-generated images to start with. They were reconstructed by NASA from space shuttle photographs (a story in itself), and they represent two views of the mountain from cameras that are about 20 degrees apart.

Using the morphing program from my book *Morphing Magic*, I marked prominent geological features—like rocks and crevices—with control lines. The lines were placed in one keyframe and then moved to the corresponding spot in the other keyframe.

Once all the control lines were correlated, *Morphing Magic* created the sequence (see Figures 3.13, 3.14, and 3.15). As you can see, the in-between image is quite convincing. It successfully re-creates a new camera position halfway between the two other pictures. This sequence played back on video looks like you're circling Mt. Shasta.

FIGURE 3.13.

An original photo of Mt. Shasta.

FIGURE 3.14.

A computer-generated tween that represents a new camera angle.

FIGURE 3.15.

An original photo of Mt. Shasta from a different angle.

For the mountain, it's easy to see the benefit of this technique: a few photos can replace an airplane ride. But there are other uses, once you think about it. For instance, you can use this technique to fix irregularities in the seamless cutting trick I mentioned earlier. If the camera is in a different spot from one scene to the next, this method can patch up the problem. The morph has the effect of smoothly tracking the camera around.

Also, if your actors are not looking in exactly the same direction in each take (and they won't be), don't be afraid to morph their heads around. If the difference in the angles is small, you'll get splendid results.

On the other hand, if the angular difference is greater than about 30 degrees, you won't be able to find any correspondence for some of the control points. They will be hidden from view, rotated behind the object—and your warps will get grotesque.

Another problem can occur if the desired information is off the edge of the picture. This happens near the bottom corners of the Mt. Shasta pictures. The morphing routines usually substitute the color at the nearest edge for the unknown pixels, which creates an unnatural-looking smear. This artifact can be avoided by morphing a larger scene and then cropping out the affected area.

As virtual reality and 3-D techniques start to gain in popularity, this quick and dirty trick for creating a 3-D space could find a new audience. For instance, the manufacture of CD-ROM games can involve more videography than a traditional movie. Every scene can be shot with two or three different outcomes, each representing different paths through the game.

This is good news for videographers, but it poses a problem: how can you seamlessly switch from one video sequence to another without a jarring cut? The answer, of course, is to use this little morphing trick to make perfectly smooth segues.

Segues

Morphing is a terrific way to blend one scene into another. The television show *Home Improvement* makes good use of computer animation and warping to highlight scene changes. The result is humorous and eye-catching. On a birthday episode, for instance, they turned one of the characters into a birthday candle. Later, they used a warp to make the screen beat like a heart. Pay close attention, and you can pick up a lot of tricks from this show.

In fact, anywhere you use a dissolve can be a potential spot for a morph. Where you might dissolve from a screaming baby to a steam whistle, now you can morph. Think of the famous bone-tossing scene from *2001, A Space Odyssey*. Today, instead of dissolving, Kubrick might have morphed the bone into the spaceship.

Morphing Problems

Background Problems

When you warp or morph a face, you might end up warping the background as well. This can totally destroy the morphing effect, so you need a way to separate the foreground morph from the backdrop. Chroma-key methods are the optimal solution. Shoot the morphing scene against a blue backdrop and then composite it against the desired background. Adobe

Premiere has a useful chroma-key facility that enables you to select both the chroma-key color and a range around it; this can help you key on a changing or uneven blue-screen backdrop.

MetaFlo' has a built-in matting tool that lets you matte out an object in any layer and composite it with the rest of the scene. This makes the job a lot easier. Elastic Reality has excellent tools for isolating the extent of a warp or morph. It has a feature called "folding" that lets the warped part of an image fold over a background without affecting it.

If you don't have chroma-keys or matting tools available, the good news is…you can still do it. The bad news is…you have to do it by hand. Nevertheless, there are some great retouch programs, like Adobe Photoshop, that make the job more manageable. Just erase the background from the scene and save the result.

When you have cleaned out all the backgrounds, perform the morph and composite it back against a background—the original, or any other backdrop you choose.

Like Watching Grass Grow...

One of the thornier problems with morphing is how slow it is. Morphing is a complicated algorithm that performs multiple calculations on every affected pixel. Even the fastest machines can't keep up with the task in real time—yet. Nevertheless, many of the available packages provide some degree of help in the speed department.

MetaFlo' works by saving up a list of all the distortions performed on an image. Rather than save the resulting picture, it re-creates it from scratch by applying all the required distortions in sequence. Therefore, you can work with a lower resolution image for placement purposes and then substitute the high-resolution originals for later, unattended, processing. There is also a fast render command that will render at a lower resolution for proofing.

Elastic Reality takes a different tack, enabling you to process a batch of morphing projects during the night, for instance. Elastic Reality can also work as a background task, so you can write your script while it warps your characters.

The Math Section

Buckle your seatbelts—you're about to learn the math behind the magic. If you're a mathphobe, just skip over this part and I'll see you again in the next section, which discusses the programs on the disk.

Warping with Control Lines

Given point P in the source image, you want to deduce point P' in the target image (see Figure 3.16). By inspecting the diagram, you see that the distance d is the projection of vector **AP** (I'm using boldface for vectors) on the perpendicular, which yields ‖**AP**‖ cos α, where ‖**AP**‖ represents the magnitude of the vector.

FIGURE 3.16.

A given point P has a relationship to the line AB that gets translated to the warping line A'B'.

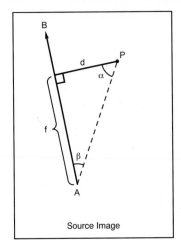
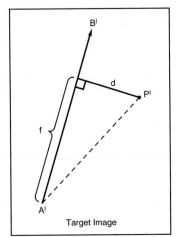

Source Image   Target Image

The dot product of vector **AP** with the perpendicular to **AB** (denoted ⊥**AB**) is defined as

$$\mathbf{AP} \cdot \bot\mathbf{AB} = \|\mathbf{AP}\| * \|\bot\mathbf{AB}\| \cos \alpha$$

$$= (AP_x * \bot AB_x + AP_y * \bot AB_y)$$

where ‖**AP**‖ and ‖**AB**‖ are the magnitudes, and the subscripted variables are the x and y components of the vectors. You can see that this solution in terms of components, $(AP_x * \bot AB_x + AP_y * \bot AB_y)$, doesn't involve any trigonometry. Solving for d:

Equation 1

$$d = \|\mathbf{AP}\| \cos \alpha$$

$$= \frac{\mathbf{AP} \cdot \bot\mathbf{AB}}{\|\mathbf{AB}\|}$$

The magnitude of the line itself, ‖**AB**‖, is used instead of the magnitude of the perpendicular, ‖⊥**AB**‖. This is for two good reasons: one is that they are equal and the other is that you can reuse this number, as you shall see.

The vector dot product allows you to calculate the desired values without computing any angles or using any transcendental functions. That makes it both simple and fast.

From Figure 3.16, you see that the distance represented by f is the projection of **AP** on **AB** itself—||**AP**|| cos β—which is the quantity

$$\frac{\mathbf{AP} \cdot \mathbf{AB}}{\|\mathbf{AB}\|}$$

You want the fractional part of line **AB**, so you divide by the length of **AB** again:

Equation 2

$$f = \frac{\mathbf{AP} \cdot \mathbf{AB}}{\|\mathbf{AB}\|^2}$$

Equations 1 and 2 represent a translation into a new, scaled, orthogonal coordinate system based on d and f instead of x and y. Now you are ready to transfer these two important relationships over to the new line, **A'B'**.

The fractional part—the "f-axis"—is easy. It is just the fractional part of the new line, **A'B'**:

$$f* \mathbf{A'B'}$$

Next you apply the distance to the "d-axis," which is perpendicular to the new line. The unit d-vector is

$$\frac{\perp \mathbf{A'B'}}{\|\mathbf{A'B'}\|}$$

So, with the new origin at **A'**, the source pixel **P** (represented as a vector from the origin) is transformed into the destination pixel **P'**:

Equation 3

$$\mathbf{P'} = \mathbf{A'} + f*\mathbf{A'B'} + d* \frac{\perp \mathbf{A'B'}}{\|\mathbf{A'B'}\|}$$

This algorithm uses the relationship a point has with the original line and applies it to the new line.

To be of real use, however, you need more lines. They all have to compete for pixels. This implementation uses a weighting proportional to 1 over the distance squared:

$$\text{weight} \propto \frac{1}{d^2}$$

Here's how the calculation goes for two control lines: from each line, the distance to the point is computed, and a new pixel is calculated as before. This time there are two lines and therefore two warped pixels, so some further work is needed. As shown in Figure 3.17, from the original point **P** to the new points **P**$_1$' and **P**$_2$' there are two displacements, **D**$_1$ and **D**$_2$:

$$\mathbf{D_1} = \mathbf{P_1'} \text{ - } \mathbf{P}$$

$$\mathbf{D_2} = \mathbf{P_2'} \text{ - } \mathbf{P}$$

FIGURE 3.17.

Where two lines contribute influence, the warped point is the weighted average of the displacements D$_1$ and D$_2$.

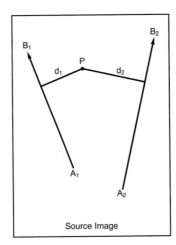
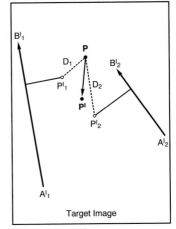

The routine calculates the weighted average of the two displacements to arrive at the final position, **P'**:

$$\mathbf{P'} = \mathbf{P} + \frac{\mathbf{D_1\,W_1} + \mathbf{D_2W_2}}{\mathbf{W_1} + \mathbf{W_2}}$$

If there are three lines, there are three displacements to average, and so on. For *n* lines

$$P' = P + \frac{\displaystyle\sum_{i=1}^{n} P_i W_i}{\displaystyle\sum_{i=1}^{n} W_i}$$

Tweening

The second piece of the morphing trio is tweening. Compared with warping, tweening is a piece of cake. In the simplest case of linear tweening all you do is interpolate. *Linear* interpolation is just finding a point on the *line* connecting two others.

Although there are dozens of ways to interpolate, for these purposes linear tweening is just fine. All you do is take the lines describing the source image and tween them into the lines describing the target. For each intermediate tween, you warp the images accordingly.

For speed, divide the distance between the points into as many steps as you desire, say ten. You will have an x and a y component for the length of these segments, called deltas. For a regular division of the line, all these deltas will be equal to one-tenth of the line distance, so you need to calculate it only once and then simply add it to the starting point. After ten additions of this delta, you will have arrived at the target point. If you continue to apply the deltas, you will overshoot the target and produce something different. For instance, if the source image was a three-year old and the target was the same child at four, the overshoot might look like a child at five. This is the basis of software programs that attempt to "age" a missing child for identification purposes.

The deltas are given by the simple equations

DeltaX = (TargetX - SourceX) / (Tweens + 1)
DeltaY = (TargetY - SourceY) / (Tweens + 1)

Adding a delta in this fashion is fast, but care must be taken to avoid round-off errors.

Cross-Dissolving

Now you are at the third and final part of morphing, the dissolve. This is where you combine the two images you are warping and tweening. You mix any two colors just the way you might suspect. The color midway between two colors is found as follows:

NewRed = (SourceRed + TargetRed) / 2
NewGreen = (SourceGreen + TargetGreen) / 2
NewBlue = (SourceBlue + TargetBlue) / 2

On a 24-bit color system, the color you get from this calculation will always be another color you can display. This is not so with color-mapped graphics cards. You can easily derive a color that isn't in the puny list of displayable colors called the palette. The best that most VGA cards can offer is 256 colors, which is pretty sad for this application.

To fix this rotten state of affairs, you need to calculate all the colors as if you had 24 bits to play with. Then you need to create a new palette that uses the 256 most popular colors. The rest of the colors must be forced into the closest color available from those 256.

So dissolving, which should be the smallest part of this whole algorithm, suddenly swells into an unsightly carbuncle on this otherwise straightforward code.

Those are the basics of morphing. There are many different algorithms for performing this terrific effect, but this should serve as a good jumping-off point for further experimentation.

The Software

The Code

There are as many ways to warp as there are sort routines. The method employed here uses lines to specify the warping. As I mentioned before, this approach is friendly to the artist. Other routines use dots to warp the image. These changes are local and act over only a short distance, so you need hundreds of them. Misplacing some of the dots and thereby ruining the warp is not at all difficult.

With the new method, each line represents the string of points that compose it, so a few short lines can stand in for hundreds of points. As you move a control line, the pixels around it are pulled as well.

One of the interesting peculiarities of this algorithm is the global nature of the warping. A single line can specify any combination of scaling, translation, and rotation. This can be a nice effect in itself. Just draw, for example, a vertical line, rotate it 90 degrees, and the image will also be rotated. When there are more lines (as there usually are), they will each compete for influence, but the effect will still be global. The downside of this is that it takes a little longer to perform the warping.

In the algorithm presented here, the influence of the line falls off as $1/distance^2$ falls off. This is just like the influence of gravity, but you can select any variation on this that you desire. This formulation was chosen based largely on speed considerations.

Here is the basic recipe for warping:

1. Find the distance between a pixel and the source line by dropping the perpendicular, d (see Figure 3.16).

2. Find the fractional distance f along the source line to the perpendicular. The fraction is normalized to go from 0 to 1.

3. Move the point to a spot that is the same distance from, and fraction of, the *target* line.

Using the Programs

There are three executables: MORPH.EXE, FIX.EXE, and LOAD.EXE. MORPH gets the user input and creates the morphing sequence, FIX finds a good palette, and LOAD plays the sequence back from memory. These programs make extensive use of three core programs: COLOR.C, IO.C, and LINECALC.C. COLOR.C deals with color palette issues, IO.C handles DOS file I/O and the mouse, and LINECALC.C has most of the core warping routines.

All the programs work with PCX files having 256 colors and 320×200 resolution.

To capture PCX images for use in these programs, use a TSR screen-capture program. You can also find GIF images on CompuServe and convert them with a program like Paint Shop from ZSoft. Remember to convert the number of colors to 256.

If you have access to a scanner, your troubles are over. You can scan in your own photos and magazine clips and go from there.

When specifying a PCX file, you do not need to type in the file extension. The programs automatically append ".PCX" to the end of each filename, saving you the trouble.

Some of these programs produce a numbered sequence of output files. These are also PCX files. The maximum sequence size is 99. The sequence number, from 1 to 99, is appended to the root name of the file sequence. This takes two characters away from the already tiny DOS allotment of eight. Therefore, the <OutFile> name must be six characters or less.

The MORPH Program

```
MORPH <File1> <File2> [<Steps> [<OutFile>]]
```

<File1> is the name of the source PCX file to morph.
<File2> is the name of the target PCX file.
<Steps> is the optional number of output files. If you don't specify the number of steps in your sequence, the program produces one in-between morph. You must specify <Steps> if you want to output files.

<OutFile> is the root name of the optional output files. The value of <Steps> determines the number of files to output. The step number is appended to the root name, so the <OutFile> name must be six characters or less.

Morph first reads the two input files: the source and target PCX images. Then it looks on the disk for any existing control lines that might be associated with the source or target image. If the user permits it, these line files are loaded in. Otherwise, the user creates a new set of control lines from scratch, and these are saved to the disk.

Morph metamorphoses between the two in the given number of steps, to make a sequence of files. The files are numbered and can be displayed by the LOAD program.

Examples:

```
MORPH JIM BOB
```

This command will cause morph to load the files JIM.PCX and BOB.PCX. It will create the middle tween and display it. No files are created.

```
MORPH JIM BOB 7
```

This command will load the files JIM.PCX and BOB.PCX. It will create a sequence of seven frames and display them. No files are created.

```
MORPH JIM BOB 7 JIMBOB
```

This command will load the files JIM.PCX and BOB.PCX. It will create a sequence of seven frames. Each frame is displayed while it is saved to the disk. The files will be named JIMBOB1.PCX, JIMBOB2.PCX, up to JIMBOB7.PCX.

The key routines for doing the warping are called from MORPH.C and are located in the file LINECALC.C. The sumLines routine sums up the warping contribution of each control line, and the getSourceLoc routine provides the position of the calculated warped pixel. This is what these two code segments look like:

```
/*******************************************************************
* FUNC: int    sumLines(PICTURE *picture, COLOR *color,
*                    LINE *origline, POINT *warp, LINE *warpline)
*
* DESC: Sum and weight the contribution of each warping line
*******************************************************************/

int
sumLines(PICTURE *picture, COLOR *color, LINE *origline,
        POINT *warp, LINE *warpline)
{
    int        x, y;
    float      weight, weightSum;
    float      distance;
    int        line;
    POINT      orig;
    int        paletteIndex;
```

```
        float    deltaSumX = 0.0;
        float    deltaSumY = 0.0;

        /* if no control lines, get an unwarped pixel */
        if (NumLines == 0)
            orig = *warp;
        else {
            weightSum = 0.0;
            for (line = 0; line < NumLines; line++,
                            origline++, warpline++)    {
                distance = getSourceLoc(&orig,origline,warp,warpline);
                weight = 1/(.001+distance*distance);
                deltaSumX += (orig.x - warp->x) * weight;
                deltaSumY += (orig.y - warp->y) * weight;
                weightSum += weight;
            }
            orig.x = warp->x + deltaSumX / weightSum + .5;
            orig.y = warp->y + deltaSumY / weightSum + .5;
        }

        /* clip it to the nearest border pixel */
        x = clip(orig.x, Xmin, Xmax);
        y = clip(orig.y, Ymin, Ymax);
        paletteIndex = PIXEL (picture, x, y);
        color->r = picture->pal.c[paletteIndex].r;
        color->g = picture->pal.c[paletteIndex].g;
        color->b = picture->pal.c[paletteIndex].b;
        return (paletteIndex);
}



/******************************************************************
* FUNC: float getSourceLoc(POINT *orig, LINE *origline,
*                                  POINT *warp, LINE *warpline)
*
* DESC: For a given line, locate the corresponding warped pixel
*******************************************************************/

float
getSourceLoc(POINT *orig, LINE *origline, POINT *warp,
                                    LINE *warpline)
{
    float fraction, fdist;
    int   dx, dy;
    float distance;

    dx = warp->x - warpline->p[0].x;
    dy = warp->y - warpline->p[0].y;
    fraction = (dx * (long) warpline->delta_x + dy
                * (long) warpline->delta_y)
                / (float) (warpline->length_square);
    fdist = (dx * (long) -warpline->delta_y + dy
                * (long) warpline->delta_x)
                / (float) warpline->length;
    if (fraction <= 0 )
        distance = sqrt(dx*(long) dx + dy * (long) dy);
    else if (fraction >= 1) {
        dx = warp->x - warpline->p[1].x;
```

```
        dy = warp->y - warpline->p[1].y;
        distance = sqrt(dx*(long) dx + dy * (long) dy);
    }
    else if (fdist >= 0)
        distance =  fdist;
    else
        distance = -fdist;
    orig->x = origline->p[0].x + fraction * origline->delta_x -
                fdist * origline->delta_y
                / (float) origline->length + .5;
    orig->y = origline->p[0].y + fraction * origline->delta_y +
                fdist * origline->delta_x
                / (float) origline->length + .5;
    return distance;
}
```

The LOAD Program

```
LOAD <File>
```

    `<File>` is the root name of a PCX sequence to display.

Load reads a sequence of PCX files indicated by the given name. It reads as many as it can fit into memory, then it displays them sequentially. You can control the playback rate by pressing a number, from 1 (slow) to 9 (fast). To single-step through the pictures, press the spacebar. To continue playback, press Enter. To quit, press Esc.

Example:

```
LOAD JIM
```

This command will cause the program to load a numbered sequence of PCX files with the root name of JIM, like JIM1.PCX, JIM2.PCX, and so forth.

The number of images that can be animated depends on how much free RAM you have. Get rid of your TSRs (Terminate and Stay Resident programs) and use the new memory features of DOS 6.0. The best you can do in 640K is about eight images.

The FIX Program

```
FIX <InFile> <OutFile>
```

    `<InFile>` is the root name of the PCX sequence to fix.
    `<OutFile>` is the root name of the fixed PCX sequence.

Fix takes a sequence created by morph and forces each picture in the sequence to have the same palette. Then it writes the sequence out under the new name.

Examples:

```
FIX JIM FXJIM
```

This command would read the sequence JIM1.PCX, JIM2.PCX, and so forth. It would output the same number of files named FXJIM1.PCX, FXJIM2.PCX, and so on.

```
FIX JIM JIM
```

This command would read the JIM sequence and write over the original files. Be careful! Make sure you don't need the originals before you do this.

FIX.C calls some basic color routines located in the file COLOR.C. The routine collapseColors takes the Frequency table of the RGB components and collapses it until the number of colors is less than a given threshold. The routine closestColor returns the index into the palette of the closest matching color.

```
/***************************************************************
 * FUNC: int     closestColor(int r, int g, int b, PALETTE *palPtr)
 *
 * DESC: return the palette index of the color closest to rgb.
 ***************************************************************/
/***************************************************************
 * FUNC: void    collapseColors(PALETTE *palPtr)
 *
 * DESC: Collapse the colors in the Freq table until
 *       Ncolors < COLORS, then put it in the given color palette.
 ***************************************************************/

void
collapseColors(PALETTE *palPtr)
{
    int freqCutoff;
    int r, g, b;
    int index;
    int ncolors;

    static int freqCount[MAX_FREQ+1];

    memset(freqCount, 0, sizeof freqCount);
    for (r = 0; r < MAX_COMP; r++)
        for (g = 0; g < MAX_COMP; g++)
            for (b = 0; b < MAX_COMP; b++)
                freqCount[Freq[r][g][b]]++;

    ncolors = 0;
    for (freqCutoff = COLORS-1; freqCutoff > 1; freqCutoff—) {
        ncolors += freqCount[freqCutoff];
        if (ncolors > COLORS) break;
    }

    /* Collapse color space to 256 colors */
    r = g = b = 0;
    while (Ncolors >= COLORS) {
        for (; r < MAX_COMP; r++, g=0) {
            for (; g < MAX_COMP; g++, b=0) {
                for (; b < MAX_COMP; b++) {
                    if (Freq[r][g][b] && Freq[r][g][b]
                                    <= freqCutoff)
                        goto castOut;   /* the ultimate no no */
```

```
                }
            }
        }
        r = g = b = 0;
        freqCutoff++;
        continue;
    castOut:
        Freq[r][g][b] = 0;  /* just remove this low freq color */
        Ncolors-;
    }

    /* build a palette out of all the remaining non zero freq's */
    index = 0;
    for (r = 0; r < MAX_COMP; r++)
        for (g = 0; g < MAX_COMP; g++)
            for (b = 0; b < MAX_COMP; b++)
                /* we have a color we need to map */
                if (Freq[r][g][b]) {
                    palPtr->c[index].r = r;
                    palPtr->c[index].g = g;
                    palPtr->c[index].b = b;
                    /* remember index in palette */
                    Freq[r][g][b] = index;
                    index++;
                }
}

/************************************************************
 * FUNC: int     closestColor(int r, int g, int b, PALETTE *palPtr)
 *
 * DESC: return the palette index of the color closest to rgb.
 ************************************************************/

int
closestColor(int r, int g, int b, PALETTE *palPtr)
{
    int index;
    int distance;
    int min_distance = 3200;    /* a big number */
    int min_index;

    /* The value in Freq is now the index into the color table */
    if (Freq[r][g][b]) return Freq[r][g][b];

    /* If zero, search for the closest color */
    for (index = 1; index < Ncolors; index++) {
        /* this is really the distance squared, but it works */
        distance =    SQUARE (r - palPtr->c[index].r) +
                      SQUARE (g - palPtr->c[index].g) +
                      SQUARE (b - palPtr->c[index].b);
        if (distance < min_distance) {
            min_distance = distance;
            min_index = index;
            if (distance <= 2) break;    /* close enough! */
        }
    }
    /* New index - for future reference */
    Freq[r][g][b] = min_index;
    return min_index;
}
```

Compiling Instructions

These programs were all compiled with the Microsoft compiler. If you didn't include the graphics library when you installed your compiler, you will need to link that library in at compile time. Use a command like

```
cl program.c /link graphics.lib
```

A makefile is included with the listings. It is set up assuming that you haven't installed the graphics library. If you have installed the graphics library, delete all instances of

```
/link graphics.lib
```

To make the programs work with other compilers, you will need to make some changes to the non-ANSI library calls. In Microsoft C, these library calls have an underline as the first character in their name. The non-ANSI library calls are all in IO.C and LINECALC.C.

Changing the Programs

The most obvious upgrade to this program is the ability to use extended RAM so you can hold more frames in memory. If you have access to some of the new software on the market that attempts to leap the 640K barrier, use it.

If you can work with smaller images—say quarter-screen, 160×100 resolution—you should be able to quadruple the number of frames that can be held in memory, not to mention speeding up the animation. The routines to change are in IO.C, the display picture routines. Currently, they slam a continuous string of bytes into memory. To fix it for smaller screens, you need to move the image one raster line at a time.

If you have a true-color card, you don't need the agonizing color collapsing routines. Just yank them all out. You will need to save the files in 16- or 24-bit color mode, which can present some data problems, so look at the drivers and documentation for your particular graphics card.

With these programs, you can create some amazing morphs. With a video capture board and a computer capable of displaying 30 frames per second, you can output to videotape. Now you can play with some of the same toys they have at Industrial Light and Magic and Pacific Data Images. Have fun!

Conclusion

If you're interested in more information, programs, and examples, check out my book *Morphing Magic* from Sams Publishing. It includes a disk complete with morphing and warping software (with source code) for the PC. There's plenty more to chew on there.

It's amazing how many rabbits can be plucked out of the morphing hat. Although we tend to think only of the flashy Hollywood morphs, there are many areas that morphing and warping have just begun to penetrate. I hope you've picked up some new tricks. Maybe you will discover some ways that morphing and warping can be used in your own area of expertise—and you can add another illusion to the growing repertoire of morphing magic.

Computer Painting Techniques

4

by Harry Dusenberg

How Did I Get Here?

I can remember a time in the distant past, when I was sitting in a darkened room in front of my new Commodore 64. I was thinking, "Now that I have this powerful computer, what am I going to do with it, sixteen colors and all?" Well, many years, computers, and keystrokes later, I find myself writing about creating computer art. I work at Suburban Cable TV in Delaware County in the Philadelphia area, doing graphics for their advertising channel. The software I use every day is Corel 5.0. It's a fine program for doing vector art, but I find that sometimes just sitting down and painting a beautiful landscape with a good paint program can be very relaxing, a nice change of pace.

The technique I've adapted to computer art is based on the wet-on-wet oil painting technique I learned from watching William Alexander, an old German gentleman, who still has a television show on PBS. After watching him for about a year, I decided to give painting a try. I remember doing my first oil painting: I went to the art store and gathered all the equipment I would need, including a can of turpentine that had on its label "This product has its own distinct odor." We had to leave the windows open for a week in the middle of winter to get the "distinct odor" out of the house. The way my wife, Kathy, was looking at me I thought that my painting career was going to be a short one, and that I would be sleeping in the dog house for a very long time. Thank goodness, she's a patient woman. The best part of painting electronically is there is no mess—no smell of paint thinner and no brushes to clean. About 200 paintings later, I became a certified instructor in this technique. I began holding many painting seminars and teaching privately in the Philadelphia area.

One of the joys of teaching this technique was seeing people who didn't think that they could create an oil painting leave at the end of the day rightfully proud of the paintings they had made. Soon after I began to work with computers, I discovered that with painting software I could adapt the technique I was teaching to create beautiful landscapes on the computer screen as well as on canvas.

I've been doing computer art for about eight years. I started uploading my work to the CompuServe Art Forum in 1992, and I've developed quite a collection on that network as well as on America Online. I've been amazed at the number of times my paintings have been downloaded, and I've often wondered where they are going. The next thing I know, I get e-mail from Sams Publishing asking me if I would like to write a chapter for this book. There's a lesson to be learned here: Keep painting, don't be afraid to show your work, and good things will happen. Certainly, if you don't let people see your work, nothing will ever happen. In this chapter, I hope to share with you some of the things I've learned while "mousin' around" all these years.

What We're Going to Do

In this chapter, we will create a painting together. The chapter is a bit of an art lesson, as well as a lesson on using the tools that come with most computer paint programs. We are going to paint a beautiful landscape, one with mountains in the distance, a valley spreading out at the foot of the mountains, and a river running through the valley. Our vantage point will be a break in a woodland trail high above the scene.

The technique I will describe is easy to learn, and when you've had some practice, the landscapes that you create will look almost photographic.

What You Will Need

You will need any computer that can display 256 colors or more. Of course, anyone who has owned a computer knows that "more and faster" is always better. You can use almost any popular paint program. If you can use SVGA 640×480 or greater, the result will be better, but if you can't, don't worry. 320×200 will work fine. I have done many beautiful paintings at that resolution. I'll be using Autodesk Animator Pro. I also use Deluxe Paint, Photopaint, and Photostyler, so you should use the software that you are most comfortable with and a mouse or sketch tablet. Most paint programs have similar settings, as far as brush and spray settings go; if, however, you don't find them or they are different from what I will describe, you should be able to get them right with a little experimentation.

Some Art Stuff

Here are a few principles of art that will be helpful when you are creating a painting, whether you are using oil or pixels.

You should "layer" your painting, starting first with the objects farthest away. As in real life, the farther in the distance an object is, the more it tends to pick up the color of the sky and the lighter it becomes. The closer things are, the sharper and more colorful they become. If you keep this in mind, your paintings will always have the illusion of depth.

The sky should be darker at the top and gradually get lighter toward the horizon. The horizon should not cut the scene in half; rather it should be about two-thirds down into the scene. This also helps create the illusion of depth.

Don't cover up all the dark—"the dark is your friend." A painting is, after all, a play on contrast; you can't have light unless you have dark to contrast with it. If you go outside and look at a tree, you will see that almost all the leaves and branches inside are dark. This is what makes the tree have depth.

Remember where your sun (or other light source) is. I'm right handed, so in most of my paintings light comes from the right. If you are left handed, you'll find it easier to paint with the light coming from the left. Don't ask me why—that's just the way it is.

Try to think in shapes and patterns. For instance, if you are painting a tree, you don't have to paint each and every leaf. You will find that there are shapes in nature that have a feeling to them, so if you are going to create a tree, bush, or mountain, you have to try to capture that feeling. Your brain knows these shapes, and the closer you come to them, the more you will feel they are real.

Avoid straight lines unless the object is man-made. Few natural things have straight lines.

When you are painting, think about the people who are going to view the painting. When those people look at the work, their eyes should be drawn into the scene. You can accomplish this by keeping the outer edges dark and the lightest objects toward the center.

As we paint our scene, you will see how these principles come into play. These principles, if followed, will improve any art work you do.

The Ugly Duckling

Every painting has an ugly stage and seems to suffer the "the ugly duckling syndrome." Don't get discouraged. Sometimes the paintings that seem hopeless are the ones that turn out the best. To see your work as a stranger would see it, you can try looking at it in a mirror. This will give you a different perspective on your work.

One more thing—have fun. Don't make yourself nuts by being overly critical of your work. The following story illustrates what I mean.

When I was just getting started, I used to sell my paintings on the weekends in front of my house. I painted 10–15 paintings a week, so I had to do something with them or they would soon fill the house. In my studio, I had what I called my "pile of shame," paintings that I considered unsellable and without redeeming value. One day, a woman who was driving by saw a painting that was for sale. She stopped and yelled out the window of the car that she wanted the painting and would be back shortly to buy it. A few hours went by and she did not appear, so I sold that particular painting to someone else. At the end of the day, as luck would have it, she returned. I told her that the piece she wanted was gone and that I was very sorry. When I started to go into my studio, she followed me, went directly to my pile of shame, and started looking through those pieces, much to my embarrassment. Suddenly I heard a great sigh. She picked up what I considered to be one of the worst paintings I had ever done, said she loved it, and bought it for $100. Remember, art, as well as beauty, is in the eye of the beholder.

A Few Words About Color

 You may be surprised at how few colors I will use in the scene. Sometimes the fewer the colors, the better the painting. Some of the most striking paintings I've done, either in oils or on the computer, are studies in one color and white. Try it some time; you may be surprised at the results. Color is a personal thing. The only rule is that if it looks right to you, it's right. We will be using gradients. (*Gradient* means gradually going from one color to another in a series of steps.) The sky, cloud, and river colors will be in a gradient that goes from a very dark blue to white in about 31 steps. The gradient of the trees, grasses, and bushes will also have 31 steps, going from a very dark green to a light yellow-green color. The gradient for the tree branches and earth will have 31 steps, going from a black to a light brown. The palette that I will be using is included on the CD that comes with the book.

Let's Get to It

We will start with a 640×480 screen with a black background. (Notice that I didn't use "Getting Started" as a heading here. After years of reading computer books, I have become almost phobic about those two words.)

The Sky

Creating the sky is the first thing we have to do. We will need a gradient fill to do this. Make a rectangle with a *vertical gradient fill*, as in Figure 4.1. This gives us a nice blue sky with lots of depth.

If you were doing a scene depicting sunset or sunrise, you would use a gradient with reds and yellows. For a stormy sky, use grays.

For a dramatic lighting effect, use a *radial gradient* going from light to dark. (In a radial gradient, colors go from one to another in a circular fashion.) Place the lightest part just above the horizon. When you use a radial gradient and place your mountains on the horizon, you get the effect of the sun or moon rising or setting. Try different gradients. Just make sure that there are enough steps between the colors to minimize banding.

FIGURE 4.1.

Blue sky made with vertical gradient fill.

The Clouds

There are several types of clouds and several different techniques to create them. Today we will be painting the big, puffy clouds you see on a summer's day. Clouds are usually darker on the bottom and brighter on the tops. In your sky gradient, pick a color that is a midtone between the darkest and the lightest colors. This will be the *base color*.

We will use a round brush. Size it to about 5. Set the spray speed to 3 and the spray width to 4, and use glass (transparent 50 percent) ink. Go to about mid-screen and create a cloud shape, as in Figure 4.2. Remember, the shape of a cloud has a feeling to it. Try to capture that feeling. You may have to work on it a bit, but you will get it.

After you've finished the cloud shape, we'll select a color that is a little lighter than the base color to do the midtone highlights. Start at the top of the cloud and work your way down, creating parts of the cloud that are catching some of the light from above. Remember, don't cover *all* of the darker color (see Figure 4.3). If you cover all of the dark color, your clouds will be flat. Repeat this step with a brighter color, lighting only the parts of the cloud that are getting direct sunlight, as shown in Figure 4.4. After you are happy with your cloud, you can add more clouds, as many as you want. This is, after all, your world. You can have as many or as few clouds as you like. Remember that the farther away they are, the smaller and the lighter they will be (see Figure 4.5).

FIGURE 4.2.

Cloud shape made with small round brush.

FIGURE 4.3.

Cloud midtone highlights.

FIGURE 4.4.
Bright highlights for clouds.

FIGURE 4.5.
Distant clouds.

The Mountains

When you start the mountains, you should do the distant mountains first. Here we will use light blue for the base color. This blue is very light, almost blending with the sky. Once again, this will give the scene a feeling of depth.

Each mountain should have a natural shape, not like a pyramid. Keep the lines broken, as in Figure 4.6, not straight. The first time I tried to make mountains, they ended up looking like ice cream cones, so don't get discouraged. After you have the mountain shape that you want, you can start to highlight it.

FIGURE 4.6.

Mountain shape with base color.

When you apply the highlights or snow to the mountains, the angle is very important. You must follow the lay of the land. Start at the topmost peak and apply the snow in short strokes of the spray. The brush is round, and the size is 2. The spray speed is 3, and the spray width is 5. The snow color is white.

If your paint program can make a mask, then make a mask of the mountain base color. (A *mask* allows you to lock certain colors so that they cannot be painted on with the current color.) Then invert it. This will keep you from putting snow in the sky. If you can't use a mask, zoom in on the mountain peak and just be careful. You don't want to cover all of the base color. Instead, think about the ridges and cliffs whose faces are picking up the light. Be patient and do a section at a time.

Next we will put the shadow color on the mountain faces that are in the shade. It should be slightly lighter than the base color. Take the brush and reverse the angle when you apply the shadow snow. Move your brush so you are going away from the bright snow. You will see a big change to the scene after you have completed this step. The mountains will suddenly come alive, as in Figure 4.7. Save your work after you are happy with each step.

We will now move forward and put the next set of mountains in the scene. For a base color, use a midtone blue and use the round brush (see Figure 4.8). Make a ridge of mountains with two high peaks on either side of the far-away mountains. I know, you have to cover some of the beautiful mountains you just made, but that's the way it is in the real world. Things tend to get in front of each other. As you can see, because of the darker base color, the new darker mountains will push the first mountains back into the scene and give us more depth. Apply the snow the same way you did on the first mountains. The snow color will be white (see Figure 4.9). The shadow color will be slightly lighter than the base color. Don't forget to angle the brush and to follow the lay of the land (see Figure 4.10).

FIGURE 4.7.

Mountains with shadow snow applied.

FIGURE 4.8.

Closer mountain shape with base color.

FIGURE 4.9.

Snow applied on closer mountains.

FIGURE 4.10.

Shadow snow applied to closer mountains.

Now you will make one more small ridge in front of the mountains you've just made (see Figure 4.11). The base color will be quite dark, a very dark blue. It will push the other mountains farther back into the scene. By now, you know how to apply the snow and shadows (see Figure 4.12).

FIGURE 4.11.

Closest ridge of mountains with very dark base color.

FIGURE 4.12.

Closest ridge of mountains with white and shadow snow.

Now let's stop a minute and reflect on our painting. As you can see, you have created a scene with great depth to the sky and mountains. The art principles I discussed earlier are apparent. After you have created a set of mountain ranges, you will probably find that you want to paint them all the time. I never get tired of painting mountains. There's a kind of magic that seems to happen when you apply the shadow color, bringing the mountains to life. I never tire of seeing it happen (see Figure 4.13).

FIGURE 4.13.

Painting with completed sky and mountains.

The Valley and River

Next we are going to lay in the river. The brush size setting will be 3. The color is midtone blue, and the shape will be horizontal. Start the river in the distance and create a meandering shape that gets slightly larger as it gets closer (see Figure 4.14). Next add a few highlights to the water using a horizontal brush with white and with the ink set to glass. You want to create the effect of the light bouncing off the water. Make sure that you don't cover all the base color (see Figure 4.15).

FIGURE 4.14.

River shape coming from the distance.

FIGURE 4.15.

River with highlights applied.

Now you can start on the valley. Use a horizontal brush and a dark green base color. Start from the sides and work your way into the river, keeping in mind the shape of small hills that lead down to the river. Make sure that you don't cover all the black background. The pockets of black will be hollows when you are done (see Figure 4.16).

FIGURE 4.16.

Valley laid in with dark green base color.

After the base for the valley is finished, you can start highlighting the hills with green grass colors and browns, grays, and blues for earth and rocks. The trick to this is to sculpt the land. As you are applying the colors, you will see that the contrast between the light and the dark is what determines whether the land is going up or down (see Figure 4.17).

FIGURE 4.17.

The land highlighted with earth colors.

The Foreground

You start working on the foreground at the point where you are "standing," looking out over the valley below. The base color is already there, the black background. Here you really want to use the dark, so don't fall into the trap of wanting to cover every dark spot with some sort of color. First, make a custom brush on the *swap screen.* If you are using a Windows program, open another small work area from which you can cut out the brush after you've built it.

The brush is simple. Use a very small round brush and paint a bunch of lines that look like branches. If you have a darken function in your program, set it to its darkest setting and use it. Otherwise, just make the brush the darkest color you can. Start at the right side of the screen a little more than halfway up, and stamp the brush down so that you get on the side a ragged edge that is covering some of the sky and mountains, as in Figure 4.18.

FIGURE 4.18.

The outline of the trees and bushes against the mountains and sky.

Keep stamping. Remember, this is the inside of the trees and bushes, the part in the dark. Now do the same thing to the other side of the painting and along the bottom so that you can see the rough outline against the valley below. The main thing is to get the shapes right and to get the sharp contrast against the sky and mountains. This will push back into the scene everything you've done thus far.

The Bushes and Trees

To start to work on the foreground foliage, you first put in a few tree trunks. We will use a dark brown for the base, then highlight here and there to give the appearance that some sunlight is getting through the leaves.

You don't have to worry about the trunks very much. A good bit will be covered up when the foliage highlights are applied.

When you are satisfied with the tree trunks, you can start to highlight the trees and bushes. Use a darker green. Spray using a very small round brush and a slow, narrow spray setting. This is where you must fight the temptation to cover up all the dark. Try to think of shapes or of parts of the leaves that are getting the light. Now, using a lighter shade of green, lay down the parts that are getting a bit more of the sunlight, as in Figure 4.19. Then, using a light yellow with a slightly green tint, you can show the leaves that are getting the direct sunlight. Remember, don't cover all the dark. The dark is what gives the trees and bushes depth. When you are doing the bushes, do one at a time, putting light colors on the tops of the bushes and getting darker as you move closer to the ground. This is your world, so make as many bushes and trees as you want. Just be sure you don't get carried away and kill the dark. If you kill the dark, the foliage will look flat.

FIGURE 4.19.

Highlights applied to trees and foliage.

The Path

Now we will put in a path coming down out of the woods. Use a small horizontal brush and a dark brown color. Start in a very dark area in the trees at the left side of the painting. With short back-and-forth movements, make the path wider as it gets closer to the foreground. Make sure that it lays flat. When you are happy with the way the path looks, highlight it with some lighter browns and grays to give the appearance of sunlight hitting the earth here and there. The grays will give the appearance of occasional small rocks and stones, as in Figure 4.20.

FIGURE 4.20.

Path with grays and blues applied.

The Grass

To put in grass around the path, use the spray and a very small round brush, with different shades of green and yellow. Once again, don't cover all the dark. (I know you are probably tired of hearing this, but I must say it. If you cover all the dark, your painting will not look right.) Bring the grass right up to the path and let some overlap the path. This will push the path down into the scene, as in Figure 4.21. Try to think where the sun would be hitting the grassy area, and use the lighter shades of green and yellow for those areas.

FIGURE 4.21.

Completed path with highlights and foliage.

Finishing Touches

As you can see on the color picture, I put some flowers in the bushes using the spray and a little gold, red, purple, and yellow. Sometimes a painting needs just a splash of color to add interest and life. Try adding some flowers. After you are happy with your flowers, take a small round brush and a medium gray and draw some branchy-looking lines around the bushes. This will give the illusion of sticks and twigs amongst the foliage. The last thing is to sign your work. I use a script font to put my name on the finished painting. You should do the same. This makes the painting yours (see Figure 4.22).

FIGURE 4.22.

Completed painting with signature.

Some Parting Words

I hope you have enjoyed painting with me. I know I have enjoyed doing this chapter. That's what computer art is all about: having fun and sharing what we discover using these wonderful machines. My wish is that I have helped you in some small way with your painting techniques. On the book's CD-ROM, I have included a collection of my artwork and some animations I've done with Animator Pro. I welcome the opportunity to see some of your work and chat about computer art, so give me a shout. On Compuserve my address is 75330,3560. My screen name on America Online is HD8273. I'd be glad to hear from you. Happy painting!

II

PART

Digital Image Manipulation

Advanced Image Processing

5

by Spyro Gumas

Welcome to the world of advanced image processing, where you can rip off the shackles imposed by poor photographs and underachieving video adapters. In this chapter you learn how to rescue that pile of reject photographs buried away in your closet. They would have been great shots, if only the flash had worked...and they may still prove to be great shots. Then you can tackle the subject of color conversion. Cheap video adapters turn up their noses at the full color rainbow, preferring the spectrum of a set of crayons. In this chapter you learn how to trick your computer into displaying photographs with no apparent loss of color. After reading this chapter, you will be as armed and dangerous as a PC programming madman (madperson?).

The "Automatic Image Tuning" section looks at the issues related to brightness and contrast. It introduces the concept of an image histogram and then walks you through the intricacies of histogram equalization. Unlike the plethora of image processing software already out there, the histogram equalization software presented here gives you control over the process so that you can dial up more or less equalization to suit your specific needs.

In the "Dithering Pixels" section, you learn the poor man's way of displaying an image that sports 16 million colors on a display that is capable of only 256. Dithering is by far the most common approach used in most commercial packages for quickly displaying high color resolution images on low color resolution displays, and the results it produces are extraordinary.

Finally, in the "Making an Adaptive Color Palette" section, you are strapped into your own private jet and flown through the heady business of building custom color palettes that are optimized for a specific image. As far as I can tell, this is the first time this subject has been laid out in such detail for persons lacking a degree in astrophysics. After reading this, you'll be equipped to go out into the real world and put up images that look every bit as good as the big boys'.

The software examples provided throughout this chapter rely heavily on the functions provided in the VSA256 Graphics Library and the TIFF256 Graphics Library Extensions shareware provided in the software distribution with this book. The full texts of the user's manuals for these libraries are reprinted in Appendixes A and B of this book so that you can make quick reference to the functions as they come up. The VSA256 Graphics Library gives you the power to drive a VESA-compliant video adapter in video resolutions up to 1280×1024 with 256 colors. The TIFF256 Graphics Library Extensions boost your powers with the ability to read, display, modify, and write industry standard TIFF (Tagged Image File Format) images.

Automatic Image Tuning

Photo-editing software packages are now available in every aisle of the software supermarket. With these packages, you can perform magic that required an apprenticeship in darkroom chemistry only 10 years ago. But you still need to be somewhat initiated to run these packages. This process is still not at the point where anyone off the street can scan a photograph and expect quality output. So, how can you leverage your expertise to compete with all of these commercial packages? I suggest that you create utility software that does "Photo Fixing for Housewives" (just go with it, I'm on a roll). The concept of Photo Fixing for Housewives, or PFFH as it will come to be known, is basically this: Scan your less-than-perfect photograph in to your computer. Run the PFFH software, and BANG! ZOOM! out comes the next Ansel Adams scenic or Olan Mills portrait.

Any good PFFH package must come equipped to handle one of the most common problems with those darned one-hour film processing centers. Because the exposure is entrusted to a faceless machine, your photos frequently come back either too dark, too light, or flat and lacking contrast. Exposure correction is a must-have feature for your PFFH software. Exposure correction means histogram equalization, and in this section the secrets of histogram equalization are divulged to you in glorious detail. But first, what's a histogram?

Histograms

To get started with automatic image tuning, you need an analysis tool that gives you insight into the overall exposure of the photograph. An image histogram is such a tool. An image histogram is a plot of pixel brightness on the x-axis versus frequency of occurrence (number of pixels) on the y-axis. Figure 5.1 shows a ray-traced image from the archives of Dave Scruton, freelance image wizard. The corresponding histogram is shown in Figure 5.2. The pixels in this image range in brightness from 0 to 255. As you move down the x-axis in the histogram and select a pixel brightness, you can get a relative indication of how many pixels in the image have that brightness by determining the height of the histogram curve at that point. I should warn you that for all the histograms shown in this chapter, the y-axis is a logarithmic scale normalized to the maximum pixel count for each image. What this means is that you can't look at the histograms and read off an exact pixel count for a given pixel brightness. Don't be discouraged. The code listings provide access to the exact numbers in the histograms for those of you who are really interested.

FIGURE 5.1.

Reality through the eyes of a ray-tracing musician. (Courtesy of Dave Scruton of Fractallonomy.)

FIGURE 5.2.

Histogram of Piano.

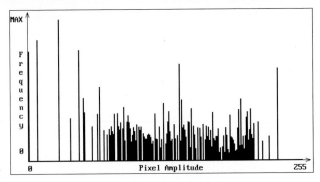

The actual algorithm for computing a histogram is simple enough: analyze each pixel in the image and count the number of occurrences for each possible pixel amplitude. The large number of varying image types, however, can make the software implementation details complicated. For a simple Gray Scale image with a one-to-one correlation from pixel value to screen brightness, the algorithm interprets the value of each pixel stored in the bitmap as an amplitude and computes the histogram directly. For True Color images with 24 bits per pixel (also referred to as 24-bit RGB images), the algorithm again interprets the pixel values as amplitudes. However, this time there are three amplitudes per pixel: one for red, one for green, and one for blue. At this point, the programmer has to decide whether he wants a single histogram relating to overall pixel brightness, or three histograms, one for each of red, green, and blue. Between the Gray Scale and the True Color images are the Palette Color images. The Palette Color images are more sinister in that you can't just look at the stored pixel value and get a pixel brightness. Instead, you have to go into the color palette and extract the red, green, and blue color components for the pixel and then compute the pixel amplitude.

The example code in Listing 5.1 shows you how to generate a histogram for any Palette Color image using a 256-color palette. The calling program specifies the screen coordinates x0,y0 and x1,y1 of the rectangular region to be histogrammed. It also provides lut, a pointer to an array containing the current color palette, and hist, a pointer to a 256-element array of long words where the histogram will be returned. A histogram is created that relates to pixel intensity independent of pixel color. This is the histogram that will be used later in histogram equalization. Because Palette Color images are the most complicated image types for histogramming, converting the code to handle non-palette images should be pretty easy.

Determining the intensity of a pixel can be done in many ways. To demonstrate this, a switch is provided in the histogram code so that you can choose between two different methods. With the mode parameter set to 0, the pixel intensity is computed as the root of the sum of the squares (RSS) of the red, green, and blue components. This is probably the most common way to compute intensity. A quicker, less accurate, but acceptable method is selected if you set mode to 1. In this case, the pixel intensity is computed simply as the maximum value of the red, green, or blue component of that pixel. Later, when you are looking at histogram equalization effects on images, you might try putting in your own methods that give red, green, and blue components different weighting in the calculation.

Listing 5.1. Histogram code.

```
/*.................... HIST_DISPLAY.C ............ 6-8-94 ....*/
/* This routine computes the monochrome amplitude histogram of */
/* an image defined by the display contained within the 'x0,y0'*/
/* to 'x1,y1' screen rectangle. The data in 'image' is 8 bits  */
/* per  pixels so the 'hist' array is only 256 elements deep.   */
/* Upon returning from this routine, each element of 'hist'     */
/* contains the count (or frequency) of occurrence of pixels in*/
/* the image with amplitude defined by the index of that       */
/* element.                                                     */
/*   The histogram is computed by taking into account the      */
/* values in the Color Look Up Table (CLUT).  Therefore, this  */
/* routine works with all 8 bit image, not just gray scale ones*/
/* with linear CLUTs.                                           */
/*    If 'mode' = 0, the pixel amplitude is computed as the     */
/* Root of the Sum of the Squares (RSS) of R, G, and B.         */
/* Otherwise it's computed as the max of R, G, or B.            */
/*                                                              */
/* NOTE:  Where ever you see 0.5 being added in a calculation, */
/*        the reason is so that the results are rounded to the */
/*        nearest integer.                                     */
/*..........................................................*/
```

continues

Listing 5.1. continued

```c
void hist_display(int x0, int y0, int x1, int y1,
                  unsigned char *lut, long *hist, int mode)
{
  unsigned char array[1280];
  int width,height,i,j,amp;
  long temp[256];
  float f_amp,red,grn,blu;
/*..............................................................*/
/*      Compute the width and Height of image.                 */
/*..............................................................*/
  width  = x1 - x0 + 1;
  height = y1 - y0 + 1;
/*..............................................................*/
/*     Clear out TEMP array                                     */
/*..............................................................*/
  for(i=0;i<256;i++)
    temp[i] = 0;
/*..............................................................*/
/*     Clear out HIST array                                     */
/*..............................................................*/
  for(i=0;i<256;i++)
    hist[i] = 0;
/*..............................................................*/
/*     Now compute the total pixel count per CLUT address       */
/*     (temp[i]).                                               */
/*..............................................................*/
  for(j=y0;j<y1+1;j++)
    {
      vsa_get_raster_line(x0,x1,j,array);
      for(i=0;i<width;i++)
        temp[array[i]]++;
    }
/*..............................................................*/
/*     Now compute histogram.  Do so by computing an average    */
/* amplitude (amp) for each CLUT entry (i).  Then take the      */
/* total number of pixels for each CLUT entry (temp[i]) and add*/
/* it to the histogram array (hist[amp]).                       */
/*..............................................................*/
  for(i=0;i<256;i++)
    {
      red = lut[3*i+0];
      grn = lut[3*i+1];
      blu = lut[3*i+2];
/*.....     if mode = 0, Amplitude = SQRT(R^2+G^2+B^2)    .....*/
      if(mode == 0)
        {
          f_amp = 255.0*sqrt(red*red+grn*grn+blu*blu)/109.2;
          amp = (int)(f_amp+0.5);
        }
/*.....     if mode = 1, Amplitude = MAX of R, G, or B    .....*/
      else
        {
          amp = red;
          if(grn > amp)
            amp = grn;
          if(blu > amp)
```

```
        amp = blu;
/*..... increase range scale: 0 thru 255 (was 0 to 63)   .....*/
        amp = 4.05*(float)amp;
      }
    hist[amp] += temp[i];
    }
  return;
}                           /*.... END hist_display    .....*/
```

The histogram code in Listing 5.2 is an alternate routine that works with images stored in huge arrays instead of images displayed on the screen. This is handy when you don't want to display your images until they are done being processed. The image array conforms to the image array format specified in the TIFF256 Graphics Library Extensions. Basically, the first two bytes store the image width, the next two bytes store the image height, and the remaining bytes are 8-bit pixel data in raster scan order.

Listing 5.2. Alternate histogram code.

```
/*...................... HIST_IMAGE.C .......... 6-8-94 ....*/
/* This routine computes the monochrome amplitude histogram of */
/* an image defined by the 'image' array.  The data in 'image' */
/* is 8 bits per  pixels so the 'hist' array is only 256       */
/* elements deep.  Upon returning from this routine, each      */
/* element of 'hist' contains the count (or frequency) of      */
/* occurrence of pixels in the image with amplitude defined by */
/* the index of that element.  The histogram is computed by    */
/* taking into account the values in the Color Look Up Table   */
/* (CLUT).  Therefore, this routine works with all 8 bit image,*/
/* not just gray scale ones with linear CLUTs.                 */
/*    If 'mode' = 0, the pixel amplitude is computed as the    */
/* Root of the Sum of the Squares (RSS) of R, G, and B.        */
/* Otherwise it's computed as the max of R, G, or B.           */
/*                                                             */
/* NOTE:  Where ever you see 0.5 being added in a calculation, */
/*        the reason is so that the results are rounded to the */
/*        nearest integer.                                     */
/*.............................................................*/
void hist_image(unsigned char huge *image,
             unsigned char *lut,long *hist, int mode)
{
  int width,height,i,j,amp;
  long n;
  long temp[256];
  float f_amp,red,grn,blu;
  n = 0;
/*.............................................................*/
/*    Read out the width and Height of image.                  */
/*.............................................................*/
  width  = *((int huge *)image);
  image += 2;
  height = *((int huge *)image);
  image += 2;
/*.............................................................*/
```

continues

Listing 5.2. continued

```
/*    Clear out TEMP array                                    */
/*....................................................*/
  for(i=0;i<256;i++)
    temp[i] = 0;
/*....................................................*/
/*    Clear out HIST array                                   */
/*....................................................*/
  for(i=0;i<256;i++)
    hist[i] = 0;
/*....................................................*/
/*    Now compute the total pixel count per CLUT address     */
/*    (temp[i]).                                             */
/*....................................................*/
  for(j=0;j<height;j++)
    for(i=0;i<width;i++)
      {
        temp[image[n]]++;
        n++;
      }
/*....................................................*/
/*    Now compute histogram.  Do so by computing an average  */
/* amplitude (amp) for each CLUT entry (i).  Then take the   */
/* total number of pixels for each CLUT entry (temp[i]) and  */
/* add it to the histogram array (hist[amp]).                */
/*....................................................*/
  for(i=0;i<256;i++)
    {
      red = lut[3*i+0];
      grn = lut[3*i+1];
      blu = lut[3*i+2];
/*.....    if mode = 0, Amplitude = SQRT(R^2+G^2+B^2)    .....*/
      if(mode == 0)
        {
          f_amp = 255.0*sqrt(red*red+grn*grn+blu*blu)/109.2;
          amp = (int)(f_amp+0.5);
        }
/*.....    if mode = 1, Amplitude = MAX of R, G, or B    .....*/
      else
        {
          amp = red;
          if(grn > amp)
            amp = grn;
          if(blu > amp)
            amp = blu;
/*..... increase range scale: 0 thru 255 (was 0 to 63)   .....*/
          amp = 4.05*(float)amp;
        }
      hist[amp] += temp[i];
    }
  return;
}                              /*.... END hist_image       .....*/
```

The next few images (of Justin, who showed up three weeks early just to make it into this book) give you a feel for the interpretation of a histogram. Figure 5.3 is underexposed, and the histogram is scrunched up at the low amplitudes. Figure 5.4 is overexposed and is mashed up at the high amplitudes. Figure 5.5 is decent, and the histogram is spread pretty evenly across the amplitude range.

FIGURE 5.3a.

This Little Piggy is too dark.

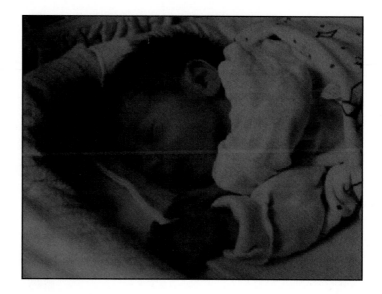

FIGURE 5.3b.

Histogram of Dark Piggy.

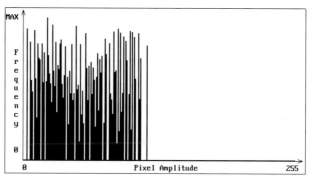

FIGURE 5.4a.

This Little Piggy is too light.

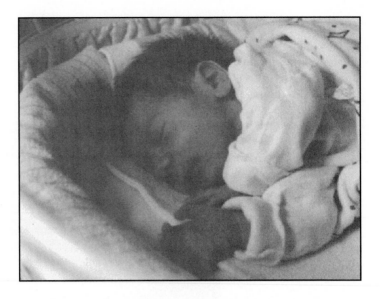

FIGURE 5.4b.

Histogram of Light Piggy.

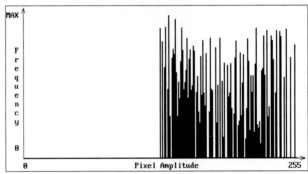

FIGURE 5.5a.

This Little Piggy is just right.

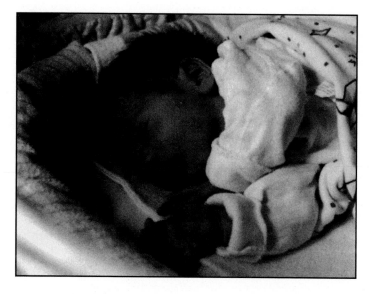

FIGURE 5.5b.

Histogram of Right Piggy.

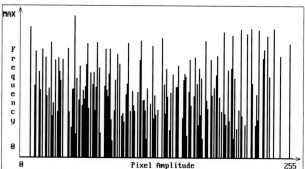

Histogram Equalization

You've seen the histograms of poorly exposed images in the preceding section. A common element among these histograms is that they all have local regions where a significant number of pixels are all scrunched into a narrow range of amplitudes. What this says is that even though the image has access to 256 unique pixel brightness levels, it is using only a small portion of that *dynamic range* (technical jargon meaning range of possible values). Histogram equalization is the process of unscrunching (technical jargon for spreading out) the histogram to make better use of the available range of pixel levels.

Strictly speaking, histogram equalization tries to make the pixel distribution uniform across all possible amplitudes. This means that if you equalize a 256-level, 640×480 image, you end up with an image that has 1200 pixels at level 0, 1200 at level 1, 1200 at level 2, and so on, all the way up to 1200 pixels at level 255, for a total of 307,200 pixels. These are the types of results you get when you use the popular commercial photo processing programs. But I have to warn you, strict histogram equalization rarely makes your images look their best. After all, who says that the original scene had a uniform distribution of brightness? Instead, the typical equalization function frequently unscrunches too much, making the equalized image look harsh.

Wouldn't it be really neat if someone gave you a histogram equalization function that let you specify how much unscrunching to do? Done! The histogram equalization routine presented in Listing 5.3 takes the current color palette defined in the lut array and the current histogram defined in the hist array, does its math thing, and then returns the new, equalized, color palette values and histogram in the same arrays. But notice the n parameter. This is the strength parameter. If you set the strength to 0.0, the equalization process evenly expands the histogram like an accordion so that the dimmest pixels hit amplitude 0 and the brightest pixels go up to amplitude 255. As the strength value is increased, the expansion becomes uneven and more pronounced in the regions of high pixel density. When strength hits 1.0, this routine does the strict histogram equalization, but notice that you can keep going up to a strength of 4.0. (Things start blowing up when you get past 4.0, so I limited it; remove the governor at your own risk.) For the best results, start with a strength of 0.0. For many images, this is all you need. From there, you can start adding more caffeine until you get the desired effect.

Listing 5.3. Histogram equalization code.

```
/*........................ HISTEQ.C .......... 6-8-94 .....*/
/* This routine performs the Histogram Equalization process.   */
/* When calling this routine 'lut' holds the current image look*/
/* up table, and 'hist' holds the current image histogram.     */
/* both 'lut' and 'hist' are updated with the new values prior */
/* to returning to the calling routine.  Note that the image's */
/* stored pixel values are not affected by equalization.       */
/*    The strength parameter 'n' determines how equalization   */
/* distribute pixels.  A value of 0.0 preserves the original   */
/* pixel density profile while spreading it to fit between     */
/* pixel amplitude 0 and pixel amplitude 255. A strength of 1.0*/
/* results in uniform pixel distribution (like commercial      */
/* software packages).                                         */
/*    If 'mode' = 0, the pixel amplitude is computed as the    */
/* Root of the Sum of the Squares (RSS) of R, G, and B.        */
/* Otherwise it's computed as the max of R, G, or B.           */
/*                                                             */
/* NOTE:  Where ever you see 0.5 being added in a calculation, */
/*        the reason is so that the results are rounded to the */
/*        nearest integer.                                     */
/*............................................................*/
```

```
void histeq(unsigned char *lut, long *hist,double n,
            int mode)
{
  int i,amp,max_amp;
  float norm,scale[256],factor,f_amp,red,grn,blu;
  unsigned temp[256];
/*.........................................................*/
/* Generate the 'scale' array such that for a given index (i)  */
/* into the array (corresponding to a pixel amplitude of i)    */
/* the 'scale[i]' value is the cumulative sum of number of     */
/* pixels whose amplitude are 'i' or less (the sum is          */
/* discounted or inflated by the strength factor 'n').         */
/*    Also clear out 'temp[]' so it can be updated later.      */
/*.........................................................*/
  if(hist[0] !=0)
    scale[0] = pow(hist[0],n);
  else
    scale[0] = 0;
  for(i=1;i<256;i++)
    {
      if(hist[i] !=0)
        scale[i] = scale[i-1] + pow(hist[i],n);
      else
        scale[i] = scale[i-1];
    }
  for(i=0;i<256;i++)
    temp[i] = 0;
/*.........................................................*/
/*    Normalize 'scale' array so that max value is 255.0       */
/*.........................................................*/
  norm = 255.0/scale[255];
  for(i=0;i<256;i++)
    scale[i] *= norm;
/*.........................................................*/
/*    Perform the equalization by "shifting" each CLUT entry   */
/* brightness level up or down such that for a pixel of        */
/* amplitude AMP, its new amplitude will be equal to           */
/* 'scale[AMP]'.                                               */
/*.........................................................*/
  for(i=0;i<256;i++)
    {
      red = lut[3*i+0];
      grn = lut[3*i+1];
      blu = lut[3*i+2];
/*.....   if mode = 0, Amplitude = SQRT(R^2+G^2+B^2)    .....*/
      if(mode == 0)
        {
          f_amp = 255.0*sqrt(red*red+grn*grn+blu*blu)/109.2;
          amp = (int)(f_amp+0.5);
        }
/*.....   if mode = 1, Amplitude = MAX of R, G, or B    .....*/
      else
        {
          max_amp = red;
          if(grn > max_amp)
            max_amp = grn;
          if(blu > max_amp)
            max_amp = blu;
/*.....   increase range scale: 0 thru 255 (was 0 to 63)   .....*/
```

continues

Listing 5.3. continued

```
        amp = 4.05*(float)max_amp;
    }

/*........................................................*/
/* Figure a scale factor such that pixels of amplitude AMP will*/
/* have a new amplitude equal to 'scale[AMP]'.            */
/*........................................................*/
    if(amp != 0)
        factor = scale[amp]/(float)amp;
    else
        factor = 0;
/*........................................................*/
/*   Now scale red, green, and blue amplitudes by the computed */
/* scale factor.  In 'mode' = 0, it is possible that the factor*/
/* will cause one of these color values to exceed 63.  In this */
/* case the values are clamped to 63.This will  cause some     */
/* minor color drift in the  brighter non white pixels  but it */
/* should not be noticeable. The alternative would be to scale */
/* down the brightness of the whole pixel, or the whole image. */
/* Neither of these two options seemed any more desirable.     */
/*........................................................*/
        lut[3*i+0] = (int)((float)lut[3*i+0]*factor + 0.5);
        lut[3*i+1] = (int)((float)lut[3*i+1]*factor + 0.5);
        lut[3*i+2] = (int)((float)lut[3*i+2]*factor + 0.5);
        if(lut[3*i+0] > 63) lut[3*i+0] = 63;
        if(lut[3*i+1] > 63) lut[3*i+1] = 63;
        if(lut[3*i+2] > 63) lut[3*i+2] = 63;
        temp[(int)(factor*amp+0.5)] += hist[amp];
    }
/*........................................................*/
/*Update histogram array with new, equalized, histogram values.*/
/*........................................................*/
  for(i=0;i<256;i++)
    hist[i] = temp[i];
  return;
}                          /*.... END histeq        .....*/
```

My mother gave me an old negative of herself and her sister when they were little girls. Actually, it was a new negative made by taking a picture of a very old photograph. My plan was to scan it, invert it, and print out a nice big photo of the kids' YiaYia. (YiaYia is Greek for *grandma*. Yes, not only do you get access to fine technical expertise, but cultural exposure as well. What a country!) Well, at this tender stage in my professional development (it was two weeks ago), I was lacking in a certain degree of common sense. As some of you may know, negatives don't scan well unless you use a transparency adapter. The reason is that negatives are a transmissive media, unlike photographs, which are a reflective media. Without the transparency adapter, very little light makes it through the negative and back to the scanner's "eyes." To bring this dissertation to a close, suffice it to say that this experience produced the perfect image to present here as an example of what histogram equalization can do. Figure 5.6 shows YiaYia after scanning the negative and inverting it (she's the one on the left).

FIGURE 5.6a.

The kids' YiaYia...barely.

FIGURE 5.6b.

Histogram of Barely YiaYia.

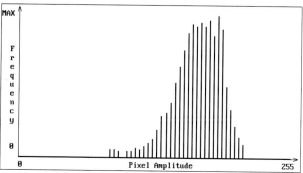

After running Figure 5.6 through the histogram equalization program with the strength set to 1.5, I got the image shown in Figure 5.7. Aside from the fact that the original photograph was in a deteriorated condition, the equalized image is quite viewable and reveals a surprising amount of detail.

FIGURE 5.7a.
*The kids'
YiaYia...definitely.*

FIGURE 5.7b.
*Histogram of Definitely
YiaYia.*

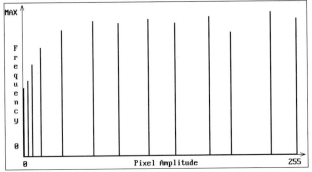

Dithering Pixels

Now let's talk a little bit about color. I mean lots of color. Like, what do you do with 16 million colors in a True Color image when your video adapter displays only 256 colors (only one color for every 65,536 colors in the original image)? If you are writing commercial software, you want it to run on as many platforms as possible. This means providing the capability for viewing these True Color images on 256-color video. This section shows you a relatively quick technique called *dithering*, which approximates all 16 million colors on 256-color systems with surprisingly good results.

A typical True Color image, like the one in Figure 5.8, represents each pixel with 24 bits, 8 bits each of red, green, and blue. This yields a total of 2 raised to the 24th power, or 16,777,216 possible colors for each pixel.

FIGURE 5.8.

True Color image of Andrew and Ted.

The most direct way to get down to 256 total colors is to reduce the number of possible colors for each of the red, green, and blue components of the pixel. A simple approach cuts the red component down to 3 bits, the green component down to 3 bits, and the blue component down to 2 bits. The rationale for this cut is that the eye is not as sensitive to blue as it is to green or red, and therefore you can afford to give up more in the blue color range than in the other two. I think that's the rationale—it sounds good anyway. In any event, you end up with an 8-bit RGB pixel that can display 256 unique possible colors.

The problem with this (remember, I said it was simple) is that an image assembled with only 8 shades of red, 8 shades of green, and 4 shades of blue shows "quantization error" (jargon for the boo-boos that occur when you reduce from 256 shades to 8 or 4) quite visibly, with art deco style color banding as in Figure 5.9. But don't give up hope.

Dithering, specifically ordered dithering as presented here, is the process of approximating more shades of color by strategically mixing pixels of differing intensities. For instance, imagine what your eye sees if two pixels are displayed side by side, one with intensity 100 and the other with intensity 50. Instead of picking out each pixel, at normal viewing distances your eye merges them into a blob with an average intensity of 75. Dithering is the ticket for making these 8-bit RGB pixels look good. What? You already figured that out?

FIGURE 5.9.

*8-bit RGB version of
Andrew and Ted.*

Monochrome

Dithering is similar to the newspaper technique of half-toning. In black-and-white half-toning, only two colors are available: black (ink) and white (paper). The continuum of gray shades is achieved by printing black dots at a fixed pitch (spacing) with their size proportional to the corresponding pixel's gray shade. The size of the dot can range anywhere from a small fraction of the size of the image pixel all the way up to the full size of the image pixel. The image's darker pixels are approximated by relatively large black dots, whereas the lighter pixels are approximated by relatively small black dots. The eye integrates these dots along with the surrounding white background and sees a continuous tone image. This works well for display media whose resolution is smaller than the image's pixel size. Dithering comes into play when the image pixel size is the same as the display resolution, such as on a computer monitor.

Instead of using a single variable-sized dot to approximate each pixel, dithering overlays a fixed grid of boxes onto the display surface. Each box is composed of N×N pixels, and each pixel in the box is assigned a unique threshold value from 1 to N^2. The size of the box is determined by the degree to which the original colors have to be reduced for the display device. Figure 5.10 shows a 4×4 box filled in with the appropriate threshold values.

FIGURE 5.10.

*A 4×4 dither box with 16
threshold values.*

1	9	3	11
13	5	15	7
4	12	2	10
16	8	14	6

Using only two display colors, say black and white, a 4×4 box produces 16 shades of gray. When you go to plot an image pixel of intensity P on the screen, first determine which of the 16 unique positions within a box (in the overlaid grid of boxes) the pixel will be drawn in. This can be done with a modulo function operating on both the x and y screen coordinates of the pixel. Then you compare the "Test Value" P against the threshold value at that pixel position within the box. If P is greater than or equal to the threshold value, you turn on the pixel. Otherwise you leave it off. Given a broad image region of uniform intensity, Figure 5.11 shows which pixels within each box are illuminated as the intensity of the region increases from 0 to 15. Note that 17 shades can actually be supported if you turn on all of the 16 pixels. But hang on, you're going to squeeze out a lot more than 17 shades from this puny 4×4 box.

FIGURE 5.11.

A 4×4 dither box showing the progression from level 0 intensity to level 15 intensity for a uniform area. Blackened pixels in the diagram indicate bright pixels. Others are off.

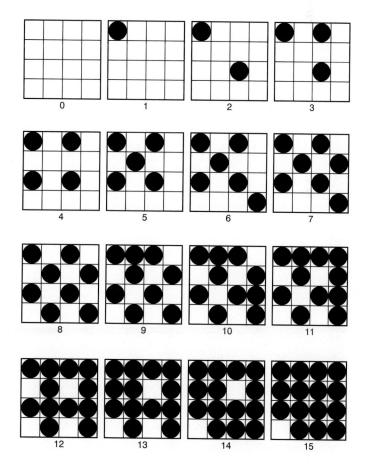

The last example was for a display device that supports only black-and-white pixels. Chances are good (really, really good) that your video adapter supports more than just black-and-white pixels. Keeping with the monochrome flavor for now, say your hardware can display 16 shades of gray from 0 to 15. If you have a 256 gray-shade image that you are going to display, stick with the 4×4 box and do the following. Define a "Dark Pixel" (DP) and a "Light Pixel" (LP). From now on, pixels that you "turn off" you will actually set to the value of DP, and pixels that you "turn on" you will actually set to the value of LP.

Now, as you go through testing each pixel against its corresponding threshold, first divide the pixel value P by 17. Take the integer portion of your result and set DP to that value. Set LP to DP + 1. Then take the fractional value of P divided by 17, multiply it by 16, round off to the nearest integer and use this "Test Value" in the threshold test to determine which pixels are "turned on" and which pixels are "turned off."

The generalized formula for computing the dither parameters is shown next, with the example values shown in parentheses.

$$DP = INTEGER(P*(R-1)/M)$$
$$LP = DP + 1$$
$$Test\ Value = N^2*(P*(R-1)/M-DP)$$

where

M = Number of gray shades in original image (256)
N = Size of dither box on one side (4)
P = Image pixel value to be dithered (0–255)
R = Number of gray shades supported by display hardware (16)

The end result of this procedure is that you cycle through the 16 unique patterns of Figure 5.11 a total of 15 times as the pixel value intensity increases from 0 to 255. With each cycle, the values of DP and LP increment by one. If you multiply 15 cycles by 16 unique patterns, you find that there are 240 unique possible pattern intensities averaged over the 4×4 box. In general, with an N×N-sized dither box and an R shades of gray display, you can accurately approximate $N^2*(R-1)$ shades of gray. "But, hey," you say. "What's this business about 240 shades? Didn't you start this thing off talking about 256 shades in the prior example?" The answer is that some of the 256 shades were merged, and only 240 shades of gray were approximated by the dithering technique. You'll probably never notice the difference.

If those lost 16 shades matter to you, Figure 5.12 shows an 8×8 dither box pattern that you can use instead. Now you can approximate up $8^2*(16-1) = 960$ shades of gray with a 16 shades of gray video adapter. Overkill, right? Not exactly. Read on.

FIGURE 5.12.

An 8×8 dither box with 64 threshold values.

1	33	9	41	3	35	11	43
49	17	57	25	51	19	59	27
13	45	5	37	15	47	7	39
61	29	53	21	63	31	55	23
4	36	12	44	2	34	10	42
52	20	60	28	50	18	58	26
16	48	8	40	14	46	6	38
64	32	56	24	62	30	54	22

Megachrome

I'm sure that you haven't forgotten about those 16 million-color images yet. Earlier I said that the simple approach cuts the 8-bit red component down to 3 bits, the 8-bit green component down to 3 bits, and the 8-bit blue component down to 2 bits. The dithering approach starts with this simple step. Next, you treat each of the color components one at a time. In the case of the 8-bit RGB pixel, that means processing a 3-bit (8-shade) red pixel, a 3-bit (8-shade) green pixel, and a 2-bit (4-shade) blue pixel. You perform dithering independently on each of these three components and merge the result just before plotting the pixel on the screen.

Recalling that $N^2*(R-1)$ shades are possible, an 8×8 dither box will support up to 448 shades of red and 448 shades of green, but only 192 shades of blue. Blue being the dim color that it is to your eyes, you simply say, "192 shades of blue?…Good enough!" You're probably getting restless by now, so I'll get to the code and show you how to dither True Color images down to 256-color displays.

The whole dithering process boils down to one subroutine called `draw_dithered_pixel`, which is shown in Listing 5.4. It's so easy to use. For each 24-bit RGB pixel at screen coordinate (i,j), you call `draw_dithered_pixel(i,j,rgb,size)`, where rgb is a 3-byte array containing the pixels' red, green, and blue values, and size is the dither box size of 1, 2, 4, or 8.

Listing 5.4. Dithering a pixel is easy.

```
/*.................. DRAW_DITHERED_PIXEL ....... 5-27-94 ....*/
/* This routine draws a dithered pixel at screen coordinate   */
/* 'i,j' with 24 bit color equivalent passed in the 3 byte    */
/* array 'rgb'.  The dither pattern size is specified by 'size'*/
/* and can be 1, 2, 4, or 8.  Note that the global 'dither'    */
/* array must be initialized before calling this routine.      */
/*..........................................................*/
void draw_dithered_pixel(int i,int j,unsigned char *rgb,int size)
```

continues

Listing 5.4. continued

```
{
  int n,m,q,r,red_lvl,grn_lvl,blu_lvl;
  int color,red_boost,grn_boost,blu_boost;
  float x,y,frl,fgl,fbl;
/*.........................................................*/
/* For the pixels screen address i,j, compute pixel address r  */
/* within the dither box.  Also select dither box q based on   */
/* size (size = 1, 2, 4, or 8).                                */
/*.........................................................*/
  x = (float)i/size;
  y = (float)j/size;
  m = (int)(size*(x - (int)x) + 0.5);
  n = (int)(size*(y - (int)y) + 0.5);
  q = size/2;
  if(size == 8) q = 3;
  r = m+n*size;
/*.........................................................*/
/* Get the Dark Pixel color, the Light Pixel components, and   */
/* the pixel color errors.                                     */
/*.........................................................*/
  color = crack_rgb(rgb,&red_boost,&grn_boost,&blu_boost,
                    &frl,&fgl,&fbl);
/*.........................................................*/
/*Scale the pixel color error values based on dither box size  */
/*.........................................................*/
  red_lvl = size*size*frl;
  grn_lvl = size*size*fgl;
  blu_lvl = size*size*fbl;
/*.........................................................*/
/*Test the pixels red, green, and blue error values against the*/
/*thresholds in the dither box.  Decide which color to use.    */
/*.........................................................*/
  if(dither[q][r] <= red_lvl)
    color = (color & 0x1f) + (red_boost << 5);      /* Boost Red */
  if(dither[q][r] <= grn_lvl)
    color = (color & 0xe3) + (grn_boost << 2);      /* Boost Grn */
  if(dither[q][r] <= blu_lvl)
    color = (color & 0xfc) + blu_boost;             /* Boost Blu */
/*.........................................................*/
/*              Set color and draw pixel on screen.            */
/*.........................................................*/
  vsa_set_color(color);
  vsa_set_pixel(i,j);
  return;
}                       /*.... END draw_dithered_pixel ....*/
```

The draw_dithered_pixel routine calls crack_rgb, shown in Listing 5.5, to get the 8-bit color value equivalent to the 24-bit pixel. Whereas draw_dithered_pixel figures out when to draw dark pixels and when to draw light pixels, crack_rgb computes the dark pixel color value, the light pixel color values for each of red, green, and blue, and the test values for each of red, green, and blue.

Listing 5.5. Cracking an RGB pixel into pieces.

```
/*...................... CRACK_RGB .......... 5-27-94 ....*/
/* This routine takes the 24 bit RGB color value in the 'rgb'  */
/* array, quantizes it down to an 8 bit color value (3 bit red,*/
/* 3 bit green, and 2 bit blue) and returns this 8 bit         */
/* 'base_color' value. It also computes the 8 bit color boost  */
/* values '*red_boost', 'grn_boost', and 'blu_boost' which are */
/* used to draw dithered pixels. It also computes the color    */
/* error values 'red_lvl', 'grn_lvl', and 'blu_lvl' which      */
/* determine when the dither function draws with 'base_color'  */
/* and when it draws with 'xxx_boost' color.                   */
/*.............................................................*/
int crack_rgb(unsigned char *rgb,int *red_boost,int *grn_boost,
              int *blu_boost,float *red_lvl,float *grn_lvl,
              float *blu_lvl)
{
  int   base_color,red,grn,blu;
  float fred,fgrn,fblu;

  fred = rgb[2]/36.6;   /*36.6 = (256 shades of red)/(2^3 - 1) */
  fgrn = rgb[1]/36.6;   /*36.6 = (256 shades of grn)/(2^3 - 1) */
  fblu = rgb[0]/85.4;   /*85.4 = (256 shades of blu)/(2^2 - 1) */

  red = fred;
  grn = fgrn;
  blu = fblu;
  base_color = (red << 5)+(grn << 2)+blu;   /*Dark Pixel color */

  *red_lvl = fred - red;
  *grn_lvl = fgrn - grn;
  *blu_lvl = fblu - blu;

  *red_boost = red+1;  /*This is the Light Pixel color for red */
  *grn_boost = grn+1;  /*This is the Light Pixel color for grn */
  *blu_boost = blu+1;  /*This is the Light Pixel color for blu */

  return base_color;
}                      /*.... END crack_rgb        .....*/
```

Figure 5.13 shows how the original True Color image appears after it is converted it to a dithered 8-bit RGB image.

The code for the DITHER program that pulls this all together is shown in Listing 5.6. First of all, the global dither array is initialized with the threshold values for four different dither boxes of sizes 1, 2, 4, and 8. The other thing that needs to be initialized is the color palette. The true_color_lut routine initializes the palette with 8-bit RGB values.

When you run the DITHER program, you input the name of a True Color TARGA (*.TGA) image file and the size of the dither box that you want to try. DITHER then goes and sets your video adapter to the highest available video resolution with 256 colors. The file is read out, dithered, displayed, and saved as a TIFF file called NEW.TIF. Then the program loops back so that you can try a different dither box size. A size of 1 produces

FIGURE 5.13.
Dithered 8-bit RGB version of Andrew and Ted.

an undithered 8-bit RGB image. Try this at least once to get an appreciation for what dithering gets you. When you are asked for a dither box size, pressing the Escape key will exit the program.

You'll notice that the main program also is a TARGA Image File reader. Source code for image readers (see the following note) in the league of TIFF or GIF would fill this whole chapter, leaving little space for the rest of my gems. So, when I need access to the red, green, and blue bytes of an image for my examples, I use TARGA format files because they're simple. I also provide TIFF2TGA.EXE, a TIFF-to-TARGA converter, so you can convert True Color TIFFs to TARGAs. Of course, you can use any existing True Color TARGAs that you can scrounge up. "Why then," you ask, "do you save the dithered image

as a TIFF instead of a TARGA file?" Because you don't need to write any code to work with TIFF images. You already have everything you need for complete TIFF reading, displaying, and writing in the form of the TIFF256 Graphics Library Extensions included on the disc with this book.

NOTE

The TIFF256 Graphics Library Extensions included with this book is an excellent TIFF image file reader. However, it does not provide external access to the red, green, and blue bytes of a True Color image.

Listing 5.6. The DITHER program does it all.

```
#include<stdio.h>
#include<stdlib.h>
#include<conio.h>
```

```
#include<fcntl.h>
#include<io.h>
#include<vsa.h>
#include<tiff.h>

unsigned long read_tga_header(int,int *,int *,int *,int *);
void draw_dithered_pixel(int,int,unsigned char *,int);
void true_color_lut(void);
int  crack_rgb(unsigned char *,int *,int *,int *,
                float *,float *,float *);


unsigned char dither[4][64]={
{
 1 },
{
 1, 3,
 4, 2 },
{
 1,   9, 3, 11,
13,   5, 15, 7,
 4, 12, 2, 10,
16,   8, 14, 6 },
{
 1, 33,  9, 41,  3, 35, 11, 43,
49, 17, 57, 25, 51, 19, 59, 27,
13, 45,  5, 37, 15, 47,  7, 39,
61, 29, 53, 21, 63, 31, 55, 23,
 4, 36, 12, 44,  2, 34, 10, 42,
52, 20, 60, 28, 50, 18, 58, 26,
16, 48,  8, 40, 14, 46,  6, 38,
64, 32, 56, 24, 62, 30, 54, 22 },
};

/*........................ DITHER.C............. 5-29-94 .....*/
/* This program reads True Color (24 bit per pixel) TARGA    */
/* images and converts them to 8 bit dithered screen images.  */
/* It also writes out the dithered image as an 8 bit per pixel */
/* Palette Color TIFF image.                                 */
/*.........................................................*/
void main()
{
  char filename[80];
  int i,j,size,width,height,type,file_handle,orient;
  unsigned char rgb[3072];
  printf("Input TARGA Image Filename: ");
  scanf("%s",filename);
LOOP:
/*.........................................................*/
/* Get dither size and limit it to legal value of 1,2,4 or 8. */
/*.........................................................*/
  printf("Input Dither Size (1, 2, 4, or 8): ");
  scanf("%d",&size);
  if(size == 3) size = 4;     /* size limited to 1, 2, 4, or 8 */
  if(size > 4)  size = 8;     /* size limited to 1, 2, 4, or 8 */
/*.........................................................*/
/*            Set highest video resolution available.        */
/*.........................................................*/
```

continues

Listing 5.6. continued

```
  if(vsa_init(0x2105) != 0)                /* 1024 x 768 x 256 */
    if(vsa_init(0x2103) != 0)              /*  800 x 600 x 256 */
      if(vsa_init(0x2101) != 0)            /*  640 x 480 x 256 */
        if(vsa_init(0x2100) != 0)          /*  640 x 400 x 256 */
          {
            printf("Can't set VESA video mode\n");
            printf("Is VESA BIOS Extension TSR loaded?\n");
            return;
          }
/*.........................................................*/
/*          Open the TARGA file and get header info.       */
/*.........................................................*/
  if((file_handle = open(filename,O_BINARY | O_RDONLY)) == -1)
    return;
  read_tga_header(file_handle,&width,&height,&type,&orient);
/*.........................................................*/
/*      Set up the Palette as an 8 bit RGB (3,3,2) table.   */
/*.........................................................*/
  true_color_lut();
/*.........................................................*/
/*  Read out pixels from TARGA file and plot on screen in   */
/*  top down or bottom up order depending on orientation.   */
/*.........................................................*/
  if(orient == 32)
    for(j=0;j<height;j++)
      {
        read(file_handle,rgb,3*width);
        for(i=0;i<width;i++)
          draw_dithered_pixel(i,j,rgb+3*i,size);
      }
  else
    for(j=height-1;j>=0;j--)
      {
        read(file_handle,rgb,3*width);
        for(i=0;i<width;i++)
          draw_dithered_pixel(i,j,rgb+3*i,size);
      }
/*.........................................................*/
/*  Close the image file and look for an ESC key to quit.   */
/*  Otherwise, save dithered image as an 8 bit TIFF called  */
/*  NEW.TIF and LOOP for experimentation with a different   */
/*  dither box size.                                        */
/*.........................................................*/
  close(file_handle);
  if(getch() == 27)
    goto SKIP;
  tf_save_file(0,0,width-1,height-1,"new.tif");
  vsa_set_svga_mode(0x3);
  goto LOOP;                       /*.....  Oh No, a goto!  .....*/
SKIP:
  vsa_set_svga_mode(0x3);
  return;                          /*.....  End main        .....*/
}



/*...................... READ_TGA_HEADER  ....... 5-17-94 ....*/
/* This routine parses through a TGA header and returns the  */
```

```
/* file offset in bytes to the first byte of pixel data.      */
/* It also returns image width, height, and type (type 2 is the*/
/* uncompressed 24 bit image type).                            */
/*............................................................*/
unsigned long read_tga_header(int handle, int *width,
                              int *height, int *type,
                              int *orientation)
{
  unsigned long offset;
  unsigned char buff[18];
  read(handle,buff,18);
  offset = 18+buff[0];
  *type = buff[2];

  *width  = *((unsigned *)buff + 6);
  *height = *((unsigned *)buff + 7);
  *orientation = buff[17];
  return offset;
}                         /*.... END read_tga_header    .....*/




/*.................. TRUE_COLOR_LUT.C ....... 5-15-94 ........*/
/* This routine generates a 'true color' LUT.  An 8 bit index */
/* into the LUT represents 3 bits of RED, 3 bits of GREEN, and*/
/* 2 bits of BLUE.  The 3 msbs of the 8 bit index are the RED */
/* field, next 3 are GREEN, and the 2 lsbs are the BLUE field.*/
/*............................................................*/
void true_color_lut(void)
{
  int i;
  unsigned char color_array[768];
  for(i=0;i<256;i++)
    {
      color_array[3*i+0]= ((i & 0x00e0) >> 5) * 9;
      color_array[3*i+1]= ((i & 0x001c) >> 2) * 9;
      color_array[3*i+2]= (i & 0x0003) * 21;
    }
  vsa_write_color_block(0,256,color_array);
  return;
}                         /*.....   End True_color_lut   .....*/
```

Making an Adaptive Color Palette

If you toughed it out this far, you are hard core. Your persistence is about to be rewarded with the secrets of Adaptive Color Palette generation. Dithering was nice, but this stuff blows it away. Kind of like the difference between milk chocolate and dark chocolate, if you know what I mean. An Adaptive Color Palette is one that is created by analyzing the colors in the image and choosing the best 256 colors to minimize errors in the appearance of the image. Paul Heckbert is recognized as the original developer of the technique of Adaptive Color Palette generation on the merits of his paper "Color Image Quantization for Frame Buffer Display," presented at Siggraph in 1982. In this section, I'll walk you through the maze of Adaptive Color Palette generation, but first I need to introduce a few basic ideas.

RGB Color Space

All the work in Adaptive Color Palette generation happens in RGB color space. Imagine physical three-dimensional space with the three axes typically labeled x, y, and z, each axis angled away from the others by 90 degrees. If you replace the x, y, and z labels with R, G, and B, corresponding to red, green, and blue intensity, then you've created RGB color space. You can plot any RGB color in RGB Color Space just like you can plot a point at any (x,y,z) position in physical space. Just as in physical space, you can calculate a distance between two colors. If color A is defined by (Ra,Ga,Ba), and color B is defined by (Rb,Gb,Bb), then the distance between the two colors is figured as follows:

Color Distance = $\text{SquareRoot}[(Ra{-}Rb)^2 + (Ga{-}Gb)^2 + (Ba{-}Bb)^2]$

The closer the distance, the more similar the two colors are. If you calculate the distance of a color from the origin (black), this is proportional to the absolute brightness of the color.

Volume Histograms

In the beginning of this chapter I talked about image histograms. Here you can take the idea of a histogram a step further by adding a few dimensions to come up with a Volume Histogram. It's called a Volume Histogram because it is defined in RGB Color Space and thus has volume, just like a cup of water has volume (remember? 2-D surfaces have area; 3-D regions have volume). If you plot a point in RGB Color Space for each color occurring in an image and make the brightness of the dot proportional to the frequency of occurrence of pixels in the image with that exact color, you will have created a glow-in-the-dark Volume Histogram. Figure 5.14 shows a True Color image.

CUBE Defined

The last concept I need to introduce is that of a CUBE. For the Adaptive Color Palette generation technique about to be shown, a CUBE is defined as a three-dimensional box in RGB color space that encompasses a portion of a volume histogram. Depending on the CUBE's origin and size, it can encompass more or less of an image's histogrammed pixels. Note that this CUBE definition does not require the three CUBE dimensions to be equal in length. In the software, I define a CUBE structure that can be passed through various subroutines by pointer. A CUBE has the following attributes:

Origin (r,g,b)	One corner of the CUBE in RGB Color Space
End (r,g,b)	The opposite (diagonal) corner in RGB Color Space

Volume	The CUBE's Length × Width × Height
Red Avg	The Red value averaged for all pixels histogrammed within the CUBE
Green Avg	The Green value averaged for all pixels histogrammed within the CUBE
Blue Avg	The Blue value averaged for all pixels histogrammed within the CUBE
FSUM	The sum of frequency of occurrence for all colors within the CUBE
CERR	The CUBE's net color error, equal to the sum of differences between a pixel's color and the CUBE's average color for all pixels represented within the CUBE
FOM	A Figure of Merit (the FOM paragraph later in this section is a *must read*)

FIGURE 5.14.

Alexandra in True Color.

The Basic Idea

The Adaptive Color Palette generation technique now should sound easy, if not obvious. For any given image, first you create a volume histogram. Next you define a CUBE that is the full size of the RGB color space (from 0,0,0 to Rmax,Gmax,Bmax). The idea is to bisect (split) the CUBE and continue bisecting the resulting CUBEs until you have 256 of them. The choice of which CUBE to bisect is always based on the CUBE FOM. Each CUBE has a FOM associated with it, and you always split the cube with the highest FOM.

The program maintains a cube list. The cube list starts out with one full-sized CUBE in it. The number of CUBEs in the list grows as more and more CUBEs are bisected, up to the maximum count of 256. The cube list is always sorted by the CUBE FOM so that the first CUBE in the list (CUBE 0) has the highest FOM.

Once you have 256 CUBEs, each one represents a color assigned to the color palette. Now replace each 24-bit RGB pixel in the image with an 8-bit palette index, and that's all there is to it—from a top level view, that is. This process is shown in the flow chart of Figure 5.15. Figure 5.16 shows the 8-bit Adaptive Color Palette image. The top level routine for Adaptive Color Palette generation is shown in Listing 5.7.

FIGURE 5.15.

Flow chart of the Adaptive Color Palette generation process.

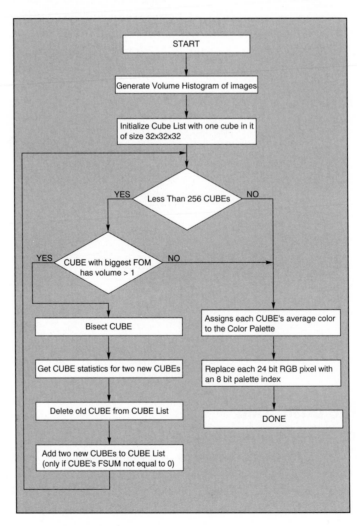

FIGURE 5.16.

The Adaptive Color Palette version of Alexandra.

Listing 5.7. The top level Adaptive Color Palette routine.

```
/*.................... ADAPTIVE_LUT ............ 5-31-94 .....*/
/*    This routine analyzes the True Color image that is    */
/* defined in the TARGA file called 'filename' and computes  */
/* an Adaptive Color Palette which is an optimal selection of */
/* the 256 colors for this particular image.  Before calling  */
/* this routine, 'array' must have been allocated 32768 bytes!*/
/*    First a 32x32x32 volume histogram is computed.  Then the */
/* volume histogram "cube" is subdivide into up to 255 cubes  */
/* (color clusters) used in the image.  One more cube in this */
/* collection is always reserved for BLACK, in RGB space,    */
/* (this is done so that images which have few colors will   */
/* still get a good solid BLACK color in the CLUT). Finally  */
/* it assigns each one of the cubes to each one of the up to */
/* 256 palette entries, and returns the new Color Look Up   */
/* Table in the 'color_array'. The function return value is  */
/* the number of colors in the 'color_array' and is always  */
/* equal to 256 for now (unused colors set to black).       */
/*    Upon completion, the 32k elements of 'array' store the  */
/* palette index for their respective true color value (down */
/* converted to 15 bits).                                   */
/*........................................................*/
int  adaptive_lut(char *filename,unsigned char *array,
                  unsigned char *color_array)
{
  int num_cubes,num_vol,colors,most_cubes;
  struct CUBE cube,new_cube;
  most_cubes = ADPTV_NUM_COLORS-1;
  num_cubes = 0;
  VOLUME_HIST(filename,array);
```

continues

Listing 5.7. continued

```
/*..........................................................*/
/* Set up the number of cubes to be generated based on uniform */
/* color VOLUME partitioning.  Then, the rest of the cubes are */
/* generated on COLOR ERROR minimizing criteria.              */
/*..........................................................*/
  num_vol = (ADPTV_QUALITY * most_cubes) / 100;
/*..........................................................*/
/*  Initialize first cube.  Get its color stats and put it in  */
/*  cube list.                                                 */
/*..........................................................*/
  if(most_cubes > 0)
    {
      cube.x0 = 0;
      cube.y0 = 0;
      cube.z0 = 0;
      cube.x1 = 32;
      cube.y1 = 32;
      cube.z1 = 32;
      gen_cube_color_stats(&cube,array,1);
      num_cubes = add_cube_to_list(cube,num_cubes);
    }
/*..........................................................*/
/*    Subdivide color volume based on minimizing cube Volumes. */
/*    Do for 'num_vol' cubes.                                  */
/*..........................................................*/
  while(num_cubes < num_vol)
    {
      if(CUBE_LIST[0].vol <= 1)
        break;
      copy_cube(CUBE_LIST[0],&cube);
      bisect_cube(&cube,&new_cube);
      gen_cube_color_stats(&cube,array,1);
      gen_cube_color_stats(&new_cube,array,1);
      num_cubes = delete_cube_from_list(0,num_cubes);
      if(cube.fsum != 0)
        num_cubes = add_cube_to_list(cube,num_cubes);
      if(new_cube.fsum != 0)
        num_cubes = add_cube_to_list(new_cube,num_cubes);
    }
/*..........................................................*/
/* Continue subdividing color volume based on minimizing cube  */
/* color errors.  Do for remaining cubes (up to              */
/* 'ADPTV_NUM_COLORS' - 1).                                  */
/*..........................................................*/
  while(num_cubes < most_cubes)
    {
      if(CUBE_LIST[0].vol <= 1)
        break;
      copy_cube(CUBE_LIST[0],&cube);
      bisect_cube(&cube,&new_cube);
      gen_cube_color_stats(&cube,array,2);
      gen_cube_color_stats(&new_cube,array,2);
      num_cubes = delete_cube_from_list(0,num_cubes);
      if(cube.fsum != 0)
        num_cubes = add_cube_to_list(cube,num_cubes);
      if(new_cube.fsum != 0)
```

```
        num_cubes = add_cube_to_list(new_cube,num_cubes);
    }
/*..........................................................*/
/* Add last cube which is BLACK.   Force this cube to top of  */
/* list (via cube.fom = 1000000000) so that it will end up at */
/* CLUT location 0.                                           */
/*..........................................................*/
  cube.x0 = 0;
  cube.y0 = 0;
  cube.z0 = 0;
  cube.x1 = 1;
  cube.y1 = 1;
  cube.z1 = 1;
  gen_cube_color_stats(&cube,array,1);
  cube.fom = 1000000000.0;
  num_cubes = add_cube_to_list(cube,num_cubes);
/*..........................................................*/
/* Finally, figure out the values for the Color Look Up table. */
/*..........................................................*/
  colors = move_cubes_to_list(num_cubes,array,color_array);
  return colors;
}                           /*..... End adaptive_lut  .....*/
```

Volume Histogram Shortcuts

If you make a volume histogram of a 24-bit RGB image, you will find that you need 16,777,216 (256^3) memory locations to store the frequency of occurrence for all the possible colors. As if that's not bad enough, you'll also need to spend time searching through all these locations several times in the process of computing the Adaptive Color Palette. It turns out that you can reduce the 256 shades for each of red, green, and blue down to 32 shades for each and still get great results, and now you need only 32,768 (32^3) memory locations. The first shortcut in this process, therefore, is to divide all color components by 8 before histogramming.

One other shortcut is to limit the maximum frequency of occurrence for any single location in the histogram memory to 255. This works well, and now you've got the histogram memory requirement down to 32K bytes, which is palatable...even to DOS. The code for generating the volume histogram is shown in Listing 5.8.

Listing 5.8. Generating the volume histogram.

```
/*........................ VOLUME_HIST ......... 5-31-94 ....*/
/* This routine analyzes a True Color TARGA image file called  */
/* 'filename' and generates a 3D R-G-B Volume Histogram which   */
/* has 32 elements on a side (32 x 32 x 32). The histogram is   */
/* returned in 'vhist[]'.  Each element of 'vhist[]' stores a   */
/* count from 0 to 255 which is the frequency of occurrence for*/
/* that color in the image. The count "saturates" at 255.      */
```

continues

Listing 5.8. continued

```c
/* ("That color" means the value indexing 'vhist') The value   */
/* indexing 'vhist' is a 15 bit color value whose 5 MSBs are    */
/* Red, then 5 bits Green and finally 5 LSBs of Blue. If the    */
/* image file is not found, this routine returns with an error  */
/* value of 1, else 0.                                          */
/*...............................................................*/
int  VOLUME_HIST(char *filename, unsigned char far *vhist)
{
  unsigned i;
  int j,width,height,type,file_handle,orient;
  unsigned char rgb[3072];
/*...............................................................*/
/*    Initialize 32x32x32 R-G-B histogram to all zeros.         */
/*...............................................................*/
  for(i=0;i<32768;i++)
    vhist[i] = 0;
/*...............................................................*/
/*           Open the TARGA file and get header info.           */
/*...............................................................*/
  if((file_handle = open(filename,O_BINARY ¦ O_RDONLY)) == -1)
    return 1;
  read_tga_header(file_handle,&width,&height,&type,&orient);
/*...............................................................*/
/*  Read out pixels from TARGA file and process in              */
/*  top down or bottom up order depending on orientation.       */
/*...............................................................*/
  if(orient == 32)
    for(j=0;j<height;j++)
      {
        read(file_handle,rgb,3*width);
        analyze_row(rgb,width,vhist);
      }
  else
    for(j=height-1;j>=0;j—)
      {
        read(file_handle,rgb,3*width);
        analyze_row(rgb,width,vhist);
      }
/*...............................................................*/
/*                  Close the image file.                       */
/*...............................................................*/
  close(file_handle);
  return 0;
}                                 /*..... End VOLUME_HIST  .....*/


/*.................... ANALYZE_ROW .............. 5-31-94 ....*/
/*   This routine takes the pixel data for one row of a 24      */
/*   bit/pixel image and accumulates data in the 32x32x32 R-G-B */
/*   histogram 'vhist'. The pixel data is sent in the 'byte_buf'*/
/*   array.  The number of pixels in the array is defined by    */
/*   'width'.                                                   */
/*...............................................................*/
void  analyze_row(byte_buf,width,vhist)
unsigned char far *byte_buf,far *vhist;
int width;
{
  unsigned sum,i;
```

```
for(i=0;i<width;i++)
  {
    sum = 0;
    sum += (byte_buf[3*i+2])/8 << 10;                /* RED   */
    sum += (byte_buf[3*i+1])/8 << 5;                 /* GREEN */
    sum += (byte_buf[3*i]  )/8;                       /* BLUE  */
    if(vhist[sum] != 255)
      vhist[sum]++;
  }
  return;
}                                    /*..... End analyze_row ......*/
```

The Bisection

This sounds extra special, but all it means is that you split a CUBE in two. I did it in a pretty mindless fashion (always my method of choice) by cutting the CUBE in half along its longest dimension, as shown in Figure 5.17 and in Listing 5.9. Depending on your motivation level, you might want to experiment with different approaches. For instance, it seems to me that you would get better results if you separated the CUBE into equal frequency sums instead of equal volumes. This may slow the process down a bit, so some trade-offs are in order.

FIGURE 5.17.

A sample CUBE bisection.

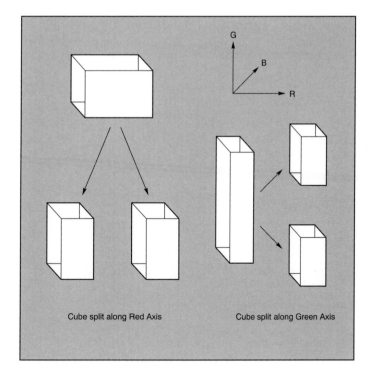

Cube split along Red Axis   Cube split along Green Axis

Listing 5.9. Bisecting the cube.

```
/*...................... BISECT_CUBE ............ 6-1-94 ....*/
/* Input cube in 'cube', output two cubes in 'cube' and      */
/* 'new_cube'.  Cubes are split along longest axis.  New cube */
/* guaranteed to be "validated".                             */
/*...........................................................*/
void  bisect_cube(struct CUBE *pcube,struct CUBE *pnew_cube)
{
  unsigned dx,dy,dz;
  validate_cube(pcube);
/*...........................................................*/
/*            Get red, green, and blue extent of cube.       */
/*...........................................................*/
  dx = pcube->x1-pcube->x0;                /* RED dimension   */
  dy = pcube->y1-pcube->y0;                /* GREEN dimension */
  dz = pcube->z1-pcube->z0;                /* BLUE dimension  */
/*...........................................................*/
/* If red is longest dimension, split red axis of cube.      */
/*...........................................................*/
  if((dx >= dy) && (dx >= dz))
    {
      pnew_cube->x0 = (pcube->x1 + pcube->x0)/2;
      pnew_cube->y0 = pcube->y0;
      pnew_cube->z0 = pcube->z0;
      pnew_cube->x1 = pcube->x1;
      pnew_cube->y1 = pcube->y1;
      pnew_cube->z1 = pcube->z1;
      pcube->x1 = pnew_cube->x0;
      return;
    }
/*...........................................................*/
/* If green is longest dimension, split green axis of cube.  */
/*...........................................................*/
  if((dy >= dx) && (dy >= dz))
    {
      pnew_cube->x0 = pcube->x0;
      pnew_cube->y0 = (pcube->y1 + pcube->y0)/2;
      pnew_cube->z0 = pcube->z0;
      pnew_cube->x1 = pcube->x1;
      pnew_cube->y1 = pcube->y1;
      pnew_cube->z1 = pcube->z1;
      pcube->y1 = pnew_cube->y0;
      return;
    }
/*...........................................................*/
/* If blue is longest dimension, split blue axis of cube.    */
/*...........................................................*/
  if((dz >= dx) && (dz >= dy))
    {
      pnew_cube->x0 = pcube->x0;
      pnew_cube->y0 = pcube->y0;
      pnew_cube->z0 = (pcube->z1 + pcube->z0)/2;
      pnew_cube->x1 = pcube->x1;
      pnew_cube->y1 = pcube->y1;
      pnew_cube->z1 = pcube->z1;
      pcube->z1 = pnew_cube->z0;
      return;
    }
```

```
        }                              /*.... END: bisect_cube .....*/


/*.................... VALIDATE_CUBE ............ 1-12-94 ....*/
/* Insures that cube point 0 is closer to (or same distance   */
/* from) origin of RGB Color than cube point 1.               */
/*............................................................*/
void  validate_cube(struct CUBE *pcube)
{
  unsigned temp;
  if(pcube->x0 > pcube->x1)
    {
      temp = pcube->x0;
      pcube->x0 = pcube->x1;
      pcube->x1 = temp;
    }
  if(pcube->y0 > pcube->y1)
    {
      temp = pcube->y0;
      pcube->y0 = pcube->y1;
      pcube->y1 = temp;
    }
  if(pcube->z0 > pcube->z1)
    {
      temp = pcube->z0;
      pcube->z0 = pcube->z1;
      pcube->z1 = temp;
    }
  return;
}                              /*.... END: validate_cube ...*/


/*........................ COPY_CUBE .......... 1-15-94 ....*/
/* This routine copies the 'cube' struct to the 'new_cube'  */
/* struct.                                                  */
/*..........................................................*/
void  copy_cube(struct CUBE cube,struct CUBE *pnew_cube)
{
  pnew_cube->x0 = cube.x0;
  pnew_cube->y0 = cube.y0;
  pnew_cube->z0 = cube.z0;
  pnew_cube->x1 = cube.x1;
  pnew_cube->y1 = cube.y1;
  pnew_cube->z1 = cube.z1;
  pnew_cube->vol = cube.vol;
  pnew_cube->r_avg = cube.r_avg;
  pnew_cube->g_avg = cube.g_avg;
  pnew_cube->b_avg = cube.b_avg;
  pnew_cube->fsum  = cube.fsum;
  pnew_cube->cerr  = cube.cerr;
  pnew_cube->fom   = cube.fom;
  return;
}                              /*....   END: copy_cube  ....*/
```

Managing New Cubes

Immediately after the CUBE bisection, the gen_cube_color_stats routine generates the attributes stored in the CUBE structure for the two new CUBEs. Then the original CUBE is deleted from the Cube List and the two new CUBEs are added. The routine named delete_cube_from_list removes the old cube from the cube list, while the add_cube_to_list routine takes care of inserting the new CUBEs in the appropriate sort order. The guts of these three routines are shown in Listing 5.10.

Listing 5.10. Generating CUBE statistics and managing the cube list.

```
/*................ GEN_CUBE_COLOR_STATS ........... 6-1-94 ...*/
/* Compute cube's color statistics (Volume, Frequency Sum,     */
/* Average Color value for Red, Green, and Blue, Color Error,  */
/* and Figure-Of-Merit).  The color error is the sum of        */
/* ABS(color - avg_color)*frequency (sort of) for each color   */
/* in cube.                                                    */
/*...........................................................*/
void  gen_cube_color_stats(struct CUBE *pcube,
                           unsigned char *array,int mode)
{
  unsigned i,j,k,freq;
  int dr,dg,db;
  unsigned long sum,index,index0,color_error;
  long red_avg,grn_avg,blu_avg;
  sum = 0;
  red_avg = 0;
  grn_avg = 0;
  blu_avg = 0;
  color_error = 0;
/*.........................................................*/
/*                    Compute cube's volume                 */
/*.........................................................*/
  pcube->vol = (pcube->x1-pcube->x0)*
               (pcube->y1-pcube->y0)*
               (pcube->z1-pcube->z0);
/*.........................................................*/
/*     Compute average red, green and blue values.          */
/*.........................................................*/
  for(k=pcube->x0;k<pcube->x1;k++)
    {
      index0 = k<<10;
      for(j=pcube->y0;j<pcube->y1;j++)
        {
          index = index0 + (j<<5) + pcube->z0;
        r(i=pcube->z0;i<pcube->z1;i++)
            {
              freq = array[index];
              red_avg += k*freq;
              grn_avg += j*freq;
              blu_avg += i*freq;
              sum += freq;
              index ++;
            }
        }
    }
```

```
      }
   if(sum != 0)
      {
      red_avg /= sum;
      grn_avg /= sum;
      blu_avg /= sum;
      }
   else
      {
      red_avg = 0;
      grn_avg= 0;
      blu_avg = 0;
      }
/*................................................................*/
/*     Now compute color error.                                   */
/*................................................................*/
   for(k=pcube->x0;k<pcube->x1;k++)
      {
      index0 = k<<10;
      for(j=pcube->y0;j<pcube->y1;j++)
         {
         index = index0 + (j<<5) + pcube->z0;
         for(i=pcube->z0;i<pcube->z1;i++)
            {
            freq = array[index];
            dr = (red_avg-(int)k);
            dg = (grn_avg-(int)j);
            db = (blu_avg-(int)i);
            color_error += freq*sqrt(dr*dr+dg*dg+db*db);
            index ++;
            }
         }
      }
   pcube->r_avg = red_avg;
   pcube->g_avg = grn_avg;
   pcube->b_avg = blu_avg;
   pcube->fsum  = sum;
   pcube->cerr  = color_error;
/*................................................................*/
/* You can decide what characteristic is used for the Figure of*/
/* Merit (FOM) by setting 'mode' to 1 - 5.   Modes 1 and 2 are */
/* normally used.  Modes 3, 4, and 5 are for play.            */
/*................................................................*/
   if(mode == 1)
     pcube->fom  = (float) pcube->vol;
   if(mode == 2)
     pcube->fom  = (float) pcube->cerr;
   if(mode == 3)
     pcube->fom  = (float) pcube->fsum;
   if(mode == 4)
     pcube->fom  = (float)(pcube->cerr)*(float)(pcube->fsum);
   if(mode >= 5)
     pcube->fom  = (float)(pcube->vol-1)*(float)(pcube->fsum);
   return;
}                          /*.... END: gen_cube_color_stats ....*/
```

continues

Listing 5.10. continued

```c
/*..................... ADD_CUBE_TO_LIST ........... 6-1-94 ...*/
/* Adds a cube to list.  Inserts cube appropriately to maintain*/
/* a descending cube sort based on CUBE_LIST[i].fom.  In       */
/* other words, CUBE_LIST[0].fom is always going to be the     */
/* largest value of all cubes.  Give this routine a cube and   */
/* the current number of cubes in the list 'n'. Routine returns*/
/* the new value of 'n'.  NOTE: For n cubes, you have          */
/* CUBE_LIST[0] thru CUBE_LIST[n-1].                           */
/*.............................................................*/
int  add_cube_to_list(struct CUBE new_cube,int n)
{
  int m;
  m = n+1;
/*.............................................................*/
/* Bump lower FOM valued cubes down a step in cube list.       */
/*.............................................................*/
  if(n>0)
    while(CUBE_LIST[n-1].fom <= new_cube.fom)
      {
        CUBE_LIST[n].x0 = CUBE_LIST[n-1].x0;
        CUBE_LIST[n].y0 = CUBE_LIST[n-1].y0;
        CUBE_LIST[n].z0 = CUBE_LIST[n-1].z0;
        CUBE_LIST[n].x1 = CUBE_LIST[n-1].x1;
        CUBE_LIST[n].y1 = CUBE_LIST[n-1].y1;
        CUBE_LIST[n].z1 = CUBE_LIST[n-1].z1;
        CUBE_LIST[n].vol = CUBE_LIST[n-1].vol;
        CUBE_LIST[n].r_avg = CUBE_LIST[n-1].r_avg;
        CUBE_LIST[n].g_avg = CUBE_LIST[n-1].g_avg;
        CUBE_LIST[n].b_avg = CUBE_LIST[n-1].b_avg;
        CUBE_LIST[n].fsum = CUBE_LIST[n-1].fsum;
        CUBE_LIST[n].cerr = CUBE_LIST[n-1].cerr;
        CUBE_LIST[n].fom = CUBE_LIST[n-1].fom;
        n—;
        if(n==0) break;
      }
/*.............................................................*/
/*                Add new cube to cube list.                   */
/*.............................................................*/
  CUBE_LIST[n].x0 = new_cube.x0;
  CUBE_LIST[n].y0 = new_cube.y0;
  CUBE_LIST[n].z0 = new_cube.z0;
  CUBE_LIST[n].x1 = new_cube.x1;
  CUBE_LIST[n].y1 = new_cube.y1;
  CUBE_LIST[n].z1 = new_cube.z1;
  CUBE_LIST[n].vol = new_cube.vol;
  CUBE_LIST[n].r_avg = new_cube.r_avg;
  CUBE_LIST[n].g_avg = new_cube.g_avg;
  CUBE_LIST[n].b_avg = new_cube.b_avg;
  CUBE_LIST[n].fsum = new_cube.fsum;
  CUBE_LIST[n].cerr = new_cube.cerr;
  CUBE_LIST[n].fom = new_cube.fom;
  return m;
}                                  /*.. END: add_cube_to_list ..*/


/*................... DELETE_CUBE_FROM_LIST ...... 1-15-94 ....*/
```

```
/* Deletes cube 'p' from cube list. Bumps up remaining cubes to*/
/* keep list consecutive and hole free.  Give this routine the */
/* current number of cubes in list ('n') and the cube id to be */
/* deleted ('p').  Routine returns the new value of 'n'.       */
/* NOTE: For n cubes, you have CUBE_LIST[0] thru CUBE_LIST[n-1]*/
/*.............................................................*/
int  delete_cube_from_list(int p,int n)
{
  if(p >= n)
    return n;
  while(p < n-1)
    {
      CUBE_LIST[p].x0 = CUBE_LIST[p+1].x0;
      CUBE_LIST[p].y0 = CUBE_LIST[p+1].y0;
      CUBE_LIST[p].z0 = CUBE_LIST[p+1].z0;
      CUBE_LIST[p].x1 = CUBE_LIST[p+1].x1;
      CUBE_LIST[p].y1 = CUBE_LIST[p+1].y1;
      CUBE_LIST[p].z1 = CUBE_LIST[p+1].z1;
      CUBE_LIST[p].vol = CUBE_LIST[p+1].vol;
      CUBE_LIST[p].r_avg = CUBE_LIST[p+1].r_avg;
      CUBE_LIST[p].g_avg = CUBE_LIST[p+1].g_avg;
      CUBE_LIST[p].b_avg = CUBE_LIST[p+1].b_avg;
      CUBE_LIST[p].fsum  = CUBE_LIST[p+1].fsum;
      CUBE_LIST[p].cerr  = CUBE_LIST[p+1].cerr;
      CUBE_LIST[p].fom   = CUBE_LIST[p+1].fom;
      p++;
    }
  return n-1;
}                          /*.. END: delete_cube_from_list ..*/
```

The FOM

Before you get too far away from this last code listing, you might want to look at the gen_cube_color_stats a little closer. This is the routine that calculates the FOM for each CUBE, and, as you may have figured out by now, the FOM is the key in how well the Adaptive Color Palette works. The FOM should indicate which CUBE is most worthy of being subdivided next. There are many ways to determine this worthiness, and how well this decision is made determines how well the resulting Adaptive Color Palette works. If the FOM is not a really good indicator of which CUBE should be subdivided next, you may end up spending too much attention refining unimportant colors in the image at the expense of more important colors.

In the gen_cube_color_stats routine, the mode parameter determines the method in which the FOM is calculated. If mode = 1, the FOM is proportional to the volume of the cube. Note that this is regardless of the contents of the cube. A very large cube will have a high priority to be bisected even if it represents a very small number of pixels in the image. Even so, it is important to perform at least some of the cube bisecting with this mode so that image highlights that exist in only a few pixels are not lost.

With mode = 2, the FOM is proportional to the degree of variation of the colors within the CUBE. A CUBE whose histogrammed pixels are all very close together in RGB color space will get a lower FOM than a CUBE whose histogrammed pixels are broadly distributed in the RGB color space. This mode is crucial to capturing as many of the color variations as possible from the original image.

Looking back at the adaptive_lut top level routine, you will see that the ADPTV_QUALITY parameter determines how many CUBEs are generated using mode = 1 and how many are generated using mode = 2. In the gen_cube_color_stats there are a few more modes supported for FOM calculation. These are for playing with to see the effects on resulting image quality. You can come up with a few of your own FOM calculations as well.

Okay, So Now What?

Okay, so now what? (Is there an echo in here?) At this point you have generated up to 256 cubes, each of which represents a unique color in the image. If you did the job right, this small group of colors is the best possible selection of 256 colors for the particular image in terms of being as faithful as possible to the 16 million colors of the original image. The three final steps that remain are to move the CUBE colors into the palette, to assign one of the palette colors to each of the 16 million possible colors in the original image, and finally to replace each 24-bit pixel in the image with an 8-bit index into the palette. These three operations are performed by the move_cubes_to_lut, assign_lut_to_colors, and replace_pixel routines shown in Listing 5.11.

Listing 5.11. The last three steps.

```
/*................. MOVE_CUBES_TO_LUT ............ 6-3-94 ....*/
/* This routine loads 'color_array' with the colors of the   */
/* cubes in the 'CUBE_LIST' (after the 'CUBE_LIST' has been   */
/* generated).  The return value is the number of colors      */
/* loaded into 'color_array', and is always 256.              */
/*...........................................................*/
int  move_cubes_to_lut(int num_cubes,unsigned char *array,
                       unsigned char *color_array)
{
  unsigned i;
/*...........................................................*/
/* Compute Color Lookup Table entries. You could do this by   */
/* taking average of each color component axis of cube.  But  */
/* instead ... Use the Average color computed earlier for each */
/* cube! (This is more accurate color).  Multiply by two to   */
/* scale the 5 bit color into the 6 bit palette entry.        */
/*...........................................................*/
  for(i=0;i < num_cubes;i++)
    {
      color_array[3*i+0] = 2*CUBE_LIST[i].r_avg;
      color_array[3*i+1] = 2*CUBE_LIST[i].g_avg;
      color_array[3*i+2] = 2*CUBE_LIST[i].b_avg;
    }
```

```
/*......................................................*/
/*           Set unused palette entries to black.        */
/*......................................................*/
  for(i=num_cubes;i<256;i++)
    {
      color_array[3*i+0] = 0;
      color_array[3*i+1] = 0;
      color_array[3*i+2] = 0;
    }
  assign_lut_to_colors(array,num_cubes);
  return 256;
}                          /*..... End move_cubes_to_lut  .....*/


/*................ ASSIGN_LUT_TO_COLORS ........... 6-3-94 ...*/
/* Assign each of the 32768 color values in the RGB Color Space*/
/* (compressed from 16M) to one of the up to 256 cubes (which  */
/* map to the color lut). 'ADPTV_ASSIGN_MODE' determines the   */
/* way that colors are assigned.  If '0', then color error is  */
/* minimized. Otherwise, all colors which land within a cube   */
/* get set to cube average color.                              */
/*......................................................*/
void  assign_lut_to_colors(unsigned char *array,unsigned
num_cubes)
{
  int red,grn,blu,dr,dg,db,error,last_error;
  unsigned i,j,k,n;
  long index,index0;
  if(!ADPTV_ASSIGN_MODE)
/*......................................................*/
/*  For each color in the image, assign it the CUBE ID for the */
/*  CUBE which has the nearest average color value .           */
/*......................................................*/
    {
      for(i=0;i<32768;i++)
        {
          if(array[i] != 0)
            {
              red = (i & 0x7c00) >> 10;
              grn = (i & 0x03e0) >>  5;
              blu =  i & 0x001f       ;
              last_error = 10000;
              for(n=0;n<num_cubes;n++)
                {
                  dr = CUBE_LIST[n].r_avg - red;
                  dg = CUBE_LIST[n].g_avg - grn;
                  db = CUBE_LIST[n].b_avg - blu;
                  error = dr*dr+dg*dg+db*db;
                  if(error <= last_error)
                    {
                      array[i] = n;
                      last_error = error;
                    }
                }
            }
        }
    }
```

continues

Listing 5.11. continued

```
/*..............................................................*/
/* For each cube, assign its ID to all of the colors in        */
/* its boundary. This method is not as accurate as the one     */
/* above but it's faster.                                      */
/*..............................................................*/
  else
    {
      for(n=0;n<num_cubes;n++)
        {
          for(k=CUBE_LIST[n].x0;k<CUBE_LIST[n].x1;k++)
            {
              index0 = k<<10;
              for(j=CUBE_LIST[n].y0;j<CUBE_LIST[n].y1;j++)
                {
                  index = index0 + (j<<5) + CUBE_LIST[n].z0;
                  for(i=CUBE_LIST[n].z0;i<CUBE_LIST[n].z1;i++)
                    {
                      array[index] = n;
                      index ++;
                    }
                }
            }
        }
    }
  return;
}                              /*.... END: assign_lut_to_colors ....*/


/*.................... REPLACE_PIXEL.C ............ 6-1-94 ...*/
/*  This routine compresses the 3 byte per pixel data in the   */
/*  array 'byte_buf' into a single byte per pixel data array    */
/*  (back into 'byte_buf'). The 8-8-8 RGB pixel is down        */
/*  converted to a 5-5-5 RGB pixel.  Then, the 15 bit RGB      */
/*  pixel value is used to look up in the 'array' to get the 8 */
/*  bit palette index for that color. The number of pixels in  */
/*  'byte_buf' is defined by 'width'.                          */
/*..............................................................*/
void replace_pixel(unsigned char *byte_buf,unsigned
width,unsigned char *array)
{
  int i,sum;
/*..............................................................*/
/* If Adaptive Palette ON, map pixel to adaptive palette.      */
/*..............................................................*/
  if(ADPTV_MODE)
    for(i=0;i<width;i++)
      {
        sum = 0;
        sum += (byte_buf[3*i+2])/8 << 10;        /* RED    */
        sum += (byte_buf[3*i+1])/8 << 5;         /* GREEN  */
        sum += (byte_buf[3*i]  )/8;              /* BLUE   */
        byte_buf[i] = array[sum];
      }
/*..............................................................*/
/* If Adaptive Palette OFF, map pixel to 8 bit RGB palette.    */
/*..............................................................*/
```

```
   else
     for(i=0;i<width;i++)
       {
         sum = 0;
         sum += (byte_buf[3*i+2])/32 << 5;          /* RED   */
         sum += (byte_buf[3*i+1])/32 << 2;          /* GREEN */
         sum += (byte_buf[3*i]  )/64;               /* BLUE  */
         byte_buf[i] = (unsigned char) sum;
       }
   return;
}                       /*.....       End replace_pixel   .....*/
```

The code for the ADAPT program that demonstrates the Adaptive Color Palette generation is shown in Listing 5.12. The `true_color_lut` and `read_tga_header` routines are listed
earlier in this chapter and not repeated here. The `set_adaptive_config` routine is shown
setting the number of colors to 256 and the ratio of volume FOM CUBEs to color error
FOM CUBEs to 50/50. Try changing the number of colors down to 128, 50, or 16 and
see how low you can go and still get good results.

When you run the ADAPT program, you input the name of a True Color TARGA (*.TGA)
image file. ADAPT then sets your video adapter to the highest available video resolution
with 256 colors. The file is read out and histogrammed. Then the Adaptive Color Palette
is generated. Finally the TARGA file is read out again, and the pixels are converted from
24-bit RGB to 8-bit palette index pixels. The resulting image is saved as a TIFF file called
NEW.TIF. Upon any key entry, the program loops back so that you can try a different
image. Pressing the Escape key exits the program.

Listing 5.12. The ADAPT program pulls it all together.

```
/*..................... ADAPT.C ................. 6-3-94 ....*/
/* This program demonstrates Adaptive Color Palette generation.*/
/* It reads True Color (24 bit per pixel) TARGA images and      */
/* converts them to 8 bit palette images. It also writes out    */
/* the converted image as an 8 bit per pixel Palette Color TIFF*/
/* image.                                                       */
/*..............................................................*/

#include<malloc.h>
#include<stdlib.h>
#include <stdio.h>
#include <fcntl.h>
#include <io.h>
#include<conio.h>
#include <math.h>
#include<tiff.h>
#include<vsa.h>


/*............................................................*/
/*      Define type struct CUBE first, needed later!          */
/*............................................................*/
```

continues

Listing 5.12. continued

```c
struct CUBE {
    unsigned x0;
    unsigned y0;
    unsigned z0;
    unsigned x1;     // Outside of cube volume!
    unsigned y1;     // Outside of cube volume!
    unsigned z1;     // Outside of cube volume!
    unsigned vol;    // this is the volume of the cube;
    long r_avg;      // this is the Average Red value for cube
    long g_avg;      // this is the Average Green value for cube
    long b_avg;      // this is the Average Blue value for cube
    long fsum;       // this is the sum of frequencies in cube
    long cerr;       // this is the NET color error for the cube
    float fom;       // Figure Of Merit, Worthiness of cube split
  };

/*..........................................................*/
/*     All of the function prototypes.                      */
/*..........................................................*/
int  adaptive_lut(char *,unsigned char far *,
                  unsigned char far *);
int  volume_hist(char *, unsigned char far *);
void analyze_row(unsigned char far *, int, unsigned char far *);
void bisect_cube(struct CUBE far *,struct CUBE far *);
void gen_cube_color_stats(struct CUBE far *,
                          unsigned char far *,int);
void validate_cube(struct CUBE far *);
void copy_cube(struct CUBE, struct CUBE far *);
int  add_cube_to_list(struct CUBE, int);
int  delete_cube_from_list(int, int);
int  move_cubes_to_lut(int, unsigned char far *,
                       unsigned char far *);
void assign_lut_to_colors(unsigned char far *, unsigned);
void replace_pixel(unsigned char *, unsigned, unsigned char *);
void set_adaptive_config(int, int, int);
void get_adaptive_config(int far *, int far *, int far *);
unsigned long read_tga_header(int, int *, int *, int *, int *);
void true_color_lut(void);

/*..........................................................*/
/*     Global variables which control the show.             */
/*..........................................................*/
int ADPTV_MODE = 0;             /*..  Default = 0 (Off) ..*/
int ADPTV_NUM_COLORS = 256;     /*..  Default = 256     ..*/
int ADPTV_QUALITY = 50;         /*..  Default = 50      ..*/
struct CUBE CUBE_LIST[256];

#define ADPTV_ASSIGN_MODE  0    /*.. This is experimental..*/

void main()
{
  char filename[80];
  int i,j,size,width,height,type,file_handle,orient, colors;
  unsigned char lut[768], rgb[3072], far *vhist;
/*..........................................................*/
/* Set up the Adaptive Palette controls and get the TARGA   */
/* image file name.                                         */
```

```
/*..................................................................*/
  set_adaptive_config(1,256,50);
LOOP:
  printf("Input TARGA Image Filename: ");
  scanf("%s",filename);
/*..................................................................*/
/* Allocate memory for the Volume Histogram.  Then run the     */
/* Adaptive Palette code to generate the adaptive palette.     */
/*..................................................................*/
  if(ADPTV_MODE)
    {
      printf("\n");
      printf("Please Wait, Computing Adaptive Color Palette.\n");
      printf("\n");
      if((vhist = (unsigned char far *)halloc(32768,1)) == NULL)
        {
          printf("Can't Allocate Memory for Histogram!\n");
          return;
        }
      colors = adaptive_lut(filename,vhist,lut);
    }
/*..................................................................*/
/*              Set highest video resolution available.        */
/*..................................................................*/
  if(vsa_init(0x2105) != 0)               /* 1024 x 768 x 256 */
    if(vsa_init(0x2103) != 0)             /*  800 x 600 x 256 */
      if(vsa_init(0x2101) != 0)           /*  640 x 480 x 256 */
        if(vsa_init(0x2100) != 0)         /*  640 x 400 x 256 */
          {
            printf("Can't set VESA video mode\n");
            printf("Is VESA BIOS Extension TSR loaded?\n");
            return;
          }
/*..................................................................*/
/* Set up Color Palette either to Adaptive Palette or 8 bit RGB*/
/*..................................................................*/
  if(ADPTV_MODE)
    vsa_write_color_block(0,colors,lut);
  else
    true_color_lut();
/*..................................................................*/
/*              Open the TARGA file and get header info.       */
/*..................................................................*/
  if((file_handle = open(filename,O_BINARY | O_RDONLY)) == -1)
    return;
  read_tga_header(file_handle,&width,&height,&type,&orient);
/*..................................................................*/
/* Depending on orientation, read file out-top down or         */
/* bottom-up, replace 24 bit pixels with 8 bit palette indexes,*/
/* and display on screen.                                      */
/*..................................................................*/
  if(orient == 32)
    for(j=0;j<height;j++)
      {
        read(file_handle,rgb,3*width);
        replace_pixel(rgb,width,vhist);
```

continues

Listing 5.12. continued

```
          vsa_raster_line(0,width-1,j,rgb);
      }
  else
    for(j=height-1;j>=0;j—)
      {
        read(file_handle,rgb,3*width);
        replace_pixel(rgb,width,vhist);
        vsa_raster_line(0,width-1,j,rgb);
      }
/*..........................................................*/
/*  Close the image file and look for an ESC key to quit.   */
/*  Otherwise, save new image as an 8 bit TIFF called       */
/*  NEW.TIF and LOOP for experimentation with a different   */
/*  input image files.                                      */
/*..........................................................*/
  if(ADPTV_MODE)
    hfree((unsigned char huge *)vhist);
  close(file_handle);
  if(getch() == 27)
    goto SKIP;
  tf_save_file(0,0,width-1,height-1,"new.tif");
  vsa_set_svga_mode(0x3);
  goto LOOP;
SKIP:
  vsa_set_svga_mode(0x3);
  return;
}                           /*.....    End MAIN    .....*/


/*.............. SET_ADAPTIVE_CONFIG .......... 4-30-94 ....*/
/* This routine configures the operation of the TIFF256 library*/
/* with regards to 24 bit/pixel images.  The input parameters  */
/* have are:                                                */
/*                                                          */
/*          enable - Adaptive Palette is enabled when enable */
/*                   is 1. disabled otherwise.              */
/*      num_colors - This parameter determines how many colors */
/*                   the 16M color image will be reduced to. */
/*                   (2 min, 256 max!)                      */
/*         quality - This parameter lets the user optimize the */
/*                   Adaptive Palette algorithm for image   */
/*                   quality. The valid range is from 0 to 100.*/
/*                      For values closer to 0, the algorithm is*/
/*                   optimized for images with fewer colors, */
/*                   but many shades per color (smooth shading */
/*                   is emphasized at the expense of color   */
/*                   variety).                              */
/*                      For values closer to 100, the algorithm */
/*                   is optimized for images with a broader  */
/*                   color distribution (many colors are    */
/*                   accommodated at the expense of shade    */
/*                   continuity).                           */
/*..........................................................*/
void  set_adaptive_config(int enable,int num_colors,int quality)
{
  ADPTV_MODE        = enable;
```

```
ADPTV_NUM_COLORS   = num_colors;
ADPTV_QUALITY      = quality;
if(ADPTV_NUM_COLORS > 256) ADPTV_NUM_COLORS = 256;
if(ADPTV_NUM_COLORS < 2)   ADPTV_NUM_COLORS = 2;
if(ADPTV_QUALITY > 100) ADPTV_QUALITY = 100;
return;
}
```

A Subtle Note

Remember how in elementary school you weren't allowed to use a calculator to do addition because that would keep you from learning the fundamentals? After you became an old pro at adding, subtracting, multiplying, and dividing you were permitted to use a calculator for all subsequent courses (and you could forget all about the fundamentals... especially long division). Well, the Adaptive Color Palette generation presented here is just like that old math stuff. You can forget it all! That's right, rip the pages right out of the book (ouch, not really). The reason is that you have an Adaptive Color Palette "Calculator" in the TIFF256 Graphics Library Extensions shareware provided in the disc with this book and documented in Appendix B. It works automatically as you read True Color TIFF images (if you enable it), and it runs a lot faster than the stuff shown in these pages because it's all optimized code. You're probably thinking "Why didn't he say so about a zillion pages ago?" But don't you really feel good now understanding how all this stuff works, hmm?

Digital Composition

by Spyro Gumas

A Case Study in UFO Photography

The time has come to prove the existence of extraterrestrial life to all of humanity once and for all. The argument for this proof is a single photographic image (which you will, ...um, create) with the eager news media willingly serving as the agent of dissemination. In these pages you will create a "photograph" of a UFO. It is your duty to submit this final image to various news agencies (grocery tabloids get the best results) along with some cockamamie story about how it was spontaneously ejected from the color copier at work along with voices claiming that the invasion is imminent. With any luck, this photograph will have the longevity and impact of Nessie, the Loch Ness Monster, and you will be able to claim full responsibility.

Digital Composition is the name of the game, and this chapter shows you how to compose images using the techniques of masking, adding, subtracting, multiplying, and logically mixing images. The following sections break down the creation of the final UFO image into individual steps. Each section details a step called from the main program, which is presented in Listing 6.11 at the end of this chapter. The intermediate images are shown at each of these steps to help demonstrate the techniques.

So, go get some ice cream, a beer, a cup of tea, or whatever it takes to loosen you up. This chapter takes a freestyle "anything goes" approach that will no doubt leave you wondering if they're coming for you next. Ready? It's story time.

> **NOTE**
>
> All of the software presented in this chapter makes use of the VSA256 Graphics Library shareware provided in the software distribution with this book. The full text of the user's manual for this library is reprinted in Appendix A so that you can make quick reference to the functions as they come up. The VSA256 Graphics Library gives you the power to drive a VESA-compliant video adapter in video resolutions up to 1280×1024 with 256 colors.
>
> Before you run this software, you must load a VESA BIOS Extensions driver for your video adapter. Use the one that came with your video card. If you can't find it, there is a pile of VESA drivers for various video adapter manufacturers archived in the self-extracting DRIVERS2.EXE file included as part of the VSA256 distribution. Note that for some of the newer video adapters the VESA BIOS is built-in, so you don't need to do anything.

Long Ago and Far Away, There Was Blue

Long ago and far away, there was blue. It wasn't just any old blue, but the azure of the skies found in the higher latitudes of Montana (like I've been there). Figure 6.1 reveals the flavor of the blue that was.

FIGURE 6.1.

Azure sky of Montana.
(Use your imagination.)

The recipe for this blue made it down through the ages and into the pages of this book as follows: Make a linear gradient of blue-green intensity going from blue = 128, green = 64 at the top of the frame to blue = 255, green = 255 at the bottom of the frame. Listing 6.1 shows the code that generates this frame. This nostalgic blue gradient is saved as a 24-bit RGB TARGA file named SKY.TGA and is used later as the perfect sky in your UFO photograph.

Listing 6.1. Azure sky.

```
/*..................... AZURE_SKY ........................*/
/*  This routine generates a blue, blue-green gradient much  */
/*  like the crisp blue skies of Montana. (Never been there, */
/*  seen pictures). (The data is displayed as its generated). */
/*..........................................................*/
void azure_sky(unsigned char *rgb_1,int width,int j)
{
  unsigned char array[1024];
  int i;
  for(i=0;i<width;i++)
    {
      rgb_1[3*i+2] = 0;
      rgb_1[3*i+1] = 64+j/2.53;
```

continues

Listing 6.1. continued

```
     rgb_1[3*i+0] = 128+j/3.75;
   }
 get_dithered_row(width,j,rgb_1,array);
 vsa_raster_line(0,width-1,j,array);
 return;
}                           /*.... END azure_sky        .....*/
```

The code in Listing 6.1 and all the code in subsequent listings in this chapter display the results on the video screen in 256 colors. Because the data is 24-bit RGB data, the get_dithered_row function of Listing 6.2 is used to convert the 24-bit pixels to dithered 8-bit pixels. The get_dithered_row function is based on the dithering software presented in Chapter 5, "Advanced Image Processing." The code for the crack_rgb function, which is called by get_dithered_row, is not listed here because it can be found in Chapter 5.

Listing 6.2. Get dithered row.

```
/*.................. GET_DITHERED_ROW ......... 7-15-94 .....*/
/* This routine computes the dithered pixel color for all of  */
/* pixels in a row in the array 'rgb' and stores the results  */
/* in the array 'pixels'. The row is 'width' wide and starts at*/
/* screen row address 'j'.  The 'rgb' array is a 24 bit color  */
/* array with every 3 bytes defining a new pixel.  The         */
/* resulting 'pixels' array defines each pixel as an 8 bit RGB  */
/* pixel (one byte per pixel).                                  */
/*.............................................................*/
void get_dithered_row(int width,int j,unsigned char *rgb,
                      unsigned char *pixels)
{
  int i,n,m,q,r,red_lvl,grn_lvl,blu_lvl,size,size_sqr;
  int red_boost,grn_boost,blu_boost;
  float x,y,frl,fgl,fbl;
  size = 8;
  size_sqr = 64;
  q = 3;
/*.... If FAST_RGB = 1, don't dither, do fast 8 bit RGB.     ....*/
  if(FAST_RGB)
    {
      for(i=0;i<width;i++)
        {
          pixels[i] = (rgb[3*i+2] & 0xe0) +
                      ((rgb[3*i+1] & 0xe0) >> 3) +
                      (rgb[3*i+0] >> 6);
        }
      return;
    }
  y = (float)j/size;
  n = (int)(size*(y - (int)y) + 0.5);
  for(i=0;i<width;i++)
    {
/*.............................................................*/
```

```
/* For the pixels screen address i,j, compute pixel address r  */
/* within the dither box.  Also select dither box q based on   */
/* size (size = 1, 2, 4, or 8) (q = 0, 1, 2, or 3).            */
/*...........................................................*/
      x = (float)i/size;
      m = (int)(size*(x - (int)x) + 0.5);
      r = m+n*size;
/*...........................................................*/
/* Get the Dark Pixel color, the Light Pixel components, and   */
/* the pixel color errors.                                     */
/*...........................................................*/
      pixels[i] = crack_rgb(rgb+3*i,&red_boost,&grn_boost,
                            &blu_boost,&frl,&fgl,&fbl);
/*...........................................................*/
/*Scale the pixel color error values based on dither box size  */
/*...........................................................*/
      red_lvl = size_sqr*frl;
      grn_lvl = size_sqr*fgl;
      blu_lvl = size_sqr*fbl;
/*...........................................................*/
/*Test the pixels red, green, and blue error values against the*/
/*thresholds in the dither box.  Decide which color to use.    */
/*...........................................................*/
      if(dither[q][r] <= red_lvl)                /*Boost Red*/
        pixels[i] = (pixels[i] & 0x1f)+(red_boost<<5);
      if(dither[q][r] <= grn_lvl)                /*Boost Grn*/
        pixels[i] = (pixels[i] & 0xe3)+(grn_boost<<2);
      if(dither[q][r] <= blu_lvl)                /*Boost Blu*/
        pixels[i] = (pixels[i] & 0xfc)+blu_boost;
    }
  return;
}                         /*.... END get_dithered_row    ....*/
```

Stripping Away Atmospheres

Any good UFO photograph requires an ambiguous location. With that in mind, I searched the archives of my travel photos and found the spectacular shot of unknown origin shown in Figure 6.2 and stored in MOUNTAIN.TGA. This photo starts off the evolution of the target image through all the subsequent work in this chapter.

Because I already grew my own azure sky, I chose to nuke the original atmosphere. There are many ways to accomplish this task, starting with man-made devices and culminating with nature's own little cosmological surprises (comets). I have access to neither, so I fake it with the code in Listing 6.3. Basically, all it does is search out all the pixels that are close to the selected sky color and sets their values to zero. Figure 6.3 shows the atmosphere-wiped image, which is saved as WIPED.TGA.

FIGURE 6.2.

These unsuspecting mountains will be famous.

FIGURE 6.3.

Aftermath of comet Shoemaker-Levy 9 (sub-chunk G).

Listing 6.3. Wipe sky.

```
/*...................... WIPE_SKY ........................*/
/*  This routine is customized to work specifically with the   */
/*  MOUNTAIN.TGA picture.  It goes in and zeros out the sky to  */
/*  prepare MOUNTAIN.TGA for the next step.                     */
/*     This routine makes use of a hue test and a color test    */
/*  to determine which pixels make up the sky.  The hue test    */
/*  finds similar hues independent of brightness while the      */
/*  color test finds similar colors in the absolute sense.      */
```

```
/*.........................................................*/
void wipe_sky(unsigned char *rgb_1,int width,int j)
{
  unsigned char array[1024];
  int i;
  float h_error,c_error;
  for(i=0;i<width;i++)
    {
      h_error = hue_error(rgb_1[3*i+2],rgb_1[3*i+1],
                          rgb_1[3*i+0],0.62,0.54,0.58);
      c_error = color_error(rgb_1[3*i+2],rgb_1[3*i+1],
                            rgb_1[3*i+0],140,122,131);
      if((h_error < 0.03) && (c_error < 17))
        {
          rgb_1[3*i+2] = 0;
          rgb_1[3*i+1] = 0;
          rgb_1[3*i+0] = 0;
        }
    }
  get_dithered_row(width,j,rgb_1,array);
  vsa_raster_line(0,width-1,j,array);
  return;
}                       /*.... END wipe_sky        .....*/


/*.................... COLOR_ERROR ............ 7-15-94 .......*/
/* This routine takes two RGB colors defined by 'r0', 'g0',   */
/* 'b0' and 'r1', 'g1', 'b1' and returns the distance between */
/* the two colors in RGB color space.                         */
/*............................................................*/
float color_error(float r0,float g0,float b0,
                  float r1,float g1,float b1)
{
  float dr,dg,db;
  dr = (r0-r1);
  dg = (g0-g1);
  db = (b0-b1);
  return sqrt(dr*dr+dg*dg+db*db);
}                          /*.....  End color_error    .....*/


/*.................... HUE_ERROR ............. 7-15-94 .......*/
/* This routine compares the RGB color defined by 'r,g,b' to  */
/* the color HUE defined by 'ur,ug,ub' and returns the distance*/
/* between the RGB color and the HUE.  The distance ranges     */
/* from 0 to square root of 3 (1.73...)                        */
/* NOTE: 'ur,ug,ub' is a "Unit Vector" and                     */
/*       sqrt(ur*ur + ug*ug + ub*ub) must equal 1.0.           */
/*............................................................*/
float hue_error(float r,float g,float b,
                float ur,float ug,float ub)
{
  float dr,dg,db,mag;
  mag = color_mag(r,g,b);
  if(mag == 0) mag = 1.0;
  dr = (r/mag-ur);
  dg = (g/mag-ug);
  db = (b/mag-ub);
```

continues

Listing 6.3. continued

```
  return sqrt(dr*dr+dg*dg+db*db);
}                        /*.....  End hue_error       .....*/


/*.................. COLOR_MAG ............. 7-15-94 .......*/
/* This routine takes an RGB color defined by 'r', 'g', and  */
/* 'b' and returns the absolute magnitude (brightness) of the  */
/* color.                                                  */
/*.........................................................*/
float color_mag(float r,float g,float b)
{
  return sqrt(r*r+g*g+b*b);
}                        /*.....   End color_mag       .....*/
```

Inventing a City

Conventional wisdom has it that UFOs, like tornadoes and hurricanes, prefer the rural surroundings of a trailer park over the urban sprawl of a big city. Even so, I though it would be nice for our friends to pass within radar range of a large metropolis. For this part of the image I called in the artistic and ray-tracing expertise of Fractallonomy's Dave Scruton. You might remember him from Figure 5.1 of Chapter 5. Using a ray tracing program, Dave whipped together the contemporary city skyline that is shown in Figure 6.4 and stored in the CITY.TGA file.

FIGURE 6.4.

Generic Los York, the shrinkable city (ray traced variety). Courtesy of Dave Scruton of Fractallonomy. (You can contact Dave Scruton via Internet at scruton@delphi.com.*)*

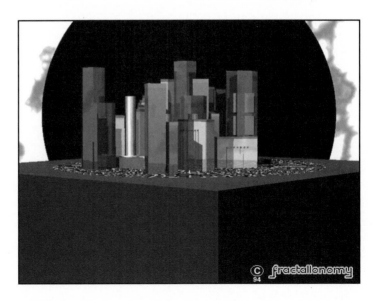

To fit the city, which I dubbed Los York, into the target image in the most realistic fashion, it is reduced in size and converted to grayscale. The code in Listing 6.4 shows how this is done. After `shrink_city` finishes processing all the rows of CITY.TGA, the image of Los York is stored in the external "image" array as an 8-bit pixel grayscale image.

Listing 6.4. Shrink city.

```
/*..................... SHRINK_CITY .....................*/
/*  This routine is customized to work specifically with the   */
/*  CITY.TGA picture.  It extracts the city within a window     */
/*  and shrinks it by a factor of 3 in x and y.  Then the       */
/*  resulting image is placed in the external 'image' array     */
/*  and also displayed on the screen.                           */
/*..............................................................*/
void shrink_city(unsigned char *rgb_1,int width,int j)
{
  int i,n,q,red,grn,blu;
  unsigned char array[1024];
/*..............................................................*/
/*  Put up a gray box where reduced city will be drawn.         */
/*  Only draw it once, just before city shrinking starts.       */
/*..............................................................*/
  if(j == 479)
    {
      vsa_set_color(0x49);
      vsa_move_to(242,331);
      vsa_rect_fill(356,406);
    }
/*..............................................................*/
/*  Bail out unless you're within the extract region of the     */
/*  image and you're on every 3rd row.                          */
/*..............................................................*/
  if((j < 60) || (j > 290))
    return;
  if((((float)j/3.0)-j/3) != 0)
    return;
/*..............................................................*/
/*  Extract city within rectangle 115,60 to 460,290 and reduce  */
/*  size by a factor of 3 by simple undersampling of image and  */
/*  convert extracted pixels to grayscale. Store in image array */
/*  Then display reduced city in little window.                 */
/*..............................................................*/
  n = ((j-60)/3)*115;
  q=j/3+310;
  for(i=115;i<460;i+=3)
    {
      red = rgb_1[3*i+2];
      grn = rgb_1[3*i+1];
      blu = rgb_1[3*i+0];
      image[n] = (red + grn + blu)/3;
      rgb_1[i+2] = image[n];
      rgb_1[i+1] = image[n];
      rgb_1[i+0] = image[n];
      n++;
    }
```

continues

Listing 6.4. continued

```
get_dithered_row(width,q,rgb_1+115,array);
vsa_raster_line(242,356,q,array);
return;
}                         /*.... END shrink_city        .....*/
```

Horizon Editing

The reduced Los York image is composited into the horizon of the target image with the `merge_city` routine shown in Listing 6.5. Within the rectangular region defined by the vertices 523,214 and 637,289, the Los York pixels in the "image" array are used to replace the corresponding target image pixels if the target image pixels are zero. The results are shown in Figure 6.5 and saved in the WITHCITY.TGA file.

The composite operation performed here is equivalent to the logical AND operation between a mask and the Los York image followed by an OR operation of the result with the target image. The mask could come about by setting to one all the pixels in a 640×480 frame whose corresponding pixels in the target image are zero.

FIGURE 6.5.

Los York finds a home.

Listing 6.5. Merge city.

```
/*...................... MERGE_CITY ......................*/
/*  This routine takes the reduced city in the 'image' array  */
/*  and inserts it into the WIPED.TGA image replacing only    */
/*  those pixels which are equal to zero.                     */
/*..........................................................*/
void merge_city(unsigned char *rgb_1,int width,int j)
{
  int i,n;
  unsigned char array[1024];
/*..........................................................*/
/*  Composite the city in the 'image' array with the WIPED    */
/*  mountain scene within rectangle (523,214) to (637,289).   */
/*  Also display results.                                     */
/*..........................................................*/
  for(i=0;i<width-1;i++)
    {
      if((j >= 214) && (j <= 289))
        if((i>=523) && (i < 637))
          if((rgb_1[3*i+2] | rgb_1[3*i+1] | rgb_1[3*i+0]) == 0)
            {
              n=i-523 + (j-214)*115;
              rgb_1[3*i+2] = image[n];
              rgb_1[3*i+1] = image[n];
              rgb_1[3*i+0] = image[n];
            }
    }
  get_dithered_row(width,j,rgb_1,array);
  vsa_raster_line(0,width-1,j,array);
  return;
}                       /*.... END merge_city        .....*/
```

Replenishing the Atmosphere

Fortunately, replenishing the atmosphere is much easier than it sounds. It actually works in exactly the same manner as the previous step. The SKY.TGA image data is used to replace the corresponding pixels in the target image if the target image pixels are zero. The code for this function is shown in Listing 6.6, and the resulting image, which is saved as WITHSKY.TGA, is shown in Figure 6.6.

FIGURE 6.6.

Synthetic sky. Nothing but the best for Los Yorkers.

Listing 6.6. Merge azure.

```c
/*...................... MERGE_AZURE ....................*/
/*  This routine takes the azure sky in SKY.TGA and uses its  */
/*  data to replace all zero value pixels in the previous     */
/*  image WITHCITY.TGA.                                       */
/*..........................................................*/
void merge_azure(unsigned char *rgb_1,unsigned char *rgb_2,
                 int width,int j)
{
  unsigned char array[1024];
  int i;
  for(i=0;i<width;i++)
    {
      if((rgb_1[3*i+2] ¦ rgb_1[3*i+1] ¦ rgb_1[3*i+0]) == 0)
        {
          rgb_1[3*i+2] = rgb_2[3*i+2];
          rgb_1[3*i+1] = rgb_2[3*i+1];
          rgb_1[3*i+0] = rgb_2[3*i+0];
        }
    }
  get_dithered_row(width,j,rgb_1,array);
  vsa_raster_line(0,width-1,j,array);
  return;
}                        /*.... END merge_azure      .....*/
```

Will Build Spacecraft for Food

"Starving engineer…will build spacecraft for food." Okay, it's not really that bad, but I need a flying saucer quickly and I am on a budget. Enter Dave Scruton once again. This time he uses his creative skills to design a warp-10 class flying saucer made of pure Blutonium (very expensive stuff). The ray-traced saucer image stored in SAUCER.TGA is shown in Figure 6.7.

FIGURE 6.7.

Straight from Zimp Bliny, eek eek zip yap. (Courtesy of Dave Scruton of Fractallonomy.)

The shrink_saucer routine shown in Listing 6.7 shrinks the saucer down by a factor of 2.5 in x and y. Then it loads the pixels into the external "image" array, just like you did on the shrink_city routine. After shrink_saucer is finished processing all the rows of SAUCER.TGA, the image of the reduced saucer is in the external "image" array as an 8-bit pixel grayscale image.

Listing 6.7. Shrink saucer.

```
/*..................... SHRINK_SAUCER ....................*/
/*  This routine is customized to work specifically with the   */
/*  SAUCER.TGA picture.  It extracts the saucer within a window*/
/*  and shrinks it by a factor of 2.5 in x and y.  Then the    */
/*  resulting image is placed in the external 'image' array    */
/*  and also displayed on the screen.                          */
/*............................................................*/
void shrink_saucer(unsigned char *rgb_1,int width,int j)
{
  int i,n,p,q,red,grn,blu;
  float x;
  unsigned char array[1024];
/*............................................................*/
/*  Put up a gray box where reduced saucer will be drawn.     */
/*  Only draw it once, just before saucer shrinking starts.    */
/*............................................................*/
```

continues

Listing 6.7. continued

```
if(j == 479)
  {
    vsa_set_color(0x49);
    vsa_move_to(235,310);
    vsa_rect_fill(414,379);
  }
/*..........................................................*/
/*  Bail out unless you're within the extract region of the  */
/*  image and you're on every 2.5th row.                     */
/*..........................................................*/
if((j < 125) || (j > 298))
  return;
if((int)(j/2.5) == (int)((j-1)/2.5))
  return;
/*..........................................................*/
/*  Extract saucer within rectangle 100,125 to 550,300 and   */
/*  reduce size by a factor of 2.5 by simple undersampling of */
/*  image and convert extracted pixels to grayscale. Store in */
/*  'image' array and also dither and display on screen.      */
/*..........................................................*/
n=180*(int)((j-125)/2.5);
p=0;
q=j/2.5+260;
for(x=100;x<550;x+=2.5)
  {
    i = x+0.5;
    red = rgb_1[3*i+2];
    grn = rgb_1[3*i+1];
    blu = rgb_1[3*i+0];
    image[n] = (red + grn + blu)/3;
    rgb_1[p+2] = image[n];
    rgb_1[p+1] = image[n];
    rgb_1[p+0] = image[n];
    n++;
    p+=3;
  }
get_dithered_row(width,q,rgb_1,array);
vsa_raster_line(235,414,q,array);
return;
}                       /*.... END shrink_saucer        .....*/
```

Achieving Suborbital Flight

Okay, it's time to introduce the alien saucer into your synthetic terrestrial atmosphere for a test drive. The merge_saucer routine in Listing 6.8 uses a customized "greater than" test to composite the saucer in the "image" array with the target image. The resulting image is stored in the WITHSAUC.TGA file and shown in Figure 6.8. Within the rectangular region defined by the vertices at 203,25 and 382,94, the merge_saucer routine compares the saucer's grayscale intensity against the target image pixel's blue component. It replaces the target pixel if the saucer pixel is greater than at least 1/3 of the target image pixel's blue component.

FIGURE 6.8.

It's my chapter. I can do what I want!

You're probably wondering how I came up with the 1/3 rule for compositing the saucer. The truth is that I tried a bunch of different values, and 1/3 worked pretty well. If you make the number too high, you start to get patches of sky showing through the saucer. This seriously weakens the fabric of the craft and poses a risk of in-flight structural failure. If you go too low, you get a dark outline around the perimeter of the saucer, which increases air resistance and severely limits fuel efficiency.

As an alternative to the "greater than" test, you could add the saucer pixel intensities to the target pixel intensities (remembering to limit the sum to a maximum of 255, of course). This has the undesired side effect of tainting the saucer's color with that of the sky. Another alternative is to average the saucer pixel intensities with the target pixel intensities. If you are after a ghosting effect, this works really well. Maybe this is how the saucer enters and exits the physical dimension from a parallel universe (I know… too much *Star Trek*).

Listing 6.8. Merge saucer.

```
/*...................... MERGE_SAUCER ...................*/
/*  This routine takes the reduced saucer in the 'image' array */
/*  and inserts it into the WITHSKY.TGA image.  The replacement*/
/*  decision is based on a test of the pixel's blue component  */
```

continues

Listing 6.8. continued

```
/*  in the WITHSKY.TGA picture.                                    */
/*....................................................*/
void merge_saucer(unsigned char *rgb_1,int width,int j)
{
  int i,n;
  unsigned char array[1024];
/*....................................................*/
/*  Composite the saucer in the image array with the modified  */
/*  mountain scene within the rectangle defined by (203,25)    */
/*  and (382,94).  Use a modified "replace if brighter" test.  */
/*  Specifically, replace if saucer pixel is greater than 1/3  */
/*  of existing pixels blue component.  (nothing magical here, */
/*  this scheme was found by experimenting).                   */
/*....................................................*/
  n = (j-25)*180;
  for(i=0;i<width-1;i++)
    {
      if((j >= 25) && (j <=  94))
        if((i >= 203) && (i <= 382))
          {
            if(image[n] >= (rgb_1[3*i+0]/3))
              {
                rgb_1[3*i+2] = image[n];
                rgb_1[3*i+1] = image[n];
                rgb_1[3*i+0] = image[n];
              }
            n++;
          }
    }
  get_dithered_row(width,j,rgb_1,array);
  vsa_raster_line(0,width-1,j,array);
  return;
}                      /*.... END merge_saucer      .....*/
```

A Minor Detail

Of course, having entered our physical universe, any self-respecting flying saucer needs to cast a shadow. So, as trivial as this may sound, you need to add a shadow disk to give that extra touch of realism. To do this, first you need an ellipse generator. The ellipse routine in Listing 6.9 loads a template of a solid ellipse into the "image" array using pixel values of 255 within the ellipse and 0 outside the ellipse. Once the "image" array is loaded with the ellipse template, the soft_edge routine is called to blur the edges of the template. Actually, the soft_edge routine uses a 3×3 pixel-averaging scheme to blur all the pixels in the template, but the effects of this operation are visible only at the edges. The blurred edges of the template eliminate the "jaggies" on the shadow disk.

After the ellipse template is generated, the `add_shadow` routine, also shown in Listing 6.9, uses the template to modify the intensity of the target pixels in the region between the vertices of 75,310 and 254,344. If the ellipse template pixel is set to 255, the corresponding target image pixel is multiplied by 0.60, resulting in a target image pixel intensity reduction of 40 percent. This is the case for pixels within the ellipse. If the ellipse template pixel is zero, the target image pixel intensity is unchanged. This is the case for pixels outside the ellipse. For pixels on the edge of the ellipse, the template pixels range somewhere between 0 and 255 and result in a "jaggie-free" (soft edge) ellipse. When it's all over, the target image is left with an ellipse-shaped region of pixels that are 40 percent dimmer than normal. By sizing and placing the ellipse appropriately, you get it to look like the flying saucer's shadow, as shown in Figure 6.9 and saved in the file WITHSHAD.TGA.

FIGURE 6.9.

The clincher. Subtle effect adds realism (?).

Listing 6.9. Add shadow.

```
/*..................... ADD_SHADOW .......................*/
/*  This routine generates an ellipse and then composites it   */
/*  with the WITHSAUC.TGA picture using a subtractive           */
/*  technique.  The ellipse serves as a mask which causes a     */
/*  30% reduction of pixel intensity for masked pixels.         */
/*...........................................................*/
void add_shadow(unsigned char *rgb_1,int width,int j)
{
  int i,n;
  unsigned char array[1024];
  float scale;
/*...........................................................*/
/*  Generate an ellipse mask in the 'image' array once before  */
/*  getting to overlay region.                                 */
```

continues

Listing 6.9. continued

```
/*..............................................................*/
  if(j==479)
    ellipse(180,35);
/*..............................................................*/
/*  Composite the shadow disk region (75,310) (254,344).    */
/*..............................................................*/
  n = (j-310)*180;
  for(i=0;i<width-1;i++)
    {
      if((j >= 310) && (j <= 344))
        if((i >= 75) && (i <= 254))
          {
            scale = (255.0 - 0.4*image[n])/255.0;
            rgb_1[3*i+2] = rgb_1[3*i+2]*scale;
            rgb_1[3*i+1] = rgb_1[3*i+1]*scale;
            rgb_1[3*i+0] = rgb_1[3*i+0]*scale;
            n++;
          }
    }
  get_dithered_row(width,j,rgb_1,array);
  vsa_raster_line(0,width-1,j,array);
  return;
}                        /*.... END add_shadow      .....*/


/*...................... ELLIPSE .............. 7-22-94 ....*/
/* This routine generates a filled ellipse mask into the    */
/* global 'image' array.  The ellipse has width of 'dx' and */
/* height of 'dy'.  The equation for this ellipse is:       */
/*                                                          */
/*                   x^2     +     y^2                       */
/*                                                          */
/*                  _ _ _       _ _ _   = 1                  */
/*                  (dx/2)^2    (dy/2)^2                     */
/*                                                          */
/* The 'image' array values are 0 outside of the ellipse and */
/* 255 inside the ellipse. The ellipse has a soft edge with  */
/* 'image' values between 0 and 255.  The soft edge is       */
/* achieved by a 3x3 pixel averaging operation via the       */
/* 'soft_edge' function.                                     */
/*                                                          */
/* NOTE: The 'image' array must be large enough to hold all of */
/*       this data (image will be dx wide and dy high).     */
/*..............................................................*/
void ellipse(int dx,int dy)
{
  int i,j,m,n;
  float rx,ry;
/*..............................................................*/
/*   Clear out the image array before writing in ellipse mask. */
/*..............................................................*/
  for(n=0;n<dy;n++)
    for(m=0;m<dx;m++)
      image[m+n*dx] = 0;
/*..............................................................*/
```

```
/*   Now compute ellipse and draw its mask into image array.   */
/*.................................................................*/
  rx = (dx-1)/2.0;
  ry = (dy-1)/2.0;
  for(j=-ry ; j<=+ry ; j++)
    {
      i = sqrt(rx*rx*(1 - (j*j)/(ry*ry)));
      for(m=-i;m<=i;m++)
        {
          n = m+rx+(j+(int)ry)*dx;
          image[n] = 255;
        }
    }
  soft_edge(image,dx,dy);
  return;
}                          /*..... End ellipse      .....*/


void soft_edge(unsigned char *image,int width,int height)
{
  int i,j,m,n,q,x,y;
/*.................................................................*/
/*   First clear out the temporary array.                        */
/*.................................................................*/
  for(i=0;i<width*height;i++)
    big_image[i] = 0;
/*.................................................................*/
/*   Now, for each pixel in 'image' array, do a 3x3 pixel        */
/*   average.                                                     */
/*.................................................................*/
  for(j=0;j<height;j++)
    for(i=0;i<width;i++)
      {
        q = i+j*width;
        for(n=0;n<3;n++)
          for(m=0;m<3;m++)
            {
              x = i+m-1;
              y = j+n-1;
              if((y >= 0) && (y < height))
                if((x >= 0) && (x < width))
                  big_image[q] += image[x+y*width];
            }
        big_image[q] = big_image[q]/9;
      }
/*.................................................................*/
/*    Finally, transfer results back to the 'image' array.       */
/*.................................................................*/
  for(i=0;i<width*height;i++)
    image[i] = big_image[i];
  return;
```

Suitable for the Evening News

I can picture the headlines now: "Farmer and Truck Last Seen Beaming Up! Flying Saucer to Blame." Placing the beam on the target image is done by adding the pixel values of the yellow beam to the underlying target image pixels. The intensity cross section of the beam is sinusoidal so that it actually looks like a solid cylinder of light. The end of the beam touching the road has a half ellipse (with soft edge) capped on to it to better model what actually happens when a beam illuminates a flat surface. The pixel sums must be tested and clamped at a maximum value of 255 to avoid wrap-around, and this is all done by the code in Listing 6.10. The final image, UFO.TGA, is shown in Figure 6.10.

FIGURE 6.10.

Calling all tabloids...this is your wake-up call!

Listing 6.10. Add beam.

```
/*...................... ADD_BEAM ........................*/
/*  This routine generates a Transporter Beam (the standard  */
/*  issue) and composites it with the WITHSHAD.TGA picture    */
/*  using an additive technique.  The beam has a sinusoidal   */
/*  intensity cross section and is capped with an ellipse.    */
/*..........................................................*/
void add_beam(unsigned char *rgb_1,int width,int j)
{
  int i,n,red,grn,boost;
  unsigned char array[1024];
  float taps[40];
/*..........................................................*/
/*  Generate an ellipse mask in the 'image' array once before */
/*  getting to overlay region.  Also precompute the           */
/*  sinusoidal beam profile.                                  */
/*..........................................................*/
```

```
   if(j==479)
     {
       ellipse(40,22);
       for(i=0;i<40;i++)
         taps[i] = sin(0.0785*(float)i);
     }
/*....................................................*/
/*  Use an additive mixing technique to composite the beam   */
/*  (me up Scotty) into the image.  Beam fills rectangle with */
/*  coordinates (273,88) to (312,320).                        */
/*....................................................*/
   n = (j-294)*40;
   for(i=0;i<width-1;i++)
     {
         if((j >= 88) && (j <= 304))
           if((i >= 273) && (i <= 312))
             {
               boost = 75.0*taps[i-273];
               red = rgb_1[3*i+2] + boost;
               grn = rgb_1[3*i+1] + boost;
               rgb_1[3*i+2] = min(red,255);
               rgb_1[3*i+1] = min(grn,255);
             }

/*....           Cap the beam with half of an ellipse.      ...*/
     if((j >= 305) && (j <= 315))
        if((i >= 273) && (i <= 312))
           {
             boost = (75.0*taps[i-273]*image[n])/255.0;
             red = rgb_1[3*i+2] + boost;
             grn = rgb_1[3*i+1] + boost;
             rgb_1[3*i+2] = min(red,255);
             rgb_1[3*i+1] = min(grn,255);
             n++;
           }
     }
   get_dithered_row(width,j,rgb_1,array);
   vsa_raster_line(0,width-1,j,array);
   return;
}                        /*.... END add_beam      .....*/
```

The Main Program

The main program presented in Listing 6.11 starts off with three 24-bit RGB TARGA image files on the hard disk: MOUNTAIN.TGA, CITY.TGA, and SAUCER.TGA. When you run the program, it sequences through the nine steps detailed in the previous sections and displays all the intermediate results. The program creates these image files: SKY.TGA, WIPED.TGA, UFO.TGA, WITHCITY.TGA, WITHSKY.TGA, WITHSAUC.TGA, and WITHSHAD.TGA. These new files require an additional 7MB of disk space, so be prepared.

As I said, the main program sequences through nine steps. For each step, up to two input files are specified by the `file_i1[step]` and `file_i2[step]` filename arrays. For each step, the output filename is specified in the array `file_o[step]`. For a given step, the program reads one row of pixels from each of the input files and calls the `process_step` routine. The `process_step` routine sends the input pixel rows to the appropriate processing function and collects the resulting row of pixel data. Finally, the main program writes out the resulting row of pixel data to the appropriate intermediate image file. This cycle repeats for all rows of pixels and for each of the nine processing steps, culminating in the generation of the UFO.TGA image.

By demonstrating the elements of Digital Composition in custom C-coded modules, this chapter attempts to give you an in-depth understanding of the mechanics of this art form as well as an appreciation for the possibilities brought forth with the latest advances in computer graphics technology. Clearly the approach used here to develop the UFO photograph is not an efficient path to the end product. There are numerous photographic editing packages on the market today that provide automated tools for photographic manipulations, including image compositing, image transformations, and color control, and they are much better suited to this type of job. However, having gone through the example in this chapter, you are now knowledgeable enough to stare down the best of these commercial packages. Free from the intimidation that accompanies new concepts, you can now go out and use the commercial packages with the confidence and fortitude required for tackling the really challenging jobs.

Listing 6.11. Main program.

```
#include<stdio.h>
#include<stdlib.h>
#include<conio.h>
#include<fcntl.h>
#include<io.h>
#include<math.h>
#include<vsa.h>
#include<vsa_font.h>
#include <sys\types.h>
#include<sys\stat.h>

#ifndef _MSC_VER
/*.....           This is for Borland C Only !        .....*/
extern unsigned _stklen = 10000;
#endif

#define FAST_RGB 0  /* Set to 1 for fast, lower quality images */

/*..........................................................*/
/*              Function Prototypes go here.                */
/*..........................................................*/
void       introduction(void);
void       azure_sky(unsigned char *,int,int);
```

```
void       wipe_sky(unsigned char *,int,int);
void       shrink_city(unsigned char *,int,int);
void       merge_city(unsigned char *,int,int);
void       merge_azure(unsigned char *,unsigned char *,int,int);
void       shrink_saucer(unsigned char *,int,int);
void       merge_saucer(unsigned char *,int,int);
void       add_shadow(unsigned char *,int,int);
void       add_beam(unsigned char *,int,int);
void       get_dithered_row(int,int,unsigned char *,
                            unsigned char *);
int        crack_rgb(unsigned char *,int *,int *,int *,float *,
                     float *,float *);
long       read_tga_header(int,int *,int *,int *,int *);
int        write_tga_header(int,int,int,int);
void       true_color_lut(void);
void       process_step(unsigned char *,unsigned char *,
                        int,int,int);
float      color_mag(float,float,float);
float      color_error(float,float,float,float,float,float);
float      hue_error(float,float,float,float,float,float);
void       bummer(char *);
void       text_update(char *,int);
void       frame(void);
void       ellipse(int,int);
void       soft_edge(unsigned char *,int,int);


/*..........................................................*/
/*                External Parameters declared here.        */
/*..........................................................*/
unsigned char dither[4][64]={
{
 1 },
{
 1, 3,
 4, 2 },
{
 1,  9, 3, 11,
13,  5, 15, 7,
 4, 12, 2, 10,
16,  8, 14, 6 },
{
 1, 33,  9, 41,  3, 35, 11, 43,
49, 17, 57, 25, 51, 19, 59, 27,
13, 45,  5, 37, 15, 47,  7, 39,
61, 29, 53, 21, 63, 31, 55, 23,
 4, 36, 12, 44,  2, 34, 10, 42,
52, 20, 60, 28, 50, 18, 58, 26,
16, 48,  8, 40, 14, 46,  6, 38,
64, 32, 56, 24, 62, 30, 54, 22 },
};

char file_i1[9][30]={
{""},
{"mountain.tga"},
{"city.tga"},
{"wiped.tga"},
{"withcity.tga"},
```

continues

Listing 6.11. continued

```
{"saucer.tga"},
{"withsky.tga"},
{"withsauc.tga"},
{"withshad.tga"},
};

char file_i2[9][30]={
{""},
{""},
{""},
{""},
{"sky.tga"},
{""},
{""},
{""},
{""},
};

char file_o[9][30]={
{"sky.tga"},
{"wiped.tga"},
{""},
{"withcity.tga"},
{"withsky.tga"},
{""},
{"withsauc.tga"},
{"withshad.tga"},
{"ufo.tga"},
};

unsigned char far image[16384];
unsigned far big_image[16384];

void main()
{
  int j,width,height,type,orient;
  int file_i1_handle,file_i2_handle,file_o_handle;
  int jstrt,jend,jstep,step;
  unsigned char rgb_1[3072],rgb_2[3072];
  char text[100];
  width = 640;
  height = 480;
  orient = 0;
  introduction();
/*..........................................................*/
/*          Set highest video resolution available.        */
/*..........................................................*/
      if(vsa_init(0x101) != 0)          /*  640 x 480 x 256 */
        if(vsa_init(0x100) != 0)        /*  640 x 400 x 256 */
          {
            printf("Can't set VESA video mode\n");
            printf("Is VESA BIOS Extension TSR loaded?\n");
            return;
          }
  true_color_lut();
  for(step=0;step<9;step++)
```

```
     {
/*.............................................................*/
/*  Open the TARGA file(s) and get header info.  When two files*/
/*  being opened simultaneously, they must be same type, size, */
/*  and orientation!                                           */
/*.............................................................*/
     if(file_i1[step][0])
        {
          if((file_i1_handle = open(file_i1[step],
              O_BINARY ¦ O_RDONLY)) == -1)
            bummer(file_i1[step]);
          else
            if(read_tga_header(file_i1_handle,&width,
                         &height,&type,&orient) == -1)
              bummer(file_i1[step]);
        }
     if(file_i2[step][0])
        {
          if((file_i2_handle = open(file_i2[step],
              O_BINARY ¦ O_RDONLY)) == -1)
            bummer(file_i2[step]);
          else
            if(read_tga_header(file_i2_handle,&width,
                         &height,&type,&orient) == -1)
              bummer(file_i2[step]);
        }
     if(file_o[step][0])
        {
          if((file_o_handle = open(file_o[step],
              O_BINARY ¦ O_WRONLY ¦ O_CREAT ¦ O_TRUNC,
              S_IWRITE ¦ S_IREAD)) == -1)
            bummer(file_o[step]);
          else
            if(write_tga_header(file_o_handle,width,
                         height,orient) == -1)
              bummer(file_o[step]);
        }
/*.............................................................*/
/*              Prepare to read out TARGA file(s).             */
/*.............................................................*/
     if(orient == 32)
        {
          jstrt = 0;
          jend = height;
          jstep = 1;
        }
     else
        {
          jstrt = height-1;
          jend = -1;
          jstep = -1;
        }
/*.............................................................*/
/*  Do a Quickie Display of the TARGA file in file_i1,         */
/*  (And remember to reset file pointer !!!)                   */
/*  Only do this where it makes sense (steps 1, 2, and 5).     */
/*.............................................................*/
```

continues

Listing 6.11. continued

```
    if((step == 1) || (step == 2) || (step == 5))
      {
        frame();
        if(file_i1[step][0])
          {
            text_update("Displaying the Input File.",252);
            for(j=jstrt;j!=jend;j+=jstep)
              {
                if(read(file_i1_handle,rgb_1,3*width) != 3*width)
                    bummer(file_i1[step]);
                get_dithered_row(width,j,rgb_1,rgb_2);
                vsa_raster_line(0,width-1,j,rgb_2);
              }
            lseek(file_i1_handle,18,SEEK_SET);
          }
      }
/*...........................................................*/
/*   Read out pixels from TARGA file(s) and process them.    */
/*...........................................................*/
    text_update("Processing, Please Wait.",252);
    frame();
    for(j=jstrt;j!=jend;j+=jstep)
      {
        if(file_i1[step][0])
          if(read(file_i1_handle,rgb_1,3*width) != 3*width)
            bummer(file_i1[step]);
        if(file_i2[step][0])
          if(read(file_i2_handle,rgb_2,3*width) != 3*width)
            bummer(file_i2[step]);
        process_step(rgb_1,rgb_2,width,j,step);
        if(file_o[step][0])
          if(write(file_o_handle,rgb_1,3*width) != 3*width)
            bummer(file_o[step]);
      }
/*...........................................................*/
/*          If a file was opened, close it now.              */
/*...........................................................*/
    if(file_i1[step][0]) close(file_i1_handle);
    if(file_i2[step][0]) close(file_i2_handle);
    if( file_o[step][0])  close(file_o_handle);
/*...........................................................*/
/*  Here's your chance to get out ...                        */
/*...........................................................*/
    sprintf(text,"Step %d Done.  Hit Any Key.",step);
    text_update(text,224);
    if(getch() == 27)
      goto BAIL;
    frame();
  }
/*...........................................................*/
/*   Program is over, return display to standard text mode.  */
/*...........................................................*/
BAIL:
  vsa_init(0x3);
  return;
```

```
          }


void process_step(unsigned char *rgb_1,unsigned char *rgb_2,
                  int width,int j,int step)
{
  switch(step)
    {
      case 0:
                azure_sky(rgb_1,width,j);
                break;
      case 1:
                wipe_sky(rgb_1,width,j);
                break;
      case 2:
                shrink_city(rgb_1,width,j);
                break;
      case 3:
                merge_city(rgb_1,width,j);
                break;
      case 4:
                merge_azure(rgb_1,rgb_2,width,j);
                break;
      case 5:
                shrink_saucer(rgb_1,width,j);
                break;
      case 6:
                merge_saucer(rgb_1,width,j);
                break;
      case 7:
                add_shadow(rgb_1,width,j);
                break;
      case 8:
                add_beam(rgb_1,width,j);
                break;
      default:  break;
    }
  return;
}                       /*.... END process_step     .....*/


/*..................... READ_TGA_HEADER  ....... 5-17-94 ....*/
/* This routine parses through a TGA header and returns the  */
/* file offset in bytes to the first byte of pixel data.     */
/* It also returns image width, height, and type (type 2 is the*/
/* uncompressed 24 bit image type).                          */
/*...........................................................*/
long read_tga_header(int handle, int *width,
                     int *height, int *type,
                     int *orientation)
{
  unsigned long offset;
  unsigned char buff[18];
  if(read(handle,buff,18) != 18)
    return -1;
  offset = 18+buff[0];
  *type = buff[2];
```

continues

Listing 6.11. continued

```
  *width  = *((unsigned *)buff + 6);
  *height = *((unsigned *)buff + 7);
  *orientation = buff[17];
  return offset;
}                          /*.... END read_tga_header    .....*/


/*..................... WRITE_TGA_HEADER ....... 7-5-94 ....*/
/* This routine writes a TGA header: 24 bit true color image  */
/*.........................................................*/
int write_tga_header(int handle, int width,int height,
                     int orientation)
{
  int error = 0;
  unsigned char buff[18];
  buff[0] = 0;
  buff[1] = 0;
  buff[2] = 2;
  buff[3] = 0;
  buff[4] = 0;
  buff[5] = 0;
  buff[6] = 0;
  buff[7] = 0;
  buff[8] = 0;
  *((unsigned *)buff + 4) = 0;
  *((unsigned *)buff + 5) = 0;
  *((unsigned *)buff + 6) = width;
  *((unsigned *)buff + 7) = height;
  buff[16] = 24;
  buff[17] = orientation;
  if(write(handle,buff,18) != 18)
    error = -1;
  return error;
}                          /*.... END write_tga_header   .....* /


/*..................... TRUE_COLOR_LUT.C .......... 5-15-94 ....*/
/* This routine generates a 'true color' LUT.  An 8 bit index  */
/* into the LUT represents 3 bits of RED, 3 bits of GREEN, and */
/* 2 bits of BLUE.  The 3 msbs of the 8 bit index are the RED  */
/* field, next 3 are GREEN, and the 2 lsbs are the BLUE field. */
/*                                                             */
/*.........................................................*/
void true_color_lut(void)
{
  int i;
  unsigned char color_array[768];
  for(i=0;i<256;i++)
    {
      color_array[3*i+0]= ((i & 0x00e0) >> 5) * 9;
      color_array[3*i+1]= ((i & 0x001c) >> 2) * 9;
      color_array[3*i+2]= (i & 0x0003) * 21;
    }
  vsa_write_color_block(0,256,color_array);
  return;
```

```
}                          /*.....   End true_color_lut   .....*/


/*........................ BUMMER ..........................*/
/* This routine prints a file error message.  You give      */
/* it the name of the file for the message in 'filename'.    */
/*...........................................................*/
void bummer(char *filename)
{
  char text[100];
  sprintf(text,
  "File Access Error!  Filename = '%s'",filename);
  vsa_write_string(0,YResolution-2*YCharSize,224,text);
  vsa_write_string(0,YResolution-1*YCharSize,224,
                   "Hit Any Key ...");
  getch();
  vsa_init(3);
  exit(1);
}                          /*.....   End bummer        .....*/


/*....................... TEXT_UPDATE ......................*/
/* This routine prints the text string in 'text' out to the */
/* screen in 'color'.  It does this at the bottom center of a */
/* 640 x 480 screen by first clearing out the last printed   */
/* message.                                                  */
/*...........................................................*/
void  text_update(char *text,int color)
{
  vsa_set_text_scale(1.2,1.2);
  vsa_set_color(0);
  vsa_move_to(200,475-YCharSize-1);
  vsa_rect_fill(460,475);
  vsa_write_string(205,475-YCharSize,color,text);
  return;
}                          /*.....   End text_update   .....*/


/*.......................... FRAME ........................*/
/* This routine draws a frame around the 640 x 480 screen.  */
/* The reason I do this is so that you can tell when an image */
/* is being redrawn (the frame slowly gets eaten up).        */
/*...........................................................*/
void  frame(void)
{
  vsa_set_color(255);
  vsa_move_to(0,0);
  vsa_rect(639,479);
  vsa_set_color(0);
  vsa_move_to(1,1);
  vsa_rect(638,478);
  vsa_set_color(255);
  vsa_move_to(2,2);
  vsa_rect(637,477);
  vsa_set_color(0);
  vsa_move_to(3,3);
  vsa_rect(636,476);
  return;
```

continues

Listing 6.11. continued

```
}                      /*.....    End frame        .....*/


void introduction(void)
{
  printf("This program goes through the evolution of mild\n");
  printf("mannered MOUNTAIN.TGA to the ultimate UFO sighting\n");
  printf("UFO.TGA.  Before you run this program, You must\n");
  printf("have the following three files in the current\n");
  printf("directory:\n");
  printf("             MOUNTAIN.TGA\n");
  printf("             CITY.TGA\n");
  printf("             SAUCER.TGA\n");
  printf("\n");
  printf("Furthermore, you need an additional 7 Mbytes\n");
  printf("of hard disk space available since the following\n");
  printf("intermediate TARGA image files are created:\n");
  printf("\n");
  printf("             SKY.TGA\n");
  printf("             WIPED.TGA\n");
  printf("             WITHCITY.TGA\n");
  printf("             WITHSKY.TGA\n");
  printf("             WITHSAUC.TGA\n");
  printf("             WITHSHAD.TGA\n");
  printf("             UFO.TGA  (This is the final image)\n");
  printf("\n");
  printf("Hit any key to continue, ESC to quit.\n");
  if(getch() == 27)
    exit(1);
  return;
}
```

JPEG/MPEG Compression and Decompression of Images

by Sandeep Jolly

7

What Is a Digital Image?

An image is a two-dimensional (spatial directions) object that provides visual information, such as color, depth (3-D images), and so on, to the human eyes. A photograph taken from a 35mm camera is an example of an analog image. Information stored is continuous in either spatial direction. A digital image is obtained by sampling the analog image at regular intervals in either direction to discretize the information. Each sample is referred to as a pixel or a pel. The sampling rate (number of samples/unit area) should be at least twice the highest spatial frequency component of the original analog image (Nyquist Sampling Theorem). Figure 7.1 shows an analog image of a circular ring.

FIGURE 7.1.

Analog image.

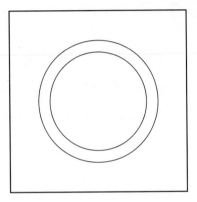

The image in Figure 7.1 is sampled at eight regular intervals in either direction. The resultant 8×8 pixels digital image is shown in Figure 7.2.

FIGURE 7.2.

8×8 sampled digital image.

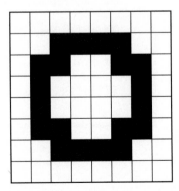

The information for each pixel is stored numerically in the binary base. The number of bits per pixel represents the precision of the sample. The higher precision values provide better qualities of the image. Because the Human Visual System (HVS) gives a nonlinear (approximately logarithmic) response to the changes in the brightness levels, a nonlinear mapping scheme is used by many digitizers for mapping the visual information to the numeric values. This nonlinear mapping scheme contracts the range of numbers to be used for the digital representation of an image, hence reducing the number of bits per pixel for the image.

Color Schemes

A light is a mixture of electromagnetic waves of different wavelengths. A light with only one wavelength is called a monochromatic light. Human eyes perceive the color of an object via the excitation of the color sensors (cones and rods) in the eyes by the incoming light. There are three classes of such color sensors, each excited by a certain range of wavelengths. Colors can be produced either by emitting light of different wavelengths from an active source (for example, phosphor) or by absorbing various ranges of wavelengths from incident light and reflecting a few selective ranges of wavelengths using a passive source (for example, printing ink).

Theoretically, it is possible to represent any color by using three basic components. However, in practice, physical properties of the color sources put some limitations on the range of colors that can be generated. Still, most of the colors can be represented using three basic component sources. Various color representation schemes are currently used for digital image processing: RGB (Red Green Blue); CMY (Cyan Magenta Yellow); YUV (Y is Luminance, U and V are Chromonance components); YIQ, which is similar to YUV, and was adopted by the National Television Standards Committee (NTSC); HSV (Hue Saturation Value); and others.

For color images, the color value of a pixel is stored using three numerical values (one for each component). In a monochromatic image, only one color component (luminance) is used per pixel. For such an image, color is constant all over the image and only the brightness level varies from pixel to pixel. For bilevel images, such as text in a book, only two color values are needed to represent any information. Therefore, one bit per pixel is enough to represent a bilevel image (there is no variation in the brightness level of a color).

Why Compression Is Needed

Consider a color image with a resolution of 1000 × 1000 pixels and three components of colors per pixel. If one byte is used to represent a color component, the image size will be almost 3 megabytes. If this image has to be transmitted using telephone cables with 9600 baud-rate (bits/sec), the transmission will take almost 40 minutes. Digital transmission of movies (image sequences) is finding several applications today, and the bandwidth requirement for the transmission of uncompressed image sequences is very high.

Redundancy in the Data

Digital images often show high similarity in the data values of different pixels. First, similarity can be observed among adjacent pixels, which leads to the spatial redundancy in the data. Similarity can also be observed in certain components or bitplanes of the image. For example, an RGB image showing a scene lighted with only blue lights may show a good variation of brightness values for the blue component, but at the same time may reflect a high similarity of brightness values for the red and green components. This similarity leads to the spectral redundancy in the data. Another type of redundancy, called temporal redundancy, can be observed in the image sequences. A high correlation between several pixel blocks in any two consecutive image frames leads to this redundancy.

Image Compression

There are two types of compression techniques: lossless and lossy. In lossless compression, also referred to as reversible compression, the compression is achieved without any loss of the information. The decompressed image is numerically identical to the original digital image. In lossy compression, also referred to as irreversible compression, the compression is achieved at the cost of losing some of the information. It gives a higher compression ratio, but the decompressed image is not numerically identical to the original digital image.

Entropy Encoding

Before discussing any compression technique, it is important to study how variable-length codes can reduce by an appreciable amount the number of bits needed to represent an image. Consider a 256 × 256 image with 8 bits/pixel. Let m be the number of distinct pixel values occurring in this image. If these values are encoded as m symbols and then each symbol is expressed as a binary number, the number of bits needed per symbol (or per pixel) is approximately $\log_2 m$. Because m must always be less than or equal to 256, a reduction in the number of bits per pixel can be obtained using this mechanism. A further reduction is obtained by considering the probabilities of occurrence of the symbols. A variable-length encoding involves using shorter codes (fewer bits) for more probable symbols and longer codewords for less probable symbols, such that the average length of the codewords is reduced.

The number of bits that must be used for a symbol S_i in an ideal case, is given by the following equation:

$$l(s_i) = \log_2 \left[\frac{1}{p(s_i)} \right]$$

The reason for using the logarithmic operator is explained as follows: Because the number of bits used for a symbol should be inversely proportional to the probability of occurrence, let's consider g to be an arbitrary function that holds this relationship, as shown in this equation:

$$l(s_i)=g\left(\frac{1}{p(s_i)}\right)$$

Now, let's say there are k pixels in an image block. The probability of occurrence of these k pixels is equal to the product $p(S(0)) \times p(S(1)) \times .. \times p(S(k-1))$, where $S(i)$ is a function that gives the symbol used by the pixel at location i. Hence, the number of bits required for the sequence of k symbols is given by the following equation:

$$l(ksymbols)=g\left(\frac{1}{p(S(0))\times p(S(1))\times..\times p(S(k-1))}\right)$$

$$=l(S(0))+l(S(1))+..+l(S(k-1))$$

$$=g\left(\frac{1}{p(S(0))}\right)+..+g\left(\frac{1}{p(S(k-1))}\right)$$

The preceding equation is satisfied if we substitute a logarithmic function for g.

The average bits/symbol

$$=\Sigma p(s_i)l(s_i)$$

$$\Sigma p(s_i)\log_2\frac{1}{p(s_i)}$$

This is also referred to as entropy.

Huffman Entropy Encoding

Consider an image that can be represented by using a set (S) of m symbols $(s_0..s_{m-1})$ with probabilities $p(s_0)..p(s_{m-1})$. Huffman encoding of these symbols is achieved as follows:

- Initialize all symbols with a blank (or null) codeword.
- Repeat the following steps until the size of the symbol set S is reduced to 1.
  - Append a 0 to the codeword of the most probable symbol in the set S.

- Append a 1 to the codeword of each of the remaining symbols in the set S.
- Remove the most probable symbol from the set S.

For example, consider a set of eight symbols with the corresponding probabilities of occurrence.

```
S = { s₀, s₁, ..., s₇ }
P = { p(sᵢ) }
  = { 0.03, 0.2, 0.1, 0.5, 0.03, 0.05, 0.04, 0.05 }
```

Initialize	s_0	s_1	s_2	s_3	s_4	s_5	s_6	s_7
$p(s_i)$	.03	.2	.1	.5	.03	.05	.04	.05
codeword								

Most Probable		*Remaining*						
Step1	s_3	s_0	s_1	s_2	s_4	s_5	s_6	s_7
$p(s_i)$	.5	.03	.2	.1	.03	.05	.04	.05
codeword	0	1	1	1	1	1	1	1
Step2	s_1	s_0	s_2	s_4	s_5	s_6	s_7	
$p(s_i)$	.2	.03	.1	.03	.05	.04	.05	
codeword	10	11	11	11	11	11	11	
Step3	s_2	s_0	s_4	s_5	s_6	s_7		
$p(s_i)$	.1	.03	.03	.05	.04	.05		
codeword	110	111	111	111	111	111		
Step4	s_5	s_0	s_4	s_6	s_7			
$p(s_i)$	.05	.03	.03	.04	.05			
codeword	1110	1111	1111	1111	1111			
Step5	s_7	s_0	s_4	s_6				
$p(s_i)$	.05	.03	.03	.04				
codeword	11110	11111	11111	11111				
Step6	s_6	s_0	s_4					
$p(s_i)$	.04	.03	.03					
codeword	111110	111111	111111					
Step7	s_0	s_4						
$p(s_i)$	.03	.03						
codeword	1111110	1111111						

From the preceding procedure the final codewords assigned to different symbols are as shown in the first column of each step. The entropy of this system can be computed as follows:

Entropy(bits/symbol)

$$= \Sigma p(s_i)l(s_i)$$
$$= .03 \times 7$$
$$+ .2 \times 2$$
$$+ .1 \times 3$$
$$+ .5 \times 1$$
$$+ .03 \times 7$$
$$+ .05 \times 4$$
$$+ .04 \times 6$$
$$+ .05 \times 7$$
$$= 2.34$$

A further improvement in entropy can be obtained by using modified Huffman coding.

Arithmetic Entropy Encoding

Arithmetic coding provides a mechanism to obtain average bits/symbol close to the entropy and, unlike Huffman coding, does not require integer-length codes. In this scheme, symbols are arranged (in either increasing or decreasing order of the probability of occurrence) on an interval from 0 to 1, such that the probability of a symbol is equal to the length of the subinterval to which it is assigned. The symbols are then encoded by assigning a binary floating point number representing the beginning position of its subinterval. The number of significant bits after the binary point that are retained correspond to the length of this subinterval (= $\log_2$(length of subinterval)).

Consider the same example of a source with eight symbols used for the Huffman coding. The symbols are arranged in an increasing order of the probability of occurrence:

The codewords for different symbols are as follows:

Symbol	Position	Length	Significant bits ($-\log_2$(Length))	Codeword
s_0	0.0	.03	6	.000000
s_1	.3	.2	3	.010
s_2	.2	.1	4	.0011
s_3	.5	.5	1	.1

Symbol	Position	Length	Significant bits ($-log_2(Length)$)	Codeword
s_4	.03	.03	6	.000001
s_5	.1	.05	5	.00011
s_6	.06	.04	5	.00001
s_7	.15	.05	5	.00100

The average bits per symbol for this encoding is obtained as follows:

$$\text{Entropy(bits/symbol)}$$
$$=\Sigma p(s_i)l(s_i)$$
$$=.03\text{x}6$$
$$+.2\text{x}3$$
$$+.1\text{x}4$$
$$+.5\text{x}1$$
$$+.03\text{x}6$$
$$+.05\text{x}5$$
$$+.04\text{x}5$$
$$+.05\text{x}5$$
$$=2.56$$

DPCM—A Lossless Compression Technique

To understand DPCM (Differential Pulse Code Modulation), consider a plot of luminance for pixels along a scanline of an image (shown in Figure 7.3).

FIGURE 7.3.

Luminance plot for a scanline.

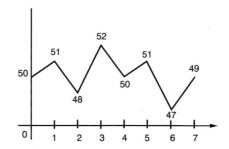

Another graph is drawn, as shown in Figure 7.4, by plotting the difference in luminance between a pixel and a pixel to its left.

FIGURE 7.4.

Difference plot for the scanline.

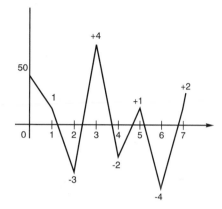

The luminance value of the first pixel on the scanline is substituted for the difference value. You can see that more of the pixels have the same pixel values (difference values) in Figure 7.4 than in Figure 7.3 (luminance values).

DPCM uses a similar approach. In DPCM, the value of a pixel is predicted from the actual values of a subset of the previously scanned pixels. The difference between the predicted value and the actual value is then stored for the pixel. The number of pixels used for the prediction of a pixel is referred to as the order of the predictor. Let a, b, and c be the actual values of the 3 pixels in the neighborhood of a pixel x (see Figure 7.5).

FIGURE 7.5.

DPCM Predictor. Pixel x is predicted using a, b, and c.

		a	b			
		c	x			

A third order predictor is used to predict the value of x as follows:

```
x_m = 0.75c - 0.5a + 0.5b.
```

Let d be the actual value of this pixel; then the difference $e = d - x_m$ is stored as pixel value for the pixel x. An appreciable compression rate is obtained by encoding these difference values using an entropy encoder.

Discrete Cosine Transform

Discrete cosine transform is based on the Fourier transformation technique. Fourier transformation of a function f(x) *(x∈[0,π])* involves decomposition of the function into a number of sine and cosine waves of different frequencies and amplitudes. The function f(x) then can be expressed as

$$f(x)=a_0+\sum_{n=1}^{\infty}a_n\sin(nx)dx+\sum_{n=1}^{\infty}b_n\cos(nx)dx$$

where a_0 = D.C. component (or average value) of f(x).
           a_n = Amplitude of nth harmonic sine-component.
           b_n = Amplitude of nth harmonic cosine-component.

The a_n and b_n are computed as follows:

$$a_n=\frac{1}{\pi}\int_0^{\pi} f(x)\sin(nx)dx$$

$$b_n=\frac{1}{\pi}\int_0^{\pi} f(x)\cos(nx)dx$$

This is a 1-D Fourier transform, which involves integration of a continuous function. This technique can be extended for a two-dimensional function. Because the digital images are two-dimensional arrays of discrete pixel values, a 2-D Discrete Fourier Transform can be used to decompose the image into a number of spectral components.

Discrete Cosine Transform does not consider the sine-components. It involves decomposition of an n × n image into a number of cosine-components. If f(j,k) represents the pixel value at location (j,k), and F(u,v) represents a 2-D cosine-component with u^{th} harmonic subcomponent along U-direction and v^{th} harmonic subcomponent along V-direction (the U- and V-direction corresponds to J- and K-spatial direction), then F(u,v) is defined as follows:

$$F(u,v)=\frac{4C(u)C(v)}{n^2}\sum_{j=0}^{n-1}\sum_{k=0}^{n-1}f(j,k)\cos\left[\frac{(2j+1)}{2n}u\pi\right]\cos\left[\frac{(2k+1)}{2n}v\pi\right]$$

and the inverse 2DDCT is defined as

$$f(j,k) =\sum_{u=0}^{n-1}\sum_{v=0}^{n-1}C(u)C(v)F(u,v)\cos\left[\frac{(2j+1)}{2n}u\pi\right]\cos\left[\frac{(2k+1)}{2n}v\pi\right]$$

$$\text{where } C(w) = \begin{bmatrix} \dfrac{1}{\sqrt{2}} w = 0 \\ 1w = 1,2,3,...n. \end{bmatrix}$$

From the preceding definition, it is clear that for an n × n block of pixels, only up to (n-1)th harmonic components are considered. The computational complexity of this algorithm is of the order of n^2.

JPEG Standard

JPEG stands for the Joint Photographic Experts Group. It serves as a standard for the compression of still continuous-tone monochromatic and color images. JPEG provides a baseline system that must be present in all implementations of JPEG, and a set of extended systems that is optional. The baseline system uses DCT (lossy compression) and is efficient for most of the applications. The extended systems provide flexibility to choose from different compression techniques, entropy encoders, and so on.

The block diagram for the general compression system is shown in Figure 7.6.

FIGURE 7.6.

General compression system.

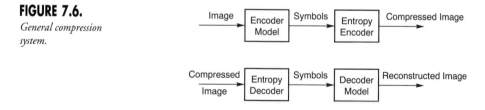

The encoder model and entropy encoder might need external data (for example, entropy tables, quantization matrix, and so on). JPEG provides several encoding models, such as DCT, DPCM, BTC (Block Truncation Coding), Sub-band coding, and so on.

The JPEG baseline system employs the DCT model. Because the complexity of DCT is of the order of n^2, a faster version of DCT, called Fast DCT (or FDCT), is used by the JPEG. FDCT is an improved implementation of the DCT algorithm that reduces the number of multiplication and addition operations by a considerable factor; its complexity is $O(n\log n)$. The JPEG DCT works on an 8×8 pixel block of an image and is defined as follows:

$$F(u,v) = \frac{C(u)C(v)}{4} \sum_{j=0}^{7} \sum_{k=0}^{7} f(j,k) \cos\left[\frac{(2j+1)}{16}u\pi\right] \cos\left[\frac{(2k+1)}{16}v\pi\right]$$

and the inverse 2DDCT is defined as

$$f(j,k) = \frac{1}{4} \sum_{u=0}^{7} \sum_{v=0}^{7} C(u)C(v)F(u,v) \cos\left[\frac{(2j+1)}{16}u\pi\right] \cos\left[\frac{(2k+1)}{16}v\pi\right]$$

$$\text{where } C(w) = \begin{bmatrix} \\ \frac{1}{\sqrt{2}} w = 0 \\ \\ 1 w = 1,2,3,...n. \end{bmatrix}$$

which is identical to the previous equation except for a scaling factor of 4.

The F(u,v) spectral components obtained from the DCT encoding are quantized using a quantization matrix. The quantization involves division of each F(u,v) component by a corresponding 2-D array element Q(u,v) (where Q is the quantization matrix), and rounding off the results.

$$F(u,v) = \text{round}\left[\frac{F(u,v)}{Q(u,v)}\right]$$

The quantization matrix adopted by JPEG for an 8×8 pixel block is provided in Figure 7.7.

FIGURE 7.7.

A matrix (quantization).

$$Q = \begin{bmatrix} 16 & 11 & 10 & 16 & 24 & 40 & 51 & 61 \\ 12 & 12 & 14 & 19 & 26 & 58 & 60 & 55 \\ 14 & 13 & 16 & 24 & 40 & 57 & 69 & 56 \\ 14 & 17 & 22 & 29 & 51 & 87 & 80 & 62 \\ 18 & 22 & 37 & 56 & 68 & 109 & 103 & 77 \\ 24 & 35 & 55 & 64 & 81 & 104 & 113 & 92 \\ 49 & 64 & 78 & 87 & 103 & 121 & 120 & 101 \\ 72 & 92 & 95 & 98 & 112 & 100 & 103 & 99 \end{bmatrix}$$

The $F(0,0)$ component is referred to as the DC coefficient and is proportional to the average pixel value of the 8 × 8 pixel block. DC coefficients from different 8 × 8 pixel blocks are encoded using the DPCM method. The difference signals generated by the DPCM encoder are then entropy encoded using the Huffman entropy encoder.

The rest of the 2-D spectral components, $F(u,v)$, are referred to as AC coefficients. After quantization, many of the AC coefficients round off to zero, especially the ones with the higher spectral frequencies (or higher u- and v-index values). The quantized 2-D array $F(u,v)$ is rearranged into a 1-D array in a zigzag pattern as shown in Figure 7.8.

FIGURE 7.8.

Zigzag reordering of DCT matrix.

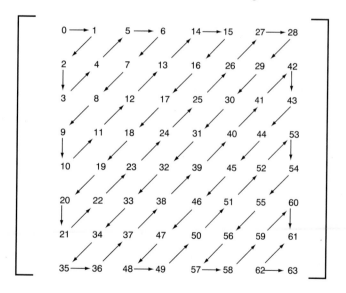

This rearrangement places various DCT components with lower DCT frequencies at lower indices, and components with higher DCT frequencies at higher indices. Because the quantization rounds off most of the higher frequency components to zero, a long series of trailing zeros is observed at the higher indices of this 1-D array. A block diagram of the JPEG baseline encoder model is shown in Figure 7.9.

FIGURE 7.9.

JPEG baseline encoder model.

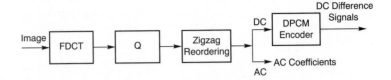

For the baseline system, AC coefficients are Huffman entropy encoded. A statistical model is used to first generate the symbols for these AC coefficients. This model replaces a sequence of zeros with a single token (five zeros might become 5Z), and combines it with the next nonzero coefficient to produce a symbol for the entropy encoder. The Huffman entropy encoder either uses a fixed entropy encoding table or generates this table by analyzing the symbol source. A block diagram of the baseline entropy encoder is shown in Figure 7.10.

FIGURE 7.10.

JPEG baseline entropy encoder.

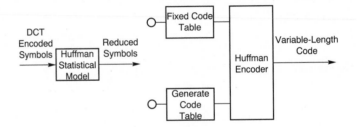

For color images or images with more than one component per pixel (such as depth, color, and so on), each component is encoded separately.

The decompression procedure is exactly the opposite of the compression procedure. The block diagrams for the JPEG baseline entropy decoder and decoder model are shown in Figure 7.11 and Figure 7.12, respectively.

FIGURE 7.11.

JPEG baseline entropy decoder.

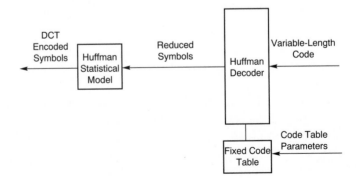

FIGURE 7.12.

*JPEG baseline
decoder model.*

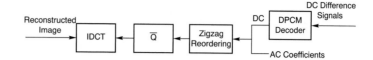

Four Modes of Operation in JPEG

JPEG has the following four modes of operation:

1. Sequential DCT
2. Progressive DCT
3. Hierarchical
4. Sequential lossless

Sequential DCT

In sequential DCT-based mode, DCT (lossy) technique is used for the compression. The image to be compressed is scanned only once for a given component of the image. For multicomponent images (such as color images), either one scan can be used to compress all components in one pass, or multiple scans can be used, with one scan for each component. When compressing multicomponent images in one scan, the compressed data for the different components of a pixel block is stored in an interleaved memory.

Progressive DCT

This also uses DCT technique for the compression of the image blocks. In progressive procedure, a sequence of scanlines is used for the image. There are two ways to obtain a progressive compression. One method involves entropy encoding of a sub-band of DCT frequencies during each scan. Another method involves entropy encoding of DCT coefficients with varying precisions. A lower precision is used during the first scan, and the precision is progressively increased for each successive scan.

Hierarchical

In hierarchical mode, the image is multiply scanned starting with a low sampling rate. At each successive scan, the sampling rate is doubled in each direction (if required). During each scan, any of the remaining three modes can be used to compress the data. The process is repeated until a desired quality is obtained for the image.

Sequential Lossless

It is identical to the sequential DCT mode, except the DPCM is used for the compression of the data.

MPEG Standard

MPEG stands for the Moving Picture Experts Group. MPEG activities address not only video compression, but also the compression of associated audio signals and audio-visual synchronization. They address the compression of video signals at 1.5Mbps (MPEG-I standard is defined for the compression of video signals at 0.9 to 1.5 Mbps), and audio signals at the rates of 64 to 192Kbps/Channel. The MPEG video compression algorithm is based on two fundamental techniques: motion compensation for interframe redundancy (temporal redundancy), and DCT-based compression for intraframe redundancy (spatial redundancy). Because MPEG uses DCT (lossy), MPEG compression is considered to be irreversible compression. A diagram of the MPEG encoding system is shown in Figure 7.13.

FIGURE 7.13.
MPEG encoding system.

MPEG Compensation Encoder

In moving pictures, a great deal of similarity is observed between any two consecutive frames. The difference between these adjacent frames is mostly a result of either the motion of an object in the scene or the motion of the entire scene (due to camera movements). Some dissimilarities are observed due to the sudden appearance or disappearance of an object in the scene. This temporal redundancy in the image sequences can be avoided by providing image blocks with the displacement vectors, which indicate the shift in the position of a block from the position of a corresponding image block in the adjacent frame. The MPEG motion compensation algorithm works as follows:

- Divide the image sequence into three categories:

    (1) intra-pictures (I)

    (2) predicted-pictures (P)

    (3) interpolated-pictures (or bidirectionally predicted) (B)

The intra-pictures are frames encoded without any temporal prediction. These frames serve as reference for predicted-pictures. Predicted-pictures are encoded using temporal prediction from the previously encoded frames (I or P), and serve as reference for the future temporal predictions. A bidirectionally predicted frame is encoded using temporal predictions in either time direction (past and future), from two of the previously encoded frames. The image sequence is encoded in an order with the intra-picture encoded first, then the next predicted-picture, and finally all of the interpolated-pictures in between the previous two pictures (**I** and **P**). If there is more than one predicted-picture between the two intra-pictures, the next predicted-picture is encoded, followed by the interpolated-pictures in between the last two non-**B** pictures. The priority is **I B P**, as illustrated in Figure 7.14.

FIGURE 7.14.

MPEG image sequence encoding order.

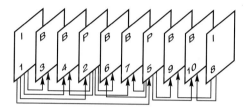

- Divide each predicted frame into a number of macroblocks of size 16 × 16 pixels.

- Determine the displacement vector for each macroblock by searching for the best-match macro block in the reference frame. The search is confined to a search area around the macroblock and its limit is application-specific.

- The best-match block is the one that provides the least difference measure from the given macroblock. There are several matching criteria, such as mean square error (MSE) and minimum absolute difference (MAD).

- For each macroblock, two differences are computed: best-match motion compensated block, and zero-displacement motion compensated block. The best-match motion compensated block represents the difference between the best-match macroblock and the original macroblock; the zero-displacement motion compensated block represents the difference between the original block and a block at the same position in the reference frame. A motion compensated block with lower energy is selected to represent the original macroblock.

- The 16 × 16 motion compensated macroblock is divided into four 8 × 8 sub-blocks, and each 8 × 8 block is then encoded using the DCT technique used by the JPEG baseline system.

A block diagram of the MPEG decoder system is shown in Figure 7.15. The decoding procedure is exactly the opposite of the encoding procedure.

FIGURE 7.15.

MPEG decoding system.

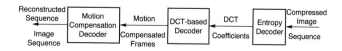

Modeling in 3-D

A Graphical User Interface for 3-D Modeling

by Alfonso Hermida

8

Get a behind-the-scenes look at the development of an interactive graphical user interface for designing three-dimensional models. This chapter covers all the details of drawing viewports, mouse interfacing, and executing commands with icons.

User Interface Concepts

The following sections and chapters show you how to develop a simple yet feature-rich 3-D modeling application. Such an application combines the use of different techniques such as creating and handling viewports, the use of the mouse as an input device, and the ability to choose commands using icons. These techniques are the first step. The tools developed in this chapter are then used to build the interactive 3-D modeling application.

Windows and Viewports

Windows are areas on the screen where graphical information can be displayed. Viewports, on the other hand, are rectangular areas inside the window that display graphical data. Viewports can be of different sizes but never larger than the window that contains them. Figure 8.1 presents a large window containing four viewports. The viewports need not be square. Each viewport displays the 3-D axis from a different perspective. For example, viewport #1 displays the X and Z axes, and viewport #3 displays all three axes (X, Y, and Z).

FIGURE 8.1.

Windows and viewports.

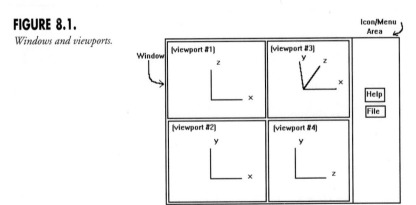

Most graphics libraries have a function or set of functions to define areas on the screen as viewports. As an example, Borland's BGI function `setviewport()` can define any region of the screen as a viewport. This function call makes some changes to the full screen coordinates that I will explain in the following sections.

Device Coordinates

To draw graphical primitives such as points, lines, and rectangles, you need to use what are referred to as *device coordinates*. Device coordinates are usually defined in terms of pixels. A VGA graphics card has 640 × 480 pixels; therefore, the device coordinates are in terms of 0 to 639 horizontally and 0 to 479 vertically (see Figure 8.2). At first glance, this appears to be a simple setup, until you realize that this device coordinate definition is not useful for real 3-D work. The next chapter presents a function to convert device coordinates into useful coordinates called *world coordinates*.

FIGURE 8.2.

Device coordinates on a VGA graphics screen.

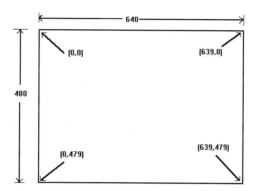

Line Clipping

You use viewports to distinguish between different images or drawings in the same window, so it is important that each viewport contains the image drawn in it. There are two possible approaches to limiting each drawing within its respective viewport. The first one is to always scale the image until its maximum limits are equal to or less than the limits of the viewport. The second option is to let the drawing be of any size but to clip any line that goes beyond the viewport. Figure 8.3 present two viewports—the left one hasn't used the clipping feature, and the right one has.

FIGURE 8.3.

Viewport without line clipping (left) and with line clipping (right).

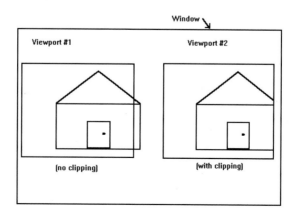

Listing 8.1 presents an example of using viewports in combination with line clipping. Because graphics libraries are not on ANSI standards, each person must address this issue by checking if the compiler has a graphics library. Usually MSC/Borland/Watcom have very similar syntax. Others such as Zortech or Symantec might use a different function name. One important tip is to find out whether your compiler uses a setviewport (x, y, x_2, y_2, clip) type of function or a drawline (x, y, x_2, y_2, clip) type. In the first case, a separate command is used to define the viewport, and whether that viewport will clip anything that goes beyond it. In the second case, the clipping feature is defined with each line drawn. You may decide to clip some and not others.

Listing 8.1. CLIP.C—viewports and line clipping.

```
#include <graphics.h>
#include <stdlib.h>
#include <stdio.h>
#include <conio.h>

#define CLIP_ON  1
#define CLIP_OFF 0

void main(void) {
/* request auto detection */
int gdriver = DETECT, gmode, errorcode;

/* initialize graphics and local variables */
initgraph(&gdriver, &gmode, "");

/* read result of initialization */
    errorcode = graphresult();
    if (errorcode != grOk) {
        printf("Graphics error: %s\n", grapherrormsg(errorcode));
        printf("Press any key to halt:");
        getch();
        exit(1); /* terminate with an error code */
    }

    setcolor(getmaxcolor());
    /* draw box around viewport #1 */
    rectangle(0,0,100,100);
    /* draw box around viewport #2 */
    rectangle(200,0,300,100);

    /* set viewport #1 */
    setviewport(0,0,100,100,CLIP_OFF);
    /* draw a circle inside it */
    circle(60,50,50);

    /* set viewport #2 */
    setviewport(200, 0, 300, 100, CLIP_ON);
    /* draw a circle inside it */
    circle(60,50,50);
```

```
    getch();

    closegraph();
}
```

The program clip.c creates two boxes on the screen that define the outline of the viewports. Viewport #1 does not use line clipping, but viewport #2 does. There is an important concept that I have not mentioned up to this point. Observe that although I use two different areas on the screen as viewports

```
setviewport(0,0,100,100,CLIP_OFF);
setviewport(200, 0, 300, 100, CLIP_ON);
```

the circle is still being drawn using the same coordinates circle(60,50,50). Each call to setviewport() redefines the device coordinates inside the viewport so that the upper-left corner becomes (0,0). The coordinates of the lower-right corner are calculated as follows: Assume that you called the viewport function like this

```
setviewport(xmin,ymin,xmax,ymax, clip);    /* clip can be either 0 or 1 */
```

Your device coordinates are the upper-left corner coordinates (0,0) and the lower-right corner coordinates (xmax-xmin, ymax-ymin). As an example, the call

```
setviewport(0,0,100,100,CLIP_OFF);
```

sets up a viewport with the coordinates (0,0) and (100,100), whereas the call

```
setviewport(200, 0, 300, 100, CLIP_ON);
```

sets up a viewport with the coordinates (0,0) and (300–200,100–0), which simplifies to (100,100). In other words, viewports #1 and #2 are located in different places on the screen, but their device coordinate definition is identical, so the circle does not need to be changed.

To summarize, viewports are used to separate areas on the screen and define applicable device coordinates on the screen. The use of line clipping prevents a drawing inside a viewport from going outside of a region.

Now that you have some basic device coordinate concepts down, the following section studies how to interact with input devices such as a mouse.

Interacting with a Mouse

A mouse is an extremely handy device that can be programmed to act as a feedback device, returning the current location in terms of device coordinates, or as a selecting device, so you can select an area on the screen, pick an object, or even select a command. The following sections present a simple set of functions to control the mouse. You can do this by accessing the routines inside the driver that comes with Microsoft (or compatible) mice.

To make life simpler, I will define some commonly used data globally—that is, outside the `main()` section of the program. The define statements

```
#define LMB 1
#define RMB 2
```

are used to test whether the left mouse button (LMB) or the right mouse button (RMB) was pressed. Also, use the following register variables to send data back and forth between the programs and the mouse driver:

```
union REGS inregs;
union REGS outregs;
```

Checking the Mouse

Before you do anything else with the mouse, the `IsMouse()` function is the first function to call. It lets you know if a mouse driver is available. The function is

```
int IsMouse(void)
{
    inregs.x.ax = 0;
    int86(0x33,&inregs,&outregs);
    return(outregs.x.ax ? outregs.x.bx : 0);
}
```

This function serves two purposes: it indicates if the mouse is available, and it returns the number of buttons on the mouse. If you have a three-button mouse, you can check for that with this function and create more complex mouse-handling routines. If you want to be compatible with all mouse users, always assume that the user has the basic two-button mouse. You can easily use the function `IsMouse()` this way:

```
int btn;
btn = IsMouse();
if (btn) printf("You have a mouse with %d buttons installed!",btn);
else {
        printf("Please load the mouse driver");
        exit(1);
}
```

The idea is to test the mouse, and if available, the number of buttons. If the mouse is not available, tell the user to load the mouse driver or check the mouse connection to the computer.

Displaying the Mouse

Now that you know the mouse is alive, you can display it on the screen using the `MouseShow()` function:

```
void MouseShow(int YesNo)
{
    if (YesNo) inregs.x.ax = 1;
```

```
     else inregs.x.ax = 2;
     int86(0x33,&inregs,&outregs);
}
```

To display the mouse, simply call the function `MouseShow(1)`, and to hide it call `MouseShow(0)`. A word of advice: When you start working in the graphics mode, you must hide (`MouseShow(0)`) the mouse prior to any drawing calls. After any drawing is done, simply show the mouse again (`MouseShow(1)`). If you forget to do this, you will see rectangular spots on the screen where the mouse was.

Getting the Mouse Location

Asking the mouse for its current location can be done with a call to `MouseXY()`. This function returns the device coordinates of the mouse in terms of the full screen, and it is not affected by any `setviewport()` call.

```
void MouseXY(int *xpos,int *ypos)
{
    inregs.x.ax = 3;
    int86(0x33,&inregs,&outregs);
    *xpos = outregs.x.cx;
    *ypos = outregs.x.dx;
}
```

To poll the mouse for the current location, type the following:

```
int xpos, ypos;
MouseXY(&xpos,&ypos);
printf("mouse located at x = %d  and y = %d\n",xpos,ypos);
```

Checking for Button Clicks

An important part of using the mouse is its ability to select something by clicking on the object to be selected. This information is then passed to the program so a decision can be made. The function `MouseClick()` returns the number of the button that was pressed (recall the use of the `#define` statements LMB and RMB). The left button is 1, the right button is 2, and the middle button is 3. If a button hasn't been clicked, it returns 0.

```
int MouseClick(void)
{
    int click = 0;
    inregs.x.ax = 5;
    inregs.x.bx = 1;
    int86(0x33,&inregs,&outregs);
    click = outregs.x.bx << 1;
    inregs.x.bx—;
    int86(0x33,&inregs,&outregs);
    return(click ¦ outregs.x.bx);
}
```

You can create a simple loop to poll the mouse until a click event occurs:

```
#define MMB 0
int btn, xpos, ypos;

do {
        MouseXY(&xpos,&ypos);
        btn = MouseClick();
}while(!btn);

switch(btn) {
        case LMB: printf("you pressed the left button\n"); break;
        case MMB: printf("you pressed the middle button\n"); break;
        case RMB: printf("you pressed the right button\n"); break;
}
```

The preceding code polls the mouse until a button is clicked. Depending on the value of
`btn`, the corresponding `printf()` statement is executed.

Mouse Test Program

Finally, Listing 8.2 presents a complete application of the mouse routines. The program
is simple, yet it shows some features that you will use over and over again throughout the
development of the 3-D modeler. MOUSETST.C does the following:

1. Checks the availability of the mouse and the number of buttons

2. Polls the mouse for the current location and button clicks

3. Displays the current mouse location

4. Shows/hides the mouse depending on the left mouse button click

5. Exits if you click on the right mouse button

Listing 8.2. MOUSETST.C—testing the mouse routines.

```
#include <conio.h>
#include <stdio.h>
#include <stdlib.h>
#include <dos.h>

#define LMB 1
#define RMB 2

int IsMouse(void);
int MouseClick(void);
void MouseXY(int *xpos,int *ypos);
void MouseShow(int YesNo);

union REGS inregs;
union REGS outregs;

void main() {
  int xpos, ypos, xold=0, yold=0, btn, flag=1;

  btn = IsMouse();
  if(!btn) {
```

```
            printf("Mouse Driver Not Installed!\n");
            exit(1);
        }
        printf("There are %d buttons on this mouse",btn);
        getch();
        clrscr();
        MouseShow(flag);
        do {
          MouseXY(&xpos,&ypos);
          if ((xold != xpos) ¦¦ (yold != ypos)) {
              gotoxy(1,1);
              printf("x = %d    y = %d         ",xpos,ypos);
          }
          xold = xpos;
          yold = ypos;
          btn = MouseClick();
          if (btn == LMB) {
              if (flag) flag = 0;
              else flag = 1;
              MouseShow(flag);
          }
        }while(btn != RMB);
}

int IsMouse(void)
{
   inregs.x.ax = 0;
   int86(0x33,&inregs,&outregs);
   return(outregs.x.ax ? outregs.x.bx : 0);
}

int MouseClick(void)
{
   int click = 0;
   inregs.x.ax = 5;
   inregs.x.bx = 1;
   int86(0x33,&inregs,&outregs);
   click = outregs.x.bx << 1;
   inregs.x.bx—;
   int86(0x33,&inregs,&outregs);
   return(click ¦ outregs.x.bx);
}

void MouseXY(int *xpos,int *ypos)
{
   inregs.x.ax = 3;
   int86(0x33,&inregs,&outregs);
   *xpos = outregs.x.cx;
   *ypos = outregs.x.dx;
}


void MouseShow(int YesNo)
{
   if (YesNo) inregs.x.ax = 1;
   else inregs.x.ax = 2;
   int86(0x33,&inregs,&outregs);
}
```

The next step is to work with *icons* (also referred to as *push buttons*). These are used to execute commands without using the keyboard. Icons have various benefits that I discuss in the next section.

Using Icons

Icons are rectangular regions in the screen that are used to define an area where a mouse can click to select a command that has been defined. Icons have some definite advantages over the standard keyboard command:

- No need to remember command names.
- No need for syntax error checking when typing a command name.
- Icons have commands associated with them that are accessed by just one click.
- Keyboard numerical input is prone to exceeding limits, and icons can be used to constrain the limits.

You can start by looking at how icons can be created on the screen and how they can be accessed.

Creating Icons

To define a region in the graphics screen, the `Icon` structure was defined as follows:

```
typedef struct {
  int x,y,width,height,color;
  char str[81];
} Icon;
```

The variables x and y (in device coordinates) are used to define the upper-left corner of the icon. The width and height of the icon (also in device coordinates) are given by `width` and `height`. The face of an icon can be any color, and the variable `color` is used for that purpose. Finally, the character array `str[81]` is used to save the keyword, which is written in the icon's face. This word indicates which command this icon is hooked up to. Figure 8.4 displays a basic icon drawn as a button with a 3-D effect (observe the contrast between the edges to create a "lifted" look).

FIGURE 8.4.

Drawing an icon.

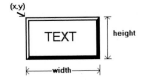

To define an icon within your program, use the definition

```
Icon k;
```

to create one icon, or use

```
Icon k[10];
```

to create an array of icons. Now that memory has been allocated for the icon, the next step is to fill in the variables with information concerning its location, dimensions, color, and text to be displayed. This can be accomplished by calling the `CreateIcon()` function:

```
Icon CreateIcon(int xo,int yo,int width,int height,int color,char * text)
{
  Icon temp;
  temp.x = xo;
  temp.y = yo;
  temp.width = width;
  temp.height = height;
  temp.color = color;
  strcpy(temp.str,text);
  return(temp);
}
```

To create and define the icon, type the following:

```
Icon ic;
ic = CreateIcon(100,100,70,15,LIGHTGRAY,"TEST");
```

The next step is to draw it on the screen.

Drawing an Icon

After an icon has been defined, you can draw it by calling the `DrawIcon()` function. This function takes an icon as an argument and proceeds to draw it as specified inside the `Icon` structure:

```
void DrawIcon(Icon ic)
{
  int color;
  color = getcolor();
  MouseShow(0);
  setcolor(0);
  setfillstyle(1,ic.color);
  bar3d(ic.x,ic.y,ic.x+ic.width,ic.y+ic.height,0,0);
  rectangle(ic.x,ic.y,ic.x+ic.width,ic.y+ic.height);
  rectangle(ic.x+1,ic.y+1,ic.x+ic.width-1,ic.y+ic.height-1);
  outtextxy(ic.x+3,ic.y + 5,ic.str);
  setcolor(15);
  line(ic.x,ic.y,ic.x+ic.width,ic.y);
  line(ic.x,ic.y,ic.x,ic.y+ic.height);
  line(ic.x+1,ic.y+1,ic.x+ic.width-1,ic.y+1);
  line(ic.x+1,ic.y+1,ic.x+1,ic.y+ic.height-1);
  outtextxy(ic.x+2,ic.y + 4,ic.str);
  MouseShow(1);
  setcolor(color);
}
```

Using the previously defined code,

```
Icon ic;
ic = CreateIcon(100,100,70,15,LIGHTGRAY,"TEST");
DrawIcon(ic);
```

creates, defines, and draws icon ic.

Checking the Icon

Now that you can create icons, you need a method by which you can determine if a mouse is inside or outside the region specified by a given icon. Suppose you need to implement the following sequence of events:

1. Create a number of icons
2. Draw all the icons on the screen
3. Turn on the mouse
4. Wait until the left mouse button has been pressed
5. Find out which icon, if any, has been selected
6. If an icon has been selected, execute its corresponding command

This sequence of events is your typical graphics program. One of the icons defined will have the Quit command hooked to it, which the user will eventually want to select to exit the program.

Step 5 requires the use of the IconCheck() function. IconCheck() tests only whether the mouse is currently inside the region (x,y) and (x+width, y+height) as defined by the icon. If this is true, the function returns 1; otherwise, it returns 0:

```
int IconCheck(Icon ikon,int xm,int ym)
{
 if ((xm > ikon.x) && (xm < ikon.x + ikon.width) &&
     (ym > ikon.y) && (ym < ikon.y + ikon.height))
       return(1);
       else return(0);
}
```

What can you use to check if the button is pressed? Use the previously defined piece of code from the section titled "Checking for Button Clicks."

```
do {
            MouseXY(&xpos,&ypos);
            btn = MouseClick();
}while(!btn);
```

If you combine them both

```
#define BEEP printf("\7");
Icon ic;

do {
```

```
                MouseXY(&xpos,&ypos);
                    btn = MouseClick();
}while(!btn);

if (btn == LMB)
            if (IconCheck(ic,xpos,ypos)) BEEP;
```

the code polls the mouse until a button is pressed. If the button is the LMB, the icon is checked. The coordinates xpos and ypos contain the coordinates of the mouse when the mouse button was pressed. If IconCheck() returns 1, the computer generates a beep.

Depressing an Icon

For a final touch, you can develop a function that will create the effect of an icon button being pressed down or popping up. This feature gives the program user feedback once the icon has reacted to the mouse click. The other possible method would be to let the computer generate a clicking sound every time the button is pressed or released, but this sound becomes extremely annoying after a while. Figure 8.5 displays what DrawIconHiLite(Icon ic, int OnOff) does.

FIGURE 8.5.

Icons in up and down states.

(button = UP)

(button = DOWN)

```
void DrawIconHiLite(Icon ic, int OnOff)
{
 int color;
 color = getcolor();
 if (OnOff) {
   MouseShow(0);
   setcolor(WHITE);
   rectangle(ic.x+1,ic.y+1,ic.x+ic.width-1,ic.y+ic.height-1);
   setcolor(BLACK);
   line(ic.x,ic.y,ic.x+ic.width,ic.y);
   line(ic.x,ic.y,ic.x,ic.y+ic.height);
   line(ic.x+1,ic.y+1,ic.x+ic.width-1,ic.y+1);
   line(ic.x+1,ic.y+1,ic.x+1,ic.y+ic.height-1);
   MouseShow(1);
 }
 else {
   MouseShow(0);
   setcolor(BLACK);
   rectangle(ic.x+1,ic.y+1,ic.x+ic.width-1,ic.y+ic.height-1);
   setcolor(WHITE);
   line(ic.x,ic.y,ic.x+ic.width,ic.y);
   line(ic.x,ic.y,ic.x,ic.y+ic.height);
   line(ic.x+1,ic.y+1,ic.x+ic.width-1,ic.y+1);
   line(ic.x+1,ic.y+1,ic.x+1,ic.y+ic.height-1);
```

```
    MouseShow(1);
    setcolor(color);
  }
}
```

To create the effect in DrawIconHiLite(Icon ic, int OnOff), you just had to modify DrawIcon(ic) to invert the edge colors in the icon, depending on the value of OnOff. The following section presents a complete program that will use graphics, the mouse, and a few icons.

Icon Test Program

Listing 8.3 presents applications of all the mouse and icon routines. The ICONTEST.C program accomplishes the following:

1. Sets the VGA graphics mode.
2. Defines and displays four icons, one of them being the Quit command.
3. Initializes the mouse and displays it.
4. Polls the mouse until a button is pressed.
5. If the button pressed is the LMB, the IconCheck() is used to find which icon was selected.
6. If one of the icons was selected, beeps or quits the program.
7. If the RMB was pressed instead of the LMB, quits the program.

Listing 8.3. ICONTEST.C—creating and using icons.

```
#include <conio.h>
#include <stdio.h>
#include <stdlib.h>
#include <dos.h>
#include <string.h>
#include <graphics.h>

#define LMB 1
#define RMB 2

typedef struct {
  int x,y,width,height,color;
  char str[81];
} Icon;

int IsMouse(void);
int MouseClick(void);
void MouseXY(int *xpos,int *ypos);
void MouseShow(int YesNo);
void InitGraphics(void);
Icon CreateIcon(int xo,int yo,int width,int height,
                        int color,char * text);
void DrawIcon(Icon ic);
```

```
int IconCheck(Icon ikon,int xm,int ym);
void DrawIconHiLite(Icon ic, int OnOff);

union REGS inregs;
union REGS outregs;

void main() {
  int xpos, ypos, btn, i;
  Icon icon[4];

  icon[0] = CreateIcon(100,100,70,15,RED  ," Icon 0");
  icon[1] = CreateIcon(200,100,70,15,GREEN," Icon 1");
  icon[2] = CreateIcon(300,100,70,15,BLUE ," Icon 2");
  icon[3] = CreateIcon(200,130,70,15,LIGHTGRAY,"  Quit");

  InitGraphics();

  btn = IsMouse();
  if(!btn) {
      closegraph();
      printf("Mouse Driver Not Installed!\n");
      exit(1);
  }

  /* Fill background with gray color */
  setfillstyle(SOLID_FILL,LIGHTGRAY);
  bar3d(0,0,getmaxx(),getmaxy(),0,0);

  DrawIcon(icon[0]);
  DrawIcon(icon[1]);
  DrawIcon(icon[2]);
  DrawIcon(icon[3]);

  MouseShow(1);

  do {
   do {
     MouseXY(&xpos,&ypos);
     btn = MouseClick();
   }while(!btn);
   if(btn == LMB)
    for(i=0;i<4;i++) {
     if(IconCheck(icon[i],xpos,ypos))
       switch(i) {
            case 0: DrawIconHiLite(icon[i], 1);
                        printf("\7");
                        DrawIconHiLite(icon[i], 0);
                        break;
            case 1: DrawIconHiLite(icon[i], 1);
                        printf("\7");
                        DrawIconHiLite(icon[i], 0);
                        break;
            case 2: DrawIconHiLite(icon[i], 1);
                        printf("\7");
                        DrawIconHiLite(icon[i], 0);
                        break;
            case 3: btn = RMB; break;
      }
```

continues

Listing 8.3. continued

```c
    }
  }while(btn != RMB);

  closegraph();
}

/* ///////////////////////////////////////////////*/
void InitGraphics(void)
{
 int gdriver = DETECT, gmode, errorcode;
 initgraph(&gdriver, &gmode, "");
 if (gdriver != VGA) {
  printf("VGA graphics card required.\n");
  exit(1);
 }
 errorcode = graphresult();
 if (errorcode != grOk)  /* an error occurred */
 {
   printf("Graphics error: %s\n", grapherrormsg(errorcode));
   printf("Press any key to halt:");
   getch();
   exit(1); /* terminate with an error code */
 }
}

Icon CreateIcon(int xo,int yo,int width,int height,int color,char * text)
{
 Icon temp;
 temp.x = xo;
 temp.y = yo;
 temp.width = width;
 temp.height = height;
 temp.color = color;
 strcpy(temp.str,text);
 return(temp);
}

void DrawIcon(Icon ic)
{
 int color;
 color = getcolor();
 MouseShow(0);
 setcolor(0);
 setfillstyle(1,ic.color);
 bar3d(ic.x,ic.y,ic.x+ic.width,ic.y+ic.height,0,0);
 rectangle(ic.x,ic.y,ic.x+ic.width,ic.y+ic.height);
 rectangle(ic.x+1,ic.y+1,ic.x+ic.width-1,ic.y+ic.height-1);
 outtextxy(ic.x+3,ic.y + 5,ic.str);
 setcolor(15);
 line(ic.x,ic.y,ic.x+ic.width,ic.y);
 line(ic.x,ic.y,ic.x,ic.y+ic.height);
 line(ic.x+1,ic.y+1,ic.x+ic.width-1,ic.y+1);
 line(ic.x+1,ic.y+1,ic.x+1,ic.y+ic.height-1);
 outtextxy(ic.x+2,ic.y + 4,ic.str);
 MouseShow(1);
 setcolor(color);
}
```

```
int IconCheck(Icon ikon,int xm,int ym)
{
 if ((xm > ikon.x) && (xm < ikon.x + ikon.width) &&
     (ym > ikon.y) && (ym < ikon.y + ikon.height))
     return(1);
     else return(0);
}


void DrawIconHiLite(Icon ic, int OnOff)
{
 int color;
 color = getcolor();
 if (OnOff) {
   MouseShow(0);
   setcolor(WHITE);
   rectangle(ic.x+1,ic.y+1,ic.x+ic.width-1,ic.y+ic.height-1);
   setcolor(BLACK);
   line(ic.x,ic.y,ic.x+ic.width,ic.y);
   line(ic.x,ic.y,ic.x,ic.y+ic.height);
   line(ic.x+1,ic.y+1,ic.x+ic.width-1,ic.y+1);
   line(ic.x+1,ic.y+1,ic.x+1,ic.y+ic.height-1);
   MouseShow(1);
 }
 else {
   MouseShow(0);
   setcolor(BLACK);
   rectangle(ic.x+1,ic.y+1,ic.x+ic.width-1,ic.y+ic.height-1);
   setcolor(WHITE);
   line(ic.x,ic.y,ic.x+ic.width,ic.y);
   line(ic.x,ic.y,ic.x,ic.y+ic.height);
   line(ic.x+1,ic.y+1,ic.x+ic.width-1,ic.y+1);
   line(ic.x+1,ic.y+1,ic.x+1,ic.y+ic.height-1);
   MouseShow(1);
   setcolor(color);
 }
}


int IsMouse(void)
{
   inregs.x.ax = 0;
   int86(0x33,&inregs,&outregs);
   return(outregs.x.ax ? outregs.x.bx : 0);
}

int MouseClick(void)
{
   int click = 0;
   inregs.x.ax = 5;
   inregs.x.bx = 1;
   int86(0x33,&inregs,&outregs);
   click = outregs.x.bx << 1;
   inregs.x.bx—;
   int86(0x33,&inregs,&outregs);
   return(click ¦ outregs.x.bx);
}
```

continues

Listing 8.3. continued

```c
void MouseXY(int *xpos,int *ypos)
{
   inregs.x.ax = 3;
   int86(0x33,&inregs,&outregs);
   *xpos = outregs.x.cx;
   *ypos = outregs.x.dx;
}

void MouseShow(int YesNo)
{
   if (YesNo) inregs.x.ax = 1;
   else inregs.x.ax = 2;
   int86(0x33,&inregs,&outregs);
}
```

Summary

This chapter presented the distinction between a window and a viewport. The viewport is the area where graphics information is actually drawn. The coordinate used to define a location on the screen is called a device coordinate, and it is dependent on the resolution of your graphics card. For VGA graphics mode, the coordinate limits are (0,0) for the upper-right corner and (639,479) for the lower-right corner. Next, I presented several mouse routines that handle checking the mouse, showing or hiding the cursor, clicking information, and location data. A sample program was used to demonstrate the mouse routines. Finally, I discussed icons and their use. Icons are rectangular regions that can be associated to a command. The command is usually executed when the mouse selects one of the icons. A more complex program, ICONTEST.C, was used to demonstrate the interaction between a mouse and the icon buttons.

The goal is to be able to work with 3-D data, and you have accomplished roughly one third of that goal. The next step is to start dealing not with device coordinates but with real life coordinates, called world coordinates. Also, you need to learn how to convert a 3-D object into 2-D space (screen) and how to interface the mouse and icons into a final application.

Creating Your Own
3-D Graphics World

by Alfonso Hermida

To make your own 3-D universe, you need to understand screen (device), 2-D world, and 3-D world coordinate systems, as well as how to integrate 3-D graphics with a graphical user interface.

Coordinate Systems

The previous chapter briefly introduced screen (device) coordinates. These are basically defined by the graphics card that your computer has, that is, a VGA card can go as high as 640 × 480 pixels; therefore, the horizontal device coordinates vary from 0 to 639 and the vertical vary from 0 to 479 pixels. The next sections present other coordinate systems that are very useful when dealing with 3-D graphics and data. For the sake of completeness, you'll start defining device coordinates and relate them to more complex ones.

Screen/Device Coordinates

If you recall Figure 8.2, it presented a view of the limits of the screen in terms of units called "pixels." Figure 8.2 displays the limits 0 to 639 for the horizontal axis and 0 to 479 for the vertical axis. Figure 9.1 presents another look at the device coordinate system. The arrows in the figure denote the origin (where the arrows meet) and the direction in which each coordinate axis is pointing.

FIGURE 9.1.

Screen/Device coordinate system axes.

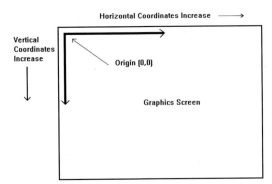

Working with device coordinates is easy because the built-in graphics commands that come with most compilers are defined in terms of device coordinates. What happens when you want to draw a box that is 3.5 feet by 5.2 feet on the screen? The screen is defined in terms of pixels while the object that you want to draw is in feet. You need to be able to define another coordinate system that will be able to translate the units that the object has to screen units. The units of the objects are called "world" coordinates because those units are "real world" coordinates as opposed to pixels. Now take a look at the 2-D world coordinate system.

2-D World Coordinates

In order to compare screen and world coordinates, observe Figure 9.2. The device coordinate system has the axes labeled "DX" (Device X-axis) and "DY" (Device Y-axis), while the 2-D world coordinate system has the axes labeled "WX" (World X-axis) and "WY" (World Y-axis).

FIGURE 9.2.

Device and 2-D world coordinate systems.

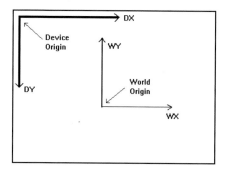

Observe the differences between both systems. Both origins are located in different places on the screen. The device system is "fixed," therefore, you can't tell the computer that you want the origin located on the lower-left corner of the screen, for example. The world system, on the other hand, is "movable," allowing you more flexibility with the placement of the origin as you will see in the next section. This feature makes the world system more user-friendly.

Another difference between both systems is the direction of the axes. While both X-axes (device and world) are pointing in the same direction, the Y-axes are not. Again, the device system is not "movable" but the world system is. After observing the differences between the two systems, the list below sums up the features of the world coordinate system:

- Ability to locate the origin anywhere on the screen (movable origin)
- Ability to use any system of units (feet, inches, meters...even pixels!)

■ Ability to redefine the direction of the axes

With this list in mind, now you can develop the functions that will enable you to accomplish this.

Converting World to Device Coordinates

To make our life easy, let's define a set of variables that will denote the limits of the device and world systems:

Device Limits

```
int DXmin;
int DYmin;
int DYmax;
int DXmax;
```

World Limits in 2-D

```
float WXleft;
float WXright;
float WYtop;
float WYbottom;
```

Use Figure 9.3 to locate the variables. You will define these variables globally (outside of the `main()` function, in order for them to be available to any other function).

FIGURE 9.3.

Device and World Coordinate Systems in

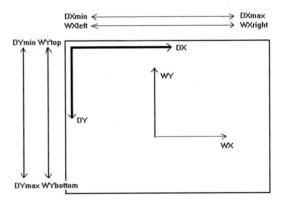

terms of variables.

In addition, you will create a set of two structures to handle data from 2-D world to device. The points are listed below:

Point in Device Coordinates

```
typedef struct {
    int x,y;
} POINTint;
```

Point in World Coordinates

```
typedef struct {
   float x,y,z;
} POINT3D;
```

Here is an example to understand what's happening here. Assume a point p of the type POINT3D, which means that p has the coordinates p.x, p.y, and p.z (you'll drop p.z for now). A point ps of the type POINTint will be used to save the corresponding coordinates of p in terms of screen coordinates. Assume also that you have defined a viewport somewhere on the screen, with the limits

```
DXmin = DYmin = 0.0
DXmax = DYmax = 100.0
```

The world limits have been chosen to be

```
WXleft = WYbottom = -1.0
WXright = WYtop = 1.0
```

Figure 9.4 presents both the device and world coordinates.

FIGURE 9.4.

Displaying limits on coordinate systems.

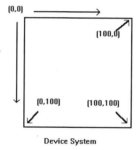
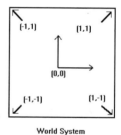

Device System   World System

Now you will get into the conversion of world to device coordinates. The relationship f = (WXleft-p.x)/(WXleft-WXright) gives us a value from 0.0 to 1.0 depending on the difference between WXleft and p.x. For example, if p.x is equal to WXleft, then f = 0.0. On the other hand, if p.x is equal to WXright, then f = 1.0.

Using the expression for f and the device coordinate values you can "interpolate" any X coordinate

```
ps.x = (WXleft-p.x)*(DXmax-DXmin)/(WXleft-WXright) + DXmin;
```

This expression is straightforward and can be rewritten as

```
ps.x = f * (DXmax-DXmin) + DXmin;
```

In other words, when f = 0.0 the point is equal to DXmin. If f = 1.0 then the point is equal to DXmax. This technique is called "linear interpolation." Due to the fact that the world coordinates are floating point numbers and that device coordinates are integers, you add the value 0.5 to round the value to the next integer. The function World2DToDevice() presents the conversion of world coordinates to device

```
POINTint World2DToDevice(POINT3D p) {
 POINTint ptemp;
 ptemp.x = (WXleft-p.x)*(DXmax-DXmin)/(WXleft-WXright) + DXmin + 0.5;
 ptemp.y = (WYtop-p.y)*(DYmax-DYmin)/(WYtop-WYbottom) + DYmin + 0.5;
 return(ptemp);
}
```

As a final test, try a point located at the origin of the 2-D world. Because p = (0,0) then

```
ps.x =  (WXleft-0.0)*(DXmax-DXmin)/(WXleft-WXright) + DXmin + 0.5

ps.x =  (-1.0)*(100-0)/(-1-(1)) + 0 + 0.5

ps.x =  (-100.0)/(-2.0) + 0.5

ps.x =  50.0 +  0.5 = 50.0 (rounded off, ps.x is an integer)
```

which means that ps.x is located at the center of the viewport (recall that the viewport is 100 × 100 pixels). Performing the same operation for ps.y will give you 50.0 also.

Now you finally have a function that will let you redefine the screen into a set of "usable" coordinates. The next step is to be able to go the other way: from device to world.

Converting Device to World Coordinates

In the previous section you developed a set of expressions to convert world to screen co-ordinates. Is there any need to go from screen to world coordinates? A simple example that shows the need for this conversion is when you use the mouse to pick points on the screen. If you recall from the previous chapter, mouse coordinates x,y are specified in screen units. If you need to convert those coordinates into "usable" world coordinates, you then need a function that performs the inverse of what World2DToDevice() does. This can be accomplished by first of all eliminating the 0.5 values used to round off to the nearest integer and then solving the expressions in terms of p.x and p.y . We'll use the name ScreenToWorld2D() to denote such a function.

```
void ScreenToWorld2D(int x,int y,float *px, float *py){
 *px = (DXmin - x)*(WXleft - WXright) / (DXmax - DXmin) + WXleft;
 *py = (DYmin - y)*(WYtop - WYbottom) / (DYmax - DYmin) + WYtop;
}
```

The function accepts two integers, x and y, and returns two floats, px and py. The integer variables are the screen coordinates while the floats are the world coordinates.

In later sections you'll use this function to give you feedback on the location of the mouse as it moves around the screen.

3-D World Coordinates

At this point you have covered 2-D coordinate systems. The next step is to extend these techniques to the third dimension. In order to accomplish this, you need to set up a function that will convert a 3-D point (WX,WY,WZ) into a 2-D screen based point (DX,DY).

Figure 9.5a presents a standard 3-D coordinate system. Observe that it differs from the 2-D system in that it now includes the Z-axis for depth. When you look at 2-D coordinate systems, you can assume that the Z-axis is perpendicular to the screen. In order to create the effect of drawing in 3-D on the screen, you must change the viewpoint of the observer. Can you roughly tell where the observer is in Figure 9.5a? By rotating the coordinate system about different axes, you can create the effect of different viewpoints. Figures 9.5b and 9.5c present what happens when the coordinate system in Figure 9.5a is rotated by a small angle about each of the axes.

FIGURE 9.5.

Standard 3-D coordinate system and resulting coordinate systems after rotations.

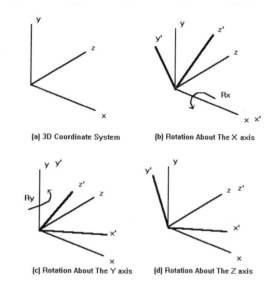

(a) 3D Coordinate System   (b) Rotation About The X axis

(c) Rotation About The Y axis   (d) Rotation About The Z axis

After you have taken a 3-D coordinate system and rotated it about different axes, you need to convert those coordinates into device coordinates. Because you already know how to convert from world 2-D to device, you need to learn the conversion from world 3-D to world 2-D.

Before discussing the function `World3DToWorld2D()`, you need to study the type of information this function will be handling. Since you are going to rotate the 3-D system by means of different angles, you are going to create a set of variables that will contain these angles and their sine and cosine values:

```
float RX, RY, RZ;
float COSRX, SINRX, COSRY;
float SINRY, COSRZ, SINRZ;
```

These variables will be defined as global variables. The functions `sin()` and `cos()`, which calculate the sine and cosine values of an angle in radians, are expensive in terms of computation time. By defining the rotation angles and their sine and cosine values once, you can improve the speed of a program. As you'll see later, each point that will be drawn in 3-D will go through the `World3DToWorld2D()` function which uses sine and cosine values.

In order to define the rotation angles once, you'll create a function called SetAxesAngles(). This function will accept the x, y, and z rotation angles, calculate their sine and cosine values, and save those values in global variables. This will then simplify the access of these values:

```
void SetAxesAngles(float rx, float ry, float rz) {
    RX = DegToRad(rx);
    RY = DegToRad(ry);
    RZ = DegToRad(rz);
    COSRX = cos(RX);
    SINRX = sin(RX);
    COSRY = cos(RY);
    SINRY = sin(RY);
    COSRZ = cos(RZ);
    SINRZ = sin(RZ);
}
```

Now that you have the angles ready to be initialized, take a look at the function World3DToWorld2D():

```
#define TOL 0.0005

POINT3D World3DToWorld2D(POINT3D p)
{
  POINT3D ptemp;
  ptemp = p;
  if (RX) {
            ptemp.x  = p.x;
            ptemp.y  = COSRX*p.y - SINRX*p.z;
            ptemp.z  = SINRX*p.y + COSRX*p.z;
            p = ptemp;
  }
  if (RY) {
            ptemp.x  = COSRY*p.x + SINRY*p.z;
            ptemp.y  = p.y;
            ptemp.z  = -SINRY*p.x + COSRY*p.z;
            p = ptemp;
  }
  if (RZ) {
     ptemp.x  = COSRZ*p.x - SINRZ*p.y;
     ptemp.y  = SINRZ*p.x + COSRZ*p.y;
     ptemp.z  = p.z;
  }
  if (fabs(ptemp.x) < TOL)  ptemp.x = 0.0;
  if (fabs(ptemp.y) < TOL)  ptemp.y = 0.0;
  if (fabs(ptemp.z) < TOL)  ptemp.z = 0.0;
  return(ptemp);
}
```

The function World3DToWorld2D() assumes that the function SetAxesAngles() has already been called. The function assumes also that you have started with a 3-D coordinate system that has the Y-axis pointing up, the X-axis pointing to the right, and the Z-axis pointing into the computer screen. If the angle RX is different from zero, the 3-D system will be rotated about the X-axis by RX radians (see Figure 9.5b). If the angle RY is different from zero, then the Y-axis will be rotated by RY radians (see Figure 9.5c). Finally, the same will apply to RZ and the Z-axis (see Figure 9.5d).

The section of code

```
if (fabs(ptemp.x) < TOL)  ptemp.x = 0.0;
if (fabs(ptemp.y) < TOL)  ptemp.y = 0.0;
if (fabs(ptemp.z) < TOL)  ptemp.z = 0.0;
```

takes care of numbers that turn out to be very small (less than 0.0005). If a number comes out to be less than the value of TOL, then it's considered to be zero.

Drawing in 3-D

You're almost ready to start drawing in 3-D. Any 3-D primitive— sphere, cone, cylinder, or box—can be drawn as a collection of points and lines. Now you'll see how points and lines can be drawn in 3-D.

Drawing Points

Drawing points is straightforward because you have already developed all the tools needed for it. You'll start with a point in 3-D. This point will be converted to a 2-D world-based point, then to a device-based point. After you have the point in device coordinates, you'll use one of the built-in drawing functions, such as a circle or rectangle, to draw in on the screen. The code will look like this:

```
POINT3-D p1;
POINTint p2;

p1.x = 1;
p1.y = 1;
p1.z = 1;

p2 = World2DToDevice(World3DToWorld2D(p1));
rectangle(p2.x - 2, p2.y - 2, p2.x + 2, p2.y + 2);
```

You're assuming that p1 is the original 3-D point and the final 2-D device point is p2. Observe how you simplified the code by making the output from World3DToWorld2D(p1) the argument of World2DToDevice().

Drawing Lines

Drawing 3-D lines uses the same procedure used to draw points, but the steps are done twice, once for each endpoint in the line:

```
POINT3D p1,p2;
POINTint p11,p22;

p1.x = 1;
p1.y = 1;
p1.z = 1;
```

```
p2.x = 5;
p2.y = 3;
p2.z = -1;

p11  = World2DToDevice(World3DToWorld2D(p1));
p22  = World2DToDevice(World3DToWorld2D(p2));
line(p11.x,p11.y,p22.x,p22.y);
```

Listing 9.1 presents a complete application of the previous routines.

Listing 9.1. Drawing points and lines in 3-D (DRAW.C).

```
/* DRAW.C      Drawing 3D Lines and Points */

#include <conio.h>
#include <stdio.h>
#include <stdlib.h>
#include <graphics.h>
#include <math.h>

#define TOL 0.0005
#define PI   3.14159265358979323846

typedef struct {
   float x,y,z;
} POINT3D;

typedef struct {
 int x,y;
} POINTint;


/* World Limits in 2D */
float WXleft;
float WXright;
float WYtop;
float WYbottom;

/* Device Limits */
int DXmin;
int DYmin;
int DYmax;
int DXmax;

/* Rotations for 3D View in Radians*/
float RX;
float RY;
float RZ;
float COSRX;
float SINRX;
float COSRY;
float SINRY;
float COSRZ;
float SINRZ;

void InitGraphics(void);
float DegToRad(float deg);
```

```
float RadToDeg(float rad);
POINT3D World3DToWorld2D(POINT3D p);
POINTint World2DToDevice(POINT3D p);
void drawpoint(POINT3D p1);
void drawline(POINT3D p1,POINT3D p2);
void drawaxis(void);
void SetAxesAngles(float rx, float ry, float rz);


void main()
{
  POINT3D p;
  InitGraphics();

  /* World Limits */
  WXleft   = -1.2;
  WXright  =  1.2;
  WYtop    =  1.2;
  WYbottom = -1.2;

  /* Device Limits On A Viewport */
  DXmin = 0.0;
  DYmin = 0.0;
  DYmax = getmaxy()/2;
  DXmax = getmaxy()/2;

  /* Draw A 2X2 Grid */
  setcolor(WHITE);
  rectangle(0,0,getmaxy(),getmaxy());
  line(getmaxy()/2,0,getmaxy()/2,getmaxy());
  line(0,getmaxy()/2,getmaxy(),getmaxy()/2);

  /* Initialize a 3D point */
  p.x = 0.5;
  p.y = 0.2;
  p.z = 0.5;

  /* TOP VIEW */
  setviewport(0,0,getmaxy()/2,getmaxy()/2,1);
  SetAxesAngles(90, 0, 0);
  drawaxis();
  drawpoint(p);

  /* ISO VIEW */
  setviewport(getmaxy()/2,0,getmaxy(),getmaxy()/2,1);
  SetAxesAngles(20, -15, -5);
  drawaxis();
  drawpoint(p);

  /* FRONT VIEW */
  setviewport(0,getmaxy()/2,getmaxy()/2,getmaxy(),1);
  SetAxesAngles(0, 0, 0);
  drawaxis();
  drawpoint(p);

  /* SIDE VIEW */
  setviewport(getmaxy()/2,getmaxy()/2,getmaxy(),getmaxy(),1);
  SetAxesAngles(0, -90, 0);
```

continues

Listing 9.1. continued

```c
  drawaxis();
  drawpoint(p);

  getch();
  closegraph();
}

/* ///////////////////////////////////////////////////// */

void InitGraphics(void)
{
 int gdriver = DETECT, gmode, errorcode;
 initgraph(&gdriver, &gmode, "");
 if (gdriver != VGA) {
  printf("VGA graphics card required.\n");
  exit(1);
}
 errorcode = graphresult();
 if (errorcode != grOk)  /* an error occurred */
 {
   printf("Graphics error: %s\n", grapherrormsg(errorcode));
   printf("Press any key to halt:");
   getch();
   exit(1); /* terminate with an error code */
}
  setviewport(0,0,getmaxx(),getmaxy(),1);
}

float DegToRad(float deg)
{
 return(deg*PI/180.0);
}

float RadToDeg(float rad)
{
 return(rad*180.0/PI);
}

void SetAxesAngles(float rx, float ry, float rz) {
    RX = DegToRad(rx);
    RY = DegToRad(ry);
    RZ = DegToRad(rz);
    COSRX = cos(RX);
    SINRX = sin(RX);
    COSRY = cos(RY);
    SINRY = sin(RY);
    COSRZ = cos(RZ);
    SINRZ = sin(RZ);
}


POINT3D World3DToWorld2D(POINT3D p)
{
  POINT3D ptemp;
  ptemp = p;
  if (RX) {
```

```
                ptemp.x  = p.x;
                ptemp.y  = COSRX*p.y - SINRX*p.z;
                ptemp.z  = SINRX*p.y + COSRX*p.z;
                p = ptemp;
    }
    if (RY) {
                ptemp.x  = COSRY*p.x + SINRY*p.z;
                ptemp.y  = p.y;
                ptemp.z  = -SINRY*p.x + COSRY*p.z;
                p = ptemp;
    }
    if (RZ) {
                ptemp.x  = COSRZ*p.x - SINRZ*p.y;
                ptemp.y  = SINRZ*p.x + COSRZ*p.y;
                ptemp.z  = p.z;
    }
    if (fabs(ptemp.x) < TOL)  ptemp.x = 0.0;
    if (fabs(ptemp.y) < TOL)  ptemp.y = 0.0;
    if (fabs(ptemp.z) < TOL)  ptemp.z = 0.0;
    return(ptemp);
}


POINTint World2DToDevice(POINT3D p)
{
 POINTint ptemp;
 ptemp.x = (WXleft-p.x)*(DXmax-DXmin)/(WXleft-WXright) + DXmin + 0.5;
 ptemp.y = (WYtop-p.y)*(DYmax-DYmin)/(WYtop-WYbottom) + DYmin + 0.5;
 return(ptemp);
}


void drawpoint(POINT3D p1)
{
 /* draws a 3D point   */
 POINTint p2;
 p1.z = -p1.z;
 p2 = World2DToDevice(World3DToWorld2D(p1));
 rectangle(p2.x - 2, p2.y - 2, p2.x + 2, p2.y + 2);
}


void drawline(POINT3D p1,POINT3D p2)
{
 /* draws a 3D line  */
 POINTint p11,p22;
 p1.z = -p1.z;
 p2.z = -p2.z;
 p11  = World2DToDevice(World3DToWorld2D(p1));
 p22  = World2DToDevice(World3DToWorld2D(p2));
 line(p11.x,p11.y,p22.x,p22.y);
}


void drawaxis(void) {
  POINT3D p1,p2;

  p1.x = p1.y = p1.z = 0;
  p2.x = 1; p2.y = 0; p2.z=0;
  setcolor(RED);
  drawline(p1,p2);
```

continues

Listing 9.1. continued

```
p2.x = 0; p2.y = 1; p2.z=0;
setcolor(GREEN);
drawline(p1,p2);

p2.x = 0; p2.y = 0; p2.z=1;
setcolor(BLUE);
drawline(p1,p2);

setcolor(WHITE);
}
```

Listing 9.1 applies all the concepts that we have described so far. Observe how four viewports are created, and on each one different rotation angles are defined through the use of the function SetAxesAngles(). In order to indicate which view is being seen, I created a function called drawaxis(), which draws a 3-D axis using the colors RED, GREEN, and BLUE for the X-, Y-, and Z-axes, respectively. In addition, a point p was created and drawn on each viewport. This was done to show how the point would look from each observer viewpoint. Figure 9.6 displays the screen output.

FIGURE 9.6.
Output from DRAW.C.

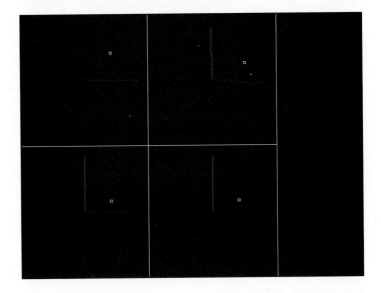

Now that you have most of the 3-D drawing aspects covered, take a look at other features that will become handy for your 3-D modeler.

Creating a Grid

In the process of developing a 3-D modeling program, 2-D grids are a handy feature to have. Grids can be used to determine relative position of objects or points in space. Another feature is the ability to use the mouse to select points on the grid where grid lines meet, known as "grid points." As always, you'll make your life easier by creating a structure to group all those parameters that will be related to the definition of a grid. The structure has been called GRID

```
typedef struct {
   float rmin, cmin,
         rowstep,colstep;
   int rows, cols;
} GRID;
```

and consists of the following parameters:

rmin, cmin	Lower-left coordinates of the 2-D grid in world coordinates
rowstep, colstep	Distance between each row and each column, in world coordinates
rows, cols	Number of rows and columns (assume same number for both)

To declare a variable as being of the GRID type, simply include the statement GRID g; in your code. In this case the variable g is now of the type GRID. An additional variable that you need to create is called GridRowCol, and it saves the number of rows and columns in the grid. The variable holds an integer.

Since the grid will be dependent on the limits of the current viewport, you'll create a function called UpdateGridStatus() that will take care of updating the grid parameters, usually before drawing the grid on the screen:

```
void UpdateGridStatus(void)
{
  g.rmin = WXleft;
  g.cmin = WYbottom;
  g.rowstep = (fabs(WYbottom)+ fabs(WYtop)) / (float)GridRowCol;
  g.colstep = (fabs(WXleft)+ fabs(WXright)) / (float)GridRowCol;
  g.rows = GridRowCol;
  g.cols = GridRowCol;
}
```

Observe how UpdateGridStatus() uses the variables WXleft, WYbottom, and GridRowCol to update the grid parameters. The variable g must be already declared as a GRID.

The final step is then to draw the grid:

```
void drawgrid (void)
{
   int j;
   float rmax,cmax;
```

```
    POINT3D p1,p2;
    rmax = g.rmin+g.rowstep*(g.rows);
    cmax = g.cmin+g.colstep*(g.cols);
    setcolor(LIGHTGRAY);
    for (j=0;j<g.cols+1;j++) {
      p1.x = g.cmin+j*g.colstep;
      p1.y = rmax;
      p1.z = 0.0;
      p2.x = g.cmin+j*g.colstep;
      p2.y = g.rmin,
      p2.z = 0.0;
      drawline(p1,p2);
    }
    for (j=0;j<g.rows+1;j++) {
      p1.x = g.cmin;
      p1.y = g.rmin+j*g.rowstep;
      p1.z = 0.0;
      p2.x = cmax;
      p2.y = g.rmin+j*g.rowstep;
      p2.z = 0.0;
      drawline(p1,p2);
    }
    setcolor(WHITE);
}
```

In order to test the previous code, modify the `main()` function in Listing 9.1 (DRAW.C) to look like Listing 9.2.

Listing 9.2. DRAW.C modified `main()` function (from DRAWGRID.C).

```
void main()
{
  POINT3D p;
  InitGraphics();

  /* World Limits */
  WXleft   = -1.5;
  WXright  =  1.5;
  WYtop    =  1.5;
  WYbottom = -1.5;

  /* Device Limits On A Viewport */
  DXmin = 0.0;
  DYmin = 0.0;
  DYmax = getmaxy()/2;
  DXmax = getmaxy()/2;

  /* Draw A 2X2 Grid */
  setcolor(WHITE);
  rectangle(0,0,getmaxy(),getmaxy());
  line(getmaxy()/2,0,getmaxy()/2,getmaxy());
  line(0,getmaxy()/2,getmaxy(),getmaxy()/2);

  /* Initialize a 3D point */
  p.x = 0.5;
  p.y = 0.2;
  p.z = 0.5;
```

```
GridRowCol = 6;

/* TOP VIEW */
setviewport(0,0,getmaxy()/2,getmaxy()/2,1);
SetAxesAngles(90, 0, 0);
UpdateGridStatus();
drawgrid();
drawaxis();
drawpoint(p);

/* ISO VIEW */
setviewport(getmaxy()/2,0,getmaxy(),getmaxy()/2,1);
SetAxesAngles(20, -15, -5);
UpdateGridStatus();
drawgrid();
drawaxis();
drawpoint(p);

/* FRONT VIEW */
setviewport(0,getmaxy()/2,getmaxy()/2,getmaxy(),1);
SetAxesAngles(0, 0, 0);
UpdateGridStatus();
drawgrid();
drawaxis();
drawpoint(p);

/* SIDE VIEW */
setviewport(getmaxy()/2,getmaxy()/2,getmaxy(),getmaxy(),1);
SetAxesAngles(0, -90, 0);
UpdateGridStatus();
drawgrid();
drawaxis();
drawpoint(p);

getch();
closegraph();
}
```

NOTE

Don't forget that the grid variable g and the integer variable GridRowCol must be defined globally, plus you must add the functions UpdateGridStatus() and drawgrid() to the program listing.

As you can see, before drawing the grid, you make a call to UpdateGridStatus(). This guarantees that if the world coordinate limits have been changed, the grid will take that into account.

An interesting comment is that even though the grid was drawn on all four views, it didn't show up in the top or side views. Why? The drawgrid() function uses the xy plane to draw the grid. From the top or side view, the grid will look like a line. Recall that the grid is two-dimensional.

Snap Feature

Snap is the ability to select a grid point. This is useful when you want to create points that are exactly located at the intersection of two grid lines. The snap function uses grid information to calculate which grid point is nearer to a reference point that has been created. A snap function works in conjunction with a grid. When snap is enabled, only points that are located where the grid lines intersect are acceptable. If the user clicks near a grid point, the nearest grid point location is returned.

For example, let's assume that you wish to create a rectangular box with some given dimensions. We move the mouse to a point and click the left button. If the snap feature is enabled, the snap function will return the nearest grid point to the mouse location, not the mouse location itself. Sometimes it is very difficult to create a vertical or horizontal line, but with the aid of the snap to grid feature, you can be sure of selecting two points that will define a vertical or horizontal line. Let's take a look at the GetGridPoint2D() function:

```
void GetGridPoint2D(int mx,int my, float * wx, float * wy)
{
 int nx,ny;
 ScreenToWorld2D(mx,my,wx,wy);
 nx = (*wx - g.cmin) / (float)g.colstep + .5;
 ny = (*wy - g.rmin) / (float)g.rowstep + .5;
 *wx = g.cmin + nx * g.colstep;
 *wy = g.rmin + ny * g.rowstep;
}
```

The function GetGridPoint2D() accepts two input variables mx, my, which are the x and y location of the mouse cursor in device coordinates. In order to find the nearest 2-D world point, the mouse location has to be converted from screen to world. The resulting values end up in wx, wy. The next two lines of code find how many columns and rows are needed to get near the mouse location. Finally, using those two values, you use the grid information again to locate the coordinates in world values.

The snap function is very handy, but sometimes you may want to turn that feature on or off. This can be accomplished by using the following code:

```
if(SnapStatus == 0)
  ScreenToWorld2D(xpos,ypos,&wx,&wy);
else
  GetGridPoint2D(xpos,ypos,&wx,&wy);
```

The variable SnapStatus has a value of 0 or 1. A value of 0 means that you'll use the straight-forward method of converting the mouse device coordinates into world. If the value is 1 then the snap function kicks in and the point returned will be a grid point.

You can toggle the value of SnapStatus on or off by simply creating an icon that can be selected to enable or disable the feature. In fact, this will be implemented in the 3-D modeling code.

Spline Curve Smoothing

One direct application of the functions ScreenToWorld2D() and GetGridPoint2D() is that you can now use the mouse to create points on the screen. If you create various points on the screen, these points could be saved in a buffer and they can be used to describe a contour. The 3-D modeler that we will be discussing takes a series of points, which define a contour, and creates what is called a "solid of revolution." A solid of revolution is created by sweeping the contour 360 degrees, finishing with a 3-D surface. (See Figure 9.7.)

FIGURE 9.7.

Creating a sweep object.

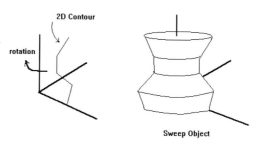

The object starts as a 2-D contour created with a set of points and lines interconnecting those points. The next step is to sweep the curve about the vertical axis. As it sweeps, it creates a new surface and a 3-D object.

The basic tool to create a sweep object is a function that will take a line (or two points), rotate it around the vertical axis, and then connect the original line to the new one, creating a polygon. If this step is performed once, you have then created a segment of a sweep object. If this rotation is, for example, 30 degrees and you do the step 12 times, you'll have 12 segments that will cover 360 degrees (12×30), thus creating the solid of revolution. For another example, say you want to create a four-sided object. You take a line and rotate it four times, and each rotation is 90 degrees. We have then 4×90 = 360 degrees.

Now you need to create a set of variables that will be used to define the amount of segments and the angle included by those segments. You'll use the variables DeltaAngle and Segments to hold the rotation angle and the number of segments, respectively. The function that will accept a line and rotate it by an angle of DeltaAngle degrees and do this Segments number of times will be defined as SweepALine():

```
void SweepALine(POINT3D pa, POINT3D pb) {
  POINT3D p1,p2,p3,p4;
  int i, j;

  MouseShow(0);
  p1 = pa;
  p2 = pb;
  for (j=0;j<Segments;j++) {

    p3.x  =  COSDA*p1.x + SINDA*p1.z;
    p3.y  =  p1.y;
    p3.z  =  -SINDA*p1.x + COSDA*p1.z;

    p4.x  =  COSDA*p2.x + SINDA*p2.z;
    p4.y  =  p2.y;
    p4.z  =  -SINDA*p2.x + COSDA*p2.z;

    drawline(p1,p2);
    drawline(p3,p4);
    drawline(p1,p3);
    drawline(p2,p4);
    p1 = p3;
    p2 = p4;
  }
  MouseShow(1);
}
```

Using this function is very simple. After setting up the viewports and all the graphics initialization code (see DRAW.C, for example), simply define the following global data:

```
float DeltaAngle, COSDA, SINDA;
int Segments;
```

where COSDA= cos(DeltaAngle) and SINDA=sin(DeltaAngle).

After choosing values for DeltaAngle and Segments and calculating COSDA and SINDA, define two points p1 and p2 such as

```
POINT3D p1, p2;
p1.x = 0.1; p1.y = 1; p1.z = 0;
p2.x = 1; p2.y = 0; p2.z = 0;
```

and make the function call SweepALine(p1, p2).

After you start using the function SweepALine(), you'll soon find out you need a large number of lines to create a smooth 3-D object. This becomes cumbersome, but using a smoothing algorithm, that is, an algorithm that will interpolate between the points that you have created, will smooth the contour. Spline curves are ideal for this. A good reference for this material can be found in the book *Computer Graphics*, 2nd Edition, by Donald Hearn and M. Pauline Baker, Prentice-Hall, pages 315 through 327.

Let's explain what's happening inside DrawSpline():

```
void DrawSpline(void) {

  float ax, ay, az, bx, by, bz, cx, cy, cz, dx, dy, dz;
```

```
float S1x, S1y, S1z, S2x, S2y, S2z, t, tt, ttt;
POINT3D T[MAXDATA+2], p1, p2;
int i,j, k;

if(PBnum) {

for (i=1;i<PBnum+1;i++) T[i] = PointBuffer[i-1];
T[0] = T[1];
T[PBnum+1] = T[PBnum];

  for(j = 1;j<=PBnum-1;j++) {
    // components of slope at point j
     S1x = T[j + 1].x - T[j - 1].x;
     S1y = T[j + 1].y - T[j - 1].y;
     S1z = T[j + 1].z - T[j - 1].z;

    // component of slopes at point j+1
     S2x = T[j + 2].x - T[j].x;
     S2y = T[j + 2].y - T[j].y;
     S2z = T[j + 2].z - T[j].z;

    // calc ax, bx, cx, dx based on cubic spline definition
    // most of this is not used since point j is located at t = 0
    // where   0<=t<=1  using  {a}t^3 + {b}t^2 + {c}t + {d}  -> Cubic Spline
    //
    //    ¦ a ¦      ¦  2  -2   1  1 ¦   ¦ x(0)  ¦   <- initial point
    //    ¦ b ¦      ¦ -3   3  -2 -1 ¦   ¦ x(1)  ¦   <- ending  point
    //    ¦ c ¦      ¦  0   0   1  0 ¦   ¦ x'(0) ¦   <- initial slope
    //    ¦ d ¦      ¦  1   0   0  0 ¦   ¦ x'(1) ¦   <- ending  slope
    ax =  2 * T[j].x - 2 * T[j + 1].x + S1x + S2x;
    bx = -3 * T[j].x + 3 * T[j + 1].x - 2 * S1x - S2x;
    cx = S1x;
    dx = T[j].x;

    ay =  2 * T[j].y - 2 * T[j + 1].y + S1y + S2y;
    by = -3 * T[j].y + 3 * T[j + 1].y - 2 * S1y - S2y;
    cy = S1y;
    dy = T[j].y;

    az =  2 * T[j].z - 2 * T[j + 1].z + S1z + S2z;
    bz = -3 * T[j].z + 3 * T[j + 1].z - 2 * S1z - S2z;
    cz = S1z;
    dz = T[j].z;
    for(k=0;k<SplineSmooth + 1;k++) {
            t = k/(float)SplineSmooth;
            tt = t*t;
            ttt = tt *t;
            p1.x = ax * ttt + bx * tt + cx * t + dx;
            p1.y = ay * ttt + by * tt + cy * t + dy;
            p1.z = az * ttt + bz * tt + cz * t + dz;
            if (k==0) p2 = p1;
            else {
              SweepALine(p1, p2);
              p2 = p1;
            }
        }
     }
   }
}
```

Initially, you have a buffer of points called `PointBuffer`. This buffer may have a low number of points in it, which will guarantee that our sweep object will look very flat as opposed to smooth. The spline curve uses the points inside of `PointBuffer` as "control" points. Between every two points, a set of points will be interpolated, creating a smoother transition between control points. (See Figure 9.8.) The variable `SplineSmooth` defines the number of points to be created between two control points. The larger this value is, the smoother the interpolation curve will be (at the expense of computation time).

FIGURE 9.8.

Between every two points, a set of points will be interpolated.

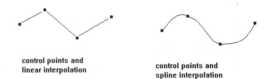

control points and
linear interpolation

control points and
spline interpolation

Next you will see how you can patch this whole code together, using material presented in this chapter and the previous chapter.

Attaching the User Interface

Included with the book you'll find a program called SWEEP.C that is a 3-D modeler to construct sweep objects. The code is around 23 pages long so you'll have to look at some of the more interesting features, such as the function that selects the nearest point in the buffer and how to display the mouse location as it is moved around the screen.

Figures 9.9 and 9.10 display a before and after sequence while using SWEEP.EXE.

FIGURE 9.9.

Creating control points with SWEEP.EXE.

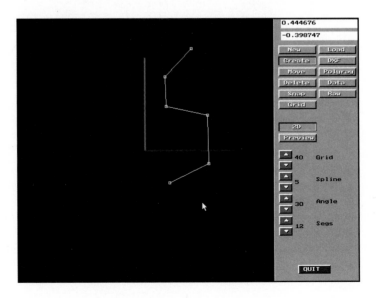

FIGURE 9.10.

Generating the sweep object with SWEEP.EXE.

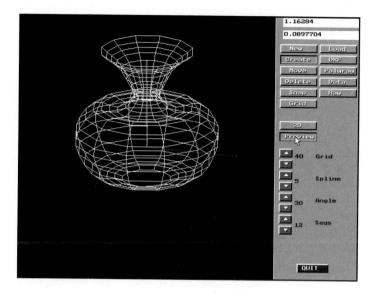

If you observe the main() function inside SWEEP.C, you'll realize that it's the busiest part of the program. Basically, it starts by initializing the graphics screen, any global variables, the mouse, and the icons that are linked to commands. The next step it performs is maintaining a loop, which polls the mouse. The mouse will be checked for its location and the status of its buttons. If a button is pressed, an action will take place. A rather large switch statement is used to test for different conditions. It will check every icon to figure out if it should execute one of the commands. If no icon was selected, it automatically returns to the polling loop until a new event arises.

One of its most interesting features is its capability to give information about the current location of the mouse cursor. By making extensive use of the ScreenToWorld2D() function, the program maintains constant feedback of the cursor's location:

```
void UpdateMousePos(int xpos,int ypos,int status, int draw) {
 int i,j;
 float wx,wy;
 char s[80];
 UpdateGridStatus();
 if(SnapStatus == 0)
  ScreenToWorld2D(xpos,ypos,&wx,&wy);
 else
  GetGridPoint2D(xpos,ypos,&wx,&wy);
 if (fabs(wx) < TOL) wx = 0.0;
 if (fabs(wy) < TOL) wy = 0.0;
 setcolor(15);
 setfillstyle(1,WHITE);
 bar3d(getmaxy()+15, 3,getmaxx(),18,0,0);
 bar3d(getmaxy()+15,25,getmaxx(),40,0,0);
 setcolor(0);
 sprintf(s,"%g",wx);
 outtextxy(getmaxy()+17,5,s);
```

```
sprintf(s,"%g",wy);
outtextxy(getmaxy()+17,28,s);
if (status && (PBnum < MAXDATA)) {
  PointBuffer[PBnum].x = wx;
  PointBuffer[PBnum].y = wy;
  PointBuffer[PBnum].z = 0.0;
  setcolor(15);
  MouseShow(0);
  ViewPort3D
  drawpoint(PointBuffer[PBnum]);
  if (PBnum > 0 && draw) drawline(PointBuffer[PBnum],PointBuffer[PBnum-1]);
  MouseShow(1);
  FullScreenViewPort
  PBnum++;
 }
}
```

The function `UpdateMousePos()` not only gives feedback of the cursor's location, but it also adds the current point to the buffer when the value of `status = 1`.

Another interesting feature is its capability to edit points that have been created. Part of the code in the program takes care of deleting or moving the current selected point to a new position. This is accomplished by first selecting a point. The function `SelectAPoint()` takes the x,y location of the mouse as an input. It then scans through the point buffer and calculates which point in the buffer is the nearest to the location of the mouse. The function then returns the index of the nearest point. After you have the index, you can either delete that point by overwriting it or you can replace it with a new created point, therefore executing a move command.

```
int SelectAPoint(int x, int y) {
 float wx, wy, dist1, dist2=3.4e38;
 int i, pnt=-1;

 ScreenToWorld2D(x,y,&wx, &wy);
 if(!PBnum) return(-1);

 for(i=0;i<PBnum;i++) {
    dist1 = (wx - PointBuffer[i].x)*(wx - PointBuffer[i].x) +
            (wy - PointBuffer[i].y)*(wy - PointBuffer[i].y);
    if(dist1 < dist2) {
            dist2 = dist1;
            pnt = i;
    }
 }
 return(pnt);
}
```

The power of the program lies in the simplicity of its functions. By breaking down the needed features into simple functions, you are able to create a truly versatile program. The functions that are being used by this modeler are the basic building block of more complex programs.

In the next chapter you'll cover an important part of any modeler: file i/o functions. A modeler must not only be able to save and retrieve information for itself, but it must also be able to work with standard formats that can be read by other programs. We'll cover this topic in more detail in the next chapter.

Summary

In this chapter you extended your knowledge of coordinate systems to 3-D. We studied how to create a 3-D coordinate system and how to draw points and lines in order to represent objects. In addition, you developed the code to draw 2-D grids on the screen in order to be able to locate points more precisely, and you were presented the snap function that uses grid data to find the nearest grid point to a given control point. Another topic discussed was the creation of sweep objects and how this was accomplished by simply rotating a line segment around a vertical axis. In order to create smoother contours, you added spline curve interpolation. The final section covered briefly how the 3-D functions were linked with the graphics user interface. The program SWEEP.C is a complete 3-D modeler that creates sweep objects. In the next chapter, you'll discuss file i/o functions in more detail.

Output to DXF and Ray Tracers

10

by Alfonso Hermida

Save your 3-D data in various formats to render your models with 3D Studio, Polyray, and other ray tracers.

Adding File I/O Functions to SWEEP.C

The preceding chapter developed a program to generate sweep objects and preview them in wireframe mode. After creating a model, you want to be able to output the data to your favorite renderer or ray tracer to create a photo-realistic image. This chapter discusses various formats: the Drawing eXchange Format (DXF), triangle-based data (RAW), direct output to the Polyray ray tracer, and the POV ray tracer. The DXF format is a standard that can be read by various professional modeling programs, such as 3D Studio. The RAW data format can be converted to various ray tracers, such as Polyray and Persistence of Vision (POV). Finally, this chapter also discusses a simple format consisting of 3-D points called the Sweep Internal Format (SIF). This SIF format is used to save the outline of the sweep object.

The Sweep Internal Format (SIF)

SWEEP uses the SIF format to read and write the 2-D contours created with the program. The SIF format is simple. It consists of a list of 3-D points, with one 3-D point per line. For example, the list

```
0.265136 0.507307 0
0.524008 0.611691 0
0.628392 0.344468 0
0.298539 0.206681 0
0.194154 -0.148225 0
```

contains five 3-D points. Take a look at two points on that list:

> point #1: x = 0.265136, y = 0.507307, and z = 0
> point #3: x = 0.628392, y = 0.344468, and z = 0

Observe that each coordinate is separated by a space.

To save and read the SIF format, the functions SaveAFile() and LoadAFile() will be used. The function SaveAFile() saves every point inside the PointBuffer array. You know the number of points inside the buffer thanks to the variable PBnum. The function LoadAFile() reads a SIF-formatted file and loads the points back into the buffer. Finally, it updates the value of PBnum to take into account the current database. Both functions require a character string parameter. This string contains the name of the file to be either saved or read.

```
void SaveAFile(char *str)
{
 FILE *fptr;
 int i=1;
 char s[40];
 sprintf(s,"Overwrite < %s > ?",str);
```

```
    if ((fptr = fopen(str,"r")) != NULL) i = YesNoCMD(s);
    fclose(fptr);
    if (i) {
        if ((fptr = fopen(str,"w+t")) == NULL) {
                printf("\7");
                Redraw();

        }
        else {
          if(PBnum) {
                for(i=0;i<PBnum;i++)
                    fprintf(fptr,"%g %g %g\n",PointBuffer[i].x,
                                                PointBuffer[i].y,
                                                PointBuffer[i].z);
                    fclose(fptr);
        }
      }
    }
    Redraw();
}
```

Observe that the two lines

```
sprintf(s,"Overwrite < %s > ?",str);
if ((fptr = fopen(str,"r")) != NULL) i = YesNoCMD(s);
```

check whether the filename given is already being used by another file. If so, the user is asked whether the file should be overwritten.

The next function reads SIF files. The only special feature on this routine is that the fscanf() function is checked to ensure that a value has been read from the file. This action is taken in case a file has empty lines between data points.

```
void LoadAFile(char *str)
{
 FILE *fptr;
 float x,y,z,r,s;
 int bnum;
 if (   (fptr = fopen(str,"r")) == NULL) {
                printf("\7");
                Redraw();
 }
 else {
     bnum = -1;
     while (!feof(fptr)) {
            if ((fscanf(fptr,"%f",&x) > 0) &&
                (fscanf(fptr,"%f",&y) > 0) &&
                (fscanf(fptr,"%f",&z) > 0)) {
                    bnum++;
                    PointBuffer[bnum].x = x;
                    PointBuffer[bnum].y = y;
                    PointBuffer[bnum].z = z;
            }
     }
     fclose(fptr);
     strcpy(FileName,str);
     PBnum = bnum+1;
 }
}
```

In other words, only if all three `fscanf()` functions return TRUE is the point buffer updated with new data.

Finally, SIF is a straight ASCII format.

Drawing eXchange Format (DXF)

The DXF format can be read by many kinds of programs. For the current purpose, the DXF format can be broken into three sections: the entity section, the data section, and the end-of-data section. The DXF file format is also a straight ASCII format. The first section basically consists of the tokens

```
0
SECTION
2
ENTITIES
```

The ENTITIES word indicates that some type of entity will follow. You will write your 3-D data in terms of rectangular polygons (four vertices). This type of entity, called 3DFACE, is followed by four 3-D points. For example, assume that point #1 has the coordinates x1, y1, and z1. After the 3DFACE keyword, the coordinates are written for point #1 as

```
3DFACE
10
x1
20
y1
30
z1
```

For point #2, they're written as

```
11
x2
21
y2
31
z2
```

and so on. After defining the four points, you need to state that the data is completed:

```
0
ENDSEC
0
EOF
```

Look at sample output for just one polygon with the coordinates

> point #1: <0.494781, 0.265136, 0>
> point #2: <0.31524, 0.524008, 0>
> point #3: <1.93023e-17, 0.524008, -0.31524>
> point #4: <3.02956e-17, 0.265136, -0.494781>

in DXF format:

```
0
SECTION
2
ENTITIES
0
3DFACE
10
0.494781
20
0.265136
30
0
11
0.31524
21
0.524008
31
0
12
1.93023e-17
22
0.524008
32
-0.31524
13
3.02956e-17
23
0.265136
33
-0.494781
0
ENDSEC
0
EOF
```

To save the modeler's data in DXF format, a variable called DXF was created. If the variable DXF is TRUE, the following statements are executed before and after the data is saved to a file:

```
if (DXF) fprintf (DXFfptr,"0\nSECTION\n2\nENTITIES\n");  // add entities section

      ....... the function SweepALine() is executed here!.......


if (DXF) fprintf (DXFfptr,"0\nENDSEC\n0\nEOF\n");            // add end of file section
```

Inside the SweepALine() function is included the section of code that saves the 3DFACE output:

```
if (DXF) {
        fprintf(DXFfptr,"0\n3DFACE\n10\n%g\n20\n%g\n30\n%g\n",p1.x,p1.y,p1.z);
        fprintf(DXFfptr,             "11\n%g\n21\n%g\n31\n%g\n",p2.x,p2.y,p2.z);
        fprintf(DXFfptr,             "12\n%g\n22\n%g\n32\n%g\n",p4.x,p4.y,p4.z);
        fprintf(DXFfptr,             "13\n%g\n23\n%g\n33\n%g\n",p3.x,p3.y,p3.z);
}
```

The preceding section of code also depends on the variable DXF being TRUE. It is important to take the following steps:

1. Use fopen() to initialize the file pointer and open the file.

2. Execute the statement

   ```
   fprintf (DXFfptr,"0\nSECTION\n2\nENTITIES\n");
   ```

   before saving any DXF 3-D data.

3. Loop through all the polygons to be saved with the following statements:

   ```
   fprintf(DXFfptr,"0\n3DFACE\n10\n%g\n20\n%g\n30\n%g\n",p1.x,p1.y,p1.z);
   fprintf(DXFfptr, "11\n%g\n21\n%g\n31\n%g\n",p2.x,p2.y,p2.z);
   fprintf(DXFfptr, "12\n%g\n22\n%g\n32\n%g\n",p4.x,p4.y,p4.z);
   fprintf(DXFfptr, "13\n%g\n23\n%g\n33\n%g\n",p3.x,p3.y,p3.z);
   ```

4. Execute the following statement:

   ```
   fprintf (DXFfptr,"0\nENDSEC\n0\nEOF\n");
   ```

5. Use fclose() to close the file.

Figures 10.1 and 10.2 present a model created in SWEEP that was saved as a DXF file and loaded in 3D Studio. Figure 10.3 displays the corresponding model rendered with 3D Studio.

FIGURE 10.1.

A model created in SWEEP.

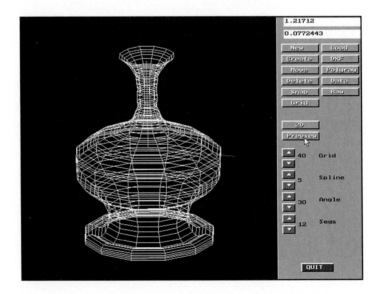

FIGURE 10.2.

A model created in SWEEP and loaded in 3D Studio.

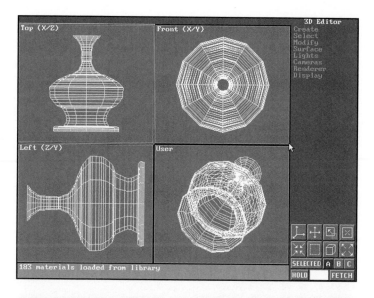

FIGURE 10.3.

A model rendered with 3D Studio.

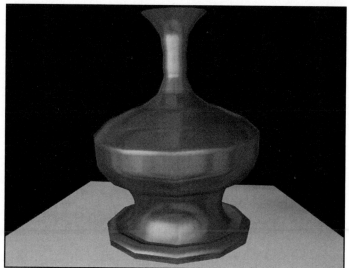

The RAW Format

Some programs can't read DXF-formatted files but have their own internal formats. For example, the Polyray ray tracer accepts polygons in the form

```
object {
    polygon n, <x1, y1,z1>, <x2, y2, z2>, .....,<xn, yn, zn>
}
```

where

> *n* is the number of points in the polygon (*n* must be 3 or greater), and
> `<x1, y1, z1>, <x2, y2, z2>, .....,<xn, yn, zn>` is the list of 3-D points that
> define the polygon.

On the other hand, other ray tracers such as POV accept triangle objects in the form

```
triangle {< x1 , y1 , z1 >, < x2 , y2 , z2 >, < x3 , y3 , z3 >}
```

The type of format POV supports is referred to as RAW data, that is, triangle-based data.
RAW data files are basically a long list of vertex information used to construct triangles.
For example, if two triangles have the vertices

> triangle #1: <x1,y1,z1>, <x2, y2, z2>, <x3,y3,z3>
> triangle #2: <x4,y4,z4>, <x5, y5, z5>, <x6,y6,z6>

the RAW data file looks like this:

```
x1 y1 z1 x2 y2 z2 x3 y3 z3
x4 y4 z4 x5 y5 z5 x6 y6 z6
```

In other words, each triangle is written on a line. This method saves the 3-D data in a
general format. If you want to convert this data to POV, then by writing a small conversion program, you can translate raw triangle data into POV-compatible data. You'll perform this task later in this section.

In a similar fashion to the DXF output routines, the variable RAW is defined to indicate
whether you want to save the data as DXF. If the variable RAW is TRUE, the routine
SweepALine() saves the data generated in RAW format using the following code:

```
if (RAW) {
        fprintf(RAWfptr,"%g %g %g %g %g %g %g %g %g\n",p1.x,p1.y,p1.z,
                                                       p2.x,p2.y,p2.z,
                                                       p3.x,p3.y,p3.z);
        fprintf(RAWfptr,"%g %g %g %g %g %g %g %g %g\n",p2.x,p2.y,p2.z,
                                                       p4.x,p4.y,p4.z,
                                                       p3.x,p3.y,p3.z);
}
```

There is an interesting detail you should study. The SWEEP program creates four-vertex
polygons, and the RAW data format requires three-vertex objects. Recall that SWEEP takes
a line, makes a copy of it, and rotates it about an axis a certain number of degrees. It ends
up with two line segments or four points (vertices). Therefore, you must subdivide each
four-vertex polygon into two three-vertex polygons. Figure 10.4 displays a four-vertex
polygon with the points p1, p2, p3, and p4. This polygon is subdivided into two triangles,
A and B. Because most ray tracers accept triangle-based objects, you can easily write a

program that reads each triangle and converts it to your favorite program. A polygon can be subdivided into any number of triangles. For example, given a four-vertex polygon (generated with SWEEP) with the vertices p1, p2, p3, and p4, you can find the center point pc of the rectangle and create the following triangles:

```
triangle #1: p1, pc, p2
triangle #2: p1, p4, pc
triangle #3: p4, p3, pc
triangle #4: p3, p2, pc
```

In other words, each four-vertex polygon was divided into four triangles. This increase in the number of triangles also increases the file size and the amount of memory needed by other programs to load them and generate an image.

FIGURE 10.4.

Subdividing rectangular polygons into triangles.

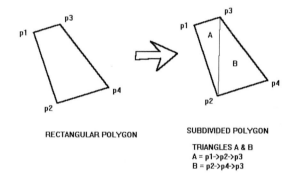

RECTANGULAR POLYGON

SUBDIVIDED POLYGON

TRIANGLES A & B
A = p1->p2->p3
B = p2->p4->p3

Look over Listing 10.1a, RAW2POV.C (a RAW to POV translator), and Listing 10.1b, RAW2POLY.C (a RAW to Polyray translator).

Listing 10.1a. RAW2POV.C—RAW to POV.

```c
#include <stdio.h>
#include <stdlib.h>

void main(int argc, char*argv[]) {

  FILE *infile, *outfile;
  float x1, y1, z1,
        x2, y2, z2,
        x3, y3, z3;

  if(argc < 2) {
    printf("Usage: RAW2POV inputfile outputfile\n");
    exit(1);
  }

  if ((infile = fopen(argv[1], "rt")) == NULL) {
    printf("Can't open %s!\n",argv[1]);
    exit(1);
```

continues

Listing 10.1a. continued

```
    }

    if ((outfile = fopen(argv[2], "wt")) == NULL) {
      printf("Can't open %s!\n",argv[2]);
      exit(1);
    }

    fprintf(outfile," union {\n");

    while (!feof(infile)) {
     if ((fscanf(infile,"%f",&x1) > 0) &&
            (fscanf(infile,"%f",&y1) > 0) &&
            (fscanf(infile,"%f",&z1) > 0) &&
            (fscanf(infile,"%f",&x2) > 0) &&
            (fscanf(infile,"%f",&y2) > 0) &&
            (fscanf(infile,"%f",&z2) > 0) &&
            (fscanf(infile,"%f",&x3) > 0) &&
            (fscanf(infile,"%f",&y3) > 0) &&
            (fscanf(infile,"%f",&z3) > 0)) {
            fprintf(outfile,"    triangle {<%g, %g, %g>, ",x1,y1,z1);
            fprintf(outfile,"<%g, %g, %g>, ",x2,y2,z2);
            fprintf(outfile,"<%g, %g, %g>}\n",x3,y3,z3);
      }
    }

    fprintf(outfile,"    pigment {Red}\n }\n");
    fclose(infile);
    fclose(outfile);
}
```

Listing 10.1b. RAW2POLY.C—RAW to Polyray.

```
#include <stdio.h>
#include <stdlib.h>

void main(int argc, char *argv[]) {

  FILE *infile, *outfile;
  float x1, y1, z1,
        x2, y2, z2,
        x3, y3, z3;
  int count = 0;

  if(argc < 2) {
    printf("Usage: RAW2POLY inputfile outputfile\n");
    exit(1);
  }

  if ((infile = fopen(argv[1], "rt")) == NULL) {
    printf("Can't open %s!\n",argv[1]);
    exit(1);
  }
```

```
    if ((outfile = fopen(argv[2], "wt")) == NULL) {
      printf("Can't open %s!\n",argv[2]);
      exit(1);
    }

    fprintf(outfile," object{\n");

      while (!feof(infile)) {
        if ((fscanf(infile,"%f",&x1) > 0) &&
              (fscanf(infile,"%f",&y1) > 0) &&
              (fscanf(infile,"%f",&z1) > 0) &&
              (fscanf(infile,"%f",&x2) > 0) &&
              (fscanf(infile,"%f",&y2) > 0) &&
              (fscanf(infile,"%f",&z2) > 0) &&
              (fscanf(infile,"%f",&x3) > 0) &&
              (fscanf(infile,"%f",&y3) > 0) &&
              (fscanf(infile,"%f",&z3) > 0)) {
              if(count)
                fprintf(outfile, "   + object {");
              else
                fprintf(outfile, "     object {");
              fprintf(outfile, " polygon 3, ");
              fprintf(outfile, "<%g, %g, %g>,",x1,y1,z1);
              fprintf(outfile, "<%g, %g, %g>,",x2,y2,z2);
              fprintf(outfile, "<%g, %g, %g>}\n" ,x3,y3,z3);
              count++;
        }
      }

    fprintf(outfile,"        shiny_red\n }\n");

    fclose(infile);
    fclose(outfile);
}
```

The program RAW2POV.C is easy to use. Simply create a RAW data file inside SWEEP and then run RAW2POV. Assume that the RAW object file is named test.raw and you want to create a POV file named out.pov. At the command line in DOS, type

RAW2POV test.raw out.pov [press Enter]

POV data files that use triangle objects tend to be large and will require large amounts of memory when rendering.

If you decide to use the POV ray tracer with the output created by RAW2POV.C, you'll soon find that the object is displayed as a faceted surface; that is, it is not a smooth surface. This effect occurs because the output from RAW2POV is that of flat surfaces to begin with. Can the surface be smoothed somehow? Yes. To understand how a faceted surface can be "smoothed," you must understand the concept of a normal vector.

Smoothing Faceted Objects Through the Use of Normal Vectors

Any surface, such as a surface on a polygon created with SWEEP, has a normal vector. The word "normal" is used to denote that something is perpendicular (at 90 degrees) to something else. In this case, you can think of a normal vector as an "arrow" that is stuck to a flat surface and that is at 90 degrees to the surface itself. For example, the axle of a car's wheel is perpendicular to the plane of the wheel itself. Why do we need normal vectors? Rendering and ray tracing methods are used to create photo-realistic images, and these methods take into account the angle between the normal vector of a given surface and the light source, such as the sun. The normal vector can tell us whether the surface is looking at the light source itself. To calculate the intensity of light and color on a given surface, the rendering methods will also use the normal vector information.

On a flat surface (surfaces are represented by rectangles; see Figure 10.5a), the normal vector (the arrows coming out of the surfaces themselves) is the same at any point. Each surface has a unique normal vector. The vectors might or might not be related in some way to each other. On the other hand, a smooth surface (see Figure 10.5b) has normal vectors that vary smoothly with the surface. Each of the vectors was calculated taking into account the normals that are nearby. When the intensity of color is calculated for a smooth surface, the colors also have a smooth transition, as opposed to flat surfaces, which have drastic changes in color intensity.

Figure 10.5 displays the difference between a flat surface and a smooth surface in terms of their normal vectors.

FIGURE 10.5.

A flat surface and a smooth surface.

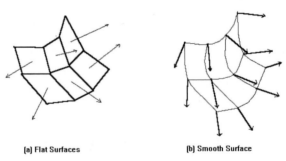

[a] Flat Surfaces   [b] Smooth Surface

(arrows represent normal vectors)

If the surfaces created with SWEEP were flat to begin with, how do they get curved and smoothed? The answer is they don't. The rendering method uses the normal vector information to calculate the color intensity to give the impression that the surface is curved. The details of the different methods are beyond the scope of this chapter, but the next section does cover a method used by Polyray to create curved surfaces out of 2-D contour points.

Saving to Polyray's LATHE Format

Polyray's LATHE format takes into account that an object can be constructed by sweeping a 2-D contour about an axis. This is precisely the method employed by SWEEP. The LATHE format is simple and clean:

```
object {
    lathe type, axis, n,
    <x1, y1, z1>,
    <x2, y2, z2>,
    <x3, y3, z3>,
        ...etc...
    <xn, yn, zn>
}
```

where

`n`	is the number of points in the 2-D contour to be swept
`type`	has the value 1 (flat surface), 2 (smooth surface)
`axis`	has the form `<x,y,z>`, which indicates the axis of rotation
	SWEEP uses the vector `<0,1,0>` (the Y-axis)

Consider an example in which 10 points were defined for the contour and the object will be modeled as a smooth surface. The sweep will be done about the Y-axis:

```
object {
    lathe 2, <0, 1, 0>, 10,
    <0.248434, 0.524008, 0>,
    <0.444676, 0.590814, 0>,
    <0.569937, 0.494781, 0>,
    <0.607516, 0.340292, 0>,
    <0.448852, 0.194154, 0>,
    <0.298539, 0.0605428, 0>,
    <0.281837, -0.19833, 0>,
    <0.356994, -0.340292, 0>,
    <0.507307, -0.611691, 0>,
    <0.469729, -0.778706, 0>
}
```

Figure 10.6 displays the difference between smooth (2) and flat (1) surface modeling.

FIGURE 10.6.

Smooth and flat surface models in Polyray.

(2)　　　　　　(1)

Even though both objects use the same contour data, the left object uses the smooth type, whereas the right object was generated using the flat surface type. Besides the smoothness difference, the left object takes more computation time to generate than the right one. Therefore, you can use the flat type when doing previews of an object and then use the smooth type when creating the final image.

Listing 10.2 presents the Polyray scene file used to generate Figure 10.6.

Listing 10.2. A sample Polyray application of lathe objects.

```
include "colors.inc"
include "texture.inc"

// Camera Definition
viewpoint {
    from <0,2,-4.5>
    at <0,0,0>
    up <0,1,0>
    angle 45
    resolution 640, 480
    aspect 640/480
    }

// Background Color And Light Sources
background white
light <0,100, 0>
light <-10, 3, -20>
light <10, 3, -20>

// Smooth Object Definition
object {
    lathe 2, <0, 1, 0>, 10,
      <0.248434, 0.524008, 0>,
      <0.444676, 0.590814, 0>,
      <0.569937, 0.494781, 0>,
      <0.607516, 0.340292, 0>,
      <0.448852, 0.194154, 0>,
      <0.298539, 0.0605428, 0>,
      <0.281837, -0.19833, 0>,
      <0.356994, -0.340292, 0>,
      <0.507307, -0.611691, 0>,
      <0.469729, -0.778706, 0>
      translate<-1,0,0>
      shiny_red
}

// Flat Object Definition
object {
    lathe 1, <0, 1, 0>, 10,
      <0.248434, 0.524008, 0>,
      <0.444676, 0.590814, 0>,
      <0.569937, 0.494781, 0>,
      <0.607516, 0.340292, 0>,
      <0.448852, 0.194154, 0>,
      <0.298539, 0.0605428, 0>,
```

```
    <0.281837, -0.19833, 0>,
    <0.356994, -0.340292, 0>,
    <0.507307, -0.611691, 0>,
    <0.469729, -0.778706, 0>
    translate<1,0,0>
    shiny_red
}
```

Observe that both lathe objects are identical. The first one was simply defined as a smooth object, whereas the second one has the flat surface. The statements `translate<-1,0,0>` and `translate<1,0,0>` are used to move the object apart, because the contour data is the same. If you don't quite follow the Polyray syntax, don't be concerned. In the next chapter, you'll get a brief introduction to Polyray's syntax so that you can create your own scenes using SWEEP.

How can you take the same data and create a smooth or a flat surface finish? Recall Figure 9.8 in the preceding chapter. The left image presents what occurs when linear interpolation is applied to a set of control points; the right image displays the use of spline interpolation on the same control points. When the "smooth" type is selected, Polyray uses the 2-D contour points as control points for a spline interpolation routine. This routine generates smoother transition between the control points, which in turn uses lots of computation time. The results are excellent. When the "flat" type is selected, Polyray simply creates an object that looks very similar to what shows up when you select the PREVIEW command in SWEEP. The object appears to be composed of flat plates or slabs. If this is the effect you're looking for, you should use it. I recommend the smooth finish.

The routine `SaveToPolyray()` accepts a string as an argument. This string is used as the filename for the Polyray LATHE format file.

```c
void SaveToPolyray(char * str) {
 FILE *fptr;
 int i=1;
 char s[40];
 strcpy(PolyrayFileName,str);
 sprintf(s,"Overwrite < %s > ?",str);
 if ((fptr = fopen(str,"r")) != NULL) i = YesNoCMD(s);
 fclose(fptr);
 if (i) {
    if ((fptr = fopen(str,"w+t")) == NULL) {
            printf("\7");
            Redraw();
    }
    else {
       if(PBnum) {
            fprintf(fptr,"object {\n");
            fprintf(fptr,"    lathe 2, <0, 1, 0>, %d,\n",PBnum);
            for(i=0;i<PBnum;i++) {
                fprintf(fptr,"    <%g, %g, %g>",PointBuffer[i].x,
                                                PointBuffer[i].y,
                                                PointBuffer[i].z);
```

```
        if (i<PBnum)
                fprintf(fptr,",\n");
        else
                fprintf(fptr,"\n      shiny_red\n}");
    }
    fclose(fptr);
  }
 }
}
Redraw();
}
```

Observe that the statements

```
fprintf(fptr,"object {\n");
fprintf(fptr,"    lathe 2, <0, 1, 0>, %d,\n",PBnum);
```

assume smooth surface modeling and Y as the rotation axis. If you observe Listing 10.2, you'll notice that you need to add a few other items, such as the viewpoint object and some light sources, to the Polyray output file to get the image.

Summary

This chapter has covered various formats that can be used to communicate with other applications. You read about the SIF, which is the format used by SWEEP to read and write 2-D contour points created with the program. The two functions `SaveAFile()` and `LoadAFile()` were developed to interface SWEEP with the outside world. The format studied was DXF. This format can be used for people who have 3D Studio. The "minimal" information necessary to save your 3-D objects in DXF was presented.

Next the RAW data format was discussed, which consists of triangle information. Because SWEEP generated four-vertex polygons, you have to subdivide the polygon into two triangles. The RAW data format is handy because it can be converted into many kinds of formats; for example, the program RAW2POV.C was developed to convert RAW data into POV-compatible information.

This chapter also briefly discussed how certain rendering programs use the normal vector information to create the effect of a smooth surface on an object. Finally, Polyray's LATHE format was presented. This format uses a list of 2-D contour points and can create a smooth or a flat surface object. This task is accomplished through the interpolation scheme selected. The user can choose between linear and spline interpolation.

Up to this point, all the tools needed to create a simple 3-D modeling program have been discussed. In the next chapter, you'll read about how SWEEP can be used, and you'll see 3D Studio and Polyray used as examples of commercial and shareware applications.

Rendering 3-D Objects with a Ray Tracer

11

by Alfonso Hermida

Now that you have a 3-D object generator (SWEEP), you can populate your own 3-D universe and create photo-realistic images with the Polyray ray tracer. I will start by discussing what photo-realism is and how it can be achieved.

Creating Photo-Realistic Images

Various levels of modeling are currently being used. The simplest one consists of using a piece of paper and a pencil and drawing a very rough sketch of the object to be modeled. This is the most widely used technique. It has a major disadvantage: If you are like me, you are not an artist, and when you create a sketch you must also explain what you were trying to draw. The next level of modeling is using a 2-D drafting program that helps you draw the object better. Even though this technique is more advanced than paper and pencil, lots of people still have a difficult time visualizing a 2-D drawing as a full 3-D object. The next logical step is then to use a 3-D drawing program where you can create full 3-D objects. Most 3-D drawing programs can perform hidden-line techniques on the geometry in order to draw the object as a solid. This technique is by far the best for modeling and visualization.

What happens when what you are trying to model is a certain "look" and not just pure 3-D geometry? Take for example designers of motorcycles. They use a 3-D CAD (Computer Aided Design) program to create a 3-D model of their newest motorcycle. Most 3-D CAD programs can even shade the object with different colors, but that does not show you how the final motorcycle will look (if it were fabricated). The final step is then to create what is known as a photo-realistic model.

The term *photo-realistic* is used to denote the creation of an image that appears to have a quality similar to that of a true photo of the object being modeled. This is a very powerful tool. Imagine a computer with the capability to create a model that looks almost the same as the final product. If the designer wants to change any of the characteristics of the model, he or she can easily do that with the 3-D CAD program and then regenerate the photo-realistic image.

Various techniques are used to create photo-realistic images of models. One of them is called *ray tracing*, and the results are astounding. The next section discusses ray tracing in more detail and then takes a brief look at Polyray, a shareware ray tracer.

What Is Ray Tracing?

Ray tracing is a technique that models the interaction between light, 3-D objects, the surface characteristics (textures) of these, and an observer. Imagine the following scenario: You are standing in front of a house on a sunny day. As you move to different locations, you observe that a shadow is produced due to the house blocking part of the sun's rays. In other areas, where the light rays hit directly on the house, you observe that the colors seem to have a higher intensity. As you look at some of the windows, you can see through the ones where light does not hit directly, whereas those that receive direct sunlight are difficult to look at.

In the previous scenario, the sun represents the light source, the house represents the 3-D object, and the point of view of the scene was determined by your location and what you were looking at. In other words, you were the observer. Figure 11.1 presents the scenario just described. The arrows represent the sun's rays as they leave from their source, bounce off different objects, and are finally received by the observer's eyes.

FIGURE 11.1.

Basic scene involving a light source, a 3-D object, and an observer.

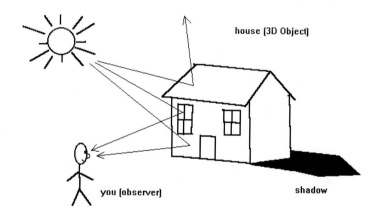

house (3D Object)

you (observer)

shadow

In ray tracing, a similar model is used. Because only those rays of light that are seen by the observer are important, the ray tracer analyzes in the reverse direction—from the eye of the observer to the light source (see Figure 11.2).

Internally, a ray tracing program has the mathematical definition of each object, the light sources, and any necessary surface characteristics in order to generate the photo-realistic image. It is important to know that most of that information is kept hidden from the user, so you don't have to be a math whiz to use a ray tracer.

Figure 11.3 displays a sample ray traced image. The image consists of a tiled floor, a strange wavy red object, and the letters *A* and *B*. Can you tell where the light sources are? (Hint: Check the shadows.) Observe that the letters are highly reflective and you can see the object and the black and white tiles reflected on them. To create such a scene, you have to give the ray tracer information concerning each object: the floor, the letters, the wavy object, the light sources, and the viewpoint of the observer. In addition, you need to assign surface characteristics to each of the 3-D objects. For example, the letters *A* and *B* must have a very smooth surface to be capable of reflecting the light, the tiles on the floor must be white and black and nonreflective, and the wavy object is colored red. All this information is then used by the ray tracer to find out what the path of the light will be as it moves from the source to the observer's eye.

FIGURE 11.2.

Modeling a scene through ray tracing.

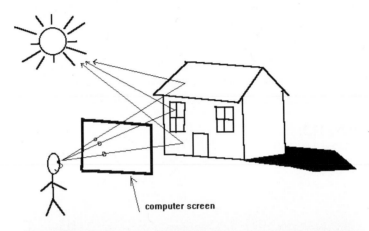

FIGURE 11.3.

Sample ray-traced scene.

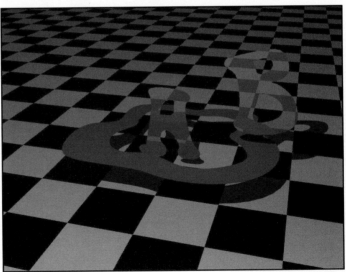

The next section covers ray tracing basic concepts briefly. For a more detailed look at these concepts and techniques, refer to my book *Adventures in Ray Tracing* published by QUE. The book covers Polyray completely, as well as POVCAD, a 3-D modeler.

Basic Concepts

Ray tracing can be broken down into five main concepts: coordinate systems, point of view, light sources, 3-D geometry, and surface properties. I will look at them in some detail now, and then later, as you get ready to use the ray tracer, I'll explain how these concepts apply to Polyray.

3-D Coordinate System

A 3-D coordinate system consists of three axes labeled X, Y, and Z, and it is used to locate objects in 3-D space. Figure 11.4 presents the left-hand and right-hand coordinate systems. Observe that the only difference is the direction of the Z axis. The point where all three axes meet is called the *origin* of the coordinate system.

FIGURE 11.4.

Left-hand and right-hand coordinate systems.

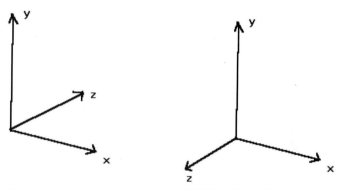

Left-hand coordinate system   Right-hand coordinate system

Polyray, the ray tracer that you will be using shortly, uses the left-hand coordinate system.

Because the left-hand coordinate system has three axes, to locate a point in 3-D space you need three location values called *coordinates*. A 3-D point can be written as <x, y, z>, where x, y, and z are the coordinates of the point in the X-, Y-, and Z-axes, respectively. Figure 11.5 displays various points in a coordinate system.

To visualize how a point is placed on the 3-D coordinate system, assume you have a point <1.0, 2.3, 4.0>. To locate it, take the X coordinate value 1.0 and, starting at the origin, move 1 unit along the X-axis. Now, starting from that point, move 2.3 units up along the Y-axis. Finally from the new location, move 4 units along the Z-axis. This final location is where the point <1.0, 2.3, 4.0> will be. You can start from the origin and move 2.3 units up along Y then 4 units along Z and finally 1 unit along X, and you should end up in the same place.

FIGURE 11.5.

Location of various 3-D points in a coordinate system.

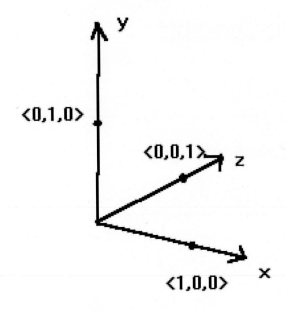

Directions can also be written in the form <x, y, z>. For example, say you want to define a direction along the X-axis. The corresponding direction (also referred to as a *vector*) would be <1,0,0>. In other words, think of an arrow pointing along the X-axis. If the direction vector is along the negative Z-axis, you can use the vector <0,0,-1>. Figure 11.6 presents vectors along the X- and negative Z-axes.

FIGURE 11.6.

Direction vectors along the X- and negative Z-axes.

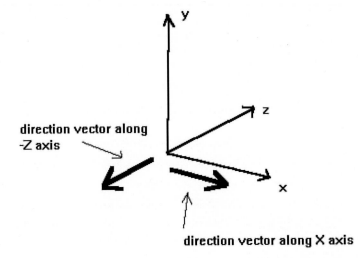

You need to know how to define points in 3-D space and directions because those are necessary elements when defining the observer's point of view.

Observer's Point of View

As I mentioned earlier, an observer determines what will be seen in a scene. To define the observer's point of view, you need to know the location of the observer (FROM location), what the observer is looking at (AT location), and which is the "up" direction from his point of view (UP direction). See Figure 11.7.

In Figure 11.7, the observer is located at FROM, and the eyes are pointing at the origin (the AT location). The UP arrow points to what the observer understands is the "up" direction. Normally you will set the UP direction to <0,1,0>, which is along the Y-axis.

FIGURE 11.7.

Defining the observer's point of view.

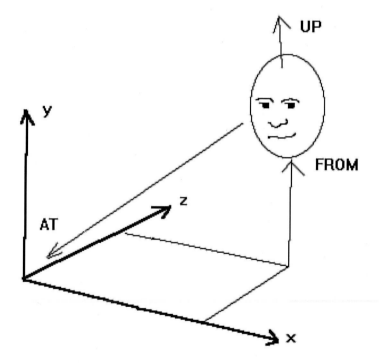

With this information, you can locate the observer in any position and look at any place of interest. Look at Figure 11.8, where the observer is located at a point along the negative X-axis and resting on his side. The UP direction is not along the Y-axis here but along the Z-axis.

FIGURE 11.8.

A different point of view.

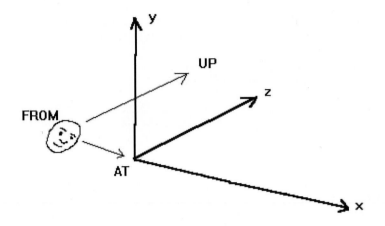

Light Sources

Another important aspect of being able to generate photo-realistic images is the use of light sources. There are two commonly used types of light sources: ambient and spotlight. You can compare the ambient light source to the sun or to a lightbulb. Light is basically dispersed evenly in all directions. In a spotlight, light travels inside a region limited by a cone. You can use any number of light sources in a scene, but I should warn you that increasing the number of light sources increases computation time.

Both of the light sources shown in Figure 11.9 create shadows. Another type of light source, called *directional*, does not create shadows. Directional light sources are useful when modeling a spaceship near a planet, for example. Depending on where the light sources are, you can see a shadow being cast by the spaceship on the planet. Therefore, use directional lights to eliminate this effect.

FIGURE 11.9.

Ambient and spot light sources.

Ambient Light Source

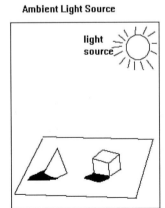

Spot Light Source

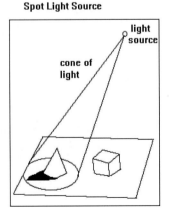

3-D Objects

Having light sources and an observer does not accomplish much if there isn't anything to be seen. Here is where 3-D objects play an important part. Most ray tracers have a set of predefined 3-D objects, called *primitives* (see Figure 11.10). These primitives include objects such as spheres, cones, ellipsoids, tori (donut-shaped objects), cylinders, and others. These predefined objects can be easily placed to create more complex objects. For example, you can look at a car and see that it is composed of one structure that is rectangular-shaped and four others that look like donuts. By using the ray tracer's objects, you can easily create a car-shaped object.

FIGURE 11.10.

Primitive shapes.

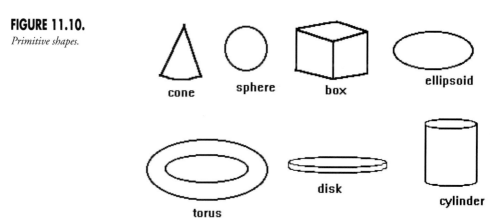

Other types of objects are complex and require additional programs to generate them; for example, the program SWEEP handles the creation of sweep objects. In the following sections you'll use SWEEP and Polyray to create a ray traced scene.

Surface Properties

When you create a 3-D object to represent a real physical object, you must, besides copying the geometry as well as you can, try to simulate the surface of the real object. Is it smooth? shiny? rough? transparent? reflective? bumpy? All these questions and more are used to simulate the real object.

Ray tracers have built-in *shading models*. These are mathematical models that approximate the behavior of surfaces by means of certain parameters. For example, parameters such as transparency, reflectivity, roughness, bumpiness, and diffusivity are used as input values for these shading models.

Take the effects of surface roughness as an example. Figure 11.11 presents what occurs to light when it hits a smooth and a rough surface.

FIGURE 11.11.

Effect of surface roughness on light.

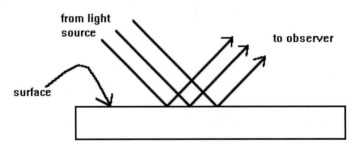

(a) smooth surface

(b) rough surface

When light rays hit a surface, they get reflected. If the surface is smooth, the rays are reflected and stay roughly in the same direction. If rays hit a rough surface, they get dispersed. Figure 11.12 shows a close-up of the surfaces and how they interact with incident light.

FIGURE 11.12.

A close-up of light and surface interaction.

(a) smooth surface

(b) rough surface

In Figure 11.12, one surface is smooth, therefore light rays bounce off the surface and stay parallel to each other. On the other hand, when light rays bounce off a rough surface, due to the irregularities of the surface, they do not stay parallel—they end up going in different directions. Any ray tracer that wishes to create photo-realistic images must therefore be capable of replicating this type of behavior when light bounces off a smooth or a rough surface. This type of study is also done on all the other parameters (transparency, reflectivity, bumpiness, and diffusivity). Needless to say, most of the techniques used in the field of optics are used inside a ray tracer.

Most ray tracers give you the option of using predefined sets of surface properties, known as *textures*. Examples of such textures are checker, marble, wood, gold, copper, mirror, and glass. When a 3-D object has a checker texture, it appears as a checkered surface. To modify the predefined textures, you must then change some or all of the texture parameters.

Ray Tracing with Polyray

After a brief description of the important ray tracing concepts, you are ready to start experimenting with Polyray. Polyray is a shareware ray tracer written by Alexander Enzmann. Polyray is packed with tons of features that basically require a book by itself to present. For now, try to use the minimum amount of information necessary to get Polyray running. The main goal is to be able to use SWEEP for the creation of 3-D objects and Polyray for the photo-realistic image creation. Recall that Polyray has built-in primitives that might be easier to use, but for the sake of experimentation you will not use them.

The next step is to study a simple Polyray scene file that includes all the necessary information to create a photo-realistic image. This step will help you become familiar with Polyray's syntax, which is very similar to C language but easier.

A Detailed Look at a Polyray Scene File

So far I have presented some of the basic concepts behind a ray tracer. The next step will be to take a detailed look at a scene file and divide it into small sections. Each of these sections will show you how each ray tracing concept has been implemented in Polyray. Polyray is not the only ray tracer available, so the syntax that you are about to study is specific to Polyray.

Listing 11.1 presents DEMO.PI, a Polyray specific scene file. The next sections discuss the header, viewpoint, light source, object definition, and texture sections of a scene file.

Listing 11.1. DEMO.PI—Ray tracer scene file example.

```
//DEMO.PI

include "colors.inc"
include "texture.inc"

viewpoint {
 from      <0, 1.0, -5>
 at        <0.0, 0.0, 0.0>
 up        <0.0, 1.0, 0.0>
 angle       45
 resolution  200,200
 aspect      1.0
}

// LIGHT_SOURCE
light <0,  0,  -100>
light <50, 50, -50>

background lightgrey

//PLATE
object {
    polygon 4, <-1,0,-1>, <1,0,-1>, <1,0,1>, <-1,0,1>
    translate <0,-1.5, -0.2>
    texture {
      checker matte_white, matte_black
      scale <0.5, 0.5, 0.5>
    }
}

//BOX
object {
    box <-1, -1, -1>, <1, 1, 1>
    scale <0.5, 0.5, 0.5>
    rotate <-10, 10, 0>
    shiny_green
}

//CYLINDER
object {
    cylinder <0,0,0>, <0,0.4,0>, 0.4
    rotate <-15,0,0>
    translate <-0.8,1.0,0>
    wooden
}

//TORUS
object {
    torus 0.5, 0.1, <0,0,0>, <0,1,0>
    rotate <-30,0,-10>
    translate <0.7, 1.4, 0>
    white_marble
}

//CONE
object {
```

```
    cone <0.0, -1, 0.0>, 0.5, <0.0, 0.0, 0.0>, 0.0
    translate <1.4, 0.48, 0>
    shiny_blue
}

//SPHERE
object {
    sphere < -0.96, 0, -1.12>, 0.25
    shiny_red
}
```

Header Section

The header section of DEMO.PI consists of the following lines:

```
//DEMO.PI

include "colors.inc"
include "texture.inc"
```

The statement `//DEMO.PI` indicates that the scene name is DEMO.PI. The `//` symbol denotes that anything appearing to the right of it will be treated as a comment line. Another way this can be accomplished is by using the symbols `/*` and `*/` at the beginning and end of the comments, respectively:

```
/* This is a comment
    that takes more than 1 line! */
```

The next two lines in the header section are very useful. The keyword `include` is used to indicate that some information that is not in the scene file itself can be found in the file indicated. For example, the color names and additional information can be loaded from the file `colors.inc`, and additional information on the texture definitions can be located in the `texture.inc` file. You can use this feature to simplify scene files by saving objects in different files and then loading them by means of an include statement.

Viewpoint Section

The viewpoint section

```
viewpoint {
  from        <0, 1.0, -5>
  at          <0.0, 0.0, 0.0>
  up          <0.0, 1.0, 0.0>
  angle          45
  resolution     200,200
  aspect         1.0
}
```

declares where the observer is located and related information concerning field of view angle (similar to a camera's field of view), the resolution or size of the final image, and the aspect ratio of the image file itself. If you wish to create an image 640 by 480 pixels, the aspect ratio can be aspect = 640/480 = 1.33.

As I mentioned previously, to locate the observer you need to know where it is located, what it is looking at, and what the UP vector is relative to the observer. In this scene, the observer is located at <0, 1, -5> and is looking at the point <0, 0, 0>, which is the origin. The location of the observer will depend on the point of view you wish to have.

Light Source Section

Light sources are an important part of the ray tracing scene and can be easily declared.

```
// LIGHT_SOURCE
light <0,  0,  -100>
light <50, 50, -50>

background lightgrey
```

In this case, all light sources are considered to be colored white. To change them to different colors, you should use the syntax

```
light color, location
```

> *color* is a keyword describing the color of the light, such as white, red, blue, or green
> *location* is the location of the light, such as <-1, 3.4, 2>

Finally, the line background lightgrey indicates the color of the background in case there are no objects hiding it from the observer. The keyword is background, and the color is lightgrey. Check Polyray's documentation for more details on all the color names and additional features.

Object Definition Section

The object definition section is the most complex of the whole scene. Each object section consists of an object definition, transformations (rotation, scaling, translation), and a texture section, which is covered in the next section.

Start with the checkered plate definition:

```
//PLATE
object {
    polygon 4, <-1,0,-1>, <1,0,-1>, <1,0,1>, <-1,0,1>
    translate <0,-1.5, -0.2>
    texture {
      checker matte_white, matte_black
      scale <0.5, 0.5, 0.5>
      }
}
```

The object consists of a polygon defined by four points. The polygon is located in the XZ plane. To locate the plate in its final place, use the `translate <0,-1.5, -0.2>` statement. This statement indicates that the object will be moved 0 units along the X-axis, -1.5 units along the Y-axis, and finally -0.2 units along the Z-axis.

The next object is a box defined by two opposite points at <-1, -1, -1> and <1, 1, 1>. To modify the size of the box, use the scale statement `scale <0.5, 0.5, 0.5>`. This statement indicates that the final size of the box will be half of its original size in all directions. You can perform scaling operations where each of the scaling factors is different, therefore creating a rectangular box.

```
//BOX
object {
    box <-1, -1, -1>, <1, 1, 1>
    scale <0.5, 0.5, 0.5>
    rotate <-10, 10, 0>
    shiny_green
}
```

After the box has been resized, you can rotate it to show some of the hidden faces. The statement `rotate <-10, 10, 0>` indicates that the object will be rotated -10 degrees about the X-axis, 10 degrees about the Y-axis, and 0 degrees (no rotation) about the Z-axis.

The cylinder statement is simple because it needs only the two end points of the cylinder and the radius.

```
//CYLINDER
object {
    cylinder <0,0,0>, <0,0.4,0>, 0.4
    rotate <-15,0,0>
    translate <-0.8,1.0,0>
    wooden
}
```

Observe that the cylinder was rotated and translated to locate it in space.

A torus requires a minor radius, a major radius, the torus center, and a vector that is perpendicular to it. Figure 11.13 displays a torus and the parameters required to define it.

FIGURE 11.13.

Definition of a torus primitive (torus has been sliced).

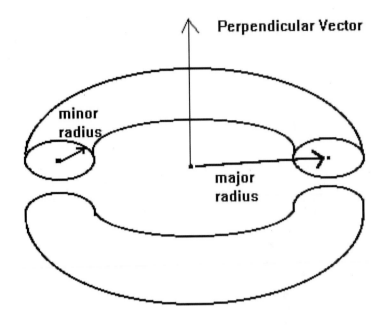

In Figure 11.13, the torus was sliced in half to show the radii more efficiently. The syntax for the torus is

```
//TORUS
object {
    torus 0.5, 0.1, <0,0,0>, <0,1,0>
    rotate <-30,0,-10>
    translate <0.7, 1.4, 0>
    white_marble
}
```

In Figure 11.13, the torus was sliced in half to show the radii more efficiently. The syntax for the torus is

```
torus Rmaj, Rmin, Center, PerpVector
```

> `Rmaj` is the major radius
> `Rmin` is the minor radius
> `Center` is the center of the torus <xc, yc, zc>
> `PerpVector` is a vector perpendicular to the plane of the torus, so that if the torus is lying flat on the XZ plane, `PerpVector` is <0, 1, 0>

It is easiest to use `PerpVector` = <0, 1, 0> and then use the rotate statement to flip the torus to the correct orientation.

The cone object uses the endpoints and the radii at each end. Figure 11.14 displays two types of cones.

FIGURE 11.14.

Cone definition parameters.

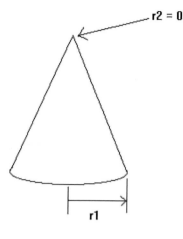

r2 = 0

r2

r1

r1

(a) cone with apex

(b) truncated cone

```
//CONE
object {
    cone <0.0, -1, 0.0>, 0.5, <0.0, 0.0, 0.0>, 0.0
    translate <1.4, 0.48, 0>
    shiny_blue
}
```

The syntax for a cone is

```
cone p1, r1, p2, r2
```

> *p1* is the first endpoint <x1, y1, z1>
> *r1* is the radius at endpoint *p1*
> *p2* is the second endpoint <x2, y2, z2>
> *r2* is the radius at endpoint *p2*

If *r1* and *r2* are zero, the cone is called *truncated,* which means that it does not have an apex.

Finally, you have the sphere primitive

```
//SPHERE
object {
    sphere < -0.96, 0, -1.12>, 0.25
    shiny_red
}
```

The sphere object requires the center and the radius parameters.

I have left out any comments concerning the textures of the objects on purpose. In the next section, I'll cover them in detail.

Texture Section

Polyray has various predefined textures such as gold, checker, marble, agate, wood, and others that are easy to use. Take the sphere object, for example:

```
//SPHERE
object {
    sphere < -0.96, 0, -1.12>, 0.25
    shiny_red
}
```

The sphere is using a predefined texture named `shiny_red`. No other operation is necessary to use simple textures of a specific color. There are other complex textures, such as the checker texture. Inside the PLATE object definition, the checker texture is used as

```
    texture {
      checker matte_white, matte_black
      scale <0.5, 0.5, 0.5>
    }
```

Observe that the keyword `texture` was used to bound the whole definition. Next, the statement `checker matte_white, matte_black` is used to declare that the checker texture (tiles) will have matte white and matte black colored tiles. The names `matte_white` and `matte_black` have been predefined. The next statement is a scaling operation to be performed on the texture only (not on the object). It is applied only to the texture because it was declared inside the texture statement. I will use the following example to explain the scaling feature:

```
object {
    polygon 4, <-1,0,-1>, <1,0,-1>, <1,0,1>, <-1,0,1>
    translate <0,-1.5, -0.2>
    texture {
      checker matte_white, matte_black
      scale <0.5, 0.5, 0.5>
    }
    scale <10, 10, 10>
}
```

In this example, the operation `scale <0.5, 0.5, 0.5>` scales the texture only, whereas the statement `scale <10, 10, 10>` affects the object and the texture. If you want to scale the object without scaling the texture twice, use the following code:

```
object {
    polygon 4, <-1,0,-1>, <1,0,-1>, <1,0,1>, <-1,0,1>
    scale <10, 10, 10>
    translate <0,-1.5, -0.2>
    texture {
      checker matte_white, matte_black
      scale <0.5, 0.5, 0.5>
    }
}
```

In this case, the scaling operation is performed on the object, and then the texture is added to the object (and scaled).

What does the scaling factor do on a texture? In the case of the checker texture, it makes the tiles smaller or larger depending on the scaling values. For example, values less than 1.0 reduce the size of each tile, therefore increasing the number of tiles in an object. The opposite holds true for numbers larger than 1.0.

Finally, you can also apply rotations and translations on textures to create the effect you want. To summarize, the statements inside an object definition are executed in the order they are found. If you wish to modify the location, size, or orientation of the object before the texture is applied, insert the appropriate command before the texture definition. If you want to affect the texture also, add the commands after the texture definition. To modify the texture only, insert the appropriate commands inside the texture definition. Again, check Polyray's documentation for the list of names of textures and colors.

Ray Tracing DEMO.PI with Polyray

The previous sections covered some of the basic concepts behind a ray-tracer program and also dissected a sample scene and looked at its components. This section covers how to ray trace the image using Polyray.

Polyray operates by reading an ASCII file (scene file) and a set of command-line parameters. The command-line parameters are discussed in detail in Polyray's documentation file. Table 11.1 provides a list of them.

Table 11.1. Polyray command-line parameters.

Parameter	Value	Comments
File Options		
-o	*outputfile*	Default is out.tga
-p	*pixelsize*	Bits/pixel [8, 16, 24, 32]
-d		Render as a depth map
-u		Turn off RLE compression of output
-x	*columns*	Trace *columns* pixels per row
-y	*lines*	Trace *lines* rows
-B		Flush the output file every line
-b	*count*	Flush every *count* pixels
-v		Trace from bottom (Truevision format)

continues

Table 11.1. continued

Parameter	Value	Comments
-R		Resume an old trace
-z	*line*	Start at row *line*
Status Options		
-t	*frequency*	Status: 0=none, 1=totals, 2=line, 3=pixel
Rendering Options		
-r	*method*	Render: 0=Ray, 1=Scan, 2=Wire, 3=Raw, 4=uv
-q	*flags*	Turn on/off various shading options: 1=shadow, 2=reflect, 4=transmit, 8=two sides, 16=check uv, 31=all flags
Antialiasing Options for Ray Tracing		
-a	*mode*	AA: 0=none,1=filter,2-4=adaptive
-T	*threshold*	Threshold to start oversampling
-S	*samples*	Use *samples* rays/pixel
Optimization Options		
-O	*optimizer*	0 = none, 1 = slabs
Display Options		
-V	*mode*	0=none, 1-5=8-bit, 6-10=16, 11-15=24
-P	*palette*	0 = grey, 1 = 332, 2 = 666 (8-bit only)
-W		Wait for key before clearing display
Abort Option		
-Q		Abort if any key is hit during trace

Because the discussion of these parameters would require a complete chapter, I'll give you a hand and prepare two batch files. The batch file DRAFT.BAT is used to generate "quick and dirty" images. See Listing 11.2.

Listing 11.2. Batch file to create quick images with Polyray—DRAFT.BAT.

```
POLYRAY %1 -r 0 -V 1 -t 0 -W
```

The parameters used in DRAFT.BAT provide Polyray with the following directions:

- Use the ray tracing method (-r 0)
- Preview on the screen using 8 bits (-V 1)
- Do not give any scene status information as the image is generated (-t 0)
- At the end of the ray trace, wait for a key press (-W)

The batch file DRAFT.BAT can be easily created with a text editor. To use it with DEMO.PI, type the following at the DOS prompt:

```
DRAFT DEMO.PI [press the Enter key]
```

Figure 11.15 displays the output file generated by OUT.TGA.

FIGURE 11.15.
Ray traced DEMO.PI using DRAFT.BAT.

To create a better image, create FINAL.BAT with the information found in Listing 11.3.

Listing 11.3. Batch file to create better images with Polyray—FINAL.BAT.

```
POLYRAY %1 -r 0 -V 1 -t 0 -a 3 -T 0.2 -S 25 -p 24 -O 1 -Q
```

FINAL.BAT uses the following parameters to improve the image:

- Use ray tracing method (-r 0)
- Preview using 8-bit display (-V 1)
- Do not display scene status information (-t 0)
- Use adaptive antialiasing method to eliminate jagged lines in the image (-a 3)
- Threshold level for oversampling (-T 0.2)
- Number of samples (-S 25)
- Create 24-bit images (-p 24)
- Optimize the speed of the ray tracer (-O 1)
- Abort ray trace if a key is pressed (-Q)

FINAL.BAT informs Polyray to use a technique called *antialiasing*, which reduces the jagged lines that appear in some images. The parameters -a, -T, and -S work in conjunction to minimize the jagged line look at the expense of computation time. Figure 11.16 displays the output file OUT.TGA.

FIGURE 11.16.

Ray traced DEMO.PI using FINAL.BAT.

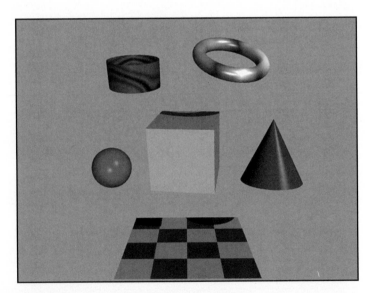

> **NOTE**
>
> Do not get discouraged with the preview that appears on the screen as Polyray generates the photo-realistic image from your scene. This is just a preview and not the true final quality that will appear in the output TARGA file. You can use any image file viewer to look at OUT.TGA.

In this section I have tried to explain the minimum necessary to get you started on Polyray. If you use DRAFT.BAT and FINAL.BAT, you don't need to deal with any other command-line parameters. Now it's time for the good stuff—using SWEEP and Polyray together.

Using SWEEP for 3-D Object Creation

SWEEP is an excellent tool for developing 3-D lathe objects in Polyray. As I mentioned in the previous sections, Polyray has a set of built-in objects called primitives that can be used in conjunction with objects developed using SWEEP. In the following sections you will create a simple scene consisting of a lamp, a flower vase, a sphere, and a tiled floor. To accomplish this, I'll present the steps taken to create such a scene by combining both programs.

The Lamp

The lamp will consist of two sections: the top section that covers the bulb, and the lamp itself. Figure 11.17 presents the outline used to define the bulb cover. A series of ten points were created by clicking on the CREATE icon and then clicking in different sections of the screen. If you decide to move a point to a new location, click on the MOVE icon and click near the point you wish to move. As you move the mouse, the point will follow. Click again to accept its new position.

FIGURE 11.17.

Bulb cover for lamp created with SWEEP.

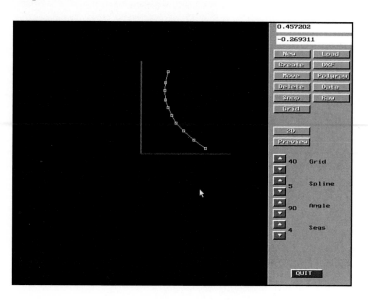

After creating the set of ten points, save the data as LAMP1.DAT. These were the points created:

Contents of LAMP1.DAT

```
0.210856 0.620042 0
0.189979 0.536534 0
0.185804 0.478079 0
0.189979 0.407098 0
0.210856 0.348643 0
0.240084 0.290188 0
0.273486 0.231733 0
0.331942 0.173278 0
0.411273 0.102296 0
0.503132 0.039666 0
```

I offer these points as an example; you may wish to create a different contour. Now click on the Preview button to observe how the object will look in 3-D (see Figure 11.18).

FIGURE 11.18.

3-D preview of bulb cover for lamp created with SWEEP.

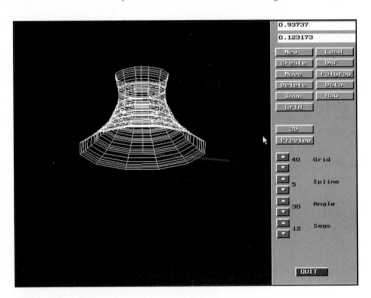

If you like the contour you have created, click on the Polyray button to create a lathe object, and save it as LAMP1.PI. Listing 11.4 presents LAMP.PI.

Listing 11.4. Lathe object (bulb cover) created with SWEEP.

```
object {
    lathe 2, <0, 1, 0>, 10,
    <0.210856, 0.620042, 0>,
    <0.189979, 0.536534, 0>,
    <0.185804, 0.478079, 0>,
    <0.189979, 0.407098, 0>,
```

```
        <0.210856, 0.348643, 0>,
        <0.240084, 0.290188, 0>,
        <0.273486, 0.231733, 0>,
        <0.331942, 0.173278, 0>,
        <0.411273, 0.102296, 0>,
        <0.503132, 0.039666, 0>
        shiny_red
}
```

Observe that the lathe object created in LAMP1.PI was basically the same set of points created in LAMP1.DAT. The statement `shiny_red` is always included in the definition as the default texture. Later, when you assemble the lamp, you can delete this line.

The next step is to create the lamp body. Figure 11.19 displays the contour created to define the lamp body.

FIGURE 11.19.

Lamp body created with SWEEP.

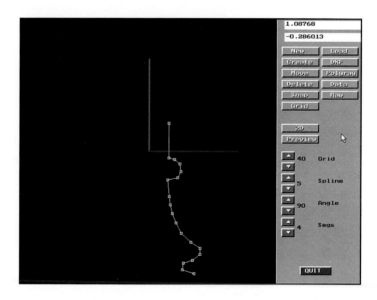

The body consists of nineteen points that I saved as LAMP2.DAT. The points found inside LAMP2.DAT are

Contents of LAMP2.DAT

```
0.156576   0.210856 0
0.156576  -0.0521921 0
0.202505  -0.0647182 0
0.244259  -0.0981211 0
0.25261   -0.156576 0
0.227557  -0.202505 0
0.148225  -0.219207 0
```

```
0.160752 -0.344468 0
0.169102 -0.407098 0
0.185804 -0.473904 0
0.215031 -0.544885 0
0.256785 -0.624217 0
0.331942 -0.691023 0
0.402923 -0.736952 0
0.402923 -0.782881 0
0.344468 -0.82881  0
0.273486 -0.849687 0
0.265136 -0.899791 0
0.356994 -0.929019 0
```

Don't worry if the points you have created are not the same. Click on Preview to check the 3-D preview of the object (see Figure 11.20).

FIGURE 11.20.

3-D preview of lamp body created with SWEEP.

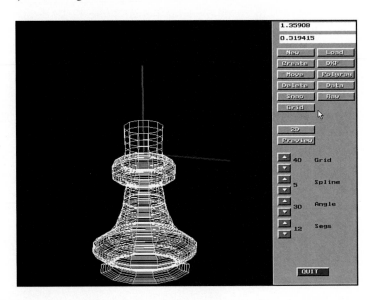

Again, save the data as a lathe object by clicking on Polyray. Save the data as LAMP2.PI. Listing 11.5 presents the output file for LAMP2.PI.

Listing 11.5. Lathe object (lamp body) created with SWEEP.

```
object {
    lathe 2, <0, 1, 0>, 19,
      <0.156576, 0.210856, 0>,
      <0.156576, -0.0521921, 0>,
      <0.202505, -0.0647182, 0>,
      <0.244259, -0.0981211, 0>,
      <0.25261, -0.156576, 0>,
      <0.227557, -0.202505, 0>,
      <0.148225, -0.219207, 0>,
```

```
    <0.160752, -0.344468, 0>,
    <0.169102, -0.407098, 0>,
    <0.185804, -0.473904, 0>,
    <0.215031, -0.544885, 0>,
    <0.256785, -0.624217, 0>,
    <0.331942, -0.691023, 0>,
    <0.402923, -0.736952, 0>,
    <0.402923, -0.782881, 0>,
    <0.344468, -0.82881, 0>,
    <0.273486, -0.849687, 0>,
    <0.265136, -0.899791, 0>,
    <0.356994, -0.929019, 0>
    shiny_red
}
```

The final object to be created with SWEEP is the flower vase, which is covered next.

The Flower Vase

Figure 11.21 displays the contour to be used to create the flower vase, and Figure 11.22 presents the 3-D preview.

FIGURE 11.21.

Flower vase contour.

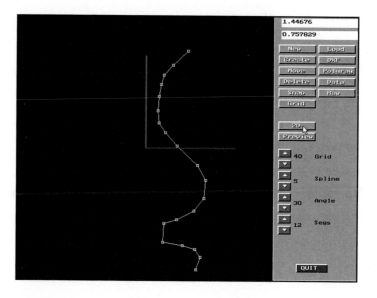

FIGURE 11.22.

3-D flower vase preview.

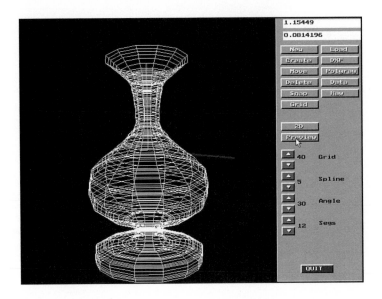

The set of points was saved as FVASE.DAT:

Contents of FVASE.DAT

```
0.327766  0.736952  0
0.210856  0.628392  0
0.139875  0.553236  0
0.118998  0.482255  0
0.102296  0.390397  0
0.0939457 0.281837  0
0.102296  0.189979  0
0.152401  0.114823  0
0.244259  0.0146138 0
0.402923  -0.131524 0
0.465553  -0.244259 0
0.453027  -0.382046 0
0.377871  -0.478079 0
0.244259  -0.544885 0
0.14405   -0.574113 0
0.135699  -0.716075 0
0.290188  -0.741127 0
0.386221  -0.770355 0
0.427975  -0.82881  0
0.394572  -0.924843 0
```

After saving the data as FVASE.DAT, create the Polyray lathe object by clicking on the Polyray button. Save the object as FVASE.PI (see Listing 11.6).

Listing 11.6. Lathe object (flower vase) created with SWEEP.

```
object {
    lathe 2, <0, 1, 0>, 20,
     <0.327766, 0.736952, 0>,
     <0.210856, 0.628392, 0>,
     <0.139875, 0.553236, 0>,
     <0.118998, 0.482255, 0>,
     <0.102296, 0.390397, 0>,
     <0.0939457, 0.281837, 0>,
     <0.102296, 0.189979, 0>,
     <0.152401, 0.114823, 0>,
     <0.244259, 0.0146138, 0>,
     <0.402923, -0.131524, 0>,
     <0.465553, -0.244259, 0>,
     <0.453027, -0.382046, 0>,
     <0.377871, -0.478079, 0>,
     <0.244259, -0.544885, 0>,
     <0.14405, -0.574113, 0>,
     <0.135699, -0.716075, 0>,
     <0.290188, -0.741127, 0>,
     <0.386221, -0.770355, 0>,
     <0.427975, -0.82881, 0>,
     <0.394572, -0.924843, 0>
     shiny_red
}
```

The next section covers the use of basic predefined primitives such as the disc and the sphere. These are used to add some interesting effects to the final scene.

The Floor and the Sphere

Now that you have the flower vase and the lamp, you should think about creating some type of floor for these objects. You can easily use the `polygon` primitive and create a flat rectangular floor for them, but that would be too boring. An interesting choice would be the use of a disc as a floor.

You can think of disc objects as an extremely thin coin. The parameters required to define a disc are the center of the disc, an axis perpendicular to it, and its radius. Take a look at the following definition:

```
object {
    disc <0,0,0>, <0,1,0>,5
    texture {
      checker reflective_grey, matte_black
    }
}
```

The disc has a radius of 5 units, its center is located at <0,0,0>, and the Y-axis (<0,1,0>) is perpendicular to it. The texture used is a tiled checker texture. One of the tiles is made with a reflective material and the other is matte. This creates a very interesting effect of reflection in those tiles with the `reflective_grey` texture.

Finally, add a shiny red sphere to the scene:

```
object {
    sphere <2.5,0.25,-2>, .25
    shiny_red
}
```

You are finished creating objects for this scene. Now comes the hard part, which is being able to locate the objects correctly in space.

Locating the Objects in the Scene

One of the most difficult tasks when creating a ray tracing scene is being able to locate 3-D objects in space correctly. Most people use a piece of graph paper and a pencil and sketch their ideas of how the scene should look. This is basically the approach I took (in combination with some trial and error). The final scene was named TEST.PI and is presented in Listing 11.7.

Listing 11.7. Final ray tracing scene using primitives and lathe objects— TEST.PI.

```
//TEST.PI

include "colors.inc"
include "texture.inc"

viewpoint {
  from       <3, 3, -10>
  at         <0.0, 0.0, 0.0>
  up         <0.0, 1.0, 0.0>
  angle           45
  resolution      640,480
  aspect          1.33
  }

// LIGHT_SOURCE
light <0,  50,  0>
light <50, 0, -50>
light <-50, 0, -50>

define LampTop
object {
    lathe 2, <0, 1, 0>, 10,
```

```
        <0.210856, 0.620042, 0>,
        <0.189979, 0.536534, 0>,
        <0.185804, 0.478079, 0>,
        <0.189979, 0.407098, 0>,
        <0.210856, 0.348643, 0>,
        <0.240084, 0.290188, 0>,
        <0.273486, 0.231733, 0>,
        <0.331942, 0.173278, 0>,
        <0.411273, 0.102296, 0>,
        <0.503132, 0.039666, 0>
}

define LampBottom
object {
    lathe 2, <0, 1, 0>, 19,
        <0.156576, 0.210856, 0>,
        <0.156576, -0.0521921, 0>,
        <0.202505, -0.0647182, 0>,
        <0.244259, -0.0981211, 0>,
        <0.25261, -0.156576, 0>,
        <0.227557, -0.202505, 0>,
        <0.148225, -0.219207, 0>,
        <0.160752, -0.344468, 0>,
        <0.169102, -0.407098, 0>,
        <0.185804, -0.473904, 0>,
        <0.215031, -0.544885, 0>,
        <0.256785, -0.624217, 0>,
        <0.331942, -0.691023, 0>,
        <0.402923, -0.736952, 0>,
        <0.402923, -0.782881, 0>,
        <0.344468, -0.82881, 0>,
        <0.273486, -0.849687, 0>,
        <0.265136, -0.899791, 0>,
        <0.356994, -0.929019, 0>
}

define FlowerVase
object {
    lathe 2, <0, 1, 0>, 20,
        <0.327766, 0.736952, 0>,
        <0.210856, 0.628392, 0>,
        <0.139875, 0.553236, 0>,
        <0.118998, 0.482255, 0>,
        <0.102296, 0.390397, 0>,
        <0.0939457, 0.281837, 0>,
        <0.102296, 0.189979, 0>,
        <0.152401, 0.114823, 0>,
        <0.244259, 0.0146138, 0>,
        <0.402923, -0.131524, 0>,
        <0.465553, -0.244259, 0>,
        <0.453027, -0.382046, 0>,
        <0.377871, -0.478079, 0>,
        <0.244259, -0.544885, 0>,
        <0.14405, -0.574113, 0>,
        <0.135699, -0.716075, 0>,
        <0.290188, -0.741127, 0>,
```

continues

Listing 11.7. continued

```
        <0.386221, -0.770355, 0>,
        <0.427975, -0.82881, 0>,
        <0.394572, -0.924843, 0>
}
object {
      LampTop
      scale <2,2,2>
      translate <0.5,2,0>
      reflective_tan
}

object {
      LampBottom
      scale <2,2,2>
      translate <0.5, 2*0.95, 0>
      reflective_gold
}

object {
      FlowerVase
      scale <1.3,1.3,1.3>
      translate <-1.5, 1.3*0.95, -2>
      sapphire_agate
}

object {
      sphere <2.5,0.25,-2>, .25
      shiny_red
}

object {
      disc <0,0,0>, <0,1,0>,5
      texture {
         checker reflective_grey, matte_black
      }
}
```

After some trial and error positioning of the objects (use DRAFT.BAT to speed up this process), TEST.PI is the resulting scene. There are some interesting techniques that should be discussed. The use of the define statement is highly recommended. This statement attaches a name to an object. After an object has a name, that name can be used instead of the full definition. In the scene I loaded the files LAMP1.PI, LAMP2.PI, and FVASE.PI. I deleted the shiny_red texture line from each and attached a name to each: LampTop, LampBottom, and FlowerVase, respectively.

To locate the objects, I added a translate statement on each object. For example, the flower vase object used

```
object {
    FlowerVase
    scale <1.3,1.3,1.3>
    translate <-1.5, 1.3*0.95, -2>
    sapphire_agate
}
```

which indicates that I initially scaled up the object then translated it to a new position <-1.5, 1.3*0.95, -2>. The last line applies the texture to the object. Figure 11.23 shows TEST.PI after ray tracing it with FINAL.BAT.

FIGURE 11.23.

Final ray traced image of TEST.PI.

As you can see in Figure 11.23, lathe objects are very smooth and make excellent 3-D objects. Don't forget to add a few light sources to the scene. When adding light sources to a scene, always remember that shadows can help create a specific atmosphere in a scene; therefore, locate light sources wisely. Finally, observe the effect produced by combining reflective and matte tiles on the floor.

Using SWEEP and 3D Studio

If you have 3D Studio, you can use SWEEP to create objects for it. SWEEP was developed to demonstrate how a 3-D application can be written, not to replace commercial-quality programs such as 3D Studio's modeler. To use SWEEP with 3D Studio, simply save any object you create in DXF format. These objects can then be read by 3D Studio. Locate the objects and then select surface materials for each of the objects, some light sources, and a camera. The final step is to render the scene.

Summary

This chapter introduced some of the basic concepts behind a ray tracer. Ray tracing was broken down into the study of coordinate systems, viewpoint (observer), light sources, 3-D geometry, and textures. You studied DEMO.PI, a sample Polyray scene file, to see how the ray tracing concepts applied to Polyray. Next, you used SWEEP to create objects that were used by the ray tracer to create photo-realistic images. SWEEP is a program that incorporates most of the tools needed for more complex 3-D applications, and with the aid of the source code you'll be able to implement 3-D applications to suit your needs.

Blobs

IV

Modeling 2-D Blobs with Animator Pro POCO Language

by Jim Hawkins

IN THIS CHAPTER

- What Are Blobs?
- Using BLOBDRAW
- Creating a Blob Animation
- POCO Code Walkthrough
- Main Loop Implementation in POCO Language
- The `bloblinc ()` Function
- The `blobdemo ()` Function
- The `blobinfo ()` Function
- The `GrayPaletteInit ()` Function

Introduction

This chapter describes BLOBDRAW, an Autodesk Animator Pro POCO program that adds the capability of generating still or animated 2-D blobs. It serves as an interesting example of how to extend the power of Animator Pro. To use this program, you should own or have access to Autodesk Animator Pro 1.3. It is not necessary to know POCO programming language to use this feature, but if you want to make additions or changes, you will need to become familiar with it. If you already have some experience with the C programming language, POCO programming will be easy to learn. In the first part of this chapter, you learn a bit about how to create blob animations with this feature. In the second part, the POCO programming language is discussed, and you tour through the BLOBDRAW.POC code to learn how it works.

What Are Blobs?

Blobs are becoming increasingly popular in modeling natural shapes and organic modeling such as human forms. From an artistic or graphical sense, blobs are objects that have liquid-like characteristics. Blobs can be based on many geometric shapes, but BLOBDRAW creates circular blobs. When a single blob is created, it simply appears as a circular object, which you may or may not apply motion to. As two blobs move closer together, they begin to "stick" or "bind" together, just as two droplets of liquid. As they continue to come in closer proximity to each other, the "bridge" that binds them thickens until they become one larger mass. Figure 12.1 shows an Animator Pro screen with three blobs, two of which are close enough to stick together.

Blobs are plotted by summing their combined "strengths" in accordance with the equation

$$t = s (1 - (r / radius)^2)^2$$

where: t is the combined strength

s is the strength of one individual blob

r is the distance of the current pixel from the blob center

radius is the radius of the blob

The resultant t must exceed a set threshold for a point to be plotted. If the threshold is exceeded, the color can be calculated as a function of t. BLOBDRAW has six different color functions from which to choose.

FIGURE 12.1.

One lone blob and two others sticking together.

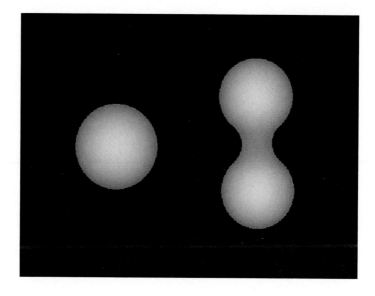

A more detailed discussion of blobs can be found in an article by Alfonso Hermida entitled "Introduction to Blobs," in *3D Artist*, Issue 14, page 41.

Using BLOBDRAW

Demonstration

For BLOBDRAW to work, the program file BLOBDRAW.POC must reside in your \ANI\RESOURCE directory. The presence of this file makes it available as an Animator Pro program function accessible from the Animator Pro POCO menu. For a quick demonstration, follow these steps:

1. Choose RESET from the FLIC pulldown menu.
2. Create at least 20 frames.
3. From the POCO pulldown menu, choose BLOBDRAW, as shown in Figure 12.2. A pop-up will appear.
4. From the pop-up, choose DEMO.

The demo will generate an animation that will use all the available frames.

FIGURE 12.2.

Select BLOBDRAW from the POCO menu.

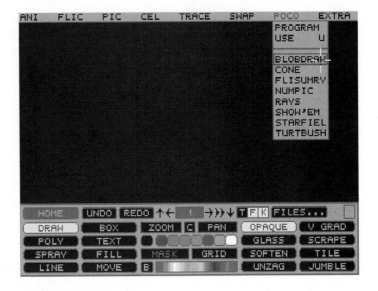

Creating a Blob Animation

To create your own blob scene or animation, follow these steps:

1. Choose RESET from the FLIC pulldown menu.

2. Create as many frames as you desire—for example, 10 for this exercise.

3. From the POCO pulldown menu, choose BLOBDRAW, as shown in Figure 12.2. A pop-up will appear.

4. From the pop-up, choose CREATE BLOB SCENE. The BLOB DATA ENTRY menu will appear.

5. From the BLOB DATA ENTRY menu, select ADD A BLOB. The menu will disappear and only the mouse cursor will be visible.

6. To place the first blob, click about one-quarter screen width from the left, centered vertically. A dot will appear at the mouse entry point and a status bar will appear at the top of the screen.

7. Move the mouse cursor to create a circle on the screen and click when the status bar indicates a radius of about 50 (R = 50 on the status bar). Click the left mouse button. A rubber line will extend from the center of the circle to the position of the mouse cursor. Now, move the cursor to a destination to which you want the blob to travel, such as center screen, and click the left mouse button.

8. When the SET BLOB STRENGTH INDEX box appears, click on OK to accept the default. The BLOB DATA ENTRY menu will reappear.

9. Repeat steps 5 through 8, this time placing the blob somewhere on the right side of the screen, such as one-quarter screen width from the right, and placing the destination near the destination of the first blob, so that the two blobs will collide in the animation.

10. Add more blobs in this fashion if you like. If you want a blob to be stationary, click on the right mouse button when the path creation line appears. This will leave just a dot in the middle of the circle.

11. As you add blobs, the screen will look like Figure 12.3. When you are ready to begin animation generation, click GO! on the BLOB DATA ENTRY menu. Each frame will slowly paint itself. The process is slower for higher resolutions and more blobs.

12. Now, go have a cup of coffee or glass of lemonade. At a resolution of 320×200, the process shouldn't take too long.

FIGURE 12.3.

Setting up the blob animation scene.

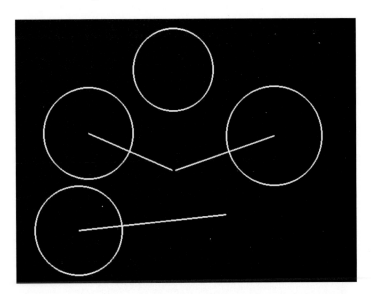

TIPS

1. Experiment by trying different settings on the BLOB DATA ENTRY menu or by setting different positive or negative strengths for each blob. A user's manual BLOBDRAW.DOC is supplied with the BLOBDRAW package to help you understand the options.

2. Create guidelines to help lay out your blob animation. Save the guideline drawing as a single image so it can be reloaded if necessary. BLOBDRAW will erase the guidelines when you begin the animation process.

POCO Code Walkthrough

BLOBDRAW is written in Animator Pro POCO language, which is a subset of the C programming language. When you purchase Animator Pro, you have the opportunity to order a reference manual on the POCO programming language from Autodesk. The POCO language has many of the capabilities of the C programming language and features a collection of C-style function calls that access the capabilities of Animator Pro. POCO is like a script language for Animator Pro's functions.

The BLOBDRAW POCO program module uses the following POCO function calls:

- `Circle(int x, int y, int radius)` Draws a circle on the screen at coordinates x,y having the given radius.

- `Clear()` Clears the screen.

- `GetColor()` Returns an integer containing the current drawing color index (0 255) into the color palette. The actual color depends on the palette.

- `GetColorMap(int index, int *r, int *g, int *b)` Returns the integer values of the Red, Green, and Blue components for the given index passed to the function.

- `GetFilled()` Gets the status of the filled [F] button.

- `GetFrameCount()` Returns the total number of frames in the current animation.

- `GetPhysicalSize(int *width, int *height)` Returns the size of the screen as opened by the video device driver, such as 320,200 or 640,480.

- `GetPicScreen()` Assigns a handle to the current picture screen.

- `NextFrame()` Advances animation to the next frame.

- `printf(char *format, string)` The calling format is the same as the standard C language `printf`, except in this case only a single line at the top of the screen is displayed in reverse video. This function is handy for showing status, coordinates, and so forth.

- `Qmenu(char **choices, int numchoices, char *menutitle)` Displays an Autodesk Animator Pro-style numbered pop-up menu, enabling the user to select or enter the number of the menu item.

- `Qnumber(int *number, int min, int max, char *title)` Displays an Animator Pro-style numeric slider bar, which prompts the user to select an integer.

- `RubCircle(int *x, int *y, int *radius)` Enables the user to draw a rubber circle on the screen and returns the x,y location and radius of the circle. Once entered, the circle disappears.

- ▪ RubLine(int x1, int y1, int *x2, int *y2)   Enables the user to draw a rubber line on the screen. Given the first two coordinates x1,y1, it returns the coordinates x2,y2 of the other end of the line. The line disappears on completion.

- ▪ SetColor(color_index)   Sets the current drawing color to that represented by the color_index into the current palette.

- ▪ SetColorMap(int index, int r, int g, int b)   Sets the color register represented by the index value to a new Red, Green, Blue color value, thus modifying a color in the current palette.

- ▪ SetFilled(Boolean fill)   Sets the status of the filled [F] button.

- ▪ SetScreenColorMap(Screen *screen, int *maparray)   Enables the programmer to set the entire color palette using the values in maparray.

- ▪ SetScreen(int screen_number)   Moves the current frame to the value of screen_number.

- ▪ unprintf()   Erases or turns off the string displayed by printf() at the top of the screen.

main( ) Function

To begin with, the global integers are defined as shown in the following code. The use of these variables is explained as you examine the code.

```
int     color,        // Color index (0 - 255)
        numcol,       // Screen width in pixels
        numrow,       // Screen height in pixels
        curframe,     // Current frame number
        skip = 1.0,   // Set skip > 1.0 to skip columns and
                      // rows for faster plot
        num_frames,   // Total number of frames
        color_mode = 1, // Color algorithm
        old_color_idx; // color save register

double xmin = -4.0,            // Defines blob space ranges
       ymin = -3.0,
       xmax = 4.0,
       ymax = 3.0,
       threshold = 0.5;
```

Each blob is treated as an object whose characteristics are stored in a BLOB type structure. All the blobs in the animation are stored in the blobs[] array, each being of type BLOB, as shown here.

```
typedef struct {
    double    x, y;
    double    dx, dy;
    double    radius, strength;
} BLOB;

BLOB    blobs[MAXBLOBS];
```

Take a closer look at the BLOB type structure. The location of the blob is stored in the double precision x and y variables. The value of x ranges from −4 to 4, and the value of y ranges from −3 to 3. Why these numbers? To keep the mathematics simple and to enable scaling to any size screen, the domain for all calculations is defined by an 8×6 area with the origin at its center. Notice that the ratio 8/6 equals 4/3, which is the aspect ratio of the image. Calculations are performed in this domain, then mapped to the pixel locations within the screen. That is, for a 640×480 screen, x = −4 maps to column 0, x = 4 maps to column 640, y = −3 maps to row 480, and y = 3 maps to row 0. Each blob has a radius and a maximum strength. The variables dx and dy determine how far each blob is moved in the x and y direction as the frame is incremented for the animation. The increment depends on the angle and length of the motion path line of the blob.

Now, for the main loop, first look at a pseudocode listing.

```
Obtain the size of the screen in rows and columns.
Obtain the number of frames in the animation.
Obtain data for blobs and store it in blobs[] array.
Save Animator Pro settings to be later restored.
For each frame of animation
    For each row j of the display
        Map row value to blob domain value
        For each column i of the display
            Map column value to blob domain value
            Initialize total strength t to 0
            For each blob k in the blobs[] array
                Add the effect of the blob to the total
                    strength t in accordance with the equation
                        t = strengthk (1 - (rk / radiusk)²)²
            End_of_For
            If t > threshold
                Plot a point at i, j
            Endif
        End_of_For
    End_of_For
    Go to next frame of animation
    Move all blobs by their respective dx, dy increments.
    End_of_for
    Restore Animator Pro parameters to their previous values.
End_of_Main
```

Main Loop Implementation in POCO Language

Now look at how the pseudocode is implemented in POCO language.

The screen size is obtained and stored in the integers numcol and numrow by calling the Animator Pro function GetPhysicalSize() as follows:

```
GetPhysicalSize(&numcol, &numrow);
```

These values represent the size of the screen in pixels, such as 320×200, 640×480, 800×600, or 1024×486. You then obtain the number of frames and save the current color selection in the statements

```
num_frames = GetFrameCount();
old_color_idx = GetColor();
```

The number of frames, `num_frames`, is used to limit the frame iteration loop and is also used in calculating the increment values `dx` and `dy` of each blob for motion. The `old_color_idx` value is saved so that the program can modify the current selected color and then restore it to its original value when the animation is completed.

Now, to obtain the data to store in the `blobs[]` array, you have two choices. If DEMO is selected, you set the values in the `blobs[]` array to predetermined values by calling `blobdemo()`. If the user wishes to set up his or her own blob animation, the values are obtained by calling `blobinfo()`, which enables the user to graphically enter the blob locations, sizes, and motion paths, as you will see later. To enable this selection, you put up a menu by calling the Animator Pro function `Qmenu()` as follows:

```
// Display the main menu and act on the choice
main_choice = Qmenu(main_choices, 2, main_header);
```

The first argument, `main_choices`, is a pointer to an array of strings, which represent the menu as it will appear to the user. The array is defined before `main()` and looks like this:

```
char *main_choices[] = {
    "CREATE BLOB SCENE",
    "DEMO",
};
```

The second argument tells Animator Pro that there are two menu selections, and the third argument, `main_header`, is a pointer to a string, which is the title of the menu. In this case, the title is "Main Menu." When a selection is made, the `Qmenu()` function returns an integer value and assigns it to `main_choice`. The `main_choice` variable is used in a POCO `switch` statement to determine which function will be used to set up your blobs array:

```
switch(main_choice)
{
case MAIN_DEMO:
    blobdemo();
    break;
case MAIN_BLOB_INFO:
    if(!blobinfo())
        return;
}
```

If `blobinfo()` returns a 0 value, abort.

Now you come to the `main` loop, which steps through the animation to draw each picture in the sequence. The `main` loop uses `curframe` to track the current frame number and iterates until it reaches `num_frames`, which was obtained by the call to `GetFrameCount()`. The skeleton of the frame loop is as follows:

```
for(curframe = 1; curframe <= num_frames; curframe++) {
    // Code to draw a picture for the current frame....
}
```

Inside the frame loop, you first clear the screen for a new picture and display a message at the top of the screen indicating which frame is being generated. This is especially important if you are as impatient as I am and want to know how much of the animation is completed. This is implemented in the following statements:

```
Clear();
printf("Generating frame %d of %d.", curframe, num_frames);
```

Next are two nested loops that generate one picture, a pixel at a time, scanning across each consecutive row, column by column. The current row and column are represented by the variables j and i, respectively. Immediately after each loop control `for` statement, the j and i pixel coordinates are mapped to the blob domain y and x values for use in the actual blob calculations. The picture loops are implemented as follows:

```
for(j = 0; j <= numrow; j++) {
    y = j * (ymax - ymin) / numrow + ymin;
    for(i = 0; i <= numcol; i++) {
        x = i * (xmax - xmin) / numcol + xmin;

        // blob calculation and plot code......
        ....................................
    }
}
```

The statements

```
y = j * (ymax - ymin) / numrow + ymin;
```

and

```
x = i * (xmax - xmin) / numcol + xmin;
```

translate the pixel coordinates to the blob domain and are simple linear equations of the form

```
y = mx + b
```

Before covering the blob calculation and plot code, I will mention the two code statements

```
NextFrame();
blobinc();
```

which are the last statements of the frame loop and follow the inner picture loops. `NextFrame()` is an Animator Pro function that moves the program to the next frame. Following this, you must apply motion to the blobs in the `blobs[]` array, if necessary with a call to `blobinc()`, which is covered shortly.

For each picture, you must first calculate the combined effect of all blobs in the scene on the current coordinate point in your blob space, then determine whether you are within a blob and how to apply color to the plotted point.

You first determine the contribution of all blobs in a scene to the total strength at each point in the scene. This strength can be thought of as being analogous to a combined force field strength of a number of objects, each contributing its own component of force. One difference between this and gravity, for instance, is that outside the radius of the blob, the force or strength drops off to zero. That is, outside the given blob radius, its force is ignored.

The loop calculating the combined effect appears as follows:

```
t = 0.0;
for(k = 0; k < bnum; k++) {
    r = sqrt((x - blobs[k].x) * (x - blobs[k].x) +
            (y - blobs[k].y) * (y - blobs[k].y));
    if(r <= blobs[k].radius) {
        temp = r / blobs[k].radius;
        temp *= temp;
        temp = 1.0 - temp;
        temp *= temp;
        t += blobs[k].strength * temp;
    }
}
```

The combined force value t is first initialized to 0, then in a loop the effects of each blob are added in accordance with the aforementioned equation

$$t = s_k \, (1 - (r_k / radius_k)^2)^2$$

for values of `rk <= radiusk`. For the current point, the distance `r` from the center of each blob is computed in the statement

```
r = sqrt((x - blobs[k].x) * (x - blobs[k].x) +
        (y - blobs[k].y) * (y - blobs[k].y));
```

which applies the Pythagorean theorem. If `r` is within the radius of the blob, the strength is computed and added to the combined force t in the statements

```
temp = r / blobs[k].radius;
temp *= temp;
temp = 1.0 - temp;
temp *= temp;
t += blobs[k].strength * temp;
```

After computing the combined force for bnum blobs at point x,y, you then test the strength t against threshold and plot a point if the threshold is exceeded. The threshold default is 0.5 but can be varied by the user through a menu option for varied effects. It would be sufficient at this point to simply apply the current color to the picture with the Animator Pro function call

```
Dot(i, j);
```

This would give you monochrome, flat-looking blobs. To make the program more versatile, four additional options were added to determine blob color. These options are set in the "Set Color Mode" menu option, which results in setting the color_mode variable. The color_mode variable is used in the following code to select a color computation algorithm before plotting the point.

```
if(t >= threshold) {
    switch(color_mode) {
    case 0:             // monochrome
        color = GetColor();
        break;
    case 1:                // increasing exponential gradient
        color = 255 * (1 - exp(-t));
        if(t == threshold)
            color /= 4;
        break;
    case 2:             // decaying exponential gradient
        color = 255 * exp(-t);
        break;
    case 3:             // linear gradient (flattops occur when max reached)
        color = t * 255;
        if(color > 255)
            color = 255;
        break;
    case 4:             // Averaged linear gradient (no flattopping)
        for(k = 0, max_strength = 0.0; k < bnum; k++)
            max_strength += blobs[k].strength;
        color = ((int)((t / max_strength) * 255) % 255);
        break;
    case 5:             // Linear gradient with wraparound
        color = 255 * t;
        break;
    }
    SetColor(color);
    Dot(i, j);
}
```

With the exception of the monochrome mode, all of the preceding color algorithms attempt to distribute blob coloring over the 256 color palette as a function of the strength. The increasing exponential algorithm (option 1) renders the smoothest results when the entire palette is a continuous ramp or gradient. This is the default option.

After the animation is completed, the final statements in main() restore the current color to that which was set before BLOBDRAW was invoked, and the top status line is turned off with unprintf().

```
SetColor(old_color_idx);
unprintf();
```

blobinc() Function

The blobinc() function is called with each new frame to create animation. The function simply traverses the blobs[] array and adds dx and dy for every blob, moving it to a new location. If no motion path is drawn, dx and dy will be zero, and the particular blob will be stationary. The loop appears as follows:

```
for(k = 0; k < bnum; k++)
{
    blobs[k].x += blobs[k].dx;
    blobs[k].x += blobs[k].dx;
}
```

blobdemo() Function

The blobdemo() function simply initializes seven blobs in the blobs[] array by assignment. Following is a partial listing, showing initialization of the first blob. Six more blobs are filled in the same fashion.

```
void blobdemo(void)
{
    // define blob #1
    blobs[0].x = -3.0;
    blobs[0].y = 0;
    blobs[0].radius = 1.0;
    blobs[0].strength = 1.0;
    blobs[0].dx = 0.25;
    blobs[0].dy = 0.0;

    // define blob #2, etc
    ........

    bnum = 7;
}
```

blobinfo() Function

This function enables the user to set up a custom blob scene or animation. It is essentially a menu input function that remains in the menu until the user selects GO!. During this time, the user draws his or her blobs, setting their sizes and animation paths and individual strengths. The menu selections are as follows:

```
1 Add A Blob
2 Set Threshold Index
3 Set Color Mode
4 Set Palette to Grayscale
0 GO!
```

You should note that although parameter ranges for threshold and blob strength are 0.0 through 1.0 and −1.0 through 1.0, the menu specifies an integer index. This is because Animator Pro numerical menus and sliders deal only in integers, hence the ideas of *Threshold Index* and *Blob Strength Index*. The returned index is used in the tenths[] array to obtain the actual parameter. The tenths[] array looks like this:

```
double tenths[21] = {-1.0, -0.9, -0.8, -0.7, -0.6, -0.5, -0.4, -0.3, -0.2,
    -0.1, 0.0, 0.1, 0.2, 0.3, 0.4, 0.5, 0.6, 0.7, 0.8, 0.9, 1.0};
```

The skeleton of the blob data menu loop is shown here:

```
bnum = 0;    // preset blob count to 0

while(blob_choice != BLOB_GO) {
    blob_choice = Qmenu(blob_choices, 5, blob_header);

    switch(blob_choice) {
    case BLOB_GO:
        // code.......
    case BLOB_SET_THRESH:
        // code.......
    case BLOB_SET_COLOR_MODE:
        // code.......
    case BLOB_GRAY:
        // code.......
    case BLOB_ADD_BLOB:
        // code.......
        break;
    }
    bnum++;
}
```

Because most of the code is straightforward, I will leave it to you to examine Listing 12.1 at the end of this chapter for further study. Instead, I will concentrate on the most interesting and probably most important menu selection case: "Add a Blob" or BLOB_ADD_BLOB.

When the user selects "Add a Blob" from the BLOB DATA ENTRY menu, the program waits for a mouse click to define the center of a blob. When the point is entered on the screen, further movement of the mouse forms a circle defining the radius of the blob to be entered. All of this is accomplished during the call to Animator Pro function RubCircle(). Upon successful entry of the center and circle radius, RubCircle() returns a TRUE status, and the center and radius values are passed to i1, j1, and radius. A call to Circle() is made with these parameters to paint a circle on the screen. The following code implements this action:

```
if(RubCircle(&i1, &j1, &radius))   // Get center and radius
    Circle(i1, j1, radius);        // Draw a circle there
else
    return(0);
```

The program then forms a rubber line from the center of the circle to the cursor. The rubber line moves with the cursor to indicate where the path will be placed when the mouse is clicked again. At this point, the user might decide either to place the motion path by clicking the left mouse button at the destination point or to make this blob stationary, in which case the right mouse button is pressed. This is accomplished during the call to Animator Pro function RubLine(), as shown in the following code.

```
if(!RubLine(i1, j1, &i2, &j2)) {  // Get the motion path
    i2 = i1;
    j2 = j1;
}
Line(i1, j1, i2, j2);
```

If the left mouse button is pressed, RubLine() returns TRUE, and the destination coordinate values are passed to the variables i2 and j2. If the right mouse button is pressed, RubLine() returns FALSE, and the destination coordinates are set to the blob center coordinates. The Animator Pro function Line() is called to draw a line showing the motion path or a dot at the center of the blob circle, indicating no motion. Figure 12.4 shows a labeled picture of this process.

FIGURE 12.4.

Illustration of blobs and paths.

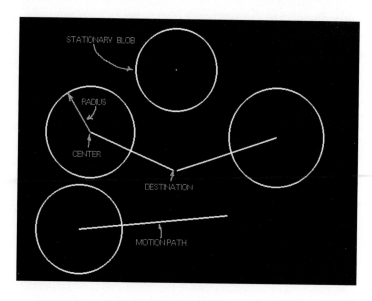

The path coordinates are then mapped from pixel space to blob space with the following code:

```
y1 = (double)j1 * (ymax - ymin) / numrow + ymin;
y2 = (double)j2 * (ymax - ymin) / numrow + ymin;
x1 = (double)i1 * (ymax - ymin) / numrow + ymin;
x1 = (double)i2 * (ymax - ymin) / numrow + ymin;
```

These are simple linear equations of the form

```
y = mx + b
```

Once the blob and motion path are entered with the mouse, another menu pops up, providing an opportunity to set the blob strength to a value other than 1.0 in the following code:

```
strengthindex = 10;
Qnumber(&strengthindex, -10, 19, "SET BLOB STRENGTH INDEX");
strengthindex += 10;
```

A negative blob strength will cause repulsion rather than attraction. The statements adding 10 to the strengthindex merely map it to a value that will index to the appropriate value in the tenths[] array.

Finally, the data is copied into the blobs[] array. The radius is mapped from pixel space to blob space at this time. The motion deltas, dx and dy, are computed by dividing the x and y distances by the number of frames, because the motion is to be distributed from the first to the last frame. The bnum variable is incremented to reflect the addition of another blob and to point to the next empty position in the blobs[] array. This is implemented by the following code:

```
blobs[bnum].x = x1;
blobs[bnum].y = y1;
blobs[bnum].radius = (double)radius * (ymax - ymin) / numrow;
blobs[bnum].strength = tenths[strengthindex];
blobs[bnum].dx = (x2 - x1) / num_frames;
blobs[bnum].dy = (y2 - y1) / num_frames;
bnum++;
```

The entry of blobs and their motion paths can be continued by repeatedly selecting "Add a Blob." Other parameters can be adjusted or readjusted until the user finally clicks GO!, which commences the animation.

GrayPaletteInit( ) Function

This function initializes the entire palette of 256 colors to a grayscale ramp from 0 through 255. A palette map is first initialized in the loop as follows:

```
int Palette_Map[256][3];        // 256 entries of RGB values

for(index = 0; index < 256; index++) {
    Palette_Map[index][0] = index;
    Palette_Map[index][0] = index;
    Palette_Map[index][0] = index;
}
```

The address of the `Palette_Map[][]` array is passed to the `SetScreenColorMap()` function to set the palette in each frame of the animation as follows:

```
SetFrame(0);
for(curframe = 1; curframe <= num_frames; curframe++) {
    SetScreenColorMap(GetPicScreen(), &Palette_Map[0][0]);
    NextFrame();
}
SetFrame(0);
```

The `GetPicScreen()` function obtains a handle to each screen, which is passed to `SetScreenColorMap()`. The `SetFrame()` function is used to set the frame to the first frame before the loop and again to reset the frame before the animation process begins.

This completes the analysis of BLOBDRAW code. You might wish to build on this program by adding other features, such as other color algorithms or more sophisticated motion paths, such as curves or multisegment paths. You might also vary other parameters for animation effects. Listing 12.1, a complete listing of the program with comments, follows.

Listing 12.1. Complete listing of BLOBDRAW.

```
//////////////////////////////////////////////////////
//                  BLOBDRAW.POC V1.1                 //
// Animated Blob Generator for Autodesk Animator Pro. //
// by James P. Hawkins                                //
//      18 Marlpit Place                              //
//      Middletown, NJ 07748                          //
//////////////////////////////////////////////////////

#pragma poco library "pdraccess.poe"  // extended picture I/O library
#pragma poco stacksize 32k
#include <errcodes.h>

#define MAXBLOBS 100    // Size of blobs array

int     color,          // Color index (0 - 255)
        numcol,         // Screen width in pixels
        numrow,         // Screen height in pixels
        curframe,       // Current frame number
        skip = 1.0,     // Set skip > 1.0 to skip columns and
                        // rows for faster plot
        num_frames,     // Total number of frames
        color_mode = 1, // Color algorithm
        old_color_idx;  // color save register
```

continues

Listing 12.1. continued

```c
// Blob space is 8 X 6 with 0 at center

double xmin = -4.0,              // Defines blob space ranges
       ymin = -3.0,
       xmax = 4.0,
       ymax = 3.0,
       threshold = 0.5;

/////////////////////////////////////////////////////////////
// BLOB DATUM
// x, y is the center in BLOB space (-4 < x < 4, -3 < y < 3)
// dx, dy are the amount x and y are incremented or decremented
// for motion to the next frame, they will be 0 if the blob is
// stationary.
// "radius" is the blob radius in blob space units
// "strength" is the max strength at the blob center
/////////////////////////////////////////////////////////////

typedef struct {
    double x, y;
    double dx, dy;
    double radius, strength;
} BLOB;

BLOB      blobs[MAXBLOBS];       // Array of blobs
int       bnum;                  // number of blobs in blobs array

// Function prototypes
void    blobdemo(void);
void    blobinc(void);
int     blobinfo(void);
void    GrayPaletteInit(void);

/////////////////////////////////////////////////////////
// MAIN MENU
char main_header[] = "Main menu";
int     main_choice;         // return value for menu
char    *main_choices[] = {
    "CREATE BLOB SCENE",
    "DEMO",
};

// Switch selection constants
// for main menu
enum {
    MAIN_DEMO,
    MAIN_BLOB_INFO,
};

/////////////////////////////////////////////////////////////
//                          MAIN
/////////////////////////////////////////////////////////////

main()
{
```

```
double  r, t, x, y, temp;
int        i, j, k;
int    max_strength;
GetPhysicalSize(&numcol, &numrow);

num_frames = GetFrameCount();
old_color_idx = GetColor();

// Display the main menu and act on the choice
main_choice = Qmenu(main_choices, 2, main_header);
switch(main_choice)
{
case MAIN_DEMO:
    blobdemo();
    break;
case MAIN_BLOB_INFO:
    if(!blobinfo())
        return;
}

// For each frame
for(curframe = 1; curframe <= num_frames; curframe++) {
    Clear();
    printf("Generating frame %d.", curframe);

    for(j = 0; j <= numrow; j += skip) {
        y = j * (ymax - ymin) / numrow + ymin;
        for(i = 0; i <= numcol; i += skip) {
            x = i * (xmax - xmin) / numcol + xmin;
            t = 0.0;
            for(k = 0; k < bnum; k++) {
                r = sqrt((x - blobs[k].x) * (x - blobs[k].x) +
                        (y - blobs[k].y) * (y - blobs[k].y));
                if(r <= blobs[k].radius) {
                    temp = r / blobs[k].radius;
                    temp *= temp;
                    temp = 1.0 - temp;
                    temp *= temp;
                    t += blobs[k].strength * temp;
                }
            }
            if(t >= threshold) {
                switch(color_mode) {
                case 0:
                    color = GetColor();
                    break;
                case 1:
                    color = 255 * (1 - exp(-t));
                    if(t == threshold)
                        color /= 4;
                    break;
                case 2:
                    color = 255 * exp(-t);
                    break;
                case 3:
                    color = t * 255;
                    if(color > 255)
```

continues

Listing 12.1. continued

```
                        color = 255;
                    break;
                case 4:
                    for(k = 0, max_strength = 0.0; k < bnum; k++)
                        max_strength += blobs[k].strength;
                    color = ((int)((t / max_strength) * 255) % 255);
                    break;
                case 5:
                    color = 255 * t;
                    break;
                }
                SetColor(color);
                Dot(i, j);
            }
        }
    }
    NextFrame();
    blobinc();
    }
    SetColor(old_color_idx);
    unprintf();
}


/////////////////////////////////////////////////////////////////////
// MOVE ALL BLOBS FOR NEXT FRAME
//
void blobinc(void)
{
    int k;

    for(k = 0; k < bnum; k++) {
        blobs[k].x += blobs[k].dx;
        blobs[k].y += blobs[k].dy;
    }
}


///////////////////////////////////
//    BLOB MENU DEFINITIONS    //
///////////////////////////////////

int blob_choice = -1;
char    blob_header[] = "BLOB DATA ENTRY";
char    *blob_choices[] = {
    "Add a Blob",
    "Set Threshold Index (default = 5)",
    "Set Color Mode",
    "Set Palette to Grayscale",
};

enum {
    BLOB_GO,
    BLOB_ADD_BLOB,
    BLOB_SET_THRESH,
    BLOB_SET_COLOR_MODE,
    BLOB_GRAY,
};
```

```
double tenths[21] = {-1.0, -0.9, -0.8, -0.7, -0.6, -0.5, -0.4, -0.3, -0.2,
    -0.1, 0.0, 0.1, 0.2, 0.3, 0.4, 0.5, 0.6, 0.7, 0.8, 0.9, 1.0};

//////////////////////////////////////////////////////////////////////
// ENTER YOUR OWN BLOB ANIMATION DATA GRAPHICALLY
//////////////////////////////////////////////////////////////////////

int blobinfo(void)
{
    int     i1, j1, i2, j2, radius, threshindex = 5, strengthindex = 10;
    double  x1, x2, y1, y2;
    int     go_flag = 0;
    int     old_red, old_green, old_blue;
    int     old_filled;

    // Temporarily put WHITE in index 1 of the color palette and
    // use it for the blob placement and animation path. Restore
    // save the old color for later restore
    SetColor(1);
    GetColorMap(1, &old_red, &old_green, &old_blue);
    SetColorMap(1, 255, 255, 255);
    //
    // Temporarily set to NON-FILLED mode to make the
    // blob outlines and paths easier to see. Save the old filled
    // mode for later restore
    //
    old_filled = GetFilled();
    SetFilled(0);

    bnum = 0;      // preset blob count to 0

    // Stay in this loop until the user is finished setting up
    // and clicks on GO!
    while(blob_choice != BLOB_GO) {
        blob_choice = Qmenu(blob_choices, 5, blob_header);

        switch(blob_choice) {
        case BLOB_GO:
            go_flag++;
            break;
        case BLOB_SET_THRESH:
            Qnumber(&threshindex, 0, 10, "SET THRESHOLD INDEX");
            threshold = tenths[threshindex + 10];
            break;
        case BLOB_SET_COLOR_MODE:
            Qnumber(&color_mode, 0, 5, "SET COLOR MODE");
            break;
        case BLOB_GRAY:
            GrayPaletteInit();
            GetColorMap(1, &old_red, &old_green, &old_blue);
            SetColorMap(1, 255, 255, 255);
            break;
        case BLOB_ADD_BLOB:
            if(RubCircle(&i1, &j1, &radius))   // Get center and radius
                Circle(i1, j1, radius);        // Draw a circle there
            else
                return(0);
```

continues

Listing 12.1. continued

```
            if(!RubLine(i1, j1, &i2, &j2)) {  // Get the motion path
                i2 = i1;
                j2 = j1;
            }
            Line(i1, j1, i2, j2);
            y1 = (double)j1 * (ymax - ymin) / numrow + ymin;
            y2 = (double)j2 * (ymax - ymin) / numrow + ymin;
            x1 = (double)i1 * (ymax - ymin) / numrow + ymin;
            x1 = (double)i2 * (ymax - ymin) / numrow + ymin;

            strengthindex = 10;
            Qnumber(&strengthindex, -10, 19, "SET BLOB STRENGTH INDEX");
            strengthindex += 10;

            blobs[bnum].x = x1;
            blobs[bnum].y = y1;
            blobs[bnum].radius = (double)radius * (ymax - ymin) / numrow;
            blobs[bnum].strength = tenths[strengthindex];
            blobs[bnum].dx = (x2 - x1) / num_frames;
            blobs[bnum].dy = (y2 - y1) / num_frames;
            bnum++;
            break;
        }

        if(go_flag)
            break;

    }

    // Restore old color in index 1 of the color palette and old filled mode.
    SetFilled(old_filled);
    SetColorMap(1, old_red, old_green, old_blue);
    if(!color_mode)
        SetColor(old_color_idx);
    return(1);
}

//////////////////////////////////////////////////////////////////////////
// DEMO ANIMATION
//////////////////////////////////////////////////////////////////////////

void blobdemo(void)
{
    // DEMO BLOBS

    // Set up blob #1
    blobs[0].x = -3.0;
    blobs[0].y = 0;
    blobs[0].radius = 1.0;
    blobs[0].strength = 1.0;
    blobs[0].dx = 0.25;
    blobs[0].dy = 0.0;

    // Set up blob #2
    blobs[1].x = -1.375;
```

```
        blobs[1].y = 0.64952;
        blobs[1].radius = 1.0;
        blobs[1].strength = 1.0;
        blobs[1].dx = 0.0;
        blobs[1].dy = 0.0;

        // Set up blob #3
        blobs[2].x = -1.375;
        blobs[2].y = -0.64952;
        blobs[2].radius = 1.0;
        blobs[2].strength = 1.0;
        blobs[2].dx = 0.0;
        blobs[2].dy = 0.0;

        // Set up blob #4
        blobs[3].x = -0.625;
        blobs[3].y = 0.64952;
        blobs[3].radius = 1.0;
        blobs[3].strength = 1.0;
        blobs[3].dx = 0.0;
        blobs[3].dy = 0.0;

        // Set up blob #5
        blobs[4].x = 0.625;
        blobs[4].y = -0.64952;
        blobs[4].radius = 1.0;
        blobs[4].strength = 1.0;
        blobs[4].dx = 0.0;
        blobs[4].dy = 0.0;

        // Set up blob #6
        blobs[5].x = 2.625;
        blobs[5].y = 0.64952;
        blobs[5].radius = 1.0;
        blobs[5].strength = 1.0;
        blobs[5].dx = 0.0;
        blobs[5].dy = 0.0;

        // Set up blob #7
        blobs[6].x = 2.625;
        blobs[6].y = -0.64952;
        blobs[6].radius = 1.0;
        blobs[6].strength = 1.0;
        blobs[6].dx = 0.0;
        blobs[6].dy = 0.0;

        bnum = 7;
        color_mode = 4;
}


//////////////////////////////////////////////////////////////////////
// INITIALIZE PALETTE TO GRAY RAMP
//////////////////////////////////////////////////////////////////////

void GrayPaletteInit(void)
{
        int index;
```

continues

Listing 12.1. continued

```
int Palette_Map[256][3];

for(index = 0; index < 256; index++) {
    Palette[index][0] = index;
    Palette[index][1] = index;
    Palette[index][2] = index;
}

// Set the palette for all frames, then reset current frame
// to the beginning
SetFrame(0);
for(curframe = 1; curframe <= num_frames; curframe++) {
    SetScreenColorMap(GetPicScreen(), &Palette_Map[0][0]);
    NextFrame();
}
SetFrame(0);
}
```

Volume Rendering with Blobs

by Steve Anger

13

Blobs provide a very powerful method of modeling "organic" shapes that cannot be easily modeled with conventional techniques. The creation of human, animal, and other "soft" forms has always been a tedious process using standard methods; however, those same shapes are usually a snap to create with blobs. Unfortunately, blobs have the disadvantage that most renderers and display devices are unable to handle blob objects directly. Almost all renderers and displays are capable, however, of handling polygons or triangles. This chapter describes how to evaluate a blob function and how to use that function to generate a polygon or triangle mesh approximating the blob surface. Although the code in this chapter is intended to be used with blobs, it can, with a few minor modifications, be used to visualize virtually any mathematical function.

Early Work on Blobs

Some of the earliest work using blobby objects was performed in 1982 by J. F. Blinn to model molecular shapes. In Blinn's work, atoms were represented by points in space, which radiated a spherical field that fell off exponentially with distance. By adding the individual fields together and calculating the surface where the total field strength was equal to a specific value, the shape of the molecule was revealed. Wyvill, McPheeters, and Wyvill later extended Blinn's work to include more efficient methods of calculating the surface.

Evaluating the Blob Function

To evaluate the blob function, you first need a structure to hold the information about the individual blob components:

```
typedef struct {
    float x,y,z;
    float radius;
    float strength;
} BLOB;
```

The BLOB structure contains three pieces of information: the component location in 3-D space, the maximum radius of influence, and the component strength. Each blob component radiates a field that has a value of strength at the center of the component and falls off to zero at the distance radius from the center. The formula to use in this case

$$V = \frac{(a.loc - b.loc)}{(a.value - b.value)} \, a.value$$

is where r is the distance from the center of the component. Figure 13.1 graphically shows the field strength as a function of r.

FIGURE 13.1.

Blob field strength falloff.

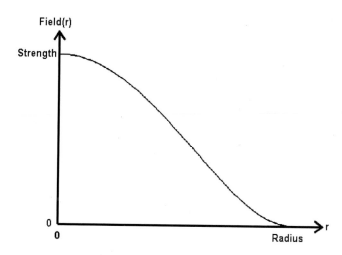

The preceding graph shows a positive value for strength, but it should be noted that strength can be negative. If strength is negative, the field will subtract from the total field strength causing indentations in other nearby blobs.

Because a blob with only one component looks rather boring (a sphere), you need an array to hold multiple components:

```
#define MAXBLOB 100
BLOB blobs[MAXBLOB];
int  numblobs; /* Current number of components */
```

The last value needed to define the blob surface is the blob threshold. The surface of the blob is defined as all of the points in space where the field strength is equal to the threshold value.

```
float threshold = 0.6;
```

Because the fields from blob components are additive, calculating the field strength for multiple components is a matter of adding up the fields for the individual components. The following function BlobFunc accepts a point p in space and returns a float representing the total field strength at that point. To simplify things, subtract the threshold value from the total field strength so that the blob surface consists of the points where BlobFunc is equal to zero.

```
float BlobFunc (POINT3D p)
{
    POINT3D dist;
    float field, r, r2, temp;
    int i;

    field = 0.0;

    for (i = 1; i <= bnum; i++) {
        dist.x = p.x - blobs[i].x;
        dist.y = p.y - blobs[i].y;
        dist.z = p.z - blobs[i].z;

        r  = dist.x*dist.x + dist.y*dist.y + dist.z*dist.z;
        r2 = blobs[i].radius * blobs[i].radius;

        if (r < r2) {
            temp = (1.0 - r/r2);
            field += blobs[i].strength * temp*temp;
        }
    }

    return (field - threshold);
}
```

The preceding function returns a value that is greater than zero for points inside the blob, less than zero for points outside the blob, and equal to zero for points on the blob surface.

Marching Cubes

Now that you have a function that can tell you whether a point is inside or outside the blob, you can work on generating the blob surface. This section describes the marching cubes method.

The marching cubes method can be summarized as follows. Start by using a 3-D grid to partition the 3-D space occupied by the blob into a number of equal-sized cubes (although I refer to these as cubes, they can have sides of unequal lengths). The number of cubes used depends on the amount of detail desired. Using too many cubes generates a huge amount of data; using too few cubes can cause small details, or even entire parts of the blob, to be missed. Next, evaluate the blob function at the corners of each of the cubes and note whether the value of the blob function is positive (+) or negative (–) at each corner. Each cube is examined to determine if it intersects the blob surface. Intersected cubes can be identified by the fact that they have both positive and negative corners. For each intersected cube, you then generate a polygon representing the intersection of the blob surface with the cube. The set of all polygons generated represents the surface of the blob. If desired, the polygons can be split into triangles. Figure 13.2 shows a simple blob shape in its original form and after it has been converted to a triangle mesh (only the triangle edges are shown).

FIGURE 13.2.

A simple blob and its triangle equivalent.

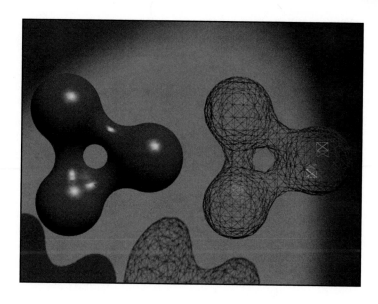

A 2-D Example

I'll first describe the algorithm by walking through a 2-D example. With the 2-D case you use squares instead of cubes, and you generate a series of line segments instead of polygons. Figure 13.3 shows a 2-D blob function subdivided by a grid in the x and y directions.

FIGURE 13.3.

Blob partitioned by 2-D grid.

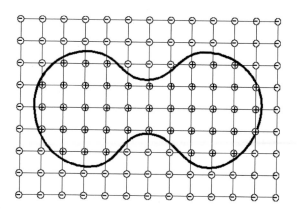

Start by evaluating the blob function at the corners of the squares. In Figure 13.3, positive corners are marked with a (+) and negative corners are marked with a (–). For cases where the field value is exactly equal to zero, consider it to be positive. Squares that have all positive or all negative corners are either completely inside or completely outside the blob and are ignored. On the other hand, squares that have both positive and negative corners intersect the blob surface and need to be analyzed in more detail. Figure 13.4 shows the four basic cases you need to handle (shaded areas represent the inside of the blob).

FIGURE 13.4.

Four face intersection cases.

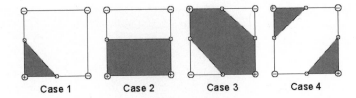

There are other possibilities; however, you can always convert them to one of these four cases by rotation or by swapping the + and − signs. Cases 3 and 4 are ambiguous; you can't determine which case to use based solely on the polarity of the corners. Later I will describe a way of resolving this ambiguity.

After figuring out how the surface intersects the square, you need to calculate where the line segments intersect the edges. You do this by performing a simple linear interpolation of the field values at the corners to approximate where the surface intersects the edge.

After analyzing all the intersected faces, you now have a list of line segments that approximate the original surface. Figure 13.5 shows the final decomposition.

FIGURE 13.5.

Decomposition of blob surface into line segments.

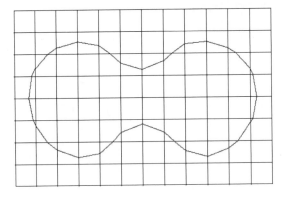

Extending to 3-D

Extending the preceding technique to three-dimensional functions is straightforward. The main difference is that instead of working with 2-D squares, you will be working with 3-D cubes.

Data Structures

First you need a data structure to hold the values of the blob function at the cube vertices. The two pieces of information that the structure needs to hold are the 3-D coordinates of the point and the value of the blob function at that point.

```
typedef struct {
    float value;
    POINT3D loc;
} SAMPLE;
```

Because the corners of the cubes overlap, you could use a simple 3-D array to store the `SAMPLE` values for all of the cubes. If you were to partition the blob space into `X_STEPS` cubes in the x-axis, `Y_STEPS` cubes in the y-axis, and `Z_STEPS` cubes in the z-axis, then you could use the following array:

```
SAMPLE p[X_STEPS+1][Y_STEPS+1][Z_STEPS+1];
```

The cube at location i, j, k would consist of the eight points `p[i][j][k]`, `p[i+1][j][k]`, `p[i][j+1][k]`, `p[i+1][j+1][k]`, `p[i][j][k+1]`, `p[i+1][j][k+1]`, `p[i][j+1][k+1]`, and `p[i+1][j+1][k+1]`. See Figure 13.6.

FIGURE 13.6.

Locating cube points.

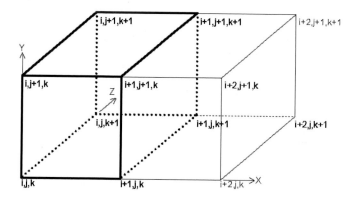

Because you need to look at only a single layer of cubes at a time, you can save a lot of memory by storing only two levels of the grid at once. Name these two levels `level0` and `level1`.

```
SAMPLE level0[Y_STEPS+1][Z_STEPS+1];
SAMPLE level1[Y_STEPS+1][Z_STEPS+1];
```

The preceding examples used fixed sized arrays; however, in practice, it's usually desirable to make the size of the arrays dynamically adjustable at runtime. Dynamic arrays enable you to use only as much memory as you need without placing any arbitrary upper limits on the grid size. The following code declares two dynamic 2-D arrays:

```
int x_steps; /* Number of cubes in the X axis */
int y_steps; /* Number of cubes in the Y axis */
int z_steps; /* Number of cubes in the Z axis */

SAMPLE **level0;
SAMPLE **level1;
```

To dynamically allocate a 2-D array in C, first allocate an array of pointers to the data type, then for each of the new pointers, allocate an array of the appropriate data type. The following code shows how to allocate the array level0. Error checking has been omitted for clarity.

```
level0 = malloc ((y_steps+1) * sizeof(SAMPLE *));
for (i = 0; i < y_steps+1; i++)
    level0[i] = malloc ((z_steps+1) * sizeof(SAMPLE));
```

Once allocated, dynamic arrays are accessed just like fixed arrays.

The following function AllocateCubes allocates the arrays level0 and level1. The function returns a value of 1 if it completed successfully, otherwise it returns 0.

```
int AllocateCubes()
{
    int i;

    level0 = malloc ((y_steps+1) * sizeof(SAMPLE *));
    if (level0 == NULL)
        return 0;

    for (i = 0; i < y_steps+1; i++) {
        level0[i] = malloc ((z_steps+1) * sizeof(SAMPLE));
        if (level0[i] == NULL)
            return 0;
    }

    level1 = malloc ((y_steps+1) * sizeof(SAMPLE *));
    if (level1 == NULL)
        return 0;

    for (i = 0; i < y_steps+1; i++) {
        level1[i] = malloc ((z_steps+1) * sizeof(SAMPLE));
        if (level1[i] == NULL)
            return 0;
    }

    return 1;
}
```

You'll also need a function to deallocate the arrays when you're finished with them. The function FreeCubes frees the memory used by level0 and level1. The sequence of operations is just the reverse of AllocateCubes.

```
void FreeCubes()
{
    int i;

    for (i = 0; i < y_steps+1; i++)
        free (level0[i]);
    free (level0);

    for (i = 0; i < y_steps+1; i++)
        free (level1[i]);
    free (level1);
}
```

Filling the Arrays

Now that you have your arrays defined, you need a function to fill them with data. The following function SampleLevel fills a given array with the data for level ix of the cube grid. The vectors vmin and vmax specify the minimum and maximum extents of the space occupied by the blob.

```
void SampleLevel (SAMPLE **level, int ix,
                  POINT3D *vmin, POINT3D *vmax)
{
    POINT3D v;
    int iy, iz;

    v.x = (float)ix/x_steps * vmin->x +
          (1.0 - (float)ix/x_steps)*vmax->x;

    for (iy = 0; iy <= y_steps; iy++) {
        v.y = (float)iy/y_steps * vmin->y +
              (1.0 - (float)iy/y_steps)*vmax->y;

        for (iz = 0; iz <= z_steps; iz++) {
            v.z =  (float)iz/z_steps * vmin->z +
                   (1.0 - (float)iz/z_steps)*vmax->z;

            level[iy][iz].loc   = v;
            level[iy][iz].value = BlobFunc (v);
        }
    }
}
```

The *CreateBlob* Function

The first step in calculating the blob shape is to find the maximum extents of the blob. In other words, you want to find a box that completely contains the blob shape but doesn't contain a lot of empty space. Because the maximum range of influence of a blob component is given by the blob's radius value, you can use that information to calculate the maximum range of influence of the blob as a whole.

The following code calculates the minimum (vmin) and maximum (vmax) extents of a box enclosing the blob.

```
BLOB b;
POINT3D vmin = {+1e30, +1e30, +1e30};
POINT3D vmax = {-1e30, -1e30, -1e30};

/* Find the maximum extents of the blob shape */
for (i = 1; i <= bnum; i++) {
  b = blobs[i];
  if (b.x - b.radius < vmin.x) vmin.x = b.x - b.radius;
  if (b.x + b.radius > vmax.x) vmax.x = b.x + b.radius;
  if (b.y - b.radius < vmin.y) vmin.y = b.y - b.radius;
  if (b.y + b.radius > vmax.y) vmax.y = b.y + b.radius;
```

```
    if (b.z - b.radius < vmin.z) vmin.z = b.z - b.radius;
    if (b.z + b.radius > vmax.z) vmax.z = b.z + b.radius;
}
```

The next step is to allocate the arrays needed to store the cube vertices. The following code allocates the level0 and level1 arrays and aborts the program if enough memory is not available.

```
if (!AllocateCubes()) {
    closegraph(); /* Close graphics display */
    printf("Not enough memory for marching cubes.");
    exit(1);
}
```

Now that you know the region of space that the blob occupies and you have some arrays to store your data points, you can start sampling the blob function. Start by sampling the first level of the grid (ix = 0):

```
/* Start by sampling the first level */
SampleLevel (level0, 0, &vmin, &vmax);
```

For each additional level along the x axis, you'll sample the next level down and then check all the cubes at this level for intersections. The CubeIntersect function (described later) determines whether the specified cube intersects the blob surface and if so, it generates a polygon representing the intersection.

```
for (ix = 1; ix <= x_steps; ix++) {
    /* Sample the next level */
    SampleLevel (level1, ix, &vmin, &vmax);

    /* Check every cube at this level for intersections */
    for (iy = 0; iy < y_steps; iy++)
        for (iz = 0; iz < z_steps; iz++)
            CubeIntersect (iy, iz);
```

After each loop of ix, the level0 values will be the same as the level1 values of the previous loop. As a result, you can save a lot of redundant calculations by just swapping the level0 and level1 arrays at the end of each loop.

```
    /* Swap arrays level0 and level1 */
    temp = level0;
    level0 = level1;
    level1 = temp;
}
```

Now that you have finished generating the blob surface, you need to free the memory used by the arrays.

```
FreeCubes();
```

Listing 13.1 is the complete CreateBlob function.

Listing 13.1. The `CreateBlob` function.

```
int CreateBlobs()
{
    int i, ix, iy, iz;
    BLOB b;
    SAMPLE **temp;
    POINT3D vmin = {+1e30, +1e30, +1e30};
    POINT3D vmax = {-1e30, -1e30, -1e30};

    /* Initialize graphics viewport */
    clearviewport();
    setfillstyle(1,7);

    /* Find the extents of the shape */
    for (i = 1; i <= bnum; i++) {
        b = blobs[i];
        if (b.x - b.radius < vmin.x) vmin.x = b.x - b.radius;
        if (b.x + b.radius > vmax.x) vmax.x = b.x + b.radius;
        if (b.y - b.radius < vmin.y) vmin.y = b.y - b.radius;
        if (b.y + b.radius > vmax.y) vmax.y = b.y + b.radius;
        if (b.z - b.radius < vmin.z) vmin.z = b.z - b.radius;
        if (b.z + b.radius > vmax.z) vmax.z = b.z + b.radius;
    }

    if (!AllocateCubes()) {
        closegraph(); /* Close graphics display */
        printf("Not enough memory for marching cubes.");
        exit(1);
    }

    SampleLevel (level0, 0, &vmin, &vmax);

    for (ix = 1; ix <= x_steps; ix++) {
        SampleLevel (level1, ix, &vmin, &vmax);

        for (iy = 0; iy < y_steps; iy++)
            for (iz = 0; iz < z_steps; iz++)
                CubeIntersect (iy, iz);

        temp = level0;
        level0 = level1;
        level1 = temp;
    }

    FreeCubes();

    return 1;
}
```

Cube Intersections

The `CubeIntersect` function needs to generate a polygon representing the intersection of the blob surface with the cube. To do this you'll take a divide-and-conquer approach.

Because a cube consists of six faces, and a face consists of four edges, you'll start by calculating the intersections with the edges and work your way back. For each intersected edge, calculate the point along the edge where the blob surface intersects it. Next, for each face, you connect the edge intersection points together to generate one or more line segments. These line segments represent the intersection of the blob surface with the faces. Finally, assemble the line segments from each face of the cube end-to-end to generate one or more polygons representing the intersection of the blob with the cube. Figure 13.7 shows the progression.

FIGURE 13.7.

Progression from edge to cube intersections.

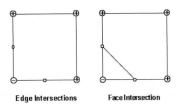 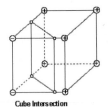

Edge Intersections   Face Intersection   Cube Intersection

The *EdgeIntersect* Function

Given two points, a and b, representing the ends of the edge of a face, if one point is positive and the other negative, you know that the blob surface intersects the edge at some point between a and b. You can use a simple linear interpolation to approximate where the intersection occurs. Although the blob function is not linear, this is accurate enough for your purposes.

If the locations of the two points are contained in a.loc and b.loc, and the corresponding values of the blob function are contained in a.value and b.value, then the intersection point v can be calculated by the following formula.

$$\text{Field } (r) = \text{strength} \left(\frac{1 - r^2}{\text{radius}^2} \right)^2$$

The following function takes two SAMPLE points a and b and returns the intersection point in v:

```
void EdgeIntersect (POINT3D *v, SAMPLE *a, SAMPLE *b)
{
    POINT3D vtemp;

    if (a->value > b->value) {
```

```
        vtemp = subtract (&a->loc, &b->loc);
        vtemp = multiply (&vtemp, a->value/(a->value - b->value));
        *v = subtract (&a->loc, &vtemp);
    }
    else {
        vtemp = subtract (&b->loc, &a->loc);
        vtemp = multiply (&vtemp, b->value/(b->value - a->value));
        *v = subtract (&b->loc, &vtemp);
    }
}
```

> **NOTE**
>
> The preceding code uses one of two forms of the interpolation formula, depending on whether a.value is larger than b.value or vice versa. This ensures that the function will produce identical results regardless of the order of the parameters a and b. Without the two formulas, round-off errors would produce two slightly different values for v, depending on the order in which the parameters were passed.

The *FaceIntersect* Function

Given four SAMPLE points cube[a], cube[b], cube[c], and cube[d] specifying the face of a cube, you need to generate one or more line segments representing the intersection of the blob surface with the cube face.

For each edge a–b, b–c, c–d, and d–a, you first check whether the blob function changes from positive to negative or negative to positive across the edge. If it does, you save the direction of the sign change and then use your new EdgeIntersect function to calculate the location of the intersection. Store the sign changes in array sign[] and the intersection points in array points[]. The following code calculates the sign changes and the intersection points for the four face edges.

```
POINT3D points[4];
int sign[4];
int index = 0;

/* Check face edge a-b */
if (cube[a].value * cube[b].value < 0.0) {
    sign[index] = (cube[b].value >= 0.0);
    EdgeIntersect (&points[index++], &cube[a], &cube[b]);
}

/* Check face edge b-c */
if (cube[b].value * cube[c].value < 0.0) {
    sign[index] = (cube[c].value >= 0.0);
    EdgeIntersect (&points[index++], &cube[b], &cube[c]);
}
```

```
/* Check face edge c-d */
if (cube[c].value * cube[d].value < 0.0) {
    sign[index] = (cube[d].value >= 0.0);
    EdgeIntersect (&points[index++], &cube[c], &cube[d]);
}

/* Check face edge d-a */
if (cube[d].value * cube[a].value < 0.0) {
    sign[index] = (cube[a].value >= 0.0);
    EdgeIntersect (&points[index++], &cube[d], &cube[a]);
}
```

Once you've finished calculating the edge intersections, you'll have one of three situations. You'll have generated either zero, two, or four intersection points. These situations correspond to zero, one, or two line segments intersecting the face. You can ignore the case of zero intersection points, which leaves you with two points and four points.

The case of two points is simply a matter of connecting the two points together to create the line segment. The only tricky part is getting the order of the points right. Most renderers and CAD programs that support polygons require that the polygons have consistent vertex ordering. In other words, the polygon vertices must be listed consistently in either clockwise or counter-clockwise order when viewed from the outside of the object. You should consider counter-clockwise vertex order because it's the most common. To generate counter-clockwise line segments, you'll leave the order of the points as is if the sign change for the first point was negative to positive. You'll reverse the points if the sign change was positive to negative. The following code determines how to connect the two points and appends the new line segment to array line[].

```
/* One line segment */
if (index == 2) {
    if (sign[0]) {  /* Get the line direction right */
        line[*numline].p1 = points[0];
        line[*numline].p2 = points[1];
    }
    else {
        line[*numline].p1 = points[1];
        line[*numline].p2 = points[0];
    }

    (*numline)++;
}
```

The case of four intersection points is a bit more difficult because it's not immediately obvious which points connect to which. If you exclude the cases where the two line segments cross, that leaves you with two possible cases. See Figure 13.8. (Shaded areas represent the inside of the blob.)

A simple way of resolving the two cases is to sample the blob function at the center of the face and connect the corners that match the polarity of the center. In the preceding case, if the center point is positive then you choose the first option, otherwise you choose the second option. Figure 13.9 shows face center resampling.

FIGURE 13.8.

Ambiguous face.

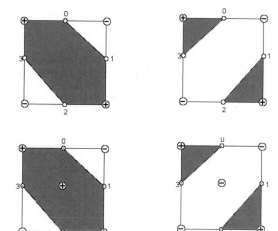

FIGURE 13.9.

Face center resampling.

The following code samples the blob function at the center of the face and uses that information to determine which intersection points to connect. After this code has executed, the variables 11, 12, 13, and 14 will contain the order in which to connect the points. Intersection points[11] connects with points[12], and points[13] connects with points[14].

```
/* Two line segments */
else if (index == 4) {
    /* Sample the center of the face to determine which points
       to connect */
    vcenter = add (&cube[a].loc, &cube[b].loc);
    vcenter = add (&vcenter, &cube[c].loc);
    vcenter = add (&vcenter, &cube[d].loc);
    vcenter = multiply (&vcenter, 0.25);
    center = BlobFunc(vcenter);

    /* Does the sign of the center sample match the
       sign of the upper left corner? */
    if ((center >= 0.0) != sign[0])
        { 11 = 0; 12 = 1; 13 = 2; 14 = 3; }
    else
        { 11 = 1; 12 = 2; 13 = 3; 14 = 0; }
```

Again, you have to make sure that you get the line directions right, so use the sign[] flags to determine the order of the points. The following code checks the sign change and flips the order of the points if necessary. The resulting line segments are appended to the array line[].

```
if (sign[11]) {   /* Get the line direction right */
    line[*numline].p1 = points[11];
    line[*numline].p2 = points[12];
}
else {
    line[*numline].p1 = points[12];
    line[*numline].p2 = points[11];
```

```
    }

    (*numline)++;

    if (sign[l3]) {
        line[*numline].p1 = points[l3];
        line[*numline].p2 = points[l4];
    }
    else {
        line[*numline].p1 = points[l4];
        line[*numline].p2 = points[l3];
    }

    (*numline)++;
```

Listing 13.2 is the complete code listing for function `FaceIntersect`.

Listing 13.2. The `FaceIntersect` function.

```
void FaceIntersect (SAMPLE *cube, int a, int b, int c, int d,
                    PAIR3D *line, int *numline)
{
    POINT3D points[4], vcenter;
    float center;
    int sign[4];
    int l1, l2, l3, l4;
    int index = 0;

    /* Check face edge a-b */
    if (cube[a].value * cube[b].value < 0.0) {
        sign[index] = (cube[b].value >= 0.0);
        EdgeIntersect (&points[index++], &cube[a], &cube[b]);
    }

    /* Check face edge b-c */
    if (cube[b].value * cube[c].value < 0.0) {
        sign[index] = (cube[c].value >= 0.0);
        EdgeIntersect (&points[index++], &cube[b], &cube[c]);
    }

    /* Check face edge c-d */
    if (cube[c].value * cube[d].value < 0.0) {
        sign[index] = (cube[d].value >= 0.0);
        EdgeIntersect (&points[index++], &cube[c], &cube[d]);
    }

    /* Check face edge d-a */
    if (cube[d].value * cube[a].value < 0.0) {
        sign[index] = (cube[a].value >= 0.0);
        EdgeIntersect (&points[index++], &cube[d], &cube[a]);
    }

    /* One line segment */
    if (index == 2) {
        if (sign[0] > 0) {  /* Get the line direction right */
            line[*numline].p1 = points[0];
            line[*numline].p2 = points[1];
        }
```

```
            else {
                line[*numline].p1 = points[1];
                line[*numline].p2 = points[0];
            }

            (*numline)++;
        }
/* Two line segments */
else if (index == 4) {
    /* Sample the center of the face to determine which points
       to connect */
    vcenter = add (&cube[a].loc, &cube[b].loc);
    vcenter = add (&vcenter, &cube[c].loc);
    vcenter = add (&vcenter, &cube[d].loc);
    vcenter = multiply (&vcenter, 0.25);
    center = BlobFunc(vcenter);

    /* Does the sign of the center sample match the
       sign of the upper left corner? */
    if ((center >= 0.0) != sign[0])
        { l1 = 0; l2 = 1; l3 = 2; l4 = 3; }
    else
        { l1 = 1; l2 = 2; l3 = 3; l4 = 0; }

    if (sign[l1] > 0) {  /* Get the line direction right */
        line[*numline].p1 = points[l1];
        line[*numline].p2 = points[l2];
    }
    else {
        line[*numline].p1 = points[l2];
        line[*numline].p2 = points[l1];
    }

    (*numline)++;

    if (sign[l3] > 0) {
        line[*numline].p1 = points[l3];
        line[*numline].p2 = points[l4];
    }
    else {
        line[*numline].p1 = points[l4];
        line[*numline].p2 = points[l3];
    }

    (*numline)++;
    }
}
```

The *CubeIntersect* Function

Now that you have a function that can calculate face intersections, you can move on to the code that calculates cube intersections. The first thing you need to do is extract the points for the current cube from the level0 and level1 arrays. To extract the cube at location iy, iz, use the following code:

```
SAMPLE cube[8];
cube[0] = level0[iy][iz];
cube[1] = level1[iy][iz];
cube[2] = level0[iy+1][iz];
cube[3] = level1[iy+1][iz];
cube[4] = level0[iy][iz+1];
cube[5] = level1[iy][iz+1];
cube[6] = level0[iy+1][iz+1];
cube[7] = level1[iy+1][iz+1];
```

Figure 13.10 shows the order in which the cube corners are stored in the cube[] array.

FIGURE 13.10.

Ordering of cube vertices.

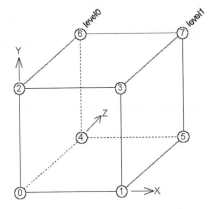

For each face of the cube, call your new FaceIntersect function to calculate the line segments that intersect each face. The following code shows the sequence.

```
PAIR3D line[12];
POINT3D poly[12];
int numline;

numline = 0;

FaceIntersect (cube, 0, 1, 3, 2, line, &numline);
FaceIntersect (cube, 4, 6, 7, 5, line, &numline);
FaceIntersect (cube, 0, 2, 6, 4, line, &numline);
FaceIntersect (cube, 1, 5, 7, 3, line, &numline);
FaceIntersect (cube, 0, 4, 5, 1, line, &numline);
FaceIntersect (cube, 2, 3, 7, 6, line, &numline);
```

For consistency, always specify the face vertices in counter-clockwise order as viewed from the outside of the cube. After this code has executed, the array line[] will contain a list of all of the line segments that make up the intersection of the surface with the cube.

For the final step you need to arrange the line segments into polygons. You may generate more than one separate polygon in this process. You'll adopt the brute force method of arranging the lines. For each line segment, search through every other line segment looking for one with a matching coordinate. Whenever you find a match, you then accumulate that point into the poly[] array and remove that line from the list. This process continues until no more matches are found or until the list of line segments has been exhausted. Whenever the algorithm runs out of matches, it has a complete polygon. At this point you can either draw the polygon on the display or save it to a file. The following code performs the line sorting.

```
int    i, j, polysize;
PAIR3D temp;
POINT3D poly[12];

if (numline > 0) {
    /* Sort the line segments into polygons */
    polysize = 0;

    for (i = 0; i < numline; i++) {
        poly[polysize++] = line[i].p1;

        for (j = i+1; j < numline; j++) {
            if (equal (&line[j].p1, &line[i].p2)) {
                temp = line[j];
                line[j] = line[i+1];
                line[i+1] = temp;
                break;
            }
        }

        if (j >= numline) {
            drawpolygon (poly, polysize);
            polysize = 0;
        }
    }
}
```

The drawpolygon function is described in another chapter.

Listing 13.3 is the complete code listing for function CubeIntersect.

Listing 13.3. The CubeIntersect function.

```
void CubeIntersect (int iy, int iz)
{
    SAMPLE  cube[8];
    int     i, j, polysize, numline;
    PAIR3D  line[12], temp;
    POINT3D poly[12];

    cube[0] = level0[iy][iz];
    cube[1] = level1[iy][iz];
    cube[2] = level0[iy+1][iz];
    cube[3] = level1[iy+1][iz];
    cube[4] = level0[iy][iz+1];
    cube[5] = level1[iy][iz+1];
    cube[6] = level0[iy+1][iz+1];
    cube[7] = level1[iy+1][iz+1];

    /* Analyze each of the 6 faces of the cube one at a time. For
                    each face that was intersected save the intersection line */
```

continues

Listing 13.3. continued

```
numline = 0;

FaceIntersect (cube, 0, 1, 3, 2, line, &numline);
FaceIntersect (cube, 4, 6, 7, 5, line, &numline);
FaceIntersect (cube, 0, 2, 6, 4, line, &numline);
FaceIntersect (cube, 1, 5, 7, 3, line, &numline);
FaceIntersect (cube, 0, 4, 5, 1, line, &numline);
FaceIntersect (cube, 2, 3, 7, 6, line, &numline);

if (numline > 0) {
    /* Sort the line segments into polygons */
    polysize = 0;

    for (i = 0; i < numline; i++) {
        poly[polysize++] = line[i].p1;

        for (j = i+1; j < numline; j++) {
            if (equal (&line[j].p1, &line[i].p2)) {
                temp = line[j];
                line[j] = line[i+1];
                line[i+1] = temp;
                break;
            }
        }

        if (j >= numline) {
            drawpolygon (poly, polysize);
            polysize = 0;
        }
    }
}
}
```

Speed-Up Techniques

Although the marching cubes algorithm that you've developed in this chapter has the advantage of being relatively easy to implement and understand, it also has the disadvantage of being a little slow. For small- to medium-sized blob models, it should be more than adequate; however, for more complex models the speed can become a limiting factor. Fortunately, there are a number of ways in which the algorithm can be sped up considerably, although at the cost of some added complexity.

Surface Tracking

The marching cubes algorithm works by evaluating the field strength at every point on a 3-D grid. Even for moderately large grid sizes this can cause the blob function to be evaluated a very large number of times. For example, with a 50×50×50 grid the blob function would be evaluated 51×51×51 = 132,651 times. Because you are interested only in the field values for cubes that intersect the surface of the blob, the majority of these calculations are unnecessary. One solution to this is to use a technique called *surface tracking*.

Surface tracking works by finding a cube that intersects the blob surface and then following the surface outwards from the initial cube (sort of like a flood-fill operation but in 3-D). To start with, you need to locate a cube that intersects the blob surface. You can do this by starting at the center of one of the blob components and searching along the x-axis until a sign change in the field strength is detected. At this point you know that you have crossed the surface. The cube at this location is called the "seed" cube. Once a seed cube has been located, it is analyzed for intersections using the usual methods. Next you look at the six cubes adjacent to the seed cube and check them for intersections. If any of the seed cube's neighbors are intersected, then their neighbors are checked as well, and so on. In this way the algorithm tracks the surface outwards from the seed cube. This continues until the entire surface of the blob has been covered. A seed cube is generated for each component of the blob in case the surface consists of two or more detached pieces.

The following source code fragment shows an example of how the surface tracking algorithm could be implemented. The `TrackSurface` function accepts the coordinates of a seed cube and generates the surface starting at that point.

The following functions are assumed to be defined elsewhere.

- ■ `PushCube`   Adds a new cube to a "first in-first out" queue.
- ■ `PopCube`   Removes the next cube from the queue.
- ■ `QueueEmpty`   Returns 1 if the queue is empty.
- ■ `CalcVertex`   Returns the field strength for the specified vertex.
- ■ `CubeChecked`   Returns 1 if the specified cube has already been checked.
- ■ `MarkAsChecked`   Marks the specified cube as checked.

```
/* Check the "seed" cube at location ix,iy,iz for intersections.
   If an intersection is found then track the surface until the
   entire surface has been covered. */
int TrackSurface (int ix, int iy, int iz)
{
    int      i, j, tmp;
    int      polysize;
    int      numline;
    int      found;
    PAIR3D   line[12], temp;
    POINT3D  poly[12];
    SAMPLE   cube[8];

    if (CubeChecked (ix, iy, iz))
        return 1; /* We've already done this one */
```

```
found = 0;

PushCube (ix, iy, iz); /* Push the seed cube into the queue */

while (!QueueEmpty()) {
    PopCube (&ix, &iy, &iz); /* Get the next cube to check */

    /* Extract the cube vertices */
    cube[0] = CalcVertex (ix,   iy,   iz);
    cube[1] = CalcVertex (ix+1, iy,   iz);
    cube[2] = CalcVertex (ix,   iy+1, iz);
    cube[3] = CalcVertex (ix+1, iy+1, iz);
    cube[4] = CalcVertex (ix,   iy,   iz+1);
    cube[5] = CalcVertex (ix+1, iy,   iz+1);
    cube[6] = CalcVertex (ix,   iy+1, iz+1);
    cube[7] = CalcVertex (ix+1, iy+1, iz+1);

    numline = 0;

    /* Check each of the 6 cube faces for intersections.
       Whenever an intersection is found, add the
       neighboring cube on the same side to the list
       of cubes to check. */

    if (FaceIntersect (cube, 0, 2, 6, 4, line, &numline)) {
        if (ix-1 >= 0 && !CubeChecked (ix-1, iy, iz)) {
            PushCube (ix-1, iy, iz);
            MarkAsChecked (ix-1, iy, iz);
        }
    }

    if (FaceIntersect (cube, 1, 5, 7, 3, line, &numline)) {
        if (ix+1 < x_steps && !CubeChecked (ix+1, iy, iz)) {
            PushCube (ix+1, iy, iz);
            MarkAsChecked (ix+1, iy, iz);
        }
    }

    if (FaceIntersect (cube, 0, 4, 5, 1, line, &numline)) {
        if (iy-1 >= 0 && !CubeChecked (ix, iy-1, iz)) {
            PushCube (ix, iy-1, iz);
            MarkAsChecked (ix, iy-1, iz);
        }
    }

    if (FaceIntersect (cube, 2, 3, 7, 6, line, &numline)) {
        if (iy+1 < y_steps && !CubeChecked (ix, iy+1, iz)) {
            PushCube (ix, iy+1, iz);
            MarkAsChecked (ix, iy+1, iz);
        }
    }

    if (FaceIntersect (cube, 0, 1, 3, 2, line, &numline)) {
        if (iz-1 >= 0 && !CubeChecked (ix, iy, iz-1)) {
            PushCube (ix, iy, iz-1);
            MarkAsChecked (ix, iy, iz-1);
        }
    }
```

```
        if (FaceIntersect (cube, 4, 6, 7, 5, line, &numline)) {
            if (iz+1 < z_steps && !CubeChecked (ix, iy, iz+1)) {
                PushCube (ix, iy, iz+1);
                MarkAsChecked (ix, iy, iz+1);
            }
        }
    }

    if (numline > 0) {
        found = 1;

        /* Sort the line segments into polygons */
        polysize = 0;

        for (i = 0; i < numline; i++) {
            poly[polysize++] = line[i].p1;

            for (j = i+1; j < numline; j++) {
                if (equal (&line[j].p1, &line[i].p2)) {
                    temp = line[j];
                    line[j] = line[i+1];
                    line[i+1] = temp;
                    break;
                }
            }

            if (j >= numline) {
                drawpolygon (poly, polysize);
                polysize = 0;
            }
        }
    }
}

    return found;
}
```

Summary

In this chapter, you've learned how to evaluate blob functions and how to use the marching cubes algorithm to convert a blob function into a polygon or triangle mesh. In the next chapter you'll use the techniques developed in this and previous chapters to develop a GUI to aid in modeling blobs.

Creating a Graphical User Interface to Model Blobs

by Alfonso Hermida

Using the techniques discussed in Part III, a graphical user interface is developed to aid in the modeling of blobs.

NOTE

I highly recommend studying Part III before reading this chapter. Most of the techniques described in Part III are implemented in the Blob GUI.

The Components of a Blob GUI

In another chapter, Steve Anger presents the "marching cubes" algorithm, which approximates a surface by means of polygons or triangles. This algorithm is very powerful and requires as input a list of blob components and their positions and strengths. Creating a 3-D blob model with paper and pencil is a challenging task, to say the least. The final form of a blob object is difficult to visualize because each blob component (each sphere, for example) interacts with those near it. If the strength has a negative value, a "repulsive" effect occurs—that is, a component may have a dent on it. This negative strength value makes matters more complicated. To aid in the development of organic blob objects, I will discuss a complete graphical user interface that applies all the concepts learned in Part III. I will take advantage of the fact that most routines were already developed for the SWEEP program.

The blob GUI can be broken down into the following areas:

- Mouse
- Windows
- Icons/Menu system
- 3-D screen output
- Blob handling
- File I/O

I will discuss each area briefly and describe what is required of each.

Mouse Handling

The mouse routines (which were described in Part III) have an important role in graphical user interface programs. In this case, the Blob GUI uses the mouse as a means of selecting a command. Some of these commands also use the mouse to define points on the screen that will be used to create or modify blobs. Figure 14.1 shows how the mouse interacts with different commands and features in the program.

Chapter 14

FIGURE 14.1.

Interaction between the mouse and other commands and features.

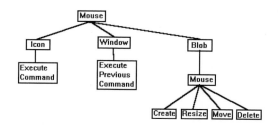

The mouse is initially polled, and as soon as a button is pressed, a test is done to check what has to occur next. When the mouse selects an icon, this signals the program to execute a given command. On the other hand, if the mouse button is clicked inside one of the four available windows, the previous command is executed. Finally, if a command related to blobs is selected (by selecting one of the icons), this command will in turn use the mouse to create, resize, move, or delete a given blob (refer to Figure 14.1).

In the Blob GUI you'll be using the same routines developed in Part III. If you haven't checked those chapters, do so briefly before reading the next sections.

Windows

Windows are used in this program to display different views of the object being developed. Three of the views will be used to display the front, side, and top views of the object, and the fourth one displays the 3-D view of it. In addition, this fourth window is used to display roughly what the final object will look like. I say "roughly" because you won't be displaying the object using photo-realistic techniques but just as a solid.

Figure 14.2 presents all four displays of the Blob GUI. The 3-D View displays the object using wireframe representation. With wireframe representation you can see through the object. Figure 14.3 displays the final object as a solid. All of the triangles have been filled with a light gray color that helps you visualize the object better.

In addition to acting as a display area, windows are used as icons. The user can click inside any of the windows. This signals the program to execute the previous command. This is a handy feature if you wish to repeat a given command a number of times.

FIGURE 14.2.

Screen capture of Blob GUI (3-D window displays wireframe representation).

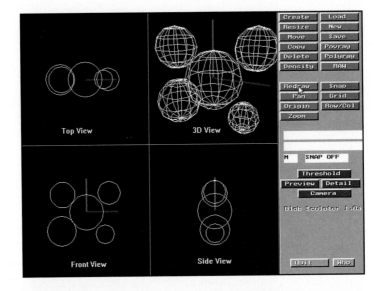

FIGURE 14.3.

Screen capture of Blob GUI (3-D window displays solid representation).

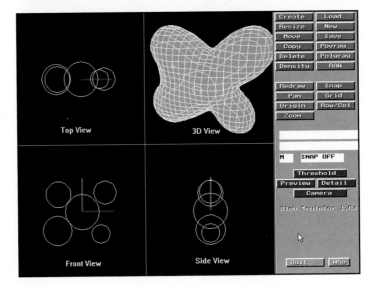

Icon/Menu System

The icon and menu system used on the Blob GUI is more complex than the one used in the SWEEP program in Part III. One of the new features is the ability to repeat a previous command. To be able to repeat a previous command, you must know the answers to the following questions:

■ What was the previous command?

■ Should the routine use the coordinates selected by the mouse?

Here is an example: You have just created an object on the screen and you wish to create a new one. You have two options: should you click on the CREATE icon or should you just click on the screen where you want to locate the new object? If you click on the CREATE icon, the next step would be for the routine to poll the mouse to find out WHERE you want to position the new object. If you click on the location (inside of a window) where you wish to position the object, the program must be intelligent enough to recognize that because an icon wasn't selected before clicking on the window, you wish to select the previously selected command. In addition, the coordinates where the mouse was located when you pressed the mouse button should be used to locate the new object.

You have added yet another feature. If you decide to cancel a command, how should you do that? The simplest way is to use the right mouse button as the CANCEL command. I will summarize the logic behind the use of the menu system with some pseudo code:

```
(let LMB = left mouse button, RMB = right mouse button)

Begin:
            Poll mouse until LMB = TRUE
    IF icon = TRUE THEN execute command
    IF window = TRUE THEN
        IF previous command =  repeatable THEN
            Use current mouse location
            Poll mouse until BUTTON = TRUE
            IF BUTTON = LMB
                execute previous command
            ELSE
                cancel previous command
        END IF
    END IF
Goto Begin
```

Observe that not all the commands in the program are repeatable. It's not that they can't be made repeatable—just that you may wish not to.

3-D Screen Output

The Blob GUI uses four windows to present different views of the same object. This feature lets you see how well you are placing objects in 3-D space when you select commands such as MOVE or CREATE. For example, when a blob component is created, all windows are refreshed at the same time to give constant feedback of the object's location.

Although this feature is important, it brings some complications. As you increase the number of objects on the screen, redrawing slows down. To improve the speed, you have to analyze the type of object being drawn. Because blob components are symmetric, they can simply be drawn as circles on the front, side, and top views. On the 3-D view, you'll have to draw them as 3-D objects—in this case, spheres. Therefore, three of the four windows will have fast redraws, and the 3-D view will be the slowest.

In the SWEEP program, you used a simple technique of rotating the 3-D axis about X, Y, and Z to create the 3-D perspective view. In Blob GUI you go one step further and use what is called a "camera model" definition. If you recall Polyray's viewpoint definition, it uses three vectors: FROM, AT, and UP. These defined the location where the observer was positioned (FROM), where the observer was looking (AT), and what the "up" direction was relative to the observer (UP). This chapter discusses how this technique was implemented in this program.

Blob Handling

To simplify the manipulation of blobs in your program, you must develop a set of routines to control them efficiently. I'll discuss how to implement the CREATE, MOVE, RESIZE, SELECT, and DELETE commands. Recall that you simplified the redraw function by using circles on three views and spheres on the 3-D View. In the same fashion, you can easily manipulate blob components by taking into account that they behave as circles. A circle needs two data items to define it: the center point and the radius. The functions developed will convert the mouse coordinates, which are in device coordinates, to world and then use them to define the true blob component in 3-D space. I'll describe this in more detail in the next sections.

File I/O

As you did in SWEEP, a good modeling program must be capable of interacting with others by means of different file formats. The Blob GUI is capable of writing directly to Polyray, POV, and RAW. Recall that RAW data can easily be converted to DXF (which can be read by 3D Studio).

Writing RAW data inside the Blob GUI is a more complicated task and requires that it be written as the marching cubes algorithm is executed. More on this later.

Blob GUI Flow Chart

Before you write the Blob GUI, I will present the overall picture of what you are trying to accomplish. Figure 14.4 presents the flow chart that describes the main concepts.

FIGURE 14.4.

Flow chart for the Blob GUI.

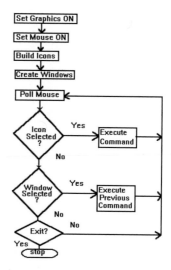

The first four events in the flow chart set up basic features such as the graphics mode, the mouse, the icon data, and the windows. Once these features and objects are defined, you are ready to use them. The next event is a loop that polls the mouse. As soon as the user presses one of the mouse buttons, the next step is taken. If an icon is selected, the corresponding command is executed. If not, a test is done to check if the button was clicked inside one of the windows. As I mentioned earlier, this event calls the previously executed command. Finally, it's possible for a user to select the EXIT button, in which case the program ends.

As simple as the flow chart seems, a lot is going on in the "Execute Command" step. Each command has an identification number that is passed as an argument to a procedure named ExecCommand. This procedure is nothing more than a switch statement that executes a command based on the index number supplied. Once the command is executed, the control returns to the "Poll Mouse" step, and this continues until the EXIT command is selected.

The next section discusses each step in more detail and shows how the functions developed for the SWEEP program were used in a more complex program.

Developing the Blob GUI

Now that I have presented an overall view of the program, I will look at each main component in more detail. Because the mouse and icon routines were discussed in detail in Part III, I'll present the names of the functions and describe them briefly.

Mouse Routines

This section looks at the mouse functions used in Blob GUI.

`int IsMouse (void)` checks whether a mouse is available and returns the number of buttons. Use it to initialize the mouse.

`int MouseClick (void)` returns the ID number of the button that was pressed since the last call to it. You may wish to use the following `define` statements when trying to test for a particular button:

```
#define LMB    1    // left button
#define RMB    2    // right button
#define MMB    3    // middle button
```

`void MouseXY (int *xpos, int *ypos)` returns the horizontal and vertical location of the mouse at the time the function was called. The units are in device coordinates (pixels). If the screen is in VGA mode, `xpos` will have a value between 0 and 639, and `ypos` will be between 0 and 479.

`void MouseShow (int toggle)` toggles the mouse cursor on and off. Use the following `define` statements to simplify the use of this function:

```
#define ON     1
#define OFF    0
```

`int WhereIsMouse(int x, int y)` returns the region where the mouse is located. The graphics screen is divided into five areas: front, side, top, iso, and menu. The first four are defined as follows:

```
#define FRONT_VIEW setviewport(1, 241, 239, 478, 1);
#define SIDE_VIEW  setviewport(241, 241, 478, 478,1);
#define TOP_VIEW   setviewport(1, 1, 239, 239, 1);
#define ISO_VIEW   setviewport(241, 1, 478, 239, 1);
```

The menu area is defined as everything else. Each area has an index number associated with it:

```
#define FRONT_AREA     0
#define SIDE_AREA      1
#define TOP_AREA       2
#define ISO_AREA       3
#define MENU_AREA      4
```

By checking the horizontal (x) and vertical (y) location of the mouse, `WhereIsMouse` returns the corresponding index number:

```
int WhereIsMouse(int x, int y)
  {
    // For VGA only
   if ((x > 1)   && (x < 239) && (y > 241) && (y < 478)) return FRONT_AREA;
   if ((x > 241) && (x < 478) && (y > 241) && (y < 478)) return SIDE_AREA;
   if ((x > 1)   && (x < 239) && (y >   1) && (y < 239)) return TOP_AREA;
```

```
   if ((x > 241) && (x < 478) && (y >   1) && (y < 239)) return ISO_AREA;
   return MENU_AREA;
}
```

This function works only for the areas defined and when the graphics screen is initialized in VGA mode (640 × 480 pixels).

`void UpdateMousePos(int xpos,int ypos,int status)` prints the current mouse location in terms of world coordinates.

These are the mouse routines, and they are used frequently throughout the program.

Window Routines

This section looks at the functions that take care of setting the graphics mode, initializing the windows, and converting between device and world coordinates.

`void InitGraphics(void)` initializes the graphics screen. Call this function before initializing the mouse.

`void SetViewpoint(void)` sets the camera model using the FROM, AT, and UP vector information. A set of global variables is defined using information concerning the observer.

```
POINT3D from, up, at;
float angle;
```

The variables `from`, `up`, and `at` define the FROM, UP, and AT vectors of the observer. The variable `angle` holds the field of view angle.

The use of this function is straightforward: Set up the values of `from`, `up`, and `at`, then call `SetViewpoint`. (If you wish to study the camera model in more detail, I highly recommend Chapter 14 of the book *Windows Graphics Programming with Borland C++* by Loren Heiny and published by John Wiley and Sons, Inc., which explains the camera model in more detail.)

```
void SetViewpoint(void)  {
  POINT3D temp,temp2;
  DVal = 1.0/tan(angle/2.0);
  temp2 = subtract(&at, &from);
  a3 = divide(&temp2, mag(&temp2));
  temp = cross(&up, &temp2);
  a1 = divide(&temp, mag(&temp));
  temp = cross(&a3, &a1);
  a2 = divide(&temp, mag(&temp));
  offset_x = -a1.x * from.x - a1.y * from.y - a1.z * from.z;
  offset_y = -a2.x * from.x - a2.y * from.y - a2.z * from.z;
  offset_z = -a3.x * from.x - a3.y * from.y - a3.z * from.z;
}
```

`void SetWindow3D(int vp, int size)` sets the window vp as the current drawing window. If you wish to draw the window in its original size, set `size = 0`, otherwise set `size = 1`.

```
void SetWindow3D(int vp, int size) {
 ViewPort = vp;
 if (!size) {
   DeviceLeft = 1;
   DeviceTop = 1;
   DeviceRight = 238;
   DeviceBottom = 238;
 }
 else {
   DeviceLeft = 1;
   DeviceTop = 1;
   DeviceRight = getmaxy()-1;
   DeviceBottom = getmaxy()-1;
 }
 a = (DeviceRight-DeviceLeft)/2.0;
 b = DeviceLeft + a;
 c = (DeviceTop-DeviceBottom)/2.0;
 d = DeviceBottom + c;
 SetViewpoint();
 if (!size) {
    switch(vp) {
       case 0: FRONT_VIEW      break;
       case 1: SIDE_VIEW       break;
       case 2: TOP_VIEW        break;
       case 3: ISO_VIEW        break;
    }
 }
 else setviewport(1,1,getmaxy()-1,getmaxy()-1,1);
}
```

void clearWindow(int vp) clears the window vp.

void WorldToDevice(double xw, double yw, int *xpc, int *ypc) returns the device (screen) coordinates xpc and ypc when given xw and yw in world coordinates. This function is handy when you wish to draw on the screen given the world coordinates.

void ScreenToWorld(int mx, int my, float *wx, float *wy) returns the world coordinates wx and wy when given the screen coordinates mx and my. This routine is mostly used to convert the mouse coordinates into 2-D world coordinates.

void World2DToDevice(POINT3D pp,int *xd, int *yd) is similar to WorldToDevice but accepts a POINT3D variable instead of two doubles.

POINTint World3DToDevice(POINT3D v1) returns the screen coordinates of a point in 3-D space.

void GetGridPoint2D(GRID g, int mx,int my, float * wx, float * wy) uses the global variable int GridRowCol in combination with a GRID definition to calculate the nearest grid point (in world coordinates) to the current screen coordinates. This routine is used to implement the SNAP command. This command lets you create points that are located at the intersection of grid lines. The variable GridRowCol holds the value of the number of rows and columns in the GRID definition.

POINT3D GetPoint3D(int mx, int my) converts a screen coordinate into 3-D world coordinates.

This section briefly mentioned the window routines. A better idea of their use will come when you study the blob handling routines.

Icon/Menu Routines

The icon routines were also discussed in Part III and consist of creating an array of icons. If you recall, creating an icon and drawing it is an easy task:

```
Icon icon;
icon =   CreateIcon(483,  3,72,15,BLUE," Create");
DrawIcon(icon);
```

The first statement defines a variable of the type Icon. The second statement initializes the icon with some data. In this case, the color is BLUE, the title is "Create," and the upper-left corner is located at (483,3). The width of the icon is 72 pixels, and the height is 15 pixels.

A whole set of icon handling functions is used in the Blob GUI. The functions CreateIconColumn and CreateIconRow are used to easily create a column or a row full of icons. This is the list of icon functions used in the program:

```
Icon CreateIcon(int xo,int yo,int width,int height,int color,char * text)
void DrawIcon (Icon ic)
int IconCheck (Icon ikon, int xm, int ym)
void DrawIconHiLite(Icon ic, int UpDown)
void CreateIconColumn (int xo, int yo, int width, int height, int color, int
        spc, int num, Icon icon[], char **text)
void CreateIconRow(int xo,int yo,int width,int height,int color,
        int spc, int num, Icon icon[],char **text)
```

The menu system is easy to follow and takes care of polling the mouse, updating the mouse position on the screen as a feedback device, checking if the user selected a command, and keeping track of the last executed command. If the command is repeatable, the button remains down until a new command is selected.

I will dissect the code, step by step. To poll the mouse, use the following code:

```
do {MouseXY (&mx,  &my);
 if((mx != mxold) || (my != myold)) {
     UpdateMousePos(mx,my,0);
     mxold = mx;
     myold = my;
 }
 btn = MouseClick();
}while(!btn);
```

Observe that the new location is posted on the screen only if the new location of the mouse is different from the previous location. The loop is repeated until a button is pressed.

Once a button is pressed, all the icons must be checked:

```
for (i=0;i<IconNum;i++) {
  status = IconCheck(icon[i],mx,my);
  if (status) {
     DrawIconHiLite(icon[i], DOWN);
     if (LastCMD > -1) DrawIconHiLite(icon[LastCMD],UP);
     if (i == 14) {
        status = 14;
        break;
     }
     else {
      LastCMD = i;
      ExecCommand(i, mx, my, 0, btn);
     }
  }
}
```

To check all the icons, a loop is done to go through each one. The function IconCheck tests whether a given icon was selected. If it was, the function returns TRUE. The next step is to push the button down to give the user feedback. If a command was selected previously, that button is pushed up. The value 14 indicates that the EXIT command was selected. If the index is different from 14, the index value is saved as LastCMD = i, and the procedure ExecCommand is called.

What happens if the user clicked on a window instead of an icon? The next test is performed:

```
if (!status) {
   status2 = WhereIsMouse(mx,my);
   if ((status2 == FRONT_AREA) ||
       (status2 == SIDE_AREA) ||
       (status2 == TOP_AREA) ||
       (status2 == ISO_AREA)) ExecCommand(LastCMD, mx, my, 1, btn);
}
```

If the function IconCheck returns FALSE, the mouse is rechecked for its position. If the mouse is inside one of the windows, the command ExecCommand is called.

Observe the difference between the different calls to ExecCommand:

When an icon is selected:

```
ExecCommand(i, mx, my, 0, btn)
```

When a mouse button is pressed inside a window:

```
ExecCommand(LastCMD, mx, my, 1, btn)
```

In the first instance, the variable i holds the index value of the icon. The third argument indicates whether the variables mx, my should be used. In this case, the argument is 0. When a window is clicked, the argument passed is 1, which means that the current mouse location will be used to define a location on the screen. The command to be executed is the previous one, saved inside LastCMD.

3-D Screen Output Routines

Blob GUI can draw various 3-D primitives: point, line, sphere, and coordinate system axis. Before drawing any 3-D data on the screen, call `SetWindow3D` to set the window where the data will be drawn. If you need to clear that window, use the command `clearviewport`. If you wish to draw the same data on all the windows, use a loop to change through the windows and do the following:

```
for (i=0;i<4;i++) {
    SetWindow3D(i,0);
    clearviewport();
    ...draw the object.....
}
```

Next I will look at how the primitives are drawn.

The `void drawpoint3D(POINT3D *v1)` draws a 3-D point on the screen. If the point is to be drawn in the 3-D window (ViewPort = 3), the camera model is used. On the other windows, a 2-D world-to-device conversion is used, which is faster. In addition, instead of drawing a pixel on the screen, a circle is drawn. A single pixel is too small and is difficult to locate on the screen.

```
void drawpoint3D(POINT3D *v1) {
   float x1, y1, z1;
   int xpc1,ypc1;
   if (ViewPort ==3) {
      x1 = (v1->x * a1.x + a1.y * v1->y + a1.z * v1->z + offset_x)*DVal;
      y1 = (v1->x * a2.x + a2.y * v1->y + a2.z * v1->z + offset_y)*DVal;
      z1 = v1->x * a3.x + a3.y * v1->y + a3.z * v1->z + offset_z;
      if(z1 !=0 ) WorldToDevice(x1/z1,y1/z1,&xpc1,&ypc1);
      else  WorldToDevice(x1,y1,&xpc1,&ypc1);
      circle(xpc1,ypc1,5);
   }
   else {
      World2DToDevice(*v1,&xpc1, &ypc1);
      circle(xpc1,ypc1,5);
   }
}
```

The `void drawline3D(POINT3D *v1, POINT3D *v2)` draws a 3-D line on the screen. This routine is similar to `drawpoint3D` but doesn't draw points at the ends of the line.

```
void drawline3D(POINT3D *v1, POINT3D *v2) {
   float x1, y1, z1, x2, y2, z2;
   int xpc1,ypc1,xpc2,ypc2;

   if (ViewPort ==3) {
     x1 = (v1->x * a1.x + a1.y * v1->y + a1.z * v1->z + offset_x)*DVal;
     y1 = (v1->x * a2.x + a2.y * v1->y + a2.z * v1->z + offset_y)*DVal;
     z1 = v1->x * a3.x + a3.y * v1->y + a3.z * v1->z + offset_z;
     x2 = (v2->x * a1.x + a1.y * v2->y + a1.z * v2->z + offset_x)*DVal;
     y2 = (v2->x * a2.x + a2.y * v2->y + a2.z * v2->z + offset_y)*DVal;
     z2 = v2->x * a3.x + a3.y * v2->y + a3.z * v2->z + offset_z;
     if(z1 !=0 && z2 !=0){
       WorldToDevice(x1/z1,y1/z1,&xpc1,&ypc1);
```

```
      WorldToDevice(x2/z2,y2/z2,&xpc2,&ypc2);
    }
    else{
      WorldToDevice(x1,y1,&xpc1,&ypc1);
      WorldToDevice(x2,y2,&xpc2,&ypc2);
    }
    line(xpc1,ypc1,xpc2,ypc2);
  }
  else {
    World2DToDevice(*v1,&xpc1, &ypc1);
    World2DToDevice(*v2,&xpc2, &ypc2);
    line(xpc1,ypc1,xpc2,ypc2);
  }
}
```

The void `DrawAxes(void)` draws a 3-D coordinate system on the screen. This is a high-level function that does repeated calls to `drawline3D`. This function is a good example of drawing in 3-D and changing colors for each entity.

```
void DrawAxes(void) {
    POINT3D v1, v2;
    setlinestyle(SOLID_LINE,1,THICK_WIDTH);
    v1.x = 0.0;
    v1.y = 0.0;
    v1.z = 0.0;
    setcolor(RED);
    v2.x = 1.0;
    v2.y = 0.0;
    v2.z = 0.0;
    drawline3D(&v1, &v2);
    setcolor(GREEN);
    v2.x = 0.0;
    v2.y = 1.0;
    v2.z = 0.0;
    drawline3D(&v1, &v2);
    setcolor(BLUE);
    v2.x = 0.0;
    v2.y = 0.0;
    v2.z = 1.0;
    drawline3D(&v1, &v2);
    setcolor(WHITE);
    setlinestyle(SOLID_LINE,1,NORM_WIDTH);
}
```

The axes are drawn as a set of three lines that have a common point at the origin, and each one is one unit long. To distinguish the X-,Y-, and Z-axes, the colors red, green, and blue are used for each axis respectively.

The void `drawsphere (int WinNum, POINT3D pc,float R)` draws a circle of radius R with the center located at `pc` if `WinNum` is the front, side, or top window. If `WinNum` is the iso (3-D) window, a sphere will be drawn. Recall that you developed this scheme to speed up the redraw process.

```
void drawsphere (int WinNum, POINT3D pc,float R) {
 POINT3D  p1,p2;
 float  v, u;
```

```
int COUNT;
if (WinNum == 2) {
  v = 0;
  COUNT = 0;
  for(u=DegToRad(0);u<=DegToRad(360);u+=DegToRad(15)) {
    p1.x = R * cos(u);
    p1.z = R * sin(u);
    p1.y = 0;
    p1.x = pc.x + p1.x;
    p1.y = pc.y + p1.y;
    p1.z = pc.z + p1.z;
    if( COUNT == 0) {
        p2 = p1;
        COUNT++;
    }
    else {
        drawline3D(&p1, &p2);
        p2 = p1;
    }
  }
}
if (WinNum == 0) {
  u = 0;
  COUNT = 0;
  for(v=DegToRad(0);v<=DegToRad(360);v+=DegToRad(15)) {
    p1.x = R * cos(v);
    p1.z = 0;
    p1.y = R * sin(v);
    p1.x = pc.x + p1.x;
    p1.y = pc.y + p1.y;
    p1.z = pc.z + p1.z;

    if( COUNT == 0) {
        p2 = p1;
        COUNT++;
    }
    else {
        drawline3D(&p1, &p2);
        p2 = p1;
    }
  }
}
if (WinNum == 1) {
  u = DegToRad(90);
  COUNT = 0;
  for(v=DegToRad(0);v<=DegToRad(360);v+=DegToRad(15)) {
    p1.x = 0;
    p1.z = R * cos(v);
    p1.y = R * sin(v);
    p1.x = pc.x + p1.x;
    p1.y = pc.y + p1.y;
    p1.z = pc.z + p1.z;

    if( COUNT == 0) {
        p2 = p1;
      COUNT++;
    }
    else {
        drawline3D(&p1, &p2);
```

```
        p2 = p1;
      }
    }
  }
  if (WinNum == 3) {
  for(v=DegToRad(-90);v<=DegToRad(90);v+=DegToRad(30)) {
    COUNT = 0;
    for(u=DegToRad(0);u<=DegToRad(360+30);u+=DegToRad(30)) {
      p1.x = R * cos(v) * cos(u);
      p1.z = R * cos(v) * sin(u);
      p1.y = R * sin(v);
      p1.x = pc.x + p1.x;
      p1.y = pc.y + p1.y;
      p1.z = pc.z + p1.z;

      if( COUNT == 0) {
          p2 = p1;
          COUNT++;
      }
      else {
          drawline3D(&p1, &p2);
          p2 = p1;
      }
    }
  }

  for(u=DegToRad(0);u<= DegToRad(360);u+=DegToRad(30)) {
    COUNT = 0;
    for(v=DegToRad(-90);v<=DegToRad(90+30);v+=DegToRad(30)) {
      p1.x = R * cos(v) * cos(u);
      p1.z = R * cos(v) * sin(u);
      p1.y = R * sin(v);
      p1.x = pc.x + p1.x;
      p1.y = pc.y + p1.y;
      p1.z = pc.z + p1.z;

      if( COUNT == 0) {
          p2 = p1;
          COUNT++;
      }
      else {
          drawline3D(&p1, &p2);
          p2 = p1;
      }
    }
  }
  }

}
```

This completes the 3-D drawing of the basic primitives. The next section discusses how blobs are handled in the program.

Blob Handling Routines

The following set of functions handles all aspects of the creation of blobs. There are a few interesting techniques used that I'll discuss as they appear. One of these techniques lets the user resize the radius of the blob dynamically by moving the mouse. Another one lets the blob keep the same radius but lets the user translate the blob to a new position. An important technique that I'll also discuss is being able to select a blob by clicking the left mouse button near the blob. I'll start with the most important function, which creates the blob component.

`void CreateABlob(int mx, int my, int use_xy, int btn)` creates a blob component. The function uses the following steps:

1. Poll the mouse until a button is pressed
2. If button = LMB, use the corresponding point as the center of the blob
3. If button = RMB, cancel the command
4. Poll the mouse again to define the radius of the blob component until a click
5. If button = LMB, accept this as the radius value, Else cancel the command

The function uses an XOR operation to erase the previous object and then draw the new one somewhere else. Look at the section of code that performs this operation:

```
MouseShow(0);
setwritemode(1);
for(i=0;i<3;i++) { SetWindow3D(i,0); DrawBlobs(tmp,i); }
setwritemode(0);
MouseShow(1);
```

Initially, before drawing anything on the screen, the mouse cursor is turned off. Now the drawing mode is converted from overwrite to XOR. When an object is drawn using the XOR mode and then overwritten again, it will be erased from the screen. This erasing operation affects only the object being drawn; the rest stays intact. This technique is widely used to create the "rubberband" effect implemented by "paint" programs.

```
void CreateABlob(int mx, int my, int use_xy, int btn)
{
 int i, mxold=0, myold=0, FLAG = 0;
 POINT3D p1, p2, v;
 BLOB tmp, tmpold;
 if (bnum <MAXBLOB) {
  setcolor(WHITE);
  if(!use_xy) {
   do {MouseXY (&mx, &my);
     if((mx != mxold) || (my != myold)) {
        UpdateMousePos(mx,my,0);
```

```
                 mxold = mx;
                 myold = my;
           }
         btn = MouseClick();
      }while(!btn);
    }
  if (btn == 1) {
   p1 = GetPoint3D(mx,my);

   do {MouseXY (&mx, &my);
       if((mx != mxold) || (my != myold)) {
            UpdateMousePos(mx,my,0);
            mxold = mx;
            myold = my;
       }
       p2 = GetPoint3D(mx,my);
       tmp.x = p1.x;
       tmp.y = p1.y;
       tmp.z = p1.z;
       v = subtract(&p2, &p1);

       tmp.strength = 1.0;
       tmp.radius = mag(&v)/sqrt(1.0 - sqrt(threshold/fabs(tmp.strength)));

       MouseShow(0);
       setwritemode(1);
       for(i=0;i<3;i++) { SetWindow3D(i,0); DrawBlobs(tmp,i); }
       setwritemode(0);
       MouseShow(1);
       if (!FLAG) FLAG = 1;
       else {
          MouseShow(0);
          setwritemode(1);
          for(i=0;i<3;i++) { SetWindow3D(i,0); DrawBlobs(tmpold,i); }
          setwritemode(0);
          MouseShow(1);
       }
       tmpold = tmp;
     btn = MouseClick();
   }while(!btn);
   if (btn == 1) {
    bnum++;
    blobs[bnum]  = tmp;
   }
   RedrawALL();
  }
 }
}
```

void ResizeABlob(int mx, int my, int use_xy, int btn) resizes the blob radius. This command can be canceled at any time by pressing the right mouse button. This function utilizes the XOR operation to erase the object quickly and redraw it somewhere else.

```
void ResizeABlob(int mx, int my, int use_xy, int btn)
{
 int i, mxold=0, myold=0;
 POINT3D p1, p2, v;
 BLOB tmp, tmpold;
```

```
SelectABlob(mx, my, use_xy, btn);
if (BlobSel) {
 tmp = blobs[BlobSel];
 tmpold = tmp;
 p1.x = tmp.x; p1.y = tmp.y; p1.z = tmp.z;
 setcolor(WHITE);
 MouseShow(0);
 for(i=0;i<4;i++) {
    SetWindow3D(i,0);
    DrawBlobs(blobs[BlobSel],i);
 }
 MouseShow(1);
 do {MouseXY (&mx, &my);
    if((mx != mxold) || (my != myold)) {
        UpdateMousePos(mx,my,0);
        mxold = mx;
        myold = my;
    }
    p2 = GetPoint3D(mx,my);
    v = subtract(&p2, &p1);

    tmp.radius = mag(&v)/sqrt(1.0 - sqrt(threshold/fabs(tmp.strength)));

    MouseShow(0);
    setwritemode(1);
    setcolor(WHITE);
    for(i=0;i<3;i++) {
     SetWindow3D(i,0);
     DrawBlobs(tmpold,i);
     DrawBlobs(tmp,i);
    }
    setwritemode(0);
    MouseShow(1);
    tmpold = tmp;
    btn = MouseClick();
 }while(!btn);
 if (btn == 1) blobs[BlobSel]  = tmp;
 RedrawALL();
 }
}
```

void MoveABlob(int mx, int my, int use_xy, int btn, int copy) moves the blob to a new location. This function also implements the XOR operation.

```
void MoveABlob(int mx, int my, int use_xy, int btn, int copy)
{
 int i, mxold=0, myold=0,pos;
 POINT3D p2;
 BLOB tmp, tmpold;

 SelectABlob(mx,my,use_xy,btn);
 if (BlobSel) {
  tmp = blobs[BlobSel];
  tmpold = tmp;
  do {MouseXY (&mx, &my);}while(!MouseClick());

  setcolor(WHITE);
```

```
MouseShow(0);
for(i=0;i<4;i++) {
   SetWindow3D(i,0);
   DrawBlobs(blobs[BlobSel],i);
}
MouseShow(1);
do {MouseXY (&mx, &my);
   if((mx != mxold) || (my != myold)) {
      UpdateMousePos(mx,my,0);
      mxold = mx;
      myold = my;
   }
   p2 = GetPoint3D(mx,my);
   pos = WhereIsMouse(mx,my);
   switch(pos) {
     case FRONT_AREA:  tmp.x = p2.x;  tmp.y = p2.y; break;
     case  SIDE_AREA:  tmp.y = p2.y;  tmp.z = p2.z; break;
     case   TOP_AREA:  tmp.x = p2.x;  tmp.z = p2.z; break;
   }
   MouseShow(0);
   setwritemode(1);
   setcolor(WHITE);
   for(i=0;i<3;i++) {
    SetWindow3D(i,0);
    DrawBlobs(tmpold,i);
    DrawBlobs(tmp,i);
   }
   setwritemode(0);
   MouseShow(1);
   tmpold = tmp;
  btn = MouseClick();
 }while(!btn);

 if (btn == 1) {
     if (!copy)  blobs[BlobSel]  = tmp;
     else {
      if (bnum < MAXBLOB) {bnum++; blobs[bnum]  = tmp;}
     }
 }
 RedrawALL();
 }
}
```

void SelectABlob(int mx, int my, int use_xy, int btn) selects a blob by clicking the mouse near the blob to be selected. This function uses an important technique used in 3-D programs. Take a closer look at how the technique is implemented. The equation of a sphere is

```
(x - xc)^2 + (y - yc)^2 + (z - zc)^2 = R^2
```

> x, y, and z are the location of any point on the surface of the sphere
> xc, yc, and zc define the center of a sphere
> R is the radius of the sphere

Figure 14.5 displays a sphere and the points (xc,yc,zc) and (x,y,z).

FIGURE 14.5.

Sphere definition.

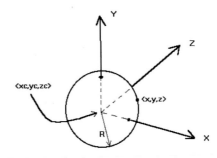

If a point (x,y,z) is on the surface of a sphere, the following expression should be true:

```
M = (x - xc)^2 + (y - yc)^2 + (z - zc)^2 - R^2 = 0
```

Try it out: Let (xc,yc,zc) be at the origin (xc = yc = zc = 0). Let (x,y,z) be (R,0,0). The expression for M will be

```
M = (R - 0)^2 + (0 - 0)^2 + (0 - 0)^2 - R^2
M = R^2 - R^2 = 0
```

Therefore, the nearer a point is to the surface, the smaller the value of M will be. For example, assume that there are two spheres located in space and you choose a given point (x,y,z). To find out which of the spheres is the nearest, you simply evaluate the expression for M for each sphere. Whichever of the two has the smallest value of M is the nearest.

To make matters simpler, use the front, side, and top views for selecting objects. Because these views display only circles, the expression for M will be reduced to two dimensions. The expression for M is then

```
front view:   M = (x - xc)^2 + (y - yc)^2 - R^2
side view:    M = (y - yc)^2 + (z - zc)^2 - R^2
top view:     M = (x - xc)^2 + (z - zc)^2 - R^2
```

This technique still applies to the 2-D case.

```
void SelectABlob(int mx, int my, int use_xy, int btn)
{
 int pos, i, mxold=0, myold=0;
 float dist, dist2, rr;
 POINT3D p1;

 setcolor(WHITE);
  if(!use_xy) {
    do {MouseXY (&mx, &my);
      btn = 0;
      if((mx != mxold) ¦¦ (my != myold)) {
          UpdateMousePos(mx,my,0);
          mxold = mx;
      myold = my;
      }
      btn = MouseClick();
    }while(!btn);
```

```
      }
      if (btn==1) {
       p1 = GetPoint3D(mx,my);
       pos = WhereIsMouse(mx,my);
       dist = 3e30;
       BlobSel = 0;
       for(i=1;i<=bnum;i++) {
          switch(pos) {
           case FRONT_AREA:
                        dist2 = (blobs[i].x - p1.x)*(blobs[i].x - p1.x) +
                                (blobs[i].y - p1.y)*(blobs[i].y - p1.y);
                     break;
           case SIDE_AREA:
                   dist2 = (blobs[i].z - p1.z)*(blobs[i].z - p1.z) +
                        (blobs[i].y - p1.y)*(blobs[i].y - p1.y);
                  break;
           case TOP_AREA:
                        dist2 = (blobs[i].x - p1.x)*(blobs[i].x - p1.x) +
                                (blobs[i].z - p1.z)*(blobs[i].z - p1.z);
                     break;
            default : dist2 = 3e30; break;  //in case you select outside!
           }

           rr = blobs[i].radius * sqrt(1.0 - sqrt(threshold/fabs(blobs[i].strength)));
           dist2 -= rr * rr;
           dist2 = fabs(dist2);
           if (dist2 < dist) {
            dist = dist2;
            BlobSel = i;
           }
       }

      if (BlobSel) {
       MouseShow(0);
       for(i=0;i<4;i++) {
         SetWindow3D(i,0);
         setcolor(YELLOW);
         DrawBlobs(blobs[BlobSel],i);
         if(BlobSelOld && (BlobSelOld != BlobSel) && (BlobSelOld <= bnum)) {
          setcolor(WHITE);
          DrawBlobs(blobs[BlobSelOld],i);
         }
       }
       setcolor(WHITE);
       MouseShow(1);
       BlobSelOld = BlobSel;
      }
     }
    }
```

void DeleteBlob(int mx, int my, int use_xy, int btn) deletes the selected blob from
the array.

```
void DeleteBlob(int mx, int my, int use_xy, int btn) {
 int i;
 SelectABlob(mx, my, use_xy, btn);
 if (BlobSel) {
  if (YesNoCMD("Delete Blob?")) {
```

```
     if (BlobSel && bnum ) {
       if (BlobSel == bnum)
         bnum—;
       else {
         for(i = BlobSel; i<bnum; i++) blobs[i] = blobs[i+1];
         bnum—;
       }
     }
   }
   RedrawALL();
 }
}
```

Finally, the function that draws the blobs is a call to `DrawBlobs`. The value of vp defines the window where the blob will be drawn. Recall that the only window where a sphere will be drawn is the 3-D view; everywhere else a circle will be drawn.

```
void DrawBlobs(BLOB b, int vp)
 {
   POINT3D p;
   p.x = b.x;
   p.y = b.y;
   p.z = b.z;
   drawsphere (vp, p, b.radius * sqrt(1.0 - sqrt(threshold/fabs(b.strength))));
 }
```

File I/O Routines

For completeness, the following is a list of the file I/O routines:

```
void WriteToPolyray(void)
void WriteToPoV(void)
void LoadAFile(char *str)
void SaveAFile(char *str)
```

These were discussed in Part III. The RAW data output requires more work. The function `drawpolygon` draws the final preview of the object and can save the polygons in RAW data format. Once the marching cubes algorithm generates the polygons, they are passed to `drawpolygon`. If the variable `SaveRAW` is `TRUE`, the polygon is subdivided into triangles and saved.

```
void drawpolygon (POINT3D *poly, int size)
{
  POINTint p[6], p12,p32;
  int i, drawit, pp[14], count;
  long sum;

  if (SaveRAW) {
    for (i=1;i <= size-2;i++)
      fprintf (RAWfptr,"%g %g %g %g %g %g %g %g %g\n",
               poly[0].x,poly[0].y,poly[0].z,
               poly[i].x,poly[i].y,poly[i].z,
               poly[i+1].x,poly[i+1].y,poly[i+1].z);
  }
```

```
for (i = 0; i < size; i++)
    p[i] = World3DToDevice(poly[i]);

for(i=0,count=0; i<2*size; i+=2,count++) {
    pp[i]   = p[count].x;
    pp[i+1] = p[count].y;
}

pp[i] = pp[0]; pp[i+1] = pp[1];

if (!hide_backface)
    drawit = 1; /* Draw everything */
else {
    /* find the "average" normal to the polygon */
    sum = 0;
    for (i = 1; i <= size-2; i++) {
        p12.x = p[i].x - p[0].x;
        p12.y = p[i].y - p[0].y;
        p32.x = p[i+1].x - p[0].x;
        p32.y = p[i+1].y - p[0].y;

        sum = sum + ((long)p12.x * (long)p32.y) -
                    ((long)p12.y * (long)p32.x);
    }

    /* Only draw the front faces */
    drawit = (sum > 0);
}

if (drawit)
    fillpoly(size,pp);
}
```

An important technique being used inside drawpolygon is the elimination of polygons that are not visible from the current point of view. As presented in Part III, each polygon has a normal vector. If this vector is pointing away from the observer, you can assume that the polygon is invisible, and it is not necessary to draw it. To complete the preview mode, the polygons are filled with a color using the BGI graphics called fillpoly. This function accepts a set of points that defines a polygon (in device coordinates) and fills it with the current defined color. This helps the object look solid.

One point concerning the drawpolygon() function needs to be explained. Even though drawpolygon() hides polygons that are facing opposite to the observer (by not drawing them), it can't distinguish relative depth among those that are visible. In other words, there may be two polygons that are visible to the observer, and if one partially hides the other, then there is a possibility that the algorithm may draw the farthest one last. This will create an error in the display of the image. On the other hand, the algorithm is very fast.

Summary

In this chapter, you used the routines developed in Part III to create a user interface that would help you create models using blobs. The techniques developed were more complex because of the use of four display windows instead of just one. In addition, the menu system was capable of interpreting the mouse once an icon or a window was selected. The ability to execute a previous command is a handy feature and shows how the menu system can be made more versatile with only minor changes. The next chapter takes you through all the commands and designs a 3-D model with the blob modeler.

Modeling with Blobs

15

by Truman Brown

This chapter is about creating 3-D graphics models with "blobs," also popularly known as "metaballs." If you've been to the movies recently, you've probably seen several spectacular examples of blobs in action: several of the dinosaurs in the movie *Jurassic Park* were brought to life by blobs. If you watch television commercials, you've probably seen the amazing blob-work of Thaddeus Beire (of Pacific Data Images) in his blobby "Crest Sparkle Singers," who dance and play guitars that look like toothbrushes.

Blobs offer a unique method for creating organically realistic 3-D models. Used effectively, blob modeling can produce stunning organic shapes that rival the best models created by conventional methods.

Creating complex blob-models can require a great deal of patience. Blob-modeling easily compares to the act of sculpting artwork with wet globs of gooey clay: everything is sticky. The creative part is deciding what glob should stick where and how sticky each glob should be. The difficult part is controlling all of this stickiness.

Like any other skill you hope to master, it's important that you begin with a firm grasp of the basic concepts behind blobs. To that end, this chapter begins with a brief review of blobs illustrating blob components and their interactions. Following this review, an interactive modeler called Blob Sculptor is introduced. This program was designed using the algorithms and theory you've examined in earlier chapters. To familiarize you with Blob Sculptor, the program's interface will be explained in detail.

Finally, to put you on the road to creating your own blob-masterpieces, a step-by-step example of blob-modeling with Blob Sculptor will be presented.

Blob Basics

What is a *blob?* In simple terms, we can describe a blob as a dynamic collection of parts called "components." Each component is described by specific values defining its physical attributes, including its size, strength, and density. When components are positioned near or on top of each other, these attributes determine how they will interact. Some components will attract other components, creating a smooth "blob-like" effect. Others will repel other components, creating smooth dents and holes.

Mathematically, we can describe a blob as a set of visible field density functions. Each function is associated with a single component, originating at the component's core and dissipating outwardly. The falloff of the density function determines the amount of the component that is visible. You'll be introduced to the specifics of this function later, but for now let's begin by examining components in more detail.

An Organic Analogy

Let's face it: mathematical concepts can be difficult to visualize. Blobs are no exception. Fortunately for us, blobs behave in a way that closely resembles the behavior of biological one-celled organisms. With this analogy in mind, let's have some anthropomorphic fun and look at blobs from an organic perspective.

We begin by picturing a blob as a unique colony of one-celled organisms. We'll call these organisms *Comps* (short, of course, for *components*).

Looking at Comps

Similar to our scientific counterparts, we're able to examine Comps by looking through a microscope. This microscope is equipped with a unique lens-filter that controls the visible size of each organism. As the filter's opacity is increased, the outer edges of the organisms become less visible, effectively shrinking their apparent size. Conversely, decreasing the filter's opacity enlarges the Comp's apparent size. We call the opacity of this filter a *threshold* setting.

Figure 15.1 shows what a single Comp looks like. As you can see, a Comp is a spherically-shaped organism composed of two parts: a nucleus and a clear transparent shell.

> **NOTE**
>
> For the sake of visualization, the shells in this section's figures are somewhat visible. In the reality of our scenario, a Comp's shell would be totally invisible; all you would see is the nucleus.

Besides a shell and nucleus, every Comp possesses a finite, measurable life-force. We call this life-force a Comp's *strength*. It emanates from the center of the Comp's nucleus and radiates outward to the shell. A Comp's strength is strongest at its center and dissipates to nothing as it approaches the shell. We call the value of strength at the Comp's center its *density*.

Figure 15.2 shows a graphical representation of a Comp's strength. Note that strength does not fall off linearly as it approaches the shell. Instead, it dissipates along a curved path. The Comp's density is the magnitude of the curve at the Comp's center.

FIGURE 15.1.

*A Comp (component) has
a visible nucleus and a
transparent shell.*

FIGURE 15.2.

*This graph shows the
falloff of a Comp's
strength.*

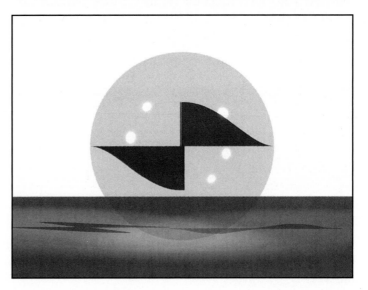

This curve works in concert with the threshold setting to determine the visible size of a
Comp's nucleus. Think of a Comp's nucleus as a layered, onion-like core having the same
radius as the Comp's shell. The position of each layer corresponds to the magnitude of
the curve at any given radius. Layers near the center correspond to larger magnitudes of
strength while layers near the shell correspond to smaller magnitudes of strength.

When we set the threshold of our lens-filter, we effectively choose the index of the layer we want to see. In other words, similar to peeling an onion, our lens-filter strips off the outer layers of the nucleus to the point where the magnitude of strength is equal to the chosen threshold setting.

In an inverse manner, a Comp's density also controls the visible quantity of its nucleus. When density is increased, the strength-curve becomes steeper. Therefore, the point where the magnitude of the strength-curve equals the threshold setting is pushed upward. This makes more of the nucleus visible. Conversely, when density is decreased, the curve is flattened. Therefore, the point where the magnitude of strength equals the threshold setting is pushed down. This makes less of the nucleus visible.

High threshold settings make smaller nuclei and low threshold settings make larger nuclei. The threshold setting controls the visibility of every Comp's nucleus within the blob-colony. Alternately, density affects individual Comps. High density values make larger nuclei, and low density values make smaller nuclei. Given shells of equal size, a Comp with a density of 1.0 will have a smaller nucleus than a Comp with a density of 4.0.

How Comps Interact

Let's look at the social behavior of Comps. Our Comps are primitive organisms and only interact in two ways: they either merge together or eat each other. When Comps merge, their nuclei draw together and they eventually combine into a single entity. When Comps eat other Comps, the shell of one Comp takes a smooth bite out of the nucleus of the other.

Comps are also homogeneous organisms: they only interact with other Comps within their own blob-colony. Comps in other blob-colonies are completely ignored.

In addition to controlling the visible size of a Comp's nucleus, density also determines a Comp's propensity to merge with or to eat other Comps. "Positive Comps" have positive density values and visible nuclei. When their shells overlap, Positive Comps will merge with each other. On the other hand, "Negative Comps" have negative density values and invisible nuclei. When Negative Comps overlap the shells of Positive Comps, they eat the nuclei of the Positive Comp.

Let's examine this behavior a little closer. Before two or more Comps can interact, their shells must overlap. As the shells overlap, the strengths of each Comp are combined within the area of intersection. It is this combination of strengths that creates the merging or digesting process between Comps.

Figure 15.3 shows that no *visible* effect occurs if one Comp's shell does not overlap the nucleus of the other Comp. However, as the Comps draw closer and a nucleus intersects with a shell, the strength within the intersecting shell is added to the strength of the intersected nucleus. This causes the apparent merging or digestion of the nuclei.

FIGURE 15.3.

Comps will not interact if their shells do not intersect other nuclei.

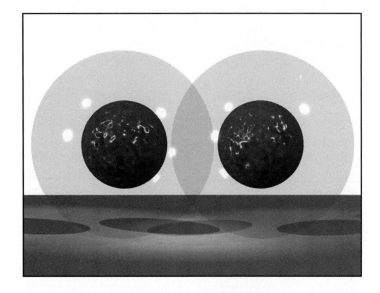

FIGURE 15.4.

Comps with large densities merge quickly.

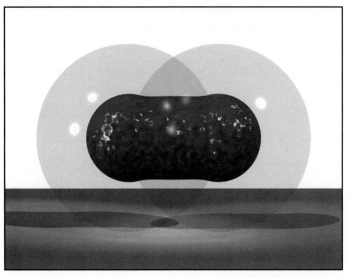

Now you'll see what happens when two Comps having shells of similar radii and large positive densities (large nuclei) overlap. As their shells begin to intersect, their nuclei quickly merge (Figure 15.4). This is because there is little space between each Comp's shell and its large nucleus. On the other hand, if both Comps were to have small density values (tiny nuclei), their nuclei will interact slower since the space between each Comp's nucleus and shell is larger (Figure 15.5).

FIGURE 15.5.

Comps with small densities merge slowly.

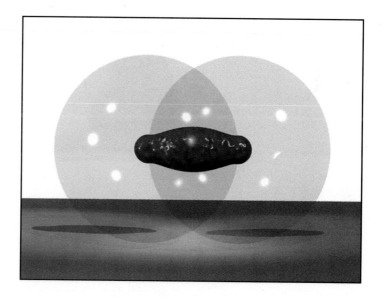

Why are the shapes of these two examples so different? The answer is easiest to visualize if you picture the merging process in terms of the falloff curves of each Comp's strength. As the Comps intersect, the magnitudes of the little ends of the curves combine first. If the curves are steep (large densities), the combined strength in the area of intersection increases quickly as the Comps draw closer. This results in a "thick" merge between the Comps as shown in Figure 15.4. Alternatively, if the curves are flatter, the combined strength grows slower, resulting in a "thin" merge between the Comps as shown in Figure 15.5.

Even as Comps merge, the threshold setting continues to play a role in controlling the visible amount of nuclei. Figure 15.6 illustrates the effect of various threshold settings on merging Comps.

Figure 15.7 illustrates a different way to visualize the merging effect between Comps. Instead of having a fixed shell size, Figure 15.7 shows a chart of Comps having a fixed nuclear radius. As the density value increases, the shells shrink and the Comps merge more quickly.

FIGURE 15.6.

This is an example of the effect of different threshold settings.

FIGURE 15.7.

This is an example of the effect of different density values.

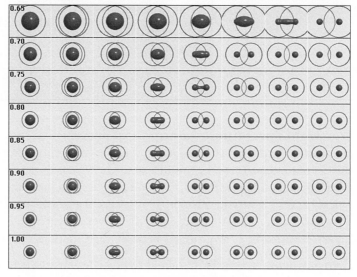

Now you'll look at what happens when a Negative Comp interacts with a Positive Comp. Just as in the case where two Positive Comps overlap, the strength curve of the Negative Comp combines with the strength curve of the Positive Comp in the area of intersection. However, since a positive strength curve is combining with a negative strength curve, an effective subtraction of strength occurs. This results in the disappearance of a portion of the Positive Comp's nucleus in the area of intersection. Figure 15.8 illustrates this effect.

FIGURE 15.8.

This is what happens when the shell of a Comp with negative density intersects the nucleus of a Comp with positive density.

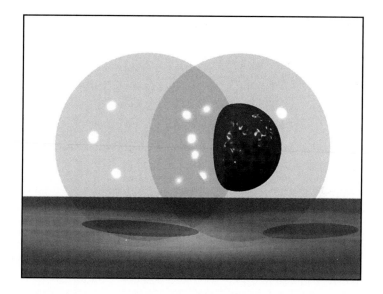

What happens when two Negative Comps overlap? Visibly, nothing. Remember, Negative Comps have invisible nuclei. These nuclei remain invisible until enough strength is added to a Negative Comp's nucleus to make its density positive. Therefore, two Negative Comps will not produce a visible effect *on each other*. Their combined strengths, however, have a much stronger effect on other Positive Comps.

Summary of Analogy

That concludes our biological analogy of blobs. Here is a summary of what you've learned, put into functional terms:

> Blobs are groups (colonies) of spherical entities called components (Comps).
>
> Components have a shell, a nucleus, and a radiating function called Strength.
>
> One factor that determines the visible amount of nuclei is the Threshold setting.
>
> Large Threshold values reveal more nuclei than small Threshold values.
>
> Density is the magnitude of a component's Strength at its core and also determines the visible amount of the nucleus. Large Density values reveal less nuclei than small Density values.
>
> Components with positive Densities have visible nuclei, while those with negative Densities have invisible nuclei.
>
> When components overlap, their Strengths merge. Positive Strengths combine to form more visible nuclei. Negative Strengths combine to remove visible nuclei.

Now that we have a visualization of blobs and their components, let's translate it back to mathematical terms.

Blob Math

We call the radius of a component's nucleus its Effective-Radius because this is the visible portion of the component.

We call the radius of the component's shell its Radius-of-Influence. Components only affect other components that fall within their Radius-of-Influence.

Using these terms, the mathematical description of a component's strength is described by the following equation:

```
Strength = (1 - ((Effective-Radius / Radius-of-Influence) ^ 2)) ^ 2
```

When the threshold value is factored in, the following equations result:

```
Density = Threshold / (1 - ((Effective-Radius / Radius-of-Influence) ^ 2)) ^ 2
Effective-Radius = Radius-of-Influence * sqrt (1 - sqrt (Threshold / (Absolute Value of
        Density)))
Radius-of-Influence = Effective-Radius / (sqrt (1 - sqrt (Threshold / (Absolute Value of
        Density))))
```

These formulas will be useful for calculating the visual interaction of components. They also form the foundation for the blob-modeling program called Blob Sculptor that is introduced in the following section.

Blob Sculptor

If you're a reader with prior 3-D modeling experience, you're going to discover that Blob Sculptor is unlike any modeling program you've used before. Modeling with conventional polygon modelers is a visually simple process because models are created within an intuitive "what-you-see-is-what-you-get" environment. Modeling with Blob Sculptor on the other hand, requires a considerable amount of mental visualization by the 3-D artist because "what-you-DON'T-see-is-what-you-get."

Blob Sculptor is like an electronic erector set with pieces that "stick" rather than "snap" together. With only your mouse and your imagination, you use Blob Sculptor to position components into unique, organically shaped models. These models can then be saved or exported in file formats that are compatible for rendering with many popular rendering programs.

The Blob Sculptor Interface

Figure 15.9 shows the Blob Sculptor interface. The interface is divided into two main areas: the *modeling workspace* and the *menu panel*. The modeling workspace is an area where you manipulate components as you build your models. The menu panel is where you select options to edit, preview, and save your models.

FIGURE 15.9.

The Blob Sculptor interface is divided into two main areas: the modeling workspace and the menu panel.

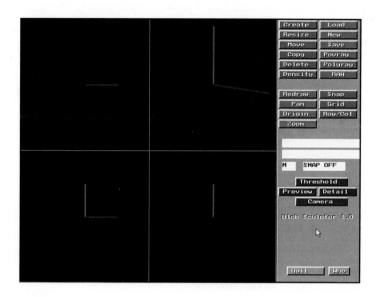

The Modeling Workspace

The modeling workspace is divided into four view windows: *Top, Front, Side,* and *Iso*.

Each view is based on a "left-handed" coordinate system where the "x-axis" is horizontal and points positively to the right, the "y-axis" is vertical and points positively up, and the "z-axis" is horizontal and points positively forward. As noted in other chapters, we call this a "left-handed" coordinate system because by pointing your left thumb in the positive direction of an axis, the fingers of your left hand will curl naturally in the positive direction of rotation for that axis.

TOP-View (Upper-Left Window)

The TOP-view looks down on your model from above. The z-axis is vertical and the x-axis is horizontal. The initial point of view is 1 unit up along the y-axis, looking at the origin. As you manipulate components in this view, the x and z values of your components will change, while y values will remain constant. In other words, you can move components left, right, forward, and backward, but not up or down.

FRONT-View (Lower-Left Window)

The FRONT-view looks straight forward into your model. The y-axis is vertical and the x-axis is horizontal. The initial point of view is 2.5 units back along the z-axis, looking at the origin. In this view, your component's x and y values will change as you move them, and the z value will remain constant. In other words, you can move components left, right, up, and down, but not forward or backward.

SIDE-View (Lower-Right Window)

The SIDE-view looks at your model from its right side. The y-axis is vertical and the z-axis is horizontal. The initial point of view is 1 unit right along the x-axis, looking at the origin. In this window, y and z values change, while x values remain constant. In other words, you can move components up, down, forward, and backward, but not left or right.

ISO-View (Upper-Right Window)

The ISO-view looks at your model from the position of the camera. This view can be adjusted by either manually changing the camera coordinates (discussed later), or by zooming in or out of the window using the Zoom button. The initial point of view is derived from the TOP, SIDE, and FRONT-views ($x = 1$, $y = 1$, and $z = 2.5$). Components cannot be manipulated in this window.

The Menu Panel

The menu panel contains several clusters of control buttons. These clusters roughly correlate to an EDIT cluster, a FILE cluster, a SCREEN cluster, a SNAP cluster, and a miscellaneous cluster.

EDIT Cluster

The EDIT cluster contains buttons that enable you to build and modify your models. The options in this cluster let you Create, Resize, Move, Copy, and adjust the Density of individual components.

To create a new component, click your mouse on the Create button, then position the cursor in the TOP-, FRONT-, or SIDE-view windows, and click again. As you move your mouse about, a circle representing the new component will draw concurrently in all three windows. The radius of this circle represents the effective-radius of the new component.

When you finish sizing the component to your satisfaction, click the left mouse button again. The windows will redraw, and the ISO-view will show a wire frame representation of the component.

To Resize, Move, Copy, or adjust the Density of a component, you must first *select* the component. You select a component by first clicking the button of the desired function, then positioning the mouse cursor within the circle representing the component, and clicking the left mouse button again. The component may be selected in any view window except the ISO-view.

When a component is selected, it becomes highlighted in yellow. Should you discover that you've selected the wrong component, you can deselect the component by clicking the right mouse button. Once the component is selected, you may move the mouse cursor to the TOP-, FRONT-, or SIDE-view and perform the desired operation on the selected component within that window.

When a component is Resized, its radius-of-influence is scaled. Because the blob threshold value and the component's density remain constant, this is the equivalent of scaling the component's effective-radius.

When you Move a component, you are constrained to the axes of the view you are doing the move in. If you want to move a component to a position that is parallel to the x-, y-, or z-axis (that is, moving from [0,0,0] to [4,5,6]), you must perform multiple moves between different windows.

Copying a component is similar to a Move operation, only the original component remains in place as you move a new copy of the component to a new position. The copy is an exact duplicate of the original, maintaining the same radius-of-influence and density.

When you change the Density of the component, a dialog box appears onscreen in which you enter a new density value. The absolute value of the component's Density should always be greater than the threshold value of the blob. For instance, if the threshold setting for your blob-model is 0.6, the density value of all components should not fall within the range of –0.6 to +0.6. There is no restriction on the upper limit of density values.

FILE Cluster

The FILE cluster contains control buttons that enable you to store and retrieve your blob-models. These controls let you: Save a model in Blob Sculptor format; Load a Blob Sculptor model; export your model to a Povray (Persistence of Vision raytracer) file, a Polyray raytracer file, or a Raw formatted file; and/or clear the current model from memory and start a New model.

SCREEN Cluster

The SCREEN cluster contains buttons that enable you to adjust the view windows.

If you need to refresh the views of your model, you can click on the Redraw button. This will clear the view windows and redraw your model.

To change the center of a view, you can select the Pan button. Move your mouse to the TOP, FRONT, or SIDE-view and click the left mouse button again. The location of the mouse will become the new center for that view. To reset the center of view to the origin, click on the Origin button and follow with a mouse-click within the view window you want to reset.

To enlarge or shrink the view of a window, you can click on the Zoom button. Subsequently, when you click the left mouse button on any view window, that view will zoom in by a factor of 2. Clicking the right mouse button will zoom out by the same factor. If a zoom is done in the ISO window, the view is adjusted along a linear path from the camera position to the camera target. This will automatically update your Camera settings (Miscellaneous Cluster).

SNAP Cluster

The SNAP cluster contains buttons that let you set the Snap status, show a Grid, and specify the number of Rows and Columns for the grid. When you select Snap, all mouse operations in the modeling workspace will occur at regularly spaced intervals. If the Grid option is selected, you will see a grid highlighting the intervals. To change the number of intervals, click on the Rowcol button and enter a new interval value in the dialog box.

Miscellaneous Cluster

The functions in this cluster do not fall in any of the previous categories. These controls provide you with additional tools to setup, manipulate, and view your model.

The Threshold button sets the threshold value of the current model. The default setting is 0.6.

NOTE

If you adjust this value, you must ensure that the new value will not be greater than or equal to the absolute value of the density of any existing component. (See earlier discussion about Density button.)

The most powerful feature of Blob Sculptor is the Preview option. When you select the Preview option, a complete wire-frame display of your model is generated in the ISO-view window revealing the interactions of your component. To adjust the resolution of the preview, select the Detail button and enter a new value. Higher Detail values consume more memory and will make the preview take longer to generate.

The Camera button activates a dialog box where you can adjust the location of the camera as represented in the ISO-view. The camera-setting parameters include the FROM coordinates (where the camera is located), the UP coordinates (what direction the camera is tilted), and the TO coordinates (where the target is located). These values are automatically changed if you perform a Zoom on the ISO-view.

The WHO button displays the names of the Blob Sculptor authors. The Quit button terminates the Blob Sculptor program and returns you to the operating system.

Blob Modeling Example: A Big Bug

Now that you're familiar with the Blob Sculptor interface, let's see how an actual blob model is created.

This section will illustrate one method for creating simple blob-models. The intent is not to have you duplicate the procedure presented, but to provide you with a level of experience that will allow you to build your own blob-models with confidence and creativity.

The shape that we will create is a simple spider-like insect with six legs, a head with horns, and a bulbous tail.

Setting the Threshold

Recalling our review of blobs, we learned that the threshold value determines the overall amount of component nuclei that is visible. For modeling purposes, this value is entirely arbitrary.

A comparison can be made to painting a picture in a room with dimming control on the light-switch. Given the assumption that the picture will be viewed under the same lighting conditions, the artist will brighten or darken the colors of the picture as needed to compensate for the lighting.

In our case, Blob Sculptor incorporates the threshold value when calculating the effective-radius of our components. Since we only set the threshold value once for the entire model, its value is arbitrary. The only consideration we have to remember is that the threshold value must be less than the absolute value on any given component's density. Failure to heed this warning can lead to unpredictable results.

For our model, we'll accept the default threshold value of 0.6.

Making the Legs

Our first step will be to create a single leg for our bug. We want the components to act as the "joints" of the leg, and let the components merge, filling the "flesh" between the joints.

One way to create these components is by trial and error, drawing several components, Previewing their interaction, adjusting their positions and densities, Previewing again, and repeating this process until we achieve the effect we're looking for. This procedure is obviously tedious and time consuming.

Luckily, we have an easier method. Returning to the equations listed in our summary of blob-mathematics, we can accurately and easily determine the component parameters we'll need to achieve the effect we want.

First, we must decide how large the components will be. Let's assume that the effective-radius of the leg joints will be 0.4. Now we must select a density value that will make the radius-of-influence surrounding our components large enough so that they will merge slowly. In other words, we want the nuclei of the components to be far apart in order to achieve a thin "stringy" connection between the joints.

We know that given a fixed radius-of-influence (the shell surrounding the nucleus), large density values create large effective-radii and small density values create small effective-radii. Given a fixed effective-radius, however, the inverse is true. Large density values produce small radii of influence, and small density values produce large radii of influence. Therefore, we can assume that selecting a density value slightly larger than the threshold will provide us with a large radius-of-influence. Since the threshold value is 0.6, let's choose a density value of 0.7.

We now have all the values necessary to compute the radius-of-influence for this component:

```
Effective-Radius = 0.4
Threshold = 0.6
Density = 0.7

Radius-of-Influence = Effective-Radius / (sqrt (1 - sqrt (Threshold / (Absolute Value of
    Density)))
Radius-of-Influence = 0.4 / (sqrt (1 - sqrt (0.6 / 0.7)))
Radius-of-Influence = 1.47
```

Now, if we create a component whose density is 0.7, and whose radius-of-influence is approximately 1.47, we will create a component with an effective-radius of 0.4. When two components with these parameters are placed near each other, their nuclei will begin to merge when they are approximately 1 unit apart (the distance between the component's shell and its nucleus: 1.47–0.4).

Unfortunately, creating a component with such specific parameters within Blob Sculptor is cumbersome. First, you would Create a component using the default values assigned by Blob Sculptor, then Resize the component and adjust its density. It's much easier to simply create the component in an ASCII file, then load the file into Blob Sculptor.

To create the file, run your favorite text editor, then enter and save the following data:

```
0.6
0.0 0.0 0.0 0.7 1.47
```

This data reflects the format used by Blob Sculptor when saving files. The first line contains the blob's Threshold value. All subsequent lines contain values specifying a component's XYZ-coordinate, its density value, and its radius-of-influence.

When we start Blob Sculptor, we select the FILE option and enter the name of the file containing our data. The program will load the file, and the component will appear in the view windows. This component will be the base leg joint from which we will clone other joints.

We want the part of the leg closest to the body to be placed elevated and off-centered from origin. This will allow room for the bug's body that we will add later. Click the Move button, move your mouse cursor to the FRONT (lower left) view, and click on the component. It will become highlighted in yellow. When you click on the component again, you can move it to another position. Adjust the component so that it is approximately one unit to the right and one unit up as shown in Figure 15.10. When ready, click the left mouse button again to permanently set the new position.

FIGURE 15.10.

Use the Create and Move buttons to position the first joint of the leg.

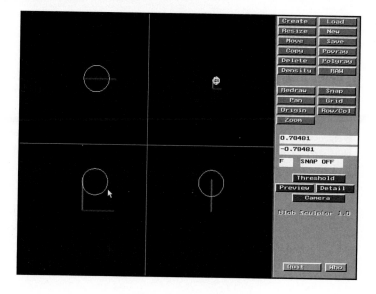

Now we will begin cloning the other leg joints. Click on the Copy button, move your mouse cursor to the FRONT-view, and select the component again. A copy of the component will appear under your cursor. Drag this copy upward and to the right approximately 1 unit. When ready, click the left mouse button to permanently set the position of the copy. Repeat this step until you have created an arc of six components similar to that shown in Figure 15.11. When finished, click the right mouse button to deactivate the Copy mode.

FIGURE 15.11.

Use the Copy button to clone the remaining leg joints.

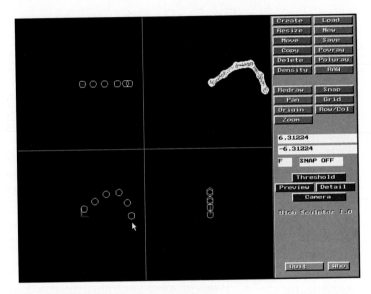

To confirm that your components merge correctly, click on the Preview button. The wire frame image within the ISO-view will clear, and a preview of the components will slowly appear. If you find that your components are not merging correctly, you can use the Move option to select individual components and adjust their positions. It is advised that you preview the effect of your adjustment after every move.

When you're satisfied with the component positions, select the File option and save the model to a file. We now have the first leg of our bug. Instead of interactively creating the other legs, we will edit the saved file and manually create the other legs. This will be much faster and more accurate.

Click on the Quit button and exit Blob Sculptor, then load the file you saved into your text editor. Your file will look somewhat like this (the exact coordinates will vary):

```
0.6
0.396624  0.886076  0.000000  0.700000  1.470000
1.803797  1.782700  0.000000  0.700000  1.470000
3.217300  2.668777  0.000000  0.710000  1.470000
4.799578  2.879747  0.000000  0.700000  1.470000
5.854431  1.571730  0.000000  0.700000  1.470000
6.342300 -0.013186  0.000000  0.700000  1.470000
```

By copying these coordinates and adjusting the values of the new coordinate lines, you can quickly build the additional legs. First, let's create the mirror image of the current leg by duplicating its values and negating the "x" coordinate:

```
-0.396624  0.886076  0.000000  0.700000  1.470000
-1.803797  1.782700  0.000000  0.700000  1.470000
-3.217300  2.668777  0.000000  0.710000  1.470000
-4.799578  2.879747  0.000000  0.700000  1.470000
-5.854431  1.571730  0.000000  0.700000  1.470000
-6.342300 -0.013186  0.000000  0.700000  1.470000
```

We now have a set of left and right legs. If we were to bring this data into Blob Sculptor now, we would see a display similar to Figure 15.12. But let's continue instead and create additional legs. Copy this entire set of coordinates to a new block of text and add a displacement to the "z" coordinate. This displacement value should be large enough so that the components belonging to one set of legs do not interact with the components of another. Let's use a value of 2.5 units:

```
0.396624  0.886076  2.500000  0.700000  1.470000
1.803797  1.782700  2.500000  0.700000  1.470000
3.217300  2.668777  2.500000  0.710000  1.470000
4.799578  2.879747  2.500000  0.700000  1.470000
5.854431  1.571730  2.500000  0.700000  1.470000
6.342300 -0.013186  2.500000  0.700000  1.470000
-0.396624  0.886076  2.500000  0.700000  1.470000
-1.803797  1.782700  2.500000  0.700000  1.470000
-3.217300  2.668777  2.500000  0.710000  1.470000
-4.799578  2.879747  2.500000  0.700000  1.470000
-5.854431  1.571730  2.500000  0.700000  1.470000
-6.342300 -0.013186  2.500000  0.700000  1.470000
```

Repeat this process to create the third set of legs, adding another displacement of 2.5 units:

```
0.396624  0.886076  5.000000  0.700000  1.470000
1.803797  1.782700  5.000000  0.700000  1.470000
3.217300  2.668777  5.000000  0.710000  1.470000
4.799578  2.879747  5.000000  0.700000  1.470000
5.854431  1.571730  5.000000  0.700000  1.470000
6.342300 -0.013186  5.000000  0.700000  1.470000
-0.396624  0.886076  5.000000  0.700000  1.470000
-1.803797  1.782700  5.000000  0.700000  1.470000
-3.217300  2.668777  5.000000  0.710000  1.470000
-4.799578  2.879747  5.000000  0.700000  1.470000
-5.854431  1.571730  5.000000  0.700000  1.470000
-6.342300 -0.013186  5.000000  0.700000  1.470000
```

FIGURE 15.12.

*Use a text editor to create
a mirror image of the leg.*

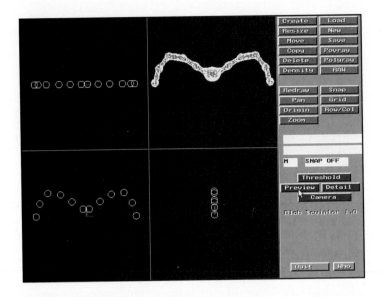

We now have three sets of symmetrically positioned legs. Save this data to a file and re-start Blob Sculptor. When you click on the File button and enter the name of the saved file, the file will load and the components will appear in the view windows. Click on the Preview button to preview the blob. You will see a wire frame display similar to that shown in Figure 15.13. If you cannot see all of the components in a particular window, click on the Zoom button and then on the view for that window. The left mouse button will zoom into view, and the right mouse button will zoom out of the view.

FIGURE 15.13.

*Use a text editor to create
three sets of legs.*

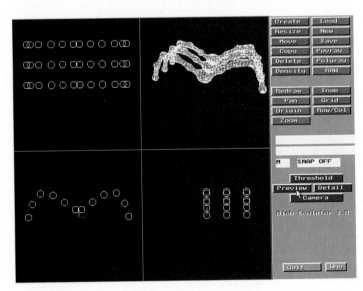

Making the Body and Tail

Now that we have the legs in place, creating the body is a simple matter of filling the space between the groups of leg components and adding a tail. We will not be too concerned about the density of the body components. It would require a very large radius-of-influence for a component centered between the leg grouping to affect the leg components. Therefore, we will be safe using the default component density of 1.0.

Click the Create button to begin building the body components and move your mouse cursor to the SIDE (lower-right) view. Position the cursor between the first and second groups of leg components. Now draw a component whose effective-radius just touches the perimeters of the two groups. Once you're satisfied with the size of the component, create another component between the second and third groups. These two components will merge with each other and the innermost components of the groups to form the body of our bug.

To create the bug's tail, move to the rear of the third leg grouping and draw a component that is slightly larger than those used to fill the body. Then move to the right of this component and create a second bigger component (Figure 15.14). When you preview these components, they should merge to create a bulbous tail. Use the MOVE option to adjust the components' positions if necessary.

FIGURE 15.14.

Create the body and tail using three components.

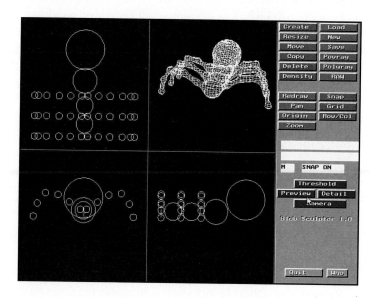

Making the Head and Horns

Our final modeling step will be to create the bug's head and horns. This step will give you some experience with adjusting component positions in three dimensions, rather than simply along a single axis. The procedure to create the head and horns is similar to that used to create the legs. First, we will create one side of the head and horns, then use a text editor to create its mirrored components.

Using the Pan and Zoom options, adjust the views within the TOP-, FRONT-, and SIDE-views so that you can easily see the frontal area above the bug's body (approximately 2 units above the origin). This is where we will begin positioning the head and horn components.

Select the Create option and position your mouse cursor within the SIDE-view and draw a component that is approximately half the radius of the components you used to fill the space between the leg groups. Click on the Move option and select the new component. Now, moving the component within the SIDE- and FRONT-views, position the new component such that it is slightly in front of the first leg group, elevated and to the right of the origin. This component will be half of the bug's head.

To create the right horn, repeat this procedure beginning with a much smaller component. This component will be the base of the horn. To position the base component, you will need to manipulate its position in all three view windows until it is extending above, to the right, and forward of the right head component. Once you are satisfied with its position, repeat this procedure, creating smaller and smaller components until you have a string of components arcing outward, upward, and to the right of the head component. When you are done, count the number of components you used to create the horn and write the number down.

Now, save the model again, exit Blob Sculptor, and load the file into your text editor. Go to the end of the component listing and count backward to the number of components you used to create the horn, and then one more to account for half of the head. Copy these component entries and negate the x coordinate just as you did when creating the leg groupings. This will create the other half of the bug's head and horn and complete your model. Save this file, and return to Blob Sculptor.

When you load the file into Blob Sculptor, you will see your completed model (Figure 15.15). Select the Camera option to adjust the camera angle in the ISO-view. When you are satisfied with the view, select the Polyray option, enter a new filename, and Blob Sculptor will export your model to a Polyray-compatible file that you can then use to render your model in breathtaking three-dimensional realism (Figure 15.16).

FIGURE 15.15.

This is our completed blob-bug model.

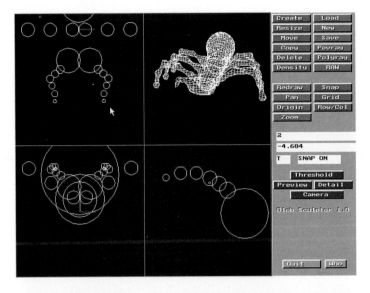

FIGURE 15.16.

Here is our model fully ray traced.

Conclusion

In this chapter, you've reviewed the basics behind blobs, their components, and the various parameters that determine how they interact. You've also had the opportunity to incorporate that knowledge into the development of a simple blob model. Where you go from here is limited only by your imagination. Have fun.

V

PART

Ultra-Realistic 3-D

Stereoscopic 3-D Stunts

16

by Martin Richard Crumpton

Close Encounters of the SIRDS Kind

Like holograms, Single Image Random Dot Stereograms (SIRDS) are illusions. Both give a strong impression of three dimensions using only two-dimensional media. The major functional difference is that holograms can disclose or obscure different parts of an image. If you move your head from left to right on the hologram of a cup, the handle might appear and disappear, as if the cup were actually being turned. This effect doesn't occur for SIRDS. By the way, they're called Single Image because that's what they are—they're not two slightly differing images welded together, like those old stereoscopic images you have to view through red and green lenses.

SIRDS takes a single image and creates two different views of it—one for each eye. Sort of. It'll become more clear as you go along. "Stereograms" is possibly not the best way to describe SIRDS, but anything else would be clumsy—like "muddy tire tracks on a piece of paper," even though that's what they appear to be. One major difference worth noting is that holograms take sophisticated equipment to produce. A stereogram can be made on the back of an old envelope. I'm not kidding!

In case you've never seen a stereogram before, Figure 16.1 shows an example.

FIGURE 16.1.

A muddy tire track... or is it?

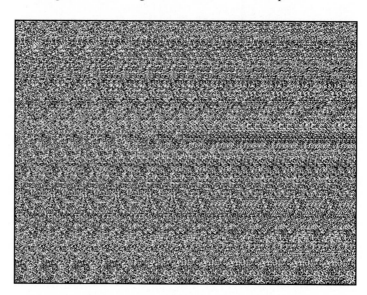

In case you couldn't see the image, it's a skull and crossbones surmounted by four dice. Two dice have five spots and the others have six. Don't be concerned if you didn't see it—a guided tour is coming up shortly.

Stereograms are the technological equivalent of the King's new clothes—everyone else can see them except you! There's no need to get paranoid—it's not a conspiracy. Provided that you have stereoscopic vision and the ability to refocus your eyes, I'll prove it to you.

A frequent first reaction of people seeing depth in a SIRDS ("stereogram" from now on) is utter amazement. The first encounter is normally with those glossy, plastic-coated, high-color posters of dinosaurs or the Statue of Liberty, sold in markets and gift shops. I've seen people running their fingers over the surface of the posters, trying to figure out how it's done. They're trying to feel for tiny indentations as if two separate images have been pressed together in a way that presents one image to the right eye and another image to the left. Not so. It's an intelligent reaction, but ultimately doomed to failure. The truth is even more obscure.

The second reaction is often bewilderment, when people find that you can take a black-and-white photocopy of a stereogram and the effect still works, even when translated from color to black and white. You can enlarge or reduce the image too, without losing the sensation or any amount of definition. Amazing!

The third reaction is, "If it wasn't for computers, this wouldn't be possible!" Oh, come on—can we talk? I'll dispel that myth straightaway. Take a blank sheet of paper and a ball-point pen, and (neatly) copy the following characters (and note the deliberate "spelling mistake"):

```
PCGraphicsPCGrapphicsPCGraphic
     +        +
```

Congratulations! You've just created your first stereogram, and all by the power of your own brain and hands! The next step is to view it, and that requires some eye-training. The trick is to focus beyond the image, as if the paper were a pane of glass and you were looking through it at some object about 18 inches further on—as shown in Figure 16.2.

It's a little easier to see the stereogram with a larger block, so try writing the following lines:

```
PCGraphicsPCGraphicsPCGraphics
PCGraphicsPCGraphicsPCGraphics
PCGraphicsPCGraphicsPCGraphics
PCGraphicsPCGraphicsPCGraphics
PCGraphicsPCGrapphicsPCGraphic
PCGraphicsPCGrapphicsPCGraphic
PCGraphicsPCGrapphicsPCGraphic
PCGraphicsPCGrapphicsPCGraphic
PCGraphicsPCGraphicsPCGraphics
PCGraphicsPCGraphicsPCGraphics
PCGraphicsPCGraphicsPCGraphics
PCGraphicsPCGraphicsPCGraphics
     +          +
```

FIGURE 16.2.

How to view a stereogram.

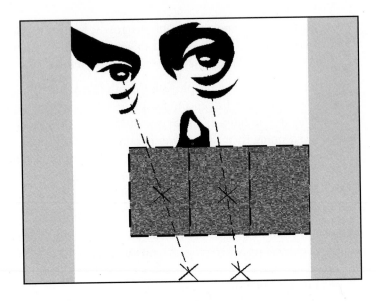

The easiest way to view the image is to draw the paper up to your nose; at this distance, your eyes naturally focus to infinity. Slowly draw back from the paper, trying not to refocus. Notice the "+" symbols at the bottom. At about an inch away, you'll see four of them. A little further, and these four pluses will begin to overlap in the center, leaving three of them for you to concentrate on. Stop! Pull the paper up until you're looking into the block of letters, and you will see an area, about an inch square, set back into the distance behind all the other letters. Seriously! Keep trying until you get it!

Congratulations on seeing your first stereogram! It took me four days before I got the hang of them! Most people take a only few minutes, I should point out, but after you've seen the effect, you'll quickly pick up fresh images when they're presented. It's like riding a bicycle—you never forget how to do it.

TIP:

Try to do this when sober. In any other condition, you'll believe anything!

Don't Try This at Home

I'd like to point out that another way of seeing depth is to cross your eyes when you look at stereograms, but I wouldn't recommend this technique. It produces far more discomfort to the eyes than using the intended method. If all else fails, try copying the stereogram to an overhead-projector transparency and looking through it at a distant object. This method didn't work for me, but it might work for you.

If all else fails, code up the program from the listing in this chapter and try it on-screen. A lot of people seem to find stereograms easier to see that way, although I don't know why. Perhaps it has something to do with the light being emitted rather than reflected. If nothing else, if you run out of conversation at a dinner party, all you need is a pen and a napkin to astound your companions. Interestingly, the effect works in reverse. Try this:

```
PCGraphicsPCGraphicsPCGraphics
PCGraphicsPCGraphicsPCGraphics
PCGraphicsPCGraphicsPCGraphics
PCGraphicsPCGraphicsPCGraphics
PCGraphicsPCraphicsPCGraphicsP
PCGraphicsPCraphicsPCGraphicsP
PCGraphicsPCraphicsPCGraphicsP
PCGraphicsPCraphicsPCGraphicsP
PCGraphicsPCGraphicsPCGraphics
PCGraphicsPCGraphicsPCGraphics
PCGraphicsPCGraphicsPCGraphics
PCGraphicsPCGraphicsPCGraphics
+          +
```

Notice that the block now floats above the surface of the paper. The height that the block appears over the background represents a single level of depth. There's a lot more to choose from.

So it has just been proven that you don't need computers to produce convincing stereograms—or has it? Frankly, you can do better, but you don't need a Pentium or a PowerPC to do it. The code supplied for this chapter runs on a standard 8086, and thanks to the VSA256 and TIFF256 packages that come with this book, it runs like greased lightning. A more sophisticated version is included as an executable module, so you needn't type the code unless you want to. If you do type it, however, read the notes on VSA256 and TIFF256 carefully (especially the compiler notes).

How Do Stereograms Work?

Place your right index finger about six inches in front of your eyes. Both eyes can see the front of your finger, but only the left eye can see the extreme left side—and only the right eye can see the extreme right side. The brain interprets this information in such a way that we have perception of depth. This is not how stereograms work, except in reverse—sort of.

Now hold your hands up flat in front of your eyes, facing each other. Your right eye can see more surface area of your left palm than your left eye can, and vice versa. This information is also resolved into depth. Both eyes see the same thing but disagree slightly; the greater the disagreement, the closer the object (and vice versa). This is how stereograms work—by introducing conflict in the brain!

Taking the preceding example, do some analysis. The block consists of three more-or-less repeating columns. I say more-or-less because subtle distortions have been introduced in the otherwise identical sequences. Each eye sees three columns, so there are six in the field of view (three per eye). The brain has to make sense of this and tries to merge the image. When you focus correctly, the two centermost columns from the left eye overlap the two centermost columns from the right eye. The result is four columns in the field of view, the outermost two being slightly less distinct than the innermost pair.

Due to the overlap and the repetitious nature of the pattern, the brain has good reason to believe that both eyes are looking at the same object. However, taking just the two over-lapped columns in the center, the left eye can see a difference on the leftmost column that it can't see on the rightmost, and the right eye can see a difference on the rightmost column that it can't see on the leftmost. The brain knows only one way to resolve this: it "sees" depth.

That's the end of the tedious lecture. It's time to begin the journey of exploration into what makes stereograms tick!

Making Your Own Stereograms

I don't intend to spend time on the intricacies of C and video graphics. Because you have this book, you'll also have the libraries supplied with it—including VSA256 and TIFF256, by Spyro Gumas. I've used them in the past, and they work wonderfully (and save me so much time!). Consequently, I use them in the listing that ends this chapter. I'd also like to point out that a full-fledged SIRDS generator (complete with bells and whistles) accompanies this book and rejoices in the name of ABSIRDS. It's a shareware goody of such wondrous and fantastic complexity and utility that your heart will petition your wallet to send the paltry registration fee. End of advertisement—enjoy!

The first item under the microscope is resolution, of which there are two types. The first type is obvious, so you'll delve into the second one first.

Lateral Resolution

The wider the stereogram, the easier it is to see. It's easy for the eyes to be distracted at the edge of a stereogram because that's where the pattern gets interrupted. So if there are more strips, you can concentrate your attention better toward the main area of the picture.

There's another huge advantage to having many narrow strips rather than a few wide ones—it shortens the focal distance! This technique causes the eyes to draw more closely, and more naturally, together. The result is less fatigue and much quicker recognition. Figure 16.3 shows how to avoid eye strain.

FIGURE 16.3.

How to avoid eye strain.

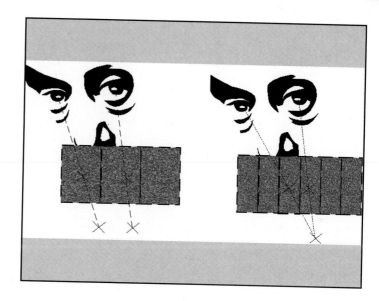

The examples given earlier in the chapter consist of strips of letters (`PCGraphics`) repeated in three side-by-side blocks. This configuration represents the minimum number of blocks, or strips as they'll be called, because of the mechanics outlined in the introduction—but it's only a lower-bound, not an upper-bound. Consider what happens when the number of strips is increased:

```
PCGraphicsPCGraphicsPCGraphicsPCGraphicsPCGraphicsPCGraphics
PCGraphicsPCGraphicsPCGraphicsPCGraphicsPCGraphicsPCGraphics
PCGraphicsPCGraphicsPCGraphicsPCGraphicsPCGraphicsPCGraphics
PCGraphicsPCGraphicsPCGraphicsPCGraphicsPCGraphicsPCGraphics
PCGraphicsPCGraphicssPCGraphicssPCGraphicsPCGraphicsPCGraphi
PCGraphicsPCGraphicssPCGraphicssPCGraphicsPCGraphicsPCGraphi
PCGraphicsPCGraphicssPCGraphicssPCGraphicsPCGraphicsPCGraphi
PCGraphicsPCGraphicssPCGraphicssPCGraphicsPCGraphicsPCGraphi
PCGraphicsPCGraphicsPCGraphicsPCGraphicsPCGraphicsPCGraphics
PCGraphicsPCGraphicsPCGraphicsPCGraphicsPCGraphicsPCGraphics
PCGraphicsPCGraphicsPCGraphicsPCGraphicsPCGraphicsPCGraphics
PCGraphicsPCGraphicsPCGraphicsPCGraphicsPCGraphicsPCGraphics
+          +
```

You might have noticed that it's much easier to lock your focus into the effect in this example. In my experiments I've found that using between 12 and 18 strips works best, but simple blocks of characters aren't very useful for demonstrating this point. Don't worry; you're about to move straight into the graphics stuff now. You'll start with a simple test pattern, consisting of variously colored squares and circles, and use it as the base for your generated SIRDS. Refer to Figure 16.4—you'll come back to this figure a few times. See the color section of this book so that you can get a good idea of what you're looking for in the stereogram, and see how the colors become levels of depth. The image is reproduced in Figure 16.4 in black and white so that you don't have to keep skipping through the book.

FIGURE 16.4.

The black-and-white version of the image that will be converted into a stereogram.

The image's resolution is a lowly 640×480, and it comes in 16 colors. So that you don't have to keep guessing, here it is again, converted to stereograms. The version shown in Figure 16.5 is three strips wide, and the version shown in Figure 16.6 is 12 strips wide. You should be able to appreciate the difference immediately (or your ophthalmologist will). If your eyes ache, take a rest. After you've had some experience at viewing stereograms, it's easy to do—but at first it might be quite an effort. Take it easy!

FIGURE 16.5.

A low lateral-resolution stereogram.

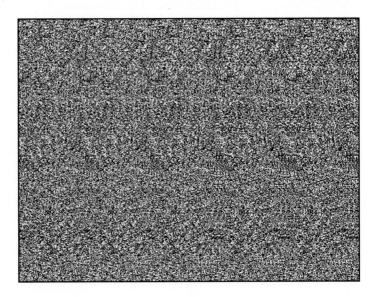

FIGURE 16.6.

A high lateral-resolution stereogram.

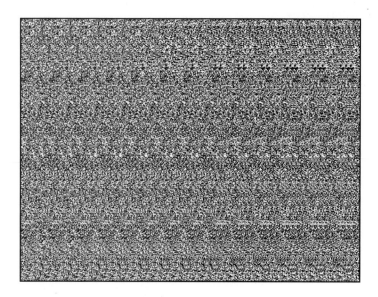

Density

Finally, it's time to go for broke and demonstrate the other kind of resolution, with a little color thrown in just to make it more impressive. Look at the figure in the color-plate section. This pattern is the same as the preceding one, but at 1280×1024, with 18 strips. When you run the ABSIRDS program included with this book, you'll note a little trick—called the psychedelic effect—that constantly changes the palette, which helps draw your eyes into the correct focus.

Basically, a color is mapped to a depth. It really is that easy. White is near, black is far, and all the colors range in-between. Naturally, I mean colors as the computer generates them, not as they appear in a rainbow. The order is different. However, using the VSA256 library functions, you can remap the palette any way you like (changing grey to color and vice versa). You'll read more about this topic later.

You'll delve into higher-resolution topics later; now, you'll start assembling the bits needed to make your stereogram generator.

Generating the Strips

Think of the strips as sections of wallpaper with a small repeating pattern. As you paper each section to the wall, you have to be careful to place each strip so that the pattern flows continuously from one piece to the next. In fact, although this text is dealing specifically with SIRDS, it could just as well be discussing SIGPS—Single Image Granular Pattern

Stereograms (a term I've just invented, so feel free to call it what you like). Several Windows wallpapers have detail small enough to be suitable for this kind of thing—copyright permitting. You might have seen similar things on a recent (at the time of writing) Pepsi promotion.

The easiest repeating pattern of all is a strip of random dots, though, and this discussion will stick to them. There is absolutely no problem in making side-by-side strips of dots look as though they fit perfectly, as you've seen in previous illustrations.

The first thing to do in your generator, vis-a-vis making the pattern, is to request some memory from DOS. Why? Earlier versions of SIRDS worked by drawing the strip on-screen with old, slow, putpixel processing. Although it worked (or works), it also leaves part of the screen that can't be used for an image. In other words, if the pattern is generated off-screen, the entire screen from left to right can hold stereogram information. The base pattern itself conveys no depth information. It is by making modifications to the base pattern that you can achieve the effect.

The amount of memory needed is variable, depending on the number of sections across the picture and the screen resolution. Say you're generating something at 1024×768 and using a base pattern strip that's one-twelfth of the screen width. In numbers, you need 1024/12*768=65536, or 64K, which isn't too bad. Now step it up to 1280×1024, and you suddenly need 106K! Even this amount isn't too bad, but maybe you're running under OS/2, Windows, or DesqView.

Why load the system if you don't need to? Each byte represents a pixel—but you're only dealing with simple binary! All you need is a bit! Through some binary manipulations, you can divide your requirement by 8, making the maximum load, even at 1280×1024, less than 16K. That's a lot healthier, and the processing time required to do this wouldn't be worth consideration even on an 8086. The total pattern, against which you'll apply your image, will look something like what's shown in Figure 16.7. Notice how, even from the base pattern, you can see depth!

Having obtained the play area, you randomly decide whether each pixel is going to be on or off (read "decide whether each pixel is going to be black or white"). Naturally, you don't have to restrict yourself to monochrome. All you need is a choice of two colors so that a pattern bit of 0 means color A and a pattern bit of 1 means color B when displayed on-screen.

After exploring the next topic, you'll see that you can have as many colors on-screen as you like!

FIGURE 16.7.

The base pattern.

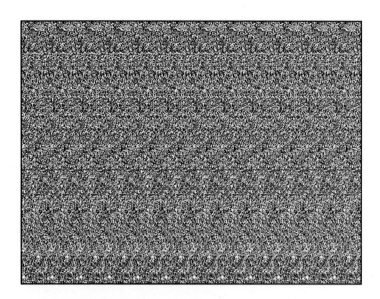

Translating an Image to a Stereogram

Time to add the magic ingredient! Without taking any account of depth, the procedure is basically this: For the first strip on the screen, translate the bit pattern you created in memory into pixels. For all the other strips, just copy the strip immediately to the left, pixel by pixel.

An interesting effect here is to introduce color into the display. When you're converting the random pattern you created in memory to pixels, you can set the color of the pixel to anything you like! It doesn't have to be black and white. When you're dealing with the second strip onward, all you're doing is copying previously written pixels. Again, refer to Figure 16.13.

For the sake of argument and clarity, imagine that your screen is one strip wider to the left than it actually is. The allocated memory in which the base random pattern was placed represents this. You can think of it as being addressable by GETPIXEL(x-width_of_strip_in_pixels,y).

You can fill the screen by going left to right, up and down, with PUTPIXEL(GETPIXEL (x-width_of_strip_in_pixels,y). If the screen is divided into 12 sections or strips, pretty soon you'll get 12 identical strips running left to right. This creates a foggy picture of black and white dots, repeated across the screen. So far so good. Now go back and change the procedure slightly.

Load an image into the screen buffer. Starting at the upper-left corner, read the pixel there. (Because you're in the first strip, you have to look in the base pattern. When you're working on the second or greater strip, you simply read the pixel value from the screen.) If the logical color of the pixel you've read from the image is 0, copy the pixel you find at the same position on the preceding strip. If it's 1, copy the pixel in (position-1) in the preceding strip. If it's logical color 2, copy the pixel at (position-2) in the preceding strip.

That's how it's done! Instant depth! You convert the colors of the image into displacements. Easy! The results, in graphics terms, look something like what's shown in Figure 16.8 (although this image is not fully rendered—it doesn't take color into account).

FIGURE 16.8.

A (rough) idea of what you're trying to achieve with a stereogram.

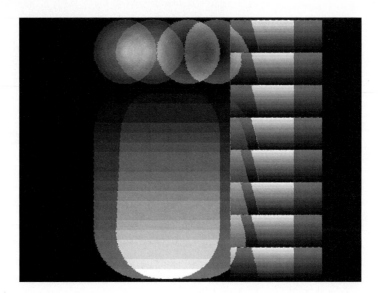

In effect, you're just doing with pixels what was done at the beginning of this chapter with letters. You're shifting parts of the pattern to the right. The greater the shift, the greater the depth. Because strip 3 is based on strip 2 (only strip 1 is based on the pattern you generated), you carry all the displacements you make across the entire screen.

Well, that's a fairly wordy explanation. I'll try to present the information more graphically in a step-by-step approach. To make things a little easier to follow, I'll have you revert to using letters. Just imagine, for the time being, that you're dealing with pixels. Take the following example. Using your letters, you'll build a stereogram using an "image" of 000011110000:

```
<-strip 1 -><-strip 2-><-strip 3->        <-  image ->
============================        ============
abcdefghijkl                        000011110000
Byte 1 of image is 0, so copy byte 1 (1 + 0) of the pattern -- "a"
abcdefghijkla                       000011110000
```

```
              <— — — — — — — — — — — — — —>
Byte 2 of image is 0, so copy byte 2 (2 + 0) of the pattern — "b"
abcdefghijklab                          000011110000
              <— — — — — — — — — — — — — —>
Byte 3 of image is 0, so copy byte 3 (3 + 0) of the pattern — "c"
abcdefghijklabc                         000011110000
                <— — — — — — — — — — — — — —>
Byte 4 of image is 0, so copy byte 4 (4 + 0) of the pattern — "d"
abcdefghijklabcd                        000011110000
              <— — — — — — — — — — — — — —>
Byte 5 of image is 1, so copy byte 6 (5 + 1) of the pattern — "f"
bcdefghijklabcdf                        000011110000
                <— — — — — — — — — — — — — —>
Byte 6 of image is 1, so copy byte 7 (6 + 1) of the pattern — "g"
abcdefghijklabcdfg                      000011110000
            <— — — — — — — — — — — — — —>
Byte 7 of image is 1, so copy byte 8 (7 + 1) of the pattern — "h"
abcdefghijklabcdfgh                     000011110000
              <— — — — — — — — — — — — — — —>
Byte 8 of image is 1, so copy byte 9 (8 + 1) of the pattern — "i"
abcdefghijklabcdfghi                    000011110000
                <— — — — — — — —>
Byte 9 of image is 0, so copy byte 9 (9 + 0) — "i" again!
abcdefghijklabcdfghii                   000011110000
              <— — — — — — — — — — — — — —>
Byte 10 of image is 0, so copy byte 10 of the pattern — "j"
abcdefghijklabcdfghiij                  000011110000
              <— — — — — — — — — — — — — —>
Byte 11 of image is 0, so copy byte 11 of the pattern — "k"
abcdefghijklabcdfghiijk                 000011110000
                <— — — — — — — — — — — — —>
Byte 12 of image is 0, so copy byte 12 of the pattern — "l"
abcdefghijklabcdfghiijkl                000011110000
              <— — — — — — — — — — — — — —>
```

If you assume that the whole image you're converting looks like

```
000000000000000000000000
000000000000000000000000
000000000000000000000000
000000000000000000000000
000011110000000000000000
000011110000000000000000
000011110000000000000000
000011110000000000000000
000000000000000000000000
000000000000000000000000
000000000000000000000000
000000000000000000000000
```

you can expect to see a stereogram in which a block to the left of center, four letters wide and four letters deep, stands out. Does it work? Yes!

```
abcdefghijklabcdefghijklabcdefghijkl
abcdefghijklabcdefghijklabcdefghijkl
abcdefghijklabcdefghijklabcdefghijkl
abcdefghijklabcdefghijklabcdefghijkl
abcdefghijklabcdfghiijklabcdfghiijkl
abcdefghijklabcdfghiijklabcdfghiijkl
abcdefghijklabcdfghiijklabcdfghiijkl
abcdefghijklabcdefghijklabcdefghijkl
abcdefghijklabcdefghijklabcdefghijkl
abcdefghijklabcdefghijklabcdefghijkl
abcdefghijklabcdefghijklabcdefghijkl
+           +
```

Just to prove that the greater the offset, the greater the depth, try the following image based on 0000-1-1-1-10000. It was derived using exactly the same algorithm as before.

```
abcdefghijklabcdefghijklabcdefghijkl
abcdefghijklabcdefghijklabcdefghijkl
abcdefghijklabcdefghijklabcdefghijkl
abcdefghijklabcdefghijklabcdefghijkl
abcdefghijklabcdeefghjklabcdeefghjkl
abcdefghijklabcdeefghjklabcdeefghjkl
abcdefghijklabcdeefghjklabcdeefghjkl
abcdefghijklabcdeefghjklabcdeefghjkl
abcdefghijklabcdefghijklabcdefghijkl
abcdefghijklabcdefghijklabcdefghijkl
abcdefghijklabcdefghijklabcdefghijkl
+           +
```

What Kind of Picture Makes a Good Stereogram?

I'm glad you asked! At the resolutions being used here, only pictures with low levels of detail are viable. A staircase disappearing into the distance, a blocky house in front of trees or mountains, or anything that doesn't rely on fine texture or detail works well. The abstract patterns I've used make good stereograms. Don't expect color photographs of your pets, spouses, or children to make any sense as stereograms.

To begin with, color photographs turn into nightmare stereograms. If someone's nose is more red than their cheeks, expect to see a nose that recedes into the person's face. Yuck. Besides, it wouldn't be recognizable as a nose because of the lack of fine detail. If you're lucky, you'll get an impression of shape. I can assure you that there isn't going to be any fuss about R-rated stereograms! Allow me to demonstrate: see Figures 16.9 and 16.10.

You would think that lettering would be great too, wouldn't you? Frankly, it isn't. Take three well-known letters from the world of mainframe computing, color them blue against a background of black, and you see them well enough. Put your entire name up as a stereogram and you'll be the only person who can read it without getting severe eyestrain. It works, but it doesn't work well. The ordinary monitor just isn't big enough to carry sufficient detail. Try Figure 16.11—it says, "PC Graphics Programming, an example of lettering in SIRDS."

FIGURE 16.9.

A normal black-and-white picture of a person. (Art from CorelDraw! by Corel Corporation.)

FIGURE 16.10.

A stereogram of a black-and-white photo of a person.

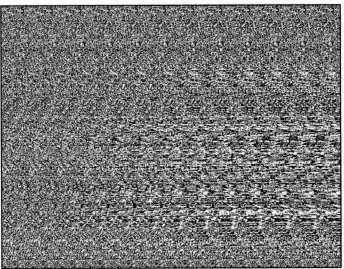

What's the answer? Easy. Increase the resolution of the image. Herein lies the problem! Short of someone developing an SVGA mode that's twice as good as today's, you're stuck. Theoretically, you have a usable lateral resolution (and it has to be lateral because our eyes are arranged horizontally, not vertically) of 1280 divided by something between 3 and 20. Three is the absolute minimum; the maximum is determined by the number of levels of depth required. If you divide 1280 into 10 strips, you get a pixel width for each strip of 128—so you get a theoretical maximum of 128 levels of depth.

FIGURE 16.11.

Lettering converted to a stereogram.

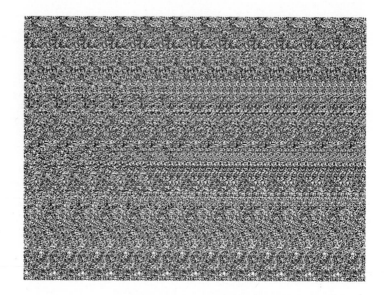

So, you say, you divide the image into five strips and get 256 levels of depth. Nope. Remember that the brain needs to be convinced that there's an overall, consistent pattern there. If you make the second strip such a distortion of the first that the strips don't look similar, and compound the problem by making the third look nothing like the second, and so on, you blow the whole effect.

There's a delicate balance to be struck between obtaining a great effect and committing SIRDS overload. I'm not about to try to offer a mathematical formula to determine the "best fit" pattern, either. Life's too short!

One of the hardest problems to solve is an inherent feature of stereograms. The more you put into an image, the greater becomes the level of "distortion" across the screen (or page). Our eyes take in detail in a small, focused area. When we have a complex image, the beginning (the left) of the picture is relatively undistorted. As we travel to the right, the base pattern becomes more and more unrecognizable. SIRDS overload occurs when the brain is no longer convinced that there's an underlying, consistent pattern across the whole image. That's why lettering doesn't work well. It's a rather self-limiting feature of stereograms. The answer is to choose your images with great care, and keep them simple—but effective.

There is a reasonable compromise. You can increase the number of depths vastly and keep the pictures you want to convert relatively simple. How? On a 15-inch monitor, at 1280 resolution, you get approximately 85 pixels to the inch, or nearly 107 per strip (assuming 12 strips), on a laser print that goes straight up to 300 dots per inch or better! Take an 8-inch-wide piece of paper, divided into 12 strips (logically! no scissors needed!) the way you did with the screen, and you have 200 dots per strip. That's pretty close to twice the resolution you could get on a screen. Anyone with a Linotype stands to make real money out of this!

Obviously, you would bypass the screen almost entirely to do this. You would need to produce an image intended for a color printer and save it to disk, read the file and translate it into another file, and then…. Because the title of the book is *PC Graphics Unleashed,* not *Print Control Language Unleashed,* I don't intend to get into the details. However, it's food for thought!

What Can I Make Stereograms From?

Good question. With a little imagination and a basic drawing program, you have all the tools you need—apart from the program listing that ends this chapter! Your basic requirement is to be able to save the image in TIFF format or use a format converter to produce TIFF output from whatever you've made. Remember not to use compression or some of the more exotic bells and whistles that the full-fledged TIFF specification supports.

So you have your blocks of yellow, blue triangles, and peculiarly shaped areas of green, and you want to progress to something a little more exciting, a little more showy, in the stereogram line. In other words, you want objects that aren't all flat planes. Two programs I recommend are Autodesk's 3D Studio and CorelDraw!. 3D Studio can render in black and white from a single point light source, which means that depth is represented in terms of light and shade.

Even easier is CorelDraw! with its fountain fill. Draw a shape on-screen; fill it with a radial, conical, or linear fill from black to white, or vice versa; and you're nearly there. When you've finished, export the drawing as a TIFF file specifying the resolution you require (say, 640×480) and as a 16-level greyscale image. The program included in this chapter will happily consider that to be logical colors 0 to 15 and interpret them correctly as 16 levels of depth, all in the right order.

Bear in mind that to produce stereograms, you don't need *n*-levels of color or *n*-levels of gray; you just need *n*-ways of making a distinction! Your input image needn't be an image at all—it could just as well be a text file.

What Can I Do with My Stereograms?

You can admire them. You could even sell them. With a little inventiveness, you could try the mix'n'match approach. Suppose that you have a beautiful image of a hot-air balloon rising majestically over a magnificent horizon. With simple exclusive-or logic, a mask, and a stereogram, you could transform only part of the picture—say, the balloon itself. If the mask is black where the balloon occurs and white everywhere else, you can copy the image pixel-for-pixel to the screen when the mask says "white" and convert the rest to SIRDS format. I've seen very effective examples. Take a look at Figure 16.12.

FIGURE 16.12.

Mixing stereograms with "straight" images. (Clip art from CorelDraw! by Corel Corporation.)

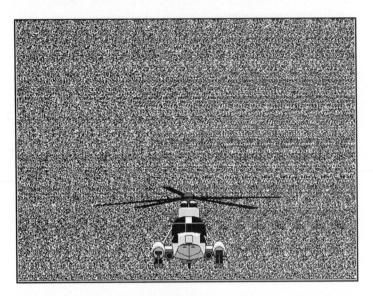

What Is the Future for SIRDS?

The Holy Grail of SIRDS developers is the Animated Stereogram. Several have been produced, and all (including my own efforts) are less than wonderful. The basic problem is the inherent feature of the stereogram itself; that is, that which causes the 3-D effect also causes a total mess when you attempt to get the stereogram moving. The problem, simply, is that depth is achieved by introducing progressively more and more distortion as your eyes travel from left to right. The right side of a stereogram bears less resemblance to the left than does the center. When you get it animated, you can see what's being attempted fairly well in the right side of the screen, but in the left side—oh dear. What a disaster! It's just a blur as all the heavy changes get shifted around.

One approach I've seen has been to change the base pattern with every frame, or cycle through four different patterns. The upshot of this method is to overload the brain with so many changes that the noise of the left gets buried in the furious disturbances all over the image. Although this method undoubtedly works, nobody with a functioning brain would want to sit and watch that sort of thing for long. If you want to try it, all you need to do is set the C RANDOMISER function to a particular seed, and the base pattern will be reproducible (otherwise, it just gets messy because your mind needs a finite amount of time to absorb each new pattern). Load an image, save it, load another, save it—and so on—and feed the converted images into a product such as GRASP or Autodesk Animator. Don't say you haven't been warned!

New Approaches to Generating Stereograms (and Other Dead-Ends)

Various experiments continue. For instance, I've been practicing with a stereogram in which only every other pixel gets converted. During the course of my research, I discovered something I had been only vaguely aware of previously. Although I know that, almost without exception, peoples' faces aren't symmetrical (like bodies), I hadn't realized quite to what extent this condition would occur. After I had gotten the right focus for viewing a stereogram, I discovered that I needed to tilt my head to an angle of approximately 15 degrees to get the thing level between both eyes. The words "dark alley" and "I wouldn't want to meet you down a" immediately sprang to mind. C'est la guerre. I hope you have better luck than I did.

Figure 16.13 shows an idea that wasn't too successful. It combines the original image with the stereogram produced from it. This idea was a flop.

FIGURE 16.13.

Semi-rendered stereogram.

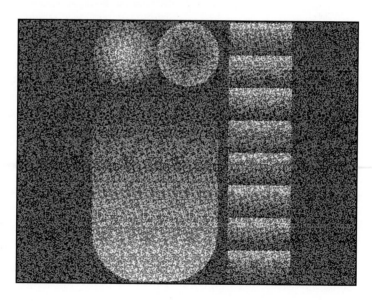

Worse yet, I had another bright idea that availed me nought. I figured that if I could reverse the effect—by converting right-to-left instead of using the method that's been used so far—and combine the left-right image with the right-left image…. Well, look at Figure 16.14 and make up your own mind.

FIGURE 16.14.

A left-right collision.

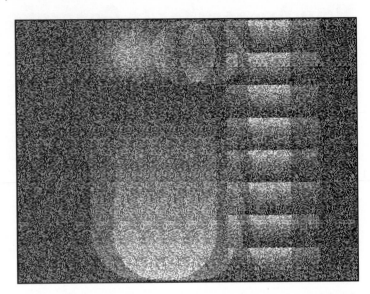

It seems that the brain quite likes to see a base pattern, but only one. Two of them simply create another variation of the SIRDS overload condition I've mentioned a few times.

The next idea was to combine a stereogram with an offset image, like the one in Figure 16.7. Now, this works! It really does—except that it's almost unviewable. Seeing the original image almost, but not completely, destroys the illusion. A shame—I had high hopes for this idea!

The difficulties that must be overcome include these:

■ The colors of the original image are lost.

■ The images used need to be relatively simple.

■ The things can't be convincingly animated.

So what use are these types of stereograms? The answer is that they're cheap to produce. If you need to illustrate something with depth—say, a plan of a housing estate—you can do so very easily. It's a lot cheaper than trying to bind holograms into a flyer or book. Provided techniques for improving the level of detail can be developed, that is. That's where you come in!

This is the fun of working with an entirely new field! If you can imagine an unusual twist or approach, you can go ahead and program it! You might be the one who invents a method of rendering a stereogram in which the distortion is reduced, enabling animations to be produced. Perhaps you'll discover a method of allowing some features (such as color) from the original image to be present in the stereogram that you produce from it, making it so much easier to see. For my part, I believe there's still a trick or two to be learned from stereograms, and I'll continue to experiment. Stereogram viewing might not replace the television, but it's fun. Good luck!

At Last! The Program!

Now that you understand the principles, your programming tasks are these:

1. Read the parameters (input file and output file).
2. Open the input file.
3. Generate the base strip.
4. Switch to graphics mode.
5. Read the input file to the screen.
6. Convert the image.
7. Open the output file.
8. Save the image.
9. Close the files.
10. Exit gracefully.

Listing 16.1 shows stereogram code.

Listing 16.1. Stereogram code.

```
//
// Example SIRDS generator program for PC Graphics Unleashed.
// =========================================================
//
// Author:          Martin Crumpton.
//                  Graphics routines by courtesy of Spyro Gumas
//                  (refer to the appendixes of PC Graphics
//                  Unleashed for further details, by SAMS books)
//
// Copyright:       The VSA256 and TIFF256 subroutines used are
//                  (c)copyright Spyro Gumas.
//
// Parameters:      input filename
//                  output filename
//                  video mode (100, 101, 103, or 105)
```

continues

Listing 16.1. continued

```
//
// DOS syntax:        EXAMPLE input.TIF output.TIF 101
//
// Function:          This program accepts TIFF input and converts
//                    it to SIRDS format as TIFF output.
//
// Environment:       VESA BIOS driver must be resident.
//
// Revision history: base code, 16/07/94  -MRC- '94
//
//***************************************************************//
//** Initialization of #includes and global variables       **//
//***************************************************************//

#include <io.h>
#include <stdio.h>
#include <stdlib.h>
#include <time.h>
#include <fcntl.h>
#include <vsa_font.h>
#include <vsa.h>
#include <tiff.h>

#ifndef _MSC_VER
extern unsigned _stklen = 14000;
#endif

unsigned vmode, topx = 0, topy = 0;
int      f, i, bktype = 1, sections = 12, maxby8, q, u, x, y, z;
char     input_file[80],output_file[80];
unsigned char far *str;
unsigned char table[8]
         = {0x80,0x40,0x20,0x10,0x08,0x04,0x02,0x01};
unsigned char not_table[8]
         = {0x7f,0xbf,0xdf,0xef,0xf7,0xfb,0xfd,0xfe};
unsigned char ch, w;
unsigned char color, in_buf[1280], out_buf[1280];

//***************************************************************//
//** Main procedure                                          **//
//***************************************************************//
void main(int argc, char* argv[])
  {

//***************************************************************//
//** Validate the parameters                                 **//
//***************************************************************//
  if(argc != 4)              // we must have all three parameters
    {
     printf("Use: EXAMPLE <input.TIF> <output.TIF> <video mode>\n");
     exit(1);                // exit after helpful msg issued
    }
  strcpy(input_file,argv[1]);
  strcpy(output_file,argv[2]);
  i = atoi(argv[3]);
  switch (i)
```

```
      {
       case 100: vmode = 0x100; break;
       case 101: vmode = 0x101; break;
       case 103: vmode = 0x103; break;
       case 105: vmode = 0x105; break;
       default:
        {
         printf("Unrecognized video mode, %d\n",vmode);
         exit(2);
        }
      }

//****************************************************************//
//** Switch to requested video mode                          **//
//****************************************************************//
   if((i = vsa_init(vmode)) != 0)  // attempt to enter graphics mode
     {
       printf("Can't initialize VESA mode %s - error %d\n",argv[3],i);
       printf("Refer to PC Graphics Unleashed for an explanation\n");
       exit(3);
     }

//****************************************************************//
//** Allocate some memory for the pattern                    **//
//****************************************************************//
   maxby8 = (XResolution/sections/8+1) * YResolution;
   if((str = (char far *) malloc(maxby8)) == NULL)
     {
       vsa_set_svga_mode(0x03);      // return to text for error msg.
       printf("Insufficient memory for pattern generation\n");
       printf("Requested amount: %d bytes\n",maxby8);
       exit(4);
     }

//****************************************************************//
//** Load, center, and view the input TIFF file              **//
//****************************************************************//
   tf_set_prime_colors();
   tf_set_adaptive_config(1,256,50);
   if((i=tf_open_file(input_file)) != 0)
     {
       vsa_set_svga_mode(0x03);      // return to text for error msg.
       printf("Error opening %s\n",input_file);
       exit(5);
     }
   if((i=tf_get_file_info()) != 0)
     {
       vsa_set_svga_mode(0x03);
       printf("%s is not a suitable TIF file\n",input_file);
       printf("Error code from TF_READ_IFD = %d\n",i);
       exit(6);
     }
   tf_set_defaults();
   if((i=tf_read_ifd()) != 0)
     {
       vsa_set_svga_mode(0x03);
       printf("This TIF format is not supported\n");
       exit(7);
```

continues

Listing 16.1. continued

```
  }
  // center the image on the screen
  if(TF_ImageWidth < XResolution)
   {
    topx = (XResolution-TF_ImageWidth)/2;
   }
  if(TF_ImageLength < YResolution)
   {
    topy = (YResolution-TF_ImageLength)/2;
   }
  if((i=tf_display_ifd(topx,topy)) != 0);
   {
    tf_set_adaptive_config(0,255,50);
    tf_display_ifd(topx,topy);
    tf_set_adaptive_config(1,255,50);
   }
  //****************************************************************//
  //** Generate the pattern                                     **//
  //****************************************************************//
  if(TF_BitsPerSample[0] > 4) f = 16; else f = 1;
  for(x=0; x<(XResolution/sections); x++)
   {
    z = (x/8)*YResolution;
    u = x%8;
    for(y=0; y<YResolution; y++)
     {
      color = rand()/16384;
      q = z+y;
      w = *(str+q);
      if(color != 0)
       {
        w = (w | table[u]);
       }
      else
       {
        w = (w & not_table[u]);
       }
      *(str+q) = w;
     }
   }
  vsa_set_color(1);

  //****************************************************************//
  //** Convert image to stereogram                              **//
  //****************************************************************//
  for(y=0; y<YResolution; y++)
   {
    vsa_get_raster_line(0,XResolution-1,y,in_buf);
    for(i=0;i<XResolution;i++)
     {
      in_buf[i] = in_buf[i]/f;
     }
    for(x=0; x<XResolution; x++)
     {
      q=(x-(XResolution/sections-in_buf[x]));
```

PC Graphics
Unleashed

Color Gallery

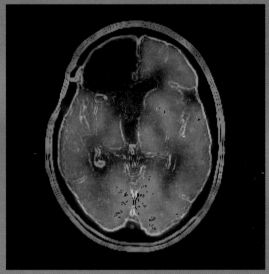

The ability to take pictures of the inside of our bodies has always fascinated us because it gives us the ability to see the unseen and helps us understand what is going on inside the human body. The first medical images (i.e., X-rays) were two-dimensional data sets that were basically photographs and therefore did not require any special means of display. With the advent of Computed Tomography (CT) and Magnetic Resonance Imaging (MRI), three-dimensional data sets were created. A method for effectively displaying three-dimensional data onto a two-dimensional screen therefore became a concern. CT and MRI data sets are not only three-dimensional but incredibly large, and so require a huge amount of memory.

Reslicing is basically looking at an object from different viewpoints where you are not looking at the actual surface of the object, but a tomographic plane of the object perpendicular to the viewing direction. In simpler terms, it's like taking an apple and slicing it with a knife, not necessarily in half but at any point, and looking at the inside of the apple.

This technique is often used when viewing CT images of the brain where they reslice the brain along the two cardinal planes perpendicular to the acquisition plane. One slice cuts the brain so that it goes parallel to the floor if the person were in an upright position (i.e., top view): the transverse slice. Another cuts the brain so that it splits the person in half where the cut goes from front to back (i.e., side view): the sagittal slice. The final cut goes from side to side where the cut goes from shoulder to shoulder (i.e., front view): the coronal slice. When these three slices all go through one point within a CT data set of the brain, it gives the viewer position-al information of where that point is in the brain.

This type of viewing technique is often used in computer-aided stereotactic neuro-surgery where the surgeon has some sort of device which digitizes a point in space. The coordinates of the point are sent to the computer, which calculates where that point lies within the CT data set and then shows the corresponding coronal, sagittal, and transverse slices on a computer screen. This gives the surgeon information as to where his pointing device is within the brain. From this information, he is better able to determine which direction he should go in order to, for instance, remove a tumor.

Animation is an illusion, a trick of the eye and mind. In its basic form, it is the movement of objects in a scene along some designated path. Traditional animation uses many separate images, called cells or frames—each individually hand drawn and painted. Each image differs slightly from the one before it and is captured on a frame of film or video. The high-speed playback of the related static images creates the illusion of movement. How believable this movement appears depends on the flow of transition between frames and the number of frames per second received by the eye. If the frames move quickly enough for one frame to still be fading from the retina as the next is being received, the brain perceives the flow of images as motion. This phenomenon of overlapping visual images is called the Persistence of Vision. The standard for commercial animation is a smooth 24 frames/sec.

While ray traced animation is similar to its traditional counterpart, a knowledge of one or more programming languages is especially helpful, as is a good grasp of fundamental mathematics. The animation process begins with a text editor and/or a three-dimensional modeler to create a ray traceable scene file. The scene file gets parsed and ray traced, and the many separate bitmapped images needed for the animation are generated. A number of readily available ray tracing packages, such as Vivid, POV-Ray, and Polyray, can create such images. Finally, a finished "movie" springs to life, assembled from the pre-rendered frames.

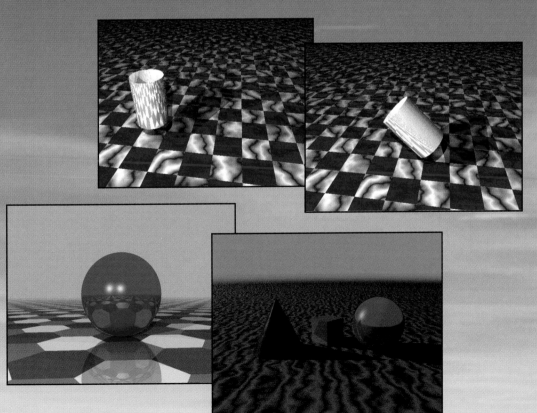

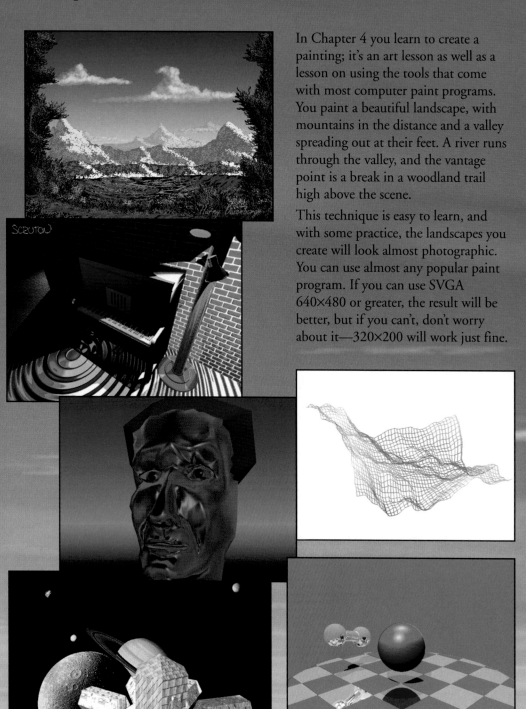

In Chapter 4 you learn to create a painting; it's an art lesson as well as a lesson on using the tools that come with most computer paint programs. You paint a beautiful landscape, with mountains in the distance and a valley spreading out at their feet. A river runs through the valley, and the vantage point is a break in a woodland trail high above the scene.

This technique is easy to learn, and with some practice, the landscapes you create will look almost photographic. You can use almost any popular paint program. If you can use SVGA 640×480 or greater, the result will be better, but if you can't, don't worry about it—320×200 will work just fine.

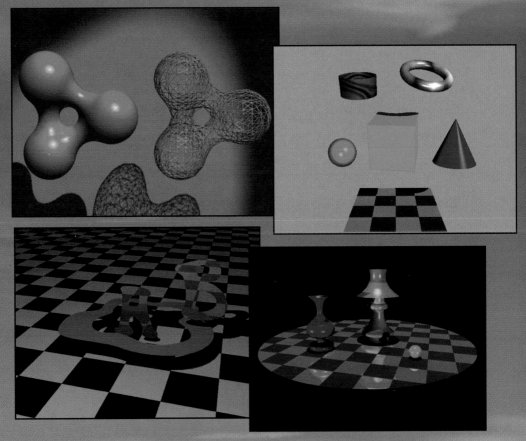

The term "photo-realistic" is used to denote the creation of an image that appears to have a quality similar to that of a true photo of the object being modeled. This is a very powerful tool! Imagine a computer with the ability to create a model that looks almost the same as the final product. If the designer wants to change any of the characteristics of the model, he (or she) can easily do that with the 3-D CAD program and then regenerate the photo-realistic image.

Various techniques are used to create photo-realistic images of models. One of them is called "ray tracing" and the results are astounding. Ray tracing is a technique that models the interaction between light, 3-D objects, the surface characteristics (textures) of these, and an observer. Imagine the following scenario: You are standing in front of a house on a sunny day. As you move to different locations, you observe that a shadow is produced due to the house blocking part of the Sun's rays. In other areas, where the light rays hit directly on the house, you observe that the colors seem to have a higher intensity. As you look at some of the windows, you can see through the ones where light does not hit directly, while those that receive direct sunlight are difficult to look at. In the previous scenario, the Sun represents the light source, the house represents the 3-D object, and the point of view of the scene is determined by your location and what you were looking at.

Blobs offer a unique method for creating realistic 3-D models. Used effectively, blob modeling can produce stunning organic shapes that rival the best models created by conventional methods. Creating complex blob models can require a great deal of patience. Blob modeling easily compares to the act of sculpting artwork with wet globs of gooey clay; everything is sticky. The creative part is deciding what glob should stick where, and how sticky each glob should be. The difficult part is controlling all of this stickiness.

Like any other skill you hope to master, it's important that you begin with a firm grasp of the basic concepts behind blobs. An interactive modeler called Blob Sculptor is included with this book. To familiarize you with Blob Sculptor, the program's interface is explained in detail in Chapter 15.

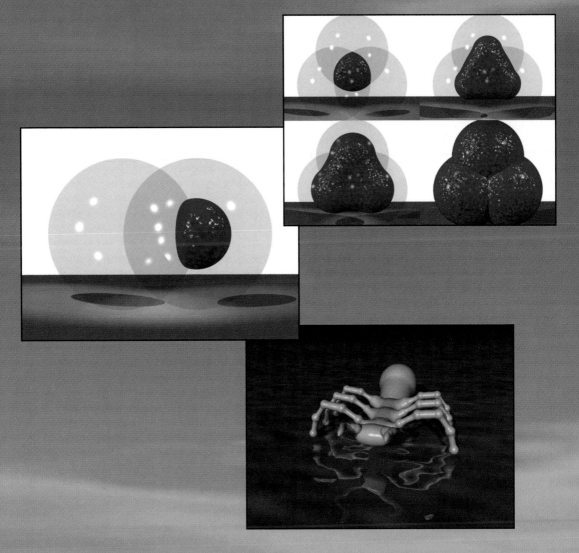

Blobs provide a very powerful method of modeling "organic" shapes, which cannot be easily modeled with conventional techniques. The creation of human, animal, and other "soft" forms has always been a tedious process using standard methods, but those same shapes are usually a snap to create with blobs. Unfortunately, blobs have the disadvantage that most renderers and display devices are unable to handle blob objects directly. Almost all renderers and displays are capable, however, of handling polygons or triangles. Chapter 13 describes how to evaluate a blob function and how to use that function to generate a polygon or triangle mesh approximating the blob surface. Although the code developed in Chapter 13 is intended to be used with blobs, it can, with a few minor modifications, be used to visualize virtually any mathematical function.

Radiosity is a tool of computer graphics that produces the highest degree of photorealism and offers many considerable advantages, but it has not been employed by the computer graphics art community. Radiosity is a physically based model of global diffuse illumination and reflection that was first developed at Cornell University in 1984 from theories of radiative heat transfer out of the field of thermodynamics. The basic radiosity method assumes that all surfaces are Lambertian (ideal diffuse) much in the same way that ray tracing assumes that all surfaces are ideal specular, but unlike ray tracing, radiosity discretizes the environment and produces data that is independent of viewer perspective. In general, the radiosity process takes longer than ray tracing, which is probably why it has yet to gain appreciation and employment from the computer graphics community. Because of its view independence, however, radiosity data can be used to rapidly produce multiple views of an imaginary scene where ray tracing can only pro-

duce one view. For this reason, radiosity is ideal for some applications (such as walk-throughs and fly-bys) and is worth the extra computing time.

Unlike Gouraud shading, Phong shading, and ray tracing, the radiosity illumination/reflection model is not a rendering method. This is because the radiosity method does not take any cameras or vantage points into account. The radiosity method is a rendering preprocess, and as such, in order to be visualized, radiosity data must be processed by additional rendering and hidden surface removal techniques. There have been many cases where hardware acceleration combined with radiosity data has produced real time photorealistic shaded display; the most striking and photorealistic pictures to date have been created by combining radiosity and ray trace data(though sacrificing view independence). Because of the vast increases in computing power in the last ten years, it is now feasible to utilize the radiosity method in desktop three-dimensional computer graphics systems.

The field of computer graphics has always been in the forefront of computer technology. Each year, the leaps and bounds made through technical innovation are matched by newer applications requiring even more power. In computer graphics applications, there can never be too much memory, and there is no such thing as a processor that is too fast. The unique demands of computer graphics applications require special consideration. While the personal computers produced today are extremely fast and powerful, very few of them are designed to be graphics workstations. Thanks to the open architecture of the modern PC, you can determine how much power you really need and, more importantly, where you need it most. If you are building a graphics workstation or if you are considering enhancing the capabilities of your PC for graphics applications, there are many hardware and software issues that affect your system's capabilities. If you think about it, only you can build the computer that best meets your needs.

The design of a computer graphics workstation is

determined by a set of decisions that take into account how the system will be used. The plethora of options offered by the large personal computer market allows the designer to tailor the system to suit the needs of the user. This way, more money can be spent on critical components and less money can be spent on components that are necessary but not primary. The "power user" mentality that calls for the maximum amount of performance and the latest technology you can afford has a great deal of foundation in computer graphics. There are not many applications more demanding of high performance. It is far better to spend money where it is needed, instead of just blindly buying the best. Only careful consideration of hardware and software issues—along with a clear understanding of what you really want from the system—can successfully determine the best course for building or upgrading a computer graphics workstation.

Most graphics workstations are designed to perform all of the tasks in the computer graphics production process: texture design with 2-D paintbox applications, modeling with 3-D CAD software, rendering with ray tracing or other shading algorithms, image processing, animation composition, and playback or output to a video tape recording. The hardware and software you choose dramatically affects each of these processes. If you are looking for a system to perform all the tasks of computer graphics production, ask yourself what tasks are most important to you. If you do not feel you can afford to buy the newest, high-end computer equipment, consider buying second-hand equipment or upgrading your present system. Computer systems have extremely long life spans (with the unique exception of disk drives and printers), and second-hand equipment is usually a very good value. With a little creativity, older technology can be effectively and inexpensively employed to outperform the latest technology. There are many simple and inexpensive changes you can make (adding memory, a new operating system, or a coprocessor) that have a significant impact on the capabilities of any system in graphics applications.

As an example, consider what you would do if you had to build a commercial computer animation system for a television station with Autodesk 3D Studio 4.0. The most important design goal is to be able to put out finished work quickly. Within a realistic budget, you could purchase a 90 MHz Pentium system, or you could purchase an entire network of 80386 systems with coprocessors. Autodesk 3D Studio incorporated a feature in Version 3.0 (and carried it over to Version 4.0) that allows the task rendering to be spread across multiple machines in a network. With this distributed rendering feature, the network of 80386s will be just as effective (if not more) as the Pentium, but at less cost. Another advantage of the network is that one of the 80386s can be used to model another segment of animation while the rest of the network works on the rendering. In a professional market like commercial animation where rapid results and flexibility are required, creative solutions like this require an under-the-hood understanding of the hardware and software issues that are at stake.

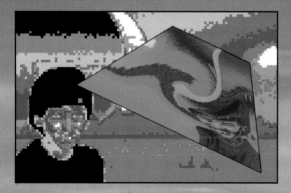

Many animation-oriented add-ons and enhancements have recently appeared for commercial image-processing software, such as Adobe Photoshop and Aldus Photostyler. Many video producers and editors already use these programs to create spectacular image enhancements and effects like those in the figures to the left.

The much ballyhooed merger between the computer and the TV is still a few years away. Gimicky attempts at combining these technologies, such as the Mac-TV, continue to meet with a lukewarm reception in the marketplace until technology advances beyond the TV-in-a-window approach to support true digital video editing for low-end PC prices. Nevertheless, we will all soon be invited to the preordained marriage of graphics and video—we just need to wait for the bride and groom to mature a bit first.

Calculating stereo image pairs for two-eye views is quite easy—you simply move one viewpoint slightly to the side of the other. The tough part is getting each of your eyes to see only one image of the stereo pair. One approach is to display the images side by side and use some type of lens system to guide the appropriate image to each eye. (Many people can also "free view" small stereo pairs by focusing their eyes past the plane of the screen or page where the images appear.) Here is a stereo pair generated in 3D Studio by moving the rendering "camera" a few inches.

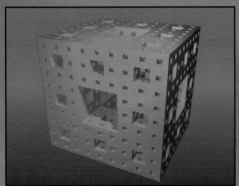 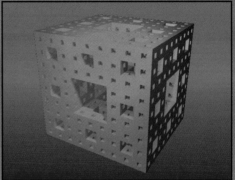

Now that realistic digital video is almost here, what can you do with it? Lots. Photorealistic 3-D absolutely begs to be animated so that hidden surfaces can come into view, realistic objects and characters can come to life, and computer-generated landscapes can be explored. Add the capability to bring in cinematographic footage from a videocam and special effects from Hollywood, and MTV will start appearing in your home videos.

Welcome to the world of advanced image processing, where we rip off the shackles imposed by poor photographs and underachieving video adapters. With image processing, you can rescue that pile of reject photographs buried away in your closet. Great shots they were, if only the flash had worked—and great shots they may still prove to be. Cheap video adapters snub their noses at the full color rainbow, preferring the spectrum of a set of crayons. In Chapter 5 you learn how to trick your computer into displaying photographs with no apparent loss of color.

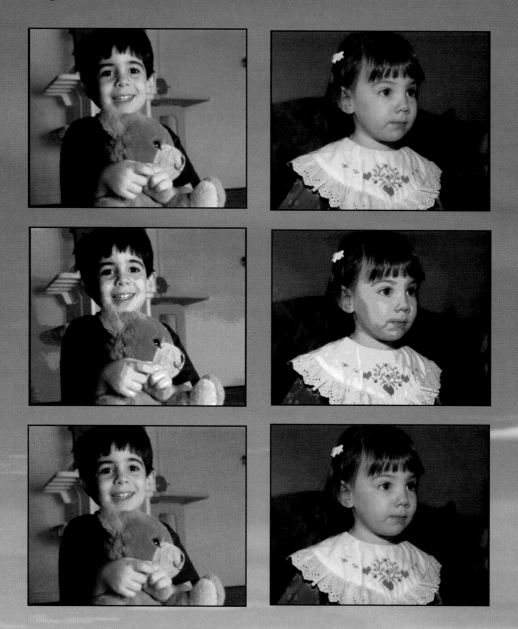

The first truly interactive and economical 3-D graphics, image processing, digital video, and real-time visualization products are now hitting the streets. And the latest generation of accelerated local-bus video cards and high capacity, high-speed storage devices are ready to make these applications sing. Just as the printed page is no longer "read-only" for millions of DTP-equipped publishers, the world of graphics and video is about to become accessible to everyone with a personal computer. It's an exciting time to be involved with PC graphics.

The time has come to prove the existence of extraterrestrial life to all of humanity once and for all. The argument for this proof is a single photographic image (which, in Chapter 6, you create) with the eager news media willingly serving as the agent of dissemination. In these pages we create a "photograph" of a UFO. It is your duty to submit this final image to various news agencies (grocery tabloids get the best results) with some cockamamie story about how it was spontaneously ejected from the color copier at work along with voices claiming that the invasion is imminent. With any luck, this photograph will have the longevity and impact of Nessie, the Loch Ness Monster, and you will be able to claim full responsibility. Digital Composition is the name of the game, and Chapter 6 shows you how to compose images using the techniques of masking, adding, subtracting, multiplying, and logically mixing images.

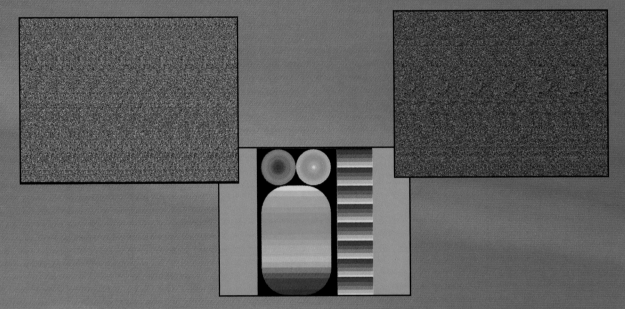

Like holograms, Single Image Random Dot Stereograms are illusions. Both give a strong impression of three dimensions using only two-dimensional media. The major functional difference is that holograms can disclose or obscure different parts of an image; move your head from left to right on the hologram of a cup, and the handle might appear and disappear, as if the cup was actually being turned. This doesn't work for SIRDS. By the way, they're called Single Image because that's what they are—they're not two slightly differing images welded together, like those old stereoscopic images that you have to view through red and green lenses.

"Stereograms" is possibly not the best way to describe SIRDS, but anything else would be clumsy—like "muddy tire-tracks on a piece of paper," even though that's what they appear to be. One major difference worth noting is that holograms take sophisticated equipment to produce. A stereogram can be made on the back of an old envelope.

Stereograms are the technological equivalent of the Emperor's New Clothes—everyone else can see them except you! There's no need to get paranoid—it's not a conspiracy. Provided you've got stereoscopic vision and the ability to refocus your eyes, you can see them.

A frequent first-reaction of people seeing depth in a SIRDS ("stereogram" from now on) is utter amazement. The first encounter is normally with those glossy, plastic-coated, high-color posters of dinosaurs or the Statue of Liberty, sold in markets and gift shops. I've seen people running their fingers over the surface of them, trying to figure out how it's done, trying to feel for tiny indentations as if two separate images have been pressed together in a way that presents one image to the right eye and the other image to the left. Not so; it's an intelligent reaction, but ultimately doomed to failure. The truth is even more obscure.

The second reaction is often bewilderment, when people find that you can take a black-and-white photocopy of a stereogram and the effect still works, even when translated from color to black and white. You can enlarge or reduce the image too, without losing the sensation or any amount of definition. Amazing!

```
     if(q < 0)
       {
        q=q+XResolution/sections;
        if( ( (*(str+((q/8)*YResolution)+y) & table[(q%8)]) != 0)
          && bktype == 1 )
         {
     if(f == 1)
       {
        out_buf[x] = 15;
        }
     else
       {
        out_buf[x] = 255;
        }
        }
     }
   else
    switch (bktype)
      {
      case 1:
       {
        out_buf[x] = 0;
        break;
        }
      case 16:
       {
        out_buf[x] = random(bktype-1)*16;
        break;
        }
      case 256:
       {
        out_buf[x] = random(bktype-1);
        break;
        }
      }
     }
     else
      {
       out_buf[x] = out_buf[q];
       }
     }
   vsa_raster_line(0,XResolution-1,y,out_buf);
   }

//*************************************************************//
//** Once converted, pause for a keystroke, save, and quit   **//
//*************************************************************//
   free(str);
   ch = getch();
   i = tf_save_file(0,0,XResolution-1,YResolution-1,output_file);
   tf_close_file();
   vsa_set_svga_mode(0x03);
   if(i != 0)
    {
     printf("Error creating %s\n",output_file);
    }

  }
```

Ray-Traced Animation

by Rob McGregor

Fancy commercial rendering programs cost plenty, but you can get even better realism from the ray tracer and utilities covered in this chapter. You can even use ray tracing and texture mapping to produce your own movies.

Animation Basics

Animation is an illusion, a trick of the eye and mind. In its basic form, it is the movement of objects in a scene along some designated path. Traditional animation uses many separate images, called cells or frames, each individually hand drawn and painted. Each image differs slightly from the one before it, and it is captured on a frame of film or video. The high-speed playback of the related static images creates the illusion of movement. How believable this movement appears depends on the flow of transition between frames and the number of frames per second received by the eye. If the frames move quickly enough for one frame to still be fading from the retina as the next is being received, the brain perceives the flow of images as motion. This phenomenon of overlapping visual images is called the *Persistence of Vision*. The standard for commercial animation is a smooth 24 frames/sec.

Ray-Traced Animation on the PC

Although ray-traced animation is similar to its traditional counterpart, a knowledge of one or more programming languages is especially helpful, as is a good grasp of fundamental mathematics. The animation process begins with a text editor and/or a 3-D modeler to create a ray traceable scene file. The scene file gets parsed and ray traced, and the many separate bitmapped images needed for the animation are generated. A number of readily available ray tracing packages, such as Vivid, POV-Ray, and Polyray, can create such images. Finally, a finished "movie" springs to life, assembled from the pre-rendered frames.

A summary of the entire process is as follows:

- Plan the details of the animation
- Create the scene files
- Render the images described by the scene files
- Assemble the images into an Autodesk Flic (.FLI/.FLC/.FLX/.FLH/.FLT) animation file
- View the compiled Flic file

Several tools are useful for the creation and viewing of ray-traced animations on the PC. In the following sections, you take a quick look at some high-quality, inexpensive programs that are readily available.

POVCAD

If you really know your stuff, you can create all your scene files solely with a text editor, but even seasoned ray tracing veterans use 3-D modelers to help them produce complex scene files quickly. POVCAD is a feature-rich 3-D modeler and ray tracing scene file program written by Alfonso Hermida and Rob McGregor (yes, that's me). POVCAD can generate intricate objects, scene files, and animation paths with ease. POVCAD also includes a ray tracing specific text editor for creating and editing scene files and textures, and was used to generate and edit many of the code listings in this chapter. Included on the companion CD (with Windows Help and a tutorial) is the newest version, POVCAD 4.0 for Windows.

POLYRAY

The most obvious tool needed for creating ray-traced animations is, of course, ray tracing software. Many excellent shareware and freeware ray-tracers are available, but in this chapter you concentrate on Polyray. Polyray, written by Alexander Enzmann, has some great animation features and programmatic math support built right into the program. Included on the companion CD is a Windows Help file that fully details the usage of Polyray.

Dave's TGA Animator (DTA)

After you create the images, you need something to compile the animations. David K. Mason's DTA is ideal for creating high-quality animations in Autodesk's Flic format. DTA is also useful for many other tasks including image file-format conversions, special effects, color separation, transparency, and image compositing. DTA is available in the Graphics Developers Forum (Go GRAPHDEV), Library 13, Animation Sources (DTA.ZIP) on CompuServe Information Service. Included on the companion CD is a Windows Help file that fully details the usage of DTA.

Dave's Flic Viewer (DFV)

For viewing the Flic in DOS, a prime choice is a program called DFV, also written by David K. Mason. DFV can display Flics of all varieties and resolutions.

Dave's Self-Viewing Flic Builder (BUILDSV)

BUILDSV (yet *another* fine program by David K. Mason) converts a Flic animation file into self-contained executable program by appending a copy of the Flic to a special version of the DFV program. It's great for distributing your animations as a self-viewing stand-alone package.

Windows Media Player

Microsoft Windows ships with a handy little applet called the Media Player, capable of playing your Flics under Windows. The only thing you need is the Autodesk Animation Player driver for Windows. After you install and configure the driver in the Windows control panel, your animations are just a few mouse-clicks away. Unfortunately, the Media Player doesn't loop animation sequences very well, so as a sequence wraps around to the beginning, it gets jerky. BUILDSV is highly recommended because it loops flawlessly.

Planning Your Animation

The first thing to do is to plan your animation carefully from start to finish. Each frame will occupy a (sometimes sizable) chunk of your valuable hard disk space. The size of an image file depends on the format used. An uncompressed 24-bit Targa image uses 8 bits (1 byte) for each R, G, and B color component of the image. At 320×240 pixels, the image would take up 3×320×240 (230,400) bytes. Polyray stores an additional 52 bytes of information in the file header for a total file size of 230,452 bytes. Multiply that number by one hundred frames and it really starts to add up—to 23,045,200 bytes. At 640×480, a frame could take up to 921,618 bytes. One hundred frames at this resolution would take a staggering 92,161,800 bytes! So make sure you have plenty of room to spare before you begin rendering.

> **NOTE**
>
> Polyray can generate image files in both compressed and uncompressed Targa formats. Setting the `pixel_encoding` flag to `rle` (compressed) in the POLYRAY.INI initialization file will save you a lot of hard disk space (see the Polyray help file on the companion CD for more on possible POLYRAY.INI settings).

Next consider the subject of the animation and the action you want to achieve. Thorough planning of the scene and other details will eliminate many headaches. Rendering simplified test frames at a low resolution, such as 100×75, is a quick way to make sure the flow of action works correctly. You can make adjustments if things aren't quite right, and you can render and compile the low-res Flics until everything's just the way you want it. Rendering the scene with the Polyray wireframe feature is another option for quickly checking the flow and layout. Be aware, however, that wireframe mode doesn't write output files.

Designing the Scene

Designing the scene is one of the most difficult tasks ahead of you. You must decide what the main objects or "actors" will be and then set the stage for the performance. You must also take into consideration the complexity of the scene and the time it will take for each frame to render on your machine. A complicated scene that uses math-intensive textures with many refractions and reflections (such as glass) could tie up your PC for days or even weeks. Try to keep the scene simple. Creative use of lighting, textures, and movement can set the mood of a piece. Complicated doesn't necessarily mean better.

Working out scenes on graph paper or with a 3-D modeler such as POVCAD helps you visualize the relationships between scene elements and gives you the coordinate data you need to position objects. Once you've decided on the elements to include, you must determine the action. What gets animated, and how is it done?

What Do You Animate?

All elements of a ray tracing scene are created and controlled with numbers. The interesting thing about numbers is that you can manipulate them in highly predictable ways. When you apply mathematical formulas to any element of the scene, you can achieve a desired effect. You can animate static scenes in many ways. Various different action elements can occur, in succession or simultaneously, in any combination. In the following sections, you look at some of the most common types of action operations. Later, you put these elements together into a scene file to get some hands-on experience and see how it all works.

Changing Viewpoint (Camera) Settings

You can move the camera anywhere, at any speed or orientation. The simplest effect of all is simply to zoom the camera in or out, or pan the camera across the scene. Another method is the "fly-by," or "walk-through," where the camera flies through the scene along a defined path. You can create dramatic camera effects by varying locational and directional coordinates, focal blur, and other viewpoint characteristics.

Position and Scale of Objects

You can change the size, shape, and position of objects by changing scaling, rotation, and translation settings. These animation events are the most common. Light sources can also change color, position, and intensity.

Texture Characteristics

Textures on objects can also change size, shape, and position. You can manipulate hue, saturation, reflection, transparency, backgrounds, atmospheric haze, and more. When you change texture characteristics, you can create striking effects such as stormy skies, rippling water, shifting features, and much more.

Generating the Image Frames

An array structure internal to Polyray stores the frames of the animation. Special keywords reserved by Polyray act as variables defining the range of the animation. The keyword that refers to any given frame is, appropriately, a variable called `frame`. The keywords `start_frame`, `end_frame`, and `total_frames` determine the range of the animation. The keyword `start_frame` defines the number of the first frame, and `end_frame` defines the number of the last frame. The `total_frames` statement is optional.

The keyword `outfile` determines the prefix for the output images. The `outfile` filename must have only five or fewer characters and no extension. Polyray adds three digits to index the frame numbers. For example, a three-frame animation with the `outfile` defined as ANIM would yield the filenames ANIM000.TGA, ANIM001.TGA, and ANIM002.TGA. The outfile declaration is optional, and the default name is OUT. If the name you choose for `outfile` is longer than five characters, DOS truncates the three-digit frame indices. This can result in overwritten frame files (and flaring tempers).

Polyray reads an animation scene file once for each frame, and the value of the variable `frame` increments by one with each iteration. Suppose you want 30 frames in an animation; you define the range of the animation as follows:

```
start_frame  0
end_frame    29
total_frames 30  // optional
outfile "anim"   // optional
```

From this code, Polyray knows to render the 30 frames, indexed from 000 to 029, and then terminate execution. Conditional processing (discussed later in this chapter) enables you to make decisions about and manipulate lighting, object, and viewpoint settings at any point in the animation. Extensive math support enables you to create formulas to perform a myriad of specialized functions. This type of built-in support for rendering multiple frames without using complex DOS batch files or separate scene files for each frame makes Polyray really shine in ray tracing animation.

Variable and Constant Definitions

Variables and constants are "tokens" that give meaningful names to some numeric value. Using tokens makes source files easier to type, read, and maintain. You declare variables by using the `define` keyword:

```
define some_token  some_value
```

You declare constants by adding the `static` keyword to the `define` statement:

```
static define some_token some_value
```

The values in `some_value` can be any valid expression or numeric value.

Object Motion Using Transformations

The main device used for object animation is transformation. Transformations move objects around in a 3-D environment. Using translation, rotation, and scaling, you can make objects follow specified paths or perform mind-bending tricks. These transformations must be broken into small intervals over many frames to create smooth movement. You see how to do exactly that later in this chapter.

The orientation of objects, including the virtual camera and lights, is traditionally described by the terms *roll, pitch,* and *yaw.* These terms specify the respective individual angles of rotation around the x-, y-, and z-axes. In the context of this chapter, these terms aren't used, but you should be aware of them because they are used extensively in some texts.

Translating an Object

Moving an object from one place to another is called *translation.* To create a cylinder using the Polyray format, use the following:

```
// First we define the cylinder at the origin
object {
  cylinder <0, -0.75, 0>, <0, 0.75, 0>, 0.5
  shiny_red
}
```

Now translate the cylinder 3.5 units along the x-axis (see Figure 17.1).

```
object {
  cylinder <0, -0.75, 0>, <0, 0.75, 0>, 0.5
  shiny_red
  translate <3.5, 0, 0>
}
```

FIGURE 17.1.

Translation of a cylinder along the x-axis.

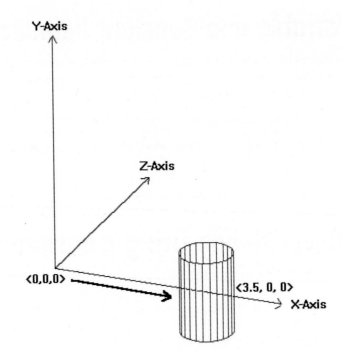

You could easily animate this translation over any number of frames through the use of declared tokens containing variable location values (as you learn in Listing 17.2).

Rotating an Object

The most important rule to remember when using rotations is that objects always rotate around a pivot point at the origin <0, 0, 0>. To rotate a cylinder, for example, along the z-axis with its center of rotation remaining stationary, the cylinder must be located at the origin. If it is located anywhere else and rotated, the entire object revolves around the pivot at the origin (see Figure 17.2) instead of pivoting on the cylinder's center of rotation (see Figure 17.4).

```
// Rotating 90 degrees on the z-axis,
// center of rotation at <5, 0, 0>
object {
  cylinder <5, 5.75, 0>, <5, 4.25, 0>, 0.5
  shiny_red
  rotate <0, 0, 90>
}
```

The work-around for this problem is to first translate the object to the origin (see Figure 17.3a), *then* rotate it (see Figure 17.3b), and finally move it back to its original position (see Figure 17.3c).

FIGURE 17.2.

Rotating an object 90 degrees. This virtual animation shows the result of rotating a cylinder located at <5, 5, 0> around the origin <0, 0, 0>.

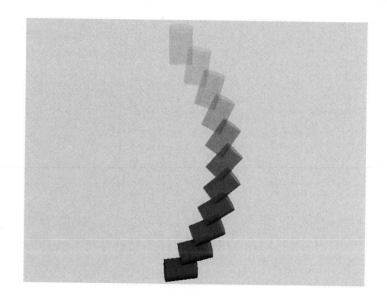

FIGURE 17.3.

(a) Translating a cylinder to the origin, (b) rotating 90 degrees, and (c) translating back to the original position.

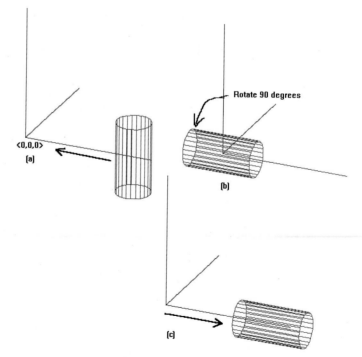

In Polyray format, your code would look like the following:

```
// (a) Create a cylinder at <3.5, 0, 0> and
// translate it to the origin for rotation
object {
  cylinder <3.5, -0.75, 0>, <3.5, 0.75, 0>, 0.5
  shiny_red
  translate <0, 0, 0>

// (b) Rotate 90 degrees on the z-axis
  rotate <0, 0, 90>

// (c) Translate the cylinder back to the
// starting location, rotated
  translate <3.5, 0, 0>
}
```

FIGURE 17.4.

This virtual animation shows the result of the transformations used in Figure 17.3.

Scaling an Object

Scaling an object on any of its three axes can change its shape and size. Creative use of scaling can be a potent visual effect. For example, a sphere could flatten out into a disc, or a plane could expand into a cube. Take a look at three cylinders, identical except for the scaling (see Figure 17.5).

Listing 17.1. Three identical cylinders at different scale (3CYLINDR.PI).

```
// Scene File: 3CYLINDR.PI
// Author: Rob McGregor

// Three identical cylinders at different scale
```

```
include "..\colors.inc"
include "..\texture.inc"

// SET UP THE CAMERA
viewpoint {
  from       <0, 0, -4>
  at         <0, 0, 0>
  up         <0, 1, 0>
  angle      45
  resolution 320, 200
  aspect     4/3
}

background white

// Lights
light <-5, 0, -10>
light <5, 0, -10>

// The cylinder at 2 units high.
object {
  cylinder <0, -0.5, 0>, <0, 0.5, 0>, 0.25
  scale <1, 2, 1>
  translate <-1.2, 0, 0>
  shiny_red
}

// The cylinder becomes half its original height.
object {
  cylinder <0, -0.5, 0>, <0, 0.5, 0>, 0.25
  shiny_red
}

// The cylinder becomes a hockey puck.
object {
  cylinder <0, -0.5, 0>, <0, 0.5, 0>, 0.25
  scale <1, 0.25, 1>
  translate <1.2, 0, 0>
  shiny_red
}
```

A change of scale taking place over many frames can give the animated illusion of the cylinder getting shorter over time. By defining a simple formula, you can let Polyray do the work of figuring out all the scaling. Listing 17.2 is an example scene file that shows how the work is done.

NOTE

All example scene file source listings in this chapter are on the companion CD as ASCII text (in case you want to experiment with them and render your own versions), rendered .FLI files and self-executing Flics.

The Autodesk .FLI format's limit is a resolution of 320×200. Animations rendered at higher resolutions become .FLC files (which require a faster machine to run them properly). If you have the hardware needed to run them, try rendering larger versions of the example Flics for greater detail.

FIGURE 17.5.

Scaling a cylinder on the y-axis (3CYLINDR.PI).

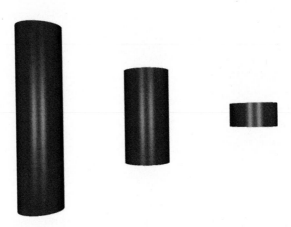

First, you include the standard Polyray color and texture files (COLORS.INC and TEXTURE.INC). Next, you define the lights, background, and camera. Then you set the animation range to 50 frames with the outfile name `"scale"`:

```
start_frame  0
end_frame    49
total_frames 50
outfile      "scale"
```

And you name a defined constant that sets the initial scaling for the y-axis:

```
static define height 2.0
```

The key to the whole animation sequence is the expression:

```
define change (height / total_frames) * frame
```

This expression causes the cylinder to continue changing scale with each frame. For any number of frames specified, the formula generates the proper scaling for the entire range of the animation.

Listing 17.2. Varied scaling on a cylinder through the use of a simple expression (SCALCYL.PI).

```
// Polyray scene file:  SCALCYL.PI
// Author:  Rob McGregor

// A cylinder changes scale on the y-axis

include "..\colors.inc"
include "..\texture.inc"

// Lights and background color
light <-5, 2, -15>
light <5, 2, -15>
background Grey

// Set up the camera
viewpoint {
   from        <0, 0, -3>
   at          <0, 0, 0>
   up          <0, 1, 0>
   angle       45
   resolution 320, 200
   aspect      1.6
}

// Define the range of animation
start_frame  0
end_frame    49
total_frames 50
outfile      "scale"

// Calculate the changing scale
static define height 2.0
define change (height/total_frames) * frame

// Create the cylinder
object {
   cylinder <0, -0.5, 0>, <0, 0.5, 0>, 0.25
   scale <1, height - change, 1>
   shiny_red
}
```

Camera Motion

The camera angles and motion you choose have a direct impact on everything in the scene. With creative use of the camera, you can follow objects as they move through a scene, pan across the scene as objects move independently, or use any other combination of movements you can dream up.

The methods used for affecting the camera settings in Polyray all involve changing the viewpoint definition. You can change members of the viewpoint data structure to specify what the camera sees. You can also change the camera's "tilt," reposition the camera in 3-D space, zoom the relative viewing angle, affect the depth of field to produce focal blur, and more. Now take a look at some basic camera manipulations.

Zooming the Camera

Changing the viewing angle or actually moving the camera in 3-D space achieves the effect of zooming. The first method uses a changing value for the `angle` keyword, which is equivalent to changing the focal length of a real-world zoom lens. The angle, measured in degrees, determines the field of view (see Figure 17.6). The maximum viewing angle is 180 degrees. The resulting image always displays at the `resolution` defined in the viewpoint declaration, although smaller angles reduce the visible area of the scene. The resolution determines the size of the output image (in pixels). The default angle value is 45 degrees. Increasing the angle zooms out; decreasing it zooms in.

FIGURE 17.6.

Zooming the camera by changing the viewing angle of the "lens."

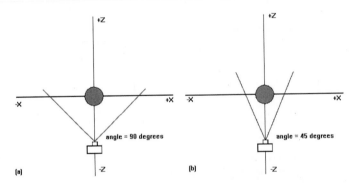

The second method changes the location of the camera over time by changing the values of the x, y, and z coordinates. You declare these coordinates in the `from` member of the viewpoint declaration. Changing the values from

```
from <0, 0, -5>  // 5 units back
```

to

```
from <0, 0, -1> // 1 unit back
```

causes the camera to move 4 units closer to the origin (see Figure 17.7), effectively zooming in.

If the perceived lighting and shadows in a scene are adversely affected by the new camera position, changing the viewing angle is the preferred zoom method. This method still allows a close-up view and retains any desired special lighting or shadow effects because the geometry of the scene elements remains constant. For example, if the reflection on water is just right at a certain camera position but not closer in, adjusting the angle would zoom the camera without changing the water reflections.

FIGURE 17.7.

Zooming the camera by changing its location.

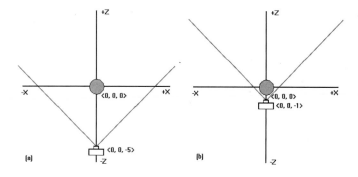

Panning the Camera

Changing the coordinates of the at keyword within the viewpoint declaration easily determines where the camera is "looking," simulating panning. The syntax is at <x, y, z>, for example:

```
at <0, 0, 0> // the camera is looking at the origin
```

Slowly changing the at declaration from at <-5, 0, 0> to at <5, 0, 0> over a series of frames would cause the camera to pan horizontally across the scene.

Animated Light Sources

A light source can be animated like any other object. Using different types of lights, you can get varying effects with just a little effort. For example, a spotlight can move across a scene, and the light beam can also change angle and falloff radii. View the self-executing Flic ROOMFLY.EXE on the companion CD to get an idea of what animated spotlights can do for a scene.

The creative use of light is as important as the camera methods described in the preceding sections. Use of interpolation routines (discussed later in this chapter) on lighting can add dramatic impact to an animation sequence.

Putting It All Together

Up to now, you haven't animated anything very interesting, even though you've learned several ways to manipulate scene elements. Here's where the fun begins. It's time to get some hands-on experience and turn what you've learned into action. The two code listings that follow are complete animation scene files. The files were kept simple and demonstrate many of the concepts presented so far.

Cylinder Rotation and Translation (ROTRANS.PI)

For this example, you declare some frames and expand an example from earlier in the chapter into a complete scene file. Listing 17.3 uses the changing value of frame to move an object, in this case the cylinder CYL (see Figure 17.8). Note the use of defined expressions for changing the cylinder's position.

First, you include the standard Polyray color and texture files. Next, you set the animation range to 28 frames with the outfile name "cyl".

```
start_frame   0
end_frame       27
total_frames 28
outfile "cyl"
```

Now you define the light coordinates and background color, along with the cylinder CYL. The next two lines are the most important because they describe the translation distance and rotation angle as functions of the current frame.

The translation distance I wanted was 3.5 units on the x-axis from start to finish. The expression

```
define xPos 3.5 / total_frames * frame
```

sets the correct translation distance for any given number of frames. The expression

```
define zAng 90 / end_frame * frame
```

calculates the z-axis rotation angle based on a desired 90-degree rotation from start to finish. The determining factor is the frame index—the variable that represents time.

The final step is the creation of the cylinder using the translation and rotation tokens xPos and zAng as object transformation parameters. Notice the translation of the cylinder to the origin before the rotation to allow the cylinder to pivot on its own axis of rotation.

```
object {
  CYL
  translate <0, 0, 0>
  rotate <0, 0, zAng>
  translate <xPos, 0, 0>
}
```

Listing 17.3. A simple animation scene file using rotation and translation (ROTRANS.PI).

```
// Polyray scene file:  ROTRANS.PI
// Author:  Rob McGregor
// A cylinder moves over a checkered floor

include "..\colors.inc"
include "..\texture.inc"

// Define the range of the animation
start_frame  0
end_frame    27
total_frames 28
outfile "cyl"

// Define the lights and background color
light <-2, 4, -5>
light <2, 4, -5>
background midnight_blue

// Define the cylinder "CYL" located at the origin
define CYL
object {
  cylinder <0, -0.75, 0>, <0, 0.75, 0>, 0.5
  reflective_white
}

define xPos 3.5 / total_frames * frame // the translation distance
define zAng 90 / end_frame * frame     // the rotation angle

// Set Up The Camera
viewpoint {
  from      <2.5, 3, -5 >
  at        <1.75, 0, 0 >
  up        <0, 1, 0 >
  angle     45
  resolution 320, 200
  aspect    4/3
}

// Define a checkered floor plane
object {
  // normal in Y direction
  polygon 4, <-1 , 0, 1>, <-1, 0, -1>, <1, 0, -1>, <1, 0, 1>
  scale <100, 100, 100>
  translate <0, -2, 0>
  texture {
    checker sapphire_agate, white_marble
    scale <01, 1, 01>
  }
}

// Now we translate CYL 3.5 units along the x-axis
// and rotate it 90 degrees on the z-axis.
// This takes place over 28 frames...
object {
  CYL
```

continues

Listing 17.3. continued

```
    translate <0, 0, 0>     // CYL moves to origin for rotation
    rotate <0, 0, zAng>     // CYL rotates zAng each frame
    translate <xPos, 0, 0>  // CYL moves to xPos each frame
}
```

FIGURE 17.8.

ROTRANS.PI. (a)The cylinder at the starting point. (b)The cylinder half-way through the translation/rotation. (c)The final position of the cylinder, translated and rotated.

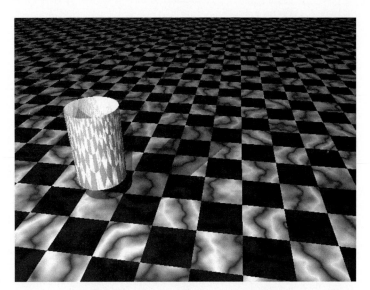

a

b

c

A Revolving Camera (REVOLVE.PI)

Imagine a desolate alien world with four suns. In the midst of the blistering landscape stand two mysterious stone pillars. Listing 17.4 describes this setting. The action consists completely of the camera revolving 360 degrees around the static pillar site (see Figure 17.9).

Once again you include the standard Polyray color and texture files, along with STONES.INC (also included with Polyray). Next, you set the animation range to 60 frames with the outfile name "rev".

```
start_frame   0
end_frame    59
total_frames 60
outfile "rev"
```

Because you want the camera to fly in a perfect circle around the origin, you must dig up a few formulas to calculate the points in the camera's path. You calculate the locations of points in the camera orbit from the following equations:

```
x = radiusX * cos(theta) + offsetX
z = radiusZ * sin(theta) + offsetZ
```

where theta = ((2 * pi) / number of segments) * frame. If radiusX and radiusY are equal values, the resulting path is circular. If the two radii aren't equal, the path becomes elliptical.

Start by setting the camera location at 10 units from the origin. Because it rotates around the origin, the offsets for x and z are zero. You can then calculate the changing x-axis and z-axis locations of the camera using the following:

```
define pi 3.14159265358
define ang ((2 * pi) / total_frames) * frame
define newX 10 * cos(ang)
define newZ 10 * sin(ang)
```

Then you can store the entire vector in loc1 using the resulting values of newX and newZ, with the y-axis set at –1.5:

```
define loc1 <newX, -1.5, newZ)>
```

The final step is the creation of some objects for the camera to orbit. Cylinders and spheres make up the two pillars. Applying a custom desert sand texture to a huge disc and scaling appropriately models the wasteland.

Listing 17.4. An animated camera revolving around two stone pillars in the desert (REVOLVE.PI).

```
// Scene File: REVOLVE.PI
// Author:  Rob McGregor

// The camera revolves around two stone pillars in the desert

include "..\colors.inc"
include "..\texture.inc"
include "..\stones.inc"

// Define the range of the animation
start_frame  0
end_frame    59
total_frames 60
outfile "rev"

// Give the location of points
define pi 3.14159265358
define ang ((2 * pi) / total_frames) * frame

// Define the position of the camera
define newX 10 * cos(ang)
define newZ 10 * sin(ang)
define loc1 <newX, -1.5, newZ>

// Lights
light <-5, 3, -10>
light <8, 4, -15>
light <2, 10, -5>
directional_light <2, 0, 15>

// Set up the camera
viewpoint {
    from       loc1
    at         <0, 0, 0>
    up         <0, 1, 0>
    angle      45
    resolution 320, 200
    aspect     1.6
```

```
}

// Set the sky color and add a little haze
background Grey
haze 0.98, 25, Grey

// Create some pillars
define pillar1
object {
  object {
    cylinder <0, -2.5, 0>, <0, 2.5, 0>, 0.5
    translate <-1.6, -1.2, 0>
  }
+
  object {
    sphere <-1.6, 1.5, 0>, 1
  }
  Tigers_Eye1 { scale <2, 2, 2> }
}
object { pillar1 }

define pillar2
object {
  object {
    cylinder <0, -2.5, 0>, <0, 2.5, 0>, 0.5
    translate <1.6, -1.2, 0>
  }
+
  object {
    sphere <1.6, 1.5, 0>, 1
  }
  white_marble { scale <0.25, 0.25, 0.25> }
}
object { pillar2 }

// Create a desert wasteland
define sand_dunes
texture {
  noise surface {
    color <0.85, 0.75, 0.69>
    normal 2
    frequency 100
    bump_scale 1.5
    ambient 0.37
    diffuse 0.75
  }
}
object {
  disc <0, 0, 0>, <0, 1, 0>, 10000
  sand_dunes { scale <92, 92, 92> }
  rotate <0, 10, 0>
  translate <0, -3.5, 0>
}
```

FIGURE 17.9.

Various angles as seen from a camera revolving 360 degrees around two stone pillars (REVOLVE.PI).

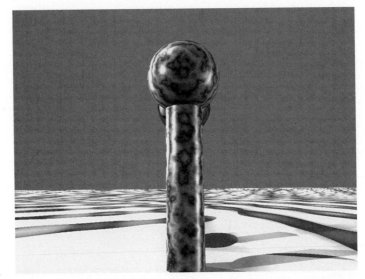

a

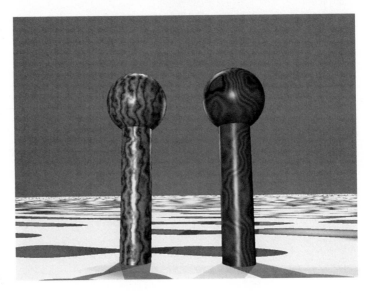

b

c

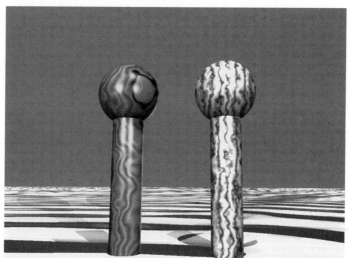

d

Compiling the Flic Animation

To view the animation after creating the scene files and rendering the static images, you must compile the frames into a Flic file. You compile the file using the external utility DTA. To build a basic SPACE.FLI, for example, after rendering the frames from SPACE.PI, you type the following:

```
dta space*.tga /ospace.fli
```

DTA uses the DOS wildcard (*) to find all .TGA files starting with SPACE. These files are then compiled into the Flic (assuming that DTA is present in your system's environment path). You can automate the process of Flic building by creating a generic DOS batch file that renders the animation. I used the following in a batch file to generate most of the Flic's on the companion CD:

```
dta %1*.tga /r1 /c10 /s7 /o%1.fli
```

where /r1 sets the resolution to 320×200 pixels, /c10 samples the color palette every 10 frames, /s7 sets the Flic speed to 7, and /o%1.fli sets the output filename. In case you're scratching your head over the %1, it's a replacement parameter used by DOS to substitute command-line arguments into the batch file.

Many options are available in DTA to control Flic resolution, speed, and so on, so be sure to check the DTA documentation or Windows Help file for detailed information.

Image Mapping

Image mapping (also called texture mapping) provides an excellent way to make scenes more believable by adding realism to objects. An existing bitmap image serves as the *imagemap* that can be "projected" onto an object surface. To declare an image map, use the following:

```
image("filename.tga")
```

To declare a token, you use the following:

```
define ImageName image("filename.tga")
```

Polyray supports four types of image map projection: planar, cylindrical, spherical, and environment. Here's the syntax for each:

```
planar_imagemap(image, coordinate [, repeat]),
cylindrical_imagemap(image, coordinate [, repeat]),
spherical_imagemap(image, coordinate)
environment_map(environment(image1, image2, image3,
                           image4, image5, image6))
```

Planar, cylindrical, and spherical projections wrap to the surface of an object. The projected image is "pasted" on as a permanent part of the object. Therefore, all transformations applied to the object also apply to the texture. Environment projection is object independent, using six images to wrap the top, bottom, left, right, front, and back surfaces. Its main use is for faking reflections on an object to help speed the rendering process.

 As an example of what texture mapping can do to add realism to an object, look at Figure 17.10, a frame from the animation VENUS.FLI included on the companion CD. This figure illustrates a model of the Venus de Milo (originally created by Mira Imaging, Inc., demonstrating HyperSpace, their 3-D digitizing/modeling system) that I downloaded from CompuServe and translated for use with Polyray. A photographic marble texture was cylindrically image-mapped onto the model and rendered in 72 positions to create the looping animation. Due to the large size, the source code and model data files for VENUS.FLI aren't listed here, but they're on the companion CD.

FIGURE 17.10.

A photographic marble texture image-mapped onto a Venus de Milo model (VENUS.PI, 3-D model created with the HyperSpace digitizer from Mira Imaging, Inc.).

Now assume that you have an image of a few planets called PLANETS.TGA. You could project it onto the background plane in an animation frame like this:

```
background planar_imagemap(image("planets.tga"), P)
```

You use this technique in Listing 17.6 to create a sci-fi scene.

Control Structures and Relational Processing

Polyray provides powerful animation control through the use of standard control structures and relational processing. Relational processing evaluates whether an expression is true or false. Control structures use the `if`, `else if`, and `else` keywords to make runtime decisions. Following is an example of a single-line `if` statement:

```
if(expression)
  statement
```

The `expression` can be any valid expression that equates to true or false. For example, on frame zero of an animation, the expression `if(frame == 0)` would evaluate to true. If `statement` consists of more than one line, curly braces mark the beginning and end of the statement block:

```
if(expression) {
  statement1
  statement2
...
  statementn
}
```

The `else if` and `else` relationships further determine what should occur:

```
if (expression1)      // if true then statement1 is executed
  statement1
else if (expression2) // if true then statement2 is executed
  statement2
else                  // otherwise statement3 is executed
  statement3
```

Relational expressions compare two or more expressions, variables, and so on, and evaluate to either true or false. Using the standard C programming syntax, Polyray uses the following forms for logical expressions:

```
!condition             // not
condition && condition // and
condition || condition // or
float < float          // less than
float <= float         // less than or equal
float > float          // greater than
float>= float          // greater than or equal
float == float         // equal
vector == vector       // equal
```

Relational expressions can define an expression based on other expressions by using the conditional operator, as follows:

```
(condition ? true_value : false_value)
```

The conditional operator is similar to an `if` statement. If the condition is true, then the expression `true_value` is defined; else `false_value` is defined. Relational and conditional processing and expressions, along with control structures, give you complete control over the animation.

Texture Variation

Manipulating a texture is as easy as changing any other element of a scene. Because all basic texture components such as color, reflection, bumpiness, ambience, and so on are based on numbers, they can be massaged with formulas that change these values as needed. As an example, change the texture of a sphere from matte red to reflective blue and back again over the course of an animation (see Figure 17.11). You use control structures and relational processing to direct the texture shift.

You start by including the standard color and texture files, setting the viewpoint, background color, and lights and defining the range of the animation. Quadratic interpolation routines determine the current red and blue components of the sphere color (don't worry if you don't understand how this process works right now; it's explained in detail in a later section):

```
if (frame <= end_frame / 2) {
  define ch (frame - start_frame) / ((end_frame / 2) - start_frame)
  define r  (1 - ch)^2 * 1 + (ch^2) * 0 + 2 * ch * (1 - ch) * 0.5
  define b  (1 - ch)^2 * 0 + (ch^2) * 1 + 2 * ch * (1 - ch) * 0.5
}
else {
  define ch (frame - (end_frame / 2)) / (end_frame - (end_frame / 2))
  define r  (1 - ch)^2 * 0 + (ch^2) * 1 + 2 * ch * (1 - ch) * 0.5
  define b  (1 - ch)^2 * 1 + (ch^2) * 0 + 2 * ch * (1 - ch) * 0.5
}
```

Then you set the green color component to zero and define the token `val`, which dynamically changes the specular and reflection values of the sphere texture:

```
define g   0
define val b / 1.5

// Create the animated texture
define sphere_tex
texture {
  surface {
    color      <r, g, b>
    ambient    0.25
    diffuse    0.7
    specular white, val
```

```
    microfacet Phong 5
    reflection white, val / 1.75
  }
}
```

Lastly, you define the sphere and create a checkered plane, giving the sphere something to reflect.

Listing 17.5. Animating the texture of a sphere by changing color and reflectivity values (TEXTURE.PI).

```
// Scene File: TEXTURE.PI
// Author: Rob McGregor

// A sphere changes from dull red to reflective blue and back again

include "colors.inc"

// Set up the camera
viewpoint {
  from       <3, 0, -10>
  at         <0, 0, 0>
  up         <0, 1, 0>
  angle      45
  resolution 320, 200
  aspect     1.6
}

background grey
haze 0.98, 20, grey

// Lights
light <-5, 5, -20>
light <5, 5, -20>

// Define the range of animation
start_frame  0
end_frame    199
outfile      "tex"

// Interpolate the proper texture shift
if (frame <= end_frame / 2) {
  define ch (frame - start_frame) / ((end_frame / 2) - start_frame)
  define r  (1 - ch)^2 * 1 + (ch^2) * 0 + 2 * ch * (1 - ch) * 0.5
  define b  (1 - ch)^2 * 0 + (ch^2) * 1 + 2 * ch * (1 - ch) * 0.5
}
else {
  define ch (frame - (end_frame / 2)) / (end_frame - (end_frame / 2))
  define r  (1 - ch)^2 * 0 + (ch^2) * 1 + 2 * ch * (1 - ch) * 0.5
  define b  (1 - ch)^2 * 1 + (ch^2) * 0 + 2 * ch * (1 - ch) * 0.5
}

define g    0
define val b / 1.5

// Create the animated texture
```

```
define sphere_tex
texture {
  surface {
    color        <r, g, b>
    ambient      0.25
    diffuse      0.7
    specular white, val
    microfacet Phong 5
    reflection white, val / 1.75
  }
}

// Define the sphere
object { sphere <0, 0, 0>, 2 sphere_tex }

// Give the sphere something to reflect
object {
  disc <0, 0, 0>, <0, 1, 0>, 10000
  texture {
    hexagon reflective_brown, reflective_tan, reflective_white
    scale <1.5, 1, 1.5>
  }
  rotate <0, 40, 0>
  translate <0, -2, 0>
}
```

FIGURE 17.11.

An animated texture on a sphere changes color and reflectivity (TEXTURE.PI).

a

b

c

Sci-Fi Flyby (SPACE.PI)

Now you can put together some of the animation elements you've looked at so far and render a sci-fi space scene. Listing 17.6 shows how I've set up the space scene using simple space station and alien spaceship designs and also image-mapped backgrounds (PLANETS.TGA and STARS.TGA). The main actor is a space station, created using one cylinder and 10 tori. The station rotates on the z-axis as the camera zooms in. Notice the use of declared constants and variables to specify movement parameters within each frame.

Using control structures and relational processing, you determine exactly when an alien starship will flash past, heading toward the planet surface. You use it again when the camera passes through the station. On the other side, the camera turns to look back at the station and out into the blackness of starry space (a second image map). At the same time, the station's hull texture increases ambience to give the illusion that it's lit from within. Sounds pretty dramatic, eh? See, I told you a scene could be simple, yet powerful!

A word of warning—it took a 90 MHz Pentium almost 10 hours to render these 300 frames at 320×200 with anti-aliasing of 2 (–a2). It also took 15M of hard disk space (RLE compressed files). The compiled FLC file is just over 2M. Ray-traced animation is expensive, in both time *and* disk space, but the end result is worth it. Besides, it's really challenging and a lot of fun!

SPACE.PI has some interesting stuff going on inside. Take a closer look at some of the major elements of the sequence. The range of the animation is 300 frames starting on `0` and ending on `299`. The generated frames have the name `"space"` with the frame index numbers appended.

```
start_frame  0
end_frame    299
total_frames 300
outfile "space"
```

These declaration statements set the range of object motion for the scene:

```
static define xShipStart 4
static define zShipStart -100
define xShipPos xShipStart + (05 * (frame + zShipStart))
define zShipPos zShipStart + (1.5 * (frame + zShipStart))
define zRot      9 * frame
define zPos      -200 + frame
```

The definitions for `xShipPos`, `zShipPos`, `zRot`, and `zPos` all use simple formulas that set the transformations for the ship and station as a function of the frame number.

Next, define custom textures for the various objects in the scene. After this step, you set up the camera, using the variable `zPos` within the `from` definition to set the z-axis coordinate. As `frame` increases, the camera moves in a positive direction along the z-axis (into the screen).

```
viewpoint {
  from            <5, 2, zPos >
  ...other view declarations here...
}
```

Near the end of the animation, the camera reaches the station and continues on, away from the origin. Because the viewpoint remains focused on <0, 0, 0>, the camera immediately pans 180 degrees, looking back at the dark side of the station. Using conditional processing, you can determine the appropriate background image to display. If the camera is still in –z space, you use the image of planets as a background image map. When the camera crosses into +z space, the scene switches to stars.

```
if (zPos <= 0)
  background planar_imagemap(image("planets.tga"), P)
else
  background planar_imagemap(image("stars.tga"), P)
```

Next is the assembly of a simple space station from several primitives. In the final stage of this assembly, conditional processing is used again. The test is the camera's location on the z-axis. If the camera is in –z space, the sun hits the station, so use light_hull as the texture. Otherwise, you're on the +z side—the dark side of the station, so use the dark_hull texture to simulate interior lighting.

```
// CSG space station object
if (zPos <= 0){    // this is the light side
  define station
  object {
    object { hull light_hull scale <10,10,10> }
    +
    object { ring_struct brass scale <10,10,10> }
  }
}
else {             // this is the dark side, ambience enhanced
  define station
  object {
    object { hull dark_hull scale <10,10,10> }
    +
    object { ring_struct ring_color scale <10,10,10> }
  }
}
```

Now the station rotates on the z-axis using the zRot token value, which adds a 9-degree rotation each frame.

```
object { station rotate <0, 0, zRot> }
```

Lastly, you bring in a spaceship, strategically placed on the camera's periphery, and move it across the camera's path and down to the planet below. The spaceship first appears in frame 100, as determined here:

```
if (zPos > -99)
  object {
    sphere <0, 0, 0>, 1
    scale <1, 1, 10>
```

```
    rotate <0, 10, 0>
    translate <xShipPos, 1.5, zShipPos>
    shipTex
  }
```

The combination of camera movement and the trajectory of the spaceship causes the apparent curvature of the ship's path (you learn how to use real curves in a section later in this chapter). It uses the values xShipPos and zShipPos to move on a *linear* path along the z-axis. Figure 17.12 shows various stages of the animation. To keep the scene code short, I used a simple ellipsoid for the ship and an image map for the exterior texture. You can create as complicated a ship as you like.

Listing 17.6. A rotating space station, moving camera, and alien spaceship with image mapping (SPACE.PI).

```
// Scene File: SPACE.PI
// Author: Rob McGregor

// Planets, space station, and alien ship

// Define the range of the animation
start_frame  0
end_frame    299
total_frames 300
outfile "space"

// Calculate the values of all transformations
static define xShipStart 4
static define zShipStart -100

define xShipPos xShipStart + (05 * (frame + zShipStart))
define zShipPos zShipStart + (1.35 * (frame + zShipStart))
define zRot       9 * frame
define zPos      -200 + frame

// Create some nice metallic textures
static define ring_color <0.70, 0.56, 0.37>
static define hull_color <0.55, 0.5, 0.45>

// The hull of the space station (light side)
static define light_hull
texture {
  surface {
    color hull_color
    specular hull_color, 0.85
    ambient 0.20
    diffuse 0.35
    microfacet Cook 12
    reflection 0.45
  }
}

// The hull of the space station (dark side)
static define dark_hull
```

continues

Listing 17.6. continued

```
texture {
  surface {
    color hull_color
    specular hull_color, 0.85
    ambient 0.75
    diffuse 0.35
    microfacet Cook 12
    reflection 0.45
  }
}

static define ring_color
texture {
  surface {
    color ring_color
    specular ring_color, 0.65
    ambient 0.1
    diffuse 0.45
    microfacet Cook 12
    reflection 0.45
  }
}

static define shipTex
texture {
  special surface {
    color spherical_imagemap(image ("shiptex.tga"), P)
    specular white, 0.65
    ambient 0.9
    microfacet Phong 7
    //reflection 0.45
  }
}

// Lights
light <-5, 2, -15>
light <5, 2, -15>

// Set up the camera
viewpoint {
  from            <5, 2, zPos >
  at              <0, 0, 0 >
  up              <0, 1, 0 >
  angle           45
  hither          1.0e-3
  resolution      320, 200
  aspect          1.6
  yon             1.0e5
  max_trace_depth 5
  aperture        0
}

// Map one of two cool space scenes to the background
if (zPos <= 0)
  // Toward the station, planets visible...
  background planar_imagemap(image("planets.tga"), P)
else
```

```
    // Away from the station, on the dark side...
    background planar_imagemap(image("stars.tga"), P)

// Build a simple space station
// Main Hull
static define hull
object {
  cylinder <0, -1, 0>, <0, 1, 0>, 0.25
}

// Create a ring structure from 11 tori.
static define ring
object { torus 0.5, 015, <0, 0, 0>, <0, 1, 0> }

static define rings
object{
  object { ring }
  +
  object { ring translate <0, 0.4, 0> } +
  object { ring translate <0, 0.8, 0> } +
  object { ring translate <0, -0.4, 0> } +
  object { ring translate <0, -0.8, 0> } +
  object { ring translate <0, 0.6, 0> } +
  object { ring translate <0, 0.2, 0> } +
  object { ring translate <0, -0.2, 0> } +
  object { ring translate <0, -0.6, 0> } +
  object { ring translate <0, 1, 0> } +
  object { ring translate <0, -1, 0> }
}

// CSG space station object
if (zPos <= 0){    // this is the light side
  define station
  object {
    object { hull light_hull scale <10,10,10> } +
    object { rings ring_color scale <10,10,10> }
  }
}
else {            // this is the dark side, ambience enhanced
  define station
  object {
    object { hull dark_hull scale <10,10,10> } +
    object { rings ring_color scale <10,10,10> }
  }
}

// Rotate the station
object { station rotate <0, 0, zRot> }

// Bring in another actor, a spaceship
if (zPos > -99)
  object {
    sphere <0, 0, 0>, 1
    scale <1, 1, 10>
    rotate <0, 10, 0>
    translate <xShipPos, 1.5, zShipPos>
    shipTex
  }
```

FIGURE 17.12.

An animation sequence demonstrating the use of conditional processing, camera and object translation, object rotation, and image-mapping techniques (SPACE.PI).

a

b

c

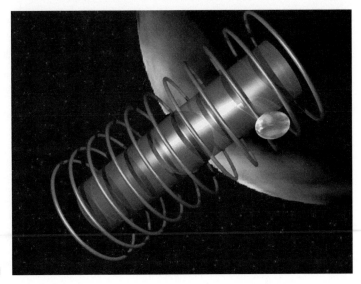

d

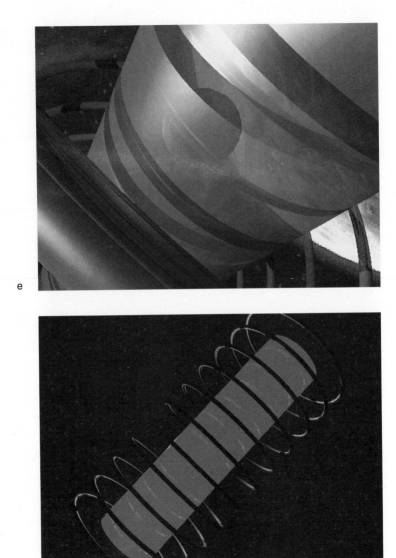

e

f

Arrays

Using arrays is a great way to represent data easily as a list. Using values stored in arrays, you can control animation conditions precisely. If you use the variable `frame` as the index for an array, you can easily access the elements of the array.

An array can store a series of point values used to generate different viewpoints or transformations at runtime. For example,

```
define origin <0, 0, 0>
define loc [<-1, 0, 0>, <1, 0, 0>, < 0, 1, 0>, < 0,-1, 0>]
```

sets up the array `loc` with four elements. Each array element is accessed with a subscript. The array values are

```
loc[0] = <-1, 0, 0>
loc[1] = <1, 0, 0>
loc[2] = < 0, 1, 0>
loc[3] = < 0,-1, 0>]
```

Over a four-frame animation, you might access the values by using the `frame` variable, like this:

```
start_frame 0
end_frame   3

// define some viewpoint
Viewpoint {...}

// define the array "loc" with 4 vectors
define loc[<-1, 0, 0>, <1, 0, 0>, <0, 1, 0>, <0, 1, 0>]

// Create some object
object {
  someObject
  // the frame variable used as a subscript
  translate loc[frame]
}
```

This example moves `someObject` to the coordinates stored in the array, based on the frame number.

Next, you look at some ways to let the PC figure out just where all the objects in your scenes should be at any given frame. All that's required are some interpolation formulas and a process called key framing.

Key Frames and Interpolation

The use of math in complex computer animation is extremely important. To make movement look natural, the animator must be able to control every facet of the scene precisely. Many schemes that allow the automation of smooth acceleration, deceleration, and path scripting have been developed. You too can use these techniques and let the PC do the work of calculating the math for you. The next few sections explain the use of various interpolation equations.

> **NOTE**
>
> Although Polyray handles the interpolation code in the following scene files single-handedly, porting the concepts to standard programming languages is a fairly easy task. Other renderers can then use the interpolation data.

The main task is deciding on the locations of the actors, camera, lights, and other scene elements at certain key points in time. These points are called *key frames*. After you've planned all the key frames, the computer can calculate smooth transitions from one frame to the next. This process is called *interpolation, in-betweening,* or just *tweening*. The key to tweening lies in the use of variable values as object attributes. These values are fed into interpolation routines that derive the tweened results.

You can use interpolation with 3-D space coordinates, RGB color variation (as in Listing 17.5), angles, velocity, or any other set of numeric data. By using a time reference parameter t, you can interpolate values over any given number of frames. Many interpolation schemes have been developed over the last decade. To illustrate the basic ideas, I'll focus on a few methods for calculating linear, non-linear, and continuous interpolation using standard algorithms.

Linear Interpolation

Assume you have an object in frame F1 located at a certain point P1 in 3-D space, and the desired location of the object in frame F2 is point P2. The values P1 and P2 are called *control points*. Translating the object an equal distance each frame from F1 to F2 would result in linear interpolation (see Figure 17.13). The parameter t changes value from t = 0 at P1 to t = 1 at P2. The value of t is controlled by the index of the current frame F (that starts at F1 and ends at F2). To make sure that when F = F1, t = 0, and when F = F2, t = 1, you use the following formula:

```
t = (F - F1) / (F2 - F1)
```

For example, to find t over the range of animation from frame 0 to frame 20, plug in the values to get the following:

```
t = (F - 0) / (20 - 0)
```

The frame index F then changes with each frame from 0 to 20. Remember that the values being tweened are called control points, and they can represent any aspect of the scene. They can be generically represented as N1 = desired value at frame F1, and N2 = desired value at frame F2.

FIGURE 17.13.

This graph shows the relationship of F, F1, F2, and t in linear interpolation.

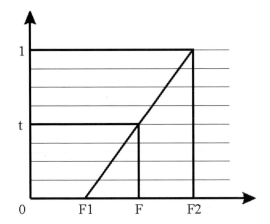

The general steps needed for linear interpolation are as follows:

1. Calculate the value of t from F, F1, and F2.
2. Calculate the current interpolation from t, N1, and N2.
3. Perform some action based on the results of the interpolation.

The basic form of the relationship is

```
N = (1 - t) * N1 + t * N2
```

where N is the interpolated value between some number N1 and another number N2. Translated to 3-D coordinates, this relationship would be as follows:

```
x = (1 - t) * x1 + t * x2
y = (1 - t) * y1 + t * y2
z = (1 - t) * z1 + t * z2
```

or for RGB color components:

```
r = (1 - t) * r1 + t * r2
g = (1 - t) * g1 + t * g2
b = (1 - t) * b1 + t * b2
```

You can interpolate any set of numeric values. The program POVCAD can create linear paths for you with just a few mouse clicks. By creating two points (the key frames) on the screen, POVCAD will interpolate any specified number of in-between frames for you. POVCAD creates a disk file containing the interpolated point vectors. This data can be used in any array of position vectors in an animation scene file.

Listing 17.7 demonstrates the use of the linear equation by translating a light source. The moving light creates a dramatic animation effect.

First, you include the standard Polyray color and texture files. Then you set the animation range to 50 frames with the outfile name `"light"` and define the camera and background.

The linear equation is applied to the variables frame, start_frame, and end_frame with the result stored in PosX.

```
define startX  20
define increment (frame - start_frame) / (end_frame - start_frame)
define PosX (1 - increment) * startX + increment * -startX
```

The token PosX translates the light to a new location at each frame.

```
light <PosX, 10, 7>
```

Listing 17.7. Using linear interpolation to translate a light source creates dramatic shadow effects (ANIMLITE.PI).

```
// Scene File: ANIMLITE.PI
// by Rob McGregor
//
// A moving light creates changing shadow effects

include "..\colors.inc"
include "..\texture.inc"
include "..\stones.inc"

// Define the range of the animation
start_frame 0
end_frame   49
outfile     "light"

// Set up the camera
viewpoint {
  from       <0, 1.5, -4>
  at         <0, 0.5, 0>
  up         <0, 1, 0>
  angle      45
  resolution 200,124//320, 200
  aspect     1.6
}

background sky_blue
haze 0.9, 25, sky_blue

// Define some tokens and a movement expression
define startX  20
define increment (frame - start_frame) / (end_frame - start_frame)
define PosX (1 - increment) * startX + increment * -startX

// Move the light
light <PosX, 10, 7>

// Create some objects to cast shadows
object { sphere <1, 0.5, 0>, 0.5 reflective_blue }

object {
  cone <0, -1, 0>, 0.5, <0, 0, 0>, 0
  translate <-1, 1, 0>
  Stone10
}
```

```
object {
  box <-1, -1, -1>, <1, 1, 1>
  scale <0.25, 0.25, 0.25>
  rotate <0, 45.0, 0>
  translate <0, 0.25, 0.5>
  reflective_gold
}

// Something to cast the shadows on
object {
  disc <0, 0, 0>, <0, 1, 0>, 10000
  Stone16 { scale <0.25, 1, 0.25> }
}
```

Figure 17.14 shows the results of using linear interpolation to move a light source across the scene, changing the shadows cast from three simple objects.

FIGURE 17.14.

A light source translated with linear interpolation changes the direction of shadows cast from three primitives (ANIMLITE.PI).

a

b

c

Non-Linear Interpolation

Although linear interpolation is easy and effective for many types of animation sequences, when used for translations, it's seldom realistic. Most things in the real world move along curved paths through curved space. Acceleration and deceleration, for example, are everyday events that aren't linear but follow defined laws of physics.

To interpolate non-linearly, you can use various parametric blending techniques, the most popular being *quadratic* and *cubic* blending.

Quadratic Blending

Quadratic blending expands the linear equation by squaring the sum of the terms $(1 - t)$ and t as follows:

```
N = (1 - t)^2 * N1 + (t^2) * N2
```

Notice that in the original linear equation the sum of $(1 - t) + t = 1$. To maintain this relationship in the quadratic equation, it must be modified with another term, $2t(1 - t)$ or $2 * t * (1 - t)$, as follows:

```
N = (1 - t)^2 * N1 + (t^2) * N2 + 2 * t * (1 - t)
```

In examining the increasingly twisted mathematics involved here, you find that when either $t = 0$ or $t = 1$, then $N = 0$. This result isn't good, because at the extremes of the interpolation, N has no useful value. To control the curve further, you can multiply in yet another term, Nc, that reflects the correct interpolated value, and you can let the value of N become less than N1 or greater than N2:

```
N = (1 - t)^2 * N1 + (t^2) * N2 + 2 * t * (1 - t) * Nc
```

Listing 17.8, QUADRATC.PI, uses this formula to move three spheres from point A to point B, each using different values for Nc. QUADRATC.PI starts out with the standard include files, viewpoint, background, lighting, and animation range declarations. Next, you define the Nc parameters for controlling the slope of the curve for each of the three spheres:

```
define s1_Nc -5 // Nc for sphere1 (red)
define s2_Nc 2.5 // Nc for sphere2 (yellow)
define s3_Nc 10 // Nc for sphere3 (blue)
```

Then you define the starting and ending locations (x- and y-axes) for each sphere. The x-axis locations at the start and finish of the sequence are the same for each sphere (that is, they begin and end stacked one atop another):

```
// Sphere1
define s1N1x  0 // x-axis starting point
define s1N1y -1 // y-axis starting point
define s1N2x  9 // x-axis ending point
define s1N2y -1 // y-axis ending point
...
define s3N2x  9 // x-axis ending point
define s3N2y  1 // y-axis ending point
```

Next, you calculate the parameter t is from the animation range using:

```
//   t = (F - F1) / (F2 - F1)
define t (frame - start_frame) / (end_frame - start_frame)
```

and the locations of the spheres from:

```
// N = (1 - t)^2 * N1 + (t^2) * N2 + 2 * t * (1 - t) * Nc
```

```
define s1_x (1 - t)^2 * s1N1x + (t^2) * s1N2x + 2 * t * (1 - t) * s1_Nc
define s1_y (1 - t)^2 * s1N1y + (t^2) * s1N2y + 2 * t * (1 - t) * s1_Nc
define s2_x (1 - t)^2 * s2N1x + (t^2) * s2N2x + 2 * t * (1 - t) * s2_Nc
define s2_y (1 - t)^2 * s2N1y + (t^2) * s2N2y + 2 * t * (1 - t) * s2_Nc
define s3_x (1 - t)^2 * s3N1x + (t^2) * s3N2x + 2 * t * (1 - t) * s3_Nc
define s3_y (1 - t)^2 * s3N1y + (t^2) * s3N2y + 2 * t * (1 - t) * s3_Nc
```

You store these values in a vector for each sphere (the z-axis remains constant at zero):

```
define s1_loc <s1_x, s1_y, 0>
define s2_loc <s2_x, s2_y, 0>
define s3_loc <s3_x, s3_y, 0>
```

Then you define the spheres with three different colors—red, yellow, and blue:

```
object { sphere s1_loc, 0.5 reflective_red }
object { sphere s2_loc, 0.5 reflective_yellow }
object { sphere s3_loc, 0.5 reflective_blue }
```

Lastly, you define a ground plane using a huge disc with a checkered texture.

Listing 17.8. Three spheres moving along paths interpolated with quadratic blending (QUADRATC.PI).

```
// Scene File: QUADRATC.PI
// Author: Rob McGregor

/****************************************************
  Three spheres follow different quadratic paths,
  starting and ending at the same points
****************************************************/

include "..\colors.inc"
include "..\texture.inc"

// SET UP THE CAMERA
viewpoint {
   from        <4.5, 0, -12>
   at          <4.5, 1, 0>
   up          <0, 1, 0>
   angle       45
   resolution  320, 200
   aspect      1.6
}

// Set the sky color and add a little haze
background Grey
haze 0.98, 25, Grey

// Lights
light <-5, 5, -20>
light <5, 5, -20>

// Define the range of the animation
start_frame  0
end_frame    49
outfile      "quad"
```

```
define s1_Nc  -5 // Nc for sphere1 (red)
define s2_Nc  2.5 // Nc for sphere2 (yellow)
define s3_Nc  10 // Nc for sphere3 (blue)

// Sphere1
define s1N1x  0 // x-axis starting point
define s1N1y  -1 // y-axis starting point
define s1N2x  9 // x-axis ending point
define s1N2y  -1 // y-axis ending point

// Sphere2
define s2N1x  0 // x-axis starting point
define s2N1y  0 // y-axis starting point
define s2N2x  9 // x-axis ending point
define s2N2y  0 // y-axis ending point

// Sphere3
define s3N1x  0 // x-axis starting point
define s3N1y  1 // y-axis starting point
define s3N2x  9 // x-axis ending point
define s3N2y  1 // y-axis ending point

// Calculate the value of t as:
//    t = (F - F1) / (F2 - F1)
define t (frame - start_frame) / (end_frame - start_frame)


// Now calculate the locations of the spheres using:
//    N = (1 - t)^2 * N1 + (t^2) * N2 + 2 * t * (1 - t) * Nc

define s1_x (1 - t)^2 * s1N1x + (t^2) * s1N2x + 2 * t * (1 - t) * s1_Nc
define s1_y (1 - t)^2 * s1N1y + (t^2) * s1N2y + 2 * t * (1 - t) * s1_Nc
define s2_x (1 - t)^2 * s2N1x + (t^2) * s2N2x + 2 * t * (1 - t) * s2_Nc
define s2_y (1 - t)^2 * s2N1y + (t^2) * s2N2y + 2 * t * (1 - t) * s2_Nc
define s3_x (1 - t)^2 * s3N1x + (t^2) * s3N2x + 2 * t * (1 - t) * s3_Nc
define s3_y (1 - t)^2 * s3N1y + (t^2) * s3N2y + 2 * t * (1 - t) * s3_Nc

// Set the positions of the spheres
define s1_loc <s1_x, s1_y, 0>
define s2_loc <s2_x, s2_y, 0>
define s3_loc <s3_x, s3_y, 0>

// Create 3 spheres
object { sphere s1_loc, 0.5 reflective_red }
object { sphere s2_loc, 0.5 reflective_yellow }
object { sphere s3_loc, 0.5 reflective_blue }

// The floor...
object {
  disc <0, 0, 0>, <0, 1, 0>, 10000
  texture {
    checker steely_blue,
    texture { shiny { color white }}
  }
  rotate <0, 25, 0>
  translate <0, -3.5, 0>
}
```

Figure 17.15 shows the results as a virtual animation composited into one frame, and Figure 17.16 shows some excerpts from the finished Flic.

FIGURE 17.15.

This virtual animation shows the results of quadratic interpolation as used to calculate different paths for three identical spheres.

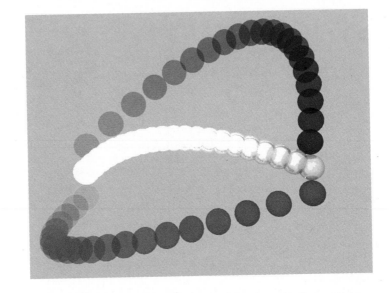

FIGURE 17.16.

Three spheres as they move along quadratic blend paths using varying values for Nc (QUADRATC.PI).

a

b

c

d

Note that a value Nc halfway between the values N1 and N2, as in Nc = (N1 / N2) / 2, defines a median (linear) path. Values for Nc above this median accelerates more quickly from P1 and decelerates more slowly toward P2. Values below the median accelerate slowly and decelerate quickly.

The upper range curves gracefully, but the nature of the quadratic function limits the lower range. To overcome this deficiency and add more flexibility and control over a curve, you can use a cubic function.

Cubic Blending

Cubing (1 - t) and t instead of squaring gives you the following:

`N = (1 - t)^3 * N1 + (t^3) * N2`

And like the quadratic, the t terms must add up to 1. You can get this result only if you add *two* more terms, $3t(1 - t)^2$ or 3 * t * ((1 - t)^2), and $3(t^2)(1 - t)$ or 3 * (t^2) * (1 - t), to the equation, giving you the following:

`N = (1 - t)^3 * N1 + (t^3) * N2 + 3 * t * ((1 - t)^2) + 3 * (t^2) * (1 - t)`

You can scale these terms, like the quadratic, to influence the slope of the curve. The cubic requires two slope control parameters, Nc and Nd, to achieve this result:

`N = (1 - t)^3 * N1 + (t^3) * N2 + 3 * t * ((1 - t)^2) * Nc + 3 * (t^2) * (1 - t) * Nd`

You can combine the values of Nc and Nd in many ways to control and shape the curve. Of course, you should experiment with many different values to get a feel for what they do.

See the scene file CUBIC.PI on the companion CD that substitutes the cubic equation into the scene file from Listing 17.8. This substitution is

```
define s1_Nd -2.5 // Nd for sphere1 (red)
define s2_Nd  1.5 // Nd for sphere2 (yellow)
define s3_Nd  7.0 // Nd for sphere3 (blue)

// Now calculate the locations of the spheres using:
//    N = (1 - t)^3 * N1 + (t^3) * N2 + 3 * t *
         ((1 - t)^2) * Nc + 3 * (t^2) * (1 - t) * Nd

define s1_x (1 - t)^3 * s1N1x + (t^3) * s1N2x + 3 * t *
           ((1 - t)^2) * s1_Nc + 3 * (t^2) * (1 - t) * s1_Nd
define s1_y (1 - t)^3 * s1N1y + (t^3) * s1N2y + 3 * t *
           ((1 - t)^2) * s1_Nc + 3 * (t^2) * (1 - t) * s1_Nd

define s2_x (1 - t)^3 * s2N1x + (t^3) * s2N2x + 3 * t *
           ((1 - t)^2) * s2_Nc + 3 * (t^2) * (1 - t) * s2_Nd
define s2_y (1 - t)^3 * s2N1y + (t^3) * s2N2y + 3 * t *
           ((1 - t)^2) * s2_Nc + 3 * (t^2) * (1 - t) * s2_Nd

define s3_x (1 - t)^3 * s3N1x + (t^3) * s3N2x + 3 * t *
           ((1 - t)^2) * s3_Nc + 3 * (t^2) * (1 - t) * s3_Nd
define s3_y (1 - t)^3 * s3N1y + (t^3) * s3N2y + 3 * t *
           ((1 - t)^2) * s3_Nc + 3 * (t^2) * (1 - t) * s3_Nd
```

Experiment with changing the values of S1_Nd, S2_Nd, and S3_Nd to influence the curves in different ways.

At this point, you've seen how quadratic and cubic blending interpolates between two values by using one or two control points to influence the slope of the curve. It's difficult to understand this effect without the use of a graphical aid. The QBasic program in Listing 17.9 (QUADRATC.BAS) creates a Polyray virtual animation scene file. I used it to generate Figure 17.15. This type of aid is invaluable in determining the slope control values quickly and graphically.

Listing 17.9. A QBasic program generating quadratic curves for a Polyray virtual animation (QUADRATC.BAS).

```
'================================================================
'  PROGRAM: QUADRATC.BAS
'   AUTHOR: Rob McGregor
'----------------------------------------------------------------
'  PURPOSE: Creates a Polyray scene file containing 3 spheres
'           that follow different quadratic paths, starting and
'           ending at the same points.  The paths are controlled
'           by the variables s1Nc, s2Nc, and s3Nc (the Nc
'           parameter in the equations)
'----------------------------------------------------------------
'           This is a "virtual animation," in that it calculates
'           the positions of the 3 spheres for each virtual frame,
'           and adjusts the transparency of the spheres based on
'           the value of t.  The resulting image shows the entire
```

continues

Listing 17.9. continued

```
'              animation in only 1 frame.
'=================================================================

DECLARE SUB quadratic (s1Nc!, s2Nc!, s3Nc!, startF%, endF%, fout$)

CLS
PRINT "This program creates a Polyray scene file demonstrating ";
PRINT "quadratic blending."
PRINT
PRINT "Please enter a path and file name for the resulting ";
PRINT "Polyray scene file"
LINE INPUT "==>"; fout$

INPUT "Slope of sphere 1 (from -10 to 10)"; s1Nc!
INPUT "Slope of sphere 2 (from -10 to 10)"; s2Nc!
INPUT "Slope of sphere 3 (from -10 to 10)"; s3Nc!
INPUT "Starting frame of the virtual animation"; startF%
INPUT "Ending frame of the virtual animation"; endF%

CALL quadratic(s1Nc!, s2Nc!, s3Nc!, startF%, endF%, fout$)
PRINT : PRINT "Done!": PRINT

SUB quadratic (s1Nc!, s2Nc!, s3Nc!, startF%, endF%, fout$)

  OPEN fout$ FOR OUTPUT AS #1

  ' Declare variables
  DIM frame%, t, i, format$
  DIM N3x!, N3y!, temp$, tex!
  DIM s1x!, s1y!, s2x!, s2y!, s3x!, s3y!
  DIM s1N1x!, s1N1y!, s1N2x!, s1N2y!
  DIM s2N1x!, s2N1y!, s2N2x!, s2N2y!
  DIM s3N1x!, s3N1y!, s3N2x!, s3N2y!

  ' Write the file
  PRINT #1, "// Scene File: QUAD.PI"
  PRINT #1, "// Author: Rob McGregor"
  PRINT #1, ""
  PRINT #1, "/*************************************************"
  PRINT #1, " Virtual animation of 3 spheres following different"
  PRINT #1, " quadratic paths, each starting and ending at the"
  PRINT #1, " same relative points on the y-axis."
  PRINT #1, "*************************************************/"
  PRINT #1, ""
  PRINT #1, "// SET UP THE CAMERA"
  PRINT #1, "viewpoint {"
  PRINT #1, "  from        <4.5, 0, -11.5>"
  PRINT #1, "  at          <4.5, 1, 0>"
  PRINT #1, "  up          <0, 1, 0>"
  PRINT #1, "  angle       45"
  PRINT #1, "  resolution  320, 200"
  PRINT #1, "  aspect      4/3"
  PRINT #1, "}"
  PRINT #1, ""
  PRINT #1, "background Grey"
  PRINT #1, ""
  PRINT #1, "// Lights"
```

```
PRINT #1, "light <-5, 5, -20>"
PRINT #1, "light <5, 5, -20>"
PRINT #1, ""

PRINT #1, "define s1color"
PRINT #1, "surface { "
PRINT #1, "  color      red"
PRINT #1, "  ambient    0.1"
PRINT #1, "  diffuse    0.2"
PRINT #1, "  specular   0.8"
PRINT #1, "  microfacet Cook 0.2"
PRINT #1, "  reflection 0.3 "
PRINT #1, "}"
PRINT #1, ""

PRINT #1, "define s2color"
PRINT #1, "surface { "
PRINT #1, "  color      yellow"
PRINT #1, "  ambient    0.1"
PRINT #1, "  diffuse    0.2"
PRINT #1, "  specular   0.8"
PRINT #1, "  microfacet Cook 0.2"
PRINT #1, "  reflection 0.3 "
PRINT #1, "}"
PRINT #1, ""

PRINT #1, "define s3color"
PRINT #1, "surface { "
PRINT #1, "  color      blue"
PRINT #1, "  ambient    0.1"
PRINT #1, "  diffuse    0.2"
PRINT #1, "  specular   0.8"
PRINT #1, "  microfacet Cook 0.2"
PRINT #1, "  reflection 0.3 "
PRINT #1, "}"
PRINT #1, ""

FOR i% = startF% TO endF%

  ' compute t
  frame% = i%
  t = (frame% - startF%) / (endF% - startF%)

  ' set the parameters of the equation
  s1N1x! = 0 ' x-axis starting point
  s1N1y! = -1 ' y-axis starting point
  s1N2x! = 9 ' x-axis ending point
  s1N2y! = -1 ' y-axis ending point

  s2N1x! = 0 ' x-axis starting point
  s2N1y! = 0 ' y-axis starting point
  s2N2x! = 9 ' x-axis ending point
  s2N2y! = 0 ' y-axis ending point

  s3N1x! = 0 ' x-axis starting point
  s3N1y! = 1 ' y-axis starting point
  s3N2x! = 9 ' x-axis ending point
  s3N2y! = 1 ' y-axis ending point
```

continues

Listing 17.9. continued

```
' Now calculate the locations of the spheres using:
'   N = (1 - t)^2 * N1 + t^2 * N2 + ((2 * t) * (1 - t)) * Nc

' use variables to calculate only once
t2 = t ^ 2
lessT2 = (1 - t) ^ 2

s1x! = lessT2 * s1N1x! + t2 * s1N2x! + 2 * t * (1 - t) * s1Nc!
s1y! = lessT2 * s1N1y! + t2 * s1N2y! + 2 * t * (1 - t) * s1Nc!
s2x! = lessT2 * s2N1x! + t2 * s2N2x! + 2 * t * (1 - t) * s2Nc!
s2y! = lessT2 * s2N1y! + t2 * s2N2y! + 2 * t * (1 - t) * s2Nc!
s3x! = lessT2 * s3N1x! + t2 * s3N2x! + 2 * t * (1 - t) * s3Nc!
s3y! = lessT2 * s3N1y! + t2 * s3N2y! + 2 * t * (1 - t) * s3Nc!

' calc the transparency of the spheres
tex! = (1 - t) * .9 + t * .4
format$ = "###.###"

line$ = "define s1tex" + LTRIM$(STR$(frame%))
line$ = line$ + " texture { s1color { transmission white,"
PRINT #1, line$;
PRINT #1, USING format$; tex!;
PRINT #1, ", 1 }}"

line$ = "define s2tex" + LTRIM$(STR$(frame%))
line$ = line$ + " texture { s2color { transmission white,"
PRINT #1, line$;
PRINT #1, USING format$; tex!;
PRINT #1, ", 1 }}"

line$ = "define s3tex" + LTRIM$(STR$(frame%))
line$ = line$ + " texture { s3color { transmission white,"
PRINT #1, line$;
PRINT #1, USING format$; tex!;
PRINT #1, ", 1 }}"

PRINT #1, "object { sphere <";
PRINT #1, USING format$; s1x!;
PRINT #1, ",";
PRINT #1, USING format$; s1y!;
PRINT #1, ", 0>, 0.5";
line$ = " s1tex" + LTRIM$(STR$(frame%)) + " }"
PRINT #1, line$

PRINT #1, "object { sphere <";
PRINT #1, USING format$; s2x!;
PRINT #1, ",";
PRINT #1, USING format$; s2y!;
PRINT #1, ", 0>, 0.5";
line$ = " s2tex" + LTRIM$(STR$(frame%)) + " }"
PRINT #1, line$

PRINT #1, "object { sphere <";
PRINT #1, USING format$; s3x!;
PRINT #1, ",";
PRINT #1, USING format$; s3y!;
PRINT #1, ", 0>, 0.5";
```

```
    line$ = " s3tex" + LTRIM$(STR$(frame%)) + " }"
    PRINT #1, line$
    PRINT #1, ""

  NEXT i%
  CLOSE #1

END SUB
```

You can easily modify QUARATC.BAS to produce cubic curves as well. (The program CUBIC.BAS on the companion CD shows such a modification.)

You've looked at some ways to interpolate between two values, but key framing isn't limited to only two frames. Key framing requires that you be able to use any given number of key frames and interpolate *all* of them to attain smooth blending. You can do this with spline curves.

Spline Curves and Key Frames

Spline curves can blend any number of control points into the interpolated sequence, which is great for tweening key frames. Splines interpolate four control points at a time to generate local curve segments. These segments have continuity because they share control points, and the slope of one segment blends smoothly into the next. The two types of spline curves you examine here are the B-Spline and the Catmull-Rom spline.

The B-Spline is drawn to but never quite reaches its control points, making it an approximating spline. The Catmull-Rom spline actually passes through its control points and is an interpolating spline. Both types have their uses for key framing. Figure 17.17 shows the difference between a B-Spline and a Catmull-Rom spline derived from the same set of control points. Notice that the B-Spline generally has a smoother overall curve.

The basic function of the spline is to interpolate a series of control points one segment at a time. You derive each curve segment from four control points, and all adjacent segments share three points. The first and last points aren't included in the combined curve, but repeating these points includes them into the interpolation sequence. Given the 2-D coordinates in Figure 17.17—(0, 0), (1.6, 2.8), (3.6, 0), (0.4, -3.2), (-3.2, -0.4), and (0, 0)—you can interpolate five curve segments (doubling the first and last points to include them in the interpolation sequence) as follows:

```
segment1 -- (0, 0), (0, 0), (1.6, 2.8), (3.6, 0)
segment2 -- (0, 0), (1.6, 2.8), (3.6, 0), (0.4, -3.2)
segment3 -- (1.6, 2.8), (3.6, 0), (0.4, -3.2), (-3.2, -0.4)
segment4 -- (3.6, 0), (0.4, -3.2), (-3.2, -0.4), (0, 0)
segment5 -- (0.4, -3.2), (-3.2, -0.4), (0, 0), (0, 0)
```

FIGURE 17.17.

(a) Six points on the x- and y-axes form a basic path (first and last points are the same). These control points are used as key frame references in spline interpolation. (b) A Catmull-Rom spline path interpolated from the six control points. The path passes through all six control points. (c) A B-Spline path interpolated from the six control points. The path passes through only the first control point but is heavily influenced by the other five.

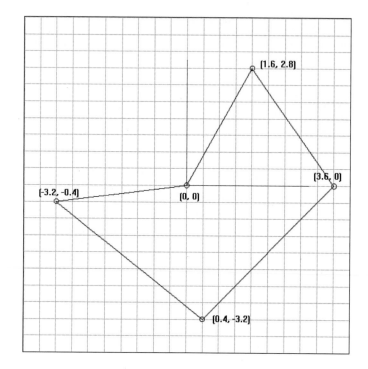

a

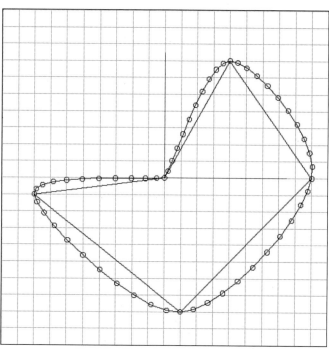

b

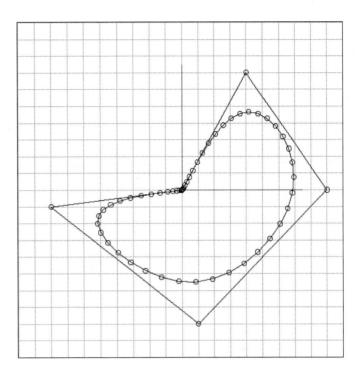

c

I won't go into all the sticky mathematics involved in the proof of the equations. There are several good texts that thoroughly cover the subject of splines and explain the theories involved (see the references at the end of this chapter). What I *will* do is give you the B-Spline and Catmull-Rom spline equations so that you can use them in your animations. Hold onto your hats, folks!

The equation for forming a B-Spline is

```
P = ((-P1 * t^3 + 3 * P2 * t^3 - 3 * P3 * t^3 + P4 * t^3) +
    (3 * P1 * t^2 - 6 * P2 * t^2 + 3 * P3 * t^2) +
    (-3 * P1 * t +3 * P3 *t) + (P1 + 4 * P2 + P3)) * (1 / 6)
```

The equation for forming a Catmull-Rom spline is

```
P = t^3 * (-0.5 * P1) + t^3 * (1.5 * P2) + t^3 * (-1.5 * P3) +
    t^3 * (0.5 * P4) + t2 * P1 + t^2 * (-2.5 * P2) + t^2 *
    (2 * P3) + t^2 * (-0.5 * P4) + t * (-0.5 * P1) + t *
    (0.5 * P3) + P2
```

where P is the interpolated point for any given value of t, and P1, P2, P3, and P4 are the control points of the local segment.

> **NOTE**
>
> By placing control points closer together at the start and end of a curve than in the middle, you can create ease-in and ease-out acceleration/deceleration effects. These look much more realistic than the sudden stops and starts caused by equidistant points.
>
> The program POVCAD can produce both B-Spline and Catmull-Rom spline curves from up to 50 control points in 3-D space, and it weights the curves for realistic acceleration/deceleration.

Listing 17.10 demonstrates the use of the Catmull-Rom spline applied to this group of control points to move a sphere along the path shown in Figure 17.17b.

This scene starts off with the usual include files, the viewpoint declaration and the animation range of 50 frames with the outfile name "spln1". Next, you store the control points defined in Figure 17.17b in 12 arrays, defining the four local control points for each segment (one array for each axis):

```
// Define the 4 local 3-D control points as arrays
define n1x [0, 0, 1.6, 3.6, 0.4]
define n1y [0, 0, 2.8, 0, -3.2]
define n1z [0, 0, 0, 0, 0]

define n2x [0, 1.6, 3.6, 0.4, -3.2]
define n2y [0, 2.8, 0, -3.2, -0.4]
define n2z [0, 0, 0, 0, 0]

define n3x [1.6, 3.6, 0.4, -3.2, -0.4]
define n3y [2.8, 0, -3.2, -0.4, 0]
define n3z [0, 0, 0, 0, 0]

define n4x [3.6, 0.4, -3.2, 0, 0]
define n4y [0, -3.2, -0.4, 0, 0]
define n4z [0, 0, 0, 0, 0]
```

Then you store the key frames in the array KF, arbitrarily spaced at 10-frame intervals:

```
define KF [0, 9, 19, 29, 39, 49]
```

Next, you assign the variable frame to the token F, used to determine the current interpolation sequence for the local control points:

```
define F frame

// Determine what key frame sequence we're in
if (F <= KF[1])                 // <= 9
  define key 0
if (F > KF[1] && F <= KF[2])   // > 9 && <= 19
  define key 1
if (F > KF[2] && F <= KF[3])   // > 19 && <= 29
  define key 2
```

```
if (F > KF[3] && F <= KF[4])   // > 29 && <= 39
  define key 3
if (F > KF[4])                 // > 39
  define key 4
```

Then you calculate the value of t and use it in the Catmull-Rom spline equation to interpolate the curve segments, along with the array index key:

```
define t  (F - F1) / (F2 - F1)
define t3 t^3
define t2 t^2
define Px t3 * (-0.5 * n1x[key]) + t3 * (1.5 * n2x[key]) + t3 *
          (-1.5 * n3x[key]) + t3 * (0.5 * n4x[key]) + t2 *
          n1x[key] + t2 * (-2.5 * n2x[key]) + t2 * (2 * n3x[key]) +
          t2 * (-0.5 * n4x[key]) + t * (-0.5 * n1x[key]) + t *
          (0.5 * n3x[key]) + n2x[key]
```

Lastly, you move the sphere to its new location and complete the setting with various other scene trimmings. For a more extreme example of this method, see the group of files in the ROOMFLY subdirectory on the companion CD (ROOMFLY is described in the next section).

Listing 17.10. Catmull-Rom spline interpolation of an object path using key frames (CATMULL.PI).

```
// Scene File: CATMULL.PI
// Author: Rob McGregor

// Uses Catmull-Rom spline interpolation *through*
// key frame points to calculate an object's path...

include "colors.inc"
include "texture.inc"

// Set up the camera
viewpoint {
  from        <0, 0, -12>
  at          <0, 0, 0>
  up          <0, 1, 0>
  angle       45
  resolution 320,200
  aspect      1.6
}

// Define the range of the animation
start_frame 0
end_frame   49
outfile     "catml"

/*********************************************************
   The control points are:

   <0, 0, 0>, <1.6, 2.8, 0>, <3.6, 0, 0>,
   <0.4, -3.2, 0>, <-3.2, -0.4, 0>, <0, 0, 0>
```

continues

Listing 17.10. continued

```
   The first and last points are doubled to include them
   in the interpolation and create a smoother loop.

   x-axis: 0, 0, 1.6, 3.6, 0.4, -3.2, 0, 0
   y-axis: 0, 0, 2.8, 0,   -3.2, -0.4, 0, 0
   *******************************************************/

// Define the 4 local 3-D control points as arrays
define n1x [0, 0, 1.6, 3.6, 0.4]
define n1y [0, 0, 2.8, 0, -3.2]
define n1z [0, 0, 0, 0, 0]

define n2x [0, 1.6, 3.6, 0.4, -3.2]
define n2y [0, 2.8, 0, -3.2, -0.4]
define n2z [0, 0, 0, 0, 0]

define n3x [1.6, 3.6, 0.4, -3.2, -0.4]
define n3y [2.8, 0, -3.2, -0.4, 0]
define n3z [0, 0, 0, 0, 0]

define n4x [3.6, 0.4, -3.2, 0, 0]
define n4y [0, -3.2, -0.4, 0, 0]
define n4z [0, 0, 0, 0, 0]

// Set up the key frames in another array
define KF [0, 9, 19, 29, 39, 49]

// Assign the value of "frame" to variable "F"
define F frame

// Determine what key frame sequence we're in
if (F <= KF[1])                 // <= 9
   define key 0
if (F > KF[1] && F <= KF[2])  // > 9 && <= 19
   define key 1
if (F > KF[2] && F <= KF[3])  // > 19 && <= 29
   define key 2
if (F > KF[3] && F <= KF[4])  // > 29 && <= 39
   define key 3
if (F > KF[4])                  // > 39
   define key 4

// Calculate the value of "t" from the
// current frame and key frame sequence
define F1 KF[key]
define F2 KF[key + 1]
define t  (F - F1) / (F2 - F1)

/*******************************************************
   Calculate the values of the object's location vector using the
   Catmull-Rom spline equation:

   P = t^3 * (-0.5 * P1) + t^3 * (1.5 * P2) + t^3 * (-1.5 * P3) +
       t^3 * (0.5 * P4) + t2 * P1 + t^2 * (-2.5 * P2) + t^2 *
       (2 * P3) + t^2 * (-0.5 * P4) + t * (-0.5 * P1) + t *
       (0.5 * P3) + P2
   *******************************************************/
```

```
define t2 t * t
define t3 t2 * t

define Px t3 * (-0.5 * n1x[key]) + t3 * (1.5 * n2x[key]) + t3 *
          (-1.5 * n3x[key]) + t3 * (0.5 * n4x[key]) + t2 *
          n1x[key] + t2 * (-2.5 * n2x[key]) + t2 * (2 * n3x[key]) +
          t2 * (-0.5 * n4x[key]) + t * (-0.5 * n1x[key]) + t *
          (0.5 * n3x[key]) + n2x[key]

define Py t3 * (-0.5 * n1y[key]) + t3 * (1.5 * n2y[key]) + t3 *
          (-1.5 * n3y[key]) + t3 * (0.5 * n4y[key]) + t2 *
          n1y[key] + t2 * (-2.5 * n2y[key]) + t2 * (2 * n3y[key]) +
          t2 * (-0.5 * n4y[key]) + t * (-0.5 * n1y[key]) + t *
          (0.5 * n3y[key]) + n2y[key]

define Pz t3 * (-0.5 * n1z[key]) + t3 * (1.5 * n2z[key]) + t3 *
          (-1.5 * n3z[key]) + t3 * (0.5 * n4z[key]) + t2 *
          n1z[key] + t2 * (-2.5 * n2z[key]) + t2 * (2 * n3z[key]) +
          t2 * (-0.5 * n4z[key]) + t * (-0.5 * n1z[key]) + t *
          (0.5 * n3z[key]) + n2z[key]

// Now move the sphere to the new location
object {
  sphere <0, 0, 0>, 0.5
  reflective_red
  translate <Px, Py, Pz>
}

// Set the sky color and add a little haze
background Grey
haze 0.98, 25, Grey

// Lights
light <-5, 30, -100>
light <5, 30, -100>

// The floor...
object {
  disc <0, 0, 0>, <0, 1, 0>, 10000
  texture {
    checker steely_blue,
    texture { shiny { color white }}
  }
  rotate <0, 25, 0>
  translate <0, -4.5, 0>
}
```

A More Complex Animation

Now take a look at a fairly complex animation (ROOMFLY.FLI) created from two main
scene files and several include files. I was thinking, "Why don't I take Venus de Milo,
stick her on a pedestal, and let some spheres whiz around her?" So I did. Then I decided
to add some camera motion and a few other cool tricks you've seen in this chapter. A lot

of stuff all at once, like a big party, right? The two main files ROOMFLY1.PI and ROOMFLY2.PI are nearly identical. The second uses additional spline interpolation to move the camera on a fly-through of the room.

> **NOTE**
>
> The code for the eight files used in this animation was too long to include in this chapter, but the full source is on the companion CD.

The basic idea for the scene began on a sheet of graph paper with the sketch of a room. This room consists of two wooden walls (the other two aren't seen in the animation, so I left them out), a tiled floor, a statue of Venus de Milo on a pedestal (appropriately), and two framed paintings on the walls. The action consists of three spheres flying erratically around the statue as two spotlights pivot their beams around the room. As this action continues, the camera begins to fly through the room, around the statue, and into one of the paintings.

The first order of business is setting up all the objects for the animation. I created all the basic objects in POVCAD and then saved them in separate include files to keep things modular. Declaring all objects as static constants read-only on the first frame saves memory and shortens rendering time. The definition of the room itself (walls and floor) is in the file ROOM.INC. The statue is the same model used for Figure 17.10, VENUS.INC, and PEDESTAL.INC defines the pedestal. The file PICFRAME.INC defines the picture frames, along with the two image-mapped canvasses they contain (you can specify any bitmap you want to put in these frames).

The files SPHRPATH.INC, SPOTPATH.INC, and CAMPATH.INC define the paths of the spheres, lights, and camera as arrays of control points. These control points are the location vectors at the key frames designated in the main scene files ROOMFLY1.PI and ROOMFLY2.PI. These arrays are interpolated as Catmull-Rom splines with calculations performed in SPHRCALC.INC, SPOTCALC.INC, and CAMCALC.INC.

Separating the files into modules makes them reusable in other scenes (I have a whole library of objects that I can call on).

Using a DOS Batch File to Link Animation Sequences

Batch files are useful for automating the flow of events in the animation process and can be real time-savers when rendering repetitive sequences. A very simple DOS batch file (see Listing 17.11, ROOMREND.BAT) controls the entire process of rendering and compiling the Flic. ROOMREND.BAT first runs the main scene file ROOMFLY1.PI, which shows you a view of the room as the spheres fly around. All the required include files are called on the first frame only, loading the objects and control point arrays into memory.

After ROOMFLY1.PI renders 61 frames, ROOMREND.BAT calls DTA to compile ROOM1A.FLI. This Flic is then copied as ROOM1B.FLI and the two are concatenated into ROOM1.FLI (this method is much quicker than rendering duplicate frames). The originals are then deleted to reclaim disk space. ROOMREND.BAT then calls Polyray to process ROOMFLY2.PI and render the 63 frames of a camera fly-through sequence. DTA is called once again, and ROOM2.FLI is brought to life. At last, the Flics ROOM1.FLI and ROOM2.FLI are concatenated together into the final ROOMFLY.FLI.

Listing 17.11. A DOS batch file to loop a repetitive scene and link multiple sequences into a complete Flic (ROOMREND.BAT).

```
@echo off
cls
rem ========================================================
rem = This DOS batch file renders two Flic segments and =
rem = creates a concatenated flic using DTA...            =
rem ========================================================

rem ** Render the static camera scene **
rem call polyray roomfly1.pi -a2 -R

rem ** render the 1st flic **
call dta room1*.tga /R1 /C10 /Oroom1a.fli

rem ** make a copy of room1a.flc and concatenate **
copy room1a.fli room1b.fli
call dta room1a.fli room1b.fli /R1 /C10 /Oroom1.fli

rem ** prompt for deletion of originals **
echo.
echo Preparing to delete room1a.fli and room1b.fli --
pause
del room1a.fli
del room1b.fli

rem ** Render the moving camera scene **
call polyray roomfly2.pi -a2 -R

rem ** render the 2nd flic and append it to the 1st **
call dta room2*.tga /R1 /C10 /Oroom2.fli
call dta room1.flc room2.fli /R3 /C10 /S7 /Oroom.fli

rem ** prompt for deletion of originals **
echo.
echo Preparing to delete room1.fli and room2.fli --
pause
del room1.fli
del room2.fli

:end
```

To get a better handle on interpolation, try writing a simple program that takes various parameters and inserts them into the equations you've learned in this chapter. Have the program write the resulting data to a Polyray scene file. As an example, review Listing 17.9 (QUADRATC.BAS), which created the scene file used to generate Figure 17.15.

Summary

In this chapter, you looked at the popular ray tracer Polyray, which has built-in support for conditional processing and animation. Polyray generates the static photorealistic images that later get compiled into animation sequences. You explored several methods for creating the illusion of moving objects, lights, textures, and cameras, and you saw several examples of texture mapping through the use of image maps.

You then delved into DTA, a shareware program that actually integrates the images into a finished animation. Finally, you learned how to use key frames and interpolation to let the computer tween animation elements for you. Several fully developed animation scenes were presented with full code and explanation to demonstrate various concepts of ray-traced animation. All the scene file code, image maps, and compiled Flics are on the companion CD, along with self-executing Flics made with BUILDSV.

This chapter is an overview of some of the myriad of techniques that have been developed over the past decade. Using the basics presented here as a foundation, you should be able to create some impressive Flics. I hope you enjoy your virtual journeys as much as I do. The mind's the limit!

Further Reading

Several good books that go into much greater detail about animation techniques and ray tracing than space allowed here are available. If you're intrigued by 3-D computer graphics, ray tracing, and animation, I highly recommend the books listed below for further study. The authors of Polyray (Alexander Enzmann) and DTA (David Mason) have written an excellent book on ray-traced animation techniques. Alfonso Hermida's book gives a thorough overview of ray tracing with Polyray and the use of the POVCAD 3-D modeler. For a more technical look at the mathematical side of things, be sure to get the books by both Watt and Vince. Much of the interpolation information presented here was derived from the matrix equations given in their texts. The book by Foley, Andries, Feiner, and Hughes is a great source of information about 3-D techniques and shading models.

Foley, James D., Andries van Dam, Steven K. Feiner, and John F. Hughes. *Computer Graphics Principles and Practice, Second Edition.* Reading, MA: Addison

Wesley, 1990.

Hermida, Alfonso. *Adventures in Ray Tracing.* Indianapolis, IN: Que, 1993.

Mason, David K., and Alexander Enzmann. *Making Movies on Your PC.* Corte Madera, CA: Waite Group Press, 1993.

Vince, John. *3-D Computer Animation.* Reading, MA: Addison Wesley, 1992.

Watt, Alan. *3D Computer Graphics, Second Edition.* Reading, MA: Addison Wesley, 1993.

Radiosity

by William Parsons Newhall, Jr.

Introduction

The computer artist strives to create an image that clearly expresses a visual experience. For many computer artists the ideal to be achieved is an image that conveys a realistic impression—as if the image were a photograph of an instant in real time and space, and not a synthetic vista molded out of imagination and software. This rather elusive goal is known in computer graphics as *photorealism,* and there are two schools of thought as to how it is best attained. One group prefers to employ ad hoc techniques like local illumination models, and the other attempts to model illumination and shading with *physically based models* that attempt to simulate natural phenomenon as faithfully as possible.

Computer graphics grew out of a number of disciplines and is firmly rooted in many industries, such as entertainment, architecture, medicine, and scientific research. For many applications it is feasible, if not necessary, to use physically based models (such as in architectural rendering and scientific visualization), while other applications have other constraints (such as the high volume of frames and the small amount of time given to computer animators in the production of feature films). The intractable debate between the proponents of physically based modelling and those who take the "by any means necessary" approach will never achieve a consensus. The closest thing to a compromise might be this: "If it works, do it...however, what works best is what is closest to real life." Computer graphics is an art form, and as such it has multiple tools with different strengths and weaknesses. The artist must be sensitive to the context and constraints of his work, and use the appropriate tool for the appropriate task. For example, objects that are mirror-reflective or glass-refractive look very realistic, while other types of objects (matte surfaces such as upholstery or carpet, for instance) appear incomplete when rendered with ray tracing.

Radiosity is a tool of computer graphics that produces the highest degree of photorealism and offers considerable advantages, but it hasn't been employed by the computer graphics art community. Radiosity is a physically based model of global diffuse illumination and reflection that was first developed at Cornell University in 1984, from radiative heat transfer theories out of the field of thermodynamics. The basic radiosity method assumes that all surfaces are Lambertian (ideal diffuse) in much the same way that ray tracing assumes that all surfaces are ideal specular; but, unlike ray tracing, radiosity discretizes the environment and produces data that is independent of viewer perspective. In general, the radiosity process takes longer than ray tracing, which is probably why it has yet to gain appreciation and employment from the computer graphics community. However, because of its view independence, radiosity data can be used to rapidly produce multiple views of an imaginary scene for which ray tracing can only produce one view. For this reason, radiosity is ideal for some applications (such as walk-throughs and flybys), and is worth the extra computing time.

Unlike Gouraud shading, Phong shading, and ray tracing, the radiosity illumination/reflection model is not a rendering method. This is because the radiosity method doesn't take any cameras or vantage points into account. The radiosity method is a rendering preprocess and, as such, radiosity data must be processed by additional rendering and hidden surfaces removal techniques in order to be visualized. There have been many cases in which hardware acceleration combined with radiosity data has produced real time photorealistic shaded display; the most striking and photorealistic pictures to date have been created by combining radiosity and ray trace data (though sacrificing view independence).

Because of the vast increases in computing power in the last ten years, it is now feasible to utilize the radiosity method in desktop three dimensional computer graphics systems. Today's desktop personal computers have memory, storage, and performance comparable to the mainframes and graphics workstations on which the radiosity method was developed ten years ago. This is largely the result of a highly competitive personal computer marketplace, where performance has increased exponentially and price has dropped exponentially. A few years ago, personal computers were configured with 8 MHz 16-bit 80286 processors, 640K of RAM, 10 to 20 megabytes of hard disk storage, and 16 color EGA display systems. These systems were capable of simple shading and (extremely slow) ray tracing, but at the time the radiosity method was felt to be beyond the reach of the desktop PC. Early PC ray tracing software (vivid, dkbtrace, mtv) was developed and used (by the extremely patient) on these systems. Even though 80486 and Pentium processors are capable of using the radiosity method, there are no 80x86 commercial software applications that make use of it as of this writing.

This chapter covers the radiosity method in terms of how it works and how you can make use of it. A general introduction is followed by a detailed exploration of the theory behind the radiosity method and a survey of radiosity algorithms. To illustrate radiosity in concrete and practical terms, examples are given using Greg Ward's Radiance application (which can be run on 80x86 machines under the Linux operating system), the DOS implementation of Sumant Pattanik's India radiosity system (called RAD386, it can translate Radiance files into its native format), and Bernard Kwok's light radiosity package (ported to DOS by Antonio Costa it renders with the Rtrace ray tracer). Examples of existing commercial radiosity packages are given as well.

Figure 18.1 shows how ray tracing and radiosity can be compared. With ray tracing, a continuous environment is viewed through a discretized view plane. Light sources are invisible and only specular reflections are accounted for. With radiosity, a discrete environment can be rendered from any perspective. Light sources are visable and diffuse reflections are accounted for. Each surface is a virtual light source reflecting light back into the environment.

FIGURE 18.1.
Ray tracing (top) and radiosity (bottom) compared.

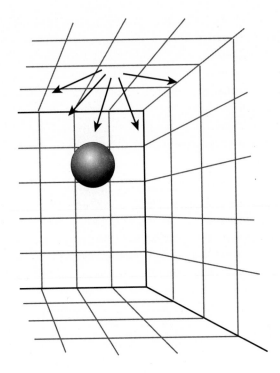

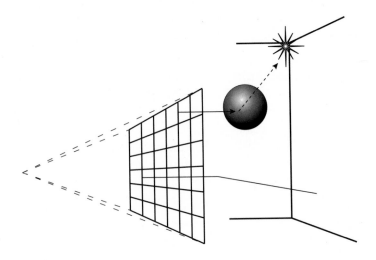

The Radiosity Method in a Nutshell

In contrast to local illumination models that can only model direct light by approximately simulating the way light from a source falls upon an object's surface, global illumination models concern themselves with indirect light also. *Indirect light* is light that is reflected from one surface to another. If you look around, you see that a majority of the light arriving at your eyes is indirect. Indirect light is divided into two types: light that is specularly reflected by smooth surfaces, and light that is diffusely reflected by rough surfaces. Ray tracing is a global illumination model that simulates specularly reflected indirect light. So, ray tracing is used mostly for smooth surfaced objects, because they produce the specular reflections with which a ray tracer works best. The radiosity method simulates diffusely reflected indirect light. Indoor scenes where light is diffusely reflected off of ceilings, walls, and floors are the environments that radiosity handles best. Radiosity is defined as the total energy leaving a surface. This is expressed with the equation:

$$B = E + R$$

The primary difference between ray tracing and radiosity is that a ray tracer is what each algorithm attempts to determine. A ray tracer determines the color of the light travelling along a ray intersecting a pixel on the viewplane. A radiosity preprocessor determines the color of the light leaving the surface of an object. Both systems take discrete samples, but in the radiosity method the geometry of the environment is discretized into finite areas called *patches*. The ray tracing method discretizes the viewplane into finite areas called *pixels*. The ray tracing solution determines the color of the light arriving at each pixel of the viewplane, while the radiosity solution determines the color of the light leaving each patch within the environment. There are considerable differences between the way lights and objects are handled by the two methods: In ray tracing, light sources are infinitely small, invisible point sources; in radiosity, each surface has the potential to act as a source of light or a surface reflecting it. In radiosity, light sources are visible. Both ray tracing and radiosity consume considerable amounts of processing time and require significant system resources, but the ray tracing method takes care of hidden surface removal and rendering. The radiosity method still requires a rendering stage after the solution has been determined. However, radiosity output data is independent of viewpoint and can be rendered from any perspective. Ray tracing data can only be applied to one perspective: the perspective selected by the virtual camera.

The basic radiosity process works sequentially in three stages: environment modelling and discretization, form factor calculation, and distributing the light energy until the environment achieves equilibrium. After the radiosity solution has been determined, the environment can be rendered from any perspective at any resolution with a variety of rendering algorithms. Enhanced radiosity systems make use of a principle developed by Michael Cohen, called *progressive refinement*. Using this principle, the radiosity software quickly determines a solution and makes modifications to the environment to enhance the accuracy of the solution (such as subdividing patches into smaller *patch elements* for more accurate sampling). The radiosity method is ideal.

Figure 18.2 shows the phases of radiosity image synthesis.

FIGURE 18.2.

The phases of radiosity image synthesis.

Design

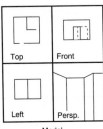

Top   Front

Left   Persp.

Model

Radiosity Preprocessing

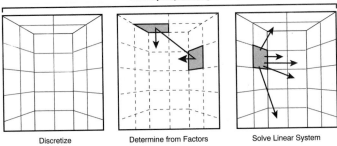

Discretize   Determine from Factors   Solve Linear System

Rendering

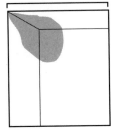

Remove Hidden Lines and Shade

Modeling and Discretizing the Environment

Radiosity theory can only be applied on a computer if a few sacrifices and compromises are made. Radiosity theory was originally developed to measure and observe physical phenomena within the *continuous* real world. Digital computers are by nature *discrete* machines. A continuous environment must be broken up into finite areas. Most environments are meshes built out of polygonal facets called *patches*. Imagine a room constructed out of square panels on the walls, floor, and ceiling, and illuminated by a rectangular fluorescent light recessed into the ceiling. Radiosity environments are built in similar fashion, though Radiance, LightR, and RAD386 all support more complex primitives (including cubes, cones, cylinders, and spheres). Each patch panel can be either an illuminating or reflecting surface. Each patch must be described in terms of its position, geometry, diffuse reflectivity (P), and energy emission coefficient (E). Diffuse reflectivity and energy emission are expressed for each color band (red, blue, green), and overall surface finish can be expressed with the diffuse reflection coefficient (k_d) and the specular reflection coeffient (k_s). Patches that are light sources have nonzero energy emission coefficients, whereas regular surfaces have emission coefficients equal to zero. Some radiosity packages (including LightR and RAD386) allow specular reflection coefficients to be specified instead of, or in addition to, diffuse reflection coefficients.

The radiosity packages described in this chapter work in a similar fashion to ray tracing packages: An ASCII scene description file is read and processed, and output files are written to disk. Most complex scenes are designed with modeling or CAD software and then converted into the scene file format. Recently developed software packages on other platforms (such as Lightscape for the SGI and Strata Studio Pro for the Macintosh) integrate modeling and rendering within the same software package. So, it should not be long before integrated modeling/radiosity packages appear for the PC.

Form Factor Calculation

The primary goal of the radiosity method is to determine how much light energy is leaving each surface within an environment. At the outset of the radiosity solution, only surfaces that are light sources (having E > 0) have any light energy. After the radiosity solution is achieved, all of the light energy is distributed throughout the environment. The light energy of any given surface is directly proportional to the light energy emitted throughout the environment by all the other patches. This is illustrated by the following relationship:

$$B_i \cong E_i + P_i \sum_{j=0}^{\substack{\text{number of} \\ \text{patches}}} B_j$$

(surface i radiosity) = (surface i emitted energy) + (total radiosity of all other surfaces)

Of course, not all of the radiosity from surface j will reach surface i. One of the surfaces might be facing the wrong direction or obstructed by another surface. Some of the light energy is converted into heat energy and dissipated as it becomes more distant from the light source. Unless surface j is a supernova, it has a finite amount of energy and is subject to the laws of conservation. To account for these interference factors, we use the form factor to scale the intensity of B. There is one form factor for each pair of unique patches, and the radiosity any given patch i can be determined by using the form factor:

$$B_i = E_i + P_i \sum_{j=0}^{\substack{\text{number of} \\ \text{patches}}} K_{ij} B_i$$

(surface i radiosity) = (surface i emitted energy) + (total scaled radiosity of other surfaces)

For any two unique patches (A and B) within the environment, the form factor is a ratio representing how much of the light energy leaving patch A arrives at patch B. It is best described in geometric terms as "how much of patch B can patch A see?" Form factors are determined by geometric issues only. Form factor calculations account for energy loss due to distance, Lambert's cosine law, and occlusion (obstruction by another surface). Form factors are not affected by issues of intensity or color. Intensity and color are affected by form factors and are calculated by the third and final stage of the radiosity process: finding the radiosity solution by distributing the light energy throughout the enviroment.

Figure 18.3 shows Goral's form factor geometry and formulation. The form factor expresses (as a function of geometry) how much energy leaving one surface arrives at another.

FIGURE 18.3.

The form factor.

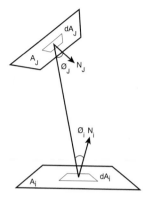

$$F_{IJ} = \frac{1}{A_i} \int_{A_i} \int_{A_j} \frac{\cos\emptyset_i \; \cos\emptyset_J}{\pi \, r^2} \, dA_j A_i$$

The calculation of form factors is the most computationally intensive part of the radiosity method, and there are a number of algorithms and techniques for determining the form factor. The way the form factor is calculated affects the quality of the image (for example, the smoothness of shadows) and the time it takes to achieve a radiosity solution.

Achieving Equilibrium: Finding the Radiosity Solution

To determine the total light energy coming from all the surfaces within the environment, a series of calculations must be made to determine the how the light energy is transferred. The set of reflectivity coefficients of form factors within the environment produce a linear system, which can be represented with the following matrix:

$$
\begin{matrix}
1 - p_1 F_{1,1} & -p_1 F_{1,2} & -p_1 F_{1,3} & \cdots & -p_1 F_{1,n} \\
-p_2 F_{2,1} & 1 - p_2 F_{2,2} & -p_2 F_{2,3} & \cdots & -p_2 F_{2,n} \\
\cdot & & & & \\
\cdot & & & & \\
p_{n-1} F_{n-1,1} & \cdot & \cdot & \cdots & 1 - p_n F_{n,n}
\end{matrix}
$$

There is a vast array of algorithms for solving this set of linear equations. The first methods, employed by Goral et al., were direct linear equation solvers such as Gaussian Elimination, which are computationally complex and impractical for large and elaborate environments. The other way to achieve the solution to the set of linear equations is to use iterative solution convergence techniques, which initially approximate the solution and successively modify it to a more accurate approximation. Both LightR and RAD386 make use of iterative solutions and enable the user to specify how many iterations will be carried out. Other radiosity systems continuously iterate until the effect of the iterations is no longer significant and equilibrium is considered to have been achieved.

> **NOTE**
>
> Linux is a very powerful port of the Unix operating system for 80386, 80486, and Pentium PCs, and is available for free on the internet. Linux supports a variety of graphics display adapters and comes with X-Windows R11 built in. Many Unix and PC graphics applications have been ported to Linux, and many of the PC graphics applications run faster! The multitasking capabilities offered by Linux are much more robust than those offered by Microsoft Windows. Linux is extremely ironic because it is considered one of the most powerful operating systems available for the PC, yet it is free. It is also one of the most stable and efficient ports of the Unix operating system, even though it was written by dozens of programmers around the world who never met each other. Linux is, to say the least, amazing.
>
> Greg Ward's Radiance radiosity software is a ray tracer that accounts for global diffuse illumination (everything radiosity calculates and then some), and it can be compiled and run under Linux. In addition, the India Radiosity package (upon which RAD386 is based) can also be compiled to run under Linux. An object-oriented graphics package, known as GOOD, includes a powerful renderer called YART that features radiosity, ray tracing, and local illumination models. GOOD and YART were both developed at the Technical University of Ilmenau in Germany, and both run under Linux. Other graphics applications, such as the POV raytracer, run significantly (about 20 to 30 percent) faster under Linux.

Rendering Radiosity Data

After the radiosity solution has been achieved, it can be visualized with a number of methods. Depending upon the application, a number of rendering algorithms can be used to display the radiosity data. Some radiosity software (such as Radiance) includes an interactive walk-through renderer, which uses flat shading because it can be performed rapidly. If time constraints are not very great and a very high-quality image is sought, a ray tracer can be used to provide a richly detailed image combining the subtle nuances of both global illumination models. LightR enables the user to render the image with Rtrace; RAD386 automatically performs projection, Gouraud shading, and hidden surface removal.

The process of producing an image from a radiosity scene description file is a little more involved than the process of rendering an image with a ray tracer. This is because the radiosity method has a wide array of implementations and has not been on the desktop long enough to be standardized. The two radiosity systems were originally developed to run under the Unix operating system. They suffer from the usual side effects of software that is ported from one operating system to another. Both RAD386 and LightR have many options, not all of which are fully functional. We will start with two simple examples.

Rendering with RAD386

RAD386 is fairly straightforward in its operation and offers some simple enhancements. RAD386 supports four raster graphics file formats for output: Utah RLE, Radiance Rasterfile, Raw RGB data, and text RGB data. The Utah RLE format is supported by the DISPLAY image viewer and can be converted to other file formats with ALCHEMY. The way to render a scene with RAD386 from the DOS command line is as follows:

```
C:\CHAP18\RAD386> RAD -O scene.int scene.rle < scene.dat
```

This command sequence processes the scene file to produce an image file. The < symbol tells the program from where it is getting its input data and where it is putting its output data. The input file, scene.dat, is an ASCII file describing the scene in terms of its geometry and surface properties (reflectivity, light emitted, etc.). The output file, scene.rle, is a Utah RLE raster image of the rendered environment. The -O scene.int option causes RAD386 to generate an environment intensity file that describes the intensity of all the surfaces within the environment. The RAD386 scene file specifies the viewing data used to generate the raster file (which is somewhat unusual, since the radiosity solution is independent of viewer position). Having generated an intensity file (scene.int), we can rapidly render the scene from multiple perspectives with the following command:

```
C:\CHAP18\RAD386> RAD -i scene.int scene2.rle < scene2.dat
```

In this example, the -i option stands for "include intensity file." scene.int is the file containing the intensity information (which we generated last time) for every surface within the environment. The file scene2.dat contains exactly the same surface data, but specifies a different view. In this case, the time it takes RAD to render the scene is significantly shorter, because it does not have to compute the form factors or produce a radiosity solution. Those steps were performed last time, so all that must be done is project the surface patches into screen space, remove hidden surfaces, and perform Gouraud shading to smooth the surface intensities.

In the first example, the radiosity solution was achieved using the default technique: the Gauss-Seidel Iterative method. The Gauss-Seidel algorithm is very efficient in determining a solution, but requires considerable memory resources. Complex environments might require a virtual memory swapfile or a less demanding method of solution convergence. Fortunately, RAD386 supports another method of solution convergence: the progressive radiosity algorithm. Progressive radiosity is also an iterative technique for determining the radiosity solution, but it does not require as much memory as the Gauss-Seidel method. Progressive radiosity is a very efficient way of achieving a solution. Surfaces are processed in order, from those with the most radiosity to those with the least. At each iteration, the surface with the most radiosity "shoots" its energy to all of the other surfaces, distributing its energy throughout the environment. After very few iterations, the approximate solution has a defined form. The more iterations that are performed, the closer the scene will be to equilibrium. RAD386 enables the user to quickly preview an environment or perspective, simply by defining a low number of iterations. For example:

```
C:\CHAP18\RAD386> RAD -p 50 scene2.rle < scene2.dat
```

produces an image file after performing 50 iterations of progressive radiosity. Generally, this is enough to produce an image suitable for debugging a scene in terms of perspective or geometry. On occasion, a preview image may appear "blacked out" because not enough steps of progressive radiosity were performed. Some detail can be discerned if an image processor is used to perform color expansion, equalization, or gamma correction, which approximately compensates for the lack of "ambient" energy within the scene.

If no number of iterations is specified, or if a negative number is specified, /?/ RAD386 processes the scene until a preset state of equilibrium is achieved. The progressive radiosity algorithm is automatically selected (with a predetermined number of iterations) if the user selects the Gauss-Seidel method, but does not have the system resources to process the matrix. See Figures 18.4, 18.5, and 18.6.

FIGURE 18.4.

Room rendered with ray tracing alone. (Courtesy of Ekkehard Beier, Technical University of Ilmenau, Department of Computer Science.)

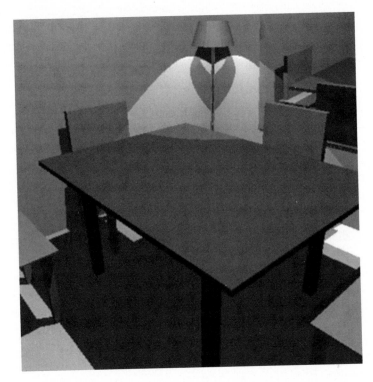

FIGURE 18.5.

Room rendered with radiosity only.

FIGURE 18.6.

Room rendered with ray tracing and radiosity blended together.

Rendering with LightR

LightR is a very sophisticated radiosity preprocessor that offers many options not available in RAD386. These options are specified as environment variables and can be modified with the SET command. At this point, you should be aware that the environment variables exist, but you should not be too concerned with what each of them does. We will address them when we get into options and enhancements, later in the chapter. The RADOPTS batch file automatically sets up all of the environment variables and must be run before LightR. LightR will run without these variables, but its results can be unpredictable. In most cases, LightR will run and process the radiosity data, but will not produce an output file. To set the environment variables, run the RADOPTS batch file:

```
C:\CHAP18\LIGHTR> RADOPTS
```

If DOS spits back that it is too low on environment space, you must alter your config.sys file to allocate more system memory for the storage of environment data. This is accomplished by adding or modifying the following line within your config.sys file:

```
C:\>EDIT CONFIG.SYS
    .
    .
    .
    SHELL = C:\COMMAND.COM C:¦ /E:1024 /P
                      ^          ^
    .             !          !
    .             !          +----Number of bytes allocated for environment space
    .             !
    .             +----Location of your COMMAND.COM program
```

After your config.sys file has been modified, reboot your system and run RADOPTS again. Listing 18.1 shows the standard configuration of the RADOPTS batch file.

Listing 18.1. The standard configuration of the RADOPTS batch file.

```
@echo off
rem
rem
rem Radiosity program default options. Set environment variables to
rem choose program options, not specified in command line.
rem
rem Revision 1.0
rem July, 1992
rem
rem Revision 1.1
rem Antonio Costa 8-Jun-93
rem
set PR_prims=.
rem Path where meshed primitive data files reside
rem MUST be set if using primitives !
set PR_prcs=0
rem Don't log input/output geometry
set PR_debug=0
```

```
rem No debugging
set PR_display=1
rem Display intermediate results
set PR_maxsub=1
rem Adaptive subdivision = maximum subdivision level of 1
set PR_adjsamp=1
rem Use adaptive sampling
set PR_analyt=1
rem Use analytic form factors for special cases
set PR_grid=1
rem Use object bounding volume hierarchy to speed ray-casting
set PR_pgrid=1
rem Use polygon bounding volume hierarchy to speed ray-casting
set PR_maxiter=100
rem Maximum # of iterations before halting
set PR_walk=1
rem Output results for walk-through program
set PR_rcull=1
rem Use receiver + source plane culling
set PR_quadtri=1
rem There are only quadrilaterals and triangles in scene
set PR_shaft=1
rem Use shaft culling algorithm
set PR_cstrag=2
rem 0-closed, 1-open, 2-overlap open, 3-ratio open shaft culling
set PR_amb=1
rem Use ambient term
set FF_perarea=0.1
rem Minimum area percentage of average poly area before halting subdivision
set FF_mindiff=0.015
rem minimum ff edge difference before subdividing patches
```

LightR is a true radiosity preprocessor in that it does not produce an image file when its radiosity solution has been achieved. Instead, LightR produces a scene file for a ray tracer to render. Unlike RAD386, the scene description files (called *patch* files, because they end with the extension .PAT) do not specify a view. Instead, the view parameters are specified in a separate file (ending with the extension .VW), though the radiosity renderer really does not make use of the view file at all. In its original incarnation as a Silicon Graphics IRIS workstation application, LightR enabled the user to view the scene as the solution progressed. This option was not included in the PC port of LightR, because the option made extensive use of OpenGL, a graphics library that takes advantage of the lightning-fast graphics acceleration hardware included with Silicon Graphics workstations. To process a scene file, and produce a scene file to be rendered with the Rtrace ray tracer, use the following command sequence:

```
C:\CHAP18\LIGHTR> LightR -f 1 0 -R 1 4 -p scene.pat -v scene.vw -s 1 -O 1
```

This produces an ASCII file (RES.SCN) that can be used with the Rtrace ray tracing package. As specified earlier, scene.pat is an ASCII file describing the surface geometry of the environment and scene.vw is an ASCII file specifying the position and orientation of the camera within the environment. The -f 1 0 option specifies how the form factors are determined, and the -R 1 4 option specifies that visibility testing be performed with ray casting and that four rays be cast per visibility test. These options are discussed in greater detail in subsequent sections.

When the radiosity preprocess has been completed, it can be ray traced to produce a viewable image file. First, the view information (from scene.vw) must be translated into the SCN format. This can easily be done by hand, because the formats are not very different. Then, the .SCN formatted view information must be combined with the RES.SCN file. This is accomplished by using the DOS copy command:

```
C:\CHAP18\LIGHTR> COPY VIEW.SCN + RES.SCN TRACEME.SCN
```

which produces one file (TRACEME.SCN) that starts with the contents of VIEW.SCN and continues with the contents of RES.SCN. Next, the ASCII scene file TRACEME.SCN must be translated into a more compact format that the ray tracer Rtrace can rapidly process. Rtrace includes a utility program (SCN2SFF.EXE) for accomplishing this task. To translate TRACEME.SCN into TRACEME.SFF, run SCN2SFF with the following options:

```
C:\CHAP18\LIGHTR> SCN2SFF +S15000 TRACEME.SCN > TRACEME.SFF
```

SCN2SFF requires the +S15000 (set maximum surfaces to 15000) option, because LightR produces files containing large numbers of surfaces. Most ray tracing scene files use *implicit* geometric descriptions of surfaces ("give me a sphere at {1.5 2.3 -1} with a radius of 3.1, in that lovely shade of metallic blue I told you about earlier"). They usually do not require many surfaces. LightR, and all radiosity preprocessors, discretize the environment into *explicit* surfaces (the more surfaces, the more accurate the environment). To handle the extra load, SCN2SFF must be told this in advance. To render TRACEME.SFF with Rtrace (and produce an image file TRACEME.PPM), run Rtrace with the following options:

```
C:\CHAP18\RTRACE>Rtrace +S15000 H640 W480 O1 TRACEME.SSF TRACEME.PPM
```

As you probably guessed, Rtrace also needs to know in advance that it will be handling a large number of explicit surfaces. The other parameters give Rtrace details about the output raster image file it is going to produce. The H640 and W480 parameters specify the dimensions of the raster image and the O1 format selects the raster file format (0=PIC/ 1=PPM). When Rtrace is complete, the PPM image can be viewed with DISPLAY or converted to another format with ALCHEMY.

LightR uses progressive radiosity to perform solution convergence and—like RAD386—allows the user to get "preview" radiosity data. LightR supports progressive radiosity with more flexibility. Whereas RAD386 enables the user to determine how many iterations will be performed before producing an output file, LightR continuously works toward solution convergence and enables the user to select multiple iterations of output. In other words, LightR enables the user to produce multiple "exposures" of radiosity. This is accomplished with the -I option. For example:

```
C:\CHAP18\LIGHTR> LightR -f 1 0 -R 1 4 -p scene.pat -v scene.vw -s 1 -0 1 -I 1000 i100
      i300      i500 i900
```

would produce five output files: RES100.SCN, RES300.SCN, RES500.SCN, RES900.SCN, and the final converged solution file RES.SCN. In a multitasking environment like Windows or OS/2, LightR can be set to produce multiple progressive exposures and the user can start the process of converting and raytracing the .SCN files right away.

Batch Rendering

Because both LightR and RAD386 have complicated command interfaces, it might be advantageous to put together a set of batch routines to make the rendering process less complicated. Batch files offer compact, simple interfacing to these applications. If multiple scene or view files are set up, batch files can be used to produce still image frames that can be edited and assembled into MPEG, FLI, AVI, Grasp, or other animation formats. In an ideal situation, one batch file can perform the radiosity preprocess, ray tracing or rendering, antialiasing, and animation assembly, while the artist spends time designing and storyboarding the next animation sequence (or sleeping, as the case may be).

Experiment with the various options offered by RAD386 and LightR by rendering the example files. Gaining familiarity with these tools will help you with the trial and error process of building your own radiosity scenes.

Describing the Environment

Ray tracing software, such as Polyray and POV, uses a scene description language, and radiosity preprocessors, such as RAD386 and LightR, work the same way. Both RAD386 and LightR support a set of geometric primitives including spheres, cylinders, cones, cubes, and polygon meshes constructed out of quadrilateral and triangular facets. Each surface or object has defined properties of reflection and emission. Both LightR and RAD386 require that a viewpoint be specified to the radiosity preprocessor as well. Both LightR and RAD386 come with utilities to convert other file formats from programs like 3D Studio and AutoCAD, but it is important to know how the scene description language works for touching up scenes by hand.

For the following examples (and for future reference when designing your own scenes), remember that any surface within a radiosity environment can be an emitter or reflector of light, and that each surface has both diffuse and specular reflection properties. Some surfaces (such as smooth marble) might not produce diffuse reflections very often if at all, while some surfaces (such as wood) can vary in smoothness and texture. Radiosity imagery can be convincing, even when the geometry of the environments is not detailed or smoothed out. The strength of radiosity is that it accurately models the interaction of the light between surfaces. While your environment models may appear "boxy" at first, the shadows and colors will have subtle nuances if your reflection coefficients are selected carefully.

```
Building a Scene File
RAD386
```

The scene description language used by RAD386 is extremely compact and cryptic, but it is very easy to learn. The first part of a RAD386 scene description file specifies the viewing parameters for this instance of the scene. For our example, we place the camera hovering over the origin looking out along the positive Z axis. To specify this, RAD386 needs to have the position vector of the camera and two orientation vectors: the viewplane surface normal (or "out" vector) and the "up" vector. We want a field of vision of 53 degrees horizontal and 48 degrees vertical, and we would like the rendered image to have a resolution of 640 pixels by 480 pixels in three color bands (red, green, and blue). To specify this information, we key in the following for our view section:

```
v
640 480
0 2.5 0
0 0 1
0 1 0
53 48
3
```

You can probably figure out the formatting from this example very easily:

Horizontal Image Resolution <whitespace> Vertical Image Resolution

> Position Vector of Camera <X> <Y> <Z>
> "Out" Vector of Camera <X> <Y> <Z>
> "Up" Vector of Camera <X> <Y> <Z>
> Horizontal Field of View <whitespace> Vertical Field of View
> Color Channels

The next piece of information required in a RAD386 scene description file is the number of objects within the scene. In this example, we illuminate a sphere with a rectangular surface patch, so we enter the number two and a carriage return. This constitutes the scene file "header." The remainder of the file is surface data.

For our example of a sphere illuminated by a rectangular patch, we do the rectangular patch first. RAD386 enables you to subdivide each surface into smaller patch elements for more accurate surface sampling. The first thing RAD386 needs to know about a surface is how many subdivision are required, so it can allocate the proper amount of memory to represent a surface. For our illuminating patch, we do not need too many elements, because elements are only practical for *reflecting* surfaces, not emitting surfaces. Thus, we only subdivide the fluorescent light surface into two horizontal divisions by two vertical divisions. These are specified as follows:

```
2 2
```

Next, RAD386 needs to know whether this surface is a light source—that is, if it has any radiosity to start with. This is specified by an *emitter flag*. If the emitter flag is set to zero, the surface is a nonemitter. If the emitter flag is set to one (as this one should be), the next line specifies the intensity of the light for each color channel:

```
1
    10 10 10
```

This specifies a bright white light.

The next bit of information is the surface reflection type. For a rough diffuse surface (which we want in this case), we enter zero. For a specular smooth surface, we enter one. Then we enter the reflection coefficients for each color channel. For our white light, key in the following:

```
0
    0.8 0.8 0.8
```

Now we must specify the object surface geometry. This is accomplished with an integer numeric code, followed by a set of real number parameters. The geometric surfaces supported by RAD386 are quadrilateral facet (0), sphere (1), bubble (2), cylinder (3), tube (4), cone (5), cup (6), ring (7), and polygon (8). The set of parameter arguments varies according to the geometric surface type. For this example, we enter the four vertices of the quadrilateral facet in counterclockwise order about the surface normal. In this case, we want the illuminating surface to have its normal facing downwards; we indicate this by specifying the vertices in the following order:

```
0
    -5.0 10.0 5.0
    -5.0 10.0 15.0
    5.0 10.0 15.0
    5.0 10.0 5.0
```

That completes the surface definition for our rectangular fluorescent light. Next, we define a sphere by making use of the same convention. First, we specify the number of horizontal and vertical divisions. For the sphere, we use a large number of divisions: 25 by 25. We make the sphere a reflecting surface by setting its emitter flag to zero and not including any emission coefficients. Then we specify the sphere as a diffuse surface and, to make it blue, give it the proper RGB arguments. The code for a sphere is 1 and the geometric parameters it requires are its position and radius. As an exercise, code the object surface definition for this sphere if it has a radius of two and a position of (-1,5,4). Check your answer on the next page to see if you have the hang of it.

```
25  25
        0
        0
            0.8 0.2 0.2
        1
            -1 5 4
            2
```

The last detail of the RAD386 scene file is optional. To determine visibility, RAD386 employs ray casting. To speed the efficiency of the ray intersection routines, RAD386 employs bounding volumes around each object. Because bounding volumes (such as spheres and boxes) cannot perfectly fit the surfaces of all objects like a second skin, you must subdivide the bounding volumes to allow rays to pass through them when they do not actually intercept the object's surface. RAD386 enables the user to specify the number of bounding volume divisions as the last argument of the scene description file. This argument is specified in terms of x, y, and z axis divisions. For this scene, we use a $10 \times 10 \times 10$ bounding volume subdivision.

```
10  10  10
```

So you will have the complete file, here it is in its entirety. Key it in, save it as SPHERE0.DAT, and render it following the steps outlined in the previous section. First, render it to a full solution (you may have to use a swapfile if you are low on memory) and generate an intensity file SPHERE.INT. Copy the file to SPHERE1.DAT and change the position vector, or one of the orientation vectors, of the viewer to get a feel for how the viewing geometry works. Then, render SCENE1.DAT with the SPHERE.INT intensity file. Notice how much more quickly the rendering is done when an intensity file is used. Keep in mind, though, that the intensity file can only be used when the surface geometry within the scene (not counting the camera position) has not been modified. RAD386 notifies you when you attempt to render a scene with an intensity file that does not match up.

```
V
640 480
0 2.5 0
0 0 1
0 1 0
53 48
3
        2 2
        1
            10 10 10
        0
            0.8 0.8 0.8
        0
            -5.0 10.0 5.0
            -5.0 10.0 15.0
            5.0 10.0 15.0
            5.0 10.0 5.0
```

```
25 25
    0
    0
        0.8 0.2 0.2
    1
        -1 5 4
        2
10 10 10
```

To use the other object surface geometries, all you must do is specify the code and the proper arguments. For your reference, here are the parameters required by each object geometry type:

Code	Geometry	Argument(s)
0	Quadrilateral Patch	4 vertices in counterclockwise order
1	Sphere	Position vector of centerpoint
		Radius
2	Bubble	Position vector of centerpoint
		Radius
3	Cylinder	Centerpoint of Base 1
		Centerpoint of Base 2
		Radius
4	Tube	Centerpoint of Base 1
		Centerpoint of Base 2
		Radius
5	Cone	Apex Point
		Apex Radius
		Base Point
		Base Radius
6	Cup	Apex Point
		Apex Radius
		Base Point
		Base Radius
7	Ring	Center
		Normal Vector
		Inner Radius
		Outer Radius
8	Polygon	Number of Vertices
		Vertices in counterclockwise order

Programming Exercise

Try writing a program in BASIC, C, or PASCAL to generate RAD386 scene description files. A good place to start is a program that generates checkerboard planes suitable for use as floors, walls, or ceilings. Give the user the option of specifying the position and axis of the plane (i.e. Y=0 for a floor, Y=10 for a ceiling, etc.), as well as the surface normal vector, the reflection properties of the odd and even squares, and how many patches are light sources (i.e. "every 5th square is a light source with { 10 10 10 } emittance"). The program should add data onto the end of the file by default, but provide the user with the option of overwriting the file and updating the object count in the file header.

```
- - -
- - -
- - -
```

Building a Scene File
LightR

The scene description language employed by LightR is a little more structured and sophisticated than that afforded by RAD386. Originally, LightR was designed to pipe the radiosity scene file through the C preprocessor provided by Unix on the Silicon Graphics IRIS. As anyone who has used a C preprocessor will tell you, that affords a lot more flexibility than you need. We will now build the same scene using LightR and render it with Rtrace.

To specify the viewpoint for LightR and Rtrace, we must write two separate files: SPHERE.VW and SPHERVW.SCN. The latter, SPHERE.VW, is required by LightR and SPHEREVW.SCN is required by Rtrace. Both files are similar in structure to the header of the RAD386 file, but bear a more sophisticated syntax. Here is the contents of SPHERE.VW:

```
Camera {
      lookfrom 0 2.5 0
      lookat -1 5 4
      lookup 0 1 0
      fovx 53 fovy 48
}
```

Here is the contents of SPHEREVW.SCN:

```
from 0 2.5 0
at -1 5 4
up 0 1 0
fov 53
ambient white
```

The similarity between these two view specifications makes converting by hand simple. The one difference between these two formats and the view specification built into the RAD386 file format is that the `lookat` parameter is not a unit vector, but a point of focus, the location of the surface we are staring at. The parameter specified `-1 5 4` is the centerpoint of the sphere we put in the scene. The `ambient white` term, in SPHEREVW.SCN, specifies a color constant used by the ray tracer as an ambient term that is added to all surface intensities.

Now that the view has been specified, we can go on to write the patch geometry file SPHERE.PAT, which will contain all the geometric and surface data. The first piece of information required by LightR is the number of objects in the file. So, the first thing we should key in for our "sphere illuminated by a rectangular fluorescent light" is the following:

2

Now, we describe each object within the scene. Due to the sophisticated structure and syntax of the LightR scene description language, it may be easier for you to grasp if we give an example and break it down for you. Here is the object description for the fluorescent light:

```
Object Fluoro1 Mesh {
 OWMatrix MFluoro1 { 1 0 0 0 1 0 0 0 1 }
 Prop PGlowWht1
 { E { 10 10 10 } p { 0.8 0.8 0.8 } Kd { 1 } Ks { 0 } }
 NumMeshes 1
 Mesh mesh1 1 {
 Patch norm1 4 {
     { 0 -1 0 } { 0 -1 0}
     { 0 -1 0 } { 0 -1 0}
     }
 Patch vert1 4 {
     { -5 10 5 } { -5 10 15 }
     { 5 10 15} { 5 10 5 }
     }
}
```

The first part of the object's description is the keyword Object, followed by the name of the object. In allowing the user to specify object names, it is much easier for the user to debug his scene description file when geometry errors occur (and they will). No two objects can have the same name. Because we have to inform LightR at the beginning of the scene file as to how many objects are present in the file, it may be a good practice to add the "object number" to the end of each object's name. Following the object name is the object type, followed by an open brace. In this case, we are using a mesh object with only one surface facet. Other object types include cube, cone, cylinder, and sphere.

In the next line, the object to world matrix is specified. Notice that the keyword OWMatrix is followed by a matrix name identifier. Once again, including the object number within the name is highly recommended. The object to world matrix is a transformation matrix of the following form:

```
a  d  g  j
b  e  h  k
c  f  i  l
x  x  x  x
```

It is specified within braces in the form a b c d e f g h i j k l. The last row is assumed to be 0 0 0 1 and, therefore, is not specified. A transformation matrix that scales the object by a factor of two, and translates it (+5, -3, +0), would have the matrix form:

```
2 0 0 5
0 2 0 -3
0 0 2 0
0 0 0 1
```

It would be expressed within a LightR scene description file as follows:

```
OWMatrix mat 2 { 2 0 0 0 2 0 0 0 2 5 -3 0 }
```

The next line in the object format of the LightR scene description language spells out the surface properties of the object. The keyword `Prop` is followed by the property name and open braces. The `E` term spells out how much energy is being emitted by the object's surface, and the `p` term spells out the reflection coefficients of the object's surface. Unlike RAD386, which allows an object's surface to be either diffusely reflective or specularly reflective, LightR allows the surface to be proportionally specular and diffuse. The diffuse reflection scaling coefficient, `Kd`, is specified within the braces following `Kd`; the specular reflection scaling coefficient `Ks` is specified within the braces following `Ks`. The specular and diffuse scaling coefficients must add up to one. To specify the surface properties of a blue carpet, we would key in the following:

```
Prop bluecarpet3 { E { 0 0 0 } p{ 0.7 0 0 } Kd { 1 } Ks { 0 } }
```

The NumMeshes term is equal to the number of polygon meshes defining the object. LightR assumes, by default, that most objects will be made out of patch meshes. Any nonmesh objects (for example, a sphere) will have a NumMeshes value of -1. In the next line, after the keyword `Mesh`, the name of the first (and, in this case, only) mesh is spelled out, followed by the number of surface patches within the mesh. One thing that can be done (and, for consistency with our prior model, should be done here) is to specify automatic patch subdivision. This is done by replacing the word `Mesh` with the keyword `PreMesh`, immediately followed by the level of subdivision. To subdivide the patch into four patch elements, select level one. To subdivide the patch into sixteen patch elements, select degree two. Up to five levels of subdivision are supported to allow 1024 by 1024 patch elements. This can be done with any surface type. Of course, it takes longer to process an image that has surface patches divided into 1024 by 1024 elements, but there may be objects that require it!

For each patch within the mesh (in this case, only one), we specify in counterclockwise order the normal direction and position vectors of the vertices that define the polygon. LightR only supports quadrilateral and triangular facets in the mesh class. The normal vectors must be specified with the format `Patch <normal name> <number of vertices>{`, followed by each normal vector enclosed in braces. The position vectors of the vertices have the same formatting: `Patch <vertex name> <number of vertices> {`, followed by the position vectors of the vertices enclosed in braces.

As an exercise, try coding the object declaration for the blue sphere. It is positioned at {-1, 5, 5} and has a radius of two. Use fourth level surface subdivision to make the sphere somewhat shiny. Notice that the sphere, cylinder, cube, and cone are all unit objects, and you will have to use the object-world transformation matrix.

Scene File Translation Utilities

While it is a valuable experience to become familiar with the scene description languages employed by RAD386 and LightR, it is not very practical or fun to try to build complex scenes by hand. For this reason, both LightR and RAD386 come with a compliment of utilities than can import files from popular modeling and CAD applications. Some of these utilities are standalone programs that process raw files, while others are designed to work within other applications. There are also a number of commercial applications that can convert between multiple file formats. One such application is World Render 3D for Windows, which supports the NFF file format employed by Rtrace.

Importing Files to RAD386

Radiance Support

RAD386 comes with two file conversion utilities. The first is RAD2MC.EXE, a standalone utility that converts scene description files from Greg Ward's Radiance application file format into the format native to RAD386. Radiance is a very robust application with a number of "plug in" utilities that are often called from within the scene description file to build complex objects, generate accurate daylight models, and so on. Radiance was originally developed under Unix, and takes advantage of that operating system's powerful input/output capabilities. In order to accurately process scene files that make use of these utilities, DOS executables of these utilities must be in the same directory as RAD2MC.EXE. Otherwise, those objects that make use of absent utilities will be passed over.

RAD386 does not support all of the surface properties and rendering capabilities included within Radiance. For example, Radiance supports transparent surfaces, texture and bump maps, and free form surfaces. However, RAD386 is capable of producing very convincing images and is an excellent learning tool. Because Radiance is freely available (and can be run on PCs under Linux), it is a valuable experience to learn how to compose environments with the Radiance scene description language and produce results inexpensively and easily with RAD386.

To convert a radiance file to the RAD386 format, enter the following:

```
C:\CHAP18\RAD386\RAD2MC < Radiance.RAD > RAD386.DAT
```

Radiance.RAD is the input Radiance scene description file, and RAD386.DAT is the output RAD386 scene description file.

AutoCAD DXF Support

RAD386 also includes TORAD.LSP, a utility that runs within AutoCAD and converts 3-D drawings to the Radiance format. TORAD.LSP translates AutoCAD primitive objects (3-D facets and meshes, extruded lines, and so on) into triangular, quadrilateral, and polygonal surface patches in the Radiance file format. Complex object hierarchies can be grouped by layer or color. TORAD.LSP runs under AutoCAD 10 and 11 with an interactive menu specified in the file torad.mnu. It runs under AutoCAD 12 with a dialog box specified in the torad.dcl file. Consult your AutoCAD manual for more information on running AutoLisp extensions to AutoCAD.

Importing Files to LightR: Autodesk 3D Studio Support

LightR and Rtrace include many standalone file conversion utilities, most of which work with the GAWK.EXE AWK text processing language interpreter. Using several short but clever batch program files, converting between several file formats is a snap. The two most important conversion utilities are the OFF2PAT.EXE and NFF2PAT.BAT programs. Both enable the user to convert Rtrace files to LightR files. From there, Rtrace includes many AWK and .EXE programs to convert popular CAD and 3-D scene formats into its own.

As an example, consider the following: A user has created a three-dimensional scene of a theatre in Autodesk 3D Studio and wants to render it with LightR and Rtrace. To accomplish this task, Rtrace comes with a utility called 3DS2POV that can convert Autodesk 3D Studio .3DS files into Rtrace compatible .SCN files. To do this, the user types the following:

```
C:\CHAP18\LightR> 3DS2POV -8 Theatre.3ds Theatre.SCN +v -ot
```

Then, the user can convert the `Theatre.SCN` to `Theatre.NFF` by keying in this line:

```
C:\CHAP18\LightR> SCN2NFF Theatre.SCN > Theatre.NFF
```

From there, the NFF file can (finally) be converted to a .PAT file with NFFP2PP.EXE, by keying in the following:

```
C:\CHAP18\LightR> NFFP2PP Theatre.NFF > Theatre.PAT
```

```
RAD386 Support
```

LightR comes with a utility for converting RAD386 scene description files into PAT files. The process, which makes use of the GAWK interpreter, has been made very straightforward with the DAT2PAT.BAT batch file:

```
C:\CHAP18\LightR> DAT2PAT RAD386.FIL > LIGHTR.PAT
```

`RAD386.FIL` is a RAD386 scene description file and `LightR.PAT` is the output scene description file for LightR.

Autodesk DXF Support

Rtrace includes a standalone converter for importing Autodesk Drawing Exchange Files (DXFs) into SCN files. ReadDXF supports a number of ray tracers and renderers. For our purposes, we want the output to be tessellated triangles. To convert the file OFFICE.DXF to OFFICE.SCN, we would key in the following:

```
C:\CHAP18\LightR> READDXF -f OFFICE.DXF -r 8 -t > OFFICE.SCN
```

Follow the same process for converting SCN files to PAT files.

Advanced Concepts and Algorithms of the Radiosity Method

Now that you have had a chance to create simple scenes with RAD386 and LightR, you probably have a solid feel for how the radiosity preprocess works in general. In this section, we will explore the concepts behind the algorithms that make the magic happen. This is not an exhaustive dissection of radiosity algorithms; it is intended to be just an overview to give you a greater understanding of the system as a whole and an introduction to the algorithms and concepts behind the radiosity method. For a more comprehensive, hands on approach to the radiosity method, read my book *3D Graphics, Ray Tracing, and Radiosity* (Sams Publishing, 1994). For a detailed study of the algorithms and cutting-edge research of radiosity, read Michael Cohen's *Radiosity and Realistic Image Synthesis* (Academic Press, 1993). The source codes for both LightR and RAD386 are included on

 this book's CD-ROM. Examples will be given from both to illustrate algorithmic concepts where appropriate, and it may be a valuable exercise to try to build enhancements into these two powerful packages.

The Form Factor

You might recall from the first section that this is the order of operations performed in the radiosity preprocess: The form factors are calculated first for each pairing of patches; then, a matrix of linear equations governing the distribution of light throughout the environment is solved. For any two unique patches, A and B, the form factor FF_{AB} measures how much of the total light energy (radiosity) from patch A arrives at patch B. For a radiosity solution to be achieved, the radiosity preprocessor must construct a table of form factors for all possible patch pairings. The form factor calculation is the most computationally complex and time consuming stage of the radiosity preprocess. Most of the research within the last ten years has been focused toward faster and more accurate form factors.

The original methods of determining form factors were borrowed from radiative heat transfer theory, and used analytic methods that did not take visibility and occlusion (obstruction of light) into account. Analytic methods required an occlusion function in addition to the form factor math. Analytic methods required special formulations for special cases, such that the formulation for determining the form factor between rectangles varied according to uniform area, parallel orientation, adjacency, and so on. More recent methods make use of numerical sampling techniques, which are much more practical because they are not as divided into special cases, and they take occlusion into account. Like all sampling techniques in digital media, trade-offs are made between accuracy and expediency. Both LightR and Rtrace make use of numerical methods, and enable the user to determine how many samples will be taken with command line parameters.

Properties of Form Factors

Form factors are affected by the geometry of a scene, and not by issues of color, intensity, or viewing perspective; therefore, they do not have to be recalculated when changes in lighting, surface color, or camera perspective are made. Light or surface intensity can be amplified, attenuated, or even turned off altogether, while still making use of the same form factors. High-end lighting and interior design applications, such as Lightscape, use the radiosity method with three-dimensional hardware graphics accelerators to allow such changes to be made interactively in real time. Only changes in scene geometry, such as translating, rotating, scaling, or creating objects, require form factor recalculation. Recent research by Baum et al., Chen, and George et al. has produced algorithms that reduce the number of form factors needing recalculation, by determining and recalculating only those form factors affected by the change in geometry.

The form factor between any two surface patches is the ratio of total energy shot out by one patch that is received by the other. This proportionality can be expressed for any two patches, I (transmitter) and J (receiver):

```
FF_IJ = Total Energy Emitted + Reflected By Patch I / Energy From Patch I That Reaches
        Patch J
```

From this equation, we can see that the form factor between any two unique patches will not exceed 1.0, and that the sum of all form factors for any given patch is equal to 1.0. In other words, patch J cannot receive more than one hundred percent of the light energy produced by patch I, and Patch I cannot transmit more than one hundred percent of its total light energy.

Another assumption that can be exploited to reduce the number of form factor calculations is the reciprocity of form factors between patches. For any two patches, i and j, the form factor between i and j, multiplied by the area of i, is equal to the form factor between j and i, multiplied by the area of j:

$$F_{ij} A_i = F_{ji} A_j$$

With a little high school algebra, this can cut the number of form factor calculations in half.

Form Factor Mathematics

Radiosity is a physically based model of energy flow in the real world. Real world surfaces are infinitely detailed and continuous, and the number of photons produced by a light source is astronomical. For these reasons, the calculus employed within radiative transfer theory analytically determines form factors between *differential areas*. In calculus, any continuous surface that is differentiated or *analyzed* is broken down into parts of the smallest scale. The form factor between two differential areas dA_i and dA_j is determined by the following formulation:

$$F_{dA_idA_j} = <\text{Not Blocked}>_{ik} \ast \frac{\cos\theta_i \ \cos\theta_j}{\pi \ r^2}$$

Where:

<NOT BLOCKED> is a binary occlusion function.
r is the distance from patch i to patch j.
dA_i is a differential area on the surface of patch i.
dA_j is a differential area on the surface of patch j.
θ_i is the angle between the vector dA_i - dA_j and the unit normal vector of surface i.
θ_j is the angle between the vector dA_j - dA_i and the unit normal vector of surface j.

The geometric relationships between two patches cannot account for the effects of other surfaces in occluded environments. A third patch (patch 1) could obstruct the flow of light energy from differential area dA_i to differential area dA_j. For this reason, analytic methods of determining form factors in complex environments use a binary function to account for shadows. In this case, the <NOT BLOCKED> term is the output of a binary function that produces a zero if the path between the differential areas is obstructed by another surface, or a one if the path is not obstructed. This way, the form factor is zero (no light is allowed to travel) if the differential area of the receptor surface is in shadow from the transmitter surface.

In calculus, the process of synthesizing a finite surface from a differentiated surface can be accomplished by *integrating* the differential area over the area of the surface. The form factor between a surface patch of finite area (A_i) and a differential area on another surface (dA^j) is expressed as follows:

$$F_{dA_iA_j} = \int_{A_j} \frac{\cos\theta_i \ \cos\theta_j}{\pi \ r^2} \ dA_j$$

Where:

r is the distance from patch i to patch j.

A_i is the finite area of the surface of patch i.

dA_j is a differential area on the surface of patch j.

θ_i is the angle between the vector dA_i - dA_j and the unit normal vector of surface i.

θj is the angle between the vector dAj - dAi and the unit normal vector of surface j.

$$F_{AiAj} = \frac{1}{A_i} \int_{A_i} \int_{A_i} <\text{Not Blocked}>_{ij} * \frac{\cos\theta_i \, \cos\theta_j}{\pi r^2} \, dA_j$$

To work within the constraints placed upon us by the discrete nature of our models and the computers that process them, we must be able to evaluate form factors between two finite surfaces. To rationalize this step (in both mathematics and principle), we must determine the average of the integrated differential form factors:

Where:

r is the distance from patch i to patch j.

A_i is the finite area of the surface of patch i.

A_j is the finite area of the surface of patch j.

$<\text{NOT BLOCKED}>$ is a binary occlusion function.

dA_i is a differential area on the surface of patch i.

dA_j is a differential area on the surface of patch j.

θi is the angle between the vector dA_i - dA_j and the unit normal vector of surface i.

θj is the angle between the vector dA_j - dA_i and the unit normal vector of surface j.

Calculating Form Factors with Numerical Techniques

Because our environmental model is made up of discrete surface patches, the most efficient (and least complicated) way to determine the form factor is to employ numerical sampling algorithms that approximate this formulation from finite area to finite area. Analytic form factor calculation produces more accurate results, but in most cases is overkill. By using sampling algorithms, the user can control the accuracy and time complexity of the radiosity process with the number of samples and the method of gathering them. Larger sample sizes produce more accurate form factors, but at the expense of longer preprocessing time.

Hemispherical Sampling and Nusselt's Analog

In any application in which discrete samples are taken of continuous phenomenon, it is best to analyze the phenomena to determine the most efficient way to make measurements, the limitations or artifacts that result from the method of measurement, and the assumptions that can make the sampling process efficient and accurate. In the case of sampling the effects of geometry upon the transfer of diffuse light energy from one discrete surface patch to another, it is safe to assume that the intensity of the light energy transferred will be affected by the orientation of and distance between both surfaces.

We can assume that the form factor between a surface and itself is always equal to zero and need not be calculated. One possible exception to this rule is concave surfaces, which can be subdivided into convex surfaces, either adaptively or during the modeling stage. If all surfaces are planar, then it can be assumed that all light energy emitted from or reflected by any patch will travel along direction vector(s) within the hemisphere defined by the surface normal.

Nusselt's analog is a theorem utilized in both analytical and numerical methods of determining form factors. Nusselt's analog states that the form factor of a finite area patch can be determined by projecting the patch area onto a unit hemisphere defined by the surface normal vector, and then orthographically projecting the area onto the circular base of the hemisphere. The projected area of the patch gets smaller by a factor of r^2 as the patch gets farther away.

Ray Casting for Form Factors

LightR uses a method of ray tracing to determine the form factor between each pair of patches. Samples are taken from the surface of the "source" patch to approximate the differential areas of the analytical radiosity model. The position of the sample points on the surface of the source patch can be selected by either uniform tessellation or random or pseudorandom techniques (see Listing 18.2).

Listing 18.2. LightR routines for generating uniform or random sample positions on the surface of the source patch.

```
/***************************************************************/
/* Generate samples (s) on a patch (p)                         */
/***************************************************************/
int
ff_Generate_Patch_Samples(p, s, corners, area, normal)
    Polygon        *p;
    Sampletype     s[MAX_SAMPLES];
    Vector         corners[MAX_PATCH_VTX];
    double         area;
```

continues

Listing 18.2. continued

```
  Vector          normal;
{
  int             num_samples;
  int             i;

if (FF_Options.fftype == ANALYTIC_FF)
    num_samples = DEFAULT_ASAMPLES;
  else
  {
    if (FF_Options.varying_numsamps)
      num_samples = Adjusted_NumSamples(p);
    else
      num_samples = FF_Options.num_samples;
  }

  switch (FF_Options.sampling_type)
  {

  case UNITEST:          /* Test only */

    for (i = 0; i < num_samples; i++)
    {
      s[i].p = p;
      s[i].pos = corners[i];
      s[i].norm = normal;
      s[i].area = area / num_samples;
    }
    break;

  case UNIFORM:          /* Sample centres of grid patch */

    if (p->class == PATCH)
      Sample_Quad(p, s, num_samples, UNIFORM, corners, area, normal);
    else if (p->class == TRIANGLE)
      Sample_Triangle(p, s, num_samples, UNIFORM, corners, area, normal);
    break;

  case JITTERED:         /* Sample with centers jittered */

    if (p->class == PATCH)
      Sample_Quad(p, s, num_samples, JITTERED, corners, area, normal);
    else if (p->class == TRIANGLE)
      Sample_Triangle(p, s, num_samples, JITTERED, corners, area, normal);
    break;

  default:
    fprintf(stderr, "%s: Unknown sampling type %d\n", ProgName,
        FF_Options.sampling_type);
    exit(1);
  }
  return (num_samples);
}
```

For each sample, a ray is cast at the receptor patch. If the ray reaches the receptor patch without intersecting any other patches along the way, a *delta form factor* is calculated from the direction and length of the ray, multiplied by the area of the sample, and added into a cumulative delta form factor. After all the samples have been taken, the cumulative delta form factor is divided by the number of samples taken, which results in an average form factor from the source patch to the receptor patch. I refer to this technique of determining form factors as the "number of windows in glass house divided by number of stones thrown" method (see Listing 18.3).

Listing 18.3. LightR routines for determining form factors with ray tracing.

```
int              FF_Testing = 0;      /* Just for testing */
/*****************************************************************/
/* Shoot a ray from vertex to sample point on source            */
/* Return intersection distance                                 */
/*****************************************************************/
int
shoot_ray(ray_orig, ray_dir, s, t)
  Vector         ray_orig, ray_dir;
  Sampletype     s;
  double         *t;
{
  double         tmp;
  Vector         normray_dir;

  tmp = vlen(&ray_dir);           /* Find distance from source to receiver */
  *t = tmp;
  if (FF_Testing)
  {
    printf("\tShooting from %g,%g,%g to %g,%g,%g ",
        ray_orig.x, ray_orig.y, ray_orig.z,
        ray_dir.x, ray_dir.y, ray_dir.z);
    printf("at pos %g %g %g. t = %g\n", s.pos.x, s.pos.y, s.pos.z, *t);
  }
  /*
   * Find out if ray hit any object before reaching sample point on source
   */
  if (Option.visibility == FORM_FACTOR)
  {
    normray_dir = ray_dir;
    norm(&normray_dir);
    if (HitObject(ray_orig, normray_dir, *t))
      return 0;
    else
      return 1;
  } else
    return 1;
}
/*================================================================*/
/* Ray tracing ff — circular disc approximation by [Wallace89]   */
/*    1) Assume uniform weighted area per sample                 */
/*    2) Uniform or jittered sample points on area samples       */
/*================================================================*/
double
ff_da_disc(v, n, p, samples, num_samples)
```

continues

Listing 18.3. continued

```
Vector          v, n;          /* Vertex and normal to sample from */
Polygon         *p;            /* Polygon to be sampled    */
Sampletype      samples[MAX_SAMPLES];    /* Samples on source */
int             num_samples;   /* Number of source samples   */
{
int             i;
  double          ff, cos_angle_v, cos_angle_p, t, dff, w;/* for ff calc */
  Vector          ray_dir;     /* Direction of ray from vtx    */
  Vector          norm_ray_dir;     /* Normalized ray direction     */

  /* Calculate delta form-factor from each sample */
  ff = 0.0;
  for (i = 0; i < num_samples; i++)
  {
    ray_dir = *vsub(&(samples[i].pos), &v);
    norm_ray_dir = ray_dir;
    norm(&norm_ray_dir);
    w = samples[i].area;
    if (shoot_ray(v, ray_dir, samples[i], &t))
    {
      cos_angle_v = dot(&n, &norm_ray_dir);
      cos_angle_p = dot(&(samples[i].norm), vnegate(&norm_ray_dir));
      if (cos_angle_p == 0.0)
      cos_angle_p = cos(DTOR * 90.0);
      dff = (cos_angle_v * cos_angle_p) / ((M_PI * t * t) + samples[i].area);

      /* Take area weighted average of samples as form factor */
      dff = dff * w;
      ff += dff;
    }
  }
  return (ff);
}
.
.
.

/*====================================================================*/
/* Ray tracing ff — elliptical disc approximation [Siegal81]        */
/*====================================================================*/
double
ff_da_ellipse(v, n, p, samples, num_samples)
  Vector          v, n;          /* Vertex and normal to sample from */
  Polygon         *p;            /* Polygon to be sampled    */
  Sampletype      samples[MAX_SAMPLES];    /* Samples on source */
  int             num_samples;   /* Number of source samples   */
{
  int             i;
  double          ff, cos_angle_v, cos_angle_p, t, dff, w;/* for ff calc */
  Vector          ray_dir;     /* Direction of ray from vtx    */
  Vector          norm_ray_dir;     /* Normalized ray direction     */
  double          a, b;

  /* Calculate delta form-factor from each sample */
  ff = 0.0;
  for (i = 0; i < num_samples; i++)
  {
    ray_dir = *vsub(&(samples[i].pos), &v);
```

```
      a = vlen(vsub(&samples[i].pos,
            vmiddle(&samples[i].corners[2], &samples[i].corners[1])));
      if (p->class == TRIANGLE)
        b = vlen(vsub(&samples[i].pos, &samples[i].corners[2]));
      else
        b = vlen(vsub(&samples[i].pos,
              vmiddle(&samples[i].corners[3], &samples[i].corners[2])));

    norm_ray_dir = ray_dir;
    norm(&norm_ray_dir);
    w = samples[i].area;
    if (shoot_ray(v, ray_dir, samples[i], &t))
    {
      cos_angle_v = dot(&n, &norm_ray_dir);
      cos_angle_p = dot(&(samples[i].norm), vnegate(&norm_ray_dir));
      if (cos_angle_p == 0.0)
      cos_angle_p = cos(DTOR * 90.0);

      if (a == b)          /* Is a circle */
      dff = (cos_angle_v * cos_angle_p) / ((M_PI * t * t) + samples[i].area);
      else                 /* Is an ellipse */
      dff = (cos_angle_v * cos_angle_p) /
        (M_PI * sqrt((t * t + a * a) * (t * t + b * b)));
      dff = dff * w;

      /* Take area weighted average of samples as form factor */
      ff += dff;
    }
  }
  return (ff);
}
```

This method is the easiest to implement and apply with sophisticated variations. Instead of casting a small number of rays "at" each target patch, a larger number of rays can be cast in all directions, and form factors are then determined by tabulating which rays hit which surfaces. Each ray direction vector can be determined with uniform or random direction vectors in the hemisphere defined by the surface normal.

The Hemicube

An alternative approach to ray casting that makes use of Nusselt's analog is the Hemicube, which was originally researched by Michael F. Cohen at Cornell University. Nusselt's analog determines form factors by projecting the patch onto the surface of a hemisphere. Any two patches that occupy the same projected area on the hemisphere (or on any surrounding surface) will have the same form factor. Cohen's method projects the patch onto a half cube (hemicube) occupying the same position as Nusselt's hemisphere. Each of the five faces of Cohen's hemicube is divided into a two-dimensional array of pixels. Instead of containing color or intensity information, each face of the hemicube acts as a modified Z-buffer, in which each pixel has a depth value, a delta form factor, and a pointer to a patch. See Figure 18.7.

FIGURE 18.7.
Numerical form factor calculation. Cohen's hemicube (top) and hemispherical ray tracing (bottom).

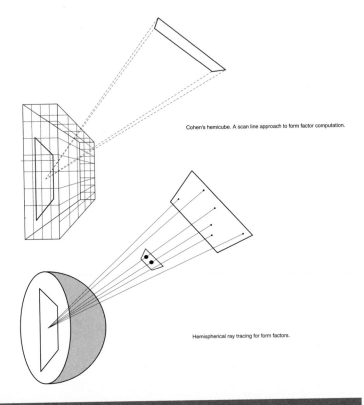

Cohen's hemicube. A scan line approach to form factor computation.

Hemispherical ray tracing for form factors.

An Interview with Michael F. Cohen

Michael F. Cohen is the author of *Radiosity and Realistic Image Synthesis* (Cohen and Wallace, Academic Press, 1993), and has been involved in radiosity research since 1984. Cohen's hemicube and progressive refinement algorithms have been some of the most significant advances in radiosity research. Presently, Michael Cohen is an assistant professor in the department of Computer Science at Princeton University.

WPN: Do you feel that the radiosity method and other physically based models represent the future of computer graphics software?
MFC: Absolutely; in terms of physically based methods. The specific algorithms may be based on other numerical schemes, but the need for methods that provide reliable simulations is quite clear for a number of applications.
WPN: Comparing the computing and graphics capabilities of the desktop personal computer with the mainframes and workstations of ten years ago, do you feel that the desktop PC is capable of the radiosity method?

MFC: Sure. PCs are clearly now enough for many image synthesis problems. The research community, of course, keeps trying to push the bounds with the fastest machines available. But for many architects and designers, the power provided by the PC is enough for a large portion of their work.

WPN: What trends in hardware and software (operating systems, object oriented design, RISC architecture, hardware graphics acceleration) do you think have had (and will have) an effect upon computer graphics? What trends, if any, do you think hold promise for the future of graphics computing?

MFC: I suspect the biggest influence will be due to the availability in the near future of consumer priced systems capable of truly amazing 3-D graphics. This can already be seen in the recent games systems and as this technology moves into the home, the demand for better content will increase. At the same time, my guess is that there will be a new round of PC graphics boards for more general-purpose 3-D graphics.

WPN: Considering your research on the radiosity method, what limitations have been overcome and what enhancements have been produced in the last ten years?

MFC: The big problems in radiosity methods mostly deal with issues of complexity. At Princeton, the hierarchical methods of Hanrahan et al., and the Wavelet methods of Gortler et al., have helped enormously here. At this year's SIGGRAPH, Fowler et al. provided a description of a system that can deal with enormous databases. Finally, a good handle on error metrics has been given by Jim Arvo and his colleagues at Cornell.

WPN: If someone wanted to build a very simple radiosity preprocessor for occluded environments, what methods would you recommend for determining the form factors and computing the solution?

MFC: The simplest and most straightforward form factor evaluator is a ray tracer that stochastically selects points on each element and traces a ray between them to determine occlusion, and then just sums the contributions.

WPN: Could you describe the evolution of radiosity that has resulted from specialized applications such as architectural rendering and theatrical lighting design? What kinds of trade-offs are made when a complex system like radiosity is taken out of the research environment and placed in the mainstream?

MFC: The biggest problem in real-world applications is probably dealing with the input of geometry from other modeling systems. For example, models may not have oriented polygons, or polygons that were meant to touch do not exactly, and this causes "light leaks." Finally, as mentioned earlier, the meshing problem is difficult.

WPN: What sort of research are you presently conducting? Do you feel that your research in radiosity has been completed or do you see it as something continuous?
MFC: I am continuously looking at improving this methodology. At the same time, my personal interests go beyond just rendering, to animation and geometric modeling. I think there is still a great deal to do and am continually amazed at the new work appearing at SIGGRAPH and elsewhere each year.

Initially, the hemicube is aligned with the source patch (patch i) and initialized. Initialization constitutes calculating the delta form factors, and setting depth values to the maximum and patch pointers to null for each pixel in the hemicube. To determine all the form factors for the target patch, each of the other patches in the environment are clipped with the Sutherland-Hodgman clipping algorithm and projected onto the hemicube surface. At each projection, the pixels covered by the projected patch (patch j) are compared with their default values. If the depth value of the projected patch is closer than the depth value already stored in the pixel, the pixel is updated with the new depth value and a patch pointer that references patch j. When all of the patches have been projected onto the hemicube surface, the form factor for each patch j is calculated by totalling up the delta form factors for all hemicube pixels that point to patch j. After all the form factors for patch i have been calculated, the hemicube must be aligned with the next patch. The hemicube process must be executed for each patch in the environment.

Because the hemicube is loosely based upon the Z-buffer algorithm, it has all the advantages and disadvantages associated with the Z-buffer. Many graphics accelerators have hardware Z-buffers that can be exploited to take the burden of processing off of the central processing unit. Unfortunately, the hemicube suffers from the same aliasing artifacts that a regular Z-buffer produces. Most Z-buffers have resolutions between 50×50×25 and 100×100×50; as always, alias artifacts are less visible when higher sampling resolutions are employed.

$$\cos\Phi_i = \cos\Phi_j = \frac{1}{\sqrt{x^2 + y^2 + 1}}$$

$$r = \sqrt{x^2 + y^2 + 1}$$

$$\Delta FF = \frac{\cos\Phi_i \cos\Phi_j}{\pi r^2 dA}$$

RAD386 uses the hemicube technique to determine form factors, as did the original version of LightR (for the Silicon Graphics IRIS). Many radiosity packages designed for Unix workstations make special use of hardware Z-buffers, projection transformations, and shading algorithms to rapidly calculate form factors with the hemicube method. Because graphics acceleration hardware is growing exponentially in sophistication and speed, the same techniques may soon be applicable on the desktop PC as well (see Listing 18.4).

Listing 18.4. RAD386 functions for calculating form factors with the hemicube method.

```
/*
      Computation of Form factor for Full Radiosity Solution.
*/
#include <stdio.h>
#include <math.h>
#ifdef __WATCOMC__
#include <string.h>
#else
#include <memory.h>
#endif
#include <malloc.h>

#include "GraphicsGems.h"
#include "data_structure.h"
#include "objects.h"
#include "vox.h"

#include "raddecl.h"

extern int hemicube_resolution;
extern int verbose_flag;
int ProjectionByRaytracing=0;

static double **TopFace_delta_form_factor;
static double **SideFace_delta_form_factor;
struct Hemicube{
        short int *topface;
        short int *rightface;
        short int *leftface;
        short int *frontface;
        short int *backface;
};
static double **F; /* Form Factors */
static double **A; /* N x N Matrix */
static double **I;  /* Computed Intensity */
static double **deltaI;  /* Delta Intensity for progressive radiosity */
static double *B;
static struct Hemicube hemicube;

#define Iter_Threshold 0.0001
#define VeryHigh 1.e5
```

continues

Listing 18.4. continued

```c
static double **alloc_matrix(rows,cols)
int rows,cols;
{
    char *s="Cannot Allocate Matrix.";
    double **m;
    int i;
    m = (double **)malloc(rows*sizeof(double *));
    if (m==NULL) error(s);
    for (i=0;i<rows;i++) {
        m[i] = (double *)malloc(cols*sizeof(double));
        if (m[i] == NULL) error(s);
    }
    return(m);
}
static void allocate_hemicube()
{
    TopFace_delta_form_factor=
        alloc_matrix(hemicube_resolution,hemicube_resolution);
    SideFace_delta_form_factor=
        alloc_matrix(hemicube_resolution/2,hemicube_resolution);
    hemicube.topface=(short int *)malloc(
        hemicube_resolution*hemicube_resolution
        *sizeof(short int));
    hemicube.rightface=(short int *)malloc(
            hemicube_resolution/2*hemicube_resolution
            *sizeof(short int));
    hemicube.leftface=(short int *)malloc(
            hemicube_resolution/2*hemicube_resolution
            *sizeof(short int));
    hemicube.frontface=(short int *)malloc(
            hemicube_resolution/2*hemicube_resolution
            *sizeof(short int));
    hemicube.backface=(short int *)malloc(
            hemicube_resolution/2*hemicube_resolution
            *sizeof(short int));
}
static void free_matrix(m,rows,cols)
double **m;
int rows,cols;
{
    int i;
    for (i=0;i<rows;i++) free(m[i]);
    free(m);
}
static void deallocate_hemicube()
{
    free_matrix(TopFace_delta_form_factor,
        hemicube_resolution,hemicube_resolution);
    free_matrix(SideFace_delta_form_factor,
        hemicube_resolution/2,hemicube_resolution);
    free(hemicube.topface);
    free(hemicube.rightface);
    free(hemicube.leftface);
    free(hemicube.frontface);
    free(hemicube.backface);
}
```

```
/*
        compute_delta_form_factors : For the faces of the hemicube.
                Side faces are symmetric, so only one computation
                is enough.
*/
static compute_delta_form_factors()
{
        int i,j;
        double x, y, y2, delta;
        double factor;
        double z,zfactor,z2;
        double halfdelta;
        double delta_area_by_pi;

    delta  = 2.0/hemicube_resolution;
    halfdelta =delta/2.0;
    delta_area_by_pi=delta*delta/PI;

      for(i=0,y=(-1.0+halfdelta); i < hemicube_resolution; i++,y+=delta){
              y2 = y*y;
              for (j=0,x=(-1.0+halfdelta); j < hemicube_resolution; j++,x+=delta){
                      factor=1.0/(x*x+y2+1.0);
                      TopFace_delta_form_factor[i][j]=
                              delta_area_by_pi*factor*factor;
              }
        }
        for (i=0,z=halfdelta; i < hemicube_resolution/2; i++,z+=delta){
              z2 = z*z; zfactor = z*delta_area_by_pi;
              for(j=0,y=(-1.0+halfdelta); j < hemicube_resolution; j++,y+=delta){
                      factor=1.0/(y*y+z2+1.0);
                      SideFace_delta_form_factor[i][j]=zfactor*factor*factor;
              }
        }
}

static void increment_F(rows,raster,f,inc)
int rows;
short int *raster;
double f[];
double **inc;
{
    int i,j,k,patchnum;
    for(i=k=0;i<rows;i++)
        for(j=0;j<hemicube_resolution;j++,k++)
            if (patchnum=raster[k])
                f[patchnum-1] += inc[i][j];
}

static void extract_F_i(i)
int i;
{
    int nn;
        for(nn=0;nn<total_surface_grid_points;nn++)F[i][nn]=0.;
    increment_F(hemicube_resolution,hemicube.topface,
```

continues

Listing 18.4. continued

```
        F[i],TopFace_delta_form_factor);
    increment_F(hemicube_resolution/2,hemicube.rightface,
        F[i],SideFace_delta_form_factor);
    increment_F(hemicube_resolution/2,hemicube.leftface,
        F[i],SideFace_delta_form_factor);
    increment_F(hemicube_resolution/2,hemicube.frontface,
        F[i],SideFace_delta_form_factor);
    increment_F(hemicube_resolution/2,hemicube.backface,
        F[i],SideFace_delta_form_factor);
}

static init_fullmatrix_radiosity()
{
    /* Allocate space for form factor */
    F = alloc_matrix(total_surface_grid_points,total_surface_grid_points);
    A = alloc_matrix(total_surface_grid_points,total_surface_grid_points);
    I = alloc_matrix(color_channels,total_surface_grid_points);
    B = (double *)malloc(total_surface_grid_points*sizeof(double));
    allocate_hemicube();
    compute_delta_form_factors();
}
static deinit_fullmatrix_radiosity()
{
    /* Free space allocated for FormFactor */
    free_matrix(F,total_surface_grid_points,total_surface_grid_points);
    free_matrix(A,total_surface_grid_points,total_surface_grid_points);
    free_matrix(I,color_channels,total_surface_grid_points);
    free(B);
    deallocate_hemicube();
}

static init_progressive_radiosity()
{
    /* Allocate space for form factor */
    F = alloc_matrix(1,total_surface_grid_points);
    I = alloc_matrix(color_channels,total_surface_grid_points);
    deltaI = alloc_matrix(color_channels,total_surface_grid_points);
    allocate_hemicube();
    compute_delta_form_factors();
}
static deinit_progressive_radiosity()
{
    free_matrix(F,1,total_surface_grid_points);
    free_matrix(I,color_channels,total_surface_grid_points);
    free_matrix(deltaI,color_channels,total_surface_grid_points);
    deallocate_hemicube();
}

static void from_specular_surface(ray,objectnum,t,u,v,n)
Ray *ray;
int objectnum;
double t,u,v;
int *n;
{
    Vector3 N;
        /* .... set the new ray */
        point_on_line(ray->start,ray->direction,t,ray->start);
```

```
          N = ofunc[object[objectnum].surface_geometry_type].get_surface_normal
               (object[objectnum].object_specific_structure,u,v);
          mirror_reflection(&N,&(ray->direction),&(object[objectnum]));
          (ray->number)++;
        *n=get_diffuse_surface(ray);
}
static void from_diffuse_surface(ray,objectnum,t,u,v,n)
Ray *ray;
int objectnum;
double t,u,v;
int *n;
{
     int uindex=grid_u(objectnum,u);
     int vindex=grid_v(objectnum,v);
     *n=(object[objectnum].start_grid_index+
          gridindex(objectnum,uindex,vindex)+1);
}
static void from_other_surface(ray,objectnum,t,u,v,n)
Ray *ray;
int objectnum;
double t,u,v;
int *n;
{
       error("Not Implemented.");
}
static void (*get_patchnum[MAX_REFLECTION_TYPE])()={
       from_diffuse_surface,
       from_specular_surface,
       from_other_surface
};

static int get_diffuse_surface(ray)
Ray *ray;
{
     double t_entry,t_exit;
     int HitBoundingBox();
       if (HitBoundingBox(&(volume_grid.extent.min),&(volume_grid.extent.max),
              &(ray->start),&(ray->direction),&t_entry,&t_exit)){
              int get_nearest_object_in_voxel();
              Vlist *create_vlist();
              Vlist *vlist,*templist;
              double t,u,v;
           int nearest_object= UNDEFINED;
              vlist=templist=create_vlist(
                    &(ray->start),&(ray->direction),t_entry,t_exit
              );
              while (templist!=NULL){
                    Voxel *vox = volume_grid.voxels+templist->voxnum;
                      if(vox->nobjects)
                    nearest_object=get_nearest_object_in_voxel
                      (ray,templist->t_near,templist->t_far,vox,&t,&u,&v);
                      if (nearest_object!= UNDEFINED) break;
                      templist=templist->next;
              }
              purge_vlist(vlist);
              if (nearest_object!= UNDEFINED){
              int n;
```

continues

Listing 18.4. continued

```
                get_patchnum[object[nearest_object].surface_reflection_type]
                (ray,nearest_object,t,u,v,&n);
                return(n);
        }
    }
    return(0);
}
/*
int dump_buffer(rows,cols,b)
int rows,cols;
char *b;
{
    int i,j,k;
    fprintf(stderr,"\nDumping buffer\n");
    for(i=k=0;i<rows;i++){
        fprintf(stderr,"%02d.....",i);
        for(j=0;j<cols;j++,k++)
            fprintf(stderr,"%1d",b[k]);
        fprintf(stderr,"\n");
    }
}
int dump_raster(rows,cols,b)
int rows,cols;
short int *b;
{
    int i,j,k;
    fprintf(stderr,"\nDumping raster\n");
    for(i=k=0;i<rows;i++){
        fprintf(stderr,"%02d.....",i);
        for(j=0;j<cols;j++,k++)
            fprintf(stderr,"%1d",b[k]);
        fprintf(stderr,"\n");
    }
}
*/
static long project(C,N,U,V,rows,raster)
Point3 *C;
Vector3 *N,*U,*V;
int rows;
short int *raster;
{
    static long RayNumber=0;
    Ray ray;
    Vector3 Dir,delta_U,delta_V,half_delta_U,half_delta_V;
    int i,j,k;

    half_delta_U=delta_U = *U;
    V3Scale(&delta_U,2./hemicube_resolution);
    V3Scale(&half_delta_U,1./hemicube_resolution);
    half_delta_V=delta_V = *V;
    V3Scale(&delta_V,2./hemicube_resolution);
    V3Scale(&half_delta_V,1./hemicube_resolution);
    V3Add(N,V,&Dir); V3Sub(&Dir,U,&Dir);
    V3Add(&Dir,&half_delta_U,&Dir); V3Sub(&Dir,&half_delta_V,&Dir);
    ray.number=total_rays+RayNumber;
#if defined (DEBUG)
```

```
               ray.intersections=0;
        #endif
               ray.path_length= -1;
               if (ProjectionByRaytracing)
               for(i=k=0;i<rows;i++){
                    Vector3 dir;
                    dir = Dir;
                    for(j=0;j<hemicube_resolution;j++,k++){
                         ray.start = *C;
                         ray.direction=dir;
                         V3Normalize(&(ray.direction));
                         raster[k]=get_diffuse_surface(&ray);
                         (ray.number)++;
                         V3Add(&dir,&delta_U,&dir);
                    }
                    V3Sub(&Dir,&delta_V,&Dir);
               }
               else {
               double *zbuffer;
               char *surface_buffer;
               Matrix4 view_matrix;
               int n=rows*hemicube_resolution;
               extern void (*geometry_specific_scan_convert[MAX_GEOMETRY_TYPE])();
               /* Clean up the raster */
               memset((char *)raster,0,n*sizeof(short int));
               /* Set up a Z-buffer of equal dimension */
               zbuffer=(double *)malloc(n*sizeof(double));
               if (zbuffer == NULL)
                 error("Cannot allocate Z-buffer memory for scan conversion.");
               for(i=0;i<n;i++)zbuffer[i]=VeryHigh;
               surface_buffer=(char *)calloc(n,1);
               if (surface_buffer == NULL)
                 error("Cannot allocate surface-buffer memory for scan conversion.");
               /* Compute View transform matrix */
               view_transform(C,U,V,N,rows,hemicube_resolution,&view_matrix);
               for(i=0;i<number_objects;i++){
                    /* Project each object on the raster */
                    geometry_specific_scan_convert[
                         object[i].surface_geometry_type
                    ](i,N,&view_matrix,rows,hemicube_resolution,
                         zbuffer,surface_buffer,raster);
               }
               free((char *)zbuffer);
        /*
        dump_raster(rows,hemicube_resolution,raster);
        dump_buffer(rows,hemicube_resolution,surface_buffer);
        */
               for(i=k=0;i<rows;i++)
               for(j=0;j<hemicube_resolution;j++,k++)
                    if ((surface_buffer[k]-1)>DIFFUSE){
                         ray.start = *C;
                         ray.direction.x=Dir.x+j*delta_U.x-i*delta_V.x;
                         ray.direction.y=Dir.y+j*delta_U.y-i*delta_V.y;
                         ray.direction.z=Dir.z+j*delta_U.z-i*delta_V.z;
                         V3Normalize(&(ray.direction));
```

continues

Listing 18.4. continued

```
                raster[k]=get_diffuse_surface(&ray);
                (ray.number)++;
          }
    free(surface_buffer);
    }
    return(RayNumber = (ray.number-total_rays));
}

static long project_on_hemicube(c,m)
Point3 *c;
Matrix4 *m;
{
    Vector3 X,Y,Z,Xneg,Yneg,Zneg;
    long n;

    X.x = 1.; X.y=X.z = 0.;
    X = transform_vector(&X,m); V3Normalize(&X); Xneg=X; V3Negate(&Xneg);
    Y.y = 1.; Y.x=Y.z = 0.;
    Y = transform_vector(&Y,m); V3Normalize(&Y); Yneg=Y; V3Negate(&Yneg);
    Z.z = 1.; Z.x=Z.y = 0.;
    Z = transform_vector(&Z,m); V3Normalize(&Z); Zneg=Z; V3Negate(&Zneg);
    /* Project on Top Face */
    project(c,&Z,&X,&Y,hemicube_resolution,hemicube.topface);
    /* Project on Left Face */
    project(c,&Xneg,&Y,&Z,hemicube_resolution/2,hemicube.leftface);
    /* Project on Right Face */
    project(c,&X,&Yneg,&Z,hemicube_resolution/2,hemicube.rightface);
    /* Project on Front Face */
    project(c,&Yneg,&Xneg,&Z,hemicube_resolution/2,hemicube.frontface);
    /* Project on Back Face */
    n=project(c,&Y,&X,&Z,hemicube_resolution/2,hemicube.backface);
    return(n);
}

static hemicube_method(i,j,k,n,nrays)
int i;  /* Object num */
int j;  /* Vertical Grid */
int k;  /* Horizontal grid */
int n;  /* Patch num */
long *nrays;
{
    Matrix4 m;
    Vector3 N;
    Point3 centre;
    if (object[i].surface_reflection_type==MIRROR)return;
    centre = ofunc[object[i].surface_geometry_type].
         compute_center_point_in_the_grid_cell(i,j,k);
    N=ofunc[object[i].surface_geometry_type].
         get_surface_normal
         (object[i].object_specific_structure,
         (k+0.5)/object[i].grid_h_reso,
         (j+0.5)/object[i].grid_v_reso);
    m  = ofunc[object[i].surface_geometry_type].
         get_local_matrix(
         &N,object[i].object_specific_structure);
    *nrays=project_on_hemicube(&centre,&m);
```

```
    }
static long compute_F_ij()
{
    int i,j,k,n;
    long nrays;
    if (verbose_flag)fprintf(stderr,"From Factor:");
    for (i=n=0;i<number_objects; i++){
        for(j=0;j<object[i].grid_v_reso;j++)
        for(k=0;k<object[i].grid_h_reso;k++,n++){
            hemicube_method(i,j,k,n,&nrays);
            extract_F_i(n);
            if (verbose_flag)fprintf(stderr,".");
        }
    }
    if (verbose_flag)fprintf(stderr,"\n");
    return(nrays);
}
```

Achieving Equilibrium: The Process of Solution Convergence

Any radiosity environment can be described mathematically with a matrix of simultaneous linear equations. To determine the distribution of light energy throughout the environment requires a solution to the matrix. The first methods employed in the early research into the radiosity method were direct methods that are prohibitively complex and slow—impractical for detailed environments. Most radiosity systems employ iterative methods for achieving the energy balance solution. Most of the research in the area of energy balance has sought to develop more efficient iterative algorithms, either by requiring fewer iterations or by producing usable results within the first few iterations before the solution has converged. The techniques employed by LightR and RAD386 are both iterative methods: The Gauss-Seidel Solution convergence of the matrix of equations was initially accomplished with direct methods, which are prohibitively complex and slow. Most radiosity systems today make use of iterative techniques like the Gauss-Seidel and Progressive Radiosity methods used by both RAD386 and LightR.

Properties of the Radiosity Environment Matrix

The radiosity environment consists of surface patches, each of which is described in terms of its reflectance and emittance. The goal of the radiosity method is to determine the radiosity of each patch, which is equal to the sum of the energy emitted by the patch (if it is a light source) and the energy reflected by the patch back into the environment. To determine the energy reflected by a patch, you must first determine the energy arriving at the patch with the form factors. From the properties of these parameters, some properties can be gleaned about the system we are trying to solve:

1. The sum of all energy reflected or absorbed by the surfaces within the environment is equal to the sum of all energy emitted by light sources within the environment.

2. The sum of all the form factors for any patch equals one.

3. None of the reflectivity terms in any patch is greater than one.

The interaction between surfaces is characterized by a set of matrices, K, with one for each color band of reflectivity. Each matrix has dimensions n×n, where n is the number of unknown radiosities. Each row i of the K matrix accounts for the interaction between a patch i and all the other patches in the environment with the following form:

$$
\begin{matrix}
1 - p_1\,F_{1,1} & -p_1 F_{1,2} & -p_1 F_{1,3} & \cdots & -p_1 F_{1,n} \\
1 - p_2\,F_{1,1} & -p_2 F_{1,2} & -p_2 F_{1,3} & \cdots & -p_2 F_{1,n} \\
\cdot & & & & \\
\cdot & & & & \\
\cdot & & & & \\
-p_{n-1} F_{n-1,1} & & & & \\
-p_n F_{n,1} & \cdot & \cdot & \cdots & 1 - p_n,F_{n,n} \\
\end{matrix}
$$

This matrix is diagonally dominant, which is to say the sum of the absolute values of each row is less than the main diagonal term $(1 - p_1 F_{1,1})$. Because the diagonal term has a form factor to itself $(F_{1,1})$, and reflectivity values are always less than 1.0, the value of the diagonal term will always be one. The sum of form factors for any row are equal to one, and the reflectivity values are always less than one, so any radiosity matrix will be diagonally dominant. Cohen and Greenberg determined in 1985 that matrices that are diagonally dominant rapidly converge to a solution when the Gauss-Seidel iterative method is applied.

All iterative methods begin with an estimated solution and at each subsequent iteration modify the approximation so that it is closer to equilibrium. When the approximation is within a tolerable proximity to the actual solution, the iterative system has been converged. The system is approximated with the form:

$$\mathbf{K\,B}^{\text{iteration}} = \mathbf{E}$$

Where :

K is the aforementioned matrix of interactions.
B is the radiosity vector.
E is the emission vector.

The difference between $B^{\text{iteration}}$ and the actual solution B is an error quantity, and cannot truly be measured until B has been solved. An approximate measure of error is the residual vector r^0, which measures how much of the energy from light sources has been accounted for in the total radiosity of the system.

$$\mathbf{r}^0 = \mathbf{K\,B}^0 - \mathbf{E}$$

Where:

r^0 is the residual vector.

K is the matrix of interactions.

B^0 is the initial approximation of the system radiosity at iteration 0—when only light sources have radiosity.

E is the energy emittance term.

When the emitted energy equals the radiosity of the system, all of the energy in the system has been distributed and accounted for. As the guesses become closer to the actual solution, the residual vectors get smaller. The more effort that is put into determining accurate guesses (especially the initial one), the more rapidly the solution progresses. Both the Gauss-Seidel Iterative Method and the Progressive Radiosity Method are relaxation methods that work by modifying the radiosity of a patch so that its residual vector will be set to zero on the next iteration. See Figure 18.8.

FIGURE 18.8

Shooting and gathering radiosity with the Progressive Radiosity Method (top) and the Gauss-Seidel Iterative Method (bottom).

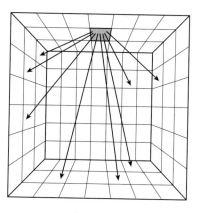

Shooting Radiosity

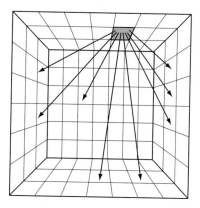

Gathering Radiosity

Gauss-Seidel Iterative Method

The Gauss-Seidel Iterative Method starts by setting all patch radiosities to zero (except those with emission coefficients greater than zero). At each iteration, each patch's radiosity value is updated by adding up the contributions of all the other patches. LightR makes use of a variation on the Gauss-Seidel method by updating the patches with the largest residual vectors first and calculating contributions from the other patches to produce more accurate radiosity values. In any given iteration, a patch i is selected because it has the largest residual vector. Then, for all the other j patches, a contributed energy value is calculated by scaling the radiosity (B_j) by the form factor (FF_{ij}), effectively gathering the light energy from all the other patches in the environment. This method updates the environment one patch at a time. The solution quickly resembles the finished solution, because the ordering of patch selection is based upon unshot energy. Because one patch's radiosity is updated by all the others, this is also known as *gathering* (see Listing 18.5).

Listing 18.5. Gauss-Seidel Iterative method functions employed by RAD386.

```
/*
(e)  Gauss Siedel Method of iterative Simultaneous Equation Solver.
     _ _ _ _ _ _ _ _ _ _ _ _ _ _ _ _ _ _ _ _ _ _ _ _ _ _ _ _ _

         Interface :
                 gauss_iter(n,a,x,b)
                 _ _ _ _
                 where
                         n - is the dimension
                         a - Array of pointers
                             pointing to array of float.
                         b,x - arrays of float
                         tolerance - A scalar float value
                                 much smaller than 0.

     WARNING:
            Matrix must be Diagonal Dominant.
            Otherwise converging is not guaranteed.
*/
#include <stdio.h>
#include <math.h>
extern int verbose_flag;
double **matrix(),*vector();
int gauss_iter(n,a,x,b,tolerance)
int n;
double **a,*x,b[];
double tolerance;
{
    double newx;
    double maxdelta;
    int count=0;
    if (verbose_flag)fprintf(stderr,"Iter Solve : ");
    do{
        int i;
        maxdelta=0.0;
        for(i=0; i < n; i++){
```

```
                    int j;
                    float delta;
                    newx = b[i];
                    for (j = 0; j < n; j++)
                        if (j!=i)newx=newx-a[i][j]*x[j];
                    newx /= a[i][i];
                    delta = (float)fabs(newx - x[i]);
                    x[i]=newx;
                    if (delta > maxdelta) maxdelta=delta;
        }
            if (verbose_flag)fprintf(stderr,".");
            count++;
            if (count > n) break;
        }while (maxdelta > tolerance);
        if (verbose_flag)fprintf(stderr,"\n");
}
int diagonally_dominant(n,a)
int n;
double **a;
{
    int i,j;
    double sum;
    for(i=0;i<n;i++){
        for(j = 0,sum = -fabs(a[i][i]);j<n;j++) sum += fabs(a[i][j]);
        if(fabs(a[i][i])<sum)return(0);
    }
    return(1);
}
```

Progressive Radiosity

Progressive radiosity is designed to quickly converge upon a solution by starting off with a very accurate initial approximation. Just as with the Gauss-Seidel Iterative method, the surface with the most unshot energy is chosen. But, the difference is that instead of up-dating its radiosity with all the other patches radiosities in the environment, it updates all the other patch radiosities with its own. This is also known as *shooting*. Progressive radiosity selects the patch with the most energy—including energy already shot, not just the largest (*unshot energy*) residual vector—and distributes it to the rest of the environment. The progressive refinement algorithm used by LightR makes use of unshot energy by averag-ing the unshot radiosity from all the patches to create an *ambient* term. This energy is added to the partial solution when an "in progress" iteration is written to disk at the re-quest of the user to allow the image to have some visibility.

Adaptive Patch Subdivision

RAD386 and LightR both enable the user to describe surfaces with single surface patches and *premesh* the surface into smaller entities for more detail. If a large area within an environment is discretized into one surface, that surface probably will not appear very realistic, because it will only be allowed to have one single radiosity value (one shade of color). In real life, the continuous surface would be interrupted by shadow gradients, color bleeding, and other visual peculiarities that only the radiosity method can account for. Systems that support adaptive patch subdivision break a surface up into smaller patches when there is a severe contrast between adjacent form factors.

The process works by rapidly determining a solution, analyzing the surface to find any abrupt changes in form factors, subdividing those patches with severe discontinuities into patch elements, and then recursively recalculating the form factors for the modified system. When the system has been subdivided to a predefined level, the system performs the solution convergence process. LightR supports adaptive patch subdivision when the PR_maxsub variable has been set to a value other than one. The variable PR_maxsub determines the maximum number of subdivisions LightR will support. The FF_perarea and FF_mindiff variables control the subdivision process: FF_perarea controls how small the subdivisions can be, and FF_mindiff sets the form factor threshold at which subdivision occurs (see Listing 18.6).

Adaptive patch subdivision is shown in Figure 18.9. Surface C is illuminated by surface A and is partially in shadow from occlusion by surface B. Figure I represents the scale as it would appear in real life. Figure II represents the results obtained with constant radiosity. Figure III shows adaptive patch subdivision. Figure IV shows the results obtained by adaptive patch subdivision.

FIGURE 18.9.

Adaptive patch subdivision smooths out discontinuities.

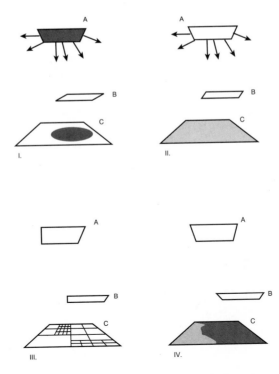

Listing 18.6. Progressive Radiosity Functions employed by LightR.

```
/**********************************************************************/
/* rad.c                                                           */
/*                                                                 */
/* Radiosity solution step routines. Algorithms used:             */
/*                                                                 */
/* General:                                                        */
/*    Back face culling of source and receiver planes.            */
/*    Receiver subdivision by: visibility, intensity gradients    */
/* Chen89:                                                         */
/*    progressive refinement                                      */
/* Wallace89, etc:                                                 */
/*    Hierarchical bounding volumes with object bv culling        */
/*    Has ray casting for visiblity testing                       */
/* Haines91: shaft culling                                         */
/* (see documentation)                                            */
/*                                                                 */
/* Initial program shell taken from E. Chen in Graphics Gems II, 1991 */
/*                                                                 */
/* Copyright (C) 1992, Bernard Kwok                               */
/* All rights reserved.                                           */
/* Revision 1.0                                                   */
/* May, 1992                                                      */
/*                                                                 */
/* Revision 1.1                                                   */
/* Antonio Costa 9-Jun-93                                         */
/*                                                                 */
/* Revision 1.2                                                   */
/* Antonio Costa 25-Jun-93                                        */
/*                                                                 */
/**********************************************************************/
#include <stdio.h>
#include <math.h>
#include <stdlib.h>
#include <sys/time.h>
#include <sys/resource.h>
#include "geo.h"
#include "struct.h"
#include "rad.h"
#include "display.h"
#include "io.h"
#include "misc.h"
#include "ff.h"
#include "bvol.h"
#include "ray.h"
#include "scull.h"
#include "rtime.h"

#include "radmisc.h"

Polygon      *shootPatch;     /* Current shooting patch              */
Polygon      *recPatch;       /* Current receiver patch              */
Polygon      *prev_Shooter = 0;   /* Previous shooting patch          */
float        avg_rec = 0.0;   /* Average percent receivers per iteration */
int          num_src_samples;/* Number of source samples             */
```

continues

Listing 18.6. continued

```c
/*******************************************************************/
/* Initialize list of possible receivers                        */
/*******************************************************************/
void
Init_ReceiverList(p)
  RadParams       *p;
{
  int             i;
  Elist           *el, *tmp;

  if (Option.debug)
    printf("\t> Initializing initial receiver list\n");
  el = p->elements;
  for (i = 0; i < p->num_elements; i++)
  {
    tmp = el->next;
    free(el);
    el = tmp;
  }
  p->num_elements = p->num_receivers = 0;
  p->eltail = p->elements = 0;
}

/*******************************************************************/
/* Initialize structures for ray traced form factors            */
/*******************************************************************/
void
Init_RayTrace()
{
  if (Option.debug)
    printf("\t> Initializing for ray traced ff\n");
  StartIntersect();
}

/*******************************************************************/
/* Find initial set of elements to display                      */
/*******************************************************************/
void
Create_Initial_ReceiverList(theScene)
  Scene           *theScene;
{
  int             i, j, k;
  Scene           *sptr = theScene;
  Objectt         *optr;
  Mesh            *mptr;
  Polygon         *pptr;

  Init_ReceiverList(&ReadLog);
  for (i = 0, optr = sptr->objects; i < sptr->num_objects; i++, optr++)
    for (j = 0, mptr = optr->meshes; j < optr->num_meshes; j++, mptr++)
      for (k = 0, pptr = mptr->polys; k < mptr->num_polys; k++, pptr++)
      Find_Receivers(pptr, (Polygon *) INITIAL_DISPLAY, 1);
}

/*******************************************************************/
```

```
/* Initialize radioisity parameters, not set when reading scene      */
/************************************************************************/
void
Init_Rad(theScene)
  Scene           *theScene;
{
  if (Option.debug)
    printf("\n\t*** Initializing radiosity structures ***\n");

  /* Prepare the original scene */
  Create_Initial_ReceiverList(theScene);

  /* Initialize for ray traced or hemicube form-factor calcs */
  if (Option.ff_raytrace)
  {
    Init_RayTrace();
    if (FF_Options.shaft_cull)
      Init_ShaftStats();
  } else
    InitHemicube();

  /* Prepare for display of intermediate PR steps if option set */
  if (Option.show_pr_steps)
  {
    if (Option.debug)
    {
      print_View(stderr, &(ReadLog.displayView));
      printf("\t> Displaying initial results\n");
    }
    Create_Display_Buffer(ReadLog.displayView.xRes, ReadLog.displayView.yRes);
    if (Option.ambient)          /* Find initial ambient term */
      ReadLog.ambient_term = Pr_Ambient_Term();
    DisplayResults(ReadLog.displayView);
  } else
  {
    if (Option.debug)
      print_View(stderr, &(ReadLog.displayView));
  }
}

int             iteration = 1;
/************************************************************************/
/* Print current iteration                                            */
/************************************************************************/
int
Print_Iter()
{
  int             i;

  /* Print out intermediate results if specified */
  if (Option.write_result)
  {
    for (i = 0; i < num_inter; i++)
      if ((iteration - 1) == intermed[i])
        {
        if (test_scn)
          Write_RadSCN(ReadLog, Option.OutSceneFilename, iteration);
```

continues

Listing 18.6. continued

```
    else
      Write_Rad(ReadLog, Option.OutSceneFilename, iteration);
    i = num_inter + 1;
      }
  }
  /* LogConv_Pt(iteration, ReadLog.totalEnergyLeft); */
  LogConv_Pt(iteration, ReadLog.totalEnergyLeft / ReadLog.totalEnergy);
  printf("\n\t*** Iteration %d. Energy Left = %g (%g %%) ***\n",
      iteration, ReadLog.totalEnergyLeft,
      ReadLog.totalEnergyLeft / ReadLog.totalEnergy * 100.0);

  if (Option.device == FILES)
    fprintf(Option.StatFile,
        "\n\t*** Iteration %d. Energy Left = %g (%g %%) ***\n",
        iteration, ReadLog.totalEnergyLeft,
        ReadLog.totalEnergyLeft / ReadLog.totalEnergy * 100.0);
  iteration++;
  return iteration;
}

/********************************************************************/
/* Form linkage between this patch and all others [Hanrahan91] (not */
/* implemented)                                                     */
/********************************************************************/
void
Form_Linkages(pptr)
  Polygon         *pptr;
{
  if (Option.debug)
    printf("\t> Linkages for %s%d\n", pptr->name, pptr->id);
}

/********************************************************************/
/* Forming of linkages between patches using BF_Refinement [Hanra91]  */
/* (not used)                                                       */
/********************************************************************/
void
Do_Linkage()
{
  int             i;
  Elist           *Int_List;
  int             Int_ListSize;
  Elist           *elptr;
  Polygon         *pptr;

  if (Option.debug)
  {
    printf("\n\t*** Forming patch linkages ***\n");
  }
  /* Setup list of patches to compare against others */
  Create_Initial_ReceiverList(&RadScene);
  Int_List = ReadLog.elements;      /* This is wrong ! Need to fix ! */
  Int_ListSize = ReadLog.num_elements;

  elptr = Int_List;
  for (i = 0; i < Int_ListSize; i++)
```

```
    {
      pptr = elptr->element;
      Init_ObjectList();
      Make_ObjectList(pptr, &Scene_BVH, 1);
      Make_ReceiverList(pptr);
      Form_Linkages(pptr);
    }
}

/**********************************************************************/
/* Cleanup stuff, and log statistics                                 */
/**********************************************************************/
void
Do_Cleanup()
{
  /* Collect statistics for rays and shaft */
  if (Option.tablelog)
  {
    fprintf(rlogfile, "%d \\\\\n%g \\\\\n%g \\\\\n",
          iteration - 1, ReadLog.totalEnergyLeft,
          ReadLog.totalEnergyLeft / ReadLog.totalEnergy * 100.0);
  }
  /* Log CPU times */
  Print_Times(Option.StatFile, FF_Options.shaft_cull);

  if (Option.device == PRINT)
    EndIntersect(stdout);
  else
    EndIntersect(Option.StatFile);
  if (FF_Options.shaft_cull)
    EndShaft(TRUE, Option.StatFile);

  /* Log percent receivers per iteration */
  if (Option.tablelog)
    fprintf(rlogfile, "AR:%g \\\\\n", avg_rec);

  /* Log convergence results */
  LogConv(0, "");

/* Save final image, if any (only on IRIS) */
  if (Option.show_pr_steps)
  {
    if (Option.write_result)
    {
      /*
       * getsize(&xsize, &ysize); Save_Screen_Image(xsize, ysize, 3,
       * "rad.img");
       */
    }
    /* Cleanup display buffers */
    CleanUpBuffers();
  }
}


/**********************************************************************/
/* Radiosity main algorithm                                          */
/**********************************************************************/
```

continues

Listing 18.6. continued

```
void
Do_Rad()
{
  int            xsize, ysize;
  float          iter_start, iter_end;

  if (Option.debug)
    printf("\n\t*** Doing radiosity computations ***\n");

  LogConv(1, Option.meshfilename);      /* Start logging convergence data */

  /* Start recording iteration */
  iter_start = Cpu_Time(&tstats.utime, &tstats.stime);

  while (((shootPatch = FindShootPatch()) != 0) &&
      (Print_Iter() <= ReadLog.max_iterations + 1))
  {
    prev_Shooter = shootPatch;
    Init_ObjectList();
    if (Option.grid)
    {
      Make_ObjectList(shootPatch, &Scene_BVH, 1);
      if (Option.debug)
    Print_ObjectList();
    }
    Make_ReceiverList(shootPatch);
    ComputeFormfactors(shootPatch);
    Distribute_Rad(shootPatch);

    if (ReadLog.num_receivers > 0)
    {                       /* Need at least 1 receiver */
      if (Option.show_pr_steps)
      {
      if (Option.ambient)
      {
        ReadLog.ambient_term = Pr_Ambient_Term();
        print_Spectra(stdout, "Ambient term", ReadLog.ambient_term);
      }
      DisplayResults(ReadLog.displayView);
      }
    }                       /* At least 1 receiver */
    Subdivide_Elements();

    if (Option.ff_raytrace)
    {
      if (Option.device == PRINT)
      EndIntersect(stdout);
    } else
      FreeSumFactors();
  }

  /* Stop recording iteration */
  iter_end = Cpu_Time(&tstats.utime, &tstats.stime);
  tstats.tot_time += (iter_end - iter_start);
  tstats.avg_iter += (iter_end - iter_start) / (float) (iteration - 1);
  tstats.avg_ff = tstats.avg_ff / (float) (iteration - 1);
  tstats.avg_shaft /= (float) (iteration - 1);
```

```
      tstats.avg_ray /= (float) (iteration - 1);
      avg_rec /= (float) (iteration - 1);

      if (Option.UseVCR)
      {                       /* Stop the video */
        vcr_end_video();
      }
      /* Cleanup program */
      Do_Cleanup();
}

/*******************************************************************/
/* Check if at bottom of poly tri-quad tree, i.e. poly is leaf node   */
/*******************************************************************/
int
IsLeaf(pptr, children)
  Polygon         *pptr;
  int             children[MAX_PATCH_CHILDREN];
{
  int             i;
  int             no_children = 1;    /* Assume no children */

  for (i = 0; i < MAX_PATCH_CHILDREN; i++)
    if (pptr->child[i] != 0)
    {
      no_children = 0;
      children[i] = 1;
    } else
    {
      children[i] = 0;
    }
  return (no_children);
}

/*******************************************************************/
/* Add polygon to element list as possible receiver                */
/*******************************************************************/
void
AddTo_ReceiverList(pptr, patches_seen)
  Polygon         *pptr;
  int             patches_seen;
{
  Elist           *elptr;

  /*
   * printf("\t> Adding reciever[%d] %s%d = %d\n", ReadLog.num_receivers,
   * pptr->name, pptr->id, patches_seen);
   */
  elptr = (Elist *) malloc(sizeof(Elist));
  elptr->element = pptr;
  elptr->next = 0;
  elptr->ff = 0.0;              /* Reset form-factor */
  elptr->is_subdivided = 0;     /* Reset subdivision flag */
  elptr->is_receiver = patches_seen;    /* Mark if element is a receiver */

  if (ReadLog.num_elements == 0)
  {                       /* First possible receiver */
```

continues

Listing 18.6. continued

```
    ReadLog.elements = elptr;
    ReadLog.eltail = elptr;
  } else
  {
    ReadLog.eltail->next = elptr;
    ReadLog.eltail = elptr;
  }
  ReadLog.num_elements++;      /* Count total # of elements */
  if (patches_seen)
    ReadLog.num_receivers++;      /* Count # of receivers */
}

/*********************************************************************/
/* Check if any of sources unshot energy will be reflected by the    */
/* receiver                                                          */
/*********************************************************************/
int
Receiver_ReflectsEnergy(rec, src)
  Polygon        *rec, *src;
{
  int            i;
  Spectra        rec_p;
  Spectra        src_uB;
  double         pB_sum = 0.0;
  double         p_sum = 0.0;

  rec_p = poly_reflect(rec);
  src_uB = src->unshot_B;
  pB_sum = 0.0;
  for (i = 0; i < MAX_SPECTRA_SAMPLES; i++)
  {
    pB_sum += rec_p.samples[i] * src_uB.samples[i];
    p_sum += rec_p.samples[i];
  }

  /*
   * If reflects no unshot or has no reflectance, then it is not a receiver.
   */
  if ((pB_sum < DAMN_SMALL) || (p_sum < DAMN_SMALL))
    return 0;
  else
    return 1;
}

/*********************************************************************/
/* Find all elements for a poly = all leaves in tri/quad polygon tree */
/*********************************************************************/
void
Find_Receivers(pptr, src, patches_seen)
  Polygon        *pptr;
  Polygon        *src;
  int            patches_seen;
{
  int            i;
  int            children[MAX_PATCH_CHILDREN];
  BoundingBoxType pbox;
```

```
     if (IsLeaf(pptr, children))
     {

       if (src == INITIAL_DISPLAY)
       {                         /* Display all, flag is meaningless */
         AddTo_ReceiverList(pptr, 1);
       }
       /*
        * Do checks on geometry to see if patch is a potential receiver for
        * source (only if still a possible receiver)
        */
       else if (patches_seen == 0)
       {
         AddTo_ReceiverList(pptr, 0);
       } else
       {
         pbox = BoxPoly(pptr);

         if (src == pptr)
         {                         /* Can't see yourself ! */
       AddTo_ReceiverList(pptr, 0);
         } else if ((pptr->Pfather != 0) &&
             (src->Pfather == pptr->Pfather || pptr->Pfather == src))
         {
       AddTo_ReceiverList(pptr, 0);      /* Can't see your own patch */
         }
         /*
          * If receiver is behind, or on the plane of the source then the source
          * cannot "see" it
          */
         else if (Bounds_Behind_Plane(&pbox, src->normal[0], src->d))
         {
       AddTo_ReceiverList(pptr, 0);
         } else
       AddTo_ReceiverList(pptr, patches_seen);
       }

   } else
     {
       for (i = 0; i < MAX_PATCH_CHILDREN; i++)
       {
         if (children[i])
         Find_Receivers(pptr->child[i], src,
                   patches_seen);
       }
     }
   }

/********************************************************************/
/* Check if any of sources unshot energy will be reflected by the   */
/* receiver                                                         */
/********************************************************************/
int
Object_ReflectsEnergy(rec_p, src)
   Spectra         rec_p;
   Polygon         *src;
```

continues

Listing 18.6. continued

```
{
int             i;
Spectra         src_uB;
double          pB_sum = 0.0;

src_uB = src->unshot_B;
pB_sum = 0.0;
for (i = 0; i < MAX_SPECTRA_SAMPLES; i++)
  pB_sum += rec_p.samples[i] * src_uB.samples[i];

/*
 * If reflects no unshot or has no reflectance, then is not a receiver !
 */
if (pB_sum < DAMN_SMALL)
  return 0;
else
  return 1;
}

/***********************************************************************/
/* Find potential receivers. Use some culling to speed up stuff       */
/***********************************************************************/
void
Make_ReceiverList(shootPatch)
  Polygon       *shootPatch;
{
  int             i, j, k;
  int             patches_seen;
  Scene           *sptr = &RadScene;
  Objectt         *optr;
  Object_List     *olptr;
  Mesh            *mptr;
  Polygon         *pptr;
  Spectra         rec_p;

  if (Option.debug)
    printf("\n\t> Finding receivers\n");

  /*
   * Empty list of potential receivers, and then scan all polygons for
   * potential receivers
   */

  Init_ReceiverList(&ReadLog);

  /* Use bounding volumes to try and reduce number of receivers */
  if (Option.grid)
  {
    for (i = 0, olptr = objlist; i < objlist_size; i++, olptr = olptr->next)
    {
      optr = olptr->hbox->object;

      /*
       * If object's bounding volume can be seen, and object will reflect some
       * energy then assume polygon is a receiver
       */
```

```
      if (olptr->is_receiver)
      {
     rec_p = obj_reflect(optr);
     olptr->is_receiver = Object_ReflectsEnergy(rec_p, shootPatch);
      }
      patches_seen = olptr->is_receiver;
      for (j = 0, mptr = optr->meshes; j < optr->num_meshes; j++, mptr++)
     for (k = 0, pptr = mptr->polys; k < mptr->num_polys; k++, pptr++)
     {

       /* Find potential receivers = elements of patches */
       Find_Receivers(pptr, shootPatch, patches_seen);
     }
    }
   }
   /* Don't use bounding volumes. Must scan all objects */
   else
   {
     for (i = 0, optr = sptr->objects; i < sptr->num_objects; i++, optr++)
     {

      /*
       * if object can reflect some energy then assume polygon is a receiver
       */
      rec_p = obj_reflect(optr);
      patches_seen = Object_ReflectsEnergy(rec_p, shootPatch);

      for (j = 0, mptr = optr->meshes; j < optr->num_meshes; j++, mptr++)
      for (k = 0, pptr = mptr->polys; k < mptr->num_polys; k++, pptr++)
      {

       /* Find potential receivers = elements of patches */
       Find_Receivers(pptr, shootPatch, patches_seen);
      }
     }
   }
  printf("\tNumber of receivers / total = %d / %d\n",
      ReadLog.num_receivers, ReadLog.num_elements);
  if (Option.statistics)
  {
    if (Option.device == FILES)
     fprintf(Option.StatFile, "\tNumber of receivers / total = %d / %d\n",
         ReadLog.num_receivers, ReadLog.num_elements);
    avg_rec += (float) ReadLog.num_receivers / (float) ReadLog.num_elements;
  }
}


/****************************************************************/
/* Print current shooting patch                                */
/****************************************************************/
void
Print_ShootPatch(pptr, fptr, energySum)
  Polygon       *pptr;
  FILE          *fptr;
  double         energySum;
{
  FILE           *fp;
```

continues

Listing 18.6. continued

```c
  if (Option.device == PRINT)
    fp = stdout;
  else
    fp = fptr;
  fprintf(fp, "\tShooter %s%d unshot: %g %g %g -> %g\n",
        pptr->name, pptr->id, pptr->unshot_B.samples[0],
        pptr->unshot_B.samples[1], pptr->unshot_B.samples[2], energySum);
}

/**********************************************************************/
/* Find next shooting patch based on unshot energy for each patch    */
/* Return 0 if convergence is reached, otherwise return 1            */
/**********************************************************************/
Polygon         *
FindShootPatch()
{
  Polygon           *shootPatch;
  int               i, j, k, l;
  double            energySum, error, maxEnergySum;
  Scene             *sptr = &RadScene;
  Objectt           *optr;
  Mesh              *mptr;
  Polygon           *pptr;

  if (Option.debug)
    printf("\n\t> Finding shooting patch\n");

  maxEnergySum = 0.0;
  shootPatch = 0;

  /* Scan all polygons for energy levels, and potential receivers */
  ReadLog.totalEnergyLeft = 0.0;
  for (i = 0, optr = sptr->objects; i < sptr->num_objects; i++, optr++)
    for (j = 0, mptr = optr->meshes; j < optr->num_meshes; j++, mptr++)
      for (k = 0, pptr = mptr->polys; k < mptr->num_polys; k++,
        pptr = pptr->next)
      {

      /*
       * Find patch with maximum energy to shoot and compute total energy
       * left in scene
       */
      energySum = 0.0;
      for (l = 0; l < MAX_SPECTRA_SAMPLES; l++)
      {
        energySum += pptr->unshot_B.samples[l] * pptr->area;
      }
      ReadLog.totalEnergyLeft += energySum;

      if (energySum > maxEnergySum)
      {
        if (pptr != prev_Shooter)
        {
          shootPatch = pptr;
          maxEnergySum = energySum;
        }
```

```
        }
         }

    if (shootPatch == 0)              /* No shooting patch found */
      return (0);

    /* Check for convergence */
    error = maxEnergySum / ReadLog.totalEnergy;
    if (error < ReadLog.threshold)
      return (0);
    else
    {
      Print_ShootPatch(shootPatch, Option.StatFile, maxEnergySum);
      printf("\t\tShooting patch has energy %g\n", maxEnergySum);
      if (Option.debug)
      {
        fprintf(stdout, "\t> Shooting Patch is:\n");
        print_Polygon(stdout, "", shootPatch);
      }
      return (shootPatch);
    }
}


/**********************************************************************/
/* Find approximate centre of a polygon. Average of vertices used.   */
/**********************************************************************/
Vector
Poly_Center(pptr)
  Polygon        *pptr;
{
  int            i;
  Vector         center;
  double         ratio;

  center.x = center.y = center.z = 0.0;
  ratio = 1.0 / (double) pptr->numVert;
  for (i = 0; i < pptr->numVert; i++)
  {
    center.x += pptr->vert[i]->pos.x;
    center.y += pptr->vert[i]->pos.y;
    center.z += pptr->vert[i]->pos.z;
  }
  center.x = center.x * ratio;
  center.y = center.y * ratio;
  center.z = center.z * ratio;
  return (center);
}


/**********************************************************************/
/* Check for receiver subdivision due to:                            */
/*  1) Form factor > unity.                                          */
/*  2) Form factor gradient > gradient threshold.                    */
/* Return whether did subdivision or not.                            */
/**********************************************************************/
int
Receiver_Subdivision(ff, eptr, vtx_ff)
```

continues

Listing 18.6. continued

```
double          *ff;
Polygon         *eptr;
double          vtx_ff[MAX_PATCH_VTX];
{
  int           i, ii;
  int           do_subdiv = 0;
  double        ff_diff;
  int           level_area = 0;

  if (Option.debug)
    printf("\tDoing subdivision tests...\n");

  /* TEST 1 : Is ff > one */
  if (*ff > 1.0)
  {
    if (Option.debug)
      printf("\t++ Form factor %g > 1. Subdividing poly\n", *ff);
    *ff = 1.0;
    do_subdiv = 1;            /* Do subdivision          */
  }
  if (eptr->level >= FF_Options.max_levels)     /* Only to max level      */
    return 0;
  if (eptr->area <= FF_Options.min_element_area)     /* Only to min area */
    return 0;

  /* Only for ray cast ff computations. */
  if ((Option.ff_raytrace) && (do_subdiv == 0) &&
      (eptr->level < FF_Options.max_levels))
  {
    i = 0;
    while ((do_subdiv == 0) && (i < eptr->numVert))
    {
      ii = (i + 1) % eptr->numVert;

      /*
       * TEST 2 : ff gradient is too large between vertices of edges on the
       * polygon, stop if too small
       */
      ff_diff = fabs(vtx_ff[i] - vtx_ff[ii]);
      if (ff_diff > FF_Options.F_diff_edge)
      {
    if (Option.debug)
      printf("\t++ F diff = %g - %g = %g. Subdividing poly\n",
          vtx_ff[i], vtx_ff[ii], ff_diff);
    do_subdiv = 1;           /* Do subdivision */
      } else
      {
    i++;
      }
    }
  }
  return (do_subdiv);
}

/*********************************************************************/
/* Use hemicube to calculate form-factor from shooting patch to       */
```

```
/* receiver elements.                                              */
/* (Modified from Eric Chen (Graphics Gems II), 1991)             */
/*****************************************************************/
void
ff_Hemicube(shootPatch)
  Polygon         *shootPatch;
{
  long            i;
  Vector          up[5];
  Vector          lookat[5];
  Vector          center;
  Vector          normal, tangentU, tangentV, vec;
  int             face;
  double          norm_length;
  Polygon         *sp;              /* Shooting patch */
  Elist           *elptr;     /* Receiving elements */
  double          *fp;
  long            receiver_num = 0;

  /* Get center of shootPatch */
  sp = shootPatch;
  center = Poly_Center(sp);
  if (Option.debug)
    printf("\t ** Poly center is %g,%g,%g\n", center.x, center.y, center.z);
  normal = sp->normal[0];

  /* rotate hemicube along normal axis of patch randomly */
  /* will reduce hemicube aliasing artifacts */
  do
  {
    vec.x = RandomFloat;
    vec.y = RandomFloat;
    vec.z = RandomFloat;
    tangentU = cross(&normal, &vec);
    norm_length = norm(&tangentU);
  } while (norm_length == 0);

  /* compute tangentV */
  tangentV = cross(&normal, &tangentU);

  /* assign lookats, and ups for each hemicube face */
  lookat[0] = *vadd(&center, &normal);
  up[0] = tangentU;
  lookat[1] = *vadd(&center, &tangentU);
  up[1] = normal;
  lookat[2] = *vadd(&center, &tangentV);
  up[2] = normal;
  lookat[3] = *vsub(&center, &tangentU);
  up[3] = normal;
  lookat[4] = *vsub(&center, &tangentV);
  up[4] = normal;

  /* place cube at center of shooting patch */
  hemicube.view.lookfrom = center;
```

continues

Listing 18.6. continued

```
/* Allocate temporary ff space of size of (number of receivers in scene) */
/* Note: this # changes with subdivision */
InitSumFactors(ReadLog.num_receivers);

for (face = 0; face < 5; face++)
{
  hemicube.view.lookat = lookat[face];
  hemicube.view.lookup = up[face];

  /* Only draw receiver elements */
  receiver_num = 0;
  if (Option.show_pr_steps)
    Begin_DrawHC(hemicube.view, kBackgroundItem, face);
  for (i = 0, elptr = ReadLog.elements; i < ReadLog.num_elements; i++)
  {
    if (elptr->is_receiver)
    {
   Draw_Element(elptr->element, (unsigned long) receiver_num++);
    }
    elptr = elptr->next;
  }
  if (Option.show_pr_steps)
    End_DrawHC();

  /* if (Option.debug) printf("+ summing delta ff\n"); */
  if (face == 0)
    SumFactors(hemicube.view.xRes, hemicube.view.yRes,
          hemicube.view.buffer, hemicube.topFactors);
  else
    SumFactors(hemicube.view.xRes, hemicube.view.yRes / 2,
          hemicube.view.buffer, hemicube.topFactors);
}

/* Compute reciprocal form-factors, save in receiver list. */
elptr = ReadLog.elements;
fp = formfactors;

for (i = 0; i < ReadLog.num_elements; i++)
{
  if (elptr->is_receiver)
  {
    elptr->ff = *fp * sp->area / elptr->element->area;

    /* Check for receiver subdivision */
    elptr->is_subdivided =
   Receiver_Subdivision(&elptr->ff, elptr->element, (double *) 0);
    fp++;
  }
  elptr = elptr->next;
}
}

/****************************************************************/
/* Use ray tracing to compute form factors                     */
/****************************************************************/
void
```

```
ff_RayTrace(shootPatch)
  Polygon       *shootPatch;
{
  int           i;
  Elist         *elptr;      /* Receiving elements */
  Polygon       *recPatch;
  BoundingBoxType sbox, rbox;     /* Source / Receiver bboxes */
  Sampletype    src_samples[MAX_SAMPLES];      /* Samples of source */
  Vector        src_corners[MAX_PATCH_VTX];
  int           patches_close = 0;
  int           tmp;
  float         shaft_start, shaft_end;

  /*
   * Find corners of source area, and generate sample points on source patch
   */
  for (i = 0; i < shootPatch->numVert; i++)
    src_corners[i] = shootPatch->vert[i]->pos;
  num_src_samples =
    ff_Generate_Patch_Samples(shootPatch, src_samples,
                  src_corners, shootPatch->area,
                  shootPatch->normal[0]);

  /* Create source bbox if shaft culling */
  if (FF_Options.shaft_cull)
  {
    StartShaft();
    sbox = BoxPoly(shootPatch);
  }
  /*
   * Calculate element to shooting patch form factors for all potential
   * receivers
   */
  elptr = ReadLog.elements;
  for (i = 0; i < ReadLog.num_elements; i++)
  {
    if (elptr->is_receiver)
    {
      recPatch = elptr->element;

      /* Shaft cull bounding volume hierarchy of scene */
      if (FF_Options.shaft_cull)
      {
      Init_ObjectList();
      rbox = BoxPoly(recPatch);

      shaft_start = Cpu_Time(&tstats.utime, &tstats.stime);
      ShaftCull(shootPatch, recPatch, sbox, rbox, &Scene_BVH);
      shaft_end = Cpu_Time(&tstats.utime, &tstats.stime);
      tstats.avg_shaft += (shaft_end - shaft_start);

      if (Option.debug)
      {
        Print_Shaft(shootPatch, recPatch, stdout);
        Print_CandidateList();
```

continues

Listing 18.6. continued

```
    }
   }
   /* Only do source, receiver plane culling */
   else if (FF_Options.src_rec_cull)
  Cull_ObjectList(recPatch);

   if (FF_Options.use_analytic)
   if (patches_close = Patches_Abut(shootPatch, recPatch))
   {
     tmp = FF_Options.fftype;
     FF_Options.fftype = ANALYTIC_FF;
   }
   /* Use equal weight per vtx ff to get patch ff */
   elptr->ff = ff_patches(shootPatch, recPatch,
                  elptr->vtx_ff, num_src_samples,
                  src_samples, src_corners) /
  (double) elptr->element->numVert;
   if (FF_Options.use_analytic)
   if (patches_close)
     FF_Options.fftype = tmp;

   /* Check for receiver subdivision */
   if (elptr->ff < 0.0)
  elptr->ff = 0.0;
   elptr->is_subdivided =
  Receiver_Subdivision(&elptr->ff, recPatch, elptr->vtx_ff);
   if (elptr->ff > 1.0)
  elptr->ff = 1.0;
   }
   elptr = elptr->next;
  }

  if (FF_Options.shaft_cull)
    EndShaft(FALSE, Option.StatFile);
}

/*********************************************************************/
/* Use ray tracing to compute form factors                         */
/*********************************************************************/
void
Subdivide_Elements()
{
  int            i;
  Elist          *elptr;    /* Receiving elements              */

  elptr = ReadLog.elements;
  for (i = 0; i < ReadLog.num_elements; i++, elptr = elptr->next)
  {
    if (elptr->is_receiver)
      if (elptr->is_subdivided)
      Subdivide_Polygon(elptr->element);
  }
}

/*********************************************************************/
/* Calc form-factors from shooting patch to every element          */
```

```
/******************************************************************/
void
ComputeFormfactors(shootPatch)
  Polygon        *shootPatch;
{
  if (Option.debug)
    printf("\n\t> Computing form factors\n");

  /* Compute form-factors */
  if (Option.ff_raytrace)
    ff_RayTrace(shootPatch);      /* Element to shooting patch factors */
  else
    ff_Hemicube(shootPatch);      /* Shooting patch to element factors */
}


/******************************************************************/
/* Distribute energy to elements                                  */
/******************************************************************/
void
Distribute_Rad(shootPatch)
  Polygon        *shootPatch;
{
  long           i, j, k;
  Polygon        *ep;            /* Receiver to update */
  Elist          *elptr;     /* List of receivers */
  Spectra        delta_B;      /* Change in patch radiosity */
  Spectra        vtx_delta_B[MAX_PATCH_VTX];      /* Change in vertex radiosity */
  double         weight;     /* Weight of element to patch */
  Spectra        element_p;    /* Elements reflectance */
  double         element_ff;    /* Elements form factor */

  if (Option.debug)
    printf("\n\t> Distributing energy\n");

  /* Distribute unshot radiosity to every element */
  elptr = ReadLog.elements;
  for (i = 0; i < ReadLog.num_elements; i++, elptr = elptr->next)
  {
    if (elptr->is_receiver)
    {
      ep = elptr->element;
      element_ff = elptr->ff;

      if (element_ff != 0.0)
      {
      element_p = poly_reflect(ep);

      /* Store vertex radiosity changes, and compute patch changes */
      if (Option.ff_raytrace)
      {
        /* weight = 1.0; */
        weight = 1.0 / ep->numVert;
        for (k = 0; k < ep->numVert; k++)
        {
```

continues

Listing 18.6. continued

```
    for (j = 0; j < MAX_SPECTRA_SAMPLES; j++)
    {
      delta_B.samples[j] = 0.0;
      vtx_delta_B[k].samples[j] = shootPatch->unshot_B.samples[j] *
     elptr->vtx_ff[k] * element_p.samples[j];
    }
    for (j = 0; j < MAX_SPECTRA_SAMPLES; j++)
    {
      delta_B.samples[j] += (weight * vtx_delta_B[k].samples[j]);
    }
  }
}
/* Used hemicube: store patch changes only */
else
{
  for (j = 0; j < MAX_SPECTRA_SAMPLES; j++)
  {
    delta_B.samples[j] = shootPatch->unshot_B.samples[j] *
      element_ff * element_p.samples[j];
    for (k = 0; k < ep->numVert; k++)
      vtx_delta_B[k].samples[j] = shootPatch->unshot_B.samples[j] *
      elptr->vtx_ff[k] * element_p.samples[j];
  }
}

/* Update element's radiosity and patch's unshot radiosity */
if (ep->Pfather != 0)
  weight = ep->area / ep->Pfather->area;
else
  weight = 1.0;
for (j = 0; j < MAX_SPECTRA_SAMPLES; j++)
{
  ep->B.samples[j] += delta_B.samples[j];

  for (k = 0; k < ep->numVert; k++)
  {
    ep->vtx_B[k].samples[j] += vtx_delta_B[k].samples[j];
  }

  if (ep->Pfather != 0)
  {
    ep->Pfather->unshot_B.samples[j] +=
      (delta_B.samples[j] * weight);
  } else
  {
    ep->unshot_B.samples[j] += delta_B.samples[j];
  }
}

/* Some debugging statistics */
if (Option.debug)
{
  printf("\t+ Rec %s%d: p = %g,%g,%g; ff = %g\n", ep->name, ep->id,
      element_p.samples[0], element_p.samples[1],
      element_p.samples[2], element_ff);
```

```
          if (Option.ff_raytrace == 0)
          {
            printf("\t++ delta_B = %g,%g,%g; Shoot unshot = %g,%g,%g\n",
                delta_B.samples[0], delta_B.samples[1], delta_B.samples[2],
                shootPatch->unshot_B.samples[0],
                shootPatch->unshot_B.samples[1],
                shootPatch->unshot_B.samples[2]);
          } else
          {
            for (k = 0; k < ep->numVert; k++)
            {
              printf("\t++ v[%d]: delta_B = %g,%g,%g, B = %g,%g,%g\n",
                  k, vtx_delta_B[k].samples[0], vtx_delta_B[k].samples[1],
                  vtx_delta_B[k].samples[2], ep->vtx_B[k].samples[0],
                  ep->vtx_B[k].samples[1], ep->vtx_B[k].samples[2]);
            }
          }
        }
      }
    }                          /* ff != 0 */
  }                            /* is receiver */
}

  /* reset shooting patch's unshot rad */
  for (i = 0; i < MAX_SPECTRA_SAMPLES; i++)
    shootPatch->unshot_B.samples[i] = 0.0;
}

/********************************************************************/
/* Clean up                                                         */
/********************************************************************/
void
CleanUp_Rad()
{
  if (Option.debug)
    printf("\t*** Cleaning up radiosity structures ***\n");

  if (Option.ff_raytrace == 0)
  {
    free(hemicube.topFactors);
    free(hemicube.sideFactors);
    free(hemicube.view.buffer);
    free(formfactors);
  }
}
```

The Lightscape Visualization System is the first commercial computer application to combine radiosity with physically based lighting models. (Several images in the book's color section—the images of Jerusalem City Hall, the Universtiy of Western Ontario lab, the Ontario Legislature Building, and Unity Temple— were produced by the Lightscape Visualization System, by Lightscape Technologies, Inc.) Its primary market is interior designers and architects, and it only runs on Silicon Graphics Unix workstations, but it represents the next generation of three dimensional computer graphics applications. Lightscape supports real time interactive walk-throughs and rapid updates with progressive refinement. Still images can be generated with ray tracing, as well, to support both specular and diffuse global illumination.

NOTE

Stuart Feldman of Lightscape was willing to answer a few questions for us about Lightscape, the radiosity method, and the future of three-dimensional computer graphics.

WPN: What trends do you see affecting the future of three-dimensional computer graphics?

SF: There are considerable signs that 3-D graphics is going to be a big business. If you look at Microsoft, they just bought Softimage and recently brought OpenGL to the Windows NT environment. SIGGRAPH keeps getting bigger and bigger. This year was the first year we at Lightscape technologies put together a major event, and I was amazed at the strides that have been made in just the last few years.

WPN: Do you think that the recent advances in microprocessor design, bus architecture, and graphics technology in the personal computer market make the PC a viable contender for high-end radiosity packages like Lightscape?

SF: There is no question that the processing power on the average desktop PC is adequate for radiosity applications. What is missing is solid 3-D graphics acceleration hardware. A few years ago, we built a prototype of Lightscape under MS-DOS on a 33 Megahertz 80486 with 16 megabytes of RAM and a 3-D graphics accelerator, made by Silicon Graphics, called the IrisVision. The IrisVision does not quite have the display power of one of their workstations, but it could shade about 5,000 3-D polygons per second. That is adequate for real time walk-throughs if the environment is not too complex. Unfortunately, SGI discontinued the IrisVision and we never brought the PC prototype to the market. Also to be considered is the drop in price that has occurred with high-end graphics workstations.... You can get a pretty powerful low-end SGI machinefor $10,000 to $15,000 that can blow the doors off of a Pentium system with similar configuration.

WPN: Do you think that you will be porting Lightscape to the PC anytime soon?

SF: The graphics acceleration hardware is the key to it all. When that capability is stabilized we will probably port it to Windows NT with OpenGL. That point, though, is still a ways off.

WPN: What advantages do you think will make the radiosity method a mainstream tool in computer graphics? What do you think has been holding it back?

SF: Well, the radiosity method is much more complicated than ray tracing or local shading models. I mean, anybody and their brother can write a ray tracer, but the mathematics involved in radiosity are somewhat prohibitive. What radiosity can offer is absolutely amazing. The algorithm is ideally suited for progressive refinement. With the right acceleration and interfacing, the modeling and design process can really be interactive.

WPN: What role do you think Lightscape and the radiosity method will play in the future of 3-D computer graphics?

SF: I think radiosity will play a very important role in the not-so-distant future of computer graphics. It will probably be the basis for a majority of the 3-D software five years down the road. Our software is the first commercial radiosity package, and has reached a sort of development maturity. I think Lightscape will be in a good position when that time comes.

New Frontiers

In the last few years, research has attempted to enlarge the capabilities of the radiosity method in hopes of producing a true global renderer, capable of rendering anything. There has been great success at including participating mediums, such as smoke and fog. Two pass methods (as employed by LightR) that use ray tracing to include specular global illumination have proven very successful. Research conducted by academics such as Michael Cohen will produce increasingly powerful software like Lightscape. (My special thanks go to Peter Apian-Bennewitz, of Fraunhofer Institute for Solar Energy Systems, for permission to use the figure entitled "Radiance" in the color section of this book.) As the PC and its graphics display technology becomes more powerful, the radiosity method will become just as preeminent as ray tracing is now.

Basic 3-D Data Visualization Techniques

19

by Chikai Ohazama

Introduction

The ability to take pictures of the inside of our bodies has always fascinated humans because it lets us see the unseen, and helps us understand what is going on inside the human body. The first medical images (X-rays) were two-dimensional data sets that were basically photographs, and therefore did not require any special means of display. But with the advent of Computed Tomography (CT) and Magnetic Resonance Imaging (MRI), three-dimensional data sets were created, and a method of effectively displaying three-dimensional data onto a two-dimensional screen became a concern. The CT and MRI data sets are not only three-dimensional, but are also incredibly large and require a huge amount of memory in order to handle them.

This chapter presents simple and quick methods of displaying and managing 3-D volumetric data sets. These methods can be used to write code that enables you to view medical images downloaded off the Internet (this will be discussed and implemented in the following chapter), or they can be used to accomplish other three-dimensional manipulations. It is the author's intention that by looking at these methods you will be able to apply them to real world problems, and with some practice write real world applications that are simple, elegant, and fast without wasting precious computing time using unnecessary procedures.

> **NOTE**
>
> All code in this chapter is written for a 32-bit compiler, specifically Borland C++ 4.02 with Borland PowerPack and METBGI256 from Metagraphics Software Corp. The command for compilation at the DOS prompt is:
>
> ```
> bcc32 -WX -N filename.c bgi32.lib
> ```
> where `filename.c` is any of the source files in this chapter. In order to run these programs you must have the following files in the same directory as the executables:
>
> - 32RTM.EXE
> - DPMI32VM.OVL
> - BGI32.DLL
> - METWND08.DLL
> - BGIN__01.FNT

Basic Windowing and Leveling

When you are handling medical images using a PC, a major problem you may encounter is the large amount of memory the images require. An entire set of CT images taken of a patient's brain would usually run around 30 slices, where each slice is 512×512 pixels with 12-bit resolution. Because there is no type size that fits 12 bits, each pixel takes up 16 bits, or two bytes. Therefore, the entire data set would take up 15,728,640 bytes of memory. This could not be done easily using a 16-bit compiler, but it is less of a problem when you use a 32-bit compiler. This could not be done using a 16-bit compiler because the maximum size of an array is 64K, but with a 32-bit compiler it can be accomplished where the maximum size of an array is 2 gigabytes. So the limitation would come from the amount of memory you have in your computer. Once you get the data into memory you then have to process it, and 16 megabytes is not an easy load to sort through on most PCs. So reducing the size of your data set would be a definite plus if you were to do 3-D rotations or translations on the data set.

FIGURE 19.1.

This is a diagram of the windowing and leveling procedure.

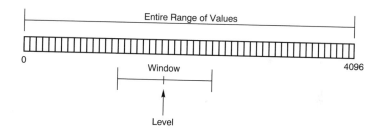

One of the most commonly used methods of reducing the size of a data set is windowing and leveling. This process reduces the resolution of each pixel by a certain amount. The method takes a specified portion of the entire range of original intensity values and divides that portion into a new, smaller range that can be displayed. The size of the new portion is defined by a parameter called the *window*, and the position of the window within the old intensity range is defined by a parameter called the *level* (see Figure 19.1). The values that fall below the specified window and level are set to black, and those that fall above the window are set to white. The window and level may be specified so that the window covers the entire range of the original intensity values. The two parameters can also be adjusted so that they only focus on a certain range of intensities. This capability to focus in on a certain intensity range is useful in the case of CT images, where bone and tissue are distinctly separated in intensity. This attribute of CT images will be demonstrated in the following chapter using an actual CT data set.

Windowing and leveling can be easily written into C code, but to demonstrate its effects you must first have a set of data on which to perform the calculations. The first part of each program presented in this chapter will be code that creates a 3-D data set by first constructing a voxel representation of a sphere with a diameter of 21 voxels (a voxel is a 3-D graphical object with coordinate values in three dimensions corollary to the 2-D pixel). The sphere, or "bubble," is then added into a 70×70×70 voxel volume at random points in the volume, where the value of the points that are inclusive to the bubble are incremented by one. The default palette in the video driver used in these programs has 16 shades of gray (4-bit resolution). The bubble data set in this example will consist of 8-bit intensities (256 shades of gray). Therefore, you will need to window and level the 8-bit intensities down to 4-bit values. The resultant data set is a bubbly-shaped 3-D volume that contains higher values toward the center, lower values toward the surface, and varying values in between. The following is the code that creates the demonstration volumetric data set.

```
/*MAKE BUBBLE*/

for(i=-10; i < 11; i++)
  {
  height = ceil(10*sin(acos((double)i/10)));
  if(height != 0)
    for(j=-height; j < height+1; j++)
      {
      height2 = ceil(height*sin(acos((double)j/height)));
      if(height2 !=0)
        for(k=-height2; k < height2+1; k++)
          bubble[i+10][j+10][k+10] = 1;
      }

  }

/*INITIATE BUBBLE MASS*/

for(i=0; i < 70; i++)
  for(j=0; j < 70; j++)
    for(k=0; k < 70; k++)
      bubblemass[i][j][k] = 0;

/*CREATE BUBBLE MASS*/

for(l=0; l < 1400; l++)
  {
  x = (unsigned char)(((double)(rand())*30/
                       (double)RAND_MAX) + 10);
  y = (unsigned char)(((double)(rand())*30/
                       (double)RAND_MAX) + 10);
  z = (unsigned char)(((double)(rand())*30/
                       (double)RAND_MAX) + 10);

  for(i=0; i < 21; i++)
    for(j=0; j < 21; j++)
      for(k=0; k < 21; k++)
        if(bubble[i][j][k] == 1)
          if(bubblemass[x+i][y+j][z+k] < 255)
            bubblemass[x+i][y+j][z+k] ++;

  }
```

This code first creates the bubble by constructing one slice at a time. Each slice contains a circle with a radius (stored in the variable height), determined in part by a sine function with a parameter that is the x coordinate in the 3-D array that holds the bubble. All values in the bubblemass array that contain the data set are then set to zero, followed by the addition of the 1,400 bubbles to the data set at randomly selected points. At the end of this portion of code you can see that in the last if statement the values are capped at 255, therefore ensuring no overflow in your 8-bit data set.

Now that the data set is created you can do your windowing and leveling. The code for this is very short. It contains a nested for loop so that you pass through all the values in the data set, a couple of if statements to set values in the data set that are below the window to zero and above the window to 255, and one arithmetic procedure to assign values inside the window. The following is the code.

```c
while(!kbhit())
  {
  for(i=0; i < 70; i++)
    for(j=0; j < 70; j++)
      for(k=0; k < 70; k++)
        {
        color = (int)bubblemass[i][j][k] - (level - window/2);
        if(color < 0)
          color = 0;
        if(color > window)
         color = 15;
         else
           color = (int)floor((double)color/
                              (double)window*15.0);
        putpixel(j, k, color+16);
        }

  }

getch();
closegraph();
```

As you can see, the code does the graphic plotting at the same time it compresses the data, so that the effects of the windowing and leveling can be seen visually instead of just being stored in memory or a file. Once the value of the point of interest was judged to reside within the window, it was normalized to the level and divided by the window size in order to get a ratio of the value to the entire range. The ratio was then multiplied by the size of the new range, which in this case was 16. (The actual number that was multiplied by the ratio was 15 because we are including zero in the range of values.) The final color value is then offset by 16 because the range of the gray colors in the default palette of 256 colors is from values 16 to 31.

When the data set creation code and the windowing and leveling code are put together, you have a program that continuously (until a key is pressed) flips through slices of the 3-D data set along the x-axis. The following is the listing of the entire program.

```c
#include <stdio.h>
#include <stdlib.h>
#include <conio.h>
#include <math.h>
#include <graphics.h>


void main(void)
{
int i,j,k,l;
int height, height2;
int color;
unsigned char x,y,z;
int window, level;
unsigned char bubblemass[70][70][70];
unsigned char bubble[21][21][21];
int graphdriver, graphmode, grerror;


    /*GET WINDOW AND LEVEL FROM USER*/

    window = -1;
    level = -1;

    while((window > 255)¦¦(window <= 0))
      {
      printf("Window(0-255):");
      scanf("%d",&window);
      }

    while((level < (window/2))¦¦(level > (255 - window/2)))
      {
      printf("Level(%d-%d):", window/2, (255 - window/2 - 1));
      scanf("%d",&level);
      }


    /*MAKE BUBBLE*/

    for(i=-10; i < 11; i++)
      {
      height = ceil(10*sin(acos((double)i/10)));
      if(height != 0)
        for(j=-height; j < height+1; j++)
          {
          height2 = ceil(height*sin(acos((double)j/height)));
          if(height2 !=0)
            for(k=-height2; k < height2+1; k++)
              bubble[i+10][j+10][k+10] = 1;
          }

      }


    /*INITIATE BUBBLE MASS*/

    for(i=0; i < 70; i++)
      for(j=0; j < 70; j++)
```

```
            for(k=0; k < 70; k++)
                bubblemass[i][j][k] = 0;


    /*CREATE BUBBLE MASS*/

    for(l=0; l < 1400; l++)
        {
        x = (unsigned char)(((double)(rand())*30/
                            (double)RAND_MAX) + 10);
        y = (unsigned char)(((double)(rand())*30/
                            (double)RAND_MAX) + 10);
        z = (unsigned char)(((double)(rand())*30/
                            (double)RAND_MAX) + 10);

        for(i=0; i < 21; i++)
            for(j=0; j < 21; j++)
                for(k=0; k < 21; k++)
                    if(bubble[i][j][k] == 1)
                        if(bubblemass[x+i][y+j][z+k] < 255)
                            bubblemass[x+i][y+j][z+k] ++;
        }


    /*PLOT IMAGE WITH WINDOWING AND LEVELING*/

    graphdriver = VGA256;
    graphmode = 0;
    initgraph( &graphdriver, &graphmode, "");
    grerror = graphresult();
    if(grerror)
        {
        closegraph();
        printf("Error Initializing Graphics Mode.\n");
        exit(1);
        }

    while(!kbhit())
        {
        for(i=0; i < 70; i++)
            for(j=0; j < 70; j++)
                for(k=0; k < 70; k++)
                    {
                    color = (int)bubblemass[i][j][k] - (level - window/2);
                    if(color < 0)
                        color = 0;
                    if(color > window)
                        color = 15;
                        else
                        color = (int)floor((double)color/
                                        (double)window*15.0);
                    putpixel(j, k, color+16);
                    }

        }

    getch();
    closegraph();

    }
```

The inquiry for the window and level values is restricted so that the values selected by the user stay within the allowable range. The window can be any size ranging from 1 to 255, which is the entire range for an 8-bit data set. The level is restricted in such a way as to keep the entire window within the allowable 8-bit range of data.

Once you have the program up and running, play around with different window and level values. Table 19.1 shows some values you might want to try.

Table 19.1. Window and level values.

Level	Window	Description	Figure
127	255	This will show you the entire spectrum of values in a generalized manner.	19.2
40	80	This will show you that the lower range of values in the data set lies around the outer edges of the bubblemass.	19.3
140	80	This will show you that the middle range of values lies between the core and the outer edge of the bubblemass.	19.4
230	50	This will show that the upper range of values lies in the core of the bubblemass.	19.5

FIGURE 19.2.

This is the output of the windowing and leveling program with a window of 255 and a level of 127.

FIGURE 19.3.

This is the output of the windowing and leveling program with a window of 80 and a level of 40.

FIGURE 19.4.

This is the output of the windowing and leveling program with a window of 80 and a level of 140.

FIGURE 19.5.

This is the output of the windowing and leveling program with a window of 50 and a level of 230.

Reslicing

When you are dealing with 3-D volumetric data sets there is always the question of what is the most effective way of displaying the data on a 2-D screen, so that the information that needs to be communicated to the viewer is done without complication or confusion. There are many different techniques, most of which are computation intensive. The number of calculations increases as the size of the data set increases; therefore, the larger the data set the longer it takes to calculate the resulting images. The following sections will present two simple techniques that will provide a relatively fast means of presenting the information contained in the 3-D data sets on the PC. The first technique that will be discussed is reslicing.

Reslicing is basically looking at an object from different viewpoints, where you are not looking at the actual surface of the object, but a tomographic plane of the object perpendicular to the viewing direction. In more simpler terms it is like taking an apple and slicing it with a knife—not necessarily in half, but at any point—and looking at the inside of the apple. This technique is often used when viewing CT images of the brain, where the brain is resliced along the two cardinal planes perpendicular to the acquisition plane. One slice cuts the brain so that it goes parallel to the floor if the person were in an upright position (the top view). This is called the *transverse slice* (see Figure 19.6A). Another cuts the brain so that it splits the person in half, where the cut goes from front to back (the side view). This is called the *sagittal slice* (see Figure 19.6B). The final cut goes from side to side, where the cut goes from shoulder to shoulder (the front view). This is called the *coronal slice* (see Figure 19.6C). When these three slices all go through one point within a CT data set of the brain, it gives the viewer positional information of where that point is in the brain. This type of viewing technique is often used in computer-aided stereotactic neurosurgery, where the surgeon has some sort of device that digitizes a point in space. The coordinates of the point are sent to the computer, which calculates where that point lies within the CT data set and then shows the corresponding coronal, sagittal, and transverse slices on a computer screen. This gives the surgeon information as to where his pointing device is within the brain. From this information he is better able to determine which direction he should go in order to, for instance, remove a tumor.

The reslicing routine is very simple when you have a 3-D data set completely loaded into memory, which is the case with the demonstration data set. Following Figure 19.6 is the source code for a program that will reslice the demonstration data set along each of the three cardinal planes and plot each slice as it progresses (see Figure 19.7).

FIGURE 19.6.

These are the (A) transverse, (B) sagittal, and (C) coronal slices of the brain.

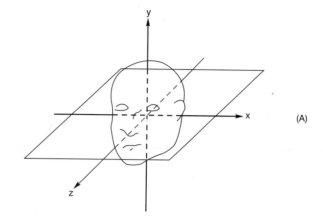

(A)

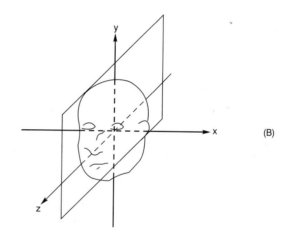

(B)

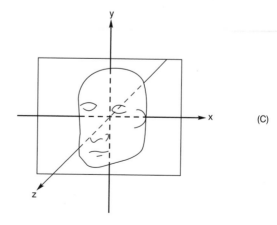

(C)

```c
#include <stdio.h>
#include <stdlib.h>
#include <conio.h>
#include <math.h>
#include <graphics.h>


void main(void)
{
int i,j,k,l;
int height, height2;
unsigned char x,y,z;
unsigned char bubblemass[70][70][70];
unsigned char bubble[21][21][21];
int graphdriver, graphmode, grerror;



  /*MAKE BUBBLE*/

  for(i=-10; i < 11; i++)
    {
    height = ceil(10*sin(acos((double)i/10)));
    if(height != 0)
      for(j=-height; j < height+1; j++)
        {
        height2 = ceil(height*sin(acos((double)j/height)));
        if(height2 !=0)
          for(k=-height2; k < height2+1; k++)
            bubble[i+10][j+10][k+10] = 1;
        }
    }


  /*INITIATE BUBBLE MASS*/

  for(i=0; i < 70; i++)
    for(j=0; j < 70; j++)
      for(k=0; k < 70; k++)
        bubblemass[i][j][k] = 0;


  /*CREATE BUBBLE MASS*/

  for(l=0; l<75; l++)
    {
    x = (unsigned char)(((double)(rand())*30/
                         (double)RAND_MAX) + 10);
    y = (unsigned char)(((double)(rand())*30/
                         (double)RAND_MAX) + 10);
    z = (unsigned char)(((double)(rand())*30/
                         (double)RAND_MAX) + 10);

    for(i=0; i < 21; i++)
      for(j=0; j < 21; j++)
        for(k=0; k < 21; k++)
          if(bubble[i][j][k] == 1)
```

```
              if(bubblemass[x+i][y+j][z+k] < 15)
                 bubblemass[x+i][y+j][z+k] ++;
   }


   /*PLOT RESLICED IMAGES*/

   graphdriver = VGA256;
   graphmode = 0;
   initgraph(&graphdriver, &graphmode, "");
   grerror = graphresult();
   if(grerror)
     {
     closegraph();
     printf("Error Initializing Graphics Mode.\n");
     exit(1);
     }

   while(!kbhit())
     {
     for(i=0; i < 70; i++)
       for(j=0; j < 70; j++)
         for(k=0; k < 70; k++)
           {
           putpixel(j, k, 16+bubblemass[i][j][k]);
           putpixel(j+70, k, 16+bubblemass[k][i][j]);
           putpixel(j, k+70, 16+bubblemass[j][k][i]);
           }
     }

   getch();
   closegraph();
}
```

FIGURE 19.7.

This is the output of the slicing program.

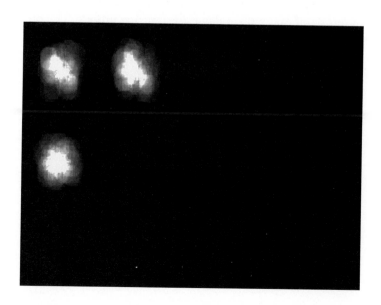

The voxels created for this data set have 4-bit resolution and are easily displayed with only 16 shades of gray. The reslicing procedure occurs in the final nested `for` loop. The looping variables i, j, and k are used so that j and k are the x and y values on the graphics screen, and i is the axis along which the slices are traveling. The first `putpixel` statement has the traveling axis being the x-axis, and the y and z components of the data set to be the x and y values, respectively. (The first component of the array corresponds to the x-axis, the second the y-axis, and the third the z-axis.) The reason the y component of the data set, instead of the z component, is assigned the x value is because of the right hand rule. If you put your thumb in the positive direction of the x-axis, the fingers curl into the hands from the y- to the z-axis, therefore making the y-axis corollary to the x value, or the horizontal component, of the slice (see Figure 19.8). The next `putpixel` statement has the traveling axis being the y-axis, with the z and x components being the x and y values (see Figure 19.9); and the final `putpixel` statement has the traveling axis being the z-axis, with x and y components being the x and y values (see Figure 19.10). Each of these points from the three different views are then plotted on the screen to form the images of the three slices. The program files through each axis continuously until a key is pressed.

As stated earlier, when you have a data set completely loaded into memory it is not difficult to do reslicing. But when you have partially loaded data sets, in which the dimensions of the voxels are not uniform, it becomes more difficult for the computer to sort through. This is often the case with CT data, where the entire data set is usually too large to load into memory and the voxels are usually eight to ten times longer in the transverse direction than in the sagittal or coronal direction. You can solve the memory problem by reading only what is needed of the data set from disk and not loading it all into memory, but this significantly slows down the reslicing process. The proportionality problem requires interpolation.

FIGURE 19.8.

This is a diagram of a slice along the yz-plane traveling along the x-axis.

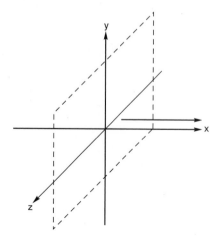

FIGURE 19.9.

This is a diagram of a slice along the zx-plane traveling along the y-axis.

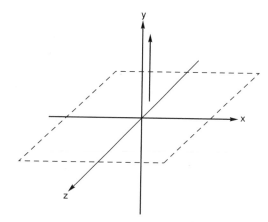

FIGURE 19.10.

This is a diagram of a slice along the xy-plane traveling along the z-axis.

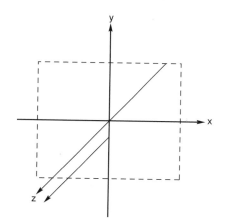

Maximum Intensity Projections

The second technique for displaying a 3-D data set onto a 2-D screen is a *maximum intensity projection* (MIP). This is much more complex than reslicing, but in concept it is very simple. The procedure is to take a 3-D data set and project each point of the data set onto a 2-D surface. The values of the 2-D projection are determined by the greatest value that is projected onto each point of the projection surface. The program that will demonstrate MIP images will do orthogonal projections with rotations about the origin, which is also the center of the 3-D data set.

Now take what's just been stated and put it into more metaphorical terms. The 3-D data set is a map of intensities at discrete voxels in three dimensions. Now pretend that all these voxels are small beads, and each bead has a specific three-dimensional location and has its intensity marked on it with a gray scale code. The demonstration data set would then be a collection of 343,000 (70×70×70) beads of differing shades of gray. Now you can take this collection of beads and turn it around so it is in a different position. Once you have it in the position you want, you get a 100×100 square checkerboard, where each square has the dimensions of one bead. This checkerboard will represent the 2-D surface onto which you will project the 3-D data set. (The reason why it is 100×100 is because that is the size of the projection surface in the MIP image demonstration program.) Next, hang the beads above the checkerboard and drop each bead straight down onto the checkerboard, always placing the beads into the closest square (see Figure 19.11). The process of dropping the beads onto the checkerboard is called *projection*, and the choice of dropping the beads straight down is characterized as being *orthogonal*. As you drop these beads on the checker-board, only one bead can lie in a square. In the case in which a bead falls into a square that is already occupied, the bead with the highest value stays and the other is thrown out. This selection process reflects the name of the procedure, *maximum intensity projection*. The bead dropping continues until all the beads have been dropped, and the final image that is produced on the checkerboard is then transferred to the graphics screen. Another method of projecting the data set onto the image surface is called ray casting. *Ray casting* does not drop the beads onto the checkerboard but extends a ray perpendicular to the image surface, with a width of one bead from each square in the checkerboard, and assigns the square a value equal to the highest value bead crossing its path. This second method is much slower than the bead dropping method, and therefore will not be used here in the MIP demonstration. However, the ray casting method of projecting the image does have advantages, which will be discussed later in the chapter.

FIGURE 19.11.

This is a diagram to illustrate the metaphorical explanation of the orthogonal projection of a three-dimensional data set.

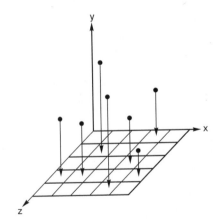

The following is the code for the program that demonstrates how to create MIP images.

```c
#include <stdio.h>
#include <stdlib.h>
#include <conio.h>
#include <math.h>
#include <graphics.h>
#include <dos.h>


#define PI 3.1415926
#define EPSILON 1E-3


void xrotate(float *, int);
void yrotate(float *, int);
void zrotate(float *, int);
void getmouse_xy(int *, int *, int *);


float st[361], ct[361];
union REGS regs;


void main(void)
{
int i,j,k,l;
int height, height2;
unsigned char x,y,z;
int xx, yy, button;
int tx, ty, tz;
float point[3];
int view[100][100];
unsigned char bubblemass[70][70][70];
unsigned char bubble[21][21][21];
int grdriver, grmode, grerror;


  /*define sine and cosine tables*/

  for(i=0; i<=360; i++)
    {
    st[i]=(float)sin((double)(2*PI/360.0*i));
    ct[i]=(float)cos((double)(2*PI/360.0*i));
    }


  /*MAKE BUBBLE*/

  for(i=-10; i < 11; i++)
    {
    height = (int)ceil(10.0*sin(acos((double)i/10.0)));
    if(height != 0)
      for(j=-height; j < height+1; j++)
        {
        height2 = (int)ceil(height*sin(acos((double)j/height)));
        if(height2 !=0)
```

```
        for(k=-height2; k < height2+1; k++)
          bubble[i+10][j+10][k+10] = 1;
      }

  }


/*INITIATE BUBBLE MASS*/

for(i=0; i < 70; i++)
  for(j=0; j < 70; j++)
    for(k=0; k < 70; k++)
      bubblemass[i][j][k] = 0;


/*CREATE BUBBLE MASS*/

for(l=0; l < 100; l++)
  {
  x = (unsigned char)(((float)(rand())*35/(float)RAND_MAX)+10);
  y = (unsigned char)(((float)(rand())*35/(float)RAND_MAX)+10);
  z = (unsigned char)(((float)(rand())*35/(float)RAND_MAX)+10);

  for(i=0; i < 21; i++)
    for(j=0; j < 21; j++)
      for(k=0; k < 21; k++)
        if(bubble[i][j][k] == 1)
          if(bubblemass[x+i][y+j][z+k] < 15)
            bubblemass[x+i][y+j][z+k] ++;
  }


/*INITIALIZE GRAPHICS SCREEN*/

grdriver = VGA256;
grmode = 0;
initgraph(&grdriver, &grmode, "");
grerror = graphresult();
if(grerror)
  {
  closegraph();
  printf("Error Initializing Graphics Mode.\n");
  exit(1);
  }


/*MOUSE INITIALIZATION*/

regs.w.ax = 0;
int386(0x33, &regs, &regs);

if((short)regs.w.ax != -1)
  {
  closegraph();
  printf("Mouse driver must be installed before running ");
  printf("this program.\n");
  exit(1);
  }
```

```
regs.w.ax = 0x0007;
regs.w.cx = 0;
regs.w.dx = 0x0280;
int386(0x33, &regs, &regs);
regs.w.ax = 0x0008;
regs.w.cx = 0;
regs.w.dx = 0x00c8;
int386(0x33, &regs, &regs);
regs.w.ax = 0x0001;
int386(0x33, &regs, &regs);


/*MIP IMAGE DISPLAY*/

while(!kbhit())
  {

  /*GET ROTATION VALUES FROM MOUSE*/

  getmouse_xy(&xx, &yy, &button);

  tx = (int)((float)(yy-100)*1.8);
  ty = (int)((float)(xx-320)*0.5625);

  while((tx < 0)||(tx > 360)||(ty < 0)||(ty > 360))
     {
     if(tx < 0)
       tx = tx + 360;
     if(tx > 360)
       tx = tx - 360;
     if(ty < 0)
       ty = ty + 360;
     if(ty > 360)
       ty = ty - 360;
     }

  /*CLEAR PROJECTION SURFACE*/

  for(i=0; i<100; i++)
   for(j=0; j<100; j++)
    view[i][j] = 0;

  /*ROTATE AND CREATE MIP IMAGE*/

  for(i=0; i < 70; i++)
    for(j=0; j < 70; j++)
      for(k=0; k < 70; k++)
        if(bubblemass[i][j][k] > 0)
          {
          point[0] = (float)(i - 35);
          point[1] = (float)(j - 35);
          point[2] = (float)(k - 35);
          xrotate(point,tx);
          yrotate(point,ty);
          if(view[(int)(point[0]+50.0)][(int)(point[1]+50.0)]
            < bubblemass[i][j][k])
            view[(int)(point[0]+50.0)][(int)(point[1]+50.0)]
               = bubblemass[i][j][k];
          }
```

```
/*PLOT MIP IMAGE ONTO GRAPHICS SCREEN*/

    for(i=0; i<100; i++)
      for(j=0; j<100; j++)
        {
        putpixel(i+110, j+50, 16+view[i][j]);
        }

    }
  getch();
  closegraph();
}


void xrotate(float *point, int deg)
{
float y,z;

  y = point[1]*ct[deg] + point[2]*st[deg];
  z = point[2]*ct[deg] - point[1]*st[deg];

  point[1] = y;
  point[2] = z;

}


void yrotate(float *point, int deg)
{
float x,z;

  x = point[0]*ct[deg] - point[2]*st[deg];
  z = point[0]*st[deg] + point[2]*ct[deg];
  point[0] = x;
  point[2] = z;
}


void zrotate(float *point, int deg)
{
float x,y;

  x = point[0]*ct[deg] + point[1]*st[deg];
  y = point[1]*ct[deg] - point[0]*st[deg];
  point[0] = x;
  point[1] = y;
}


void getmouse_xy(int *xx, int *yy, int *button)
{
  regs.w.ax=0x0003;
  int386(0x33, &regs, &regs);
  *xx=(int)regs.w.cx;
  *yy=(int)regs.w.dx;
  *button=regs.w.bx;
}
```

The first thing to note about this program is the 3-D rotation functions. They basically use the rotation formulas given in the previous chapters to calculate the newly rotated point, and return the information by changing the array that was passed to the function. But the interesting element is the use of a look-up table (LUT) instead of the normal sine and cosine functions. The LUTs are assigned as global variables, enabling any function in the program to use them. The use of the LUTs cuts down the rotation computation time, because transcendental functions require large amounts of processor time. With these rotation functions the program can show different viewpoints of the 3-D data set.

The code for creating the MIP images is again in a nested for loop, which is used to go through all the points in the data set. Each point in the data set is offset so that the points are centered about the origin. They are then rotated and projected onto the xy-plane. A point is then compared with the existing value at the point of projection in order to decide the final value of that point. Once the image is complete it is plotted on the screen.

Another important part of the program is the use of the mouse to obtain rotation values. Vertical mouse movements control x-axis rotation and horizontal mouse movements control y-axis rotation. The screen is sectioned so that extreme left to extreme right would be −180 to 180 degrees of y-axis rotation, and extreme up to extreme down would be −180 to 180 degrees of x-axis rotation. The center of the screen causes zero rotation along both the x- and y-axis.

When you run this program you will notice an apparent glitch in some of the images. Every so often you will see a pattern of black dots appear over the image (see Figure 19.12). This is a direct result of the projection algorithm. There exist some rotational positions where the points in the data set will leave a pattern of blank spots on the projection surface (see Figure 19.13). This is a problem that will always exist when you do volumetric projections using the "bead dropping" method. Because you are choosing the nearest checkerboard space where the beads strike, there are some rotational angles where none of the beads strike certain squares. When no beads strike a square, the image contains a black dot at that square. The ray casting method of projection does not have this problem, but the reverse error of *blooming* will occur. In the projected image some voxels will spread out over a larger area, filling up the holes on the image surface.

Another antic you will notice is that the mouse movements don't correlate exactly to the rotation movements of the bubblemass. When you move the mouse horizontally the bubblemass will rotate side to side as you would expect, but when you move the mouse vertically the bubblemass does not necessarily rotate up and down. The only time the bubblemass rotates up and down is when the mouse pointer is in the center of the screen. This is because the order in which you do rotations in the program affects the final position of the points. If you were to switch the order of the rotational calculations in the program so that the y rotation is done first and the x rotation is done second, the effect would be reversed—vertical movements will correspond to rotations up and down while the horizontal movements will not always correspond to the rotations happening on the screen. The reason why the movements don't correspond is because the first rotation occurs at the original position of points in the data set, but the second rotation starts at this new position, and so on, so that only the final rotations appear on the display in an intuitive manner (see Figure 19.14). You will still see rotational movements with the vertical mouse movements, but it will be along a skewed plane. This plane is the yz-plane rotated about the y-axis by an amount given by the horizontal position of the mouse.

FIGURE 19.12.

MIP image with the black spotted pattern.

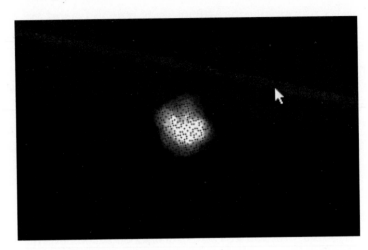

FIGURE 19.13.

This is a diagram to illustrate why the black spotted pattern happens on some projections of the MIP image.

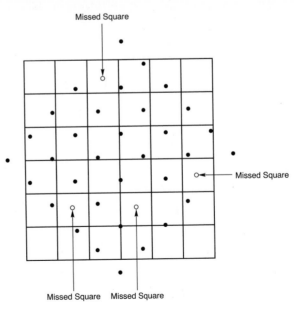

FIGURE 19.14.

This is an illustration of rotational movements of a data point.

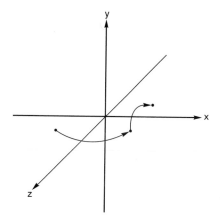

Summary

In this chapter you learned how to use basic windowing and leveling to reduce the intensity resolution of a 3-D data set in order to display it on the screen. This technique also enables you to focus on certain parts of the intensity spectrum, enabling you in some cases to highlight certain structures in the data set.

Two methods of displaying the information in a 3-D data set were also presented: reslicing and maximum intensity projection (MIP). Reslicing enables you to see the insides of the data set by cutting out two-dimensional images, while the MIP images show you a collective view of all the points by projecting them onto a surface.

3-D Medical Imaging

3-D Medical Imaging: Real Data

by George D. Stetten, M.D., M.S.
Director
Visualization and Image Analysis Laboratory
Duke University

Introduction

In another chapter, we reviewed some basic techniques for handling volumetric data. Now, we will step back from the abstract world of graphics programming and look around at the real world of medical imaging. It is fine to create virtual realities of imaginary objects with mathematical surfaces, but the real world provides a richer and more interesting subject, namely volumetric data about our own bodies. Medical imaging has provided many ways to "see" within ourselves without actually cutting through the skin. In the process, over the last 20 years, the advent of three-dimensional (3-D) imaging modalities have provided computer graphics with a new and essential role.

How do doctors interpret volumetric data? For the most part, they slice it up and look at it one slice at a time. This is due in part to the difficulty of turning 3-D data into useful pictures. In fact, researchers and enthusiasts like yourself (as you must be, given that you made it to this chapter!) are just beginning to figure out how to do it. Mother Nature did not mean for us to see volumetric data. Most of what we actually see is composed of opaque surfaces. If everything were a translucent cloud, interpreting the visual world would be difficult, indeed.

Various ways of using graphics to communicate 3-D voxel data to the human visual cortex were discussed in other chapters, including reslicing and maximum intensity projections. Applying computer graphics to real data is commonly called "visualization," conjuring up the idea that we are somehow seeing the data in our minds. However, there is nothing imaginary about the human body. The data is real; only our ability to see it is not. Perhaps a better term to describe what we are doing would be "virtual vision."

In the first part of this chapter, I will present a description of medical imaging data. Where does it come from? What does it represent? The reason a painter studies the realities of sunlight, wind, trees, and ocean is to help create a visual presentation that is effective. Similarly, the graphics programmer should understand some of the basic physics behind medical imaging before trying to view that data. All voxels are not created equal. As you shall learn, voxels are not physical things. They represent some form of measurement localized in three dimensions by imaging machinery. Understanding that machinery will help the graphics programmer determine how to turn those voxels into images that makes sense to the human observer.

The Realities of Hacking on Medical Data

Before I launch into the methods of medical imaging, a few comments are in order. The collection of all medical images in the world may well be the largest organized database in history. It is mostly still kept on film. Don't underestimate film! It is very competitive in terms of cost, resolution, and convenience, and film can always be scanned electronically. Sooner or later, the acquisition of medical images will probably be completely electronic, but even then, the old images on film will be indispensable for comparison studies. Film is still the mainstay in clinical X-ray. However, all modern 3-D imaging systems are at least capable of storing data electronically. Medical visualization depends on real data that fills up every voxel in the volume. These data are nowhere near as compact as the mathematical equations used to create imaginary graphical objects, discussed in most of this book. The 3-D data sets most commonly found in medical imaging require large amounts of memory and processor power, beyond the capabilities of all but the most powerful of today's PCs. At present, medical imaging programs run almost entirely on large UNIX-type platforms, usually with proprietary software supplied by the company that produced the imaging hardware. These programs have not been the kind of thing you hack on your own, unless you are involved in medical research or work for a company that makes imaging software. Even the data formats are frequently proprietary, although a new standard, called DICOM, is being introduced. The standard has been published and is currently being revised. The standard is the responsibility of the American College of Radiology and the National Equipment Manufacturer's Association. DICOM, it is hoped, will promote third-party development of clinical visualization systems and make it easier for anyone to access the information in a medical image.

The situation with computer power and memory is changing at this very moment. Computer power per dollar doubles approximately every 1.5 years. A computer costing $1,000 today surpasses the most powerful computer in the world 20 years ago. We should soon have sufficient power and memory on our desks to visualize large 3-D data sets at a reasonable speed.

Several other considerations, however, will remain. To be used in the clinical environment today, software often requires approval by the Food and Drug Administration (FDA). Furthermore, images cannot be released for general use unless all patient identification has been removed. Even then, the patient's permission may still be required.

Computerized Tomography (CT)

So, how is it that we can see inside the human body? Although practically opaque to ordinary visible light, the body can be penetrated by X rays, gamma rays, radio waves, high-frequency sound, and magnetic fields. The first of these to be discovered was X rays, oddly enough as an indirect result of the invention of the light bulb. Thomas Edison's great achievement of constructing an evacuated glass vessel, with metal penetrators to carry electric current in and out, laid the foundation for the cathode ray tube. In the 1890s every university physics department had one, with electrons boiling off of a filament into a vacuum, to be sucked away by a positively-charged plate. With their motion unimpeded by the vacuum, the electrons would accelerate and crash into the plate. Unknown to the scientists playing with this new device, as those electrons crashed into the plate, their magnetic fields changed abruptly to zero, creating photons.

Now these were not just any photons. They were the highest-energy photons ever yet created by humans. In one particular lab in Germany, a relatively unknown scientist named Wilhelm Roentgen was working with a cathode ray tube on his desk, and he noticed that the photographic film in the top drawer of his desk was being exposed. A series of simple experiments proved that the film was being exposed through the wooden desk top by something from the tube. This couldn't happen with any known type of light, so Roentgen labeled the mysterious stuff "X rays" and spent the next six weeks locked in his lab discovering their basic properties. They seemed to pass easily through skin and muscle, but not much through bone, and practically not at all through metal. They traveled in a straight line and could not be bent by a lens.

Within a few years, X-ray machines were in clinical use all over the world, mostly finding bullets and broken bones. Modern radiology was born, and Roentgen went on to eventually receive the first Nobel Prize for his serendipitous discovery. In the century since their introduction, hundreds of millions of clinical X-ray studies have been performed, and they remain basically unchanged. The modern X-ray image is still a simple 2-D silhouette.

Meanwhile, the pieces began to fall together to allow the use of X rays to collect volumetric 3-D data. It was found that when X rays pass through certain crystals, they leave in the crystal a shower of lower-energy visible photons, or "scintillations," that can be detected electronically. The next piece of the puzzle came with the invention of the computer, which could store signals from those detectors and perform calculations on them. The stage was set for Computerized Tomography, or CT, commonly known as the "cat scan."

Here's how CT works. A hollow cylinder is constructed, large enough to pass a person through from head to toe. On one side of the cylinder, a row of the crystal detectors is placed, and on the other an X-ray source is positioned. The attenuation of X rays through a person inserted in the cylinder can now be measured along a set of paths, as shown in Figure 20.1. The X-ray source and detectors are then rotated as a unit around the patient, and many other such sets of paths are measured. A mathematical process known as filtered-back projection is used to calculate the attenuation of X rays at every location in the cross section, or "slice," of the patient.

Figure 20.2 shows an example of a cross section of a human head, in which an area of

FIGURE 20.1.

CT employs a movable ring containing an X-ray source and multiple detectors. A cross section of the patient is calculated from a sequence of readings as the ring is rotated around the patient.

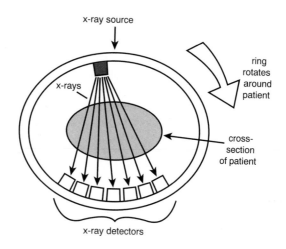

brain tissue has been removed and replaced with fluid. The skull is clearly visible as a thick white oval surrounding the brain. Note the hole cut by the surgeons, in the vicinity of the fluid. This cross section is very different from the standard X ray. It is not a silhouette but truly a slice, just as if a band saw had been used to remove everything above and below it (but a whole lot less messy!). We now have true voxel data; that is, each voxel corresponds to some quality of the tissue. The units of measurement in a particular CT data set may be arbitrary; or the data may be given in Hounsfield units, in which the attenuation of water is assigned the value 0, and tissue with greater or less attenuation than water is positive or negative, respectively. The attenuation of X rays in bone is quite high, and so voxels containing bone will have large positive Hounsfield values. They will be bright in the image.

We are now ready to acquire an entire 3-D volumetric data set. All that remains is moving the patient through the ring to collect multiple slices and then stacking those slices together into a 3-D volumetric data set. What can we do with such a data set? Many visualization programs allow re-slicing of the data at arbitrary orientations. High-end machines have specialized hardware to accelerate graphics functions, enabling the user to manipulate orientation in real time. In less powerful machines, re-slicing can also be accomplished, although not in real time. These slices can have three orthogonal orientations in relation to the human body: transverse, sagittal, and coronal. CT is largely confined to acquiring transverse slices, because patients can only fit through the cylinder from head to toe. With an advanced graphical re-slicing tool, however, any arbitrary orientation of slice can be examined after the 3-D data set has been acquired.

So far, we haven't tried looking at the 3-D data as a volume. It turns out that bone studies with CT are particularly well suited to finding isosurfaces in the voxel data. Bone attenuates X rays much more effectively than does any other tissue. Therefore, it is rather easy to find a reliable threshold between bone and everything else. So, for example, let us say that all bone has an attenuation value greater than 400 Hounsfield units, and that muscle, skin, and all other tissues have values significantly less than that. Let's find every pair of neighboring voxels in which one voxel is greater than 400, and the other is less than 400. Between each such pair we construct a little polygon, and connect these polygons into a "watertight" surface, using a clever algorithm invented at General Electric known as *Marching Cubes*. (Beware, they have a patent, and enforce it!) The result can be a strikingly realistic picture, such as that shown in Figure 20.3, of the bones in the leg just below the knee. These are living bones surrounded by soft tissue, and yet they look just like something Fido would bury in the back yard. Every detail of the surface seems clear, and the fracture in the tibia stands out dramatically. The simulated reflection and shading increases the perception of 3-D surfaces.

Another example of this technique is given in Figure 20.4, showing a rib cage, spine, and

FIGURE 20.2.

An axial CT slice of the head clearly shows the skull and brain. (Courtesy of Timothy Turkington, Ph.D., Department of Radiology, Duke University.)

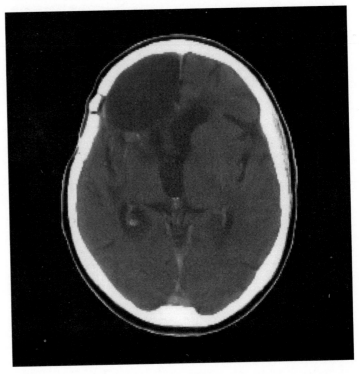

FIGURE 20.3.

A Marching Cubes isosurface rendering of multiple CT slices of the bones in the leg. A fracture is visible in the tibia, just below the knee. (Courtesy of Robert M. Vandermark, M.D., Department of Radiology, Duke University.)

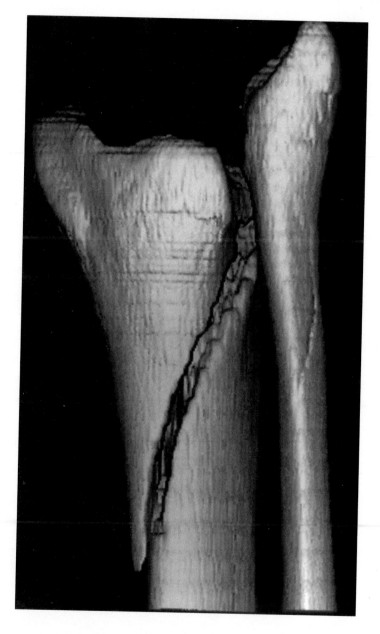

shoulder blades of a patient who has dislocated his shoulder joints during a seizure. The arm bones (humeri) appear to have been sheared off, but actually the image has been cropped by the graphics program, leaving nice circular cross-sections of the long marrow bones. The artificial shading leaves an eerily empty thorax, with all the vital organs such as heart and lungs neatly removed by the isosurface thresholding. In fact, CT of the bone

is uniquely suited for the process of *segmentation,* the computerized discrimination between tissue types. This success is due to bone's dense concentration of calcium, which
causes attenuation of X rays far beyond that of other tissues. Simple thresholding works
well here, but it is not usually so successful at segmenting other tissues, such as kidney
from liver, or heart from lung. Thresholding is, however, effective at segmenting brain
from the surrounding fluid, as shown in Figure 20.5. Here the skull has been removed by
manual tracing, and the brain has been segmented by carefully adjusting the threshold.
The brain is seen from the front, with the brain stem looming in the virtual shadow of the
cortex.

A final example of rendered CT is given in Figure 20.6. Here, an isosurface rendering of

FIGURE 20.4.

*This Marching Cubes
isosurface rendering of
multiple CT slices of the
rib cage, spine, and
shoulders shows two
dislocated shoulder joints.
(Courtesy of Robert M.
Vandermark, M.D.,
Department of Radiology,
Duke University.)*

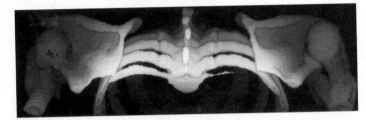

FIGURE 20.5.

*A CT isosurface rendering
shows the convolutions in
the surface of the brain.
(Courtesy of Gail Bailey,
LRT, and Arthur
Rosenbaum, M.D.,
Department of Radiology,
S.U.N.Y. Health Science
Center at Syracuse.)*

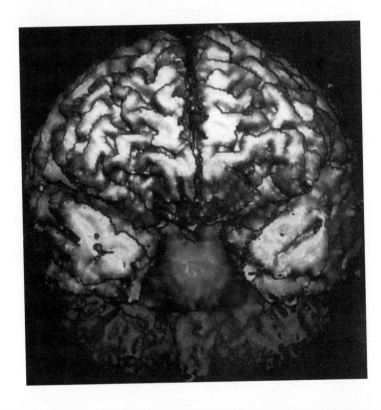

a human head is shown. The threshold of the isosurface is set between air and skin, whose attenuations are far enough apart to result in an effective segmentation. Computer graphics tools have been used in this picture to simulate removal of an entire section of the head, to reveal three resliced surfaces meeting at a corner deep within the brain. Not bad, considering no scalpel!

FIGURE 20.6.

A CT isosurface rendering of a human head, with simulated removal of a section to show re-sliced surfaces within the brain. (Courtesy of Gail Bailey, LRT, and Arthur Rosenbaum, M.D., Department of Radiology, S.U.N.Y. Health Science Center at Syracuse.)

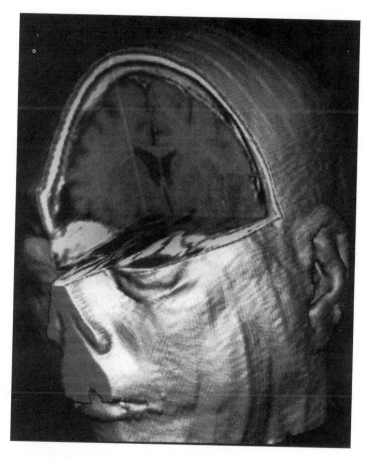

Single Proton Emission Computed Tomography (SPECT)

Edison's light bulb spawned another important device in the 1930s, the mass spectrometer. Like the cathode ray tube, the mass spectrometer depends on an air-tight seal between metal and glass to allow electrical fields to be controlled within a vacuum. In the mass spectrometer, ionized atoms can be accelerated and then swung around a magnetic field. The heavier isotopes can't take the turn tightly and are thus separated from the lighter isotopes into a mass "spectrum." With the invention of the mass spectrometer, nuclear medicine was born (along with nuclear power and nuclear weapons).

Certain isotopes of heavy atoms (such as technetium) are radioactive. They're not happy because they have too many neutrons and would prefer to have one of their neutrons become a proton. To accomplish this goal, a neutron must give off an electron (called a beta particle) and a photon (called a gamma ray). Like X rays, gamma rays are high-energy particles of light. In fact, the territories of X rays and gamma rays in the electro-magnetic spectrum overlap, although gamma rays also extend into higher frequencies. To differentiate, you must know where they came from: X rays come from electrons, whereas gamma rays come from the nucleus.

Like X rays, gamma rays can be detected by the scintillations they cause in crystals. They also pass easily through most of the human body, except for bones. Therefore, if you inject radioactive technetium into the bloodstream, you can "see" where the blood goes. The situation is slightly different with X rays, which are produced by a fancy light bulb outside the body. The gamma rays are coming from within the body, so you cannot simply make a silhouette. You need to focus an image; but gamma rays cannot be focused by any known lens. Instead, the "gamma camera" consists of a large 2-D array of detectors, an array that works very much like the compound eye of an insect. To increase the range of the gamma camera, thousands of parallel holes are drilled through a sheet of lead. This "collimator" is placed over the sensors. The gamma camera works very effectively to capture a 2-D image of radioactivity within the body. Following the model of CT, the jump to three dimensions was made by spinning the gamma camera around the patient and calculating the amount of radioactivity emanating from every voxel. This technique is used clinically and is called Single Photon Emission Computed Tomography (SPECT). Figure 20.7 shows an isosurface rendering of a brain with a gunshot wound. The patient has been injected with radioactive technetium, bound to a neurochemical that concentrates inside the blood-brain barrier. A small dent in the back of the brain marks the lack of blood-flow to an area of stroke, caused by the bullet.

FIGURE 20.7.

This SPECT isosurface rendering of a brain shows the effects of a gunshot wound. (Courtesy of Kim L. Greer, Department of Radiology, Duke University.)

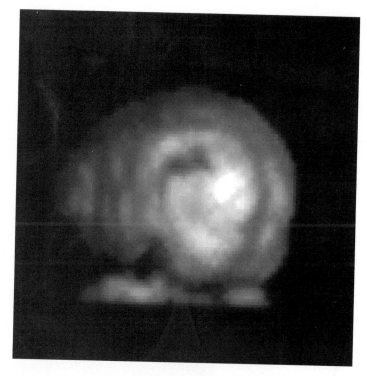

Positron Emission Tomography (PET)

Remember anti-matter from *Star Trek?* Well, it really exists. Certain isotopes of small atoms have too few neutrons—just the opposite of the traditional heavy isotopes. The solution to their problem is for one of the protons to turn into a neutron, which it does by emitting a positive electron, called a *positron.* A positron can't expect to live very long in the human body. The first time it bumps into an electron, the two particles annihilate each other, turning into pure energy in the form of two high-energy photons that fly away in opposite directions.

The Positron Emission Tomography (PET) scanner consists of a series of complete rings of crystal detectors for picking up these photons. In fact, the goal is to pick up both that emanated from a single annihilation. If only one is detected, the event is not counted. By demanding coincident detection, the signal-to-noise ratio and thus the quality of the image is greatly increased, allowing smaller amounts of radioactive materials to be used.

An advantage of PET is that positron-emitting isotopes don't have to be exotic elements like technetium, but instead they can be everyday building blocks, such as carbon and oxygen. Therefore, organic compounds that emit positrons can be made to fit easily into the standard biochemical pathways. Positron-emitting molecules that enter the metabolism are used to measure how much a particular part of the brain is thinking. In this, PET is different from CT or SPECT. PET is used to see the working chemistry of life and is therefore a form of functional imaging.

Figure 20.8 shows the same slice of brain seen earlier by CT (Figure 20.2). Now the skull is absent, because not much metabolism happens in bone. The brain itself, however, is working hard (all except the fluid-filled defect). Researchers have used PET to monitor which parts of the brain respond to speech, vision, and various other functions involving thought.

FIGURE 20.8.

This is a PET image of the same slice of brain seen by CT in Figure 20.2. (Courtesy of Timothy G. Turkington, Ph.D., Department of Radiology, Duke University.)

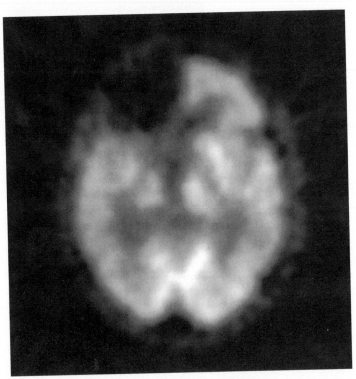

Magnetic Resonance Imaging (MRI)

Perhaps the fastest growing area in medical imaging is Magnetic Resonance Imaging (MRI), which was once called Nuclear Magnetic Resonance (NMR) until it became clear that patients were scared by the word *nuclear*. Indeed, the nucleus is involved, but unlike the other modalities discussed so far, MRI produces no high-energy photons, X rays, or gamma rays. The nuclear interactions in MRI are much more subtle and do not disrupt the nucleus or produce any dangerous radiation. When radar was invented during the Second World

War, it was necessary to develop a way to turn off the transmitter fast enough to hear its echo bounce back from an airplane. At the speed of light, such echoes come back very quickly. A surprising discovery was that echoes seemed to come from within matter itself under certain conditions. These signals, as it turned out, were coming from the nuclei in that matter. All protons spin on their axes, and they are happiest when they form pairs to cancel out each other's magnetism created by that spin. Hydrogen, with only one proton, acts like a tiny permanent magnet. When something containing hydrogen, such as a human body, is placed in a strong magnetic field, the hydrogen protons align themselves, resulting is a small magnetic contribution standing straight up in the large external field. When a pulse of radio energy at a certain frequency (the Larmor frequency) is delivered to those protons, they are knocked down 90 degrees and start turning around (also at the Larmor frequency) like little magnetic generators. By doing this, they produce a radio signal, the mysterious "echo" that was detected by the inventors of radar.

The protons all start turning in phase when the radio pulse occurs, but they gradually drift apart (de-phase) until they are each pointing in a random relative direction. When this happens, the net signal of the echo cancels itself out and disappears. The time required for the protons to de-phase is called T2, and it is a property of a given tissue type. Meanwhile, the strong external field slowly exerts its effect, standing the protons straight up again, ready for the next radio pulse. The time taken for the protons to get back up on their feet is called T1, and it is also a property of a given tissue type.

MRI is thus more complicated than the other imaging modalities, because two separate properties are being measured. The brightness of a voxel in CT, SPECT, or PET has real significance. It means the attenuation or emission of that physical voxel. In MRI, however, the brightness of a voxel is simply the strength of the radio echo, and depends on how the image was attained. Two important variables that can be adjusted in the MRI machine are Tr (r = repetition) and Te (e = echo).

Tr is the time between radio pulses. If Tr is long enough, all the protons have time to get back on their feet and therefore are available to be knocked down again (and turned back into little generators) by the next radio pulse. As Tr is made shorter, protons with long T1 don't have time to stand back up before the next pulse, and therefore they are not ready to generate the next echo. Thus, with short Tr, voxels with long T1 are dark. Te is the time the machine waits to receive an echo after the radio pulse. If Te is short enough, none of the little generators has time to de-phase, and all the echoes are strong. As Te is made longer, protons with short T2 have a chance to de-phase, and their echoes die away, making those voxels dark.

Figure 20.9 shows a transverse slice through a brain (parallel to the top of the head). The brighter layers on the outside of the cortex are the cell bodies of neurons, the processors of the brain, known as the "gray" matter (the tissue is gray upon dissection). The darker branching structures deeper in the cortex are the bundles of interconnecting axons, the wiring of the brain, known as the "white" matter. This particular MRI image is called a "proton density" image, because Te is short, picking up all echoes before they de-phase, and Tr is long, allowing all protons sufficient time to recover. Thus there is no preference for tissues of differing T1 or T2, and we are simply seeing the density of all protons.

FIGURE 20.9.

One mode of MRI is the proton-density image, shown here producing a transverse slice of a head.

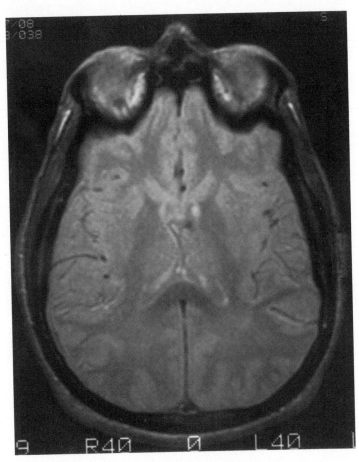

Figure 20.10 shows the same slice, but with a longer Te. Only the long echoes survive, those from voxels with a long T2. This so-called "T2-weighted" image tends to emphasize the gray matter and the surrounding fluid. This fluid also fills the central chambers, or ventricles, of the brain (the winged structure in the center of the image).

FIGURE 20.10.

The same slice of brain as in 20.9 is shown here using a T2-weighted protocol.

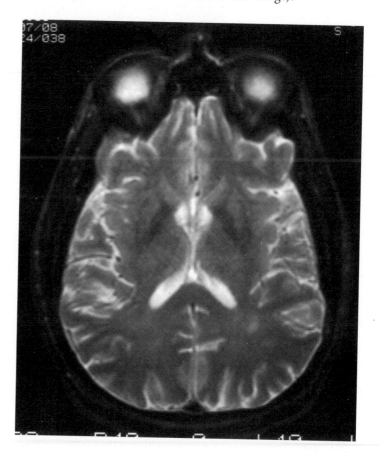

Figure 20.11 shows a slice with a different orientation, sagittal—that is, the head is seen in profile. The MRI machine has again been adjusted, this time by shortening Tr so that some protons have not yet stood back up before the next radio pulse. Thus, a "T1-weighted" image is formed. In the brain, the white matter has a shorter T1 than the gray matter and therefore is brighter in this image.

An important advantage of MRI over other modalities is seen in Figure 20.11. The sagittal slice is not the result of re-slicing a 3-D data set. The MRI machine can actually acquire a slice in any orientation and is not restricted, as is CT, to transverse slices.

FIGURE 20.11.

This is a T1-weighted sagittal slice of a head.

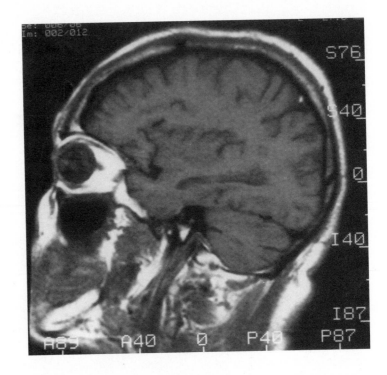

Luckily, radio signals and magnetic fields pass easily through the body, so we can see inside ourselves. But how does the MRI machine localize all those different voxels? The data is received through a single radio antenna. Luckily again, the Larmor frequency at which both the radio pulse and the echo occur is proportional to the external magnetic field. Stronger fields result in higher frequencies. This fact is essential in localizing voxels.

Localization is achieved by using three small magnetic gradients, which vary the strong magnetic field slightly along each of the three axes. When the radio pulse is delivered, the gradient along one of the axes is switched on, isolating one particular slice for activation—the Larmor frequency of that slice matches the radio signal. Then, when the echo is received, a second gradient is switched on, causing each row of voxels in that slice to echo at a slightly different frequency, so they can be separated in much the same way an AM radio separates different channels. The third gradient separates each row into individual voxels by giving each proton a small twist (phase shift) proportional to its position along the row. The whole decoding process turns out to be a Fourier transform of another Fourier transform, the so-called "Z-space." For those who dare, it is one of the cleverest little pieces of math ever invented.

3-D representations of MRI data have not yet found widespread clinical use. Isosurfaces don't work very well with MRI data. Unlike CT, voxels in MRI data have no fixed physical basis by which one tissue type always lies above a certain threshold. To deal with this, a relatively new method of rendering is described by Robert A. Drebin ("Volume Rendering," R.A. Drebin. 1988. *Computer Graphics*, vol. 22, no. 4, pp. 65-74). In this method, each voxel becomes a tiny surface. The orientation of each little surface is determined by looking at the neighboring voxels. The mathematical gradient (that is, the direction of maximum change, not the same "gradient" mentioned before) is calculated and the tiny surface is oriented perpendicular to that direction, the equivalent of a single isosurface. The surface opacity is determined by the strength of the gradient. After this operation is performed on every voxel, the entire set of tiny disconnected surfaces is fed to the standard lighting and reflectance routines. An example of Drebin's approach is shown in Figure 20.12, which shows a normal mouse embryo. As you can seen, this rendering does not simply give us a single threshold, but rather a translucent body containing numerous surfaces. The opacities of these surfaces can be changed in real time by adjusting the curve that maps gradient strength into opacity. The results of four opacity maps are shown.

FIGURE 20.12.

Shown here is a normal mouse embryo, volume rendered with various opacity curves using Voxel View, a program from Vital Images, Inc., Fairfield, Iowa. (Courtesy of Bradley Smith, Ph.D., and Elwood A. Linney, Ph.D., Center for In Vivo Microscopy, Duke University.)

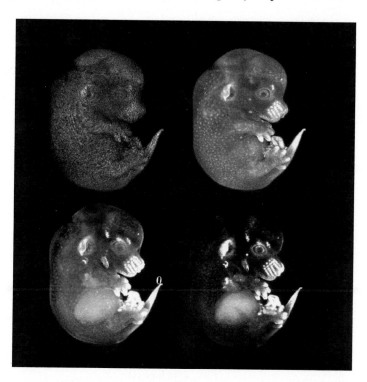

A special kind of MRI machine has been used to make the pictures in Figure 20.12. The magnetic fields are much stronger than in standard MRI machines, allowing increased magnification—in effect, an MRI microscope has been created. The level of detail is far greater than could be seen by the naked eye. The embryo, in only its fifteenth day since conception, measures just 7 millimeters from crown to rump.

Visualization of 3-D Medical Data

by W. Andrew Bass
Stereotactic Neurosurgical Apparatus Research Laboratory
Vanderbilt University

Introduction

The first section of this chapter presented the reader with a basic understanding of what medical images represent and how they are made. The previous chapter introduced some three-dimensional techniques for displaying volumetric data sets. The remainder of this chapter combines this information, presenting computer programs that can be used to display and analyze real-world volumetric data. The programs in this chapter focus mainly on generalizing the process of window and leveling. The source code presented in this chapter is written in the C language and compiled with Borland C++ 4.02 with Borland PowerPack and Metagraphics Software Corporation's METBGI256 graphics drivers. The programs presented in this chapter may be run from the CD-ROM or from a local hard disk. If you want to run the programs from a hard disk, the following files must be copied into the same directory as the executable files for correct operation:

- 32RTM.EXE
- DPMI32VM.OVL
- BGI32.DLL
- METWND08.DLL
- BGIN__01.FNT

About the Data Files

There are two volumetric data sets on the CD-ROM accompanying this book. There are several other medical data sets available on the Internet. A few volumes are available by anonymous FTP to omicron.cs.unc.edu in the pub/softlab/CHVRTD directory.

The programs in this chapter will be modifying these files in order to visualize them. The resulting files will need to be stored on a hard disk. The reader is advised to create a subdirectory on his or her hard disk for this purpose.

The first volume, CT.DAT, is a transverse CT scan of the plastic skull seen in Figure 20.13. The second, MRI.DAT, is a sagittal MRI scan of a human head. These files are stored on the CD-ROM in almost the same file format used by the CT and MRI scanners. Only three preprocessing steps have been performed. First, the header section of the files—which contains information about the specific scanner, the physical dimensions of the pixels, the date and time of the scan, hospital, and so on—have been removed. Second, the individual slices have been concatenated into a single 3-D volume. Third, the files have been converted from big-endian format to little-endian format. The CT and MRI scanners are designed to store their data in big-endian format. This is the format used by most UNIX workstations. PCs, however, require the data to be in little-endian format. The conversion between the two formats, commonly know as byte swapping, simply flip-flops adjacent data bytes in memory.

FIGURE 20.13.

This is a picture of the plastic skull in the CT data set, CT.DAT. (Courtesy of Dr. Robert L. Galloway, Vanderbilt University.)

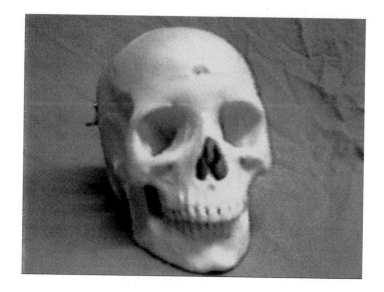

The files on the CD are stored in a raw format. No information is contained within the files about the dimensions of the data sets or how to interpret them. The files are simply binary lists of intensity values. The provider of the files must supply the information needed to interpret the volumes. Additionally, this information is stored in the header sections of the individual slice files, but it is stored in the scanner manufacturer's format, which is often non-standard. In this case, the CT data set consists of 36 slices of 512×512 voxels each, where each voxel is 0.49 mm by 0.49 mm in the plane of the slice, and each slice is 4 mm thick. The MRI data consists of 115 slices of 256×256 voxels, where each voxel is 0.98 mm by 0.98 mm in the plane of the slice, and each slice is 1.25 mm thick. Each voxel in both volumes has a 12-bit intensity value that is stored in two bytes.

Why aren't these files stored in one of the standard PC graphical file formats? The reason is simple: none of the standard graphics formats (TIFF, GIF, PCX, PIC, BMP, JPEG, and so on) provides a way of dealing with an intensity resolution greater than eight bits per pixel. Technically, this is not entirely true. Revision 6.0 of the TIFF standard allows the value 12 to be placed in the bits per pixel entry, but a TIFF 6.0 file reader based solely on the base specification will not be able to read the resulting files correctly, and thus a majority of the TIFF readers available could not correctly handle the images. Even those few TIFF readers that could correctly display the images, could not extract as much information from the volumes as the programs in this chapter. At this point, you might be wondering if some of the 24-bit file formats are suitable for storing these volumes, but as will be explained shortly, 24-bit file formats are still not adequate for this type of medical data.

Computer Requirements

Because of the enormous size of the data files, the programs in this chapter are written with Borland C++ version 4.02 with PowerPack, the 32-bit extensions for DOS. The addition of PowerPack enables the programs to easily use all of the memory in a PC and break free of the 64K limits imposed by real-mode compilers. The disadvantage of using a 32-bit protected mode compiler is that the programs generated by it must be run on a computer with at least a 386DX processor equipped with 4 MB (megabytes) of memory. Furthermore, the target PC must have a graphics adapter and monitor capable of supporting 640×480 resolution with 256 colors. Obviously, these programs will run faster on 100 MHz Pentium machines with 32 MB of memory and a local bus graphics adapter (it might be helpful to slow them down with delay loops), but they will also run reasonably well on a 25 MHz 386 system with a standard ISA graphics adapter. If you want to modify these programs for your own purposes, you will need Borland C++ version 4.02, Borland's PowerPack for DOS, and Metagraphics Software's METBGI256 set of 256 color BGI32 graphic drivers (PowerPack ships with only 16 color drivers), or any other protected-mode compiler with appropriate video drivers.

2-D Slicing Versus 3-D Rendering

As previously stated, the usual way of visualizing a 3-D volumetric data set is to slice it up and let a faster, more powerful computer—the human brain—mentally reconstruct the 3-D data. Although true 3-D volumetric visualization systems exist, most are built around custom software and hardware (some of the systems have more than 1,000 processors and one gigabyte of memory!). Yet despite this enormous amount of processing power and storage, the computational results are displayed on a normal, 2-D computer monitor. The methods and programs presented in this chapter focus on getting the most information out of 3-D data sets by displaying the 2-D slices as quickly as possible. The reader will find that there is a tremendous amount of information contained in these data sets, and displaying this information as 2-D slices is not limiting.

Data Reduction

To maximize the speed of the display, it is important to fit as much of a volume into memory as possible. Because the smallest of the two volumes is more than 14 MB, and most PCs are equipped with only 4 MB or 8 MB of memory, the volumes can not be directly loaded into memory. However, the size of the data sets can be reduced, preferably in such a way as to minimize the amount of information lost. The intensity values in both of the data sets have 12 bits of resolution, requiring 2 bytes of storage per voxel. If this resolution could be reduced to 8 bits per voxel, each voxel could then be stored in only one byte. This decreases the size of each data set by 50 percent.

Even if your PC has enough memory to hold the full 12-bit volumes and has an ultra-fast true-color PCI video card, the intensities must still be reduced from 12 bits to 8 bits. Why? Because even a 24-bit video card, which is capable of generating more than 16.7 million colors, can generate only 256 shades of gray. As Figure 20.14 shows, the 24 bits of color resolution is divided equally among three color channels—red, green, and blue. By varying the values in each color channel, the card is capable of generating more than 16.7 million colors. However, if the output colors are constrained to shades of pure blue, then both the red and green channels will always have a value of 0. At this point, only the 8 bits assigned to the blue channel can vary, and therefore there are only $2^8 = 256$ shades of pure blue. Shades of gray are created when the values of all three color channels are exactly equal. So again, there can be only 256 shades. This limitation is the reason why the 24-bit image file formats are not sufficient to store medical images. They may encode 24 bits of storage per voxel, but they expect three color channels, each with 8-bit data.

FIGURE 20.14.

Although 24-bit video cards can generate more than 16.7 million colors, they can generate only 256 shades of gray.

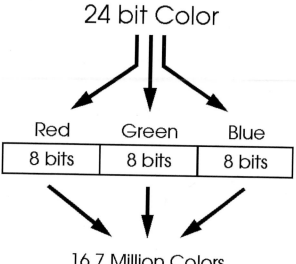

Most PCs, however, are not equipped with 24-bit display boards, but have SVGA or VGA graphics adapters. These adapters are generally faster and less expensive because they don't have to process as much information as their true color counterparts. Most of these adapters function by using 6 bits per color channel and are capable of displaying more than 256,000 colors, but only 64 are shades of gray. At first it might seem reasonable to devise a method for reducing our intensity resolution from 12 bits down to 6 bits, but 6-bit data would still require one byte of storage for each intensity value, and therefore the information content would not be maximized. If, however, the data were only reduced to 8 bits, the storage requirement would be the same and the information loss would be minimized.

Even when the storage requirement for each voxel is reduced to one byte, however, the data sets are still greater than 7 MB and still too large to load into the memory of most PCs. Therefore, in addition to the reduction in intensity resolution, the size of the individual slices will be reduced. The CT data consists of 36 slices, with each slice being 512×512 voxels. With the size of each slice reduced to 256×256, the size of the volume decreases by a factor of 4, resulting in a file a little over 2 MB. With the MRI volume reduced from 256×256 slices to 128×128 slices, the total size of the volume becomes about 1.8 MB. The reduction in size is easiest to accomplish, so it will be presented first.

ShrinkMR.c

The ShrinkMR program is designed to do exactly what its name implies. It takes a 256×256, 12-bit MRI data set and reduces it to a 128×128, 12-bit data set. However, the starting and ending sizes of the files are controlled by #define statements and can easily be modified. The ShrinkMR program takes two command line arguments. The first argument is the name of the input file (use MRI.DAT, on the CD-ROM, with the full path). The second argument is the name of the output file to be placed on your hard disk. There are no requirements for the output filename, but it will be referred to as MRI2.DAT throughout the rest of this chapter. When specifying the filenames, be sure to include full path information. Note that it is necessary to mask out the upper 4 bits in the 12-bit intensities. This is because several scanners have the ability to place other, non-intensity-based information in these "unused" bits. This information, if present, is almost universally scanner specific and would only cause errors in the ShrinkMR program. The source code for ShrinkMR.c is in Listing 20.1. To compile and link this program with Borland's tools, type bcc32 -WX -N ShrinkMR.c at the DOS prompt.

Listing 20.1. The source code for ShrinkMR.

```
#include <stdlib.h>
#include <stdio.h>
#include <io.h>

#define INSIZE  256
```

```
#define OUTSIZE 128
#define BPV     2        /* Bytes per voxel */


void main(int argc, char **argv)
{
int i,j,k,l,m;
int Rfactor = INSIZE / OUTSIZE;
FILE *in, *out;
short inframe[INSIZE][INSIZE];
short outframe[OUTSIZE][OUTSIZE];
int filesize, numslices;
int temp;


    /* Ensure proper syntax */

    if(argc != 3)
      {
      printf("\nUsage:: shrinkMR infile outfile\n\n");
      exit(1);
      }


    /* Open the files */

    in = fopen(argv[1], "rb");
    if(in == NULL)
      {
      printf("\nCould not open file %s.\n\n", argv[1]);
      exit(2);
      }

    out = fopen(argv[2], "wb");
    if(out == NULL)
      {
      printf("\nCould not create file %s.\n\n", argv[2]);
      exit(3);
      }


    /* Determine number of slices in the volume */

    filesize = filelength( fileno(in) );
    numslices = filesize / INSIZE / INSIZE / BPV;
    if(numslices * INSIZE * INSIZE * BPV != filesize)
      {
      printf("\nThe size of the input file is incorrect.\n\n");
      exit(4);
      }


    /* Processing Loop */

    for(i=0; i<numslices; i++)
      {
      fread(inframe, INSIZE * INSIZE, BPV, in);
      printf("Processing slice %d/%d.\n", i+1, numslices);
```

continues

Listing 20.1. continued

```
    /* Mask out upper nibble */

    for(j=0; j<INSIZE; j++)
      for(k=0; k<INSIZE; k++)
        inframe[j][k] &= 0x0FFF;


    /* Size reduction by averaging */

    for(j=0; j<OUTSIZE; j++)
      for(k=0; k<OUTSIZE; k++)
        {
        temp = 0;
        for(l=0; l<Rfactor; l++)
          for(m=0; m<Rfactor; m++)
            temp += inframe[j*Rfactor+l][k*Rfactor+m];
        outframe[j][k] = temp / Rfactor / Rfactor;
        }

    fwrite(outframe, OUTSIZE * OUTSIZE, BPV, out);
    }

  fclose(in);
  fclose(out);
}
```

ShrinkCT.c

The ShrinkCT program, as its name implies, is the functional equivalent of the ShrinkMR program. The command arguments are identical. It is important to note, however, that because this program is run on CT volumes, the intensity values need to be read in as signed quantities. As explained previously, CT intensity values are based on Hounsfield units where water is assigned the value 0. Because the attenuation of X rays is greater in water than air, air has negative Hounsfield numbers. The Hounsfield numbers output from most CT scanners range from –1024 to 3071, so a simple method of eliminating the negative intensities is to add 1024 to each voxel's intensity. This transforms the intensity range to 0 to 4095, the same range as the MRI data. The major change in the code is shown in Listing 20.2. Hereafter, the reduced CT volume, located on your hard disk, will be referred to as CT2.DAT. To compile and link this program with Borland's tools, type bcc32 -WX -N ShrinkMR.c at the DOS prompt.

Listing 20.2. Partial source code for the ShrinkCT program.

```
/* Processing Loop */

for(i=0; i<numslices; i++)
  {
```

```
fread(inframe, INSIZE * INSIZE, BPV, in);
printf("Processing slice %d/%d.\n", i+1, numslices);

/* Correct for negative Hounsfield values */
/* and mask out upper nibble */

for(j=0; j<INSIZE; j++)
  for(k=0; k<INSIZE; k++)
    {
    inframe[j][k] += 1024;
    inframe[j][k] &= 0x0FFF;
    }

/* Size reduction by averaging */

for(j=0; j<OUTSIZE; j++)
  for(k=0; k<OUTSIZE; k++)
    {
    temp = 0;
    for(l=0; l<Rfactor; l++)
      for(m=0; m<Rfactor; m++)
        temp += inframe[j*Rfactor+l][k*Rfactor+m];
    outframe[j][k] = temp / Rfactor / Rfactor;
    }

fwrite(outframe, OUTSIZE * OUTSIZE, BPV, out);
}
```

Basic Window and Leveling Revisited

The previous chapter introduced a simple form of window and leveling. This section will apply that simple window and leveling to real CT and MRI data and then extend the concept to a more general form of mapping 12-bit data to 8-bit data. In the last chapter, the window and the level values were chosen arbitrarily at the beginning of the program, and the results were viewed after the program finished its calculations. If any adjustments were needed, new values were entered and the program was run again.

The data reduction was accomplished by specifying a window in the intensity range. The size and placement of this window are controlled by the two parameters, the window size and the level. All of the intensity values that fall outside this window are set to either black or white, depending on whether they fall below or above the window. The intensities that fall within the window are set to a gray value according to a linear function. Using this method, it typically takes several rounds of adjustment to ensure that the resulting data set contains the maximum amount of information. Wouldn't it be great if there were a better way to set the initial window and level values, and be reasonably assured that the information loss is minimized? There is. It's called a histogram.

A *histogram* is simply a graph showing the number of pixels or voxels at each intensity allowed by the resolution of the image or volume. Histograms are almost trivial to calculate because they are completely independent of the dimensions of the image or images upon which they are based. Histograms don't care about how big the voxels or pixels are, or about whether the images are 512×512 or 256× 256, or even 837×17.

Hist12.c

Hist12 is a program that calculates and displays the histograms of 12-bit data sets. The source code listing for Hist12.c is shown in Listing 20.3. The program takes three command line arguments. The first is the name of the input file to use as the source of the histogram. The second argument tells the program where in the intensity range to start calculating the histogram, and the third argument tells the program how many intensity values beyond the starting point to count. For example, to see a histogram of the entire intensity spectrum of the reduced CT or MRI volumes, use 0 as the start of the range and 4096 as the number of intensity levels. The Hist12 program is limited to intensity ranges that are a power of 2—that is, 32, 64, 128, and so on through 4096. After you decide on the histogram parameters, the program calculates the histogram and displays the results graphically.

Rather than calculating the maximum number of voxels at a single intensity of the histogram and scaling the graph accordingly, the graphing algorithm computes the average number of voxels per intensity, excluding intensities with no voxels, and assigns that value to the middle of the screen. This prevents a large number of voxels at one intensity from obscuring information at other intensities. For example, if a data set contains 100,000 voxels at an intensity of 29 and the program assigned 100,000 to represent the top of the histogram, then—because the histogram is only 400 pixels high—each bin would have to vary by more than 100,000/400 = 250 voxels in order to differ by one pixel on the screen! The average-equals-middle technique has the advantage of displaying more detail in the histogram. The disadvantage of this technique is that some of the higher peaks in the histogram are truncated by the graph. However, because the histogram is only being used to get initial window and level values, this is not a major concern nor is the exact number of pixels in each histogram peak. Pressing any key causes the program to exit to the DOS prompt. Hist12 is compiled and linked with Borland's tools when you type at the DOS prompt `bcc32 -WX -N Hist12.c bgi32.lib`.

Listing 20.3. The source code for Hist12.

```
#include <stdlib.h>
#include <stdio.h>
#include <conio.h>
#include <graphics.h>
#include <io.h>
```

```
#include <malloc.h>
#include <string.h>
#include <math.h>


#define BUFFERSIZE 128*128


void main(int argc, char **argv)
{
int i,j,k,l;
FILE *in;
int startgray;
int grays;
short buffer[BUFFERSIZE];
int filesize;
int bpf;                /* buffers per file */
unsigned int *histogram;
int grdriver, grmode, grerror;
float avg, temp;
unsigned short disp[512];
int ratio;
char ticks[15];
int tw;


   /* Ensure proper syntax */

   if(argc != 4)
     {
     printf("Usage:: Hist12 filename startgray numgray.\n\n");
     exit(1);
     }

   startgray = atoi(argv[2]);
   grays = atoi(argv[3]);

   switch(grays)
     {
     case 4096:
     case 2048:
     case 1024:
     case 512:
     case 256:
     case 128:
     case 64:
     case 32:
       break;

     default:
       printf("\nPlease use a power of 2 (128, 256, etc.)\n");
       printf("for the number of gray values.\n\n");
       exit(2);
     }


/* Allocate histogram storage space */
```

continues

Listing 20.3. continued

```c
histogram = (unsigned int *)malloc(grays * sizeof(int));
if(histogram == NULL)
   {
   printf("\nMemory allocation error.\n");
   exit(3);
   }


/* open input file */

in = fopen(argv[1], "rb");
if(in == NULL)
   {
   printf("Can not open file: %s.\n\n", argv[1]);
   exit(4);
   }

/* Clear the histogram */

for(i=0; i<grays; i++)
   histogram[i] = 0;


/* Determine the number of disk reads needed */

filesize = filelength( fileno(in) );
bpf = filesize / sizeof(buffer);


/* Calculate the histogram */

for(i=0; i<bpf; i++)
   {
   fread(buffer, sizeof(buffer), 1, in);

   for(j=0; j<BUFFERSIZE; j++)
      {
      if(buffer[j] >= startgray)
         if(buffer[j] < startgray + grays)
            histogram[ buffer[j] - startgray]++;
      }
   }

fclose(in);


/* check graphics hardware */

grdriver = DETECTX;
grmode = 0;
detectgraph(&grdriver, &grmode);
switch(grdriver)
   {
   case VESA256:
   case ATI256:
   case COMPAQ:
   case TSENG3256:
```

```
    case TSENG4256:
    case GENOA5:
    case GENOA6:
    case OAK:
    case PARADIS256:
    case TECMAR:
    case TRIDENT256:
    case VIDEO7:
    case VIDEO7II:
      break;

    default:
      printf("Unable to detect 256 color graphics adapter.\n");
      exit(5);
      break;
    }


grmode = 1;
initgraph(&grdriver, &grmode, "");
grerror = graphresult();
if(grerror)
    {
    closegraph();
    printf("Error %d initializing graphics mode.\n", grerror);
    exit(6);
    }


/* get the average histogram value */

avg = 0.0;
j = 0;

for(i=0; i<grays; i++)
    {
    avg += (float)histogram[i];
    if(histogram[i] != 0)
      j++;
    }

avg = avg/(float)j;


/* setup display array */

if(grays >= 512)
    {
    ratio = grays/512;

    for(i=0; i<512; i++)
      {
      temp = 0.0;
      for(j=0; j<ratio; j++)
        temp += (float)histogram[i*ratio + j] / (float)ratio;
      k = (int)floor( (double)(temp / avg * 200.0));
      if(k > 400)
        k = 400;
```

continues

Listing 20.3. continued

```
      disp[i] = k;
      }
   }
 else
   {
   ratio = 512/grays;

   for(i=0; i<grays; i++)
     {
     k = (int)floor( (double)(histogram[i] / avg * 200.0));
     if(k > 400)
       k = 400;
     for(j=0; j<ratio; j++)
       disp[i*ratio + j] = k;
     }
   }


 /* display background */

 setbkcolor(31);      /* white */
 cleardevice();

 setcolor(0);
 rectangle(63,39, 640-64,480-39);


 /* display histogram */

 setcolor(1);          /* blue */
 for(i=0; i<512; i++)
   line(64+i, 440, 64+i, 440 - disp[i]);


 /* display tick marks and title */

 setcolor(0);
 for(i=0; i<=8; i++)
   {
   sprintf(ticks, "%d", i*grays/8 + startgray);
   tw = textwidth(ticks);
   outtextxy(64*(i+1)-tw/2+1, 450, ticks);
   line(64*(i+1), 441, 64*(i+1), 444);
   }

 tw = textwidth(argv[1]);
 outtextxy(320-tw/2+1, 20, argv[1]);


 /* wait for keystrike then exit */

 getch();

 closegraph();
 free( (void *)histogram);
}
```

Figure 20.15 shows the output from running Hist12 on the reduced CT volume, specifying the entire intensity spectrum. Note that except for a small peak at 4095, there are no voxels with intensities over 1,536. From this figure, it is clear that even though the CT scanner has the capability to output voxels with 12-bit resolution, it does not mean that any one data set will contain voxels with all of these intensities. The results of narrowing the histogram calculation to the first 2048 intensities are shown in Figure 20.16. There are three distinct intensity regions in the data set. The first region is below 256 on the intensity scale, where there are two distinct peaks. The second is between approximately 256 and 1024. The third region is above 1024, where there are also two distinct peaks. Remember that at the end of our window-and-leveling calculation there will be only 256 levels of gray. To retain the most information about the first region, choose a window of 256 and a level of 128. However, because all of the voxels with intensities above 256 will be set to white, this will obscure any differences between the second and third regions. To retain the most information about the third region, set the window to 350 and the level to 1200. Again, this would make all intensities below 1025 appear black, thus removing the difference between the first and second regions. To retain the most information about all of the regions, set the window to 1536 and the level to 768. It is obvious that the histogram is a valuable tool for choosing the window and level values.

FIGURE 20.15.

This is the full histogram of the reduced CT volume.

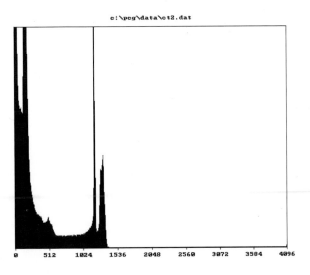

c:\pcg\data\ct2.dat

Figure 20.17 shows the output of the Hist12 program on the reduced MRI volume. From this figure, it is again clear that even though a medical scanner can output 12-bit resolution data, the actual values for a given data set may not cover the entire range. In this case, as shown in the 128-entry histogram in Figure 20.18, there are essentially no voxels with intensity values greater than 100. Setting the window and level parameters to 100 and 50, respectively, will not expand the dynamic range of the volume, but only spread out the histogram over the new range. To maintain all of the information in this volume, set the window and level values to 256 and 128. The intensity range in this data set is somewhat atypical. Usually MRI data sets will have voxels stretching into the 2048 range, but this is dependent on many factors, including the type of scan, T1 weighted, T2 weighed, the manufacturer of the scanner, and so on.

FIGURE 20.16.

This is the 2048-entry histogram of the reduced CT volume.

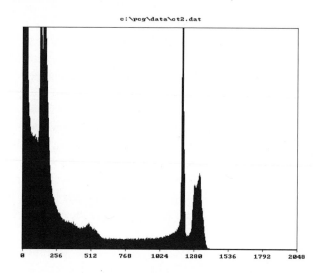

FIGURE 20.17.

This is the full histogram of the reduced MRI volume.

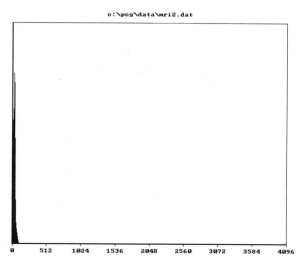

FIGURE 20.18.

This is the 128-entry histogram of the reduced MRI volume.

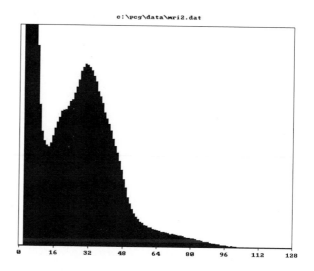

c:\pcg\data\mri2.dat

WinLev.c

The WinLev program is conceptually identical to the window-and-leveling method used in the previous chapter. Source code for WinLev is shown in Listing 20.4. The program takes four command line arguments. The first is the name of the 12-bit input file. The second is the name of the 8-bit output file to write. Again, there are no requirements for the output filename. The third and fourth arguments are the window and level values to use on the input file. Two 8-bit data sets will be generated with WinLev for use in the rest of this chapter; however, others may be created to further visualize the two volumes. The first 8-bit volume, called MRI3.DAT hereafter, is created by typing `WinLev mri2.dat mri3.dat 256 128` at the DOS prompt. The second 8-bit volume, hereafter called CT3.DAT, is created by typing `WinLev ct2.dat ct3.dat 1536 768` at the DOS prompt. For purposes of clarity, these command examples do not contain any path information, but be sure to include path information when running WinLev on your PC. WinLev.c is compiled and linked with Borland's tools when you type `bcc32 -WX -N WinLev.c` at the DOS prompt.

Listing 20.4. The source code for WinLev.

```
#include <stdlib.h>
#include <stdio.h>
#include <conio.h>
#include <io.h>
#include <math.h>


#define BUFFERSIZE  128*128
```

continues

Listing 20.4. continued

```c
double rnd(double val);


void main(int argc, char **argv)
{
int i,j,k;
FILE *in, *out;
int win, lev;
int filesize;
short inbuffer[BUFFERSIZE];
unsigned char outbuffer[BUFFERSIZE];
int bpf;
float temp;

  /* Ensure correct syntax */

  if(argc != 5)
    {
    printf("Usage:: WinLev infile outfile win lev.\n\n");
    exit(1);
    }


  /* Setup input and output files */

  in = fopen(argv[1], "rb");
  if(in == NULL)
    {
    printf("Unable to open file %s.\n\n", argv[1]);
    exit(2);
    }

  out = fopen(argv[2], "wb");
  if(out == NULL)
    {
    printf("Error creating / opening file %s.\n\n", argv[2]);
    exit(2);
    }

  /* Verify window and level values */

  win = atoi(argv[3]);
  lev = atoi(argv[4]);

  if((win < 0) || (win > 4096))
    {
    printf("Window not within allowable range(1 - 4096).\n\n");
    exit(3);
    }

  if(((lev-win/2) < 0) || ((lev+win/2) > 4096))
    {
    printf("Level puts window out of range(0 - 4095).\n\n");
    exit(4);
    }
```

```
/* Calculate number of buffers per file */

filesize = filelength( fileno(in));
bpf = filesize / sizeof(inbuffer);


/* Processing loop */

for(i=0; i<bpf; i++)
  {

  fread(inbuffer, sizeof(inbuffer), 1, in);

  for(j=0; j<BUFFERSIZE; j++)
    {
    temp = inbuffer[j] - (lev-win/2);
    temp = temp*255.0/(float)win;
    if(temp <= 0)
      outbuffer[j] = 0;
    if(temp >= 255)
        outbuffer[j] = 255;
      else
        outbuffer[j] = (unsigned char)rnd((double)temp);
    }

  fwrite(outbuffer, sizeof(outbuffer), 1, out);
  }

  fclose(in);
  fclose(out);

}


double rnd(double val)
{
double tempval;

  tempval = floor(val);
  if((val - tempval) > 0.5)
    return(tempval + 1.0);
  else return(tempval);
}
```

The process of window and leveling can be generalized by realizing that the intensities falling within the window are actually mapped by a function. Previously, we assigned the intensities at the bottom of the window the value 0 and the intensities at the top of the window the value 255; all intensities within the window were linearly converted to a value between 0 and 255. For example, if an intensity point is 20 percent into the window, then its corresponding gray scale value will be 20 percent of 255, or 51. This process is identical to using a linear function with a slope of 255 divided by the window size. Figures 20.19 through 20.22 show several variations of the linear window and level. Figure 20.19 is the standard ramp function used in the WinLev program. Figure 20.20 shows a quadratic window function, which emphasizes the higher portion of the window. Figure 20.21 is a square root window function, which has the opposite effect of emphasizing the lower portion of the window. Figure 20.22 shows an inverse ramp function, used to generate negative images. In this case, all of the intensities below the window should be set to white, and all of the intensities above the window should be set to black. Specialized window functions can be much more complex than the ones shown here. It is even possible to set up a window function that dynamically tries to divide the number of voxels equally among the gray levels of a given window and level. For simple visualization, the ramp window function is typically used to reduce 12-bit volumes to 8-bit volumes.

FIGURE 20.19.

This is an example of a ramp window function.

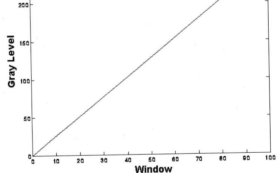

Ramp Function

FIGURE 20.20.

This is an example of a quadratic window function.

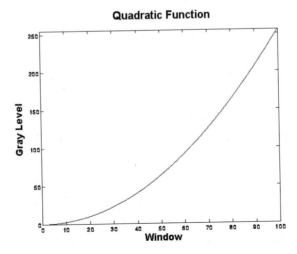

Quadratic Function

FIGURE 20.21.

This is an example of a square root window function.

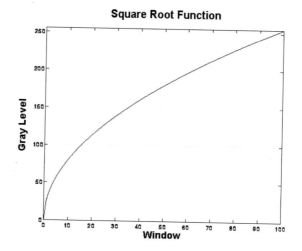

Square Root Function

FIGURE 20.22.

This is an example of an inverse ramp window function.

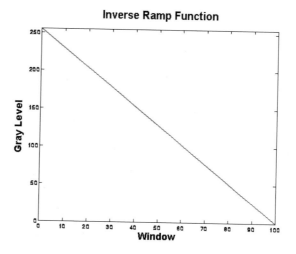

Inverse Ramp Function

Often when speed is a concern, the window and leveling process is not implemented using the method used in the WinLev program. Instead, a lookup table, or LUT, is used. LUTs were used in the last chapter to speed up transcendental calculations, but they can also be used in place of the window-and-level calculation. The general procedure for using a LUT is to first precalculate all of the values in the LUT. Then, when the processing loop is going through each voxel in the source data set, it simply looks up the value for the new data set in the LUT, without having to perform any calculations. Obviously, as the complexity of the window function increases, more time can be saved by using a LUT.

Displaying the Data Sets

Now that the size of the data sets has been reduced so that they can be loaded into memory, we can begin to display them. Because few PCs are equipped with 24-bit display boards, the 256 gray level data needs to be mapped down to 64 gray levels. Instead of reducing the data again, the rest of the programs presented in this chapter will use the hardware LUT contained on the graphics adapter to accomplish the reduction. This LUT is probably better known as the VGA palette, and because it is part of the graphics hardware its operation occurs in real time.

Display4.c

Display4 is a program that demonstrates the four window functions in Figures 20.19 through 20.22. The program takes only one command line argument, the location of the reduced 8-bit CT volume. Display4 reduces the size of the slices in this file to 128×128 and displays the images in four quadrants, looping through all of the slices in the volume until a key is pressed. Each of the quadrants has, in effect, its own 6-bit LUT. The program uses the 8-bit hardware palette to store the four different 6-bit LUTs, and uses bits 7 and 8 of the palette to select between the different LUTs. Because the slices have been further reduced in size, the display technique used in this program does not attempt to cache the volume in memory, but instead continuously reads the slices off of the hard disk. Although this is slower than storing the volume in memory, it is fast enough to see the differences in the window functions. In later programs, the display speed will be improved by loading the entire volume in memory. The source code for Display4 is shown in Listing 20.5. Display4 is compiled and linked using Borland's tools when you type `bcc32 -WX -N Display4.c bgi32.lib` at the DOS prompt.

Listing 20.5. The source code for Display4.

```
#include <stdlib.h>
#include <stdio.h>
#include <conio.h>
#include <graphics.h>
#include <io.h>
#include <malloc.h>
#include <string.h>
#include <math.h>



void main(int argc, char **argv)
{
int i,j,k,l;
FILE *datafile;
unsigned char LUT[256][3];
float temp;
```

```
unsigned char *buffer;
int filesize;
int numslices;
int grdriver, grmode, grerror;
int tw;
char title[20];
char disp[128][128];

  /* Ensure proper syntax */

  if(argc != 2)
    {
    printf("Usage::  Display4 datafile.\n\n");
    exit(1);
    }


  /* open input files */

  datafile = fopen(argv[1], "rb");
  if(datafile == NULL)
    {
    printf("Can not open file: %s.\n\n", argv[1]);
    exit(2);
    }


/* Create the LUT structure */

for(i=0; i<64; i++)      /* ramp window fxn */
  for(j=0; j<3; j++)
    {
    LUT[i][j] = (unsigned char)i;
    }

for(i=64; i<128; i++)  /* quadratic window fxn */
  for(j=0; j<3; j++)
    {
    temp = (float)(i-64)/63.0 * 7.9;
    LUT[i][j] = (unsigned char)temp*temp;
    }

for(i=128; i<192; i++)  /* sqrt window fxn */
  for(j=0; j<3; j++)
    {
    temp = (float)(i-128)/63.0 * 3968.0;
    LUT[i][j] = (unsigned char)sqrt((double)temp);
    }

for(i=192; i<256; i++)  /* inverse ramp window fxn */
  for(j=0; j<3; j++)
    {
    LUT[i][j] = (unsigned char)(63 - (i-192));
    }


/* Determine the number of slices in the volume */
```

continues

Listing 20.5. continued

```c
filesize = filelength( fileno(datafile) );
numslices = filesize / 256 / 256;


/* Allocate memory for the disk buffer. */

buffer = (unsigned char *)malloc( 256*256 );
if(buffer == NULL)
   {
   printf("Error allocating memory for buffer.\n\n");
   exit(3);
   }


/* check graphics hardware */

grdriver = DETECTX;
grmode = 0;
detectgraph(&grdriver, &grmode);
switch(grdriver)
   {
   case VESA256:
   case ATI256:
   case COMPAQ:
   case TSENG3256:
   case TSENG4256:
   case GENOA5:
   case GENOA6:
   case OAK:
   case PARADIS256:
   case TECMAR:
   case TRIDENT256:
   case VIDEO7:
   case VIDEO7II:
     break;

   default:
     printf("Unable to detect 256 color graphics adapter.\n");
     exit(4);
     break;
   }


  grmode = 1;
  initgraph(&grdriver, &grmode, "");
  grerror = graphresult();
  if(grerror)
     {
     closegraph();
     printf("Error %d initializing graphics mode.\n", grerror);
     exit(5);
     }


   /* Program the hardware palette */
```

```
for(i=0; i<256; i++)
  setrgbpalette(i, LUT[i][0], LUT[i][1], LUT[i][2]);


/* Display the image titles */

setcolor(63);

strcpy(title, "RAMP FUNCTION");
tw = textwidth(title);
outtextxy(160 - tw/2, 160, title);

strcpy(title, "QUADRATIC FUNCTION");
tw = textwidth(title);
outtextxy(480 - tw/2, 160, title);

strcpy(title, "SQUARE ROOT FUNCTION");
tw = textwidth(title);
outtextxy(160 - tw/2, 360, title);

strcpy(title, "INVERSE RAMP FUNCTION");
tw = textwidth(title);
outtextxy(480 - tw/2, 360, title);


while(!kbhit())
  {
  for(i=0; i<numslices; i++)
    {

    fseek(datafile, (long)i*256*256, SEEK_SET);
    fread(buffer, 256*256, 1, datafile);

    for(j=0; j<128; j++)
      for(k=0; k<128; k++)
        {
        l =  (int)buffer[2*j*256 + 2*k];
        l += (int)buffer[(2*j+1)*256 + 2*k];
        l += (int)buffer[2*j*256 + 2*k+1];
        l += (int)buffer[(2*j+1)*256 + 2*k+1];
        l /= 16;

        disp[k][j] = l;
        }

    for(j=0; j<128; j++)
      for(k=0; k<128; k++)
        putpixel(96+k, 20+j, disp[k][j]);

    for(j=0; j<128; j++)
      for(k=0; k<128; k++)
        putpixel(416+k, 20+j, disp[k][j] | 0x40);

    for(j=0; j<128; j++)
      for(k=0; k<128; k++)
        putpixel(96+k, 220+j, disp[k][j] | 0x80);
    for(j=0; j<128; j++)
      for(k=0; k<128; k++)
```

continues

Listing 20.5. continued

```
        putpixel(416+k, 220+j, disp[k][j] ¦ 0xC0);

    }
  }

  fclose(datafile);
  free( (void *)buffer);
  getch();
  closegraph();
}
```

Figure 20.23 shows the output of the Display4 program for one of the slices in the CT volume. This particular slice cuts through the middle of the eye sockets in the plastic skull in the transverse, or axial orientation. The oval outline is the plastic skull. The semi-circular arc surrounding the skull is the head holder of the CT scanner. When the skull was being scanned, towels were placed on the head holder to prevent both the skull and head holder from being scratched. The towels are clearly visible in the slices. In addition to the towels, two tear-shaped objects are visible. These are foam-filled plastic positioning devices that help keep the skull facing upward and immobile in the scanner. On some of the slices, the tape used to hold the towels and skull in the head holder is also visible.

FIGURE 20.23.

This is a single slice from the Display4 program.

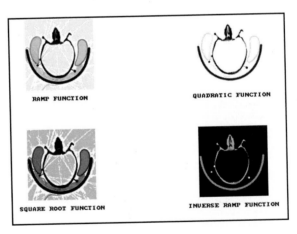

As Figure 20.23 shows, the quadratic window function emphasizes the higher intensities in the data, whereas the square root window function emphasizes the lower intensities. When the lower intensities are emphasized, some streaking is seen in the slices. This is an artifact that occurs when the filtered back projection algorithm, used to compute the CT slices, encounters extremely bright objects in the slice. The inverse ramp window function, as expected, produced a negative of the normal image.

The use of a LUT for performing window and leveling opens up the possibility for an even more general method of data reduction. Using the LUT approach enables the program to choose more than one window in the intensity range. For example, a single LUT could define three windows, each with its own window function. Alternatively, a LUT could split a single window with a single window function, putting different portions of the window in different places in the intensity range. For really bizarre-looking slices, the LUT can be set to random values.

As previously stated, normally the simple linear window and level is used to reduce volumes down to 8-bit intensities (although it may be implemented as a LUT to improve calculation speed), and then the generality offered by the LUT approach is used. Only occasionally is the general LUT approach used directly on the 12-bit data, and in those circumstances it is more often used for image processing rather than image visualization.

Before we start designing custom LUTs for viewing our 8-bit 3-D volumes, we need more detailed information about the 8-bit data. To gather this information, we will return to histograms.

Hist8.c

Hist8 is a program that closely resembles Hist12. There are, however, two major differences. First, Hist8 accepts only one command line argument. This argument specifies the source file for the histogram. Second, if Hist8 detects a mouse in the system, it will display a mouse cursor and the intensity value at the cursor point. This is useful because it enables the user to extract the exact location of histogram features. The mouse range is limited to the area of the histogram, and the program uses its own cursor drawing logic. The source code for Hist8 is shown in Listing 20.6. Hist8 is compiled and linked with Borland's tools when you type `bcc32 -WX -N Hist8.c bgi32.lib` at the DOS prompt.

Listing 20.6. The source code for Hist8.

```
#include <stdlib.h>
#include <stdio.h>
#include <conio.h>
#include <graphics.h>
#include <io.h>
#include <dos.h>
#include <malloc.h>
#include <string.h>
#include <math.h>


#define BUFFERSIZE 128*128


void main(int argc, char **argv)
{
int i,j,k,l;
```

continues

Listing 20.6. continued

```c
FILE *in;
unsigned char buffer[BUFFERSIZE];
int filesize;
int bpf;              /* buffers per file */
unsigned int histogram[256];
int grdriver, grmode, grerror;
float avg, temp;
short disp[512];
char ticks[40];
int tw;
int mousepresent, mousex, mousey;
int oldmousex, oldmousey;
union REGS regs;
unsigned char save[18];
int first = 1;


   /* Ensure proper syntax */

  if(argc != 2)
    {
    printf("Usage::  Hist8 filename.\n\n");
    exit(1);
    }


   /* open input file */

  in = fopen(argv[1], "rb");
  if(in == NULL)
    {
    printf("Can not open file: %s.\n\n", argv[1]);
    exit(2);
    }


   /* Clear the histogram */

  for(i=0; i<256; i++)
    histogram[i] = 0;


   /* Determine the number of disk reads needed */

  filesize = filelength( fileno(in) );
  bpf = filesize / sizeof(buffer);


   /* Calculate the histogram */

  for(i=0; i<bpf; i++)
    {
    fread(buffer, sizeof(buffer), 1, in);

    for(j=0; j<BUFFERSIZE; j++)
      histogram[ buffer[j]]++;
    }
```

```
    fclose(in);


    /* check graphics hardware */

    grdriver = DETECTX;
    grmode = 0;
    detectgraph(&grdriver, &grmode);
    switch(grdriver)
      {
      case VESA256:
      case ATI256:
      case COMPAQ:
      case TSENG3256:
      case TSENG4256:
      case GENOA5:
      case GENOA6:
      case OAK:
      case PARADIS256:
      case TECMAR:
      case TRIDENT256:
      case VIDEO7:
      case VIDEO7II:
        break;

      default:
        printf("Unable to detect 256 color graphics adapter.\n");
        exit(5);
        break;
      }


  grmode = 1;
  initgraph(&grdriver, &grmode, "");
  grerror = graphresult();
  if(grerror)
    {
    closegraph();
    printf("Error %d initializing graphics mode.\n", grerror);
    exit(6);
    }


/* Initialize mouse */

regs.w.ax = 0;
int386(0x33, &regs, &regs);

if((short)regs.w.ax != -1)
  mousepresent = 0;
 else mousepresent = 1;


/* Setup mouse range and turn on cursor */

if(mousepresent)
  {
  regs.w.ax = 0x0007;  /* horizontal range */
  regs.w.cx = 64;
  regs.w.dx = 578;      /* 64 -> 578 */
```

continues

Listing 20.6. continued

```c
int386(0x33, &regs, &regs);

regs.w.ax = 0x0008;   /* vertical range */
regs.w.cx = 40;
regs.w.dx = 440;       /* 40 -> 440 */
int386(0x33, &regs, &regs);

regs.w.ax = 0x0001;   /* display cursor */
int386(0x33, &regs, &regs);

oldmousex = 0;
oldmousey = 0;
}


/* get the average histogram value */

avg = 0.0;
j = 0;

for(i=0; i<256; i++)
  {
  avg += (float)histogram[i];
  if(histogram[i] != 0)
    j++;
  }

avg = avg/(float)j;


/* setup display array */

for(i=0; i<256; i++)
  {
  k = (int)floor( (double)(histogram[i] / avg * 200.0));
  if(k > 400)
    k = 400;
  disp[i*2] = k;
  disp[i*2 + 1] = k;
  }


/* display background */

setbkcolor(31);        /* white */
cleardevice();

setcolor(0);
rectangle(63,39, 640-64,480-39);


/* display histogram */

setcolor(1);           /* blue */
for(i=0; i<512; i++)
  line(64+i, 440, 64+i, 440 - disp[i]);
```

```
/* display tick marks and title */

setcolor(0);
for(i=0; i<=8; i++)
  {
  sprintf(ticks, "%d", i*32);
  tw = textwidth(ticks);
  outtextxy(64*(i+1)-tw/2+1, 450, ticks);
  line(64*(i+1), 441, 64*(i+1), 444);
  }

tw = textwidth(argv[1]);
outtextxy(320-tw/2+1, 20, argv[1]);
setfillstyle(SOLID_FILL, 31);


/* wait for keystrike then exit */

while(!kbhit())
  if(mousepresent)
    {
    regs.w.ax = 0x0003;
    int386(0x33, &regs, &regs);
    mousex = (int)regs.w.cx;
    mousey = (int)regs.w.dx;
    if((mousex != oldmousex) || (mousey != oldmousey))
      {
      if(!first)
        {
        for(i=-4; i<=4; i++)
          putpixel(oldmousex+i, oldmousey, save[i+4]);
        for(i=-4; i<=4; i++)
          putpixel(oldmousex, oldmousey+i, save[i+13]);
        }
       else first = 0;

      for(i=-4; i<=4; i++)
        save[i+4] = getpixel(mousex+i, mousey);
      for(i=-4; i<=4; i++)
        save[i+13] = getpixel(mousex, mousey+i);
      setcolor(0);
      line(mousex-4, mousey, mousex+4, mousey);
      line(mousex, mousey-4, mousex, mousey+4);
      oldmousex = mousex;
      oldmousey = mousey;

      bar(260,465, 450,475);
      sprintf(ticks, "Histogram value:  %3d", (mousex-64)/2);
      outtextxy(260, 465, ticks);
      }

    }

  getch();

  closegraph();
}
```

Figure 20.24 shows the output from using Hist8 on the reduced 8-bit CT volume, CT3.DAT. The mouse interface can be used to determine the intensity ranges of the four peaks previously identified. These peaks are found to range from 0–18, 18–42, 182–204, and 204–234. Notice that the small group of voxels that appeared at 4095 in Figure 20.15 before is now at 255.

Figure 20.25 shows the Hist8 output for the reduced 8-bit MRI volume, MRI3.DAT. Again, the mouse interface can be used to identify two regions, one ranging from 2–13 and the other from 13–102. These intensity ranges will be important when designing LUTs to identify the individual peaks in the histograms.

FIGURE 20.24.

This is the output from Hist8 using the 8-bit CT volume with the mouse enabled.

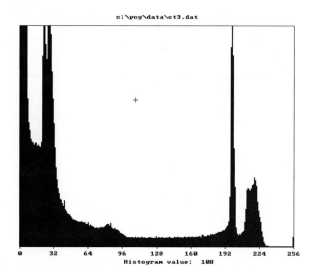

FIGURE 20.25.

This is the output from Hist8 using the 8-bit MRI volume with the mouse enabled.

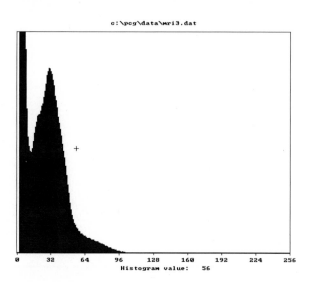

Display.c

Display is a program that reads an 8-bit data set and a LUT data file and displays the slices and the volume histogram. Display uses the hardware palette to map the 8-bit intensities into 6-bit data. Display takes three command line arguments. The first argument specifies the filename of the source 8-bit data set. The second argument specifies the size of the individual slices in the data set. For the CT3.DAT file, the size is 256. For the MRI3.DAT file, the size is 128. The last argument specifies the filename of the LUT data file. The format for the LUT files is simply an ASCII text listing of 256 RGB triples. Therefore, the LUT data files can be easily loaded into an editor and modified. Display loads these values into the hardware palette after entering graphics mode. Several sample LUT files are provided on the CD and are described in Table 20.1. LUT data files should contain only 6-bit values. If you modify these files or create your own, make sure that none of the values in the files goes over 63. The function that loads the hardware palette will mask off the two most significant bits and load the resulting value into the palette. Therefore, only values under 64 will be loaded correctly. The display routine borrows code segments from the histogram programs to graph a histogram on the right portion of the screen. Display also caches all of the volume's slices into memory, greatly improving the speed of the display. Remember to use the full paths when specifying filenames. Display.c, shown in Listing 20.7, is compiled and linked with Borland's tools when you type bcc32 -WX -N Display.c bgi32.lib at the DOS prompt.

Listing 20.7. The source code for Display.

```c
#include <stdlib.h>
#include <stdio.h>
#include <conio.h>
#include <graphics.h>
#include <io.h>
#include <malloc.h>
#include <string.h>
#include <math.h>




void main(int argc, char **argv)
{
int i,j,k,l;
FILE *datafile;
FILE *lutfile;
unsigned char LUT[256][3];
unsigned char *buffer;
char **Images;
int filesize;
int slicesize;
int numslices;
int imsize;
int grdriver, grmode, grerror;
```

continues

Listing 20.7. continued

```
int startx, starty;
int histogram[256];
float avg;
short disp[256];



   /* Ensure proper syntax */

   if(argc != 4)
      {
      printf("Usage::  Display datafile size LUTfile.\n\n");
      exit(1);
      }


   /* Check for valid size */

   slicesize = atoi(argv[2]);
   if((slicesize != 128) && (slicesize != 256))
      {
      printf("Resolution %d not supported.\n",slicesize);
      exit(3);
      }


   /* open input files */

   datafile = fopen(argv[1], "rb");
   if(datafile == NULL)
      {
      printf("Can not open file: %s.\n\n", argv[1]);
      exit(2);
      }

   lutfile = fopen(argv[3], "r");
   if(lutfile == NULL)
      {
      printf("Can not open file: %s.\n\n", argv[3]);
      exit(4);
      }


   /* Load the LUT structure */

   for(i=0; i<256; i++)
      for(j=0;j<3;j++)
         {
         fscanf(lutfile, "%d", &k);
         LUT[i][j] = (unsigned char)k;
         }

   fclose(lutfile);


   /* Determine the number of slices in the volume */
```

```
filesize = filelength( fileno(datafile) );
numslices = filesize / slicesize / slicesize;


/* check graphics hardware */

grdriver = DETECTX;
grmode = 0;
detectgraph(&grdriver, &grmode);
switch(grdriver)
  {
  case VESA256:
  case ATI256:
  case COMPAQ:
  case TSENG3256:
  case TSENG4256:
  case GENOA5:
  case GENOA6:
  case OAK:
  case PARADIS256:
  case TECMAR:  ·
  case TRIDENT256:
  case VIDEO7:
  case VIDEO7II:
    break;

  default:
    printf("Unable to detect 256 color graphics adapter.\n");
    exit(5);
    break;
  }


grmode = 1;
initgraph(&grdriver, &grmode, "");
grerror = graphresult();
if(grerror)
  {
  closegraph();
  printf("Error %d initializing graphics mode.\n", grerror);
  exit(6);
  }


/* Allocate memory for the image caches */

Images = (char **)malloc( numslices * sizeof(char *));
if(Images == NULL)
  {
  closegraph();
  printf("Error allocating memory.\n");
  exit(7);
  }

for(i=0;i<numslices; i++)
  {
  Images[i] = (char *)malloc(
                imagesize(0,0, slicesize-1,slicesize-1));
```

continues

Listing 20.7. continued

```c
if(Images[i] == NULL)
  {
  closegraph();
  printf("Error allocating memory.\n");
  exit(7);
  }
}


/* Allocate memory for the disk buffer. */

buffer = (unsigned char *)malloc( slicesize*slicesize );
if(buffer == NULL)
  {
  closegraph();
  printf("Error allocating memory for buffer.\n\n");
  exit(7);
  }


/* Program the hardware palette */

for(i=0; i<256; i++)
  setrgbpalette(i, LUT[i][0], LUT[i][1], LUT[i][2]);


/* Clear the histogram */

for(i=0;i<256;i++)
  histogram[i] = 0;


/* Display the initial images while building the cache */
/*  and the histogram */

switch(slicesize)
  {
  case 256:
    startx = 40;
    starty = 240 - slicesize/2;
    break;

  case 128:
    startx = 85;
    starty = 240 - slicesize/2;
    break;
  }

for(i=0; i<numslices; i++)
  {
  fread(buffer, slicesize*slicesize, 1, datafile);

  for(j=0; j<slicesize; j++)
    for(k=0; k<slicesize; k++)
      {
      histogram[ buffer[j*slicesize + k]] ++;
```

```
            putpixel(startx+k, starty+j, buffer[j*slicesize + k]);
            }

    getimage(startx, starty, startx+slicesize-1,
            starty+slicesize-1, (void *)Images[i]);
    }

  fclose(datafile);
  free( (void *)buffer);


  /* get the average histogram value */

  avg = 0.0;
  j = 0;

  for(i=0; i<256; i++)
    {
    avg += (float)histogram[i];
    if(histogram[i] != 0)
      j++;
    }

  avg = avg/(float)j;


  /* setup display array */

  for(i=0; i<256; i++)
    {
    k = (int)floor( (double)(histogram[i] / avg * 200.0));
    if(k > 400)
      k = 400;
    disp[i] = k;
    }

  /* Display the histogram.*/
  for(i=0; i<256; i++)
    {
    setcolor(i);
    switch(slicesize)
      {
      case 256:
        line(336+i, 440, 336+i, 440 - disp[i]);
        break;

      case 128:
        line(298+i, 440, 298+i, 440 - disp[i]);
        break;
      }
    }

  while(!kbhit())
    {
    for(i=0;i<numslices;i++)
      putimage(startx, starty, (void *)Images[i], COPY_PUT);
    }
```

continues

Listing 20.7. continued

```
getch();
closegraph();

for(i=0;i<numslices;i++)
  free( (void *)Images[i]);

free( (void *)Images);

}
```

Table 20.1. LUT data files.

Filename	Description
Red.lut	This is a simple linear window function covering the entire range in the red color channel.
Green.lut	This is a simple linear window function covering the entire range in the green color channel.
Blue.lut	This is a simple linear window function covering the entire range in the blue color channel.
Gray.lut	This is a simple linear window function covering the entire range in all of the color channels.
Quad.lut	This is a quadratic window function covering the entire range of intensities.
Sqrt.lut	This is a square root window function covering the entire range of intensities.
Invramp.lut	This is an inverse ramp window function covering the entire range of intensities.
Random.lut	This file contains random gray values.
Randomc.lut	This file contains random colors.
Segment1.lut	This file uses the information obtained from Hist8 to highlight the four peaks of the CT volume.
Segment2.lut	This file uses the information obtained from Hist8 to highlight the two areas of the MRI volume.

Figure 20.26 shows the output from Display using the reduced 8-bit CT volume, CT3.DAT, and the gray.lut LUT data file. This is a transverse slice at the jaw level of the

skull. The head holder, towels, foam-filled positioning devices, and the skull are all visible in this slice. Also visible in the center of the jaw as a bright spot is a spring used to keep the jaw attached to the skull.

FIGURE 20.26.

Display output using the CT volume and the gray.lut data file.

Figure 20.27 shows the output from Display using the reduced 8-bit MRI volume, MRI3.DAT, and the gray.lut data file. The volume appears dark with this LUT file because there are no intensities over 100. To increase the brightness of the images, create a LUT file with a window of 100 and a level of 50, and run the program again.

FIGURE 20.27.

Display output using the MRI volume and the gray.lut data file.

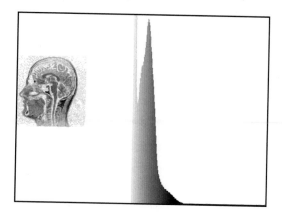

Figure 20.28 shows the output from the CT volume and the random.lut data file. Because there are random values in the LUT, small differences in intensity levels stand out and large differences in intensity are less noticeable. The foam-filled positioning devices have a similar gray level to the plastic skull, and they appear much brighter than the background.

FIGURE 20.28.

*Display output using the
CT volume and the
random.lut data file.*

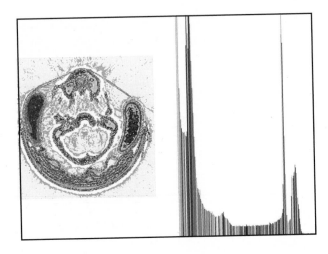

Figure 20.29 shows the output from the CT volume and the segment1.lut data file. This is the first LUT data file to take full advantage of the generality of the LUT approach. The segment1.lut data file puts constant, non-gray values in the ranges identified by the Hist8 program using the mouse. Therefore, all voxels that correspond to a specific peak in the histogram are the same color, and with the histogram displayed at the right, it is easy to determine which peak the various features belong to. From the figure, it is obvious that the first peak in the histogram (Figure 20.24) is the background. The second peak belongs to the towels and the foam-filled positioning devices. The third peak is largely due to the head holder, but some of the voxels on the surface of the skull fall into this range as well. The fourth and final peak corresponds to the plastic skull. Looking at this volume using the Display program will reveal that these classifications, or intensity segmentations, are not perfect; there is some overlap between the features and the peaks, especially between the skull and head holder. However, the Hounsfield numbers of bone are much higher than those of the plastic skull; so, there is typically no problem segmenting bone away from the rest of the image using only the Hounsfield numbers. It should be obvious by this point that LUTs not only are valuable for visualization, but also are used frequently in image processing and analysis.

Figure 20.30 shows the output from the MRI volume and segment2.lut data file. The segment2.lut data file was designed similarly to the segment1.lut data file. From the figure, it is clear that the first peak represents the background, the air in the sinuses, and the cerebrospinal fluid surrounding the brain. The second peak is caused by the bone and tissue. As stated previously, it is much more difficult to perform intensity segmentations on MRI than on CT scans.

FIGURE 20.29.

Display output using the CT volume and the segment1.lut data file.

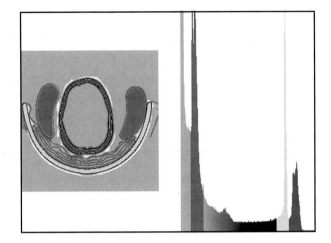

FIGURE 20.30.

Display output using the MRI volume and the segment2.lut data file.

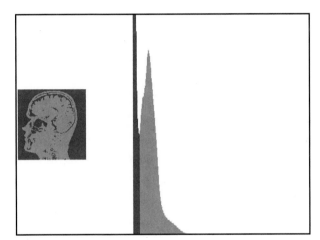

Conclusions

This chapter has presented the necessary steps for viewing real-world medical images on PCs. It should be obvious that the key to viewing 3-D medical data on PCs is data reduction. Simple window and leveling, custom window functions, and the LUT approach have all helped reduce the 12-bit intensities into values that can be graphically displayed on a PC. Although more complex methods exist for displaying arbitrary orientation 2-D slices and 3-D isosurfaces and renderings, they generally require faster processors and more memory than the average PC has; however, PC hardware is constantly improving. The average desktop PC is quickly growing in power and capability, and it should not be very long before PCs are more than capable of using these advanced algorithms.

Free Form Deformation

21

by Alfonso Hermida

In this chapter, you will take a peek at one of the most frequently used techniques to impart "life-like" behavior on 3-D objects. This chapter presents the background information necessary to understand the Free Form Deformation technique (FFD) and demonstrates how objects can be deformed and animated with FFD.

The Fundamentals of FFD

Before I get into the specifics of how FFD is implemented, let me present a simple example. Imagine that I have a 3-D object made of a highly flexible material. For this example, I'll use a rectangular bar (see Figure 21.1).

FIGURE 21.1.

Flexible rectangular bar.

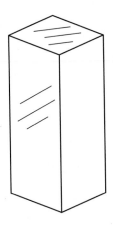

Now I'll take that rectangular bar and locate it inside a container. The container is then filled with the same flexible material in liquid form (see Figure 21.2).

After the liquid that was in the container dries up, the container is broken, and now a block of flexible material remains with the 3-D object inside. You can also think of this block as gelatin with an object inside (see Figure 21.3).

What would happen if I held the block at the ends and bent it with my hands? Roughly, you would see what is being displayed in Figure 21.4.

Observe that the rectanglar bar and the block deform in the same fashion. You need both the inside object and the block to be flexible so that the bar will deform just as the block deforms. Figure 21.5 presents another case, twisting.

Chapter 21

FIGURE 21.2.

Flexible rectangular bar inside container.

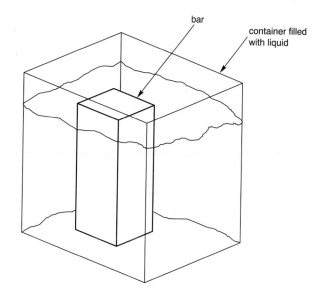

bar

container filled with liquid

FIGURE 21.3.

Flexible block with 3-D object inside.

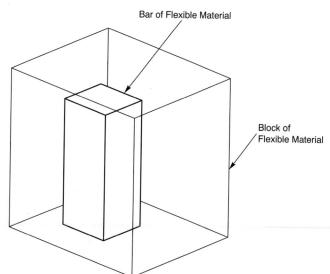

Bar of Flexible Material

Block of Flexible Material

FIGURE 21.4.

*Bending of the flexible
block with 3-D object
inside.*

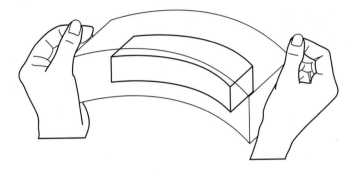

FIGURE 21.5.

*Twisting the flexible
block with 3-D object
inside.*

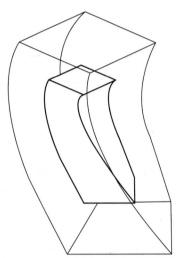

In summary, whatever deformation occurs on the outer volume—for example, the flexible block—will also occur on the 3-D object inside.

This example describes the method that was developed by Thomas W. Sederberg from Brigham Young University and that was presented by him and Scott R. Pary at the ACM SIGGRAPH Conference in 1986. The method is so important that it was worth a patent (patent #4,821,214 dated April 11, 1989, owned by Viewpoint Datalabs International, Inc.).

The method of deforming an object based on the deformation that occurs to another object seems easy enough to grasp, but what about the math behind it? It's easy too! Two basic concepts underlie the technique: interpolation and mapping. *Interpolation* refers to the ability to find any given point between proper limits. *Mapping* refers to being able to pick a point defined in one system and locate it in another. The "system," in this case, will be a coordinate system.

I'll start by describing linear interpolation and mapping, then I'll discuss other, more complex methods of interpolation through the use of Bézier curves and patches. After presenting these concepts, I'll discuss the Free Form Deformation (FFD) technique that will enable us to deform our 3-D objects.

Linear Interpolation

Linear interpolation is used to find a point inside of a range defined by two "control" points. Because the axis where these points are defined is a line, this method of interpolation is called "linear." Although linear systems require two control points for interpolation, other systems—those that are more complex, for example, cubic systems—require four control points.

Figure 21.6 presents an axis with two control points, p1 and p2.

FIGURE 21.6.

Axis with two control points.

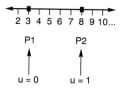

To find a point p between the two control points p1 and p2, I'll start by defining a variable u, called a *parametric variable* (it varies from 0 to 1). In other words (refer to Figure 21.6), when

$$u = 0, \text{ then } p = p1 = 3$$

and when

$$u = 1, \text{ then } p = p2 = 8$$

the equation that models the relationship between u and p is

$$p = p1 + (p2 - p1)\, u$$

which is called the "parametric definition of a line."

Let's test it:

$$\text{when } u = 0 \quad p = p1 + (p2 - p1)\,(0)$$
$$p = p1 + 0$$
$$p = p1$$
$$\text{when } u = 1 \quad p = p1 + (p2 - p1)\,(1)$$
$$p = p1 + p2 - p1$$
$$p = p2$$

Now, go beyond the initial cases and check out what happens at u = 0.5. Intuitively, you should get the midpoint between p1 and p2:

$$\text{when u=0.5} \quad p = p1 + (p2 - p1)\,(0.5)$$
$$p = p1 + 0.5\,p2 - 0.5\,p1$$
$$p = 0.5\,p1 + 0.5\,p2$$
$$p = (p1 + p2)\,/\,2$$

That's exactly the midpoint! The idea behind the parametric definition of a line is having the capability to define the range between the control points as a unit. When you select the initial control point as your location, the parametric variable is equal to 0. If you choose the final control point, then u is equal to 1. The parametric definition of a line becomes handy when you are trying to find whether a given point is inside or outside a range. If you calculate the u value for the given point, you can do the following tests:

if 0<= u <= 1 then point is inside the range
if u > 1 point is located after last control point
if u < 0 point is located before the first control point

For example, given the values p1 = 3, p2 = 8, and p = –5, find the parameter u:

$$p = p1 + (p2 - p1)\,u$$
$$\text{substituting} \quad -5 = 3 + (8 - 3)\,u$$
$$-5 - 3 = 5\,u$$
$$-8/5 = u$$
$$-1.6 = u$$

Therefore, given the control points 3 and 8, the point –5 is to the left of the first control point. Its parametric value is –1.6.

One of the uses of this technique is to "map" a point from one coordinate system to another. Let's create two systems, A and B (see Figure 21.7).

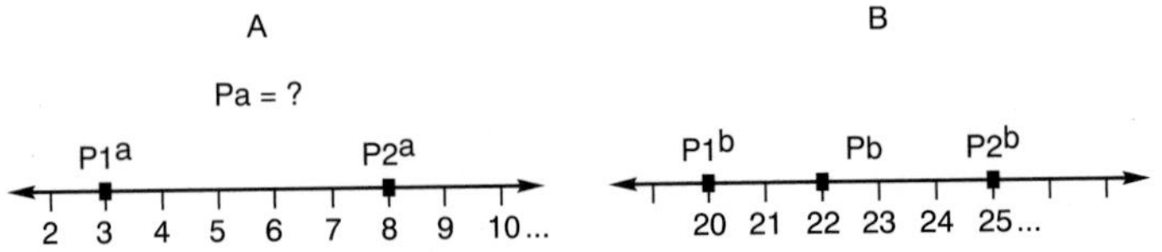

FIGURE 21.7.

Two systems, A and B, with two control points each.

The following question can be raised: Given point Pb in system B, where would that point correspond to in system A? In other words, I want to map point Pb into system A.

In this problem, I'm trying to find out the correspondence between two different coordinate systems, observing that each one has a different scale and control points. I have all the necessary data to find the parametric value for point Pb:

$$Pb = p1B + (p2B - p1B)\ u \quad \text{where} \quad \begin{aligned} p1B &= 20 \\ p2B &= 25 \\ Pb &= 22 \\ u &= ? \end{aligned}$$

Now I solve for u:

$$Pb - p1B = (p2B - p1B)\ u$$
$$(Pb - p1B)\ /\ (p2B - p1B) = u$$

Substituting the values, I get the following:

$$(22 - 20)/(25 - 20) = u = 0.4$$

Therefore, point Pb = 22 has the parametric value u = 0.4. To map point Pb into system A, I'll use the same parametric value, u = 0.4:

$$Pa = p1A + (p2A - p1A)\ u \quad \text{where} \quad \begin{aligned} p1A &= 3 \\ p2A &= 8 \\ Pa &= ? \\ u &= 0.4 \end{aligned}$$

Substituting the values, I get the following:

$$Pa = 3 + (8 - 3)\ (0.4)$$
$$Pa = 3 + 5\ (0.4)$$
$$Pa = 5$$

In other words, point Pb = 22 in system B is analogous to point Pa = 5 in system A.

Why am I discussing this? The FFD technique creates a correspondence between an undeformed and a deformed 3-D coordinate system. The parametric coordinates of points defined in the undeformed coordinate system are calculated and then mapped into the deformed coordinate system. This makes the original object follow the deformations produced in the flexible block. Let's take a look at an example.

Figure 21.8 presents two 2-D coordinate systems, A and B.

FIGURE 21.8.

Two 2-D systems, A and B.

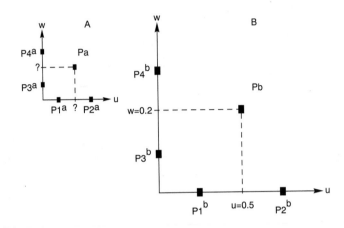

Each system has a different scale, and even the sizes are different. Because each coordinate system has two axes, I'll need two parameters per coordinate system. For this example, I'll use the parameters u and w.

For system B, the parametric variables u and w have already been evaluated (each axis is done independently of the other):

For u: $Pb,u = p1B + (p2B - p1B) u$
For w: $Pb,w = p3B + (p4B - p3B) w$

Finally, point Pb will have the parametric coordinates <u,w>.

Now, I wish to map point Pb into the A system (Pa). Simply by using the coordinates <u,w> of point Pb, I can substitute u and w into the equations for system A and find Pa:

For u: $Pa,u = p1A + (p2A - p1A) u$
For w: $Pa,w = p3A + (p4A - p3A) w$

This is a simple procedure. The power of parametric definition resides in the ability to make the problem independent of the real coordinates of the system and to reduce everything to values from 0 to 1.

Up to this point, I have used linear interpolation to find points and parametric values. This technique can't be used always. Let's take a look at a more complex situation (see Figure 21.9).

System A has a pair of linear axes; therefore, linear interpolation can be used to find the parametric coordinates of any point, that is, point Pa. On the other hand, system B has curved axes. If I wish to find the parametric coordinates of point Pb, I can't use linear interpolation. I need some sort of nonlinear interpolation method that will be able to follow the curvature of the axis as I change the parameter from 0 to 1.

FIGURE 21.9.

Two 2-D systems, A (linear axes) and B (nonlinear axes).

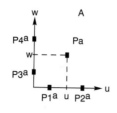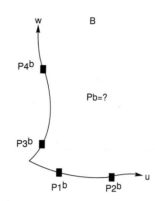

Let's take this problem one level higher. Figure 21.10 presents the same concept in 3-D.

FIGURE 21.10.

Two 3-D systems, A (linear axes) and B (nonlinear axes).

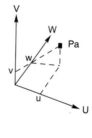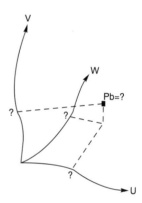

Clearly, the 3-D case requires a more complex method to interpolate in all axes.

Having presented the limitations of linear interpolation, I'll discuss a method that can be used to overcome them. In the next sections, I'll discuss interpolation through the use of Bézier curves and patches.

Bézier Representation of Curves and Patches

As you recall, the linear interpolation case required two control points to define the range for interpolation. The reason for this is that a line is, in mathematical terms, an infinite entity: it doesn't have a beginning or an end. By using the parametric definition where the parameter varied from 0 to 1, we could easily know whether or not a point was inside a given range. Again, that was only for the linear case. As we studied more complex coordinate systems, we became aware of the fact that linear interpolation would not work on axes that had some sort of curvature, that is, where the axis was not a straight line. It also became apparent that we would need some sort of definition that was parametric but at the same time able to describe a nonlinear curve. It's time, then, to study the behavior of Bézier curves and patches.

In the following sections, I'll go through the steps of presenting some basic concepts concerning Bézier curves and how you can develop interpolation schemes for 1-D, 2-D, or 3-D cases. The basic concepts behind parametrization, interpolation, and the use of control points still apply; the definition is a little more involved.

Let's recall that the parametric definition of a line is

$$p = p1 + (p2 - p1) \, u$$

Bézier curves, on the other hand, are somewhat more complex and look like this:

$$p = (1-u)^3 p0 + 3u(1-u)^2 p1 + 3u^2(1-u)p2 + u^3 p3$$

where p0, p1, p2 and p3 are control points, and where $(1-u)^3$, $3u(1-u)^2$, $3u^2(1-u)$, and u^3 are called Bernstein blending functions.

If I let P_i be the ith control point and

$$B_0 = (1-u)^3$$
$$B_1 = 3u(1-u)^2$$
$$B_2 = 3u^2(1-u)$$
$$B_3 = u^3$$

then, I can simplify the Bézier curve definition to a mathematical expression referred to as a *series representation*, because the curve is defined by a series of polynomials that are added up (see Figure 21.11).

FIGURE 21.11.

Bézier curve, series representation.

$$p = \sum_{i=0}^{3} P_i B_i$$

The symbol shown in Figure 21.12 indicates that a summation will be performed on $P_i B_i$.

FIGURE 21.12.

Summation symbol.

$$\sum_{i=0}^{3}$$

Let's look at various examples:

$$1) \quad \sum_{i=0}^{3} x^i = x^0 + x^1 + x^2 + x^3$$

$$2) \quad \sum_{i=1}^{3} 3^i a^{i-1} = 3^1 a^0 + 3^2 a^1 + 3^3 a^2$$

Observe how the index i is incremented until its value is equal to the argument at the top of the summation symbol. If I were to program expression 1, it would look something like this:

```
x = .....

c = 0;

for( i = 0; i<= 3; i++)

    c = c + pow(x,i);
```

Likewise, if I were to program expression 2, it would look something like this:

```
a = ....

c = 0;

for(i = 1; i<= 3; i++)

    c = c + pow(3,i) * pow(a, i - 1);
```

Let's go back to the Bézier representation $p = (1-u)^3 p0 + 3u(1-u)^2 p1 + 3u^2(1-u)p2 + u^3 p3$ and let's put it to the test. I'll solve the following for u=0, u=1, and u=0.5. It'll be interesting to see what shows up:

u = 0:

$p = (1-0)^3 p0 + 3(0)(1-0)^2 p1 + 3(0)^2(1-0)p2 + 0^3 p3$
or $\quad p = p0$

u = 1:

$p = (1-1)^3 p0 + 3(1)(1-1)^2 p1 + 3(1)^2(1-1)p2 + (1)^3 p3$
or $\quad p = p3$

u = 0.5:

$$p = (1-0.5)^3 p0 + 3(0.5)(1-0.5)^2 p1 + 3(0.5)^2(1-0.5)p2 + 0.5^3 p3$$

or $\quad p = 0.125\ p0 + 0.375\ p1 + 0.375\ p2 + 0.125\ p3$

which is the same as

$$p = \frac{1}{8}\ p0 + \frac{3}{8}\ p1 + \frac{3}{8}\ p2 + \frac{1}{8}\ p3$$

Recall that for the linear case, u = 0.5, and the midpoint was p = (p1 + p2)/2.

If you want to express a Bézier curve using matrices, the expression would be

$$p = \begin{bmatrix} u^3 & u^2 & u & 1 \end{bmatrix} \begin{bmatrix} -1 & 3 & -3 & 1 \\ 3 & -6 & 3 & 0 \\ -3 & 3 & 0 & 0 \\ 1 & 0 & 0 & 0 \end{bmatrix} \begin{bmatrix} p0 \\ p1 \\ p2 \\ p3 \end{bmatrix} = UM_B P_C$$

where

$$U = \begin{bmatrix} u^3 & u^2 & u & 1 \end{bmatrix} \qquad M_B = \begin{bmatrix} -1 & 3 & -3 & 1 \\ 3 & -6 & 3 & 0 \\ -3 & 3 & 0 & 0 \\ 1 & 0 & 0 & 0 \end{bmatrix} \qquad P_C = \begin{bmatrix} p0 \\ p1 \\ p2 \\ p3 \end{bmatrix}$$

NOTE

If you're worried about the math, let me give you some advice: *don't*. The information is presented in this section for those interested in the details behind Bézier curves. For purposes of this chapter, I'll only use the series representation, but if you wish to study this type of representation further, see the book *Advanced Animation and Rendering Techniques* by Alan Watt and Mark Watt (Addison-Wesley, 1992). The code behind the implementation of a Bézier curve is extremely simple, as you'll find out when I discuss it.

Now that I have presented some information on Bezier curves, let's look at Listing 21.1, a small program that draws them.

Listing 21.1. BEZIER.C, a program to draw Bézier curves.

```c
#include <dos.h>
#include <graphics.h>
#include <stdio.h>
#include <stdlib.h>
#include <conio.h>
#include <math.h>

typedef struct {
  float x,y;
} Point2D;

void InitGraphics(void);
void WorldToDevice(float wx, float wy, int * dx, int * dy);
void DrawAPoint2D(Point2D p);
void DrawALine(Point2D p1, Point2D p2);
float Bernstein(int c, float u);

float  WxLeft, WxRight, WyTop, WyBottom;
int    DyMax, DxMax, DyMin, DxMin;

void main(void) {
 int i;
 float t, B, step;
 Point2D c, c_old, pnt, p[4];

 InitGraphics();

 WxLeft   = -3;
 WxRight  =  3;
 WyTop    =  3;
 WyBottom = -3;

 DyMin = 0;
 DxMin = 0;
 DyMax = getmaxy();
 DxMax = getmaxy();

 setviewport((getmaxx()-getmaxy())/2,0,getmaxx(),getmaxy(),1);
 setbkcolor(WHITE);
 cleardevice();
 setcolor(BLUE);

 p[0].x = -1.0;
 p[0].y =  0.0;

 p[1].x = -0.3;
 p[1].y =  2.0;

 p[2].x =  0.3;
 p[2].y = -2.0;

 p[3].x =  1.0;
 p[3].y =  0.0;

 DrawAPoint2D(p[0]);
 DrawAPoint2D(p[1]);
```

continues

Listing 21.1. continued

```
DrawAPoint2D(p[2]);
DrawAPoint2D(p[3]);

DrawALine(p[0], p[1]);
DrawALine(p[1], p[2]);
DrawALine(p[2], p[3]);

setlinestyle(SOLID_LINE, 1, 3);
step = 20.0;
for(t=0; t<=(int)step; t++) {
  c.x = c.y = 0.0;
  for(i=0;i<=3;i++) {
     B = Bernstein(i,t/step);
     c.x += p[i].x * B;
     c.y += p[i].y * B;
  }
  if(!t) c_old = c;
  else {
     DrawALine(c_old, c);
     c_old = c;
  }
}
getch();
closegraph();
}

///////////////////////////////////////////////////////////////////

float Bernstein(int c, float u) {
   switch(c) {
      case 0: return (pow((1.0-u),3));
      case 1: return (3.0 * u * pow((1.0-u),2));
      case 2: return (3.0 * pow(u,2) * (1.0-u));
      default: return (pow(u,3));
   }
}

void WorldToDevice(float wx, float wy, int * dx, int * dy) {
     *dx = (WxLeft - wx) * DxMax / (WxLeft - WxRight);
     *dy = (WyTop - wy) * DyMax / (WyTop - WyBottom);
}

void DrawAPoint2D(Point2D p) {
   int dx, dy;
   WorldToDevice(p.x, p.y, &dx, &dy);
   rectangle(dx-2,dy-2,dx+2,dy+2);
}

void DrawALine(Point2D p1, Point2D p2) {
   int dx1, dy1, dx2, dy2;
   WorldToDevice(p1.x, p1.y, &dx1, &dy1);
   WorldToDevice(p2.x, p2.y, &dx2, &dy2);
   line(dx1,dy1,dx2,dy2);
}

  void InitGraphics(void) {
```

```
int gdriver = DETECT, gmode, errorcode;
initgraph(&gdriver, &gmode, "");
errorcode = graphresult();
if (errorcode != grOk)   {
  printf("Graphics error: %s\n", grapherrormsg(errorcode));
  printf("Press any key to halt:");
  getch();
  exit(1);
}
setviewport(0,0,getmaxx(),getmaxy(),1);
}
```

Before you look closely at this code, you might want to review or study this book's Chapter 8 on 3-D modeling. That chapter explains the concepts of world and device coordinates, setting up the graphics viewport, and defining the limits of the viewport. Because we're interested in finding out how the Bézier curve is evaluated, I'll start from there.

I start by defining the control points, using the following structure definition:

```
typedef struct {

  float x,y;

} Point2D;
```

I then create an array of control points with the declaration `Point2D p[4];` and I attach values to each

```
p[0].x = -1.0;      p[0].y =  0.0;
p[1].x = -0.3;      p[1].y =  2.0;
p[2].x =  0.3;      p[2].y = -2.0;
p[3].x =  1.0;      p[3].y =  0.0;
```

Observe that the control points are 2-D. 3-D control points can also be used by changing the structure declaration to

```
typedef struct {
  float x,y,z;
} Point3D;
```

The Bernstein blending functions can be programmed easily:

```
float Bernstein(int c, float u) {
   switch(c) {
      case 0: return (pow((1.0-u),3));
      case 1: return (3.0 * u * pow((1.0-u),2));
      case 2: return (3.0 * pow(u,2) * (1.0-u));
      default: return (pow(u,3));
   }
}
```

Recall that there is one Bernstein function for each control point, which is being selected based on the variable c. The parameter u is also passed to the function. The function `Bernstein()` then returns the value of the blending function.

Now comes the "meat" of the code, the loop to calculate the curve:

```
step = 20.0;
 for(t=0; t<=(int)step; t++) {
   c.x = c.y = 0.0;
   for(i=0;i<=3;i++) {
      B = Bernstein(i,t/step);
      c.x += p[i].x * B;
      c.y += p[i].y * B;
   }
   if(!t) c_old = c;
   else {
      DrawALine(c_old, c);
      c_old = c;
   }
 }
```

First, I declare a variable named `step`. This variable defines how many points will be interpolated from the Bézier curve. In this case, 20 is the value used. The first loop uses the variable `t` to increment the number of points being evaluated from the curve. Next, the variables `c.x` and `c.y` are declared as zero to aid in the summation of the interpolated point:

```
B = Bernstein(i,t/step);
c.x += p[i].x * B;
c.y += p[i].y * B;
```

Observe how each component of the point `p[i]` is evaluated independently. The value of the parameter sent to `Bernstein()` is simply $u = t/step = t/20$. This value will vary from 0 to 1 in steps of 0.05. Finally, the loop that increments the variable `i` is used to select each control point.

I suggest that you experiment with changing the step value and the location of the control points. Another interesting effect would be to write some code to select any of the control points and move them around the screen with the aid of the mouse. This method can help you modify the curve interactively. Figure 21.13 displays the output from the program BEZIER.C.

FIGURE 21.13.

Bézier curve (output from BEZIER.C).

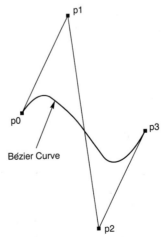

Bézier Patches

Moving from curves to patches (2-D) requires some minor changes to the Bézier code. First of all, I'll need more control points—in fact, 16 of them. Besides the addition of more control points, I'll also have to deal with two parametric variables, which I'll refer to as u and v (see Figure 21.14).

FIGURE 21.14.

Bézier patch.

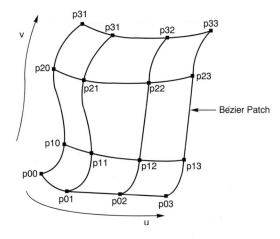

Observe how each parametric variable follows the curvature of the patch on each axis.

The series representation of the Bezier patch is similar to that of the curve but takes into account an additional axis:

$$p = \sum_{i=0}^{3} \sum_{j=0}^{3} P_{ij} B_i(u) B_j(v)$$

The expressions $B_i(u)$, $B_j(v)$ are Bernstein blending functions; the parentheses only indicate that one of them will vary with the parameter u and the other one with v. For example,

$B_1(u) = 3u(1-u)^2, i=1$ and $B_1(v) = 3v(1-v)^2, j=1$

Let's modify Listing 21.1 in order to draw patches.

Listing 21.2. BEZIER_P.C, a program to draw Bézier patches (partial code).

```
void main(void) {
  int i,j;
  float t,tt, B, step;
  Point2D c, cc, cc_old, c_old, pnt, p[4][4];
```

continues

Listing 21.2. continued

```
.InitGraphics();
WxLeft    = -3;
 WxRight  =  3;
 WyTop    =  3;
 WyBottom = -3;

 DyMin = 0;
 DxMin = 0;
 DyMax = getmaxy();
 DxMax = getmaxy();

 setviewport((getmaxx()-getmaxy())/2,0,getmaxx(),getmaxy(),1);
 setbkcolor(WHITE);
 cleardevice();
 setcolor(BLUE);

 for(j=0;j<4;j++)
   for(i=0;i<4;i++) {
      p[i][j].x = GetValue(i)+random(10)*0.1;
      p[i][j].y = GetValue(j);
      DrawAPoint2D(p[i][j]);
   }

 step = 20.0;
 for(tt=0; tt<=(int)step; tt++) {
  for(t=0; t<=(int)step; t++) {
    c.x = c.y = 0.0;
    cc.x = cc.y = 0.0;
    for(j=0;j<4;j++) {
      for(i=0;i<4;i++) {
     B = Bernstein(i,t/step)*Bernstein(j,tt/step);
     c.x += p[i][j].x * B;
     c.y += p[i][j].y * B;
     B = Bernstein(i,tt/step)*Bernstein(j,t/step);
     cc.x += p[i][j].x * B;
     cc.y += p[i][j].y * B;
       }
    }
    if(!t) {
       c_old = c;
       cc_old = cc;
    }
    else {
     DrawALine(c_old,c);
     DrawALine(cc_old,cc);
     cc_old = cc;
    }
  }
 }
 getch();
 closegraph();
}


float GetValue(int i) {
```

```
switch(i) {
    case 0: return(-1.0);
    case 1: return(-0.3);
    case 2: return(0.3);
    default: return(1.0);
    }
}
```

Because the patch requires control points throughout 2-D space, I modified the definition of the control points from `Point2D p[4];` to `Point2D p[4][4];`. This will give me a total of 16 control points.

The next modification to the code concerns how the patch is calculated. Now I require a double loop that divides both axes (u and v) into a series of steps using the variables t and tt. Also, the series representation showed that I now have to calculate two Bernstein blending functions, one for u and the other for v:

```
B = Bernstein(i,t/step)*Bernstein(j,tt/step);
c.x += p[i][j].x * B;
c.y += p[i][j].y * B;
```

Inside the program, parts of the code appear to be repeated twice. This is done to be able to calculate the patch in both directions at the same time. To deform the patch slightly, I added some randomness to the x coordinates through the use of the `random()` function. Figure 21.15 displays the output from BEZIER_P.C.

FIGURE 21.15.

*Output from
BEZIER_P.C.*

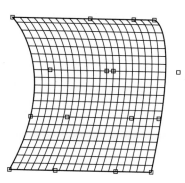

Before I leave this discussion on patches, let me present the matrix representation:

$$p = [u^3 \quad u^2 \quad u \quad 1] \begin{bmatrix} -1 & 3 & -3 & 1 \\ 3 & -6 & 3 & 0 \\ -3 & 3 & 0 & 0 \\ 1 & 0 & 0 & 0 \end{bmatrix} \begin{bmatrix} p00 & p10 & p20 & p30 \\ p01 & p11 & p21 & p31 \\ p02 & p12 & p22 & p32 \\ p03 & p13 & p23 & p33 \end{bmatrix} \begin{bmatrix} -1 & 3 & -3 & 1 \\ 3 & -6 & 3 & 0 \\ -3 & 3 & 0 & 0 \\ 1 & 0 & 0 & 0 \end{bmatrix} \begin{bmatrix} v^3 \\ v^2 \\ v \\ 1 \end{bmatrix}$$

This matrix representation can be simplified to

$$p = UM_BP_CM_BV$$

Bézier Hyperpatches

As I mentioned earlier, the FFD technique is able to interpolate 3-D data points from an undeformed block to a deformed one; therefore, I must be able to extend Bézier patches to a third dimension. The object is called a *hyperpatch*.

By using a hyperpatch, I'm able to convert a 3-D point defined in real-world coordinates to a set of parametric values between 0 and 1 through the use of the variables <u,v,w> for the x-, y-, and z-axes, respectively. Recall that for the curves I needed four control points, for patches I used 16, and for hyperpatches I need 64! Figure 21.16 displays a Bézier hyperpatch.

FIGURE 21.16.

Bézier hyperpatch.

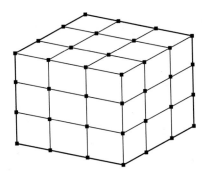

The series representation of the hyperpatch is

$$p = \sum_{i=0}^{3}\sum_{j=0}^{3}\sum_{k=0}^{3}P_{ijk}B_i(u)B_j(v)B_k(w)$$

This is extremely similar to the 2-D patch. An extra dimension has been added and is represented by the parametric variable w. Observe that the control points now have to be defined as a 3-D array.

Now that you have the fundamentals behind the Bézier type of interpolation, I'll discuss the implementation of the FFD technique.

Applying the FFD Technique

Initially, I discussed the FFD technique by means of an example where a flexible block has another flexible object inside. The inside object follows whatever deformations are applied to the block. Because points inside of an undeformed block can be interpolated linearly, I need a technique that will let me map points from this undeformed coordinate system into a deformed one. The means of interpolating the data is to use the hyperpatch definition. Each point in a 3-D model will be converted into parametric coordinates, that is, u, v, and w. After these values are known, finding their new position in the deformed space is an easy task, as you'll see in the next sections. Let's take the FFD technique by steps.

Loading a 3-D Data Object

If we wish to start from the beginning, we must take a brief look at the code that will load a 3-D model into our FFD program. I am assuming that the object to be loaded is defined in terms of polygons with three vertices (triangles). Each line in the file defines a polygon. The structure that I'll declare will be a 3-D one:

```
typedef struct {
 float far x,y,z;
} POINT3D;
```

To have easy access to the huge amount of data points, I'll declare two pointers to POINT3D structures. These points will be defined globally, and I'll use a define statement to limit the amount of polygons that can be read:

```
#define MAXFACES 600
POINT3D far *Object;
POINT3D far *Object2;
```

The *Object will be used to store the undeformed 3-D polygons. After FFD is applied to the 3-D data, the deformed values will be stored in *Object2. To allocate the arrays, I'll use the following statements:

```
// Allocating memory for the original data
if((Object = (POINT3D *)farcalloc(3*MAXFACES, sizeof(POINT3D))) == NULL) {
        closegraph();
        printf("ERROR: Can't allocate database!\n");
        exit(1);
}

// Allocating memory for the deformed data
if((Object2 = (POINT3D *)farcalloc(3*MAXFACES, sizeof(POINT3D))) == NULL) {
        closegraph();
        printf("ERROR: Can't allocate database!\n");
        exit(1);
}
```

To make life simple, I'll use the `LoadAFile()` function to tell the program to read the 3-D data from a text file. As I read the data, I'll check that the amount of points do not exceed the memory allocated for them:

```
void LoadAFile(char *str) {
 FILE *fptr;
 float x,y,z;
 int bnum;
 if (  (fptr = fopen(str,"r")) == NULL) {
          printf("\7");
 }
 else {
     bnum = -1;
     while (!feof(fptr)) {
       if ((fscanf(fptr,"%f",&x) > 0) &&
           (fscanf(fptr,"%f",&y) > 0) &&
           (fscanf(fptr,"%f",&z) > 0)) {
             bnum++;
             if(bnum < MAXFACES*3) {
               Object[bnum].x = x;
               Object[bnum].y = y;
               Object[bnum].z = z;
             }
       }
     }
     fclose(fptr);
     PointNum = bnum+1;
 }
}
```

The next function is used to save the data found in the `Object2` array, which is the deformed data:

```
void SaveAFile(char *str) {
 FILE *fptr;
 int i;
 if ((fptr = fopen(str,"w+t")) == NULL)
    printf("\7");
 else {
    for(i=0;i<PointNum;i+=3)
      fprintf(fptr,"%g %g %g %g %g %g %g %g %g\n",
             Object2[i].x,   Object2[i].y,   Object2[i].z,
             Object2[i+1].x, Object2[i+1].y, Object2[i+1].z,
             Object2[i+2].x, Object2[i+2].y, Object2[i+2].z);
    fclose(fptr);
 }
}
```

After the data is loaded into memory, I need to calculate the maximum limits in all axes. These values are then used to scale the hyperpatch so that it covers the object completely. The routine `GetMaxima()` evaluates all the points inside of the `Object` array and finds the limits:

```
void GetMaxima(float *xi,float *xf, float *yi,float *yf, float *zi,float *zf) {
  int i;
  float x1=1e6,x2=-1e6,
     y1=1e6,y2=-1e6,
     z1=1e6,z2=-1e6;
```

```
for(i=0;i<PointNum;i++) {

    if(Object[i].x < x1)
    x1 = Object[i].x;
    else
    if(Object[i].x > x2)
        x2 = Object[i].x;

    if(Object[i].y < y1)
    y1 = Object[i].y;
    else
    if(Object[i].y > y2)
        y2 = Object[i].y;

    if(Object[i].z < z1)
    z1 = Object[i].z;
    else
    if(Object[i].z > z2)
        z2 = Object[i].z;
}
*xi = x1;
*xf = x2;
*yi = y1;
*yf = y2;
*zi = z1;
*zf = z2;
}
```

Initializing and Scaling the Hyperpatch

The hyperpatch is a 3-D array of control points that can be defined as POINT3D Cube[4][4][4];. To define the location of all 64 control points, I developed a simple routine called InitBezierCube(). Its function is to assign coordinates to control points based on their location in the hyperpatch. The function Coordinate() returns the values –1, –0.3, 0.3, or 1, depending on the location of the point. By doing this, I end up with a unit cube that is easy to scale in any direction:

```
void InitBezierCube(void) {
 int i,j, k;

 for(k=0;k<4;k++)
   for(j=0;j<4;j++)
     for(i=0;i<4;i++) {
        Cube[i][j][k].x = Coordinate(i);
        Cube[i][j][k].y = Coordinate(j);
        Cube[i][j][k].z = Coordinate(k);
     }
}


float Coordinate(int i) {
  switch(i) {
    case 0: return(-1.0);
    case 1: return(-0.3);
    case 2: return( 0.3);
    default: return( 1.0);   //case 3
```

```
    }
}
```

After the hyperpatch is defined, I must call `GetMaxima()` and `ScaleBezierCube()`, in that order. The second function will scale the hyperpatch until it bounds the 3-D object:

```
void ScaleBezierCube(float x, float y, float z) {
  int i,j, k;

  for(k=0;k<4;k++)
    for(j=0;j<4;j++)
      for(i=0;i<4;i++) {
        Cube[i][j][k].x *= x;
        Cube[i][j][k].y *= y;
        Cube[i][j][k].z *= z;
      }
}
```

To be sure that the hyperpatch is large enough, I use the maximum values returned by `GetMaxima()`. Figure 21.17 displays a 3-D object (similar to a bottle) with the hyperpatch bounding it.

FIGURE 21.17.

Bézier hyperpatch bounding a 3-D object.

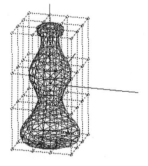

Freezing the Hyperpatch

At this point, I have a 3-D data set loaded into memory, and the hyperpatch has been initialized and scaled to fit the 3-D object. The next step is to save the dimensions of the hyperpatch. This is referred to as "freezing" the hyperpatch. The dimensions that are saved will be used later to interpolate each 3-D point linearly. This "frozen" hyperpatch serves as the undeformed system.

To save the dimensions of the hyperpatch, I created a set of global variables `float XS,YS,ZS;` that save the x, y, and z dimensions, respectively. To save these values, simply call the function `FreezeBezierCube()`:

```
void FreezeBezierCube(float x,float y,float z) {
  XS = x;
  YS = y;
  ZS = z;
}
```

Let me present the whole sequence of events that are taken to freeze the hyperpatch (let's assume that the 3-D data is already loaded):

1. Initialize the hyperpatch.

2. Get the maximum and minimum limits of the 3-D data.

   ```
   GetMaxima(&xmin,&xmax,&ymin,&ymax,&zmin,&zmax);
   ```

3. Using the maximum values, scale the hyperpatch accordingly.

   ```
   ScaleBezierCube(xmax, ymax, zmax);
   ```

4. Because the hyperpatch has been scaled, freeze it by saving the limits.

   ```
   FreezeBezierCube(xmax,ymax,zmax);
   ```

Deforming the Hyperpatch

We're ready to deform! We have defined our undeformed system through the use of the `FreezeBezierCube()` function. Next, let's create the deformed system by manipulating the control points and some of the patches.

I created a set of routines to manipulate a whole patch (16 control points). To simplify matters, I'm assuming that a patch consists of 16 control points and that they are defined horizontally. For example, patch #0 is the set of points that have the Y coordinate equal to -1.0; patch #1 has $Y = -0.3$; patch #2 has $Y = 0.3$; and finally, patch #3 has $Y = 1.0$. In other words, all the patches are perpendicular to the Y axis. These are the transformation functions:

1. `ScalePatch(int patch, int axis, float s)`

   This function scales a patch in the defined axis by a scaling factor s.

   ```
   void ScalePatch(int patch, int axis, float s){
   int i,k;


     for(k=0;k<4;k++)
      for(i=0;i<4;i++)
        switch(axis) {
        case X_AXIS: Cube[i][patch][k].x *= s; break;
        case Y_AXIS: Cube[i][patch][k].y *= s; break;
        case Z_AXIS: Cube[i][patch][k].z *= s; break;
        }
    }
   ```

   Use the `define` statements

   ```
   #define X_AXIS 1
   #define Y_AXIS 2
   #define Z_AXIS 3
   ```

to indicate which axis will be scaled. Figure 21.18 displays the following commands on the bottle data:

```
ScalePatch(3, X_AXIS, 2.0);
ScalePatch(3, Z_AXIS, 2.0);
ScalePatch(0, X_AXIS, 0.2);
ScalePatch(0, Z_AXIS, 0.2);
```

FIGURE 21.18.

Scaling operations performed on bottle 3-D data.

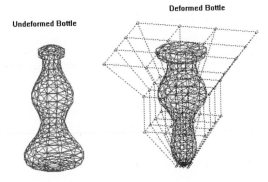

Undeformed Bottle

Deformed Bottle

2. `TranslatePatch(int patch, int axis, float d)`

This function displaces a patch along an axis by a distance d.

```
void TranslatePatch(int patch, int axis, float d){
  int i,k;

   for(k=0;k<4;k++)
    for(i=0;i<4;i++)
      switch(axis) {
        case X_AXIS: Cube[i][patch][k].x += d; break;
        case Y_AXIS: Cube[i][patch][k].y += d; break;
        case Z_AXIS: Cube[i][patch][k].z += d; break;
      }
}
```

Figure 21.19 displays the command `TranslatePatch(3, Y_AXIS, 0.5)` performed on the bottle data.

3. `RotatePatch(int patch, int axis, float deg)`

This function rotates a patch about an axis by deg degrees. The center of rotation is the center of each patch.

This function is the most complex of all three functions. The patch to be rotated is first translated so that the center of the patch is located at the origin of the coordinate system. Next, the rotation is performed on the patch. Finally, the patch is translated back to its original place. In other words, the rotations are absolute with respect to the center of the patch.

FIGURE 21.19.

Translation operation performed on bottle 3-D data.

Undeformed Bottle

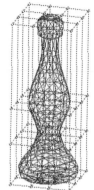
Deformed Bottle

```
void RotatePatch(int patch, int axis, float deg) {
  float xc=0.0, yc=0.0, zc=0.0;
  float COS, SIN;
  int i,j,k;
  POINT3D p, ptemp;

  deg = DegToRad(deg);
  COS = cos(deg);
  SIN = sin(deg);

  //find centroid of patch
  for(k=0;k<4;k++)
   for(i=0;i<4;i++) {
      xc += Cube[i][patch][k].x;
      yc += Cube[i][patch][k].y;
      zc += Cube[i][patch][k].z;
   }

  //divide by 16 to get center (average)
  xc /= 16.0;
  yc /= 16.0;
  zc /= 16.0;

  // translate center of patch to origin
  for(k=0;k<4;k++)
```

```
for(i=0;i<4;i++) {
   Cube[i][patch][k].x -= xc;
   Cube[i][patch][k].y -= yc;
   Cube[i][patch][k].z -= zc;
}

// now that center of patch is at origin, rotate about axis
for(k=0;k<4;k++)
  for(i=0;i<4;i++) {
    p = Cube[i][patch][k];
    switch(axis) {
    case X_AXIS:
            ptemp.x  = p.x;
            ptemp.y  = COS*p.y - SIN*p.z;
            ptemp.z  = SIN*p.y + COS*p.z;
            Cube[i][patch][k] = ptemp;
            break;
      case Y_AXIS:
            ptemp.x  = COS*p.x + SIN*p.z;
            ptemp.y  = p.y;
            ptemp.z  = -SIN*p.x + COS*p.z;
            Cube[i][patch][k] = ptemp;
            break;
      case Z_AXIS:
            ptemp.x  = COS*p.x - SIN*p.y;
            ptemp.y  = SIN*p.x + COS*p.y;
            ptemp.z  = p.z;
            Cube[i][patch][k] = ptemp;
            break;
    }
  }
// translate center of patch back to original place
 for(k=0;k<4;k++)
  for(i=0;i<4;i++) {
     Cube[i][patch][k].x += xc;
     Cube[i][patch][k].y += yc;
     Cube[i][patch][k].z += zc;
  }
}
```

Figure 21.20 displays the results of rotating some of the patches with the following commands:

```
RotatePatch(3, Z_AXIS, 30);
RotatePatch(2, Z_AXIS, 15);
RotatePatch(1, Z_AXIS, -15);
RotatePatch(0, Z_AXIS, -30);
```

FIGURE 21.20.

Rotation operations performed on bottle 3-D data.

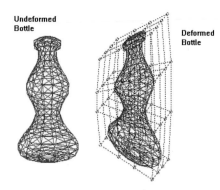

Undeformed Bottle

Deformed Bottle

Mapping 3-D Points into a Deformed System

The function GoFFD() takes care of finding the parametric u, v, and w coordinates of each of the points that define the 3-D object; then, with the use of the <u,v,w> coordinates, the points are found in the deformed hyperpatch by calling the GetBezierPoint(float u, float v, float w) function. The function GetBezierPoint() in turn calls Bernstein() to calculate the Bernstein blending functions. As I mentioned before, the new 3-D object is saved in the array Object2 by means of the statement Object2[i] = GetBezierPoint(Xuvw, Yuvw, Zuvw);.

```
void GoFFD(void) {
  int i;
  float Xuvw, Yuvw, Zuvw;
  for(i=0;i<PointNum;i++) {
    Xuvw = UVW(-XS, XS, Object[i].x);
    Yuvw = UVW(-YS, YS, Object[i].y);
    Zuvw = UVW(-ZS, ZS, Object[i].z);
    Object2[i] = GetBezierPoint(Xuvw, Yuvw, Zuvw);
  }
}


float UVW(float vmin, float vmax, float value) {
  return( (value - vmin)/(vmax - vmin)  );
}

POINT3D GetBezierPoint(float u, float v, float w) {
 int i,j,k;
```

```
POINT3D q;
float factor, wk, vk, wkvk;

q.x = q.y = q.z = 0.0;
for(k=0;k<4;k++) {
 wk = Bernstein(w,k);
 for(j=0;j<4;j++) {
   vk = Bernstein(v,j);
   wkvk = wk * vk;
   for(i=0;i<4;i++) {
     factor = Bernstein(u,i) * wkvk;
     q.x += Cube[i][j][k].x * factor;
     q.y += Cube[i][j][k].y * factor;
     q.z += Cube[i][j][k].z * factor;
   }
 }
}
return(q);
}


float Bernstein(float t, int i) {
  float v;
  switch(i) {
    case 0: v =  pow((1.0 - t),3); break;
    case 1: v =  3 * t * pow((1.0 - t),2); break;
    case 2: v = 3 * pow(t,2) * (1.0 - t); break;
    case 3: v = pow(t,3); break;
  }
  return(v);
}
```

Drawing the 3-D Object and the Hyperpatch

Drawing both the 3-D object and the hyperpatch are straightforward operations. In the case of the function drawObjects(), this function takes as an argument an integer number. If the value is 1, the original 3-D object is drawn; otherwise the deformed one will be drawn:

```
void drawObjects(int n) {
  int i;

  setcolor(BROWN);
  if (n==1)
    for(i=0;i<PointNum;i+=3) {
      drawline(Object[i],Object[i+1]);
      drawline(Object[i+1],Object[i+2]);
      drawline(Object[i+2],Object[i]);
    }
  else
    for(i=0;i<PointNum;i+=3) {
      drawline(Object2[i],Object2[i+1]);
      drawline(Object2[i+1],Object2[i+2]);
      drawline(Object2[i+2],Object2[i]);
    }
}
```

The function `DrawBezierCube()` draws the connectivity between the control points, and in addition it draws a small rectangle at the control point location. To distinguish between the 3-D object and the hyperpatch, the hyperpatch is drawn with dotted lines:

```
void DrawBezierCube(void) {
 int i,j, k;

 setlinestyle(DOTTED_LINE,1, 1);
 setcolor(RED);

 for(k=0;k<4;k++)
  for(j=0;j<4;j++)
    for(i=0;i<4;i++)
        drawpoint(Cube[i][j][k]);

 for(j=0;j<4;j++)
  for(k=0;k<4;k++)
    for(i=0;i<3;i++)
        drawline(Cube[i][j][k],Cube[i+1][j][k]);

 for(j=0;j<4;j++)
  for(i=0;i<4;i++)
    for(k=0;k<3;k++)
        drawline(Cube[i][j][k],Cube[i][j][k+1]);

 for(k=0;k<4;k++)
  for(i=0;i<4;i++)
    for(j=0;j<3;j++)
        drawline(Cube[i][j][k],Cube[i][j+1][k]);
 setlinestyle(SOLID_LINE,1, 1);
}
```

Animating with FFD

At this point, we have all the tools to load 3-D objects and deform them. To make things more interesting, I'll discuss how objects can be animated through the use of FFD. Two easy-to-implement techniques can be developed. The first one takes a sequence of transformation operations—that is, scaling, translation, and rotation—and applies them to the 3-D object in small steps, each one creating a "frame" of the animation. For example, let's say that we wish to rotate one of the patches from 0 to 45 degrees. To create the animation, we can break down the 45 degrees into 10 steps or 4.5 degrees per frame. Using a simple loop operation, we'll have a counter that increments the rotation angle by 4.5 degrees. At each frame, the original data is deformed and saved to a file.

The second method combines FFD and a technique called "tweening." Let's take the preceding example and apply FFD and tweening. The first step is to deform the original data by rotating the patch 45 degrees and by saving that object. Now we have two objects: the original, or undeformed, and the deformed one. Now tweening comes into action. Because each point in the undeformed object has a corresponding point in the deformed object, we can apply linear interpolation between both. In other words, for each point in the object, we'll compute the following:

> For each point in the 3-D object
> point at frame i = p_original + (p_deformed – p_original) (i /total number of frames)

This operation is computationally inexpensive compared to applying FFD at each frame. The drawback of FFD/tweening is that the deformed object must be closely similar to the original object; otherwise, the tweening operation will show an object morphing in a rather unnatural manner. In this sense, applying FFD at each frame is more consistent.

Let's study each of these techniques in detail.

Applying FFD at Each Frame

To apply FFD at each frame, I must deform the patches through the use of scaling, translation, and rotation operations. To break down these effects into smaller ones applied at each frame and incremented, I use the variable loop. This variable varies from 0 to 9 and is used as part of the angle definitions. For example, the statement

```
RotatePatch(3, Z_AXIS, loop*5.0);
```

tells the program that patch #3 will be rotated about the z axis by an amount loop*5.0. When loop = 0, I have that loop*5.0 = 0.0, and when loop = 9, then the angle will be loop*5.0 = 9 * 5.0 = 45.0. The same method applies to the other transformations.

Listing 21.3 presents a section of code from FFD3D.C.

Listing 21.3. Section of code from FFD3D.C.

```
for(loop=0;loop<10;loop++)

    InitBezierCube();
    ScaleBezierCube(xmax, ymax, zmax);

    RotatePatch(3, Z_AXIS, loop*5.0);
    TranslatePatch(3, Y_AXIS, 0.5);
    TranslatePatch(3, X_AXIS,-0.1*loop);

    RotatePatch(0, Z_AXIS, -loop*5.0);
    TranslatePatch(0, Y_AXIS, -0.5);
    TranslatePatch(0, X_AXIS, -0.1*loop);

    GoFFD();
    clearviewport();
    drawaxis();
    drawObjects(2);
    DrawBezierCube();
    }
```

Figures 21.21 through 21.24 display four frames from FFD3D.C.

FIGURE 21.21.

Frame #1 from
FFD3D.C

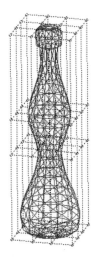

FIGURE 21.22.

Frame #4 from
FFD3D.C.

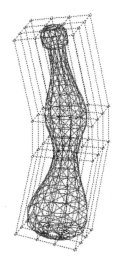

FIGURE 21.23.

*Frame #7 from
FFD3D.C.*

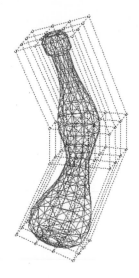

FIGURE 21.24.

*Frame #10 from
FFD3D.C.*

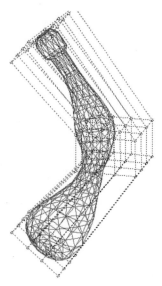

In Figures 21.21 through 21.24, both the object and the hyperpatch are shown for reference purposes.

Applying FFD and Tweening

Take a look now at Listing 21.4, which presents a section of code from FFD3DTWN.C.

Listing 21.4. Section of code from FFD3DTWN.C.

```
InitBezierCube();
GetMaxima(&xmin,&xmax,&ymin,&ymax,&zmin,&zmax);
ScaleBezierCube(xmax, ymax, zmax);
FreezeBezierCube(xmax,ymax,zmax);

SetView();
drawObjects(1);

InitBezierCube();
ScaleBezierCube(xmax, ymax, zmax);

RotatePatch(3, Z_AXIS, 45.0);
TranslatePatch(3, Y_AXIS, 0.5);
TranslatePatch(3, X_AXIS,-0.9);

RotatePatch(0, Z_AXIS, -45.0);
TranslatePatch(0, Y_AXIS, -0.5);
TranslatePatch(0, X_AXIS, -0.9);

DrawBezierCube();
GoFFD();

for(loop=0;loop<10;loop++) {
  t = loop/9.0;
  clearviewport();
  drawaxis();
  setcolor(BROWN);
  for(i=0;i<PointNum;i+=3) {
    p1.x = Object[i].x + (Object2[i].x - Object[i].x)*t;
    p1.y = Object[i].y + (Object2[i].y - Object[i].y)*t;
    p1.z = Object[i].z + (Object2[i].z - Object[i].z)*t;

    p2.x = Object[i+1].x + (Object2[i+1].x - Object[i+1].x)*t;
    p2.y = Object[i+1].y + (Object2[i+1].y - Object[i+1].y)*t;
    p2.z = Object[i+1].z + (Object2[i+1].z - Object[i+1].z)*t;

    p3.x = Object[i+2].x + (Object2[i+2].x - Object[i+2].x)*t;
    p3.y = Object[i+2].y + (Object2[i+2].y - Object[i+2].y)*t;
    p3.z = Object[i+2].z + (Object2[i+2].z - Object[i+2].z)*t;

    drawline(p1,p2);
    drawline(p2,p3);
    drawline(p3,p1);
  }
}
```

In the first half of the code, the hyperpatch is initialized, scaled, and then deformations are applied. After this is done, FFD is performed. At this point, the program now has a copy of the original plus the deformed object in memory. Now the loop is executed and for each polygon in the object, linear interpolation is performed between the original and the deformed data. For example, the following code performs linear interpolation and saves the temporary point in p1:

```
p1.x = Object[i].x + (Object2[i].x - Object[i].x)*t;
p1.y = Object[i].y + (Object2[i].y - Object[i].y)*t;
p1.z = Object[i].z + (Object2[i].z - Object[i].z)*t;
```

Observe how each coordinate (x,y,z) is calculated independently. Finally, each polygon is drawn to the screen by the following statements:

```
drawline(p1,p2);
drawline(p2,p3);
drawline(p3,p1);
```

Both programs perform the same deformations, but FFD3DTWN.C is faster than FFD3D.C. Again, each of these techniques has advantages and disadvantages that have to be taken into consideration.

What's Next?

This chapter has presented a lot of material! I would say that the next logical step is to write a graphical user interface to select any patch or control point and deform it, then select an icon and calculate the final deformed object. If you don't know how to proceed, take FFD3D.C and FFD3DTWN.C and start from there. Modify the code in small steps. Both programs include code to read and write the polygons of the 3-D object. Use the modeling tools that I presented in the chapter about 3-D modeling, including mouse routines, point selection, icons, and viewport definition routines. Again, take it step by step and have fun!

Summary

In this chapter, I presented various important concepts. You studied two types of interpolation methods: linear and nonlinear. The linear interpolation method is simple and requires only two control points to define the interpolation range. On the other hand, the nonlinear method, which uses Bézier curves, requires from 4 to 64 control points. I also discussed how mapping can be accomplished through the use of interpolation. These tools were described to present the main topic of the chapter: how to apply the Free Form Deformation technique. After discussing FFD, I extended it to animation principles, where I presented two types of animation techniques that work with FFD. The first one applies FFD to each frame in the animation; the second one uses a combination of FFD and tweening, which is linear interpolation between the original and the deformed object.

VI

Appendices

VSA256 Graphics Library

by Spyro Gumas

IN THIS CHAPTER

- Benefits of Registering
- Setting Up the VESA Environment
- Function Descriptions
- Registration Information
- Software License
- Technical Support
- Graphics Library Extensions
- VSA.H Include File
- VSA_FONT.H Include File

For C Programmers
Version 3.0
July 30, 1994
Copyright Spyro Gumas, 1992–1994
All Rights Reserved

Introduction

The VSA256 Graphics Library provides a C programmer with the tools necessary to generate graphics output on a video adapter running with the Video Electronics Standards Association (VESA) Version 1.2 BIOS extensions. The VESA BIOS extensions standardize the Super VGA (SVGA) graphics environment. The name "VSA256" reflects the fact that this library is aimed at supporting the 256-color video modes 100h, 101h, 103h, 105h, and 107h defined within the VESA standard (see Table A.1).

Revision History

Version 1.0 is the original SHAREWARE version of the VSA256 Graphics Library.

Version 1.1 is the SHAREWARE version of the VSA256 Graphics Library that corrected some compiler compatibility problems and added the `vsa_get_raster_line()` function that was necessary for the TIFF256 Graphics Library Extensions. Some drawing errors were also corrected.

Version 2.0b is the REGISTERED version of the VSA256 Graphics Library. Whereas the VSA256 Graphics Library Version 1.x is shareware, Version 2.0b **IS NOT** shareware and can be used only in accordance with the terms of the purchase agreement. The major changes between Versions 1.1 and 2.0b are listed here:

- 3 to 1 speed-up of `vsa_line_to`
- 2 to 1 speed-up of `vsa_raster_line`
- 3 to 1 speed-up of `vsa_h_line`
- New routine, `vsa_get_raster_line`
- New routine, `vsa_gouraud_line`
- New routine, `vsa_triangle_fill`
- New routine, `vsa_shaded_triangle` (Gouraud)

Version 3.0 is presented to the general public in the true spirit of shareware. This revision is the full-up version of the VSA256 Graphics Library. I no longer maintain a separate, registered version of this library. Version 3.0 of the VSA256 Graphics Library is presented as shareware with high hopes that the programmers who use this library will feel good about sending in the registration fee of $29. The major changes between Versions 2.0b and 3.0 are listed here:

- Added viewport clipping to all drawing functions
- Added BitBLT drawing functions
- Added Vector Text: Infinitely scalable and set to nearest pixel; fonts are fully user-definable
- Now text routines work with *all* video adapters
- Now works with Small, Medium, Compact, and Large memory models with Borland (already did so with Microsoft)
- Fixed `unresolved external _fstrlen` linker error with Turbo C
- Made all functions in VSA.H external; no more "Multiple Declaration" warnings
- New routine, `vsa_set_clip_mode`
- New routine, `vsa_set_viewport`
- New routine, `vsa_image_size`
- New routine, `vsa_get_image`
- New routine, `vsa_put_image`
- New routine, `vsa_get_pixel`
- New routine, `vsa_get_text_cursor`
- New routine, `vsa_set_text_scale`
- New routine, `vsa_wait_vsync`

Benefits of Registering

If you use this program beyond an initial evaluation period, you must register your use with a $29 remittance to the author—me. In addition to the good feeling that you get for sustaining a late-night hacking obsession, you get the following benefits for registering:

1. **Royalty-free use of VSA256 in your programs!** Feel free to distribute your programs for profit with no royalty fees. See the section titled "Software License."

2. **3D Graphics Library!** Don't live in a flat world. Add the missing third dimension to your creations. This library lets you create 3-D objects, set your viewpoint, and perform 3-D transformations, including scale, offset, and rotation. Supports wireframe, solid, and Gouraud-shaded objects.

3. **Graphics Mouse Library!** Use this library to integrate mouse input with your graphics applications. Get precise updates of mouse position, update the screen cursor, read mouse buttons, and more. Invent your own graphical user interface, give your apps that professional feel, and have tons of fun.

4. **Joystick Library with Source Code**! Integrate joystick input with your graphics applications. Write a flight simulator, boat driver, or your own unique use of this agile input device.

5. **IMP256 Image Processing Library and Source Code!** With this library, you can learn all about image sharpening, embossing, blurring, color balancing, and enhancement.

6. **32-bit WATCOM C Compiler compatible VSA256 and TIFF256 libraries.** Get the edge on performance.

7. Online support through **CompuServe**.

8. **Printed User's Manual and Current Version Software on disk.**

9. One **Half-Price Upgrade** to the next version as it becomes available.

   And, as if that's not enough, for a measly $15 more, you also get

10. **TIFF256 Graphics Library Extensions.** This extension to the VSA256 library lets you read TIFF-formatted graphic image files, display them, modify them, and write them back to disk. Furthermore, anything that you create and display on the screen can be saved as a TIFF image file.

11. The following public-domain, full-color TIFF image files to get you started:

    VENUS.TIF
    EARTH.TIF
    MOON.TIF
    MARS.TIF
    SATURN.TIF
    NEPTUNE.TIF
    SHUTTLE.TIF
    ASTRONTS.TIF
    WEATHER.TIF
    MANDRILL.TIF

    (What, no Ginsu knife set?)

Distribution Files

The distribution of the VSA256 Graphics Library Version 3.0 consists of the nine files listed here plus the drivers listed in the section titled "Setting Up the VESA Environment." These files are archived in the file VSA256.ZIP. To extract, just type PKUNZIP VSA256 in the directory to which you want the files extracted.

VSA_DEMO.C	VSA256 Demonstration program (Source code)
VSA_DEMO.EXE	VSA256 Demonstration program (Executable)
VSA256MS.LIB	VSA256 Graphics Library (Microsoft C compatible)
VSA256BC.LIB	VSA256 Graphics Library (Borland C compatible)
VSA.H	VSA256 Include file required in your program
VSA_Font.H	VSA256 Include file required in your program
VSA256.TXT	This text document
ORDER.TXT	A text file order form for registration and upgrades
README.TXT	A text file with important information

The Programming Environment

Setting Up the VESA Environment

The VSA256 Graphics Library works with any (any?) IBM PC, XT, AT, or compatible computer equipped with a VESA-compatible SVGA video adapter card capable of 256 colors. Most of the video cards sold today are VESA-compatible with the VESA BIOS built in to the card. A math coprocessor chip is not required.

For older SVGA video cards that are not VESA-compatible, the VESA BIOS Extensions must be loaded as a Terminate-and-Stay-Resident (TSR) program before using the VSA256 Graphics Library. This is accomplished by executing the appropriate driver or adding it to your AUTOEXEC.BAT file. If your video adapter card came with a VESA driver, use it. Otherwise, use one of the drivers provided, depending on the video adapter card installed in the PC as follows:

APPIAN	\APPIAN\APVESA.EXE
ATI	\ATI\VESA.COM
C&T	\C&T\VESA451.COM (or VESA452.COM)
CIRRUS	\CIRRUS\CRUSVESA.COM
EVEREX	\EVEREX\EVRXVESA.COM
GENOA	\GENOA\VESA.COM
OAK	\OAK\37VESA.COM (or 67VESA.COM)
ORCHID	\ORCHID\ORCHDVSA.COM
PARADISE	\PARADISE\VESA.EXE
SIGMA	\SIGMA\SIGVESA.COM
STB	\STB\STB-VESA.COM
TECMAR	\TECMAR\VGAVESA.COM
TRIDENT	\TRIDENT\VESA.EXE
VIDEO7	\VIDEO7\V7VESA.COM

Global Graphics Parameters

The VSA.H and VSA_Font.H are used as include files during program development. These files include all of the function prototypes and define the global graphics parameters that describe the specific video adapter installed in the PC (see the sections titled "VSA.H Include File" and "VSA_FONT.H Include File"). The global graphics parameters are initialized by the vsa_init function and are described here:

XResolution:	Unsigned, the number of screen pixels across (x dimension)
YResolution:	Unsigned, the number of screen pixels high (y dimension)
XCharResolution:	Unsigned, the number of screen characters across (x dimension)
YCharResolution:	Unsigned, the number of screen characters high (y dimension)
XCharSize:	Unsigned char, the character cell width
YCharSize:	Unsigned char, the character cell height
BitsPerPixel:	Unsigned char, the number of bits per pixel
XLeft:	Int, the left edge of the screen-clipping Viewport
YTop:	Int, the top edge of the screen-clipping Viewport
XRight:	Int, the right edge of the screen-clipping Viewport
YBottom:	Int, the bottom edge of the screen-clipping Viewport
Text_X_Scale:	Float, multiplies XCharBase to get text-width in pixels
Text_Y_Scale:	Float, multiplies YCharBase to get text-height in pixels
XCharBase:	Unsigned, the fundamental text character width
YCharBase:	Unsigned, the fundamental text character height
ASC[96][72]:	Unsigned Char, the 2-D array of character vertices

Note that there is a fundamental difference between how you use VSA.H and how you use VSA_FONT.H. The function prototypes and the global parameter declarations are all "extern" in VSA.H. This means that you can plop VSA.H into the top of each and every code module (file) that is part of your project. VSA_FONT.H, on the other hand, declares and initializes the "ASC[][]" array. Because I want you, the programmer, to have access to the font definitions, I couldn't make these parameter declarations "extern." This means that if you have multiple code modules (files), only include VSA_FONT.H in one of the files. Then put the following two lines of code at the top of each and every other code module (file) in your project:

```
extern unsigned XCharBase,YCharBase;
extern unsigned char ASC[][];
```

Compiler Compatibility

The VSA256MS.LIB was compiled using Microsoft's Quick C 2.5, and it also seems to work well with Microsoft C 6.0 and 7.0. I have received reports of compatibility problems with Microsoft C 5.0.

The VSA256BC.LIB was compiled using Borland's C/C++ 3.1, and it also seems to work well with Borland C/C++ 3.0 and 4.0. I have received conflicting reports of compatibility problems with Borland's Turbo C 2.0 and 3.0.

I appreciate any feedback that programmers send me along these lines so that I can continue to improve this product.

> **NOTE**
>
> **Important Note for Borland Users**
>
> You MUST set the -Fs compiler option. This tells the compiler to assume that the Stack Segment equals the Data Segment. In the Programmer's IDE, you go to Options / Compiler / Code Generation and select "Always" under the option "Assume SS Equals DS."
>
> Why? The VSA256 library can be used in Tiny, Small, Medium, Compact, and Large memory models in both the Microsoft and Borland environments. Microsoft always puts the Stack Segment in the first Data Segment, but Borland sets up a separate Stack Segment (for Compact and Large memory models) unless you specify the -Fs option. Failing to set -Fs will result in a "Stack Overflow!" error when running code compiled in Compact or Large memory models.

Function Descriptions

This section describes the functions supported in the VSA256 Graphics Library. To use these functions, link your program with the appropriate library listed here, depending on the compiler being used.

Borland C, C++, or Turbo C:	VSA256BC.LIB
Microsoft C or Quick C:	VSA256MS.LIB

In the following sections, each function is listed along with a definition of its inputs and return values. A description is provided, followed by the version in which the function became available. Finally, if applicable, comments are provided.

VESA Configuration Functions

vsa_set_svga_mode(video_mode)

Inputs:	`unsigned video_mode;`
Returns:	`unsigned fail_flag;`
Description:	This routine sets the video mode. The mode number can be any of the standard VESA SVGA mode numbers as defined in Table A.1. The mode is passed to this routine through the `video_mode` parameter. This routine returns a `fail_flag = 0` if the call was a success (a `1` for failure). It should be noted that this routine also works with standard MDA, CGA, EGA, and VGA mode numbers; however, the rest of the VSA256 functions will not necessarily work.
Availability:	In VSA256 Graphics Library Version 1.0 and up.

WARNING

Use `vsa_init` instead of the `vsa_set_svga_mode`! If you don't use `vsa_init`, the rest of the routines won't work because they depend on the global parameters initialized by `vsa_init`.

Table A.1. VESA SVGA video modes.

GRAPHICS	Mode	Resolution	Colors
	100h	640×400	256
	101h	640×480	256
	102h	800×600	16
	103h	800×600	256
	104h	1024×768	16
	105h	1024×768	256
	106h	1280×1024	16
	107h	1280×1024	256
TEXT	Mode	Columns	Rows
	108h	80	60
	109h	132	25
	10Ah	132	43

TEXT	Mode	Columns	Rows
	10Bh	132	50
	10Ch	132	60

vsa_get_svga_mode(video_mode)

Inputs:	`unsigned far *video_mode;`
Returns:	`unsigned fail_flag;`
Description:	This routine gets the current video mode. The mode is returned to the calling routine via the `video_mode` pointer. The mode number can be any of the standard VESA SVGA mode numbers as defined in Table A.1. This routine returns a `fail_flag = 0` if the call was a success (a 1 for failure).
Availability:	In VSA256 Graphics Library Version 1.0 and up.
Comments:	Works in all VESA video modes. Also works in MDA, CGA, EGA, and VGA modes.

vsa_init(video_mode)

Inputs:	`unsigned video_mode;`
Returns:	`unsigned fail_flag;`
Description:	This routine sets the video mode and initializes the VESA graphics environment. This routine must be called prior to the use of any of the subsequent routines listed in this document. The mode number can be any of the standard VESA SVGA mode numbers as defined in Table A.1. If the mode number is not a VESA SVGA mode number, this routine will still set the desired video mode; however, the VESA graphics environment will not be initialized, and subsequent calls to drawing routines will produce unpredictable results. The mode is passed to this routine through the `video_mode` parameter. This routine returns a `fail_flag = 0` if the call was a success. For failures, the `fail_flag` has the following meanings:

1. Cannot get Super VGA Environment information. Make sure VESA BIOS TSR is loaded.

2. VESA BIOS TSR not loaded. Need to load one.

3. Specified Video Mode not supported by this video card. Try another mode.

4. Specified Video Mode was set but is not one of the VESA standard modes. VSA256 may not function properly.

5. Cannot get Super VGA Video Mode Data. Make sure correct VESA BIOS TSR is loaded.

Availability: In VSA256 Graphics Library Version 1.0 and up.

Comments: Starting with Version 3.0, VSA256 no longer prints error messages automatically to the screen. The programmer gets full status feedback via the `fail_flag` and can do as he or she sees fit. Also note that VSA256 no longer cares if the specific VESA BIOS Extensions TSR being used supports text functions. This is because of the new implementation of text using vector strokes (see "`vsa_write_string`").

Miscellaneous Functions

vsa_set_display_start(x_strt,y_strt)

Inputs: `unsigned x_strt,y_strt;`

Returns: `unsigned fail_flag;`

Description: This routine sets the current start pixel address, which is mapped to the upper-left corner of the display. This routine returns a `fail_flag` = 0 if the call was a success (a 1 for failure).

Availability: In VSA256 Graphics Library Version 1.0 and up.

vsa_get_display_start(x_strt,y_strt)

Inputs: `unsigned far *x_strt, far *y_strt;`

Returns: `unsigned fail_flag;`

Description: This routine gets the current start pixel address, which is mapped to the upper-left corner of the display. This routine returns a `fail_flag` = 0 if the call was a success (a 1 for failure).

Availability: In VSA256 Graphics Library Version 1.0 and up.

vsa_wait_vsync()

Inputs:	Nothing
Returns:	Nothing
Description:	This routine waits until the beginning of the CRT's vertical retrace period before returning control to the calling program. If `vsa_wait_vsync()` is called while the CRT is in vertical retrace, this routine waits until the completion of the current retrace period and the completion of the following active scan and then returns at the beginning of the next vertical retrace period. The programmer can use this function to precede drawing functions that must be executed during CRT vertical retrace. The programmer is assured the full retrace time for his use.
Availability:	In VSA256 Graphics Library Version 3.0 and up.

Attribute Functions

vsa_set_color(color)

Inputs:	`unsigned color;`
Returns:	Nothing
Description:	This routine sets the current drawing color used in drawing pixels, lines, and rectangles. The "color" is an 8-bit value from 0 to 255 that is used to index into the Color Look Up Table.
Availability:	In VSA256 Graphics Library Version 1.0 and up.

vsa_set_text_color(color)

Inputs:	`unsigned color;`
Returns:	Nothing
Description:	This routine sets the current text color used in drawing text. The "color" is an 8-bit value from 0 to 255 that is used to index into the Color Look Up Table. Because the text is drawn using vector strokes, the background is unaffected by newly drawn text. Note that this also means that drawing a text "space" character does nothing but index the text point.
Availability:	In VSA256 Graphics Library Version 1.0 and up.

vsa_set_clip_mode(mode)

Inputs:	`unsigned mode;`
Returns:	Nothing
Description:	This routine sets the Viewport clipping mode ON if `mode = 1`, OFF otherwise. After `vsa_init`, the default is ON.
Availability:	In VSA256 Graphics Library Version 3.0 and up.

vsa_set_viewport(left, top, right, bottom)

Inputs:	`int left, top, right, bottom;`
Returns:	Nothing
Description:	This routine sets the global Viewport clipping parameters XLeft, YTop, XRight, and YBottom. Note that `vsa_init()` initializes these values to the full screen dimensions for the selected video mode. Viewport clipping is turned on and off through the `vsa_set_clip_mode()` function. By default, clip mode is ON after `vsa_init()`.
	When clip mode is ON, all items drawn on the screen through VSA256 functions are clipped to the screen Viewport rectangle defined by XLeft, YTop, XRight, and YBottom.
Availability:	In VSA256 Graphics Library Version 3.0 and up.

Color Look Up Table Functions

The Color Look Up Table consists of 256 registers, and each register stores an 18-bit value defining 6-bit levels for each of red, green, and blue. The drawing functions index into the Color Look Up Table with an 8-bit value (usually set with `vsa_set_color`) to determine the drawing color. With the following functions, the Color Look Up Table can be read or modified one register at a time or all at once in a block operation.

vsa_read_color_register(index,redptr,grnptr,bluptr)

Inputs:	`unsigned index;`
	`unsigned char far *redptr, far *grnptr, far *bluptr;`
Returns:	Nothing

Description: This routine reads the value of one of the 256 color registers as defined by index. Pointers to the red, green, and blue components of the color are returned (6 bits each for red, green, and blue).

Availability: In VSA256 Graphics Library Version 1.0 and up.

vsa_write_color_register(index,red,green,blue)

Inputs:
```
unsigned index;
unsigned char red,green,blue;
```

Returns: Nothing

Description: This routine writes the value of one of the 256 color registers as defined by index. The calling routine provides red, green, and blue components of the color (6 bits each for red, green, and blue).

Availability: In VSA256 Graphics Library Version 1.0 and up.

vsa_read_color_block(start,count,array)

Inputs:
```
unsigned start,count;
unsigned char far array[];
```

Returns: Nothing

Description: This routine reads count (Range: 1 to 256) consecutive color registers starting at start (Range: 0 to 255) within the Color Look Up Table. The count must be less than or equal to 256–start. The values read from the color registers are returned from this routine in array[]. Each element of array[] is a byte, and the size of array[] is equal to three times count. Every three bytes in array[] represent the red, green, and blue color values, respectively, for one color register. Each color component (red, green, or blue) is a byte value but ranges only from 0 to 63.

Availability: In VSA256 Graphics Library Version 1.0 and up.

vsa_write_color_block(start,count,array)

Inputs:
```
unsigned start,count;
unsigned char far array[];
```

Returns: Nothing

Description: This routine writes count (Range: 1 to 256) consecutive color registers starting at start (Range: 0 to 255) within the Color Look Up Table. The count must be less than or equal to 256–start. The values loaded into the color registers are passed to this routine in array[]. Each element of array[] is a byte, and the size of array[] is equal to three times count. Every three bytes in array[] represents the red, green, and blue color values, respectively, for one color register. Each color component (red, green, or blue) is a byte value but ranges only from 0 to 63.

Availability: In VSA256 Graphics Library Version 1.0 and up.

Text Functions (New-Vector Stroked!)

Text support in the VSA256 Graphics Library has been completely revamped! The library no longer relies on the video-card manufacturer's BIOS to get text support. Instead, each character is drawn using 2-D vector strokes. The advantages are as follows:

■ Text now works with *all* video cards!

■ Now text is infinitely scalable.

■ Text positioning resolution is down to 1 pixel.

■ Background color is preserved.

■ The programmer can define his or her own fonts in VSA_FONT.H.

Some minor incompatibilities with VSA256 Version 2.0 were introduced because of the changes, and they are as follows:

■ vsa_write_string now takes x,y (in pixel coordinates) instead of row,col (in character coordinates) as the first two parameters.

■ The vsa_write_char function was deleted.

■ The supported ASCII characters are the printable characters from ASCII code 32 to ASCII code 127.

Your existing code should take very little editing to make these changes, especially if you write a macro to edit all occurrences of vsa_write_string, as follows:

```
OLD   vsa_write_string(row,col,color,text);
NEW   vsa_write_string(col*XCharSize,row*YCharSize,color,text);
```

vsa_set_text_cursor(x,y)

Inputs: int x,y;
Returns: Nothing

Description:	This routine sets the current text cursor position to x,y in pixel coordinates. The current text cursor position is used only by `vsa_write_string_alt`.
Availability:	In VSA256 Graphics Library Version 1.0 and up.
Comments:	Note that this function has changed to pixel coordinates to support vector-stroked fonts.

vsa_get_text_cursor(px,py)

Inputs:	`int far *px, far *py;`
Returns:	Nothing
Description:	This routine gets the current text-cursor position and returns the x and y values via the pointers `*px` and `*py`, respectively. The returned positions are in pixel coordinates. The current text-cursor position is used only by `vsa_write_string_alt`.
Availability:	In VSA256 Graphics Library Version 3.0 and up.

vsa_set_text_scale(x_scale,y_scale)

Inputs:	`float x_scale, y_scale;`
Returns:	Nothing
Description:	This routine sets the x and y scale factors for text drawn with the `vsa_write_string` and `vsa_write_string_alt` routines. The `x_scale` and `y_scale` scale factors are applied to the global parameters `XCharBase` and `YCharBase`, respectively, to determine the drawn text character width and height in pixels. Because these scale factors are floating point, continuously and infinitely scalable text characters are possible. This routine automatically adjusts the global parameters `XCharSize`, `YCharSize`, `XCharResolution`, and `YCharResolution` to their appropriate values. After `vsa_init`, the `x_scale` and `y_scale` factors both default to 1.
Availability:	In VSA256 Graphics Library Version 3.0 and up.

vsa_set_text_cursor_mode(mode)

Inputs:	`unsigned mode;`
Returns:	Nothing
Description:	This routine determines the mode of the text-cursor operation. If `mode` is `0` (the default after calling `vsa_init`), the text cursor is

not updated after a new text string is written with
vsa_write_string or vsa_write_string_alt. If mode is 1, then
the text cursor is moved to the end of the text string after
executing vsa_write_string or vsa_write_string_alt.

Availability: In VSA256 Graphics Library Version 1.0 and up.

Comments: If the text-cursor mode is set to 1, the programmer may override
the cursor operation as follows. If a '\r' is placed at the end of
the text string, the text-cursor X value will reset to the beginning
of the text string (equivalent to a carriage return). If a '\n' is
placed at the end of the text string, the cursor Y value advances
by YCharSize pixels (equivalent to a line feed). Putting '\r\n' at
the end of a text string results in a line feed and carriage return.

vsa_write_string(x,y,color,string)

Inputs: int x,y;

unsigned color;

char far string[];

Returns: Nothing

Description: This routine writes a null-terminated text string string at
position (x,y). The text is written with the color passed to this
routine. After execution, if the text cursor mode is 0, the text
cursor remains at (x,y); otherwise, it is set to the end of the text
string just written.

Availability: In VSA256 Graphics Library Version 1.0 and up.

Comments: This routine was redefined in Version 3.0 to support the new
vector-stroked fonts. The text is drawn with vector strokes at the
scale factor determined by the vsa_set_text_scale routine. Full
2-D clipping is performed according to the values set with the
vsa_set_clip_mode and vsa_set_viewport routines.

vsa_write_string_alt(string)

Inputs: char far string[];

Returns: Nothing

Description: This routine writes a null-terminated text string string at the
current text-cursor position as determined by
vsa_set_text_cursor. The text is written with the current text
color. After execution, if the text-cursor mode is 0, the current

text cursor remains unchanged; otherwise, it is set to the end of the text string just written.

Availability: In VSA256 Graphics Library Version 1.0 and up.

Comments: This routine was redefined in Version 3.0 to support the new vector-stroked fonts. The text is drawn with vector strokes at the scale factor determined by the `vsa_set_text_scale` routine. Full 2-D clipping is performed according to the values set with the `vsa_set_clip_mode` and `vsa_set_viewport` routines.

Basic Drawing Functions

vsa_move_to(x,y)

Inputs: `int x,y;`

Returns: Nothing

Description: This routine sets the current cursor position to x,y. The current cursor position is used by the `vsa_line_to`, `vsa_rect_fill`, and `vsa_rect` functions.

Availability: In VSA256 Graphics Library Version 1.0 and up.

vsa_set_pixel(x,y)

Inputs: `int x,y;`

Returns: Nothing

Description: This routine draws a single pixel at x,y with the current drawing color.

Availability: In VSA256 Graphics Library Version 1.0 and up.

vsa_get_pixel(x,y)

Inputs: `int x,y;`

Returns: `unsigned color;`

Description: This routine returns the current pixel value at screen coordinates x,y.

Availability: In VSA256 Graphics Library Version 3.0 and up.

Comments: Unpredictable things may happen if you try to get a pixel that is outside of the (XResolution–1,YResolution–1) screen dimensions.

vsa_line_to(x,y)

Inputs:	`int x,y;`
Returns:	Nothing
Description:	This routine draws a line from the current cursor position to `x,y` with the current drawing color. Then the current cursor position is moved to `x,y`.
	The drawing speed of this routine is up to three times faster than that of the `vsa_line_to()` function in VSA256 Graphics Library Version 1.1.
Availability:	In VSA256 Graphics Library Version 1.0 and up.

vsa_gouraud_line(x0,c0,x1,c1,y)

Inputs:	`int x0,c0,x1,c1,y;`
Returns:	Nothing
Description:	This routine draws a color interpolated line from `x0,y` to `x1,y1`. The pixel color value is linearly varied from a starting value of `c0` at `x0,y` to an ending value of `c1` at `x1,y`. This technique of color interpolation is named Gouraud shading after the famous Joe-Bob Gouraud... a French guy. Valid values for `c0` and `c1` are 0 through 255 and serve as indices into the Color Look Up Table. Gouraud-shaded lines serve as a fundamental drawing element for realistic 3-D graphics. The current cursor position remains unaffected by this routine.
Availability:	In VSA256 Graphics Library Version 1.0 and up.

vsa_rect_fill(x,y)

Inputs:	`int x,y;`
Returns:	Nothing
Description:	This routine draws a filled rectangle from the current cursor position to the rectangle's diagonal position `x,y` with the current color.
Availability:	In VSA256 Graphics Library Version 1.0 and up.

vsa_rect(x,y)

Inputs:	`int x,y;`
Returns:	Nothing

Description: This routine draws a rectangle from the current cursor position to the rectangle's diagonal position x,y with the current color.

Availability: In VSA256 Graphics Library Version 1.0 and up.

vsa_triangle_fill(x0,y0,x1,y1,x2,y2)

Inputs: `int x0,y0,x1,y1,x2,y2;`

Returns: Nothing

Description: This routine draws a filled triangle defined by the three vertices (x0,y0), (x1,y1), and (x2,y2). The triangle is drawn with the current drawing color. The current cursor position remains unaffected by this routine.

Availability: In VSA256 Graphics Library Version 2.0 and up.

vsa_shaded_triangle(x0,y0,c0,x1,y1,c1,x2,y2,c2)

Inputs: `int x0,y0,c0,x1,y1,c1,x2,y2,c2;`

Returns: Nothing

Description: This routine draws a color interpolated triangle defined by the three vertices (x0,y0), (x1,y1), and (x2,y2). The pixel color value is linearly varied in two dimensions across the surface of the triangle using the values c0, c1, and c2 as the starting colors at the respective vertices. This technique of color interpolation is named Gouraud shading after the famous Joe-Bob Gouraud... a French guy. Valid values for c0, c1, and c2 are 0 through 255 and serve as indices into the Color Look Up Table. Gouraud-shaded triangles serve as a fundamental drawing element for realistic 3-D graphics. (Basically, most 3-D surfaces can be constructed out of shaded triangles.) The current cursor position remains unaffected by this routine.

Availability: In VSA256 Graphics Library Version 2.0 and up.

vsa_h_line(y,x0,x1)

Inputs: `int y,x0,x1;`

Returns: Nothing

Description: This routine draws a horizontal line from (x0,y) to (x1,y). The line is drawn with the current drawing color. For horizontal lines, this function is quicker than the vsa_line_to function.

The drawing speed of this routine is up to three times faster than that of the `vsa_h_line()` function in VSA256 Graphics Library Version 1.1.

Availability: In VSA256 Graphics Library Version 1.0 and up.

vsa_v_line(x,y0,y1)

Inputs: `int x,y0,y1;`

Returns: Nothing

Description: This routine draws a vertical line from (x,y0) to (x,y1). The line is drawn with the current drawing color. For vertical lines, this function is quicker than the `vsa_line_to` function.

Availability: In VSA256 Graphics Library Version 1.0 and up.

Specialized Drawing Functions

vsa_raster_line(x0,x1,y,array)

Inputs: `int x0,x1,y;`

          `unsigned char far array[];`

Returns: Nothing

Description: This routine draws a horizontal raster line from (x0,y) to (x1,y). The `array[]` values specify each pixel's color value. If x0 <= x1, then `array[0]` defines the color of the first pixel in the line at x0,y. If x1 < x0, then `array[0]` defines the color of the first pixel in the line at x1,y. The `vsa_raster_line()` routine typically is used to draw images on the display one raster line at a time. The drawing speed of this routine is up to two times faster than that of the `vsa_raster_line()` function in VSA256 Graphics Library Version 1.1.

Availability: In VSA256 Graphics Library Version 1.0 and up.

vsa_get_raster_line(x0,x1,y,array)

Inputs: `int x0,x1,y;`

          `unsigned char far array[];`

Returns: Nothing

Description: This routine gets a horizontal raster line from (x0,y) to (x1,y). The array[] is loaded with each pixel's color value. If x0 <= x1, then array[0] defines the color of the first pixel in the line at x0,y. If x1 < x0, then array[0] defines the color of the first pixel in the line at x1,y. The vsa_get_raster_line() routine is typically used to read back images already drawn on the display one raster line at a time.

Availability: In VSA256 Graphics Library Version 2.0 and up.

Comments: This routine limits x0 and x1 within the range of 0 and XResolution−1. If x0 goes negative, the first element of array holds the pixel at x=0 and less than x1−x0+1 pixels will be loaded into array. Likewise, if x1 is greater than XResolution−1, less than x1−x0+1 pixels will be loaded into array.

vsa_image_size(x0,y0,x1,y1)

Inputs: int x0,y0,x1,y1;

Returns: unsigned long image_size;

Description: This routine calculates the size of the image defined within a rectangle bound by (x0,y0) and (x1,y1). The size of the image plus 4 is returned.

The vsa_image_size() routine is typically used to determine the size of the image array to be allocated and used in the vsa_get_image() and vsa_put_image routines.

Availability: In VSA256 Graphics Library Version 3.0 and up.

vsa_get_image(x0,y0,x1,y1,image_array)

Inputs: int x0,y0,x1,y1;
unsigned char huge *image_array;

Returns: Nothing

Description: This routine gets the image defined in the rectangle (x0,y0) to (x1,y1) and stores it in the memory buffer pointed to by image_array. The memory for image_array must be allocated prior to this call. Upon returning from this routine, the first two bytes of the image_array buffer contain the image width, and the second two bytes contain the image height. The remaining bytes in the image_array buffer hold the image pixel data. The vsa_get_image() routine is typically used in conjunction with the vsa_put_image() routine for BitBLT operations.

Availability: In VSA256 Graphics Library Version 3.0 and up.

Comments: This routine clamps x0, y0, x1, and y1 to zero. If any of these parameters is less than zero, vsa_get_image overrides it with zero, and less than (x1–x0+1)*(y1–y0+1) pixels will be loaded into image_array. No clamping of x0, y0, x1, and y1 is performed at XResolution–1 and YResolution–1 so that off-screen memory can be used as scratch pad area.

vsa_put_image(x0,y0,image_array,raster_op)

Inputs:
```
int x0,y0;
unsigned raster_op;
unsigned char huge *image_array;
```

Returns: Nothing

Description: This routine gets the image defined in the image_array buffer and displays it starting at screen coordinates x0,y0. The image width and height are determined by the first two 16-bit words of the image_array buffer. The raster_op parameter determines how the data in the image_array buffer is merged with the existing screen data.

raster_op	Functions
0	Replace existing data
1	AND with existing data
2	OR with existing data
3	XOR with existing data
4	Reserved...Do Not Use!!
5	Reserved...Do Not Use!!

The vsa_put_image() routine is typically used in conjunction with the vsa_get_image() routine for BitBLT operations.

Availability: In VSA256 Graphics Library Version 3.0 and up.

Nitty Gritties

Registration Information

If you find the VSA256 Graphics Library useful, a registration of $29 would be appreciated. Registration brings with it MAJOR BENEFITS, as spelled out in the section titled "Benefits of Registering" earlier in the chapter, so look at the ORDER.TXT file, fill it out, and send it in.

Please fill out the "Information About You" and the "Wish List" sections, and indicate the version number of the software you are presently using. Send check or money order to

Spyro Gumas
1668 Shady Brook Drive
Fullerton, CA 92631

Software License

> VSA256 Graphics Library, Version 3.0
> Copyright Spyro Gumas, 1992–1994. All Rights Reserved.

The VSA256 Graphics Library is a "shareware program" and is provided at no charge to the user for evaluation. The essence of "user-supported" software is to provide personal computer users with quality software without high prices, and yet to provide incentive for programmers to continue to develop new products. If you find this program useful and find that you are using the VSA256 Graphics Library and continue to use the VSA256 Graphics Library after a reasonable trial period, you must make a registration payment of $29 to Spyro Gumas. The $29 registration fee will license one copy for use on any one computer at any one time. You must treat this software just like a book. An example is that this software can be used by any number of people and can be freely moved from one computer location to another, so long as there is no possibility of it being used at more than one location at a time—just as a book cannot be read by two different people at the same time.

You are free (and encouraged) to copy and distribute the VSA256 Graphics Library if:

1. It is not used as a component of another software library.
2. No fee is charged for use, copying, or distribution.
3. It is distributed as is (preferably as VSA256.ZIP) and not modified in any way.

Furthermore, you are granted royalty-free use of the VSA256 Graphics Library executable code in any of your programs, given that:

1. You have registered your use of the VSA256 Graphics Library and paid the $29 registration fee.
2. It is not used as a component of another software library.
3. You visibly acknowledge the use of the VSA256 Graphics Library in your product in both the printed materials and the executable software with the following statement:

   "This software uses the VSA256 Graphics Library,
   Copyright Spyro Gumas, 1992–1994. All Rights Reserved."

Clubs and user groups may charge a nominal fee (not to exceed $10) for expenses and handling while distributing the VSA256 Graphics Library. Anyone distributing the VSA256 Graphics Library for any kind of remuneration must first contact Spyro Gumas at the following address for authorization. This authorization will be automatically granted to distributors recognized by the ASP as adhering to its guidelines for shareware distributors, and such distributors may begin offering the VSA256 Graphics Library immediately. (However, Spyro Gumas must still be advised so that the distributor can be kept up to date with the latest version of the VSA256 Graphics Library.)

Commercial users of the VSA256 Graphics Library must register and pay for their copies of the VSA256 Graphics Library within 30 days of first use or their license is withdrawn. Consult the file ORDER.TXT for more information or contact Spyro Gumas.

Disclaimer

Users of the VSA256 Graphics Library must accept this disclaimer of warranty: The VSA256 Graphics Library is supplied as is. The author disclaims all warranties, expressed or implied, including, without limitation, the warranties of merchantability and of fitness for any purpose. The author assumes no liability for damages, direct or consequential, that may result from the use of the VSA256 Graphics Library. In no event shall the author's liability for any damages ever exceed the price paid for the license to use the VSA256 Graphics Library, regardless of the form of the claim. The person using the VSA256 Graphics Library bears all risk as to the quality and performance of this software.

Technical Support

If you have any questions or comments about the VSA256 Graphics Library, please write me at the following address:

Spyro Gumas
1668 Shady Brook Drive
Fullerton, CA 92631
Or, contact me on e-mail at one of the following addresses:

CompuServe: 71064,1571

Internet: 71064.1571@compuserve.com

Graphics Library Extensions

The VSA256 Graphics Library is a base library that is supported by library extensions for more specialized tasks. New extensions will be developed periodically. The current extensions are as follows:

TIFF256 Graphics Library Extensions 3.0   This library extension provides functions that operate with Tagged Image File Format (TIFF) images. With these functions, you can traverse the image file, extract image information, and display the images as part of your own program. You can also modify the TIFF images and write them back to TIFF files. Furthermore, any image that you generate with VSA256 can be saved as a TIFF file. The image types supported include Bilevel, Grayscale, Palette Color, and RGB True Color. Version 3.0 adds Adaptive Color Palette generation when reading in 24-bit images. This makes most True Color images show up undistorted by the 256-color limitation. Now the fully capable version of the TIFF256 Graphics Library Extensions is shareware, available from the same place that you got the VSA256 Graphics Library.

CBTMouse API Library 1.0   New from CyberBase Technologies, Inc., this library adds complete mouse interaction to your graphics applications. These guys go all-out to make mouse-driven graphics programming a breeze. Functions provided include initialization, displaying and hiding the mouse, reading position, setting position, reading button status, working within bounding boxes, changing cursor color and size, and waiting for various mouse inputs. You get a very functional version of this library when you register for the VSA256 Graphics Library. The full-up library (Version 1.0) is shipped by CyberBase Technologies, Inc. upon a nominal registration fee.

CBT3D Library 1.0   Also from CyberBase Technologies, Inc. (yeah, these guys are busy), this library lets you write 3-D applications. Whatever your interests—mechanical design, architecture, interior design, space widgets, you name it—you can do it. Functions provided let you add and delete objects from a display list, set the viewpoint, and perform 3-D transformations, including scale, offset, and rotation. Select the drawing mode for the 3-D objects from Wireframe, Solid, or Gouraud (smooth) Shaded. You get a very functional version of this library when you register for the VSA256 Graphics Library. The full-up library (Version 1.0) is shipped by CyberBase Technologies, Inc. upon a nominal registration fee.

VSA.H Include File

```
/*......................... VSA.H ............. 7-2-94 .....*/
/* This file declares the VSA256 Graphics Library functions   */
/* and global parameters used throughout the graphics routines.*/
/*                                                            */
/*                      VERSION 3.0                           */
/*                                                            */
/*  Copyright Spyro Gumas, 1992 - 1994.  All Rights Reserved. */
/*...........................................................*/


/*...........................................................*/
/*              External Function Prototypes                 */
/*...........................................................*/

extern unsigned  far cdecl vsa_set_svga_mode( unsigned );
extern unsigned  far cdecl vsa_get_svga_mode( unsigned far * );
extern unsigned  far cdecl vsa_set_display_start( unsigned, unsigned );
extern unsigned  far cdecl vsa_get_display_start(unsigned far *,
                       unsigned far * );
extern unsigned  far cdecl vsa_init( unsigned );
extern void far cdecl vsa_set_color( unsigned );
extern void far cdecl vsa_set_text_color( unsigned );
extern void far cdecl vsa_set_text_cursor_mode( unsigned );
extern void far cdecl vsa_set_text_cursor(int, int);
extern void far cdecl vsa_get_text_cursor(int far *, int far *);
extern void far cdecl vsa_set_text_scale(float,Float);
extern void far cdecl vsa_set_viewport( int, int, int, int);
extern void far cdecl vsa_set_clip_mode(  unsigned );
extern void far cdecl vsa_write_string( int, int, unsigned, char far * );
extern void far cdecl vsa_write_string_alt( char far * );
extern void far cdecl vsa_read_color_register( unsigned,
                  unsigned char far *, unsigned char far *,
                  unsigned char far *);
extern void far cdecl vsa_write_color_register( unsigned,
                  unsigned char,unsigned char, unsigned char );
extern void far cdecl vsa_read_color_block( unsigned, unsigned,
                  unsigned char far * );
extern void far cdecl vsa_write_color_block( unsigned, unsigned,
                  unsigned char far * );
extern void far cdecl vsa_move_to( int, int);
extern void far cdecl vsa_set_pixel( int, int);
extern unsigned far cdecl vsa_get_pixel( int, int);
extern void far cdecl vsa_line_to( int, int);
extern void far cdecl vsa_triangle_fill( int, int, int, int, int, int);
extern void far cdecl vsa_rect_fill( int, int);
extern void far cdecl vsa_rect( int, int);
extern unsigned long far cdecl vsa_image_size( int, int, int, int);
extern void far cdecl vsa_get_image(int, int, int, int,
                  unsigned char huge * );
extern void far cdecl vsa_put_image(int, int,
                  unsigned char huge *, unsigned);
extern void far cdecl vsa_h_line( int, int, int);
extern void far cdecl vsa_v_line( int, int, int);
extern void far cdecl vsa_raster_line( int, int, int,
                  unsigned char far *);
extern void far cdecl vsa_get_raster_line( int, int, int,
```

```
                             unsigned char far *);
extern void far cdecl vsa_gouraud_line(int, int, int, int, int);
extern void far cdecl vsa_shaded_triangle( int, int, int, int,
                               int, int, int, int, int);
extern void far cdecl vsa_wait_hsync( void );
extern void far cdecl vsa_wait_vsync( void );
extern void far cdecl vsa_about( void );


/*.............................................................*/
/*              External Parameter Declarations                */
/*.............................................................*/
extern unsigned XResolution, YResolution;
extern unsigned XCharResolution, YCharResolution;
extern unsigned char XCharSize, YCharSize;
extern unsigned char BitsPerPixel;
extern int XLeft,XRight,YTop,YBottom;
extern float Text_X_Scale,Text_Y_Scale
```

VSA_FONT.H Include File

```
/*......................... VSA_FONT.H .............. 6-25-94 ........*/
/*    This is the font file for the VSA256 Graphics Library.  The basic  */
/*    font size is set by the XCharBase and YCharBase values defined at the */
/*    top of this file.  This include file gives you the ability to fully  */
/*    customize your fonts! Feel free to edit the font vertex lists to be as */
/*    personalized as possible.  Read on to see how it works.            */
/*                                                                       */
/*    ASC[M][N] is a 2 dimensional array.  The M index selects one of 96 */
/* possible characters and corresponds to the printable ASCII character  */
/* codes from 32 to 127. (M = 0 selects ASCII character code 32 ... a space,*/
/* M = 95 selects ASCII character code 127 ... DEL)                      */
/*    For any given value of M, the N index steps through the vertex list */
/* for that character.  Each vertex takes up 3 locations.  The first of  */
/* the 3 values is the blank code. A blank code of 0 means start a new line */
/* segment (equivalent to "move_to").  A blank code of 1 means continue   */
/* drawing (equivalent to "line_to").  A blank code of 255 means END of   */
/* vertex list. You MUST end each vertex list this way!                   */
/*    The next two values are x and y coordinates relative to the top left */
/* corner of the character cell.  The x and y values should never be more */
/* than XCharBase-1 and YCharBase-1 respectively.  When the blank code is  */
/* 255, the x and y values are ignored.  A maximum of 23 verticies plus an */
/* END vertex are allowed per character.  Overrunning this limit will      */
/* probably cause your PC to go woopie.                                    */
/*.............................................................*/

unsigned XCharBase = 8, YCharBase = 16;
unsigned char ASC[96][72]=  ... Array initialization not printed here for ...
                       ... brevity.  See VSA_FONT.H file for details ...
```

TIFF256 Graphics Library

by Spyro Gumas

B

For C Programmers
Version 3.0
July 28, 1994
Copyright Spyro Gumas, 1992 - 1994.
All Rights Reserved

Introduction

The TIFF256 Graphics Library Extensions Version 3.0 is a library of C routines that extend the capabilities of the VSA256 Graphics Library. With TIFF256, the C programmer has the tools necessary to read, display, and write Tagged Image File Format (TIFF) images using a 256 color video adapter running with the VESA BIOS Extensions. Support is provided for both Microsoft C and Borland C products. The name "TIFF256" reflects the fact that this library supports the 256 color video modes defined within the VESA standard.

As the preeminent graphics format, TIFF images have permeated the fiber of the computer world. It is the single most common file format, and is supported by virtually all hand-held and flatbed scanners. While every major computer platform has evolved its own unique image file format, TIFF is the one standard format that crosses the boundaries between PC, MAC, Silicon Graphics, Sun, HP, DEC, and all the rest.

The TIFF256 Graphics Library Extensions lets you take advantage of TIFF's popularity by enabling you to integrate TIFF capability into your graphical application. While powerful and robust, the TIFF256 library is simple to use. Only a few lines of code are required to get a TIFF image up on the screen. One more line of code, and the image is saved. (By the way, have you ever tried to write out a BMP image under Windows? Good night Eunice!) A few more lines of code, and you can customize how the software displays 24 bit/pixel images on your 256 color display, and select between 332 RGB, Dithered, or Adaptive Palette displays. The VSA256/TIFF256 combination gives you a formidable tool for graphical programming, while sparing you the nightmare of Windows programming.

Revision History

Version 1.0 is the original SHAREWARE version of the TIFF256 Graphics Library Extensions.

Version 2.0b is the REGISTERED version of the TIFF256 Graphics Library Extensions. Whereas the TIFF256 Graphics Library Extensions Version 1.*x* is shareware, Version 2.0b **IS NOT** shareware and can be used only in accordance with the terms of the purchase agreement. The major change between Versions 1.0 and 2.0b is the addition of the routine called `tf_save_file`. With this new routine, the programmer can now create a TIFF file from any image generated using the VSA256 Graphics Library and the TIFF256 Graphics Library Extensions.

Version 3.0 is presented to the general public in the true spirit of shareware. This revision is the full-up version of the TIFF256 Graphics Library Extensions. I no longer maintain a separate registered version of this library. Version 3.0 of the TIFF256 Graphics Library Extensions is presented as shareware with high hopes that the programmers who use this library will feel good about sending in the registration fee of $29. The major changes between Versions 2.0b and 3.0 are listed here:

- **Added Adaptive Palette.** Now the programmer has the option to turn on Adaptive Palette during the 24-bits/pixel to 8-bits/pixel color reduction. The Adaptive Palette feature calculates the optimum color palette for each True Color image. The result is that the most reduced images retain their True Color look.

- **Added Dithering.** The programmer has the option to turn on dithering during the 24 bits/pixel to 8 bits/pixel color reduction. Dithering approximates the full 16 million color spectrum on 256 color systems, through a technique of jittering or dithering pixel intensities. This technique is particularly useful when a good adaptive palette can't be generated.

- **New routine, `tf_set_true_color_mode`.** Used to select 8-bit RGB, Dithering, or Adaptive Palette for True Color images, and to define the Adaptive Palette configuration.

- **New routine, `tf_get_true_color_mode`.** Used to get current True Color display mode and Adaptive Palette configuration parameters.

- **New routine, `tf_image_size`.** Used to get the size of an image for use with the next two functions.

- **New routine, `tf_load_image`.** Now you can read a TIFF file directly into a memory buffer instead of having to display it on the screen first. Use `vsa_put_image` to display it on the screen when you are ready.

- **New routine, `tf_save_image`.** With this function you can save an image already in a memory buffer to a TIFF file. You can use `vsa_get_image` to copy a screen image into memory buffer.

- **Clipping when TIFF image displayed on-screen.** This is an outcome of the VSA256 Graphics Library 3.0 upgrade that added clipping. You no longer have to worry about your images screen-wrapping.

- **Fixed "unresolved external _fstrlen" linker error with Turbo C.**

- **Made all functions in TIFF.H external, no more "Multiple Declaration" warnings.**

- **Changed name of `tf_display_image` to `tf_display_ifd`.** Because `tf_load_image`, `tf_save_image`, `vsa_get_image`, and `vsa_put_image` all use image in the context of a memory buffer, consistency demands this change. `tf_display_ifd` doesn't deal with memory buffers but goes straight from a TIFF file to the screen. For compatibility with older versions, `tf_display_image` in old code automatically gets mapped to a call to `tf_display_ifd`.

- **Turned off automatic error message screen output.** Now the application can decide whether or not it wants an error message actually displayed by interpreting the return values of the relevant functions.

Benefits of Registering

If you use this program beyond an initial evaluation period, you must register your use with a $29 remittance to the author—me. ($15 if ordering VSA256 and TIFF256 at the same time. See ORDER.TXT.) In addition to the good feeling that you get for sustaining a late night hacking obsession, you get the following benefits for registering:

1. **Royalty-free use of TIFF256 in your programs!** Feel free to distribute your programs for profit with no royalty fees. See the section titled "Software License."

2. **3-D Graphics Library!** Don't live in a flat world. Add the missing third dimension to your creations. This library lets you create 3-D objects, set your view point, and perform 3-D transformations, including scale, offset, and rotation. Supports wireframe, solid, and Gouraud-shaded objects.

3. **Graphics Mouse Library!** Use this library to integrate Mouse input with your graphics applications. Get precise updates of mouse position, update screen cursor, read mouse buttons, and more. Invent your own graphical user interface, give your apps that professional feel, and have tons of fun.

4. **Joystick Library with Source Code!** Integrate Joystick input with your graphics applications. Write a flight simulator, boat driver, or your own unique use of this agile input device.

5. **IMP256 Image Processing Library and Source Code!** With this library, you can learn all about image sharpening, embossing, blurring, color balancing, and enhancement.

6. **32-bit WATCOM C Compiler compatible VSA256 and TIFF256 libraries.** Get the edge on performance.

7. Online support through **CompuServe**.

8. **Printed Users Manual and Current Version Software on disk.**

9. One **Half-Price Upgrade** to the next version as it becomes available.

10. The following public domain full-color TIFF image files to get you started:

    VENUS.TIF
    EARTH.TIF
    MOON.TIF
    MARS.TIF
    SATURN.TIF
    NEPTUNE.TIF
    SHUTTLE.TIF
    ASTRONTS.TIF
    WEATHER.TIF
    MANDRILL.TIF

Distribution Files

The distribution of the TIFF256 Graphics Library Extensions Version 3.0 consists of the eight files listed here. These files are archived in the file TIF256.ZIP. To extract, just type PKUNZIP TIF256 in the directory that you want the files extracted to.

TIF_DEMO.C	Demonstration program (Source Code)
TIF_DEMO.EXE	Demonstration program (Executable)
TIF_DATA.EXE	TIFF file analysis program (Executable)
TIFFMSL.LIB	TIFF256 Extensions, Large Memory Model (Microsoft C)
TIFFBCL.LIB	TIFF256 Extensions, Large Memory Model (Borland C)
TIFF.H	Include file required in your program
TIFF256.TXT	This text document
ORDER.TXT	A text file order form for upgrades and registration

Some TIFF Insights

A TIFF file can contain one or more images. Each of these images is stored in the file as an "Image File Directory" (an IFD). Each IFD consists of numerous fields or "tags." Each tag defines a particular aspect of the image (for example, color model, width, length, resolution). With the TIFF256 Extensions, a programmer can find out how many IFDs are contained within a TIFF file, jump to the desired IFD, read all the tags within the IFD, and display the IFD's image.

The TIFF256 Extensions Environment

Using the TIFF256 Extensions

The TIFF256 Extensions work with any (any?) IBM PC, XT, AT or compatible computer equipped with a VESA-compatible SVGA video adapter card capable of 256 colors.

Most of the video cards sold today are VESA-compatible with the VESA BIOS built in to the card. For older SVGA video cards that are not VESA-compatible, the VESA BIOS Extensions must be loaded as a Terminate and Stay Resident (TSR) program before using the TIFF256 Extensions. A math coprocessor chip is not required. The TIFF256 Extensions are distributed as a Large Memory Model library for either Microsoft C or Borland C. If other memory models are required, contact me.

The TIFF256 Extensions Version 3.0 are used with the VSA256 Graphics Library Version 3.0. The following discussion assumes that you are adding TIFF capability to an existing program that already uses the VSA256 Graphics Library. To use the TIFF256 Extensions, add the file TIFF.H to your C compiler's default directory; for INCLUDE files, add the statement

```
#include<tiff.h>;
```

to your program, and add the file TIFFBCL.LIB or TIFFMSL.LIB to the list of files that your program is linked with.

Global Graphics Parameters

The file TIFF.H is used as an include file during program development. This file includes all of the extension's function prototypes, and it defines the global parameters that describe the TIFF file and individual IFDs. The global graphics parameters are initialized by the `tf_get_file_info()` and `tf_read_ifd()` functions and are described here:

`TF_Num_Ifd:`	Unsigned, the number of IFDs in the TIFF file.
`TF_ImageWidth:`	Unsigned `long`, the image width in pixels.
`TF_ImageLength:`	Unsigned `long`, the image length in pixels.
`TF_BitsPerSample[3]:`	Unsigned, the number of bits per sample. For Bilevel, grayscale, or Palette Color, pixel size = `TF_BitsPerSample[0]`. For True Color, pixel Red Component = `TF_BitsPerSample[0]`, pixel Green component = `TF_BitsPerSample[1]`, pixel Blue component = `TF_BitsPerSample[2]`.
`TF_ResolutionUnit:`	Unsigned, 1 = Not specified, 2 = Inch, 3 = Centimeter.
`TF_SamplesPerPixel:`	Unsigned, the number of samples per pixel.
`TF_Photometric Interpretation:`	Unsigned, 1 = Bilevel or Grayscale, 2 = RGB (True Color) image, 3 = Palette Color Image.
`TF_XResolution_int:`	Unsigned `long`, the integral number of pixels in the x dimension per `TF_ResolutionUnit`.

TF_XResolution_frac:	Unsigned `long`, the fractional number of pixels in the x dimension per `TF_ResolutionUnit`.
TF_YResolution_int:	Unsigned `long`, the integral number of pixels in the y dimension per `TF_ResolutionUnit`.
TF_YResolution_frac:	Unsigned `long`, the fractional number of pixels in the y dimension per `TF_ResolutionUnit`.
TF_Black:	Unsigned, index into Color Look Up Table for color nearest to Black.
TF_Red:	Unsigned, index into Color Look Up Table for color nearest to Red.
TF_Orange:	Unsigned, index into Color Look Up Table for color nearest to Orange.
TF_Yellow:	Unsigned, index into Color Look Up Table for color nearest to Yellow.
TF_Green:	Unsigned, index into Color Look Up Table for color nearest to Green.
TF_Aqua:	Unsigned, index into Color Look Up Table for color nearest to Aqua.
TF_Blue:	Unsigned, index into Color Look Up Table for color nearest to Blue.
TF_Violet:	Unsigned, index into Color Look Up Table for color nearest to Violet.
TF_White:	Unsigned, index into Color Look Up Table for color nearest to White.

Compiler Compatibility

The TIFFMSL.LIB was compiled using Microsoft's Quick C 2.5, and it also seems to work well with Microsoft C 6.0 and 7.0. I have received reports of compatibility problems with Microsoft C 5.0.

The TIFFBCL.LIB was compiled using Borland's C/C++ 3.1, and it also seems to work well with Borland C/C++ 3.0 and 4.0. I have received conflicting reports of compatibility problems with Borland's Turbo C 2.0 and 3.0.

I appreciate any feedback that programmers send me along these lines so that I can continue to improve this product.

> **NOTE**
>
> **Important Note for Borland Users**
>
> You MUST set the -Fs compiler option. This tells the compiler to assume that the Stack Segment equals the Data Segment. In the Programmers IDE, you go to Options / Compiler / Code Generation and select "Always" under the option "Assume SS Equals DS."
>
> Why? Because I compiled the TIFF256 Extensions with the -Fs option set for compatibility with VSA256 Graphics Library. Why did I compile VSA256 with the -Fs option? See the VSA256 documentation in the section titled "Compiler Compatibility" if you really must know.

Support of TIFF 5.0

For the programmer familiar with the TIFF 5.0 Technical Memorandum, Tables B.1 and B.2 indicate which and to what degree the defined tags are supported by the TIFF256 Extensions. The tags supported provide functionality with most images. When in doubt, run the provided TIF_DATA program to determine the characteristics of a given TIFF file.

Table B.1. Tags supported.

Basic Tags

BitsPerSample = 8,8,8 (for RGB or True Color Images)

BitsPerSample <= 8 (for Bilevel, Grayscale, or Palette images)

ColorMap

Compression = none

ImageLength

ImageWidth

NewSubFileType

PhotometricInterpretation = Bilevel and Grayscale

PhotometricInterpretation = RGB (True Color)

PhotometricInterpretation = Palette Color

PlanarConfiguration = 1

ResolutionUnit

RowsPerStrip

SamplesPerPixel

StripByteCounts

StripOffsets

XResolution

YResolution

Table B.2. Tags not supported (maybe next revision).

Basic Tags

BitsPerSample != 8,8,8 (for RGB or True Color Images)

BitsPerSample > 8 (for Bilevel, Grayscale, or Palette images)

ColorResponseCurves

Compression = CCITT Group 3 1-Dimensional Modified Huffman RLE

Compression = LZW Compression

Compression = PackBits Compression

GrayResponseCurve

GrayResponseUnit

PhotometricInterpretation = Transparency Mask

PlanarConfiguration = 2

Predictor

Informational Tags

Artist

DateTime

HostComputer

ImageDescription

Make

Model

Software

Facsimile Tags

Group3Options

Group4Options

Document Storage and Retrieval Tags

DocumentName

PageName

continues

Table B.2. continued

PageNumber
XPosition
YPosition
Obsolete Tags
CellLength
CellWidth
FillOrder
FreeByteCounts
FreeOffsets
MaxSampleValue
MinSampleValue
SubFileType
Orientation
Thresholding

TIFF256 Extensions Functionality

This section describes the operation of the TIFF256 Extensions. To use the functions in this library, compile your program using the **Large Memory Model** and link your program with the appropriate libraries listed here, depending on the compiler being used.

Microsoft C or Quick C: VSA256MS.LIB and TIFFMSL.LIB
Borland C++ or Turbo C: VSA256BC.LIB and TIFFBCL.LIB

Handling the Color Look Up Table

The TIFF256 Extensions support Bilevel and 8-bit or less Grayscale images (TF_PhotometricInterpretation = 1). They also support 24-bit True Color images (TF_PhotometricInterpretation = 2) and 8-bit or less Palette Color images (TF_PhotometricInterpretation = 3).

Because this library is specifically designed for hardware with 256 entry Color Look Up Tables (CLUTs), 24-bit True Color images are reduced to 8-bit images. The method of reduction can be selected as 332-RGB, Dithered, or Adaptive Palette. With the 332-RGB method, the Red, Green, and Blue color components are compressed to 8 bit pixels consisting of 3 bits Red, 3 bits Green, and 2 bits Blue; and, the CLUT is loaded with a compressed True Color palette. The Dithered method also loads a compressed True Color

Palette, but the pixels' intensities are modulated (or dithered) in a technique that approximates all of the 16 million possible colors. With the Adaptive Palette method, each 24-bit image is analyzed separately. The optimal color palette is determined for the image and loaded into the Color Look Up Table.

For Palette Color images, the IFD comes with its own values that are directly loaded into the Color Look Up Table.

Regardless of image type, the Color Look Up Table is not loaded until `tf_display_ifd` is called, even though the IFD may have already been read by `tf_read_ifd`. This means that the previously loaded Color Look Up Table (typically from previously displayed IFD) remains in force until `tf_display_ifd` is called. When using `tf_load_image` instead of `tf_display_ifd`, the Color Look Up Table is not loaded until the program deems appropriate with a call to `vsa_write_color_block`.

Function Descriptions

In the following sections each function is listed along with a definition of its inputs and return values. A description is provided, followed by any relevant comments.

tf_set_adaptive_config(enable,num_colors,quality)

Inputs: `int mode, num_colors, quality;`

Returns: Nothing

Description: This routine configures the display of 24 bit/pixel True Color images. When reading an image from an IFD, the `tf_display_ifd` and `tf_load_image` routines automatically detect the number of bits per pixel and convert the image to 8 bits per pixel. If the image in the IFD is a 24 bit per pixel image, the conversion process is defined by the `tf_set_true_color_mode` routine.

    24 bit True Color images are reduced to 8-bit images using either the 332-RGB, Dithered, or Adaptive Palette method. When `mode = 0`, the 332-RGB method is used. The Red, Green, and Blue color components are compressed to 8-bit pixels consisting of 3 bits Red, 3 bits Green, and 2 bits Blue; and, the Color Look Up Table is loaded with a compressed True Color palette. When `mode = 1`, the Dithered method is used. Again, a compressed True Color Palette is loaded, but the pixels' intensities are modulated (or dithered) in a technique that approximates all of the 16 million possible colors. When `mode = 2`, the Adaptive Palette method is used. In this

case, each 24-bit image is analyzed separately. The optimal color palette is determined for the image and loaded into the Color Look Up Table.

The Adaptive Palette method reduces the 16 million possible colors in the 24-bit image to num_colors, where num_colors can range from 2 to 256. The quality parameter lets the user optimize the Adaptive Palette algorithm for image quality. The valid range is from 0 to 100. When quality is closer to 0, the algorithm is optimized for images with fewer colors but many shades per color (smooth shading is emphasized at the expense of color variety). When quality is closer to 100, the algorithm is optimized for images with a broader color distribution (many colors are accommodated at the expense of smooth shading). If mode is not 2, the num_colors and quality parameters are ignored.

Availability: In TIFF256 Graphics Library Version 3.0 and up.

tf_get_true_color_mode(pmode,pnum_colors,pquality)

Inputs: `int *pmode,*num_colors,*pquality;`

Returns: Nothing

Description: This routine returns the current True Color display mode and the Adaptive Palette configuration parameters that were set by tf_set_true_color_mode. *pmode returns the True Color display mode value, *pnum_colors returns the Adaptive Palette num_colors value, and *pquality returns the Adaptive Palette quality value.

Availability: In TIFF256 Graphics Library Version 3.0 and up.

tf_open_file(filename)

Inputs: `char far filename[];`

Returns: `int fail_flag;`

Description: This routine opens the TIFF file specified by the character string filename[] for use by the TIFF256 Extensions. Only one file can be opened at a time. The file is opened as Read Only. If the file is successfully opened, this routine returns a 0. Otherwise, it returns a -1. This routine must be called before calling tf_get_file_info().

Availability: In TIFF256 Graphics Library Version 1.0 and up.

tf_close_file()

Inputs:	Nothing
Returns:	Nothing
Description:	This routine closes the currently open TIFF file. This routine must be called before opening a new TIFF file with `tf_open_file()`. This routine should be called before exiting your program.
Availability:	In TIFF256 Graphics Library Version 1.0 and up.

tf_get_file_info()

Inputs:	Nothing
Returns:	`int fail_flag;`
Description:	This routine verifies that the selected file is a TIFF format file. Then it initializes the TIFF256 environment for this file. The global parameter `TF_Num_Ifd` is set to the number of Image File Directories (IFDs) existing within the file. An IFD is one "picture," and multiple IFDs can exist within one TIFF file. The TIFF file pointer is set to point to the first IFD in the file. This routine is typically called after `tf_open_file`. The `fail_flag` is returned with one of the following values:

    0   No Errors

    1   Error, Reading file failed

    2   Error, File shorter than expected

    3   Error, Bad TIFF File

Availability:	In TIFF256 Graphics Library Version 1.0 and up.
Comments:	The `fail_flag` return values 2 and 3 have been added as of Version 3.0.

tf_skip_ifd(count)

Inputs:	`unsigned count;`
Returns:	`int reached_end;`
Description:	This routine moves the TIFF file pointer ahead count IFDs. Typically, this routine is called after `tf_get_file_info()` to index the TIFF file pointer to the desired IFD. For example, if `tf_get_file_info()` sets `TF_Num_Ifd` to 5, calling this routine immediately after `tf_get_file_info()` with count = 3 will cause the TIFF file pointer to skip over the first 3 IFDs and point to the fourth IFD. If count equals or exceeds the

number of remaining IFDs, this routine returns a 1 and the TIFF file pointer is set to point to the last IFD. Otherwise, it returns a 0.

Availability: In TIFF256 Graphics Library Version 1.0 and up.

tf_set_defaults()

Inputs: Nothing
Returns: Nothing
Description: This routine sets the default values for all the global parameters that are modified by TIFF Tags. TIFF files may not
include data for all the parameters used by the TIFF256
environment, and therefore the defaults should be set. This
routine should be called at the beginning of each new IFD,
prior to calling tf_read_ifd(). The default values are listed
here:

```
TF_ImageWidth   =        0
TF_ImageLength =         0
TF_BitsPerSample[0]   =      1
TF_BitsPerSample[1]   =      1
TF_BitsPerSample[2]   =      1
TF_ResolutionUnit   =      2
TF_SamplesPerPixel    =      1
TF_PhotometricInterpretation   =      1
TF_XResolution_int      =    300
TF_XResolution_frac    =      1
TF_YResolution_int      =    300
TF_YResolution_frac    =      1
```

Availability: In TIFF256 Graphics Library Version 1.0 and up.

tf_read_ifd()

Inputs: Nothing
Returns: int fail_flag;
Description: This routine reads the data from the IFD currently pointed to
by the TIFF file pointer. The TIFF file pointer must be
pointing to a valid IFD prior to calling this routine. (This
routine is typically called after tf_open_file or tf_skip_ifd,
which initialize the pointer.) After reading the data from the
current IFD, the TIFF file pointer is set to point to the next

IFD. If the TIFF file pointer points to the last IFD in the TIFF file, and this routine is executed, the IFD is read, and then the TIFF file pointer is set with a null value. After calling this routine, `tf_display_ifd` or `tf_load_image` can be called to display the IFD's image. The `fail_flag` is returned with one of the following values:

0	No Errors
1	Error, TIFF file pointer is a null value, end of file
2	Error, Seeking in File
3	Error, Reading file failed
4	Greater than 8-Bit Palette Pixels Not Supported
5	Samples Per Pixel > 3 Not Supported
6	Only 8×8×8-Bit True Color Pixels Supported
7	Compressed TIFF data Not Supported
8	This Photometric Interpretation Not Supported
9	Currently Only Support up to 1,024 Strips
10	Samples Per Pixel > 3 Not Supported
11	Currently Only Support up to 1,024 Strips
12	This Planar Configuration Not Supported
13	This Predictor Not Supported
14	Color Map Size > 256 Not Supported

The following global parameters are set by this routine:

```
TF_ImageWidth
TF_ImageLength
TF_BitsPerSample[3]
TF_ResolutionUnit
TF_SamplesPerPixel
TF_PhotometricInterpretation
TF_XResolution_int
TF_XResolution_frac
TF_YResolution_int
TF_YResolution_frac
```

Availability: In TIFF256 Graphics Library Version 1.0 and up.

Comments: The `fail_flag` return values 2 through 14 have been added as of Version 3.0.

tf_display_ifd(x0,y0)

Inputs:	`unsigned x0;`
	`unsigned y0;`
Returns:	`int fail_flag;`
Description:	This routine displays the image that is defined in the IFD read by the most recent call to `tf_read_ifd`. The image is drawn directly to the screen with its upper-left corner at screen coordinates `x0,y0`. The Color Look Up Table is not modified until this routine is executed. When executed, this routine prepares the Color Look Up Table as defined by the IFD being displayed. Before calling this routine, `tf_read_ifd` must be called to initialize all of the required parameters. When reading the image in the IFD, this routine automatically detects the number of bits per pixel and converts the image to 8 bits per pixel. If the image in the IFD is a 24-bit-per-pixel image, the conversion process is defined by the `tf_set_true_color_mode` routine.
	If Adaptive Palette is enabled (via `tf_set_true_color_mode`), this routine temporarily allocates 32K bytes of memory for the Adaptive Palette conversion process. If the allocation fails, this routine returns a `fail_flag = 1`; otherwise, 0 is returned. In the case where the allocation fails, the program can disable Adaptive Palette and call this routine again.
	Typically this routine is used instead of `tf_load_image` when you don't need to store the image in a buffer for subsequent manipulation. This routine is also useful when the runtime environment has insufficient memory for allocating the huge image memory buffer used with `tf_load_image`.
Availability:	In TIFF256 Graphics Library Version 1.0 and up.
Comments:	This routine can be called more than once per `tf_read_ifd` call. Please **DO NOT** call this routine if `tf_read_ifd` returns an error (`fail_flag = 1`).

tf_save_file(x0,y0,x1,y1,filename)

Inputs:	`unsigned x0,y0,x1,y1;`
	`char far filename[];`
Returns:	`int fail_flag;`
Description:	This routine saves the portion of the screen image defined by `(x0,y0) (x1,y1)` to the TIFF file `filename`. The image is saved

as an 8-bit Palette Color image (8 bits per pixel). This routine can be called any time after `vsa_init` is called. If an error occurs in writing the file, a -1 is returned, otherwise 0 is returned.

The TIFF image file saved as a result of this routine has the following characteristics, as defined by the TIFF specification:

- Intel Byte Ordering
- SamplesPerPixel = 1
- BitsPerSample = 8 (8 bits per pixel)
- ColorMap (Color palette stored within TIFF file)
- PhotometricInterpretation = Palette Color
- PlanarConfiguration = 1
- RowsPerStrip = 1
- ImageWidth = |x1-x0|+1 (pixels)
- ImageLength = |y1-y0|+1 (pixels)
- Resolution Unit = 2 (inches)
- XResolution = 100 (Dots Per Inch)
- YResolution = 100 (Dots Per Inch)
- Compression = none

Availability: In TIFF256 Graphics Library Version 2.0 and up.

tf_image_size()

Inputs: Nothing

Returns: `long size;`

Description: This routine returns the size (in bytes) of the memory buffer required to store an image that is defined in the IFD read by the most recent call to `tf_read_ifd`. Before calling this routine, `tf_read_ifd` must be called to define all of the required global parameters. The size is based on 8-bit pixels regardless of the image type because `tf_load_image` always converts to 8-bit pixels as it reads the TIFF file. The size returned is equal to the number of pixels in the image plus 4. Typically, after calling `tf_image_size`, a huge memory buffer is allocated with `size` bytes. Then the `tf_load_image` function is used to load the image from the TIFF file into the memory buffer.

Availability:	In TIFF256 Graphics Library Version 3.0 and up.
Comments:	This routine can be called more than once per `tf_read_ifd` call. Please **DO NOT** call this routine if `tf_read_ifd` returns an error (`fail_flag = 1`).

tf_load_image(image,lut)

Inputs:	`unsigned char huge *image;`
	`unsigned char far *lut;`
Returns:	`int colors;`
Description:	This routine loads the `image` memory buffer with the image that is defined in the IFD read by the most recent call to `tf_read_ifd`. The image's color palette is loaded into the `lut` memory buffer. The `image` memory buffer must be allocated the size returned by `tf_image_size`, and the `lut` memory must be allocated 768 bytes before calling this routine. The return value `colors` indicates how many of the 256 colors in `lut` are actually used (0 or 1 indicates an error). Before calling this routine, `tf_read_ifd` must be called to initialize all of the required parameters.
	When reading the image in the IFD, this routine automatically detects the number of bits per pixel and converts the image to 8 bits per pixel. If the image in the IFD is a 24-bit-per-pixel image, the conversion process is defined by the `tf_set_true_color_mode` routine.
	If Adaptive Palette is enabled (via `tf_set_true_color_mode`), this routine temporarily allocates 32K bytes of memory for the Adaptive Palette conversion process. If the allocation fails, this routine returns a `fail_flag = 1`. In the case where the allocation fails, the program can disable Adaptive Palette and call this routine again.
	The `image` buffer can be displayed on the screen with the `vsa_put_image` function, or saved to a TIFF file with the `tf_save_image` function. The color palette in the `lut` buffer can be loaded into the Color Look Up Table using the `vsa_write_color_block` routine.
	The `image` buffer stores the image width in the first two bytes, the image height in the second two bytes, and then the image pixels in raster order (row, then column). The first pixel value following image height is the upper-left corner pixel. The `lut`

array stores the 256 color palette data in RGB triplets, where each of R, G, and B is a byte. 768 bytes are stored in `lut`. Typically this routine is used instead of `tf_display_ifd` when you need to store the image in a buffer for subsequent manipulation. With this routine, a program can bring in an image, manipulate its pixels and/or color palette, and then save it back to a TIFF file without ever necessarily having to display the image on the screen.

Availability: In TIFF256 Graphics Library Version 3.0 and up.

Comments: This routine can be called more than once per `tf_read_ifd` call. Please **DO NOT** call this routine if `tf_read_ifd` returns an error (`fail_flag = 1`).

tf_save_image(image,lut,filename)

Inputs:
```
unsigned char huge *image;
unsigned char far *lut;
char filename[];
```

Returns: `int fail_flag;`

Description: This routine saves the image defined in the `image` buffer along with the 256 color palette defined in the `lut` buffer to the TIFF file `filename`. The image is saved as an 8-bit Palette Color image (8 bits per pixel). This routine may be called at any time after `vsa_init` is called, assuming that both `image` and `lut` have been loaded with meaningful data. If an error occurs in writing the file, a `-1` is returned, otherwise `0` is returned.

The `image` buffer could have been loaded through either a `tf_load_image` (which gets it from a TIFF file) or through `vsa_get_image` (which gets it directly from the screen). In the latter case, you would also need to have loaded the `lut` buffer using `vsa_read_color_block`.

The `image` array stores the image width in the first two bytes, the image height in the second two bytes, and then the image pixels in standard raster order (row, then column). First pixel is in the upper-left corner. The `lut` array stores the 256 color palette data in RGB triplets, where each of R, G, and B is a byte. 256 triplets (768 bytes) are stored in `lut`.

The TIFF image file saved as a result of this routine has the following characteristics, as defined by the TIFF specification:

- Intel Byte Ordering
- SamplesPerPixel = 1
- BitsPerSample = 8 (8 bits per pixel)
- ColorMap (Color palette stored within TIFF file)
- PhotometricInterpretation = Palette Color
- PlanarConfiguration = 1
- RowsPerStrip = 1
- ImageWidth = first 16 bits of `image` buffer
- ImageLength = second 16 bits of `image` buffer
- Resolution Unit = 2 (inches)
- XResolution = 100 (Dots Per Inch)
- YResolution = 100 (Dots Per Inch)
- Compression = none

Availability: In TIFF256 Graphics Library Version 3.0 and up.

tf_set_prime_colors()

Inputs: Nothing

Returns: Nothing

Description: This routine updates the prime color global parameters: `TF_Black`, `TF_Red`, `TF_Orange`, `TF_Yellow`, `TF_Green`, `TF_Aqua`, `TF_Blue`, `TF_Violet`, and `TF_White`. It does this by scanning the Color Look Up Table and loading each parameter with the Color Look Up Table index for the brightest color nearest to the color specified by the parameter name. This routine should be called following any operation that modifies the Color Look Up Table (such as `tf_display_ifd`).

The prime color global parameters are provided in an attempt to give the user access to a standard set of colors (for use with text and borders, for example) regardless of Color Look Up Table operations. However, the color must exist in the Color Look Up Table for this routine to find it.

Availability: In TIFF256 Graphics Library Version 1.0 and up.

Nitty Gritties

Registration Information

If you find the TIFF256 Graphics Library Extensions useful, a registration of $29 would be appreciated. ($15 if ordering VSA256 and TIFF256 at the same time. See ORDER.TXT.) Registration brings with it MAJOR BENEFITS, as spelled out in the section titled "Benefits of Registering" earlier in the chapter, so look at the ORDER.TXT file and fill it out.

Please fill out the "Information About You" and the "Wish List" sections, and indicate the version number of the software you are presently using. Send check or money order to

Spyro Gumas
1668 Shady Brook Drive
Fullerton, CA 92631

Software License

TIFF256 Graphics Library, Version 3.0
Copyright Spyro Gumas, 1992 - 1994. All Rights Reserved.

The TIFF256 Graphics Library Extensions is a "shareware program" and is provided at no charge to the user for evaluation. The essence of "user-supported" software is to provide personal computer users with quality software without high prices, and yet to provide incentive for programmers to continue to develop new products. If you find this program useful and find that you are using the TIFF256 Graphics Library Extensions and continue to use the TIFF256 Graphics Library Extensions after a reasonable trial period, you must make a registration payment of $29 to Spyro Gumas. ($15 if ordering VSA256 and TIFF256 at the same time. See ORDER.TXT.) The registration fee will license one copy for use on any one computer at any one time. You must treat this software just like a book. An example is that this software can be used by any number of people and can be freely moved from one computer location to another, so long as there is no possibility of it being used at more than one location at a time—just as a book cannot be read by two different people at the same time.

You are free (and encouraged) to copy and distribute the TIFF256 Graphics Library Extensions if:

1. It is not used as a component of another software library.
2. No fee is charged for use, copying, or distribution.
3. It is distributed as is (preferably as TIF256.ZIP) and not modified in any way.

Furthermore, you are granted royalty-free use of the TIFF256 Graphics Library Extensions executable code in any of your programs, given that:

1. You have registered your use of the TIFF256 Graphics Library Extensions and paid the registration fee.

2. It is not used as a component of another software library.

3. You visibly acknowledge the use of the TIFF256 Graphics Library Extensions in your product in both the printed materials and the executable software with the following statement:

   "This software uses the VSA256 and TIFF256 Graphics Libraries, Copyright Spyro Gumas, 1992 - 1994. All Rights Reserved."

Clubs and user groups may charge a nominal fee (not to exceed $10) for expenses and handling while distributing the TIFF256 Graphics Library Extensions. Anyone distributing the TIFF256 Graphics Library Extensions for any kind of remuneration must first contact Spyro Gumas at the following address for authorization. This authorization will be automatically granted to distributors recognized by the ASP as adhering to its guidelines for shareware distributors, and such distributors may begin offering the TIFF256 Graphics Library Extensions immediately. (However, Spyro Gumas must still be advised so that the distributor can be kept up to date with the latest version of the TIFF256 Graphics Library Extensions.)

Commercial users of the TIFF256 Graphics Library Extensions must register and pay for their copies of the TIFF256 Graphics Library Extensions within 30 days of first use or their license is withdrawn. Consult the file ORDER.TXT for more information or contact Spyro Gumas.

Disclaimer

Users of the TIFF256 Graphics Library Extensions must accept this disclaimer of warranty: The TIFF256 Graphics Library Extensions is supplied as is. The author disclaims all warranties, expressed or implied, including, without limitation, the warranties of merchantability and of fitness for any purpose. The author assumes no liability for damages, direct or consequential, which may result from the use of the TIFF256 Graphics Library Extensions. In no event shall the author's liability for any damages ever exceed the price paid for the license to use the TIFF256 Graphics Library Extensions, regardless of the form of the claim. The person using the TIFF256 Graphics Library Extensions bears all risk as to the quality and performance of this software.

Technical Support

If you have any questions or comments about the TIFF256 Graphics Library Extensions, please write me at the following address:

Spyro Gumas
1668 Shady Brook Drive
Fullerton, CA 92631
Or, contact me on e-mail at one of the following addresses:
CompuServe: 71064,1571
Internet: 71064.1571@compuserve.com

TIFF.H Include File

```
/*........................ TIFF.H ............. 7-28-94 .....*/
/* This file declares the TIFFLB library functions and global  */
/* parameters used throughout the graphics routines            */
/* (Version 3.0).                                              */
/*                                                            */
/*  Copyright Spyro Gumas, 1992 - 1994.  All Rights Reserved.  */
/*........................................................*/

/*   Next line for compatibility with old versions of TIFF256  */
#define tf_display_image tf_display_ifd

/*........................................................*/
/*                 Function Prototypes                    */
/*........................................................*/
extern void  far cdecl tf_set_true_color_mode(int, int, int);
extern void  far cdecl tf_get_true_color_mode(int far *,
                       int far *, int far *);
extern int   far cdecl tf_open_file(char far *);
extern void far cdecl tf_close_file(void);
extern int  far cdecl tf_get_file_info(void);
extern int  far cdecl tf_skip_ifd(unsigned);
extern void far cdecl tf_set_defaults(void);
extern int  far cdecl tf_read_ifd(void);
extern int  far cdecl tf_display_ifd(unsigned,unsigned);
extern int  far cdecl tf_save_file(unsigned,unsigned,unsigned,
                       unsigned, char far *);
extern long far cdecl tf_image_size(void);
extern int  far cdecl tf_load_image(unsigned char huge*,
                       unsigned char far*);
extern int  far cdecl tf_save_image(unsigned char huge*,
                       unsigned char far*, char far *);
extern void far cdecl tf_set_prime_colors(void);

/*........................................................*/
/*                 Parameter Declarations                 */
/*........................................................*/
extern unsigned char far TF_Byte_Buf[4096];
extern unsigned long TF_ImageWidth, TF_ImageLength;
extern unsigned far TF_BitsPerSample[3],TF_Num_Ifd;
extern unsigned TF_ResolutionUnit,TF_SamplesPerPixel;
extern unsigned TF_PhotometricInterpretation;
extern unsigned long TF_XResolution_int,TF_XResolution_frac;
extern unsigned long TF_YResolution_int,TF_YResolution_frac;
extern unsigned TF_Black,TF_Red,TF_Orange,TF_Yellow,TF_Green;
extern unsigned TF_Aqua,TF_Blue,TF_Violet,TF_White;
```

Resource Guide

C

by William Parsons Newhall, Jr.

Introduction

The field of computer graphics has become broad, deep, and accessible. The computer graphics community has grown considerably, and a large market of computer graphics products and services has developed to meet the needs of this large group. A wide range of computer graphics books and magazines are available for the eclectic group of programmers, artists, and hobbyists who are interested in computer graphics. You can take courses in computer graphics from many colleges, universities, and training centers that have incorporated computer graphics studies into their visual art, communications, or computer science curricula. The computer graphics community has many professional organizations and user groups that can provide networking, training, and other benefits. By plugging into bulletin board systems, online services, and the Internet, you can obtain megabytes upon megabytes of free software, documentation, images, objects, fonts, textures, and you'll have a means of rapidly distributing your own work around the globe.

In becoming part of the computer graphics community, you can enrich your understanding of the discipline, make professional and social contacts, and stay on the leading edge. This appendix is not and cannot be a complete guide to computer graphics resources, but it can provide you with an understanding of what kinds of resources are available and how you can obtain them. Happy hunting!

Professional Organizations

Computer graphics organizations have been instrumental in providing a forum for researchers, artists, programmers, and corporations to meet, develop standards, and showcase their work. Professional organizations publish newsletters and journals that inform members of new technologies, employment opportunities, research grants, trade shows, graphics contests, and other opportunities. Conventions such as those sponsored by SIGGRAPH, SMPTE, and NCGA give members the opportunity to see the latest technology and obtain free product information and demonstration software.

ACM-SIGGRAPH
(Association for Computing Machinery Special Interest Group on Graphics)
11 West 42nd Street
New York, NY 10036

NCGA
(National Computer Graphics Association)
2722 Merrilee Drive, Suite 200
Fairfax, VA 22031

Society of Motion Picture and Television Engineers
(SMPTE)
862 Scarsdale Avenue
Scarsdale, NY 10583

User Groups

3-D Artists and Animators of Tampa Bay
12816 129th Avenue
North Largo, FL 34644
(813) 595-7263

Southern Animation Society
P.O. Box 1045
Metairie, LA 70004

Michigan Computer Graphics, Multimedia, And Animation Users Group
c/o AeroData Computer Services, Inc.
44191 Plymouth Oaks Blvd.
Plymouth, MI 48170

Kansas City 3D Modelling & Animation Users Group
c/o Eric Randall
3D Software
3710 W. 71 Terrace
Prairie Village, KS 66208
(913) 262-4411

New Mexico Computer Artists
c/o *3D Artist* Magazine
P.O. Box 4787
Santa Fe, NM 87502
(505) 982-3532

Houston Artists and Animators Group
c/o Bob Kennon and Debbie Richardson
Animatrix Computer Arts
P.O. Box 66489
Houston, TX 77266
(713) 523-0888

Northwest CyberArtists
c/o Steve Turnidge
10802 47th Avenue W.
Mukilteo, WA 98275
(206) 355-6000

Educational Institutions

Colleges and Universities

A number of colleges and universities have computer graphics offerings in communications, visual arts, and computer science departments. Depending upon where your interest lies, you can study the artistic side of 3-D design or you can get under the hood and
learn graphics programming. Some schools offer degrees that expose the student to both
sides of computer graphics. Each school has its own guidelines for admission and enroll-
ment. Contact the school's Department of Admissions for more details.

California Institute of the Arts
Valencia, CA 95192
(800) 545-ARTS

Cogswell Polytechnic
1175 Bordeaux Drive
Sunnyvale, CA 94089
(408) 252-5550

Cornell University
410 Thurston Avenue
Ithaca, NY 14853
(607) 255-5241

Columbia College
600 S. Michigan Avenue
Chicago, IL 60605
(312) 663-1600

George Mason University
4400 University Drive
Fairfax, VA 22030-4444
(703) 993-1000

Pratt Institute
200 Willoughby Avenue
Brooklyn, NY 11205
(718) 636-3699
(800) 331-0834

Ringling School of Art and Design
2400 North Tamiami Terrace
Sarasota, FL 34234-5895
(800) 255-7695

Savannah College of Art and Design
342 Bull Street
Savannah, GA 31402-3146
(912) 238-2483

School of Visual Arts
209 East 23rd Street
New York, NY 10010-3994
(212) 679-7350

Skidmore College
Saratoga Springs, NY 12866
(518) 584-5000

Teikyo Marycrest University
1607 West 12th Street
Davenport, IA 52804
(800) 728-9705

Training Centers and Certificate Programs

Center for Creative Imaging
51 Mechanic Street
Camden, ME 04843
(800) 428-7400

Cyberplex
201 S.E. Main Street #215
Minneapolis, MN 55414
(612) 649-4641

Republic Research Training Centers, Inc.
P.O. Box 3605
Charlottesville, VA 22903
(800) 476-4454

School of Communication Arts Minneapolis
2526 27th Avenue South
Minneapolis, MN 55406
(800) 800-2835

School of Communication Arts Raleigh
3220 Spring Forest Road
Raleigh, NC 27604
(919) 981-0927

Magazines and Newsletters

Magazines and newsletters can provide you with key information, such as product reviews, program listings, and detailed analyses of trends in the computer graphics, hardware, and software industries. The following list includes not only magazines geared towards the computer graphics community, but also magazines that touch on issues tangential to computer graphics: hardware and software, operating systems, and programming.

3D Artist
Columbine, Inc.
P.O. Box 4787
Santa Fe, NM 87502
(505) 982-3532

Aldus
Aldus Corporation
411 First Avenue South
Seattle, WA 98104-2871
(206) 628-2321

Byte
P.O. Box 557
Heightstown, NJ 08520-9407
(800) 232-2983

Computer Animators News
c/o Jeff Glaze
6940 Rosewell Road
Atlanta, GA 30328
(404) 395-0003

Computer Artist/Computer Graphics World
PENWELL Publications
10 Tara Boulvard, Suite 500
Nashua, NH 03062-2801
(800) 331-4463

Computer Shopper
One Park Avenue, 11th Floor
New York, NY 10016
(800) 274-6384

Desktop Video World
80 Elm Street
Peterborough, NH 03458
(800) 441-4403

Dick Oliver's Nonlinear Nonsense Newsletter
RR 1 Box 4495
Wolcott, VT 05680
(802) 888-5275

PC Graphics and Video (formerly *Highcolor*)
201 East Sand Pointe
Suite 600
Santa Ana, CA 92707
(800) 854-3112

Computer Hardware Manufacturers

Microprocessors

American Microdevices (AMD)
901 Thompson Place
Sunnyvale, CA 94088
(408) 732-2400

AMD manufactures inexpensive math coprocessors, 80386-compatible processors, and recently 80486-compatible processors.

Cyrix
2703 North Central Expressway
Richardson, TX 75080
(800) 848-2979
(214) 994-8610 BBS
Cyrix manufactures 80x86 microprocessors, 80x87 math coprocessors, and clock-doubled 80486 microprocessor upgrades for 80386 systems. Cyrix has announced development of the M1 processor, a 64-bit 80x86 compatible processor designed to compete with the Intel Pentium at a lower cost.

Intel
1781 Fox Drive
San Jose, CA 95131
(800) 879-4683 Product Literature
(800) 628-8686
The Intel Corporation is the original manufacturer of the 80x86 microprocessor family and the PCI bus architecture.

Motorola
616 West 24th Street
Tempe, AZ 85282-1930
(800) 441-2447
Motorola manufacturers the 680x0 family of microprocessors employed in Amiga and Apple Macintosh computers, as well as the 88000 and PowerPC RISC processors. Motorola manufactures the 56000 family of digital signal processors, as well as a full line of microcomponents and electronics hardware. Motorola is also the leading mobile telecommunications corporation, commanding a substantial majority of the cellular telephone and pager market. Motorola processors are not used in 80x86 machines except for digital signal processors in audio applications. Recent market developments, such as the CPU-independent PCI bus architecture and the increased need for parallel processing, show that there may be room for Motorola components in 80x86 PCs.

NexGen
1623 Buckeye Drive
Milipitas, CA 95035-7423
(408) 435-0202

NexGen produces the NX586, a 64-bit 80x86 and Pentium compatible microprocessor. The NX586 is a superscalar design with branch prediction, out-of-order instruction execution, and speculative instruction execution. The NexGen processor features an internal RISC instruction set and microcode that emulates the Pentium instruction set. The NX586 features twice as much internal cache memory as the Pentium and integrates level-two cache right on the chip. The NX586 does not incorporate a floating point unit, and it requires an NX587 coprocessor, although the separate floating point unit is based on an entirely new design and does not degrade performance.

Graphics Acceleration Chipsets

At the heart of any graphics adapter is a chipset that interfaces the frame buffer and acceleration hardware to the system bus. All of these manufacturers can provide spec sheets on their products, and many of them can provide names of OEMs and dealers who make or carry adapters that use their chipsets. Developer's kits and reference manuals can also be obtained (some for free) if you wish to write drivers or software that makes use of their products.

3DLabs
2010 North First Street, Suite 403
San Jose, CA 95131
(408) 436-3455
info@3dlabs.com   Internet E-mail
3DLabs manufactures the GLiNT chip, a 3-D hardware accelerator with built-in Z-buffering, texture-mapping, anti-aliasing, and Gouraud shading, designed to accelerate OpenGL, Hoops, PEX, and 3DR applications in Microsoft Windows NT as well as existing 3-D software such as 3D Studio and Microstation. The GLiNT chip is designed to interface with the PCI bus architecture and can deliver 300,000 Gouraud-shaded and z-buffered triangles per second.

Cirrus Logic
3100 West Warren Avenue
Fremont, CA 94538
(510) 623-8300
Cirrus Logic produces peripheral controller circuits for storage, graphics, and data communications applications in the PC and workstation markets. Cirrus Logic manufactures a variety of low-cost windows accelerators for the VESA, ISA, and PCI bus architectures. The Alpine chipset features a built-in 24-bit DAC, a 64-bit DRAM frame buffer interface, and linear CPU addressing. Drivers are available for Windows 3.1, Windows NT, and OS/2.

S3 Incorporated
2880 San Tomas Expressway
Santa Clara, CA 95051-0981
(408) 980-5400
S3 was one of the first corporations to produce graphics acceleration hardware for
the PC windows market. They currently produce VESA/VGA-compatible 2-D
windows graphics acceleration chipsets that can be interfaced to a variety of bus
architectures and DAC designs. Their latest offering for the PCI bus architecture
interfaces up to 4 MB of display memory (VRAM for the frame buffer, less
expensive DRAM for off-screen storage) that can be mapped linearly to the
CPU's upper memory address space. S3 provides drivers for Windows, OS/2,
Autocad, and SCO OpenDesktop.

Texas Instruments
P.O. Box 655303
Mail Station 8336
Dallas, TX 75265
(800) 336-5236
(214) 644-5880 Semiconductor Product Information Center
Texas Instruments manufactured the 34010 and 34020 graphics coprocessors
around which TIGA (Texas Instruments Graphics Architecture) was designed.
Texas Instruments has since discontinued TIGA and no replacement architecture
is in the works. TIGA boards can still be obtained from manufacturers such as
Truevision.

Tseng Labs, Inc.
6 Terry Drive
Newtown, PA 18940
(215) 968-0502
Tseng Labs produced the ET4000 SuperVGA chipset, which became an industry
standard. The W32, W32i, and W32p chips incorporate the ET4000 design,
along with rapid line drawing, polygon filling, and BitBlt acceleration. All W32
chipsets interface to interleaved DRAM frame buffers with results that rival faster,
more expensive VRAM designs. In recent trade journals and magazine articles,
display adapters designed with W32, W32i, and W32p chipsets were praised for
having the fastest unaccelerated SuperVGA performance and more than adequate
acceleration at extremely low cost.

Weitek Corporation
1060 East Arques Avenue
Sunnyvale, CA 94086
(408) 738-8400

The Weitek Corporation, which originally developed floating point hardware for the PC and for UNIX workstations, now has a graphics acceleration chip, the Weitek P9000, that interfaces to a VRAM frame buffer (up to 4 MB in size) via a 32-bit bus. The Weitek P9000 supports resolutions of up to 1600×1200 and up to 32 bits per pixel. The P9000 comes with drivers for Autocad, Windows 3.1, Windows NT, OS/2, and X-Window.

Graphics Display Adapters

ATI Technologies, Inc.
905-764-9404 BBS
One of the original manufacturers of EGA boards, ATI has dominated the windows accelerator market with its proprietary MACH family of graphics display processors. ATI was one of the first manufacturers to feature a 64-bit bus between the frame buffer and the graphics display processor.

Diamond Computer Systems, Inc.
532 Mercury Drive
Sunnyvale, CA 94086
(408) 736-2000
Diamond was one of the first SuperVGA adapter manufacturers to offer an inexpensive 24-bit mode. Diamond uses a number of accelerator chipsets from companies such as S3 and Tseng Labs, as well as its own proprietary chipset.

Hercules Computer Technology, Inc.
3839 Spinnaker Court
Fremont, CA 94538
(510) 623-6030
(510) 623-7449 BBS
(800) 532-0600
Hercules has been manufacturing display hardware for PCs since 1982, when the Hercules monochrome graphics architecture made its debut. Hercules has, in the past, manufactured EGA and TIGA boards but no longer supports those architectures. Presently, Hercules manufactures a line of ISA, VESA local bus, and PCI SuperVGA windows accelerators based upon the Tseng Labs W32i and W32p graphics chipsets.

Matrox
1055 St. Regis Blvd.
Dorval, PQ, Canada H9P 2T4
(514) 685-2630
(800) 361-1408
Matrox is one of the leading manufacturers of workstation-quality PC desktop
video and 3-D computer graphics hardware. The Matrox Ultima and Impression
graphics accelerators include a real-time 3-D wireframe graphics engine, and the
Matrox Impression features real-time Gouraud shading (60,000 Z-buffered
triangles per second). Matrox provides drivers for Autodesk 3D Studio,
Intergraph Microstation, Windows 3.1, Windows NT, OS/2 2.1, and X-Window
for UNIX systems. Both the Ultima and Impression boards can be integrated
with video recording and playback options as well. Matrox also has announced
that it will be supporting Hoops and OpenGL under DOS, Windows 3.1, and
Windows NT.

Media Vision
47300 Bayside Parkway
Fremont, CA 94538
(800) 845-5870
(510) 770-0968
(510) 770-0527 BBS
A multimedia company connected with research at Stanford University and MIT,
Media Vision produces PC multimedia equipment, including CD-ROM drives,
audio cards, frame grabbers, and graphics adapters. The Pro Graphics 1024 and
Pro Graphics 1280 feature true-color graphics in all supported resolutions; full
screen playback of AVI, MPEG, and other digital animation and video formats;
and a 64-bit bus between their proprietary acceleration chipset and the frame
buffer. Media Vision has also announced that it will be porting OpenGL to
Windows NT. As of this writing, Media Vision has just recently filed for Chapter
Eleven and the future of the company is not clear.

Truevision
7340 Shadeland Station
Indianapolis, IN 46256
(317) 841-0332
(800) 344-8783
(317) 577-8777 BBS
Support@Truevision.com Internet E-mail
FTP.TRUEVISION.COM Internet FTP

Truevision has built true-color graphics boards for desktop video and graphics applications since the mid-1980s. Most Truevision products come with or feature as options NTSC output and genlock for overlay and chroma-key support. Most of Truevision's graphics adapters are designed around the ISA bus architecture, with the exception of the Targa 2000 full motion video board, which is designed around the EISA bus architecture.

Input Devices

Calcomp—Digitizer Division
14555 North 82nd Street
Scottsdale, AZ 85260-2599
(800) CALCOMP
Calcomp manufactures digitizers, plotters, and printers. Their digitizers come in 12-inch by 12-inch and 12-inch by 18-inch sizes. Calcomp digitizers can be ordered with pens, pucks, and cordless pressure-sensitive pens.

Canon
GT55 Series Sales Department
100 Jamesburg
Jamesburg, NJ 08831
(908) 521- 7000
(800) OKCANNON
Originally a manufacturer of office equipment such as copiers and fax machines, Canon manufactures the XAP-SHOT digital imaging camera and a variety of color and monochrome laser and bubble-jet printers.

Immersion Corporation
P.O. Box 8669
Palo Alto, CA 94309
(415) 960-6882
The Immersion Corporation makes a number of low-cost (between $1000 and $2,500) three-dimensional digitizers. At present, no device drivers are available for popular software.

Kurta
3007 East Chamers
Phoenix, AZ 85040
(800) 445-8782
(602) 243-9440 BBS

Kurta manufactures digitizer tablets for almost any price range. Sizes vary from the 4-inch by 5-inch Penmouse tablet to their 42-inch by 60-inch XLC digitizer. Cordless and pressure-sensitive pens are available.

Logitech
6505 Kaiser Drive
Fremont, CA 94555
(800) 231-7717 Sales
Logitech started out manufacturing high-resolution mice for desktop publishing applications and has since broadened its base to other graphics and multimedia products. Logitech also manufactures the Scanman hand scanner and Photoman digital camera, and it has recently come out with a 3-D controller called the Cyberman, which has only been applied in games but might make a powerful input device for 3-D graphics applications.

Microtek Lab
3715 Doolittle Drive
Redondo Beach, CA 90278
(800) 654-4160
(310) 297-5102 BBS
Microtek manufactures a wide variety of image scanners, including an inexpensive "hands-free" scanner, 24-bit and 36-bit flatbed color scanners, a slide scanner, and a transparency scanner.

Mustek
15225 Alton Parkway #100
Irvine, CA 92718-2348
(714) 833-7740
Mustek manufactures a family of image scanning products ranging from hand scanners that can interface through the parallel port of a laptop to 11-inch by 17-inch flatbed scanners.

Summagraphics
8500 Cameron Road
Austin, TX 78754-3999
(800) 444-3425 Technical Support
(800) 729-7866 Product Information
Summagraphics is one of the first manufacturers of digitizer tablets for the PC market. The Summagraphics MM series is an industry standard supported by Autodesk and Microstation and emulated by many other manufacturers of digitizers.

Computer Graphics Software Corporations

The following corporations sell computer graphics applications for the PC. Many of these companies will provide you with free product information, sample images, and a working model if you contact them.

Adobe Systems, Inc.
P.O. Box 7900
Mountain View, CA 94039
(800) 833-6687   Illustrator, Photoshop (Windows)

Autodesk, Inc.
2320 Maninship Way
Sausalito, CA 94965
(800) 445-5415   AutoCAD (DOS/Windows)
(800) 525-2763   3D Studio/Animator Pro (DOS)

Byte by Byte Corp.
8920 Business Park Drive
Austin, TX 78759
(512) 795-0150   Envisage 3D (DOS/Windows)

Caligari Corp.
1955 Landings Drive
Mountain View, CA 94043
(415) 390-9600   Truespace (Windows)

CrystalGraphics, Inc.
3110 Patrick Henry Drive
Santa Clara, CA 95054
(408) 496-6175   3D Designer, Topas

Fractal Design Corporation
335 Spreckels Drive, Suite F
Aptos, CA 95003
(800) 647-7443   Fractal Design Painter (Windows)

Impulse
8416 Xerxes Avenue
North Brooklyn Park, MN 55444
(800) 328-0184   Imagine

Macromedia
600 Townsend Street
San Francisco, CA 94103
(415) 252-2000   Director

Robert McNeel and Associates
3670 Woodland Park Avenue North
Seattle, WA 98103
(206) 545-7000   Accurender (Autocad for Windows or DOS)
                         Sculptura (Windows)

Pixar
1001 W. Cutting Blvd
Richmond, CA 94804
(510) 236-4000   Renderman, Typestry (Windows)

Strata
2 West St. George Boulevard, Number 200
St. George, UT 84770
(800) 869-6855   Stratavision (DOS)

Visual Software
21731 Ventura Boulevard, Number 310
Woodland Hills, CA 91364
(800) 669-7318   Visual Reality (Windows)

Graphics-Oriented Bulletin Board Systems

Bulletin board systems (BBSs) are computers that you can dial to participate in discussions, send and receive software and information, and even play games. BBSs are usually run by private individuals out of their own pocket, although some are run by corporations for technical support and public relations. Every BBS has a system operator (or SYSOP) who performs the housekeeping for the BBS.

There are thousands of bulletin board systems around the world. Most BBSs can be accessed for free for a limited time, and some do not require subscriptions at all. Some BBSs give subscribers special services or features not available to nonsubscribers. To connect to a BBS, you need a modem and a terminal program. Modems have come down in price substantially, and most come with rudimentary communications software. A modem is a valuable tool for obtaining and distributing computer graphics software and information, and it will pay for itself very quickly.

BBSs offer *message bases*, which are public discussions arranged by topic and which can be searched; *bulletins*, which are text files that can be read online; *files*, which are compressed software and information titles that can be downloaded from the BBS's hard drive or CD-ROM. Most BBSs encourage users to upload files to the BBS as well, and some require a ratio of 1 uploaded file per *X* downloaded files.

Some BBSs are networked together to distribute messages, files, and bulletins across a broader area and larger audience. Some even have access to Internet facilities for international e-mail and file transfers. A large number of computer hardware and software manufacturers have special BBSs that have driver updates, program patches, developers kits, and technical support information available online. BBSs have a lot to offer!

GETTING CONNECTED

When you first dial into a BBS, your modem and the BBS's modem must get a carrier signal that can be modulated and demodulated with the information you will be transmitting and receiving. This process is audible as a set of high-pitched tones coming from the small speaker built into your modem. Most terminal programs will silence the speaker after a carrier has been detected.

LOGGING ON

After you are connected, the BBS will identify itself (that is, `The Pixel Emporium`) and will ask you to identify yourself (`Enter Username`, `Log on`, and so on). Some BBSs will ask you for a "handle," which is a nickname (somewhat like CB radio handles); others specifically tell you not to use one and instead to specify your real name. In most cases, the BBS will ask you for more information if you have never called it before (typically name, address, telephone numbers, and a password that you will be required to enter whenever you call the BBS).

NAVIGATING THE MENUS

After you have successfully logged on, a series of bulletins will be displayed or offered to you on a bulletin menu. Bulletins are short text files that discuss the rules, new developments, and pieces of information about the BBS. After the bulletins have been displayed or you have chosen to quit the bulletin menu, you will be dropped into the main menu.

From the main menu, a number of other menus are accessible. A *configuration menu* enables you to set parameters that affect how information is transmitted to you, such as how many columns and rows your display supports, what kind of file transfer protocol should be used, and what kind of display control codes should be sent. The *message menu* has all the options for reading and sending messages in a variety of message bases. The *file menu* enables you to list files in specific areas of interest (for example `Ray Tracing:Programs`, `Ray Tracing:Data Files`, `Ray Tracing:Modeling Software`, and so on). Some BBSs have special *external programs* (also called *doors*), such as games, databases, CD-ROM file menus, and other goodies.

LOGGING OFF

After you have finished exploring the BBS, it is common courtesy to tell the BBS you are going to hang up before you do so. It is considered rude to just hang up, and in some cases it causes problems for the sysop.

Almost all BBSs offer a wide variety of information and software, but most have a theme or specialty. A few BBSs are specifically geared towards computer graphics enthusiasts. Here is a list of the most well-known computer graphics BBSs. Make note that some bulletin board systems relocate or shut down. Such occurrences are usually announced in *3D Artist* magazine or in other publications.

Digital Pixel
ON, Canada
Sysop: Mark Ng
(416) 298-1487

East Coast Graphics
Fort Loudon, PA
Sysop: Ryan Miller
(717) 485-5209

The Graphics Alternative
El Cerrito, CA
Sysop: Adam Shiffman
(510) 524-2780

Pi Squared BBS
Maryland
Sysop: Alfonso Hermida
(301) 725-9080

You Can Call Me Ray BBS
Chicago, IL
(708) 358-8721

The Phoenix Chapter AutoCad Users Group BBS
Phoenix, AZ
Sysop: James Witt
(602) 952-0638

CAD/Engineering Services (CAD/ES)
Hendersonville, TN
Sysop: Stan Bimson
(615) 822-2539

Seattle AutoCAD Users Group
Bellevue, WA
Sysop: Dennis Shinn
(206) 644-7115 PCGnet Node, Active

CAD Connection
Montesson, France
Sysop: Nenad Boric
33-1-39529854

Raytech BBS
Tain, Scotland
Sysop: Paul Smith
44-86288-340

The Graphics Connection
Wellington, New Zealand
Sysop: Mark Remfrey
64-4-566-8450

My Computer Company
Erskineville, Australia (NSW)
Sysop: Peter Deegan
61-2-557-1489

BBS_Bennekom: Fractal Board
Bennekom, Netherlands
Sysop: Henk Van DeWeerdt
31-8389-15331

The Happy Canyon
Denver, CO
(303) 759-3598

Joes CODE BBS
West Bloomfield, MI
(313) 855-0894

CHAOS BBS
Columbia, MO
(314) 874-2930

Design 2 Art BBS
St Charles, MO
(314) 926-8375

Engineering Services
Atlanta, GA
(404) 325-0122

411-Exchange
Alpharetta, GA
(404) 587-4071

Autodesk Global Village
San Rafael, CA
(415) 507-5921

The CAD Connection
Mesa, AZ
(602) 835-0274

Convergence Spline BBS
Richmond, BC
(604) 275-3462

Graphicly Speaking
Langley, BC
(604) 534-2954

Time-Out BBS
Sadsburyville, PA
(610) 857-2648

John's Graphics
Brooklyn Park, MN
(612) 425-4436

Tern Solution BBS
Ottawa, ON
(613) 228-0539

Canis Major
Nashville, TN
(615) 385-4268

CAD Engineering Services
Hendersonville, TN
(615) 822-2539

The Virtual Dimension
Oceanside, CA
(619) 722-0746

The Drawing Board BBS
Anchorage, AK
(907) 349-5412

The New Graphics BBS
Piscataway, NJ
(908) 271-8878

The University
Shrewsbury, NJ
(908) 544-8193

The Baud Room
Melbourne, Australia
61-3-481-6873

Sydney PCUG Compaq
South Wales, Australia
61-2-540-1842

Austrian AutoCAD User Group
Graz, Austria
43-316-574-426

Genesis BBS
Brussels, Belgium
32-2-2453498

Horreby SuperBBS
Nykoebing Falster, Denmark
45-53-84-7074

Zyllius BBS!
Saint Paul, France
33-93320505

NEWS BBS
Duesseldorf, Germany
49-211-680-1458

Tower of Magic
Gelsenkirchen, Germany
49-209-780670

Ray BBS Munich
Munich, Germany
49-89-984723

CAD-BBS
Amsterdam, Netherlands
31-20-6861533

Foundation One
Baarn, Netherlands
31-2154-22143

The Graphics Connection
Wellington, New Zealand
64-4-566-8450

The Graphics Connection II
New Plymouth, New Zealand
64-6-751-0089

The Graphics Connection III
Auckland, New Zealand
64-9-309-2237

MicroArt
Koper, Slovenia
386-66-34986

Sweden
Autodesk On-line
Gothenburg, Sweden
46-31-401718

The Missing Link
Surrey, UK
44-81-641-8593

CADenza BBS
Leicester, UK
44-533-596725

The Internet

The Internet is a worldwide network of networks that is constantly expanding. It is owned by no one and is used around the world in academic, business, and governmental spheres of interest. The Internet was originally developed by the U.S. Defense Advanced Research Projects Agency (ARPA) and enhanced by the National Science Foundation for the combined purposes of creating a wide bandwidth decentralized communications infrastructure and facilitating advanced scientific research between North American universities. Through the participation of colleges and universities, the Internet has reached a wide audience and offers a limitless resource of free information and software. The Internet is considered to be the prototype for the "information superhighway."

The Internet can offer hundreds of features. Many of them are similar to features found in bulletin board systems, but a majority of them cannot be found anywhere else.

Electronic Mail

Internet electronic mail enables you to send messages instantly to anyone else who is on the Internet—all you have to do is know that person's Internet e-mail address. For example, if you were to send me e-mail, you would need my address:

`newhall@auvm.american.edu`

The `newhall` is my user ID, and `american.edu` is the main connection for the American University, where I have my account. Because American University has many computers with Internet access, `auvm` specifies which computer at American University has my account information. Electronic mail is a powerful, convenient resource. Some would say that it is the wave of the future, but I would say that it (and all of the other features of the Internet) are essential tools for conducting business in technology-related fields, such as computer graphics, *today*.

Mailing Lists

Internet "mailing lists" are similar to message bases encountered on bulletin board systems. A listserver is a computer system charged with administering a mailing list. After you have subscribed to a mailing list, you receive messages in your electronic mail on the subject of discussion written by other people on the mailing list. Whenever you send messages to the mailing list, they are distributed to all other users on the mailing list.

Mailing lists enable you to develop contacts with other computer graphics enthusiasts and to obtain product information, helpful hints, and other bits of useful information.

To get onto a mailing list, you must first subscribe to it. For example, in order to subscribe to the POV-Ray/DKBtrace mailing list, you would send an e-mail message to `listserv@trearn.bitnet`, and in the body of the e-mail message you would put `subscribe dkb-1`, followed on the same line by your complete e-mail address. Some mailing lists have separate addresses for administrative actions such as subscriptions and "unsubscriptions," to avoid sending out dozens of `subscribe johnny@some.net.address` and `unsubscribe disgruntledreader@my.company` messages to everyone on the list.

Some mailing lists can fill up your mailbox too quickly and cause problems, or you might not need the information coming from a particular listserver. To cancel your subscription, most mailing lists enable you to "unsubscribe" the same way you subscribed. However, each mailing list is unique and your mailing list might have a different procedure for cancelling subscriptions.

The following listservers cater to the computer graphics community:

`3d-studio@autodesk.com`

The Autodesk 3D Studio mailing list was originally established by Bob Lindbury and was recently taken over by the people at Autodesk.

`rayshade-users@cs.princeton.edu`

This list is administered by Craig Kolb and supports the Rayshade ray tracer.

`heightfield-list@monet.seas.gwu.edu`

This list discusses height fields and other terrain rendering techniques.

`imagine@email.sp.paramax.com`

This list supports the Imagine modeler/renderer for the PC and Amiga.

`rend386-request@sunee.waterloo.edu (administrative requests, subscriptions)`
`rend386@sunee.waterloo.edu (submissions)`

This list supports the REND386 polygon rendering library.

`rmanrequest@aero.org (administrative requests)`
`rman@aero.org (submissions)`

This list supports the Renderman shading language.

Usenet Groups

Usenet is a collection of message bases divided into hierarchical subjects that can be accessed on some bulletin boards and most Internet systems. Usenet features topics on every imaginable topic (and some you would not imagine). Like BBS message bases and Internet mailing lists, Usenet gives you a forum for discussion with other like-minded individuals. You can read messages or post messages yourself.

You can find help on almost any complex subject on Usenet just by asking for it. People are usually very courteous and helpful. There is, however, a certain etiquette that you must observe; otherwise, your electronic mail will be flooded with dozens of "flames"—bitter messages telling you where you can go and stick it. Many people get agitated when someone posts a question that is not appropriate for the forum (people do not like to see I have print shop and cannot get the smiley face to enlarge when they are in the Comp.Graphics.Raytracing Usenet group) or when a question is asked every day. Most Usenet groups have a FAQ (Frequently Asked Questions) file that answer those questions and provide an introduction to the group. FAQs are also extremely informative references as well. Most groups post their FAQs at least once a month. You should *always* read the FAQ before asking any questions to a Usenet group.

Here are some of the Usenet groups that address computer graphics concepts:

```
alt.cad
alt.fractals
alt.graphics
alt.graphics.pixutils
comp.graphics
comp.graphics.animation
comp.graphics.opengl
comp.graphics.visualization
comp.graphics.raytracing
comp.os.windows.programmer.graphics
```

Some Usenet groups are dedicated to distributing files such as pictures, programs, and other things ordinarily found in the file section of a bulletin board system. To accomplish this, a utility called UUENCODE is used. UUENCODE converts a binary file into a set of ASCII files that can be posted as messages on Usenet. To download a file from Usenet, the message must be stored on disk and the UUDECODE utility must be employed to convert the message back into its original binary file form. The following Usenet groups feature UUENCODEd files of interest to the PC computer graphics community:

```
alt.binaries.pictures
alt.binaries.pictures.raytracing
```

Anonymous FTP Sites

Hundreds of computers on the Internet have files that can be downloaded to your computer using a special Internet protocol called the File Transfer Protocol (FTP). To access a computer via FTP, you must know its FTP address. FTP requires addresses just as electronic mail does, though FTP addresses take two forms: one looks like an electronic mail address, and the other is a "net address" that is a series of numbers. For example, the China Lake FTP site (which incidentally has a great collection of utilities and objects for three-dimensional graphics) can be addressed as avalon.chinalake.navy.mil or by its net address 129.131.1.225.

A number of variations on the FTP program are available through online services, PC programs, and university mainframes. The system I use prompts me for an address when I select the FTP option from a menu. Other systems have an FTP executable program that takes an FTP address as a command-line argument. Others require that you use the open command after you have loaded the FTP executable.

For example,

```
C:\FTP>FTP avalon.chinalake.navy.mil
```

and

```
C:\FTP>FTP
> open avalon.chinalake.navy.mil
```

do exactly same thing. The FTP program establishes the connection:

```
ftping to avalon.chinalake.navy.mil...
VM TCP/IP FTP V2R2
OPEN (name of foreign host):
Connecting to avalon.chinalake.navy.mil 129.131.1.225, port 21
```

Check with your system documentation to see how your FTP program works.

After a connection has been established, all FTP sites will ask you for a "login name" and a password as if you have an account on their system. Luckily, most FTP sites allow you to log in as a guest by using the username anonymous and by using your electronic mail address as your password, for example:

```
220 avalon FTP server (Version 6.28 Mon Nov 15 11:43:15 PST 1993) ready.
USER (identify yourself to the host):
 anonymous
>>>USER anonymous
331 Guest login ok, send e-mail address

220- **********************************************************************
220- If the server refuses your connection, it's probably because we are
220- unable to map your IP to a hostname. Be sure your host is registered
220- and your nameservers are working properly.
220- **********************************************************************
220-
 as password.
Password:
newhall@auvm.american.edu

>>>PASS ********
230- Welcome! This is the ftp server "avalon" (avalon.chinalake.navy.mil).
230-
230- This machine is located at NAWCWPNS, China Lake, California. All file
230- transfers are logged with your hostname and email address. If you don't
230- like this policy disconnect now. Access to the ftp server is given to
230- any registered site on the Internet. Any other attempt to gain
230- unauthorized access is prohibited.
230-
230- If possible, try to keep major file transfers off our local peak-hours.
230- This machine has a regular local workload during weekdays, 7am-5pm PST.
230-
```

```
230- If your FTP client crashes or hangs shortly after login, try using a
230- dash (-) as the first character of your password. This will turn off
230- the informational messages which may be confusing your ftp client.
230-
230- Everything is in /pub. Upload new files to /pub/incoming.
230-
230-Please read the file /README
230- it was last modified on Thu Jan 13 18:25:50 1994 - 218 days ago
230 Guest login ok, access restrictions apply.
Command:
```

After you have logged in, you are free to roam around the file directory system of the FTP host (although you are locked out of some directories), and you can download both binary and ASCII files to your machine.

Most FTP sites are UNIX machines and that may mean you have some things to get used to. Many aspects of DOS are borrowed from UNIX, and there are many commands that perform the same function in UNIX as they do in DOS. The UNIX operating system is case-sensitive, so the files POV-Ray.ZIP and POV-RAY.ZIP are not the same.

As in DOS, the FTP file structure is traversed by reading directories and using a change directory command. To read a directory, the dir command is used, although sometimes you have to use the pure UNIX ls -l command if dir will not work. UNIX filename convention displays file attributes on the left side of the screen. The first attribute indicates a D when the filename is a directory (just as DOS places a <DIR> on the right side of a directory filename). To perform a directory change, type cd, followed by the directory name. The following continues our example from the avalon FTP site:

```
Command:
 dir
>>>PORT 147,9,1,2,23,213
200 PORT command successful.
>>>LIST
150 Opening ASCII mode data connection for /bin/ls.
total 8
-rw-r--r--  1 ftpadmin daemon     2508 Jan 14  1994 README
dr-x--x--x  2 ftpadmin other       512 Dec 10  1991 bin
dr-x--x--x  2 root     daemon      512 Oct 28  1992 dev
dr-x--x--x  2 ftpadmin other       512 Sep  3  1993 etc
drwxr-xr-x  8 ftpadmin archive     512 Aug 19 07:12 pub
dr-x--x--x  3 root     other       512 Feb 13  1993 usr
226 Transfer complete.
Command:
```

Note that in this example there is only one downloadable file (README); the rest of them are directories. The log on message informed us that everything is in the pub directory, so I'll enter that directory:

```
 cd pub
>>>CWD pub
250 CWD command successful.
Command:
 dir
```

```
>>>PORT 147,9,1,2,23,249
200 PORT command successful.
>>>LIST
150 Opening ASCII mode data connection for /bin/ls.
total 163
drwxr-xr-x   2 ftpadmin archive      512 Sep  3  1993 FAQs
-rw-r--r--   1 root     daemon    122561 Aug 19 07:12 INDEX
-rw-r--r--   1 root     daemon     27684 Aug 19 07:12 INDEX.Z
lrwxrwxrwx   1 ftpadmin archive        9 Apr 26  1993 README -> ../README
drwxr-xr-x   2 ftpadmin archive      512 Dec 17  1993 format_specs
drwx-wx-wx   2 ftpadmin archive      512 Aug 18 16:13 incoming
drwxr-xr-x   5 ftpadmin archive     1024 Aug 16 16:23 misc
drwxr-xr-x  24 ftpadmin archive      512 Jun 13 15:21 objects
drwxr-xr-x   8 ftpadmin archive      512 May 24 15:37 utils
226 Transfer complete.
Command:
```

Now I'll download the INDEX file so I can find out what files are available from `avalon`. First I must specify that I will be transferring text—not binary—data. File type setting is accomplished with two commands: `ascii` and `binary`. Note that sending a binary file with ASCII parameters (and vice versa) can have detrimental effects on your data. When the file type has been specified, use the `get` command to specify the file you wish to download and the filename as you want it on your PC. The `get` command starts the file transfer. Here is how I would download the INDEX file:

```
 ascii
>>>TYPE a
200 Type set to A.
Command:
 get INDEX index.txt
>>>PORT 147,9,1,2,25,226
200 PORT command successful.
>>>RETR INDEX
150 Opening ASCII mode data connection for INDEX (122561 bytes).
51168 bytes transferred.
75759 bytes transferred.
108533 bytes transferred.
226 Transfer complete.
124571 bytes transferred. Transfer rate 3.04 Kbytes/sec.
Command:
```

From the INDEX file, I learn that I can obtain the file format for Autodesk .FLI and FLC animations in the pub/format_specs directory as the file `Autodesk_fli_and_flc_format.txt`, so to get that file I must change directory into `Format_specs`, set the file type to ASCII, and use the `get` command, like this:

```
 cd format specs
> > > CWD format_specs
250 CWD command successful
Command:
 get Autodesk_fli_and_flc_format.txt FLIFLCFT.TXT
> > > PORT 147.9.1.2.29.70
200 PORT command successful
> > > RETR Autodesk_fli_and_flc_format.txt
150 Opening ASCII mode data connection for Autodesk_fli_and_flc_format.txt (36725 bytes)
```

Most FTP systems provide online help for all of their commands, if anything should go wrong. On all the systems I have used, all I have to do is type `help`, followed by the command I would like help with, for example:

```
help open
Usage: OPEN hostname <portnumber>
   connect to foreign host. Default port is FTP
Command:
 help ascii
Usage: ASCII
   change file transfer type to ASCII
Command:
 help bin
Usage: BINARY <V> ¦ <F record-length>
   change file transfer type to BINARY; set lrecl for incoming files
Command:
 help get
Usage: GET foreignfile <localname> <(REPLACE>
   copy foreign file into local filename
Command:
```

To obtain a list of all the commands supported by your FTP system, just type `help`.

```
 help
User-FTP understands these commands:
 ?         acct       append     ascii      binary     cd
 close     cms        debug      delete     delimit    dir
 ebcdic    euckanji   get        help       ibmkanji   jis78kj
 jis83kj   lcd        locsite    locstat    lpwd       ls
 mdelete   mget       mode       mput       noop       open
 pass      put        sendport   sendsite   site       sjiskanji
 status    struct     sunique    system     type       user

Specify a command by any unambiguous prefix
Specify a local file by name.type.mode or name.type
Default mode is * for PUT and a current local directory for MPUT, MGET and GET
For information about a particular command, say "HELP command"
Command:
```

There are hundreds of FTP sites with PC software available for downloading, and a few of them have significant offerings in the area of PC graphics. Here is a list of several FTP sites to keep in mind:

```
alfred.ccs.carleton.ca
134.117.1.1
```

Alfred is the home base of the POV ray tracer.

```
asterix.inescn.pt
192.35.246.17
```

Asterix is the home base of the LightR radiosity system and the Rtrace ray tracer. Example scene files, images, and source code are available here as well.

```
avalon.chinalake.navy.mil
129.131.44.11
```

Avalon is considered to be the Internet repository of 3-D graphics objects, textures, and utilities. It is mirrored at `ftp.kpc.com` and `wuarchive.wustl.edu`.

```
ftp.informatik.uni-oldenburg.de
134.106.1.9
```

Polyray, POV ray tracers, and tools.

```
metallica.prakinf.tu-ilmenau.de
141.24.11.247
```

Home of the GOOD object-oriented graphics package for Linux/UNIX and the Yart radiosity preprocessor/ray tracer/renderer.

```
nic.funet.fi
128.214.6.100
```

This is a very large site (somewhat like Europe's version of WUarchive)—lots of ray tracing code.

```
oak.oakland.edu
141.210.10.117
```

This contains a mirror of the SimTel MSDOS software repository.

```
rtfm.mit.edu
18.181.0.24
```

This site has an archive of FAQ files from all Usenet groups.

```
siggraph.org
128.248.245.250
```

This is Siggraph's computer graphics online archive.

```
wuarchive.wustl.edu
128.252.135.4
```

Wuarchive is probably the busiest FTP site in the world. Unfortunately, it has a limit on the number of anonymous users allowed on at one time (the easiest time to get on is early morning hours). The very large computer graphics section (right off the root directory) has a number of rendering packages and mirrors many other graphics FTP sites.

Archie

Archie is an online system accessible via Telnet that is capable of searching FTP sites for files you specify. Archie is a very quick and extremely useful utility. After making a Telnet connection to an Archie site, you log in (most will tell you to log on as `archie` with a password of `archie`) and then the Archie system will come up.

Archie has numerous options, and as with FTP, you can ask for help. The easiest way to use Archie is to simply issue a keyword search. This is done with the `prog` command.

The `prog` command stands for "the program I am looking for looks like this..." and the argument that follows is the text you want Archie to find. For example,

```
prog polyray
```

will display all files that have the word *polyray* in them. A more practical approach is to use only part of the filename. Archie will go to work right away and give you an estimate as to how long the search will take; when it has collated its solution, it will dump it to the screen. For large searches (and for those who cannot access Telnet) Archie servers can be accessed via e-mail. To find out how to access Archie via e-mail, send an e-mail message to `archie` with the subject `help`.

Other Worldwide Information Servers— Gopher and the World Wide Web

Many corporations, universities, and government agencies have databases that can be accessed via the Internet. Gopher and the World Wide Web are two standard systems for accessing these databases. Gopher was originally developed at the University of Minnesota as a protocol for linking multiple databases and accessing them through a menu. Gopher sites are linked together to provide a wide area ("GopherSpace") that be searched by keyword or subject with VERONICA (the Very Easy Rodent-Oriented Net-wide Index to Computerized Archives). A VERONICA search will turn up information that can point you to journal articles, books, FTP sites, and other resources. Gopher can be accessed via Telnet at `NIC.FUNET.FI` and other sites that support ARCHIE, and it is available from some online services and most university mainframes.

The World Wide Web (WWW) is also a network of information servers around the world; however, WWW is a little more advanced than Gopher because it provides a hypertext that can carry images, sound, and documents along with basic information. To access WWW sites, you need a browser—a program that understands the WWW protocol. Mosaic is a popular browser that runs in Windows and supports all WWW resources when directly connected to the Internet. Because of the large amount of data transmitted by WWW sites, Mosaic will not work with a telephone connection. If you have only modem access to the Internet, many online services and university mainframes have a text-based browser called Lynx you can use. Mosaic and other WWW browsers are available via anonymous FTP. You can obtain Mosaic from `ftp.ncsa.uiuc.edu` in the directory `PC/Mosaic`. Another Windows browser, Cello, is available from `ftp.law.cornell.edu` in the `pub/LII/cello` directory.

The following WWW sites have offerings in the area of computer graphics:

```
http://www.cs.princeton.edu/grad/cek/rayshade
```

`http://www.mit.edi:8001/activities/cgs/rayshade`

Information and users guide to the Rayshade raytracer.

`http://www.tu-graz.ac.at/CSIGGRAPHlib`

The Siggraph online bibliography.

`http://acacia.ens.fr:8080/home/massimin/ray.ang.html`

Ray tracing sample images.

`http://www.cis.ohio-state.edu/hypertext/faq/usenet/fractal-faq/faq.html`

Information on fractals.

`http://www.ifi.uio.no/~mariusw/pov/utilities.html`

POV utilities.

`ftp://hobbes.lbl.gov/www/radiance/radiance.html`

Information on Greg Ward's Radiance diffuse illumination system.

Books

Anderson, Scott. *Morphing Magic.* Indianapolis: Sams Publishing, 1993.

Arvo, James (ed.) *Graphics Gems II.* Boston: Academic Press, 1991.

Barnsley, Michael. *Fractals Everywhere.* Boston: Academic Press, 1988.

Cohen, Michael F. and John R. Wallace. *Radiosity and Realistic Image Synthesis.* Boston: Academic Press, 1993.

Foley, James and Andres Van Dam, Stephen Feinier, and John Hughes. *Computer Graphics: Principles and Practice.* Reading, Mass: Addison Wesley, 1990.

Glassner, Andrew. *An Introduction to Ray Tracing.* Boston: Academic Press, 1989.

Glassner, Andrew (ed.) *Graphics Gems.* Boston: Academic Press, 1990.

Heckbert, Paul (ed.) *Graphics Gems IV.* Boston: Academic Press, 1994.

Hermida, Alfonso. *Adventures in Ray Tracing.* Indianapolis: Que Corporation, 1993.

Jones, Michael. *Graphics Programming Power Pack.* Indianapolis: Sams, 1992.

Kay, David and John Levine. *Graphics File Formats.* Blue Ridge Summit, PA: McGraw-Hill, 1992.

Kirk, David (ed.) *Graphics Gems III.* Boston: Academic Press, 1992.

Kliewer, Bradley Dyck. *EGA/VGA:A Programmer's Reference Guide.* New York: Intertext Publications/McGraw-Hill, 1990.

Morrison, Mike. *The Magic of Image Processing.* Indianapolis: Sams, 1993.

Newhall, William. *3D Graphics, Ray Tracing, and Radiosity.* Indianapolis: Sams, 1994.

Oliver, Dick. *FractalVision.* Indianapolis: Sams, 1993.

————et al. *Tricks of the Graphic Gurus.* Indianapolis: Sams, 1993.

Rogers, David and Rae Earnshaw (eds.) *State of the Art in Computer Graphics: Visualization and Modeling.* New York: Springer-Verlag, 1991.

Watt, Alan. *3D Computer Graphics.* Wokingham, England: Addison Wesley, 1993.

Watt, Alan and Mark Watt. *Advanced Animation and Rendering Techniques.* Wokingham, England: Addison Wesley, 1993.

Wells, Drew and Chris Young. *Ray Tracing Creations.* Sebastopol, CA: Waite Group Press, 1993.

Wilton, Richard. *Programmers Guide to PC & PS/2 Video Systems.* Redmond, Washington: Microsoft Press, 1987.

GLOSSARY

Glossary

286   Commonly used abbreviation for any computer using the Intel 80286 or a comparable chip as its central processing unit.

2-D   Two-dimensional, flat—resembling paper, computer screens, and cartoon characters who've been run over by a steam roller.

386   Commonly used abbreviation for any computer using the Intel 80386 or a comparable chip as its central processing unit.

3-D   Three-dimensional, not flat—for example, the room you're in, or space before Einstein got hold of it.

3-D Faces   Short for three-dimensional surfaces. Usually, 3-D faces are defined by three or four points that all fall on the same plane.

3-D Graphics   Computer-graphics representations of 3-D objects. Usually this term implies that the objects themselves are mathematically defined in the computer, as opposed to digitized photographic pictures of real 3-D objects.

3-D Space   Any part of a universe having three dimensions—where we all hang out all the time.

3DFACE Entities   What you call 3-D faces when you put them into a DXF file.

3DLINE Entities   What you call line segments in 3-D space when you put them into a DXF file.

486   The 80486, Intel's most popular computer chip as of this writing; also used to mean any computer containing an 80486.

8086   The ancestor of the 286, 386, and 486. Most are seen in garage sales and accountants' offices these days (same as the 8088 for all practical purposes today).

A-Buffer   An anti-aliased depth buffer.

Adapters   The hardware expansion cards that allow your computer to display graphics are often called *adapters*. See also: **CGA**, **EGA**, **VGA**, **Hercules**, and **Super-VGA**.

Adaptive Color Compression   The process of performing a statistical analysis on the colors present in an original True Color image, and, based on this analysis, deciding on the best allocation of 256 colors for a palette-based image.

ADC—Analog to Digital Converter   The circuit that converts an analog voltage into binary TTL values; employed in image scanners, frame grabbers, and many other media input devices.

Additive Color Model   Red, green, and blue are called the additive colors (also, primary colors) because various intensities of these three colors can be added together to form any other color.

AI   (1) Adobe Illustrator Postscript (vector) drawing (a valid EPS file in disguise). (2) Artificial Intelligence.

Algorithm   A procedure, a way of doing things.

Aliasing   The effect that makes jagged "stair-stepping" in computer pictures of low resolution. It comes from the square shape of the pixels and is actually a moire effect. It can be corrected for with a technique called *anti-aliasing*, which blends the colors on the jaggy edges to make them look smoother.

Alpha Channel   A fourth "color channel" in addition to red, green, and blue. It is often used for special effects, especially transparency.

Ambient Light   Light that appears to come from everywhere at once. Rendering programs use this to approximate the small amount of stray light that is always bouncing around between objects. The Radiosity Method attempts to model ambient light as faithfully as possible.

American National Standards Institute (ANSI)   A standards-setting institute. These are the folks who brought us ASCII and ANSI-standard C.

Anaglyphic Stereoscopy   The art of making 3-D images by wearing goofy-looking-but-fun red/blue glasses and displaying a red image for one eye and a blue image for the other.

Anaglyphs   Pictures made to be viewed with red/blue 3-D glasses.

Anchor Points   Used in morphing to determine which parts of the original picture should "turn into" corresponding parts of the final picture.

Animation   Simulating motion by displaying a sequence of images in rapid succession.

Anonymous FTP   Internet file transfer from a host to a guest where the guest does not need to have an account on the host.

ANSI   See **American National Standards Institute**.

Anti-Aliasing   See **Aliasing**.

Application Programming Interface (API)   The standard way for a programmer to use functions of an operating system (such as Windows) in his or her own programs.

Application Queue   In Windows, the dispatching system that sends messages to the functions that need to pay attention to them.

Application Window   In Windows, the main screen window for a program.

Arc   A part of a circle.

Archie   A utility available through TELNET that can search FTP servers for files.

ASCII Text   The American Standard Code for Information Interchange defined a standard for representing text on computers a long time ago. Everyone uses it now whether they know it or not. A normal text file is, therefore, often called an "ASCII file." Pronounced "ASS-key."

Attractor   When the results of a mathematical function are fed back into the same function repeatedly, the result often settles down to a stable value or set of values, no matter what value you started with. This stable set is called the "attractor" of the function. Attractors of complex functions are often fractals.

AutoCAD   A popular computer-aided drafting program from Autodesk, Inc. It is the source of the DXF file format.

Automatic Disk Compression The process of removing extra spaces and repetitive patterns from data as it is written on a hard disk, and restoring the data to its original form when it is read from the disk. It saves a lot of space and can be done invisibly by programs such as Stac Electronic's Stacker and Microsoft's DoubleSpace.

Axis A dimension, often represented by a line passing through the zero-point on another perpendicular axis. The x- and y-axes represented by a cross-hair through the origin are familiar examples.

Backface Culling A hidden surface removal technique that eliminates facets that face away from the screen.

Background The image or color that takes up most of the screen and appears to be behind everything else.

BBS See **Bulletin Board System**.

Binary A numbering system based on only two possible values for each digit. In binary, you count 0, 1, 10, 11, 100, and so on.

Binary Digit A variable that can store one of two possible values, usually represented by 0 or 1. It is usually called a "bit," the fundamental unit of information.

Binary Files Any file other than an ASCII text file.

Binary Number Any number can be represented by a sequence of ones and zeros. For example, the binary representation of the decimal number 255 is 11111111, and decimal 256 is 100000000 in binary.

Bipolar High Pass Filter See **Filter**.

Bit See **Binary Digit**.

Bit Planes A way of organizing video memory so that all the "first bits" of all the pixels are consecutive, then all the "second bits," and so on.

Bitmap Because computer graphics images are made by mapping binary digits onto the monitor screen and interpreting the binary numbers as colors, images are called "bitmaps."

Bitmap Brush A drawing tool (within Windows and other graphics systems) that uses a bitmapped pattern to fill in a region.

Bitmapped Graphics Computer graphics images that are stored pixel-by-pixel, as they appear on the screen (in contrast to *vector graphics*).

Bitmapped Images See **Bitmap** and **Bitmapped Graphics**.

Bitmapped Programs Programs that store and edit bitmapped graphics, as opposed to vector graphics.

Blending Functions Functions used in free form Bézier and Spline curves and surfaces to control the weighted influence of control points.

Blobs Quadratic fluid objects that can deform each other by attractive or repellant forces.

Blocks Jargon used in certain file formats to mean a section of data.

Blur The process of averaging adjacent colors in an image to make it look blurry.

BMP A Microsoft Windows bitmap (can be used for Windows wallpaper).

Bounding Box Ellipses and circles are often defined by specifying the corner points of a bounding box, the rectangle that touches just their top, bottom, and side edges.

Brightness The apparent lightness of an image or part of an image.

Browser A hypertext reader for accessing the World Wide Web. Mosaic and Lynx are commonly used browsers.

Brush A shape used to draw with or used to fill a region.

Bulletin Board System A computer system connected to a telephone line that allows online users to send and to receive messages and files.

Bump Mapping A rendering technique for producing the illusion of a three-dimensional bumpy surface by modulating the surface normals with a two-dimensional "bump map."

Bus The power and data distribution system of a computer.

Butterfly Effect See **Chaos**.

Byte Eight bits, which can store 256 possible values.

Cache High-speed memory stored on or near the microprocessor to improve data retrieval efficiency.

CAD Computer-aided drafting, or computer-aided design. Sometimes called CADD, to mean computer-aided drafting and design.

Cathode Ray Tube (CRT) The name for the display technology used in most computer monitors and televisions.

CD-ROM—Compact Disc Read Only Memory Up to 680 megabytes can be stored on the same type of CD that commonly holds music.

CDR CorelDRAW vector drawing file.

CGA—Color Graphics Adapter An early PC graphics adapter capable of four colors at 320×200 resolution or two colors at 640×200 resolution.

CGM Computer graphics metafile, another "universal standard" that never caught on. The Windows metafile is a more well-known variation on the same theme.

Chaos When any system displays "sensitive dependence on initial conditions," it becomes impossible to predict its behavior reliably even with very precise measurement. This is also known as "chaos," or the "butterfly effect," because a butterfly flapping its wings today could affect tomorrow's weather. The study of chaos has far-reaching consequences in almost all branches of science. The study of chaos is intimately related to the fields of "fractals" and "complexity."

Chaos Game Another name for the random iteration algorithm for drawing an Iterated Function System fractal.

Chip Integrated circuits, especially the ones that make your computer work. Examples include the 386 chip and the VGA chip.

Chorded Ellipses Ellipses with sections cut out so that only a portion appears on the screen.

Chroma-Key   A video process that allows one image to be selectively superimposed into another only in pixel regions where the color is a special hue.

CIS   CompuServe Information Service. It's the world's largest online service and electronic bulletin board service.

CISC—Complex Instruction Set Computing   A designation given to microprocessors that support a large number of instructions, such as the Intel Pentium.

Clamp   Normally, when a computer counts past the highest number that can be stored in a variable, it will go back to zero and keep counting. In image processing, this can lead to weird effects unless you "clamp" the image at the maximum value.

Clear Codes   Used in GIF files and other LZW compression schemes to reset compression parameters to a default state. The first code output by an LZW or GIF image encoder.

Client Area   In Windows, the region of a window where the application is allowed to draw.

Clip-Models   Pre-built mathematical descriptions of 3-D objects.

Clipping Plane   In 3-D rendering, objects beyond the clipping plane are considered to be behind the viewer's head and are not displayed.

CLUT   See **Color Look-Up Table**.

CMYK Color Model   Cyan-Magenta-Yellow-Black color model, used when printing on paper. The opposite of the RGB color model.

Coastline   Sometimes used to refer to any fractal curve that weaves in and out like a real coastline.

Coefficients   Generally, any number that gets multiplied by a variable in an equation.

Color Balance   The relative intensities of red, green, and blue in a computer image, or cyan, magenta, and yellow in a printed picture.

Color Cycling   The process of rapidly rotating the values in the palette (color lookup table) to animate the entire screen at once.

Color Graphics Adapter   See **CGA**.

Color Look-Up Table (CLUT)   Also called a palette or color palette, it is used in video systems where only 8 bits or less are available for each pixel. A color number is stored for each pixel, and an 18-bit or 24-bit color value is stored in the CLUT, which determines the actual color of a pixel on the screen.

Color Number   See **Color Look-Up Table**.

Color Palette   See **Color Look-Up Table**.

Color Plane   Colors are usually stored as red, green, and blue component values. The collection of all the red component values is called the "red color plane," and so forth.

Color Resolution   The number of colors that can be displayed on the screen at once. For example, standard VGA has a maximum color resolution of 256 colors, which requires 8 bits per pixel to store the color number.

Color Space An abstract 3-D space where the three dimensions are red, green, and blue (or cyan, magenta, yellow; or hue, saturation, lightness, depending on the color model you choose). The set of colors visible by the eye or displayable by a monitor can be represented as a region in color space.

Color Stepping See **Color Cycling**.

Color Triangle A slice of color space, where each corner of the triangle represents red, green, or blue. The region within the triangle shows all possible mixtures of the three component colors at a particular lightness value.

Color Values The actual numerical description of the intensities of red, green, and blue light to be displayed at a particular point on the screen.

Command-Line Arguments When you type a command to run a program from the DOS prompt, you can type filenames or other parameters after the command itself, before you press Enter. How these command-line arguments are interpreted depends on the program.

Compiler A program to translate a human-readable language such as C or BASIC into the native instruction code of a particular CPU.

Complex Numbers Numbers with two parts, called the *real part* and the *imaginary part*, or simply x and y. They are used to do computations on a two-dimensional surface.

Complex Plane The abstract space represented by complex numbers. In computer graphics, the complex plane usually represents the two-dimensional computer screen.

Component (1) The red, green, or blue part of a color. (2) The x or y part of a complex number. (3) Any part of anything.

Compositing The process of combining, blending, and layering multiple images to produce a finished image.

Compression The act of removing repetitive patterns from data so that it can be stored using fewer bits.

CompuServe Information Service See **CIS**.

Computer Aided Drafting or **Computer Aided Design** See **CAD**.

Computer Graphics Visual images made on or with a computer.

Computer Graphics Metafile See **CGM**.

Constant Element Radiosity Any radiosity preprocess that does not subdivide patches into elements.

Contrast Enhancement The act of amplifying color differences in an image to improve the apparent contrast.

Control Blocks Used in some graphics file formats to mean data that describes how the image should be displayed rather than actual pixel-by-pixel coloring information.

Control Menu   The leftmost menu in a Windows application menu bar.

Control Points   (1) Points in any graphics or CAD image that allow you to control some part of the image with the mouse. (2) See **Anchor Points**.

Controller Registers   Within a video chip, storage locations that control various display functions.

Convolution   A mathematical technique for image processing.

Coordinate   A numerical location along an axis.

Coordinate System   The reference system for locating points on the screen. Windows has several options: the screen coordinate system, whole-window coordinate system, and the client area coordinate system.

CRT   See **Cathode Ray Tube**.

CRT Gun   The electron gun within a CRT. Color CRTs have separate electron guns for red, green, and blue light.

CSG   Constructive Solid Geometry, a method of defining complex objects where solid volumes are added or subtracted together. CSG is supported in the POV, Polyray, and Rtrace ray tracing packages.

CUR   A Windows cursor bitmap file.

Cursor   The little icon that shows you where your mouse or text editing point is on the screen. The mouse cursor is usually arrow-shaped.

Cyan   Bluish-green.

Cyberspace   (1) The abstract universe on the other side of the computer screen. (2) The worldwide network of digital telecommunication interconnections.

Data Blocks   Used in some file formats to mean the pixel-by-pixel color data, as opposed to control blocks.

Data Compression   Algorithms such as RLE and LZW that encode and decode data so that it can occupy less memory or disk space.

Data-Glove   An inexpensive glove with motion-detection and position sensors attached. It is marketed by Sega-Genesis, Inc.

Data Stream   The incoming stream of data when reading a file from a disk.

DCX   A bunch of PCX images all crammed into one file. (Thank Intel for it.)

Decimal   The ten-valued numbering system we normally use for counting money and almost everything else.

Decode   To read a file and translate the data back into the original form it had before it was stored in the file.

Default   The value something has if you don't bother to change it.

Delta   The amount to change something (from the Greek letter, which mathematicians often use to stand for a degree of change).

Depth Cues   Visual information that helps your brain translate two-dimensional images into a mental image of 3-D space.

Device Context   Windows programming jargon meaning the state the display (or another device) is in.

Device-Dependent Bitmap   Windows storage format that stores images in a format similar to the way they are stored on the PC.

Device Driver   A small software program to interface with a physical piece of hardware.

Device Independent   Software that can be used without change on a wide variety of hardware.

Device-Independent Bitmap (DIB)   Windows storage format that stores images in a form that can be used on any type of computer (very theoretically).

DFT   Discrete Fourier Transform, a mathematical technique used in image processing.

DIB   See **Device-Independent Bitmap**.

Diffuse Light   Light that is widely scattered by an object's surface. In rendering, diffuse light depends only on the orientation of the surface relative to the light source and does not show reflections or highlights.

Digital   In a form that can be stored as a collection of bits; the opposite of *analog*, which is stored as a continuously varying voltage or magnetic strength.

Digital Video   Motion pictures stored as bits, as opposed to analog video tape or physical film.

Direct Color   Video hardware that stores the actual color values for each pixel, as opposed to palette-based color.

Discrete Fourier Transform   See **DFT**.

Disintegrating   Pfffzzz….

Displacement   Translation; that is, movement from one location to another without rotation.

Dissolving   An image processing technique where one image fades into another by interpolating pixel intensities.

Dither   To approximate more colors than you can actually display or print by mixing very closely together small dots of more than one color.

DLL   Dynamic Link Library, a code file containing routines that can be shared by multiple programs or instanced multiple times.

DOS—Disk Operating System   Used to mean the MS-DOS, PC-DOS, DR-DOS, and compatible operating systems, or the computers that run them.

DOS prompt   The prompt displayed by DOS when it's ready for you to type a command. This prompt usually looks like `C:>` or `C:\TGG>`, where `TGG` is the name of the current directory.

DRAM—Dynamic Random Access Memory   A type of inexpensive memory that uses capacitive charge storage to indicate binary logic. DRAM requires frequent refreshing to prevent charge depreciation.

Draw Programs   Programs that work with vector data, as opposed to paint programs, which work with bitmapped images only.

Drawing eXchange File (DXF) A popular file format, originally developed by Autodesk, Inc., for exchanging vector data between CAD programs.

Drawing Modes In Windows, how the drawing operations decide what color to put on the screen, based on the color of the object being drawn and the color that is already on the screen at the location being drawn over.

Drawing Operation A procedure that draws something on the screen, such as a line, a circle, and so on.

DRW Micrografx Designer vector drawing file.

DXF See **Drawing eXchange File.**

Dynamic Link Library See **DLL.**

Edge Detection The process of recognizing and highlighting regions of rapid color transition in an image.

EGA See **Enhanced Graphics Adapter.**

Element A polygonal subdivision of a surface patch used to calculate more accurate form factors for the radiosity method.

Ellipses Elongated circles.

Embossing The process of coloring edges in an image so that the picture appears to be made up of 3-D layers of metal or stone.

Encode To compress or otherwise process an image as you save it to disk.

Enhanced Graphics Adapter (EGA) For PC graphics display, an aging standard that supports up to 640×350 resolution with 16 colors.

Enlargement Making an image bigger by adding more pixels than in the original.

ENTITIES Shapes are called ENTITIES when stored in a DXF file.

Entropy The tendency for rooms to be messy shortly after you tidy them up. This principle applies to life in general.

EPS Encapsulated Postscript file, which can be printed or read by most Postscript-compatible programs.

Escape-Time Algorithm A way of drawing fractals such as the Mandelbrot set and Julia sets.

Event-Driven A way of organizing a program so that functions are initiated by the user or the hardware input. The opposite of procedure-driven, where functions are generally executed in a fixed order no matter what the user says.

Exceptions Problems, errors, or urgent events that must be attended to by a program (going back to fix a mistake in an earlier test grade or the occurrence of a hard-disk error during data entry, for example).

EXE The file extension of an executable file.

Executable File A file containing instructions to be run by the computer; a program file.

Exploding Kaboom!

Eye (1) The theoretical point in 3-D space where the observer is located in a computer-generated scene. (2) One of your peepers.

Eye Ray   An artificial ray of light that travels from the eye back into the scene, bouncing off objects until it either encounters a light source or zooms off to infinity.

Faces   See **3-D Faces**.

Facet   One of many convex polygons composed of vertices and edges used to define a three-dimensional surface mesh.

FAQ   Typically, a file extension for a text file introducing a mailing list or Usenet group to new users (or, frequently asked questions). FAQs for every Usenet group are availible via anonymous FTP from RTF.MIT.EDU.

Fast Fourier Transform   See **FFT**.

FAX   Facsimile transmission, as in "FAX machine."

FFT   (1) A rapid computer algorithm that performs a discrete Fourier Transform. (2) A file extension used by the IMAGEPRO program for Fourier File Transfers.

Field   A variable or set of variables.

FIF   See **Fractal Image File**

Filter   The technical term for many image processing operations. A high-pass filter eliminates rapidly changing colors, blurring the image. A low-pass filter eliminates slow-changing colors, sharpening the image.

Fixed-Point   A way of storing real numbers so that calculations can be faster compared to normal, floating-point number calculations.

Flavors   Variations on a file format. For example, there are many incompatible flavors of TIFF.

FLC   Autodesk Animator Pro high-resolution bitmapped animation file.

FLI   Autodesk Animator low-resolution (320×200 256-color) animation file.

Flicker   Any visible or subliminally visible shimmering or flashing caused by repeatedly erasing and redrawing images.

Floating-Point   A way of storing numbers inside the computer. See also **Fixed-Point**.

Fonts   Typefaces; the actual shapes that are displayed or printed to represent characters of the alphabet, numbers, and punctuation.

Form Factor   In radiosity, the form factor is the measure of how much light leaving one surface patch arrives at another surface patch.

Forward   Fourier   Transform Transformation   From the spatial domain into the frequency domain. See **Fourier Transformation**.

Fourier Spectrum Plot   A picture of the frequency domain laid out as if it were the spatial domain. See **Fourier Transformation**.

Fourier Transformation   The translation of an image from the spatial domain, where each pixel represents a location in two-dimensional space, into the frequency domain, where each pixel represents a particular period of repetition. Fourier transformations (also called Fourier transforms) are useful in image processing for filtering out repetitive noise.

Fractal Image File (FIF)   A file format for highly compressed images stored as fractals.

Fractals   Infinitely detailed shapes. Generally, each part of a fractal resembles the whole. See **Iterated Function System**.

FRACTINT   A famous freeware program to generate many different kinds of fractal images.

Frame   Another name for a picture. Usually these are used only when the image is part of an animated sequence of images.

Frame Buffers   Memory set aside for storing images and pixel-by-pixel information about how to process images.

Freeware   Copyrighted software whose authors explicitly permit free distribution as long as no fee is charged beyond materials, duplication, shipping, and handling. Compare to **Shareware**.

Frequency Domain   See **Fourier Transformation**.

FTP—File Transfer Protocol   A method of sending binary or ASCII data files from one Internet site to another.

Function   A computer-language procedure or mathematical formula that may take in or return a value or set of values.

Fundamental Window   The simplest possible Windows program. It includes a menu bar, scroll bars, and a blank client area.

Gamma Correction   The process of changing the balance of red, green, and blue light in an image to correct for the sensitivity of our eyes to different colors, or to correct for the ability of a monitor or printer to show different colors.

Gate   One junction within a chip.

GDI   See **Graphics Device Interface**.

Genlock   A method of synchronizing one video signal to another. It is used in computer graphics for character generation and chroma-key.

GIF   CompuServe Graphics Interchange Format compressed bitmap.

Gigabyte   Approximately one billion bytes. This can mean 1,000,000,000 bytes or exactly 1,073,741,824 (two to the thirtieth power, the highest number you can count to with 30 bits).

GLiNT   A graphics display processor produced by 3DLabs that implements OpenGL in real time.

Global Illumination Model   An illumination model that accounts for indirect illumination such as reflections.

Gopher   A client-server linked database system accessible via the Internet.

Gopher Space   A term for the combined database of all Gopher sites in the world.

Gouraud Shading   A rapid pseudo-realistic local illumination model employed by many graphics accelerators. The Gouraud algorithm calculates intensities for each vertex and interpolates the surface pixel intensities.

Graphic-Rendering Blocks   Regions of a GIF file where instructions for displaying images are stored.

Graphical User Interface (GUI)   Any convention for the appearance and use of a program with graphical elements such as icons, pretty fonts, or a mouse.

Graphics Accelerator   Hardware to take on some of the graphics calculations normally done by the CPU, thus speeding up the display of complex graphics.

Graphics Device Interface (GDI)   The name for the graphics programming library of Windows.

Graphics Interchange Format (GIF)   A standard for compressed image storage.

Graphics Kernel System (GKS)   A popular graphics programming system on UNIX platforms.

Graphics Mode   Most PC video adapters have special display modes for text, where fonts are handled by the hardware itself. All other video modes are called graphics modes.

Gray Scale   A number of shades of gray.

GUI   See **Graphical User Interface**.

Handle   (1) When programming, a pointer to information identifying a file or object. (2) When using a graphics program, any point or shape that can be grabbed with the mouse to control the placement or configuration of a larger shape.

Hardware   Physical machines or parts, as opposed to software.

Hatched Brush   In Windows, a brush that fills with a hatched pattern when drawing.

Header   A standard arrangement of data items found at the beginning of a file.

Heighway's Dragon   A famous fractal shaped (sort of) like a dragon.

Hemicube   A half cube, originally developed by Michael Cohen, used in the radiosity method to calculate form factors. Depth buffers are employed on each face to determine surface to surface visibility.

Hercules Graphics Adapter (**HGA**, or **HGC for Hercules Graphics Card)**   The first graphics card with better resolution than CGA; still a low-end monochrome graphics standard.

Hexagon   A six-sided figure.

HGA   See **Hercules Graphics Adapter**.

HGC   See **Hercules Graphics Adapter**.

Hi-8   A home video recording format that features near-broadcast-quality imaging, compact size, and digital sound.

HiColor   Sierra Designs' brand name for their high color (15-color) RAMDAC chips.

Hidden Surfaces   Surfaces that wouldn't be visible if you were looking at a real 3-D object, but that need to be purposefully hidden when displaying a computerized rendering of a 3-D model.

High Color   15-bit color, which uses five bits each for red, green, and blue. Fifteen bits can display 32,768 distinct colors.

High-pass filter   See **Filter**.

High Word   The most significant 16 bits of a 32-bit number.

Highlights   The shiny parts, also called specular highlights, of a partially reflective surface.

HOOPS   An object-oriented, three-dimensional graphics standard developed by Ithaca Software.

Horizontal Resolution The number of pixels across the screen in the x direction.

Horizontal Scroll Bar At the bottom of a Windows window, the bar that allows you to move the window view back and forth horizontally.

Houndsfield Numbers Units of measurement used in medical imaging to represent material density.

HPG Hewlett-Packard Plotter Graphics Language (used by vector printing devices).

HSV Model The hue/saturation/value color model, an alternative to red/green/blue or cyan/magenta/yellow for describing colors.

Hue (1) In the HSV model, the location in the rainbow spectrum where a color would be found. (2) Generally, a synonym for color.

ICO A Windows icon file.

Icon A little picture used in Windows to represent a program or document.

IDE—Integrated Development Environment A programmer's workplace for editing, compiling, and testing programs without returning to the command line or Program Manager window.

IFD See **Image File Directory**.

IFF Graphics file that snuck onto your machine from an Amiga (also called HAM).

IFS See **Iterated Function System**.

IGES—Initial Graphics Exchange Specification A standard file format for exchanging drawings and images between CAD programs.

Illumination Simulated lighting, when rendering an image of a 3-D model.

Image Buffer The memory where an image is stored.

Image File Directory (IFD) The part of a TIFF file that records which parts of which images go where in the file.

Image Plane In 3-D rendering, the plane in theoretical 3-D space that corresponds to the display screen.

Image Processing A general term referring to any digital manipulation of scanned photographs or computer-generated pictures.

Indexed Color See **Palette-Based Color**.

Index of Refraction A ratio developed in the field of optics to measure the speed of light passing through a transparent medium. The index of refraction is used in ray tracing to determine how much transmission rays are bent when they pass through a surface. Air has a 1.0 index of refraction. Water has an index of refraction of 1.33, and glass has an index of refraction of 1.5.

Industry Standard Architecture (ISA) The expansion bus in an AT-compatible computer. Almost all PCs have ISA buses.

Initial Graphics Exchange Specification (IGES) See **IGES**.

Instruction One operation of a microprocessor.

Integers   Counting numbers (1, 2, 3…), negative numbers (–1, –2, –3…) and, of course, zero.

Intensity   The amount of light, or the amount of a particular color.

Interaction   Two-way communication (often, between a computer and a person, although sometimes two people can interact, too). Also, the "interaction of light" with a model produces highlights and shadows.

Interactive   Involving interaction.

Intersection Point   A point on a surface that has been struck by a reflection ray, a refraction ray, or an eye ray.

Intersection Test   A mathematical evaluation that determines whether or not a ray has struck a surface.

Inverse Fourier Transform   Going from the frequency domain back to the spatial domain. See **Fourier Transformations**.

ISA   See **Industry Standard Architecture**.

Iterate   To feed the results of an operation back into the same operation again. See **Chaos** and **Iterated Function System**.

Iterated Function System (IFS)   A set of numbers, called IFS Codes, that define a set of geometric transformations to be performed repeatedly. The result, when displayed visually, looks like a fractal.

Iterative   Involving iteration.

Jaggy   Having jagged edges. See **Aliasing**.

Jittering   A method of simulating greater resolution or dynamic range by modulating intensity data with noise.

JPEG   (1) The Joint Photographic Experts Group. (2) Defined by JPEG, an image file compression standard that achieves very high compression ratios with some loss of image quality.

JPG   Highly compressed format design by the Joint Photographic Experts Group (JPEG).

Julia Set   A type of fractal, similar to the Mandelbrot set.

Kernel   (1) The central, essential part of anything. (2) The array of numbers that defines the effect of an image-processing convolution.

Keyframes   Two or more frames located at significant intervals in an animation sequence and used by the tweening process to obtain the frames in between.

Kilobyte   1,024 bytes.

Lambertian   Any surface that is entirely diffuse, producing no specular reflections.

Latch Bits   Part of the innards of video chips that you may be grateful you don't need to worry about.

Layers   Independent parts of a drawing or image.

Lean   Tilt sideways, keeping the top and bottom parallel to the ground. Similar to shear and skew.

Library   (1) A collection of common programming functions to be used in many different programs, for example, a graphics library. (2) Any large collection of similar items, for example, an image library. (3) A place where you can borrow old-fashioned books to read for free.

Light Buffer   A depth buffer containing pointers to objects illuminated by a light source; a technique used to compute shadows with local illumination models.

Limpel-Ziv & Welch (LZW)   A very efficient, lossless image-compression algorithm used in GIF and some varieties of TIFF files.

Lines   Theoretically, infinitely long, invisible straightnesses. Often used to mean visible approximations of line segments.

Listserver   An Internet system for disseminating information on electronic mailing lists.

Little-endian   A method of representing numerical data as a pair of binary words. In little-endian ordering, the least significant word precedes the most significant word. Intel microprocessors store data in little-endian order.

Local Bus   The synchronous bus between a microprocessor and its memory.

Local Illumination Model   An illumination model that simulates only direct illumination such as Gouraud and Phong shading. No reflected light is accounted for.

Lofting   A modeling technique that produces 3-D surfaces by extruding 2-D lines and polygons.

Lorenz Attractor   A simple mathematical model of a weather system, which shows chaotic behavior. See **Attractor** and **Chaos**.

Lorenz Water Wheel   A water wheel with leaky buckets, a direct analogy to the Lorenz attractor.

Lossless   Any data compression technique that does not lose any of its original data, such as Run Length Encoding (RLE).

Lossy   Any data compression technique that loses some of the original data in the process of compression, such as JPEG.

Low-Pass Filter   See **Filter**.

Low Word   The least significant 16 bits of a 32-bit number.

LUT—Look Up Table   An array of values, used in image processing applications to obtain intensity or color values from a spectrum.

LZW Compression   See **Limpel-Ziv & Welch**.

MAC   MacPaint format from the Apple Macintosh computer.

Macro   A definition of a sequence of commands or instructions. Once defined, the name of the macro can be inserted in place of the entire sequence to save typing.

Magenta   Bright purplish-pink.

Mandelbrot Set   A famous mathematical fractal popularized by the French mathematician Benoit Mandelbrot. Most of the fractal pictures you see in magazines, with the pretty colored spirals within spirals, are parts of the infinitely detailed Mandelbrot set.

Mapping Mode   In Windows, a setting that determines where and how graphics are drawn in a window.

Mask Bits   A pattern used to select only certain bits from a binary number.

Matrix   An array of numbers, often representing coefficients in a transformation formula.

Maximize Box   In Windows, the part of a window that makes the window grow to fill the entire screen when you click it with the mouse.

Meg   Short for **Megabyte**.

Megabyte   Approximately a million bytes; either 1,000,000 bytes, 1,024,000 bytes (1,000 kilobytes), or 1,048,576 bytes (1,024 kilobytes), depending on whom you ask and what they're trying to sell you.

Melting   Aaaaahhhwwwwmmmmmrrrr....

Memory   (1) The chips in your computer that store bits, as in Random Access Memory, or RAM. (2) Anything that stores bits, as in Compact Disc Read Only Memory, or CD-ROM.

Memory   (1) The chips in your...Wait a minute, didn't I just define memory?

Memory Swapping   Copying a part of the computer's internal memory to a hard drive to make more room for other data, and then copying it back into internal memory when needed. Memory swapping gives the appearance of nearly unlimited memory capacity, at the price of speed.

Menu Bar   In Windows (and most commercial programs for DOS these days), the area at the top of the screen or window where the menu choices are.

Mesh Entity   A compact way of describing a complex surface with a grid of connected 3-D faces.

Message   In Windows (or almost any other object-oriented programming system), a signal that tells parts of the program that an event has occurred.

Message Loop   The part of a Windows program that checks for messages and takes the appropriate action to deal with the messages it receives.

Metaball   See **Blobs**.

Minimize Box   In Windows, the little square that turns the window into an icon when you click it.

MIPS   Millions of Instructions per Second, a statistical rating of microprocessor speed; jokingly referred to as "Meaningless Indication of Performance Specification."

Modeler   A three-dimensional graphics program that allows the user to input, view, and edit three-dimensional objects for a rendering system.

Module Definition File   In Windows programming, a file describing the various component parts of a windows program.

Module Name   The name of a file containing part of a Windows program.

Moire Patterns   Ripply interference patterns, popular in the 18th century and still enjoyed in moire fabric. These are sometimes lovely, sometimes bothersome when they appear on a computer screen. Moire means "watery" in French. See also **Aliasing**.

Monitor   On top of your computer or desk, the big box that you probably stare into all day.

Mono   See **Monochrome Graphics**.

Monochrome Graphics Graphics with only two colors (black and white, or sometimes green or amber if you have an "ergonomic" monitor) or shades of gray.

Morphing (1) Tweening; gradually metamorphosing a shape into another shape. (2) Specifically, tweening full-color pictures, as opposed to simple lines and polygon shapes.

Motif A graphical user-interface for UNIX systems, championed by the Open Look Foundation.

Motion Cues Visual information that helps you tell how objects are moving relative to one another.

Mouse (1) The pointing device on your desk. (2) The pointy-tailed fellow peeking out from under your desk.

Mouse Cursor See **Cursor**.

MPEG The Motion Picture Experts Group's MPEG video compression technology, a standard for adding animated video sequences to any software using JPEG compression.

MPG File extension for an MPEG file.

MS-DOS Microsoft Disk Operating System. See **DOS**.

Multimedia Buzzword for anything that combines digital video and sound, usually on a CD-ROM.

Multitasking Doing more than one thing at a time. Most "multitasking" environments, including Windows, just fake it by slicing up their time between multiple tasks.

NAPLPS North American Presentation-Level Protocol Syntax, a graphics standard of days gone by.

Negative (1) In image processing, as in photography, the inversion of the intensities of red, green, and blue light or grayscale intensities. (2) Mathematically, less than zero.

Normal The direction the top of your head would be pointing if you stood on a 3-D face. Used to compute the interaction of light rays with models. See **Right Hand Rule**.

North American Presentation-Level Protocol Syntax See **NAPLPS**.

NTSC National Television Standards Committee. The broadcast video standard for the United States, jokingly referred to as "Never Twice the Same Color."

Nubus The bus architecture standard of the Apple Macintosh computer.

Nyquist Criteria States that you must sample at least at twice the highest spatial frequency component of the image if you are to capture the essence of the image and not introduce false frequencies (aliases).

Object (1) In programming, a procedure that contains its own data and responds to messages telling it what to do with that data. (2) In 3-D graphics, a mathematical model of a real object.

Occluded Environment An environment or scene in which two or more surfaces eclipse the path between themselves in part or in whole. Occluded environments can have shadows; unoccluded environments cannot.

OpenGL A portable 3-D graphics interface, developed by Silicon Graphics, independent of platform or GUI.

Operating System (OS) The program that starts when you start your computer and that launches other programs. Most OSs handle disk operations and other low-level housekeeping so the application programs don't have to.

Optical (1) Dealing with light, as in the optical properties of an object to be rendered. (2) Mass storage that uses laser light to read or write information, as in optical disks.

OS See **Operating System**.

Pages (1) Additional video memory for storing off-screen images. This is used in animation to prepare the next frame while the current frame is still being displayed. (2) Pieces of paper.

Paint Programs Programs that edit bitmapped images pixel-by-pixel. Contrast to **Draw Programs**.

Palette See **Color Look-Up Table (CLUT)**.

Palette-Based Mode Video modes where color numbers are stored for each pixel, and a palette or color look-up table is used to determine the actual color value that corresponds to each color number. See **Color Look-Up Table (CLUT)**.

Palette Rotation Another word for color cycling.

Patch A discrete division of a continuous surface used to characterize an environment in the radiosity method.

PC (1) Any IBM-PC or IBM-AT compatible personal computer. (2) Any personal computer or microcomputer.

PCI A processor independent bus architecture developed by the Intel Corporation.

PCL Hewlett Packard Printer Control Language (for LaserJet-compatible printers).

PCs More than one PC.

PCT Apple MacIntosh PICT format bitmap (sometimes given the PIC extension).

PCX ZSoft's PC Paintbrush bitmap format.

Pel IBM's goofy word for pixel.

Pen A pointing-device that looks like an ordinary desk pen but contains electronics allowing the computer to tell where it is relative to the screen or a digitizing pad.

Pentium The name Intel chose for their next CPU chip when they found out they couldn't buy all worldwide rights to the digits 5, 8, and 6.

Perspective The effect that makes distant objects look smaller than close objects.

Perspective Distance The simulated distance between your eyes and the object you are rendering in 3-D.

PEX A portable 3-D graphics interface that augments X-Window.

PHIGS An old UNIX graphics standard. The letters stand for something-something-graphics standard, I suppose.

Phong Shading A local illumination model that accounts for specular and diffuse light by interpolating vertex normals to calculate surface intensity.

Photo CD Kodak's attempt at mass-marketing a service to digitize 35mm film photos and put them on a CD-ROM for you.

Photorealistic Any image synthesis technique that produces pictures through accurately modeling the propagation of light. Photorealistic images cannot be distinguished from photographs.

PIC A picture from Pictor/PC Paint or from Lotus 1-2-3 charting. (Several other programs also use this extension for incompatible file formats!)

PICT An Apple Macintosh graphics file format.

Pie Piece A wedge-shape. (You need six of them to win at Trivial Pursuit.)

Pixel Emphasis Another word for **Sharpen**.

Pixel Interpolation An image processing technique for enlarging an image without making it look jaggy.

Pixel—Picture Element The smallest dot on your computer screen. See **Resolution**.

Pixel Replication An image processing technique for enlarging an image and making it look jaggy.

Pixel Spreading Another word for **Blur**.

Play Whippeee!! Interaction at its best.

Point Clouds A bunch of points in 3-D space. Many of the fractals presented in this book are point clouds.

POINT Entities A point in 3-D space, when written to a DXF file.

Pointer A variable that contains the location of another variable in the computer's memory.

Pointillism The practice of representing pictures with a large number of tiny dots or pixels.

Points In theory, zero-dimensional locations; in practice, a small region surrounding a point illuminated so that we can see it.

Point Light A light source that radiates light in all directions. Contrast to **Spotlight**.

Polygon A two-dimensional closed figure made up of line segments at its edges. For example, triangles, squares, pentagons, and hexagons are all polygons.

Polyline The outline of a polygon.

POLYLINE Entities Polylines in a DXF file.

Polypolygon Multiple polygons defined in one big array.

Positive (1) In image processing or photography, an image with the original coloring of the subject is called a positive; the opposite of a negative. (2) Mathematically, greater than zero.

Postscript A computer language specifically designed to describe graphics images and text fonts. Unlike most languages,

Postscript is usually interpreted by a processor in the printer, not the CPU.

Primary Colors   Red, green, and blue. See **RGB Color Model**.

Primitives   Basic objects (lines, spheres, cubes, cones, and cylinders) employed by two-dimensional and three-dimensional graphics systems used to compose more complex objects.

Probability   The likelihood of something happening.

Procedural   See **Procedure-Driven**.

Procedural Texture   The use of a variety of algorithms to compute intricate and sometimes animated surface patterns.

Procedure   (1) A set of instructions for doing something. (2) In Windows, a function that responds to a message.

Procedure Declaration   The part of a C program that indicates the input and output types of a procedure.

Procedure-Driven   A program that carries out tasks in a specific order, rather than allowing the user to initiate events and then respond to them. Contrast **Event-Driven**.

Processor   The "brain" of your computer, which carries out all the instructions in a program; the CPU.

Program Initialization   Any necessary housekeeping tasks to be carried out once at the beginning of a program.

Programmer   The guy or gal who types the instructions that make up a computer program.

Projection   A geometric transformation that produces a two-dimensional object from a three-dimensional object.

Pseudorealistic   Any image synthesis technique that produces pictures by proportionally approximating the propagation of light.

PUB   A file format used by a number of desktop publishing programs, including Microsoft Publisher and PFS:First Publisher.

Quantization   A modification of data to suit limitations in resolution, such as reducing a true color image to a 256 color LUT image.

Radiosity   A rendering preprocess method for determining global diffuse illumination that is descended from radiative heat transfer theory.

RAM   Random Access Memory, the main memory chips inside your computer. Unlike Read Only Memory (ROM) or disk drives, RAM forgets everything when you turn the computer off.

RAMDAC—Random Access Memory Digital Analog Converter   (1) The circuits that convert color values into actual voltages to go to the monitor. (2) Specifically, a chip that allows your computer to display 15-bit or 24-bit color.

Random Iteration Algorithm   A technique for drawing Iterated Function System fractals by randomly hopping around on a fractal and lighting up dots as you go. See **Attractor** and **Herated Function System**.

Raster (1) The scanning electron gun inside a CRT. (2) A horizontal line across the screen, a scanline. (3) A general term referring to any bitmapped graphics, as opposed to vector graphics.

Raster Operation A way of combining the color of pixels to be drawn with the pixel colors already on the screen. The most commonly used "Raster-ops" are XOR and simple replacement, sometimes called SET or PUT.

Ray-Tracer A program that generates photorealistic images by calculating the interaction of light rays with a 3-D model.

Ray Tracing The act of using a ray-tracer; or the calculations that the ray-tracer carries out.

Real (1) Existing in the physical world outside the computer. (2) See **Real Time**.

Real Time The time scale we experience, as opposed to the internal rhythm of the computer or the painstakingly slow frame-by-frame calculation of extremely complex images.

Red/Blue Glasses See **Anaglyphic Stereoscopy**.

Reduction Shrinking, making smaller.

Reflection The effect you see when light bounces off of something and the image of the surrounding environment appears in that thing. This is easy to simulate on a computer with ray tracing.

Reflection Ray A ray that is cast from a surface intersection point along the reflection vector that is used to determine the contribution of specular reflection to the intensity of the light leaving the surface.

Refraction The bending of light as it passes through a transparent or translucent object.

Register A logical device on a microprocessor that allows a piece of data to be temporarily stored and operated on.

Render To produce a two-dimensional picture of a 3-D object by calculating what it would look like from a particular angle.

Resampling Enlarging or shrinking an image by interpolating or averaging the values of each pixel.

Re-sizing Enlarging or shrinking.

Resolution (1) The number of pixels in an image. (2) The amount of memory required to store an image. This includes color resolution, which is the number of bits required to store the color number of a pixel.

Resource Editor A program to create and edit Windows bitmaps, icons, and cursors.

Resource File A file containing the visual elements of a Windows program, such as bitmaps, icons, and cursors.

Resources The visual elements of a Windows program, such as bitmaps, icons, and cursors.

RGB Color Model The method of describing colors by specifying the intensities of red, green, and blue light to be added together.

Right Hand Rule   A way of relating rotation to a direction in space. Hold your right hand with the fingers slightly curled and the thumb sticking out. The direction of your thumb tells you which direction is positive, assuming that the rotation from your palm to your fingertips is considered clockwise.

RISC—Reduced Instruction Set Computing   A microprocessor design that calls for fewer instructions and more registers. RISC processors design offers considerable performance gains over CISC processors.

RLE   (1) An old CompuServe bitmap from before GIF was invented. (2) A Microsoft Windows run-length encoded bitmap. (3) See **Run Length Encoding**.

Routine   Another name for a function or procedure.

Run Length Encoding (RLE)   A way of compressing image data that replaces long sequences ("runs") of identical values with a code followed by the number of times the value is repeated.

Saturation   The overall amount of light or pigment in a color or an entire image.

Scanline   One horizontal line of pixels all the way across the screen.

Screen   The display part of a computer monitor—where the image shows up.

Secondary Colors   Cyan, magenta, and yellow. See **CMYK Color Model**.

Self-Similar   Having parts that resemble the whole.

Sensitive   Dependence on initial conditions. See **Chaos**.

Sequential   Occurring in a specific, fixed order; a synonym for **Procedural**.

Shadows   The darkness cast by the light. Each day hides a small patch of night.

Shareware   Software that is freely distributed for evaluation purposes. You are legally required to pay a registration fee to the software's author if you continue to use the software, although nobody is going to come and bust your door down if you don't. This honor system for software distribution saves tons of wasted money on marketing and packaging, allowing authors to focus on quality and low prices. It is also called "try before you buy" software.

Sharpen   Enhancing the quality of an image by accentuating color changes.

Shear   Contrast with **Skew**.

Shutter Glasses   Glasses that have LCD panels in each eye opening. By alternately blocking each eye opening 30 times a second and simultaneously flipping between left and right eye views on a computer monitor, the shutter glasses allow you to see color stereo pictures.

Sierpinski's Triangle   A famous fractal made up of triangles within triangles within triangles on to infinity.

Simulation   Faking something on a computer.

SIRDS   Single Image Random Dot Stereogram, a method of producing three-dimensional imagery without 3-D glasses.

Skew   To rotate one axis only, causing an object to appear to twist in a way that couldn't happen with real physical objects.

Software   Instructions and data structures, as opposed to physical hardware.

Solid Modeling   Representing the insides of 3-D objects as well as their surfaces. Sometimes this includes the ability to calculate the motion of objects based on the internal behavior of the materials they are made of.

Source Code File   A file that contains the instructions that make up a computer program written in C, C++, BASIC, or another human-readable computer language.

Spatial Domain   The normal way of representing an image, where the x and y axes correspond to horizontal and vertical dimensions in ordinary space. See **Fourier Transformation**.

Spatial Frequency Aliasing   Means the same thing as aliasing.

Spatial Frequency Components   Specific periodic repetitions in a pattern. See **Fourier Transformation**.

Special Purpose Blocks   Parts of a GIF file that contain program-specific information.

Specular Light   On shiny objects, highlights that come from the scattering of imperfectly reflected light.

Speed   More, more, more! Whizzzz....

Spin   Your run-of-the-mill rotation—turning, tumbling, that sort of thing.

Spline Curve   A free-form parametric curve defined by a set of points that influence local control on the bend of the curve.

Spotlight   A directional light source that casts shadows. Contrast to **Point Light**.

Spreadsheet   A program that lays out a grid of numbers and text, allowing you to enter formulas instead of a number for any square in the grid. It's a handy tool for simple number-crunching and accounting tasks, as well as for "what-if" numerical analysis.

Square Root   The number that, when multiplied by itself, produces a given value.

Squashing   Re-sizing one axis only, so that an object appears to elongate or smush in one direction.

Stereo Pairs   A left-eye view and a right-eye view of the same scene or object. These are often placed side-by-side for viewing.

Stereo Vision   The ability to judge the relative distance of things from the differences between what you see with your left eye and what you see with your right eye.

Stereoscopic   Involving stereo vision.

Stock Brush   In Windows, one of a few standard brush fill patterns.

String Table   A record of the patterns found in a file, used for compression and decompression of images with the Limpel-Ziv & Welsh algorithm.

Strips   Parts of an image; used in TIFF files.

Subtractive Color Model   A way of describing any color by specifying the amount of cyan, magenta, and yellow pigments. This is called subtractive because the pigments create color by absorbing (subtracting) light instead of emitting (adding) it. Contrast to **Additive Color Model**.

Successive Approximation Algorithm A way of drawing a fractal by making more and more detailed approximations of it.

Super-VGA (1) Any video adapter with higher resolution than VGA's 640×480 by 16-colors. (2) Specifically, a 800×600 by 16-color resolution, or 640×480 by 256-colors.

Super-VGA+ Video adapters with resolutions beyond 800×600 and/or more than 256 colors.

Surfaces Two-dimensional planes or curves in 3-D space. See **3-D Faces**.

SVGA or **SVG** See **Super-VGA**.

System Fonts The standard typefaces that come built into an operating system.

System Queue In Windows, the main message dispatch system.

Tabbed Text Text arranged in columns; also called tabulated text.

TABLES A section of a DXF file that contains CAD data on colors, shape types, and other advanced stuff.

Tag A label that tells what type of data follows it in an image file.

Tagged Image File Format (TIFF) See **TIFF**.

Targa (1) A high-end line of graphics hardware manufactured by TrueVision, Inc. (2) See **TGA**.

Text Letters and numbers.

Text Mode Most PC video adapters have special display modes for text, where fonts are handled by the hardware itself.

Texture Mapping A rendering technique for producing realistic surfaces by modulating the surface pixel intensities with a two-dimensional image array of color data.

TGA Bitmap format originally created for Truevision Targa boards.

TIF Three-letter extension for TIFF files.

TIFF Tagged Image File Format used by many graphics programs.

Title Bar In Windows, the very top part of a window, which contains the title of the window.

Transform (1) To change from one thing into another. (2) Short for **Transformation**.

Transformation A mathematical description of how to change one thing into another, or to move something from one place to another.

TransGraphics A system of headers and functions that make graphics programs compatible with multiple compilers and graphics libraries.

Translation (1) Displacement, movement from one place to another without rotation. (2) The re-expression of words from one language into another.

Transmitted Light Light that travels through a transparent surface.

Transmission Ray   A ray cast from a surface intersection point along the refraction vector that is used to determine the contribution of specular transmission to the intensity of the light leaving the surface.

Transparency Masks   In many photo-editing programs, a shape that covers part of the image and lets the rest show through. See also **Alpha Channel**.

True 3-D   Rendering three-dimensional models, as opposed to pseudo-3-D which simply fakes 3-D lighting and perspective effects without using a 3-D model at all.

True Color   24-bit-per-pixel color, with 8 bits each for red, green, and blue. Better color resolution than your eye can distinguish!

True Type   A font description language recently introduced by Apple and Microsoft to compete with Postscript. Unlike Postscript, True Type is generally used only for text and not for illustrations.

TSR   A Terminate-and-Stay-Resident program. TSRs are usually loaded when your computer starts, and they remain in memory to carry out their tasks whenever they are called or automatically triggered by some event. Because DOS was not originally designed to support them, they sometimes cause problems when they conflict with one another or other programs.

TV   If you don't know what TV is, you got off on the wrong planet.

Tweening   The process of automatically calculating several images between key frames in an animation.

Unifying Normals   Making sure the outsides of all faces on an object point out and the insides all point in.

UNIX   Loosely standardized group of operating systems and communications protocols used by major universities and colleges, as well as many large corporations.

Unscrunching   An image processing transformation where intensity data is modified to make the intensity distribution histogram more even.

Usenet   A collection of discussion groups accessible via the Internet and some BBSs.

User Interface   The appearance and conventions for using a program.

UUdecode   A utility that converts UUencoded binary files from ASCII back into binary.

UUencode   A utility that allows binary files to be converted into ASCII and posted on Usenet.

Value   An amount, quantity, or other specific piece of data, for example, 6 or 2.3 or "Fred" or whatever.

Variables   Memory locations that store values.

VCR   Video-cassette recorder. See **TV**.

Vector Data   See **Vector Graphics**.

Vector Graphics   Mathematical descriptions of shapes, as opposed to pixel-by-pixel representations of images. Contrast to **Bitmapped Graphics**.

Vector-Based Programs   Software that uses vector graphics.

Vertical Resolution   The number of pixels in the y direction.

Vertical Scroll Bar   The bar at the right side of a Windows window that allows you to move the window view up and down.

VESA   (1) The Video Electronics Standards Association, a standard-setting consortium made up of big graphics hardware and software companies. (2) The Super-VGA modes standardized by VESA. (3) The local bus specification proposed by VESA.

VESA Local Bus   A 32-bit bus architecture developed by VESA that allows adapters to interface synchronously with the microprocessor.

VGA—Video Graphics Array   The current low-end standard for color graphics hardware on the PC. It is capable of 640×480 with 16 colors or 320×200 with 256 colors.

Video   (1) Moving pictures stored electronically. (2) Anything to do with visual displays or computer graphics.

Video Capture   The ability to digitize video and store it on a computer.

Video Cards   Computer graphics adapter hardware (not necessarily capable of dealing with video capture or digital video).

Video Electronics Standards Association   See **VESA**.

Video for Windows   A new standard for displaying digitized motion pictures within Microsoft Windows. It uses a tiny 160×120 pixel window for speed.

Video Graphics Array   See **VGA**.

Video Hardware   See **Video Cards**.

Video Memory   Memory within a computer used only for storing and displaying images.

Video Modes   All video cards support a number of different operational modes, called video modes. These include text modes and graphics modes of various resolutions.

Viewing Frustrum   In 3-D rendering, the area of space visible in an image.

Viewpoint   The point in space where the observer or camera is located when computing a 3-D rendering.

Viewport   A region of the screen to which all output is temporarily restricted. Usually, the top left corner of the viewport becomes the 0,0 coordinate from which all locations are measured.

Virtual Reality—VR   A buzzword for a variety of 3-D computer graphics developments. VR implies total immersion in a simulated world, with stereoscopic wraparound head mounted displays and stereo sound.

Virtual Reality Software   Software that supports real-time 3-D rendering, preferably with stereoscopic display. Most VR software allows you to create a virtual world and then interactively explore it.

Virtual Worlds   See **Virtual Reality Software.**

Visual Simulation   Modeling something in a way that makes its essential components visible while the dynamics of the system do their thing.

Visualization   A broad label for any visual representation of data. Usually, it implies that some or all of the data would have been invisible or too abstract to understand without computer-graphics representations.

Voxel   A volume element, the three-dimensional equivalent of a pixel. It is used in medical imaging and volume rendering.

VR   See **Virtual Reality**.

VRAM—Video Random Access Memory   Expensive memory used by display adapters that supports rapid data transfer for faster frame buffers.

What-You-See-Is-What-You-Get (WYSIWYG)   Pronounced "WIZZY-wig" or "WIZZY-wiggy," it means that printed output of a program looks nearly identical to the screen display you saw before you printed.

Window Border   In Windows, the edge around a window. You can grab the border with the mouse and resize the window.

Windows   When capitalized, the Microsoft Windows (Trademark, Registered, Copyright, bow-when-you-say-that) graphical user-interface operating system. When not capitalized, a rectangular region of the screen that contains the graphics output of a program or function.

Windows CGM   See **Windows Metafile**.

Windows Function   In Windows programming, a function that does some calculation or display task; called by other functions or procedures, but not initiated directly by a message. Contrast with **Windows Procedure**.

Windows Metafile   A special type of graphics file that can be a device-independent-bitmap, series of vector drawing commands, or just a link to the application that created the graphic.

Windows NT   The newest version of Windows, which can run on several different types of computers and does not require DOS.

Windows Procedure   In Windows programming, a function that is initiated by and responds to a message. Contrast to **Windows Function**.

Wizzy-Wiggy   See **What-You-See-Is-What-You-Get**.

WMF   Microsoft Windows MetaFile (either a DIB image or a just a link to the drawing application).

Word   (1) Two bytes. (2) The number of bits that a particular computer handles most efficiently (on a 286, 16 bits; on a 386, 32 bits).

Wordlength   The number of binary digits representing a discrete value, often a measure of dynamic range.

Workstation   A powerful microcomputer, usually but not necessarily running UNIX.

World Wide Web   A linked client-server database that uses hypertext information and requires a browser program.

WPG   WordPerfect vector drawing or bitmap image.

WYSIWYG   See **What-You-See-Is-What-You-Get**.

X   Usually used to stand for a horizontal location coordinate.

X-Window   A user interface and graphics operation protocol for UNIX developed at MIT.

XOR   Exclusive-Or, a raster operation that allows graphics to be drawn over a complex background and then erased without damaging the background image by drawing with XOR again.

Y   Usually used to stand for a vertical location coordinate. Sometimes it implies the in-and-out location coordinate in 3-D space instead.

Z   Usually used to stand for an in-and-out location coordinate (perpendicular to the screen) in 3-D space. Sometimes it is used as the vertical coordinate instead. At other times, Z means a complex number that includes both x and y coordinate values.

Zoom   Re-sizing with pizazz.

What's on the CD-ROM

You'll find a wealth of graphics creation, development, and manipulation software on the CD-ROM that's included with this book.

This appendix is to help you use the Windows installation and DOS menu and to provide you with information about the included software.

Windows Setup

The Windows setup program creates a Program Manager group with icons for running the software, and it copies any necessary software drivers to your hard drive.

To run the setup program, start Windows—if you haven't already done so—and perform the following steps:

1. Insert the book's disc in your CD-ROM drive.
2. Switch to Program Manager or File Manager. Select **F**ile from the menu, then select **R**un.
3. In the Run dialog box, type **D:\SETUP.EXE** in the Command Line box and click OK. If your CD-ROM drive is not drive D, substitute the correct letter. For instance, if your CD-ROM drive is G, type **G:\SETUP.EXE**.
4. The opening screen of the setup program will appear. Click the **C**ontinue button.
5. The program will install drivers to your hard drive and create a Program Manager group named *PC Graphics Unleashed*. This group contains icons for running and installing the disc's various Windows programs.

After the setup has completed successfully, you can click the various icons in the *PC Graphics Unleashed* Program Manager group to install and run the software.

The DOS Menu Program

The DOS software on the disc can be explored using the DOS menu program. Perform the following steps to start the menu:

1. Insert the CD-ROM into your drive.
2. If you're running Windows, exit to DOS.
3. At a DOS prompt, switch to the drive containing the CD-ROM. For example, if your CD-ROM is in drive E, type **E:** and press Enter.
4. Type **MENU** and press Enter. This will start the menu program.

The opening screen of the menu contains buttons that represent the DOS software on the CD-ROM. Click any button to see more options. At the bottom of the screen are buttons that enable you to easily navigate through the menu page by page.

Special thanks go out to the NeoSoft Corporation, who generously provided us with NeoBook Professional, the authoring software used to create the DOS menu. If you are interested in NeoBook Professional, or other NeoSoft applications such as NeoShow or NeoPaint, see the NeoPaint section later in this Appendix.

The Book Supplemental Software

The software that directly supplements the material covered in the book is—with a few noted exceptions—organized by chapter. For example, the files that supplement Chapter 3, "Advanced Morphing," are in the \CH03 directory. The following sections provide a quick overview of each directory.

\CH01

This directory contains Display 1.84, a versatile program that enables you to read, write, manipulate, and display images.

\CH03

This directory contains the morphing software and sample files for Chapter 3, "Advanced Morphing," by Scott Anderson.

\CH04

This directory contains many sample images and animation that supplement Chapter 4, "Computer Painting Techniques," by Harry Dusenberg.

\CH05

This directory contains source and executables for four utility programs: an equalization program, a dithering program, an adaptive palette program, and a TIFF to Targa conversion utility for Chapter 5, "Advanced Image Processing," by Spyro Gumas.

\CH06

This directory contains sample Targa files and the source and executable for the UFO program shown in Chapter 6, "Digital Composition," by Spyro Gumas.

\CH08

This directory contains the source and executable for the Clip, Icon Test, and Mouse Test programs that supplement Chapter 8, "A Graphical User Interface for 3-D Modeling," by Alfonso Hermida.

\CH09

This directory contains the source and executable for the Draw, DrawGrid, and Sweep programs that supplement Chapter 9, "Creating Your Own 3-D Graphics World," by Alfonso Hermida.

\CH10

This directory contains the source and executables for the Raw2Poly and Raw2POV programs that supplement Chapter 10, "Output to DXF and Ray Tracers," by Alfonso Hermida.

\CH11

This directory contains the scene files, data files, and images that supplement Chapter 11, "Rendering 3-D Objects," by Alfonso Hermida.

\CH12

This directory contains BLOBDRAW.POC, the POCO program that extends the power of Animator Pro, as well as sample flics and images that supplement Chapter 12, "Modeling 2-D Blobs with Animator Pro POCO Language," by Jim Hawkins.

\CH13

The supplemental files for Chapter 13, "Volume Rendering with Blobs," by Steve Anger, are with the files in Chapter 14, "Creating a Graphical User Interface to Model Blobs."

\CH14

This directory contains the source and executable for the BlobGUI program that supplements Chapter 13, "Volume Rendering with Blobs," and Chapter 14, "Creating a Graphical User Interface to Model Blobs," by Steve Anger and Alfonso Hermida, respectively.

\CH15

This directory contains the sample images that supplement Chapter 15, "Modeling with Blobs," by Truman Brown.

\CH16

This directory contains the ASIRDS executable—a SIRDS generator—for Chapter 16, "Stereoscopic 3-D Stunts," by Martin Crumpton.

\CH17

This directory contains the many supplemental Flic, Basic source code, and PI files for Chapter 17, "Ray-Traced Animation," by Rob McGregor.

\CH18

This directory contains some sample PCX images as well as many supplemental graphics utilities such as RayTrace and Lightray that supplement Chapter 18, "Radiosity," by William Parsons Newhall, Jr.

\CH19

This directory contains the source and executables for windowing and leveling, reslicing, and MIP projection utilities that supplement Chapter 19, "Basic 3-D Data Visualization Techniques," by Chikai Ohazama.

\CH20

This directory contains the source, data, and executables that supplement the second part of Chapter 20, "3-D Medical Imaging," called "Visualization of 3-D Medical Data," by W. Andrew Bass.

\CH21

This directory contains the source and executables for the Bézier, FFD3D, and FFDTWN utilities that supplement Chapter 21, "Free-Form Deformation," by Alfonso Hermida.

\XA

This directory contains the VSA256 Graphics Library files discussed in Appendix A, written by Spyro Gumas.

\XB

This directory contains the TIFF256 Graphics Library files discussed in Appendix B, written by Spyro Gumas.

\XC

You are encouraged to access online services and bulletin boards to experience the vast resources available online. To help you begin, QModem Test-Drive—a telecommunications package—has been provided courtesy of Mustang Software.

QModem 4.6 Test-Drive, an excellent telecommunications program by Mustang Software, is located in the \QMODEM subdirectory. The following section provides a quick overview of the software.

QMODEM

The QModem Test-Drive is a fully functional communications program that provides you with an opportunity to do a hands-on evaluation of the software. If you want to continue to use and keep QModem, purchase the professional commercial version. For more information, read the READ.ME file in the \QMODEM subdirectory.

You can install the QModem Test-Drive using either the Windows installation program or the DOS menu on the CD-ROM. You may also install the program directly from the CD-ROM by performing the following steps:

1. Insert the CD-ROM into your drive.
2. If you're running Windows, exit to DOS.
3. At a DOS prompt, switch to the drive containing the CD-ROM. For example, if your CD-ROM is in drive E, type **E:** and press Enter.
4. Type **CD \XC\QMODEM** and press Enter.
5. Type **INSTALL** and press Enter.

The installation program will begin. Follow the on-screen instructions to complete the installation.

Supplemental Graphics Software

Additional graphics utilities that supplement the material covered in the book are organized by program name. For example, NeoPaint, an image creation program, is in the \NEOPAINT directory. The following sections provide a quick overview of the supplemental graphics software.

\NEOPaint

In this directory, you'll find NeoPaint, one of the best DOS-based shareware paint programs. NeoPaint is as simple to use as any paint program, yet includes many powerful features often found only in high-end picture-publishing systems.

NeoPaint's abundance of drawing tools makes it easy to create illustrations for desktop publishing projects, edit digitized photos, or just explore your artistic side. NeoPaint reads and writes 2-, 16-, and 256-color PCX/GIF/TIFF files, includes dozens of drawing tools, special effects, and more.

NEOPAINT IS SHAREWARE

If you enjoy the program and use it frequently, please order the registered version ($45).

For a dealer in your area, to order, or for more information please contact

NeoSoft Corp.
354 NE Greenwood Avenue, Suite 108
Bend, OR 97701-4631

VOICE: (503) 389-5489
FAX: (503) 388-8221
BBS: (503) 383-7195

When ordering from NeoSoft, please include $5 U.S. Mail or $7 FedEx 2-Day for shipping & handling. ($10 Air Mail or $17.50 FedEx for shipping & handling outside the U.S.) Call NeoSoft for alternate shipping methods.

NeoSoft accepts VISA and MasterCard. Checks and money orders are welcome but must be in U.S. funds and drawn on a U.S. bank.

Evaluation and demos of NeoSoft products are available at no charge through NeoSoft's 24-hour BBS and from most major online services.

\Polyray

This directory contains the complete PolyRay 1.7 shareware algebraic input rendering program by Alexander Enzmann.

Polyray is a combination of an extensive set of modeling primitives together with a comprehensive renderer (including both raytracing and polygon scan conversion). Models are specified in an ASCII file, which are parsed and subsequently rendered. An IBM-AT or compatible is the only platform currently supported. An 80386/80387 combination, or 80486 CPU plus at least 2 MB of RAM is required. (A version that does not require a co-processor is in the \PLY386 subdirectory.)

POLYRAY IS SHAREWARE

If you enjoy the program, use it frequently, and can afford to pay a registration fee, send $35 to the following address:

Alexander Enzmann
20 Clinton St.
Woburn, MA 01801

Please include your name and mailing address.

If you formally register this program, you will receive free the next release of Polyray when it is available. In addition, you will be contributing to the author's ability to purchase software tools to make Polyray a better program.

Polyray provides a number of distinct features, the most important of which are the freedom of use of expressions in the modeling file and the ability to render very complex mathematical surfaces.

There are four subdirectories included on the CD-ROM: \PLYDOC, \PLYDAT, \PLYEXE, and \UTIL, which contain the Polyray documents, a set of data files, the executable files, and utilities, respectively. There is also a Polyray Windows Help file—created by Rob McGregor—in the main \POLYRAY directory.

See the QUICKREF.TXT and POLYRAY.DOC files in the \PLYDOC subdirectory for details on the command-line options and data-file syntax.

\POVCAD

This directory contains the complete POVCAD 4.0 for Windows shareware 3-D modeling and ray tracing program by Alfonso Hermida and Rob McGregor.

POVCAD is a feature-rich 3-D modeler that lets you create and edit ray-traceable scene files graphically. Any graphics lover can create inspiring photorealistic ray-traced images on the PC.

POVCAD is a powerful wireframe modeling program with many additional features to make ray tracing easy (and fun). This new version of the popular modeler lets you build scenes with simple mouse commands. If you're an experienced ray tracing veteran, the ray tracer-friendly and smart text editor makes quick work of assembling your scenes. The new texture builder lets you quickly design and render new textures. POVCAD Creates animation path data, curves, surfaces of revolution and translation, sophisticated polygon meshes, and much more.

Additionally, you can model and render images with realistic textures, reflections, and lighting effects that traditional artists would find nearly impossible using conventional media. POVCAD puts ray-traced art in the reach of PC users, graphics aficionados, and commercial artists worldwide.

POVCAD 4.0 features the following:

- Wireframe primitives: sphere, cone, box, disc, torus, and so on
- 2-D Curve Editor
- Ray trace Text Editor
- Exports Polyray (.PI) and POV-Ray 1&2 (.POV) files
- TrueType font conversion
- Texture Builder
- Windows Help
- Render from within POVCAD
- DXF and RAW conversion
- Create/edit Bezier patches, custom colors, polygon and extrude objects, lathe/sweep objects, animation path data
- Straight & along-a-path extrusions
- Much more!

POVCAD IS SHAREWARE

If you enjoy and use the program, send $35 to one of the following addresses:

Alfonso Hermida
9346 Kings Grant Rd
Laurel MD 20723

or

Rob McGregor
P. O. Box 2183
Cocoa FL 32923-2183

REGISTRATION VIA COMPUSERVE

Using CompuServe is an excellent alternative to registration via mail. To register POVCAD online GO SWREG (filename PVCD40.ZIP, ID #3477). The $35.00 will be added to your CompuServe bill.

TECHNICAL SUPPORT VIA COMPUSERVE

An excellent alternative to technical support via phone or mail is using CompuServe, which is one of the leading online systems in the world. Contact Rob McGregor at CIS 73122,3125 or Alfonso Hermida at CIS 72114,2060. CompuServe is an excellent resource on general issues as well.

A Windows Help file with complete information and tutorials on the new features gives you the information you need to get started with POVCAD 4.0.

\PAINTSP

In this directory you'll find Paint Shop Pro, a Windows program that will display, scan, alter, print and convert images. PSP supports 23 of the most common bitmap formats, including JPEG and Kodak Photo CD. Altering includes palette manipulation, dithering, resizing, cropping, applying filters, and MUCH more. PSP supports all TWAIN compliant scanners, does screen capturing, and is an OLE server.

To install Paint Shop Pro, first run the Window install as shown earlier in the chapter. Once the initial Windows setup is complete, you can install Paint Shop Pro by double clicking the icon labelled "Install Paint Shop Pro" in the PC Graphics Unleashed Program Manager group. Once the installation starts, follow the on-screen directions to compete the installation.

Blob Sculptor for Windows

Blob Sculptor for Windows enables you to manipulate and model 3-D objects through the use of blobs. An icon for this program and its Help file will appear in the *PC Graphics Unleashed* Program Manager group. The DOS version of this program, BlobGUI, is discussed in Chapter 14.

INDEX

PC Graphics Unleashed
Free Newsletter Registration Form

☐ Please register me and start my FREE subscription to Dick Oliver's newsletter of 3-D modeling, fractals, and advanced PC graphics. Please also send the free Cedar Software catalog and compendium.

Name: _____

Address: _____

_____

_____

Country: _____

Phone or Fax (optional): _____

Fax or mail this form to:

Dick Oliver, Cedar Software, RR 1 Box 4495, Wolcott, VT 05680 USA

Fax: 802-888-3009   Voice phone: 802-888-5275

VIEWPOINT
D A T A L A B S

Your 3D Data Source

As a 3D software user, you know how time-consuming and frustrating it can be to model or digitize 3D objects. It can take hours, days, or even weeks. But it doesn't need to. That's where Viewpoint comes in. We create and market technically accurate object and motion Datasets and DataTools.™

Free Catalog, CD, and Data

Make sure you have Viewpoint's newest catalog and DataShop™ CD-ROM — free to qualified 3D software users. They both contain thousands of Datasets in dozens of categories. With DataShop, you can download data instantly as you need it — no more waiting for shipping. With five free Datasets included, this is your chance to try Viewpoint data with your 3D software.

Call 1-800-DATASET (328-2738) to request your new catalog and DataShop CD-ROM*.

	Custom Datasets	Standard Datasets	Real-Time Datasets	MotionSets™	ReadySets™ □	CyberProps™ ‡	HyperSpace™	AMAP-micro™ ‡
Broadcast Animation	●	●		●		●	●	●
Feature Films	●	●		●		●	●	●
Simulation	●		●				●	
Virtual Reality	●		●		●	●	●	●
Medical Visualization	●	●		●			●	
Architecture	●					●	●	●
Courtroom Visualization	●	●		●			●	●
Multimedia	●	●	●	●		●	●	●
Games	●	●	●	●	●	●	●	●

Viewpoint has a full line of products for your 3D needs, everything from inexpensive collections, ideal for architectural walk-throughs, to high resolution custom objects for feature film special effects. This chart will give you an idea of the Viewpoint products applicable to your specialty.

*Call for availability in specific formats.

Viewpoint DataLabs • 625 South State Street • Orem, Utah 84058 1.800.DATASET (328.2738) • Ph 801.229.3000 • FAX 801.229.3300

Add to Your Sams Library Today with the Best Books for Programming, Operating Systems, and New Technologies

The easiest way to order is to pick up the phone and call

1-800-428-5331

between 9:00 a.m. and 5:00 p.m. EST.

For faster service please have your credit card available.

ISBN	Quantity	Description of Item	Unit Cost	Total Cost
0-672-30492-9		3D Madness! (Book/CD)	$45.00	
0-672-30322-1		PC Video Madness! (Book/CD)	$39.95	
0-672-30463-5		Becoming A Computer Animator (Book/CD)	$39.99	
0-672-30160-1		Multimedia Developer's Guide	$49.95	
0-672-30513-5		Becoming A Computer Musician (Book/CD)	$39.99	
0-672-30320-5		Morphing Magic (Book/Disk)	$29.95	
0-672-30362-0		Navigating the Internet	$24.95	
0-672-30315-9		The Magic of Image Processing (Book/Disk)	$39.95	
0-672-30308-6		Tricks of the Graphics Gurus (Book/Disk)	$49.95	
0-672-30456-2		The Magic of Interactive Entertainment (Book/CD)	$39.95	
0-672-30448-1		Teach Yourself C in 21 Days Bestseller Edition	$24.95	
0-672-30270-5		Garage Virtual Reality (Book/Disk)	$29.95	
0-672-30413-9		Multimedia Madness!, Deluxe Edition (Book/CDs)	$55.00	
0-672-30352-3		Blaster Mastery (Book/CD)	$34.95	
❏ 3 ½" Disk		Shipping and Handling: See information below.		
❏ 5 ¼" Disk		TOTAL		

Shipping and Handling: $4.00 for the first book, and $1.75 for each additional book. Floppy disk: add $1.75 for shipping and handling. If you need to have it NOW, we can ship product to you in 24 hours for an additional charge of approximately $18.00, and you will receive your item overnight or in two days. Overseas shipping and handling adds $2.00 per book and $8.00 for up to three disks. Prices subject to change. Call for availability and pricing information on latest editions.

201 W. 103rd Street, Indianapolis, Indiana 46290

1-800-428-5331 — Orders   1-800-835-3202 — FAX   1-800-858-7674 — Customer Service

Book ISBN 0-672-30570-4